AF647660

INTERNATIONAL ECONOMICS

About the Author

Dr. O.S. Shrivastava took education in the faculties of Commerce and then Economics. He had first class educational career. He obtained first position in the State and a State competitive examination; third position in CBSE in India and third position in a State PSC and fifth in the University. Dr. Shrivastava taught while in service for 40 calendar years and was Professor, Head and Chairman of Economics in Bhopal (now known as Barkatullah) University, Bhopal. He is still a visiting Professor in Management Institutes and has taught 49th calendar year batch. He is taking the paper of Managerial Economics since 1978 (along with some other papers of MBA). Dr. Shrivastava was appointed Director of CRIM (University Institute of Management), a charge he did not take concurrently with being Head of Economics Department of the University.

Dr. Shrivastava worked concurrently for 3½ years as State Bank of India Chair Professor. Dr. Shrivastava evaluated the implementation of IRDP in six districts of Madhya Pradesh under a Government of India scheme. He was also commissioned by DFID of the UK to undertake a research work for them.

Dr. Shrivastava was adviser to the Government of Madhya Pradesh for the preparation of the "Human Development Reports" of the State. Dr. Shrivastava was also involved in the all-India and States level competitive selection processes. He selected University Professors, Readers and Lecturers; not to speak of selection of lecturers in government and private colleges. He was involved in the selection of even bank managers and one of the 40 books written by him is on Bank Management. He wrote reference books, text books and joint-authorship books (other than 40, his own). He wrote course material for two Open Universities. He was Visiting Faculty for IGNOU centre at Bhopal. Hundreds of his papers were published in research journals and newspapers. He supervised the work of hundreds of M.Phil, M.A. and MBA dissertations/term papers. One IAS officer, one NDDB officer, one Australian citizen, many college lecturers and others took Ph.D. degree under him.

INTERNATIONAL ECONOMICS

(Covering syllabi of all the Universities of India).
(Also UGC syllabus of 2002)
For
M.A. and M. Phil.
Economics

O.S. Shrivastava
Professor & Head., Chairman of Economics (R)
Dean, Faculty of Social Sciences, (Ex)
Ex-State Bank of India Chair Professor in
Bhopal (now Barkatullah) University,
Bhopal (MP) India

CONCEPT PUBLISHING COMPANY PVT. LTD.
NEW DELHI-110059

© O.S. Shrivastava

All rights reserved. No part of this work may be reproduced, stored, adapted, or transmitted in any form or by any means, electronic, mechanical, photocopying, micro-filming recording or otherwise, or translated in any language, without the prior written permission of the copyright owner and the publisher. The book is sold subject to the condition that it shall not, by way of trade or otherwise, be lent, resold, hired out, or otherwise circulated without the prior publisher's written consent in any form of binding or cover other than that in which it is published.

The views and opinions expressed in this book are author's own and the facts reported by him have been verified to the extent possible, and the publishers are not in any way liable for the same.

ISBN-13: 978-81-8069-791-3 (PB)

First Published 2011

Published and Printed by

Concept
Since 1974

Concept Publishing Company Pvt. Ltd.
Regd. Office:
A/15-16, Commercial Block, Mohan Garden
New Delhi-110059 (India)
Phones : 25351460, 25351794, *Fax* : 091-11-25357109
Email : publishing@conceptpub.com
Website: www.conceptpub.com

Editorial Office:
H-13, Bali Nagar, New Delhi-110 015, India.

Cataloging in Publication Data--*Courtesy:* D.K. Agencies (P) Ltd. <docinfo@dkagencies.com>

Shrivastava, O. S. (Omkar Sharan), 1936-
International economics / O.S. Shrivastava.
p. cm.
Includes index.
ISBN 9788180697906

1. International economic relations. 2. International trade. I. Title.

DDC 337 22

Preface

This book was first published in 1985. Thereafter it was revised six times. This is 2010 edition.

This book has been tailor-made for the students of M.A. and M.Phil. Economics. It not only covers the latest UGC syllabus of 2002 but also all the variants of all the Universities of India. We have so arranged the units of this book that there is more or less equal loading of the units. The topics relating to the commercial policies (tariffs, quotas, devaluation, subsidies, exchange rates management, exchange control, protection, etc.) have now become less relevant in the sense that the world has moved full circle from interventionist regimes to the free trade regimes under WTO. However, these topics are still of academic interest; they have not been consigned to the "economic museum". The emphasis has now become different. These are presented in various syllabi as (i) issues of commercial policies, (ii) exchange control, (iii) intervention modes of the governments, (iv) methods of correcting adverse balance of payments (v) (or simply as) balance of payment and balance of indebtedness. We have made our arrangements clear. Under the WTO regime (World Trade Organization), the orientation had to be changed.

The author has written 21 books on international economics, international finance and international business for MBA, M.Com., M. Phil (Economics), MA (Economics) BBM etc. and this book was the first of them. A legion of literature was consulted before writing this book. Wikipedia sites were also browsed. In the first edition of the book, chapterwise references were given but they extended to 16 pages. We have withdrawn the long list but whosoever is mentioned in the book his works were thoroughly consulted before writing this book. No plagiary was ever intended. We have presented the chapters in such a way that the students can prepare their own version of the topic to be written in the examination.

This book will also be found useful by those who are appearing in the UPSC, State PSCs, Bank PO, SLET, and NET examinations. The UPSC syllabus mentions only two topics viz., (i) comparative cost theory and subsequent developments and (ii) balance of payment. These two topics, however, cover the entire book. The first covers all topics of pure-theory and the second topic covers all topics of commercial policies, including Indian vista.

I thank my publishers for taking up the publication of this book. I used to receive in the past letters from esteemed members of the faculty as well as from the students. I shall be grateful if they care to write to me.

O.S. Shrivastava
M.A. B.Com., Ph. D.
88 Sector A, Kasturbanagar, Bhopal-24.

Contents

Unit I

Theory of International Trade

"Pure" Theories

1 International Economics: Subject Matter and Importance: Points of Similarities between National and International Trade: Cases for Free Trade Versus Protection

INTERNATIONAL TRADE AND INTERNATIONAL BUSINESS. DEFINITIONS: NATURE AND IMPORTANCE

International trade is trade of the visibles i.e., "commodities" (which come from the primary sector) and "goods" (which come from the manufacturing sector). "Business" includes trade in the "visibles and invisibles" i.e., services. Banking transactions, middlemen functions, use of transport services etc. are transactions of 'business'. Global trade and business require that trade be with countries covering all the continents but not necessarily all countries of the world. Trade between Tamil Nadu and Tripura involves very long distance but is still be domestic trade, while trade between Bihar and Nepal is international trade not involving long distances. The national boundaries should be crossed for international trade and or business. Now a days "insourcing" and "outsourcing" are also part of the international business as the transfers of capital (FDI; foreign direct investment and FII foreign institutional investment) are. Transfers of money in currency futures or forwards are part of international business. Commodities and goods go; money comes. Commodities and goods come; money goes out. Ultimately international trade and business are exchanges of commodities, goods and services from one side with the commodities goods and services from the other side with the help of a vehicle currency (as the US $). Money facilitates transactions. If there are no exports, there can be no imports. International trade and business involve exchange of a country's surpluses with the necessary, which in turn are the surpluses of the other country/countries.

International trade maximises the exchange values (prices) as well as the "utils" (units of utilities) or use values of the country. Producers, consumers and all stake holders in the trade and business get benefits.

Without international trade and business all countries of the world would have been (even in the 21st century) in the primitive stages of development. Developed countries could not have got their raw materials and the developing countries would not have got the advance technology and technology goods. International flows of capital enrich every country with thicker streams of commodities goods and services. *International economics teaches about all the topics listed in this book.* We know about the pure theories applied aspects policy issues and vista of international trade and business. *International economics is the study of the trading of merchandise and services between different countries as also of the capital movement, transfer of the components and instruments of internationals liquidity and international grants subsidies loans and unrequited remittance.*

The scope of international economics will cover the following:

(A) *The pure theory:* International economics has its own theory in which algebra and geometry are used extensively. It is archaic at times. However each theory gives a policy point. Theories are based on certain assumptions but they are not irrelevant. Theories emphasize why should nations trade and to what extent they should trade. Theory tells us that the comparative advantage and specialisation should be the bases of international trade. Offer curve analysis is the best of the best of theoretical formulations. It is the theory which tells us where to stop trading.

(B) *Commercial policies*: They relate to the issues of free trade versus protection. Exchange control, tariffs, quotas, devaluation, exchange rate mechanism and convertibility are all parts of commercial policies. We now discuss under this topic "what remains of the protectionism".

(C) *Applied international economics*: This is mainly addressed to the topics of international balance of payment and international balance of indebtedness. What is discussed under commercial policy can be discussed under this topic also. Infact this topic is much more comprehensive than the commercial policy. The topic addresses to the issues relating to converting adverse balance of payment to favourable balance of payment so that balance of indebtedness is brought down to zero. The objective is there but most countries seldom realise that. All micro and macro issues relating to the management of zero base balance of payment can be included under this.

(D) *International liquidity and economic integration.* Once paucity of international liquidity used to be a great issue and a topic of discussion. Now the shortage of international liquidity has eased. The world is moving towards greater economic integration due to transfer of technology and such arrangements as mergers and acquisitions joint ventures and franchise. There is trading in currency futures. There is trading in options and derivatives. Risk coverage is there through hedging and arbitrage. There is business also in them. If intellectual property rights are respected and payment of royalty is there then most advanced technology can be in the hands of the poor countries as well.

International economics teaches us about the applied aspects of free trade versus protection about tariffs and quotas about being member of a trading bloc, (not to be written as "block") about transfers of money, importance of hedging and arbitrage, about trading in options and derivatives, about exchange control, about free versus fluctuating exchange rates and about convertibility versus full or fuller (fuller is less than full) convertibility. International economics teaches us how a small and a big country can secure advantages from free trade. Present day studies in international economics and conducting international business address the "environment concerns" of the world. International economics teaches us how to minimise risks and maximise gains through competitive efficiencies. International economics teaches us how can all countries experience diffusion of technology and upgradation of all production lines. International economics teaches us the advantages of specialisation. It also teaches how to remove the bottlenecks in the expansion of international trade and business. Ultimately the global divergences that lead to international trade bring countries towards convergence. We also address questions of manpower development, transfer of technology anti-dumping measures, capital formation and investment.

International business is the consequence of upgradation of sectoral activities which, in turn get a boost from international trade and business. In the short run it may be the case of "trade replacing production"; in the long run more persons are gainfully employed. The world moved from ponies to supersonics and from smoke signals to multifaceted cell phones. *The importance of international trade and business can be understood if we thinks for a moment that there is no international trade and business. We will shudder to think about that.*

POINTS OF SIMILARITIES BETWEEN NATIONAL AND INTERNATIONAL TRADE

The fact that the two types of trade must be different is obvious. Everyone knows that there should be more differences than similarities. Management of two trades is very different. However the underlying principles are the same. Trade is trade. The main basis of trade is that things are purchased at a lower price and sold at a higher price for profits. In case of production the price is higher than the cost of production. In perfect competition we say that the "price is equal to the cost of production". In this case the normal profit is included in the cost of production. The cost of production covers (i) payment for raw materials and inputs (ii) payment of rent (iii) payment of wages and salaries (iv) payment of interest and (v) normal and reasonable residual recompense (profit) from price to the entrepreneurs and stake holders. Both types of the trades involve selling of the surplus and getting what is necessary but is not with us. The two trades are based upon minimisation of costs and maximisation of the receipts. Infact maximisation is aimed at reaching the point of, what may be called "maximum maximorum".

1. *The first point of similarity is that both types of trade are based upon specialisation. In domestic economic activities people, firms, companies etc.* specialises. A car company will not manufacture bicycles in the same plant. A doctor specialises in either general surgery or in ear nose and throat ENT ...... It is in the case of those who cannot get sufficient employment and income in one line of economic activity that two vocations may be there. Companies can also have broad banding i.e. may have two or more factories in different lines of activities. TATAs and Ambanies have stakes in many lines of economic activities. International export and import houses can also involve themselves in more than one line. However specialisation rather than multiple diversification is the rule in the same plant.

   Specialisation leads to trade; trade further strengthens specialisation. No one can produce everything. No country can practise autarky (self sufficiency on the basis of using/consuming only what is produced).

2. *Secondly, regions of the country and different countries specialise according to their factor endowments and sometimes what can be procured easily.* Bangladesh specialises in the export of jute and India in the export of tea due to factor endowments. Tea plants require iron rich land which should be slopy so that water

does not stagnate in the roots. Hence hilly regions with ampie rainfall are the necessary "factors" of production.

India procures diamonds and gold from South Africa and exports jewellery. Japan and Korea import iron and export things based on that.

(3) *Thirdly, the cardinal principle of trades is that immobilities lead to specialisation; specialisation leads to trade, and trade leads to mobilities, but never to the extent of perfect mobilities Land is totally immobile.* Labour is less mobile. So are entrepreneurs. Capital is more mobile. These immobilities are responsible for all countries not being able to produce all things. Hence people trade what they cannot produce with what they produce. Immobilities are overcome by international trade but not completely. Hence specialisation and trades continue inside and outside the countries.

(4) *Fourthly, both domestic and, international trade take place for maximising utilities as consumers and exchange values that bring profits) as producers.* Both types of trade are based upon the principles of minimum of sacrifice and maximum of gains whether as producer or consumer.

(5) *Fifthly, both types of trade take place in the difference between costs and prices.* This difference decides the direction of trade. If there is higher profit margin abroad the goods will be sold outside the country till the domestic prices rise. Inequalities in prices lead to trade; equalities of prices in two countries will stop the trade.

Points of Dissimilarities Between Domestic and International Trade

These dissimilarities are more in number as well as in effects. Bertil Ohlin (to be pronounced as OLEEN), wrote "international trade is a special case of inter-regional trade". He saw these dissimilarities. *(1) First, different monies (moneys) are used.* Even if some countries have the same name of the currency the exchange rates differ. India, Pakistan, Indonesia, and Seychelles have the name of their currency as "rupee". The exchange rate of Indian and Pakistani rupee was 1:1 at the time of Independence but in August 2008 one Indian rupee was equal to 1.78 Pakistani rupees. Indian rupee appreciated *vis a vis* Pak rupee. But it depreciated *vis a vis* US Dollar from $ 1. Rs. 4.5, to Rs. 43 in Aug. 2008 and to $ 1=Rs. 46.69 in Nov. 2009. Cheaper rate promotes exports. Dearer rate promotes imports. *(2) Secondly, international trade takes place on two prices.* One is the price of the goods in two countries and the second is the exchange rate. Even if the US charges the same amount of dollars for something they export to India, Indians will find the goods becoming dearer if the exchange rate of rupee falls. However the real exchange rate is important. If there is a fall in exchange rate to the tune of 10 p.c. when inflation difference is also 10 p.c. the real exchange rate is the same. (See chapter on exchange rates *(3) Thirdly, methods of remittances and exchange restrictions also create differences in the two types of the trade.* There are no restrictions for transfer of money between Tripura and Gujarat or Tamilnadu. But there can be restrictions on remittances between certain countries. That can influence the direction of the international trade. *(4) Differences in the mobility of the factors of production and trade.* The *degree* of mobility of factors differs from country to country. Englishmen were more mobile than the past Indians. Africans were less mobile than the Europeans. Imperfect mobilities exist but differ in degrees. Therefore rent, wages, interest and salary structures differ from country to country. That brings differences in the cost of productions and hence in prices. The extent and volumes of trade differ between countries and countries as prices differ. *(5) Fifthly the political factors also differ.* India granted to Pakistan the status of "MFN" i.e., the most favoured nation long back. But Pakistan did not grant the same status to India even by 2010. Hence India imports from Pakistan without restrictions. Pakistan puts restrictions on India's export to the country. There is a lot of money laundering between different countries. Smuggling allso differs from countries to countries and so do the "havala" transactions.

Even labour can be 'smuggled '. If a country is considered to be dream destination for livelihood (as the USA), then people go as tourists and then disappear. They may be caught some day but then they continue to work with changed identity. (6) Sixthly *there. are differences in exchange controls,* though the World Trade Organisation (WTO) has introduced the regimes of uniform pattern of import export taxes. Quotas and other measures of exchange controls, differ between country to country (though at lower level now) and they cause differences in trade between various countries. A day will come when the tariffs may be just upto 3.5 p.c. and there may be no quotes. The "caps" (maximum rates) of customs duties are already low. (7) Seventhly, the rates of exchange change daily now, difference between them are seldom equal to 0.5 rupees. The difference is less. (In India the rates prevailing at 4 p.m. are quoted as the rates of the day). If India's exchange rate falls, the exports become cheaper and imports dearer. If the exchange rate rises, imports become cheaper and exports dearer. There are no exchange rates of the domestic currency between the States of the country. (8) Eighthly, rates of inflation differ between countries. If the rate of inflation in India is 14 p.c. and in the USA it is 2 p.c. then Indian goods become costly to Americans. The exports will go down unless Indian exchange rate is allowed to fall by 12 p.c. (14-2=12) (9) Ninthly macro economic policies for, development differ. India and the USA may have different policies about subsidising agriculture, about protection of wages, about differential rates of interest, about rates of income tax, about rates of taxes on production, about quotas etc. The rates of unemployment and inflation differ. All these differences cause greater differences in international trade than in the domestic trade (10) Tenthly, differences in socio cultural values bring greater differences across the borders than inside the borders. Beef cannot be imported in India as pork cannot be imported in Pakistan. All countries have dress codes. Nigerian dress cannot be imported in India as 'mundu' cannot be exported to African countries. (11) Eleventhly, transport costs are more important in international business than in national business. There are traded and non-traded goods in international business. House construction brick is not traded between countries because it cannot bear the transport costs. Gold brick can bear the transport costs because it is a small percentage of the total value. India could not export its coal to Kenya and lost business to Australia (which is farther than India) because big ships could berth there in big ports end harbours (12) Twelvethly, stages of development affect international trade more profoundly than the domestic trade. A very backward region can trade with the most developed region inside the country. But a very poor country will find that it cannot export to a very rich country unless the rich country is taking the precious mineral from the country otherwise poor. The poor country may not be given enough foreign exchange by the exploiting country.

Types of International Trade

First we have "comparative advantage centric international trade. India sells spokes of bicycles to the USA though USA can export the most advanced bomber to India. The USA concentrates on the production of the goods that command high values. *Secondly, there is geocentric international trade.* It is promoted by the geographical advantages that a country has. Bangladesh has no coal so it imports. It produces a lot of jute and hence exports jute goods. *Thirdly there is ethnocentric international business.* Where ever Indians reside the shopkeepers/mall owners import things from India that are required by the Indians. China is a past master in producing goods needed by the Indians. *Fourthly, there is region centric international trade.* India's Bengal exports jute good. Kerala exports spices and cashew nuts. All socio economic, cultural and other traits are peculiar to different regions. The patterns of exports and imports of different regions of a country differ. *Fifthly, there are polycentric aspects that enter international trade.* This type of trade means that all the above factors are important and they determine the pattern of imports and exports of a country. India is a 'vast' country than Russia, though not in area but in all aspects of varied life. Hence India's exports and imports are much more varied than that of Russia.

Top Ten Reasons why International Trade is advantageous

[Advantages of free trade or case for tree trade].

(1) First, international trade has made the world a village and has promoted international cooperation. No country need produce everything. It can afford to specialise and take greatest possible advantage. Some other countries would produce things needed by it other than the goods of specialisation. In practice however most of the countries produce most of the goods, most of them for domestic consumption. India's domestic production profile is not limited to the goods exported. Infact most of the goods produced can be non internationally traded goods. Comparative advantage rules the international trade however.

(2) Secondly, producers maximise their exchange values (prices) and revenue (from the multiplication of prices with the goods involved). The consumers maximise their use values (utilities). Countries export what is surplus to them over and above their consumption requirements. They import those things which cannot be produced or cannot be produced in sufficient quantities. Thus goods of low value are exported and of high value (in terms of utilities) are imported. A country gets the double advantage. The counterpart country also gets the double advantage. Thus international trade becomes four cornered advantageous. Specialisation promotes international trade and international trade further promotes specialisation.

(3) Thirdly international trade elevates the consumers to the status of kings and queens. There is a popular saying in trade economics viz. "consumer is the king". Since the purchasing decisions are mostly taken by the ladies of the house we can say "consumer is the queen". Or we can safely say consumers are kings and queens. Demand decides which production lines can be sustained.

(4) Fourthly, international trade makes it possible to import the factors of production. Even India has for example invited foreigners to invest in infrastructure to the tune of $15000 crore. A country can import raw materials machines, turn-key projects, capital goods, heavy engineering goods, technology technocrats, wage goods or

other consumption goods. If we look around us we will find that all things around us were invented and improvised by the foreigners mostly.

(5) Fifthly, international trade alone makes it possible for a country—to improve the domestic production base which enables a country to have imports compression/ replacement and exports promotion. That enables a country to substantially reduce its adverse balance of payment. With luck and labour a country can bring its balance of payment to zero base i.e. neither surplus not deficit. Favourable balance of payment can be achieved by some countries mostly highly developed, or practising autarky to a large measure.

(6) Sixthly, free international trade increases employment generation and income propagation in a big~way. Initially there may be loss of employment as "trade replace production in some lines". But in the long run both employment and income generation improve. Long term technological unemployment is a myth. Weak units are eliminated (sun set industries) and emerging sun rise units prosper. Enduring employment and rising incomes improve levels of living.

(7) Seventhly, free international trade gives rise to a healthy circuit of capital formation and investment. Savings increase due to increase in income. Capital formation increases due to savings. Investment increases due to capital formation. The circuit can continue. Foreign direct investment (FDI) and foreign institutional investment (FII) also reinforce the formation of bigger and healthier circles of this circuit.

(8) Eighthly severe inflation and deflation get auto-corrected. If there is deflation/ depression lower prices help in the exports picking up. Money comes and deflation can end. If there is inflation foreign goods prove cheaper and imports can close the goods gap. Prices can come down.

(9) Ninthly, franchise, joint ventures, mergers and acquisition, etc, will improve the levels of technology. All the three sectors viz., the primary sector, the secondary sector and the tertiary sector will develop in unison.

(10) Tenthly, over all economic welfare increases. The socio-economic chasm gets bridged. Many island countries have become totally developed due to being tourists destinations of the rich. Many countries have shed the totem gods tribal economy and have become developed. Both economic and non-economic aspects develop. We can conclude by saying that free trade like honesty is the best policy. With some interventions from the State the countries can experience inclusive growth which provides benefits to all or which does not pass the disadvantaged and challenged persons or groups thereof in a country

Arguments in Favour of Protection, Case Against Unbriddled Free Trade

Free trade and globalisation have now become the order of the day. The world cannot move towards high degree of protectionism now. Some protectionism remains and surprising part is that the developed countries practise that more. It is a case of cat seeking protection against mouse.

(1) First is the infant industry argument. It is argued that infant industries need protection against the old industries. Old industries may indulge in dumping. The infant or the new industry may have to close down. The old industries will then raise the

prices and will recover the cost of price war. Mill had argued that only when protection is needed it should be given. It should not be given because the industry is new. Then protection should be ended as soon as possible. The dictum should be "nurse the baby", "protect the child", "advise the adolescent" and "leave the adult free".

(2) Secondly, free trade may mean a lot capital consumption. Hence to protect the capital investment protection may be given. That can, however, be done only when there is 'unfair' competition.

(3) Thirdly, self sufficiency becomes the casualty in competition. This is not correct because if we take the world in a broad perspective it is silly to use a costly thing when cheaper is available.

(4) Fourthly, free trade seldom permits poor countries to have favourable balance of payment. This may be true but favourable balance of utilities, pleasure, consumption, and input use are more important.

(5) Fifthly, balance of indebtedness increases and protection may be necessary. Adverse balance of payment on current account is there even in the USA. But free trade keeps a country better off than otherwise.

(6) Sixthly, multinational corporations flourish more, that is true but they can be kept under control if the administration is honest.

(7) Seventhly, free trade over-exploits the natural resources. Protection can help in their utilization for domestic production, as in the case for Bailladeela and Kudremukh iron ore mines in Chhatisgarh and Karnataka respectively.

(8) Eighthly, protection may be necessary sometimes somewhere if outflows are more than inflows of money,

(9) Ninthly, terms of trade go adverse and can be made favourable with protection. This is not true in the sense that mere protection can ensure that.

(10) Tenthly, defense of the country may be jeopardized, Defense of the country depened upon overall development and inner strength of the citizens and is not a function of protection.

2 Adam Smith's Theory of 'Absolute Difference in Costs' with M.E. Porter supporting, Ricardo's theory of comparative Advantage in Costs and Porter's Empirical Evidence

I. SMITH'S THEORY

Adam Smith was a 'free trader'. He was a liberal economist. He can be regarded as the founding father of the modern supply side economics. Adam Smith was an academic disciple of the physiocrats—who were liberal economists of France. Smith believed that the good of the world as a whole and the good of the individual nations cannot be separated. Similarly the good of the producers and the good of the consumers also cannot be separated – though Smith is sometimes accused of caring more for the good of the producers than of workers and consumers. Smith believed that the policy of non-interference in the economic affairs of the people—production, trade, price setting or consumption—can secure maximum exchange-values and use-values for all. Profits and satisfaction (and hence welfare) will increase most under the system of unbridled free enterprise. Economic freedom will also see that it does not lead to selfishness. If people want that their good should be promoted that will also see that no body can do something bad to them. This is the best guarantee that no body can do bad to others because others will not allow this to happen. Competition will ensure survival of the most efficient and weeding out of the inefficient. Weeding out of the inefficient is no doubt painful and inflicts losses but it will be good in the long run. Smith believed that there cannot be any under-production and over-production in the long run. No restrictions on international and external commerce (including on flow of gold) were necessary.

Adam Smith wanted that a country should export a commodity in which its cost advantage is the highest and should import that commodity in which the cost advantage (purchasing cheaper from outside) is again the highest.

Smith thus advocated both-way advantage. Later on Ricardo— as we shall see in succeeding pages of this chapter itself—advocated that if in importing something from abroad some loss is incurred, it may be incurred, provided this helps in diverting resources and manpower to that commodity in which the specialization advantages are the highest. This will bring the largest possible gain in net terms.

Smith made use of labour costs to illustrate the theory. In fact, his 'labour theory of value' which was later on developed more elaborately by Ricardo and was later on 'perfected' by Karl Marx can be traced to have its roots in Smith's writings. Smith was, however, aware of the limitations of using labour-costs as basis of illustrations. He regarded them the true costs (real costs which can be measured in terms of disutilities or pains experienced in production or leisure sacrificed) but was of the opinion that the concept is relevant only in those economies where people are "wood-cutters and draw out water from wells."

Two commodities exchange in proportion to the manhours contained in them or in terms of congealed labour. Commodities are embodiments of labour. He wrote:

"If among a nation of hunters, it usually costs twice the labour to kill a beaver which it does to kill a deer, one beaver should naturally exchange for or be worth two deer. If we assume this ratio to alter, say one beaver for three deer, then more people will concentrate on killing a larger number of beavers to take advantage of this altered ratio. This will increase the supply of beavers and reduce that of deer, causing a shift in the exchange ratio against beavers and in favour of deer, till once again the original ratio of exchange prevailed."

Adam Smith opined that an exporting industry must be able to produce, with a given amount of capital and labour, a larger output than any rival. This absolute advantage can be illustrated with the help of the following table:

Table 2.1: Cost of production in labour hours

Country	*Cloth*	*Wheat*	*Domestic exchange ratios (DERs) LH*	
America	20	10	20 : 10	or 2 : 1
Britain	10	20	10 : 20	or 1 : 2
				or ½ : 1

It is clear from the above, that America has absolute advantage in the production of wheat and Britain in the production of cloth. If both countries exchange at the ratio of 1: 1, then both the countries can get that commodity in which the other country has the absolute advantage in 10 hours.

Appreciation M.E. Porter recently wrote that if we import (say) cars, we compare *only absolute prices* for different qualities. We do not compare the bicyle versus the car prices *or their ratios*. Hence smith is *also* correct.

CRITICAL ESTIMATE

It seems Adam Smith never exercised his mind fully on *pure theory of* international trade. He probably was more interested in expounding the *philosophy* of free trade. His theory of absolute advantage in cost was probably merely illustrative. He probably meant that an exporting country must be able to produce with a given amount of capital and labour a larger output than any rival.

Smith's theory goes against the concept of specialisation and extension of territorial division of labour because a less developed country cannot hope to possess absolute advantage over a developed country either in agriculture or in industry. A developed country cannot allow it to compete in this way. It means a less developed country can never hope to export to any developed country. If this is so the developed country can also not hope to export anything to less developed country because the latter will not possess any international purchasing power. After all, capacity to import depends on the capacity to export.

A less developed country which has no absolute advantage in the production of anything will have to perforce follow the policy of autarky at low level of production and consumption. Pursuit of absolute advantage will probably completely stop multilateral trading rather than promote it.

Smith's implicitly assumed perfect competition and considered labour to be perfectly mobile. (These aspects are examined with reference to comparative cost theory, expounded hereafter.)

Smith's 'theory' was soon superseded by the Ricardian theory of comparative advantage. However, it is not the intrinsic merit of the theory that entitles it to have a place in international economics but the fact that it is the starting point of the comparative cost theory of international trade, that entitles it to be included in the study. Ricardo's theory removed the basic defect of the Smith's theory and is now universally regarded as the starting point of pure theory of international economics.

II. RICARDIAN THEORY OF COMPARATIVE ADVANTAGE IN COSTS: THE CLASSICAL THEORY

A. Introduction.
B. Factors that lead to specialisation and international trade and business.
C. History: Theory in nut-shell. Assumptions.
D. Diagrammatic illustrations of comparative differences in advantage/cost.
E. Explanations and examples.
F. Critical estimate of the theory:

(a) Criticisms that are valid in themselves but do not invalidate the theory (seven),
(b) Criticisms which invalidate the theory but only partially. (five).

Ricardo was one of the Trinity that created the classical economics; the other two were Adam Smith and Malthus. Smith is "father of economics," Ricardo is "father of international economics" and Malthus is the "father of demography" as well as "anticipator" of the Keynesian theory of effective demand, which was regarded as the "modern" economics of the 20th Century. Mill was apogee of classicism. Ricardo's theory of C.A. is simple:

(a) export that in which the comparative advantage in costs in the highest,
(b) follow the same principle for import as or if the imports are costlier than the domestics prices, the loss should be the least provided this enables the country to divert resources to the products of the highest advantage in costs.

Ricardo developed his theory of rent which explained that rent is the creation of value and not wealth. Rent goes on increasing due to rising population and diminishing returns in agriculture. Rent was regarded by him as unearned increment that accrues to the landlord. He regarded rising rent as the sole cause of falling profits. He was of the opinion that rising rent (function of rising population and falling agriculture productivity) will retard economic growth and in fact bring stationary state.

It was in this context that he advocated "free trade". Free trade—trade without restrictions, without punitive type tariffs and without quota restrictions—shall enable a country to import cheap corn from abroad. This will check the prices of corn going up and thus arrest the rise in rent. Thus Ricardo became a champion advocate of free trade. He wrote:

> "As it is disadvantageous to a single consumer to be restricted in his dealings to one particular shop, so is it disadvantageous for a nation of consumers to be obliged to purchase of one particular country."

Ricardo saw healthy circular relationship between free trade and economic development. Free trade helps in specialisation and specialisation is the result of free trade. International trade takes place between two countries because different countries differ in factor endowments. Some countries may be rich in natural resources, others in human resources (labour) and still others in capital resources. This will make them specialize in different types of goods. The first category country will produce goods which will have more natural resource contents in the goods (agricultural goods, plantation produce, ores etc.) The second category country will produce and export those goods which make intensive use of labour (such as handicraft goods) and the third category country will produce those goods which have more capital-contents (machinery).

B. Factors That Lead to Specialisation and International Trade

International trade takes place because factors of production are not mobile between different countries, and thus different countries have different structures of cost of production for the same commodities.

Factors of production can be assumed to be perfectly mobile (except land) but they cannot be so mobile between the two countries. Thus Ricardo assumes that there will be one cost of production in the entire country for one commodity but the cost of production for the same commodity between various countries cannot be the same. Hence costs differ. There can be one wage rate, one interest rate or one price of (say) cotton in a country but the wage rates, interest-rates and commodity prices will differ from country to country. Thus cost of production may be the same inside the country but will be different between the two countries.

Mobility of factors equalizes the cost of production and immobility of factors creates differences in costs. If there are differences in costs because of various reasons (including the reason of differences in natural endowments) then trade will take place. If people cannot produce some goods at the same cost at which others produce, they will have to leave the production of those goods. This will promote specialization. Specialization is the opposite of autarky. If every country can produce all goods (of equally good quality) at the same cost, then there is no need for trade. All countries can produce all goods and thus become self-sufficient, or can practise autarky. Since this does not happen, international trade takes place and should take place.

International trade, according to Ricardo, helps in producing various things at the cheapest cost and also enables the producers to obtain the highest possible prices. At the same time free international trade enables a buyer to obtain things at the cheapest possible prices. Free international trade, according to Ricardo, makes importation of cheap raw materials and food possible and this helps in maintaining the real wage-level at stationary level. Free trade stimulates industry, rewards ingenuity, helps in using most efficaciously the peculiar powers bestowed by nature and thus helps in distribution of labour most economically. Free trade makes it possible to extend division of labour at international level. World income too is raised by a more efficient utilisation of resources. Income from foreign trade helps capital accumulation and further investment and growth.

Ricardo pointed out that immobility of factors, particularly of labour, is the sole cause of differing exchange ratios between 'A' and 'B' goods in two countries. This immobility makes it impossible for applying the "labour cost theory of value" in international trade. If labour were to be perfectly mobile between the two countries, then different commodities would exchange in the ratio of the quantities of labour congealed in different commodities. Thus the exchange ratio (selling price) will be the same as cost-ratio (including normal profit). Nobody can charge a exchange ratio which is higher than the cost-ratio. If one does, market mechanism will make this difficult. If exchange value is higher than the cost-ratio, it means labour will find it lucrative to move to this industry. If exchange ratio is lower than the cost-ratio (loss), then the labour shall move out of this industry. Thus price will always equal to the labour cost of production. Perfect mobility of labour will equalize the labour-contents of goods and thus wages. When factors of production become immobile between the two countries, the exchange ratios of two countries will differ which give rise to international trade.

C. Theory in Nut-Shell; Assumptions

Torrens is credited for first conceiving the theory of comparative advantage in international trade. His theory came two years earlier in 1815 than of Ricardo. Schumpeter wrote that the theory of comparative advantage was baptised by Torrens but was elaborated by Ricardo.

The great economist Marshall has, however, after studiously examining the contributions of all economists, come to the conclusion that Ricardo deserves the rightful place for being credited as the *Father of International Economics*. Marshall wrote:

"The masterly genius of Ricardo, like that of Adam Smith, was largely occupied with the supreme task of building up a number of fragmentary truths into a coherent doctrine. Such a doctrine has constructive force, because it is organic whole."

Theory and its Assumptions

The essence of the Ricardian theory of international trade is that trade should be based upon comparative advantage. International trade cannot take place if the domestic exchange ratio (DERs) or barter terms of trade (BTT) or domestic exchange ratios (DERs) of two countries are the same. The cost ratios must differ. The cost difference must be in comparative terms. It has been emphasized that even if absolute advantage exists in both commodities, trade cannot take place unless the advantage is at the same time comparative. Comparative advantage involves absolute advantage, but the opposite of this need not always be true.

Ricardo wanted international trade to be free. He gave two principles: (i) a country should export that commodity in which the relative advantage is the highest and (ii) can import a commodity even if there is disadvantage in doing so, provided this enables the country to divert the resources to specialized commodity; however, in this case the disadvantage should be the least.

Ricardian theory of comparative advantage is based upon certain assumptions.

(1) Costs are to be calculated in labour terms. They can be calculated thus, because even if machines are used in manufacturing, machine hours can be converted into labour hours. Labour is the true measure of value in Ricardian theory. (However, even if costs are to be calculated in money terms, the theory remains valid).

(2) There is free competition in the factor and product markets. All factors of production are rational, knowledgeable and mobile. There is full employment. The theory is spelled out in terms of 'long period'.

(3) Constant labour costs are assumed. Thus, a neutral production function is assumed.

(4) For the sake of convenience, two countries and two commodities model is developed by Ricardo.

(5) Labour units are considered to be of homogeneous quality and almost completely mobile inside the country but not so between the two countries. Immobility gives rise to differences in cost hence to specialisation and trade.

(6) Since inputs vary with commodities, different commodities have different values inside and outside the countries. All cost differences are not equalized.

(7) Transport costs are assumed away. They are treated as being equal in both way trade, or it is assumed that comparative advantage is calculated after taking them into account.

(8) Demand is not considered to be deficient for either international market or national market. No one produces but for the purpose of consumption of the goods produced by others and self.

The principal cause of the emergence of international trade is the existence of comparative advantage in costs of production. For example, if 'a' and 'b' commodities cost 4 and 8 labour hours respectively in 'A' country while the same commodities cost 6 and 12 hours in 'B' country, there is absolute advantage in costs in 'A' country but the advantage is not comparative. In both the countries the ratio is 2: 1 between two commodities. Hence there will be no trade because the absolute advantage is not comparative also.

The principles of trade are:

(A) Export the commodity in which the comparative advantage is the highest i.e., that commodity which is produced cheapest in this country. This will ensure world-wide demand. It is in this commodity that specialisation should be strengthened.

(B) Import that commodity in which the comparative advantage is again the highest i.e., that commodity which is produced most dearly in this country and most cheaply in other country, provided this advantage is at the same time comparative also.

(C) However, if circumstances so require then a country can import a commodity at loss also, provided this enables the diversion of our scarce resources to the commodity of our specialisation.

In this case, *import that commodity in which the loss is the least*. In other words, this commodity should be imported from that country which is next to our country in terms of producing it cheaper.

A few examples can be given. A botanist can be a good gardener also. Yet, he would find it more profitable to engage himself in the best suited activity viz., the activity of doing researches as botanist, and engage a gardener. Engagement of gardener involves costs, the same way as import of a dearer commodity. However, the time and energy that a botanist can save, can be utilised in better pursuits. This will be true 'economy'. Doing both jobs can be false economy. Similarly, a physician can be a good compounder but the physician should always keep himself engaged in the specialised job of a physician. A university teacher can very well teach his primary school-going children, but it will be prudent to engage a tutor so that the university teacher can devote more time to those activities which will increase his efficiency in the main job.

This principle ensures that opportunity gains far exceed the opportunity costs of specialisation. This is the true principle of specialisation on which the. principle of comparative difference in cost is based upon.

D. Diagrammatic Illustrations of Comparative Differences/ Advantages in Cost

The production possibility curves can be used to illustrate the comparative advantage.

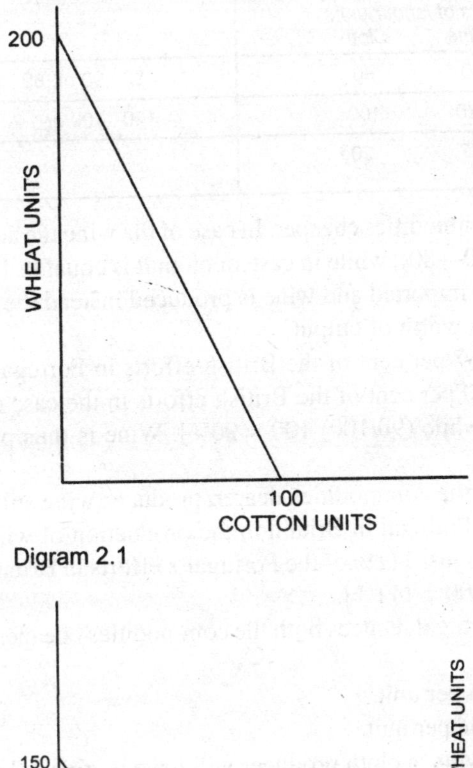

Digram 2.1

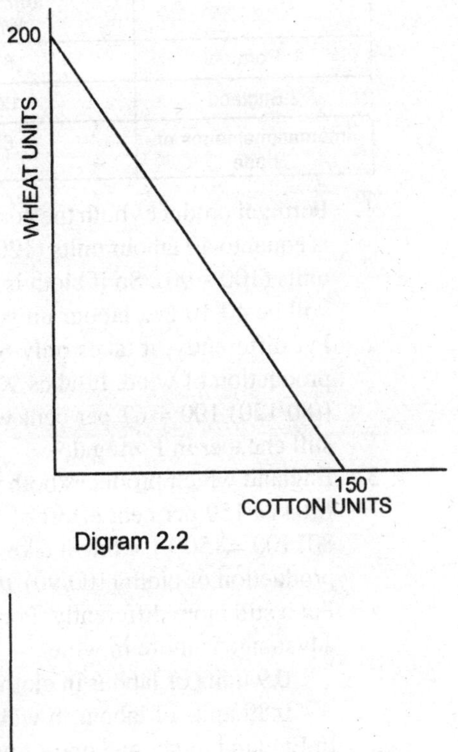

Digram 2.2

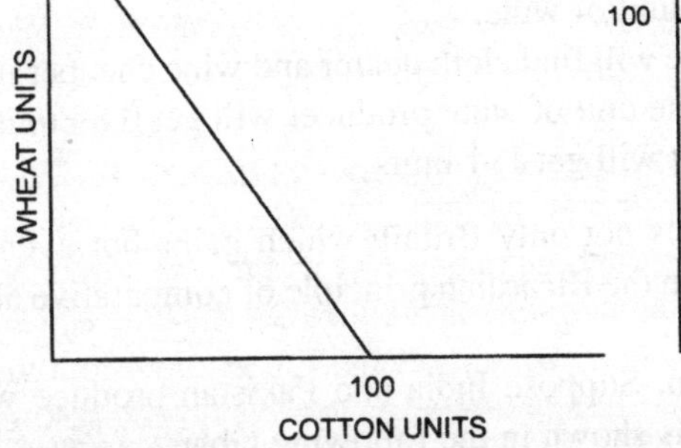

Digram 2.3

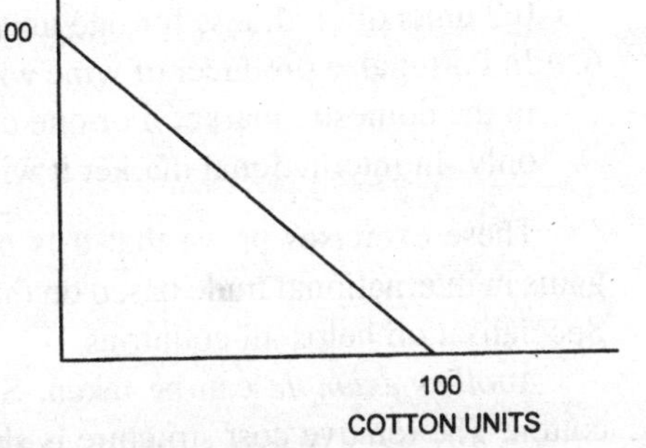

Digram 2.3

In the second set, it is shown that with the same amount of inputs (costs), 'A' country produces more wheat. This gives comparative advantage of cost in wheat to 'A' country.

E. Explanation and Examples

Suppose there are two countries, Britain and Portugal, both producing wine and cloth. The cost position is as under:

Table 2.2:

Country	Cost of production per unit of commodity in terms of labour units Wine	Cloth	Domestic exchange ratios
1. Portugal	80	90	80 : 90 or .89 : 1
2.England	120	100	120 : 100 or 1.2 : 1
International terms of trade	.67	.90	

1. Portugal produces both the commodities cheaper. In case of the wine the advantage is equal to 40 labour units (120—80), while in case of cloth it is equal to 10 labour units (100—90). So if cloth is imported and wine is produced instead the net gain will be 40-10 i.e., labour units worth of output.
2. Put differently, it takes only 67 per cent of the British efforts in Portugal for the production of wine. It takes 90 per cent of the British efforts in the case of cloth. [(80/120) 100 = 67 per cent while (90/100) 100 = 90%]. Wine is thus produced still cheaper in Portugal.
3. England which produces both the commodities dearer, produces wine still dearer. It takes 150 per cent effort of Portugal in Britain in the production of wine (120/80) 100 = 150%], while it takes just 111% of the Portugal's efforts in Britain in the production of cloth (100/90) 100 = 111%].
4. Put it still more differently, Portugal reduces both the commodities cheaper but the advantage is more in wine.
   0.9 units of labour in cloth per unit.
   0.89 units of labour in wine per unit.
5. In England to get one unit of wine, a cloth producer will have to give 1.2 units of cloth. In international trade (when the exchange will be 1: 1) England will sacrifice 0.2 units of cloth less for one unit of wine.
6. In Portugal, a producer of wine will find cloth dearer and wine cheaper if disposed in the domestic market. For one unit of wine producer will get 0.89 units of cloth only. In international market it will get 1: 1 units.

These exercises prove that it is not only Britain which gains but even Portugal gains in international trade based on the Ricardian principle of comparative advantage. Specialisation helps all countries.

Another example can be taken. Suppose India and Pakistan produce wheat and cotton. The relative cost structure is shown in the following table:

Table 2.3

	Country	Number of man-days required for producing 1 unit of	
		Wheat	cotton
1.	India	8	9
2.	Pakistan	12	10

(1) In the above example, Pakistan produces both the things dearer compared with India but its "inefficiency" and "circumstantial disadvantages" are more pronounced in wheat. The disadvantage in cotton is lower than is in wheat. India has greater comparative advantages in wheat, therefore. So India should leave cotton growing for Pakistan and incur a small loss in importing the same. This will enable India to divert its capital, labour and land to the production of wheat and gain still more.

(2) In India wheat is being produced at 0.66: 1 ratio while 0.9: 1 ratio obtains in cotton vis-a-vis Pakistan. International terms of trade are more favourable in wheat for India. In India cotton is 'costlier' because more mandays are required to produce it. Hence in India the DERs are such that less of cotton is available for wheat:

1 unit of wheat exchanges for 0.89 units of cotton or
1 unit of cotton exchanges for 1.13 units of wheat.

(3) In Pakistan the loss in wheat is greater (12/8 is greater than10/9) than in the production of cotton. The domestic exchange ratio in Pakistan are:

1 unit of wheat exchanges for 1.2 units of cotton or
1 unit of cotton exchanges for 0.83 units of wheat.

Wheat is costlier and cotton cheaper because more man-days are required to produce wheat in Pakistan.

Let it be presumed that labour cost of production are:

wheat in India........................ C_1
wheat in Pakistan...................... ..C_2
cotton in India..................................C_3
cotton in Pakistan.............................C4

There is comparative difference in cost if the condition

$$\frac{C_1}{C_2} < 1; \frac{C_3}{C_4} < 1 \text{ holds good.}$$

In our example 0.66 < 0.9 < 1, shows that while India has absolute advantage over Pakistan in the production of both the commodities, the comparative advantage of India (or the comparative disadvantage of Pakistan) is greater in wheat.

International trade does not take place under the condition of equal difference in cost.

Table 2.4: Equal Difference in Cost: Costs in Labour Terms

	Wheat	*Cotton*
India	8	16
Pakistan	12	24

In the above example, India has absolute advantage in the production of both the commodities. *But the absolute advantage is not comparative is not comparative.*

In India the domestic exchange ratio between wheat and cotton will be the same as in Pakistan. Wheat is cheaper in both the countries because it is less costly. The D.E.Rs in both the countries are 2: 1. Neither country will find it profitable to import or export. Any commodity can be had inside the country at the same price (in terms of the other commodity), as prevails in the other country. There is no opportunity cost involved nor there is any opportunity gain. By not trading no country gains or loses anything.

The above difference in cost which is absolute without being comparative may probably be due to differences in the efficiency of the factors of production. Factors of production in India are apparently more efficient and hence less number of labour hours are required to produce a given output.

If differences in efficiency do not lead to comparative differences in costs, they are irrelevant for international trade. This theme was taken up in the theory of international trade by Heckscher and Ohlin (discussed in a separate chapter). They are of the opinion that it is the difference in the factor endowments (quantities and not merely in qualities) that causes differences in the comparative cost structure. These differences bring differences in the domestic exchange ratios of the two countries and the flow of trade will be towards that direction where the IER or ITT (international exchange ratio or international terms of trade) are higher than DER or DTT or BTT (barter terms of trade).

F. Critical Estimate of the Theory

Alterations and Extensions

The comparative cost theory of international trade is the starting point of all further speculations and discussions in this regard. We divide the criticisms of the theory into two types:

(a) criticisms which are valid in themselves but do not invalidate the theory, if the effect of criticism is incorporated in the theory;

(b) criticisms which are valid and make the theory partially invalid.

The former category of the criticisms can be regarded as additions and alterations or even extensions. The opportunity cost theory of international trade (developed by Haberler and also known as the neo-classical theory of international trade) and the Heckscher-Ohlin theory of international trade (also known as the modern theory of 20th century of international trade) belong to the first category.

However, Mill and Marshall developed theories which cannot be regarded merely alterations but have to be regarded as independent theories. Ricardo, Haberler, Heckscher and Ohlin emphasized the supply (cost) aspects in international trade while Mill and Marshall emphasized the demand aspects. This is not to say that either of them was neglecting the other aspect. They simply took one aspect explicitly and the other one was taken implicitly. We cannot expect the economists of their eminence to be unaware of the second aspect of a theory.

(A) Criticisms which are Valid in themselves but do not Invalidate the Theory:

1. *First, the theory wrongly uses labour costs. Mill's criticism:* Expression of costs in terms of labour hours is a crude method. Labour is the only factor of production only in a very rudimentary economy—where tribals eat what they find rather than what they grow. In modern round-about system of production, land, capital, organisation, technology and enterprise elements enter into costs. Theoretically even machine costs can be converted into labour costs because after all "capital is stored up labour", but from practical point of view this is simply unworkable. Ricardo believed that imputed value of all other costs can be expressed in terms of labour-costs but this was a useless exercise. Costs should, therefore, be expressed in money terms.

Defense. Even if the costs are expressed in money terms the theory stands. The theory emphasizes that a country should export that commodity in which the comparative advantage is the highest and import that commodity in which the disadvantage is the least. This proposition is valid whether the costs are expressed in labour terms or in money terms.

2. *Secondly, the comparative cost theory disregards heterogeneous character of labour.* Ricardian theory of comparative advantage is based upon the assumption of homogeneous character of labour. Labour is assumed to be perfectly mobile in a perfectly competitive labour and product market. These assumptions are not correct. Labour differs in skill (there are several skill groups), and therefore wages differ. Existence of non-competitive groups and imperfections in mobility keep wage differentials. In modern day set-up where trade unions exist, in fact there are both centripetal and centrifugal tendencies in wage differentials. Language barriers, cost of migration, uncertainties relating to employment, high cost of living elsewhere, discriminations of various sorts, socio-cultural differences in living, climatic differences, love of one's surroundings are responsible for various types of barriers on inter-regional mobility of labour.

Thus the concept of real cost used by Ricardo (measurement of costs in terms of disutilities) was incorrect. The classical economists had assumed that disutilities involved in the production of various goods were proportional to the amount of labour embodied in their production. This was incorrect assumption.

Defense. Some economists have tried to prove that despite the above criticism the theory can generally be regarded as valid. If the hierarchy of different grades in two countries is the same i.e., if the relative position of labour groups is the same, then Ricardian theory is not invalidated. If trade union pressures are alike in all free countries, the relative position remains the same. *Taussig* advanced this plea. It can be seen that while Taussig's defense may have validity if we compare conditions in developed countries versus other developed countries, but the same will not hold good in case of say USA and a poor country. Thus the criticism and the defence are only partially valid or, to put it differently partially invalid.

3. *Comparative cost theory neglects transport costs as well as capital charges.* It was pointed out that India lost coal market in east Africa (now Kenya) to Australia because big ships could berth in Australia and this reduced transport costs. Transport costs matter, while in the comparative cost theory it was assumed that they do not matter. Transport costs can alter the trade pattern. During the 19th century and even in the early 20th century some regions of Germany used to import coal from England because of lower transport costs, while some regions of Germany were producing and exporting coal. It was probably assumed by Ricardo that exporter bears the cost of transport.

It is also pointed out that there are capital charges. Wages are not the only costs of production. There is interest payment also, particularly when there are storage charges due to time-lag between production and sale.

Defence: In this case also the criticism does not invalidate the theory. All that is to be done is to calculate the comparative advantage after-taking into account the transport cost. Costs may be assumed to be inclusive of the transport costs (as they are assumed to include normal profits). It is quite correct that the comparative advantage can be wiped off by transport costs, but the true nature of the comparative costs may be said to be revealed after they are taken into account.

Similarly if the interest rate and capital-labour ratio on the same range of commodities bear the same ratio between different commodities in two countries, the theory is not invalidated. Even otherwise, the probable storage (interest) charges are added in costs. Hence the comparative advantage can be calculated after adding this cost. Thus the theory is not invalidated. As written earlier, its truism viz., export that commodity in which the comparative advantage is the highest and import that commodity in which the comparative inefficiency is the least, stands.

4. *The theory is based on a very narrow assumption of two countries and two commodities.*' It has been pointed out that it is highly restrictive assumption to limit the examples of the theory to two countries and two commodities. Trade takes place in thousands of commodities and between over hundred countries.

Defence: The neo-classical writers, notably Haberler, Edgeworth and Mangoldt, have demonstrated the validity of the theory in multi-commodity and multi-country set-up. They are of the opinion that the criticism of Ricardian theory being too restrictive is valid, but it does not invalidate the theory. Even if the model is extended to several countries and several commodities, it stands.

Haberler explained this thus: 'The following paras are adaptations).

Suppose there are two countries, India and Pakistan. There are five commodities 'A', 'B', 'C, 'U and 'E'. Let us now consider about the cost and price aspects of commodities.

Cost is equal to man-hours congealed in a commodity (h) or (m) for India and Pak. multiplied by wages per hour (w).

Money cost or price will be equal to the above multiplied by the rate of exchange (R)." hw. R

For various goods we can use the subscripts 1, 2, 3, 4 and 5 for both countries and for wages we can use subscripts I for India and P for Pakistan.

Table 2.5:

Commodity	*Prices in India*	*Prices in Pakistan*
A	h_1. W_I R	m_1. W_P
B	h_2. W_I. R	m_2. Wp
C	h_3. W_I. R	m_3. Wp
D	h_4. W_I. R	m_4. W_P
E	h_5. W_I. R	m_5. W_P

h. depicts man-hours in India while m depicts man-hours in Pakistan.

In the above example R exchange rate has been used for India only and not for Pakistan because the exchange rate expressed the units of currency of Pakistan which exchange one unit of currency of India. If Pakistani currency is expressed in terms of Indian currency, then we will use R for Pakistan.

Pakistan can export those commodities in which its export price (also known as supply price or money costs) is lower than the export price of India, and shall import that commodity in which India is in similar position. If commodity 'A' is to be exported from Pakistan, the following conditions of inequality (equality condition will not permit trade) should prevail.

$$m_1.wp < h_1.w_1.r$$

$$\text{or} \quad \frac{m_1}{h_1} < \frac{w_{1.r}}{wp}$$

For 'B' commodity the same equation can be modified by substituting the subcript (2) or (1). Thus if Pak. imports 'B'

$$m_2 wp > h_2.w_1.r$$

$$or \quad \frac{m_2}{h_2} > \frac{w_{1.r}}{wp}$$

$$\text{Then} \quad \frac{m_1}{h_1} > \frac{m_2}{h_2}$$

Pakistan has comparative advantage in the commodity 'A' over India. Samuelson opined that the commodities can be arranged in order of comparative advantage as "the beads in a string". Thus:

$$\frac{m_1}{h_1} < \frac{m_2}{h_2} < \frac{m_3}{h_3} < \frac{m_4}{h_4} < \frac{m_5}{h_5}$$

WHERE WILL THE DIVIDING LINE OF TRADE LIE?

The question is that where there are several commodities where will the dividing line lie ? Naturally the cost data will decide this. However, the demand conditions play a very important part in this. Naturally if the demand for goods produced in Pakistan is high in India (inelastic also), the list will get more commodities included despite little cost differences.

It can also be imagined that R or rate of exchange will also decide the dividing line. If the foreign exchange rate rises (in the sense that the foreign country's currency becomes costly), then costs alter—become costlier to the importing country. Comparative advantage may also shift.

If more working hours are required in manufacturing a commodity and if the wages rise, then also the costs rise. An example can by given:

Table 2.6:

Costs	Commodities									
	A	B	C	D	E	F	G	H	I	J
India	20	18	17	16	15	14	13	12	11	10
Pakistan	30	28	25	20	15	10	8	7	6	4

In the above example the dividing line is at 15 on commodity 'E'. This will not enter in trade. India will export 'A', 'B', 'C and 'D', while Pakistan will export 'F', 'G', T and 'J'. (This example has nothing to do with the previous example of 'A', 'B', 'C,'D' and 'E' goods.)

The cost structure changes when man-hour ratio; wage-ratio and exchange rates undergo change i.e., when *m/h*, W_1/Wp and R change. Some additional observations can be made.

(a) If balance of payments becomes adverse against India, then India loses gold to Pakistan. Pakistan gains gold and its currency expands. The export multiplier (see chapter on foreign trade multiplier) in Pakistan will raise income. In Pakistan both the money supply and monetary incomes rise. Wage will rise. Cost of production will go up. Thus the wages ratio will go against Pakistan. In other words, as WP go up relative to WJ, the WP/WI.R goes up. Costs rise in Pakistan and they go down (relatively) in India. Thus the export line of India will shift to the right.

(b) If wages in India rise due to trade union pressure (competitive model is distorted), then the dividing line will shift to the left. If wages in Pakistan rise relativeiy, the dividing line will shift to the right.

(c) If the exchange rate of India improves (Indian currency becomes costly to Pakistan), things become costly to Pakistan and the dividing line will shift to the left.

Conclusion. Though it is correct that even in multi-commodity model, the comparative cost theory stands, it will be erroneous to regard this as mere 'defense' of the theory. Haberler's theory is an extension of the theory. The entire elaboration is an improvement over the Ricardian theory of comparative advantage in international trade.

5. *Fifthly, the theory of comparative advantage in international trade is based on two-country model and hence is unsuitable for multi-country setup.*

Defence: This is also a valid criticism, which, however, does not invalidate the theory. All that is to be done is to treat all other countries as "rest of the world." For example, if there are 'A', 'B', 'C, 'D' countries producing respectively 'a', 'b', 'c', 'd' goods then the hierarchy of countries on the basis of comparative advantage is to be established. For example, if it is established that 'a' commodity can be imported from 'A' country (because 'A' possesses the greatest comparative advantage in cost over other countries), then for the purpose of the import and export of 'a' commodity in" 'B' countries, only 'A' country exists; all other countries are ignored. Here bilateral trade conditions will rule supreme and demand conditions will also play important part.

Conclusion: This is a definite improvement over the theory.

6. *The comparative cost theory expresses cost in terms of labour unit. Neither this nor the expression of costs in terms of money is correct. Haberler is of the opinion that costs should be expressed in "opportunity-cost*" terms. (See chapter (5) The cost of producing additional wheat in India will be that less of cotton can be produced. Therefore, opportunity cost shows true sacrifice.

Defence: This *may* be regarded as valid criticism and cost may be expressed in terms of "opportunity costs". However, it may be doubted whether this will be practical way of expressing the costs. Even if this is considered more correct on pedagogic grounds, the criticism does not invalidate the theory. In the words of *Lipsey:*

"A country has a comparative advantage vis-a-vis a second country in the production of the commodity in which it has a lower opportunity cost"

The fundamental principle of trade shall remain the same; viz, export that commodity in which "opportunity gain" is the highest and import that commodity in which the loss of such "opportunity loss" is the lowest.

7. It has been argued that the comparative cost or advantage theory of international trade unrealistically assumes that costs are constant. It is wrong to assume in the modern dynamic world—and the world was not less dynamic relatively in Ricardo's time—that production follows constant production function. Technological developments are not neutral. It is not correct to assume that the cost of production remains the same in any size of the scale of production. The usual pattern of production is that producers try for increasing returns to scale by several methods. They innovate, rationalize or develop appropriate technology. However, ultimately diseconomies overcome the economies. Thus while increasing returns to scale may be normal in the 'short period', decreasing returns to scale shall operate in the 'long period'. Increasing costs may gradually wipe off the comparative advantage. Decreasing costs may give emergence to comparative advantage where comparative disadvantage existed in the past.

Defence: This argument too may be regarded as valid but this does not invalidate the theory. Suppose there were two countries 'A' and 'B' exporting respectively 'a' and 'b' goods. If the law of decreasing returns applies in both countries, then the relative position does not change. If it applies in different proportions, and the comparative advantage gets 'distorted', then it is quite possible that 'A' country may export 'b' good and the 'B' country may export 'a' good. The fundamental prepositions remain the same.

(B) Criticisms which Invalidate the Theory, at Least Partially:

1. The theory of comparative advantage as developed by Ricardo is one-sided theory after all. Only supply aspects have been taken into account and the *theory completely neglects the demand aspects.* With regard to the multi-commodity and multi-country cases, only the inclusion of demand conditions comes to the rescue of the theory. Consumer tastes change the production function. The income and expenditure (also savings) pattern in a country changes the demand pattern and hence the production and costs pattern. Demand conditions change the quality and quantity of things produced.
2. *Graham, Heckscher and Ohlin have proved that, it is not the complete specialisation that is necessary or desirable.* From practical point of view, complete specialisation is harmful from the defence standpoint. Complete specialisation will neither utilize the natural resources of the country fully nor shall provide full employment to either labour or capital of the country. Partial specialisation will provide not only full employment but shall also be desirable from other socio-political points of view. Partial autarky and partial specialisation is now the order of the day. (see chapter on Heckscher-Ohlin theorem).
3. *Specialisation also depends on the type of commodity.* It is scarcely possible for a country producing low-value bulky goods and to specialize in comparison to another country producing high-value light goods.
4. *According of Graham the theory is valid only when two countries trade in two commodities of approximately equal total consumption value and the two countries are of equal economic importance.* However, here smallness and bigness do no mean small or big in area but in economic output. Now India and Japan are unequal competitors, the latter being bigger.

Graham has made an interesting observation *viz.*, the smallness of a country is an advantage rather than disadvantage in one respect. A big country has to diversify its production to meet various domestic needs, while a small country can specialise with *relative* ease. There is an additional advantage. A small country cannot absorb all the exportable surplus of the big country but the rich country can. Thus, being small is beautiful.

5. *The theory of comparative advantage is not so relevant now in these days of restrictive trade practices.* A theory will be a mere tautology if we find nothing in the world supports it. East Pakistan (now Bangladesh) could import very cheap coal from India just across the border, yet it imported coal at a very high price from China. East Pakistan used to deny India its raw jute (99 per cent jute mills remained in India after partition, while 95 per cent jute growing area remained in East Pakistan) and India had to grow jute at high cost in Bengal, Orissa and even in some patches in Southern India.

III. EMPIRICAL EVIDENCE. MICHEAL E. PORTER'S THEORY OF "NATIONAL ABSOLUTE ADVANTAGE" IN INTERNATIONAL BUSINESS

Porter tried to prove that at national level the exporters and the importers do not bother to know about the domestic exchange ratios of different commodities and goods. They compare the absolute differences in the costs. [Say, if the same or the similar car comes in $ 1000 less than the other, people will go in for the cheaper car of the same quality]. Absolute differences in costs matter; they decide the business... both national and international.

Secondly, he based his theory upon four corner-stones viz., (i) factors of production, (ii) demand, (iii) competitive advantage and (iv) strategies.

Porter argued that the factors and resources of a nation are "general" in their original form. They are to be made specific and specialised when discovered and made of quality. Skilled labour brings goods of high quality and they enter into international business. Demand of course is another factor to match with the supplies. Supplies have to be abundant and of quality. Goods of technology supplied at competitive prices create market *i.e.,* create demand.

A nation can have competitive edge over others if the industries of the nation are developed in clusters where supplementary and complementary relations develop between industries. Then only they can find important place in the domestic and/or international market. Porter does not use the words "comparative advantage" but "competitive advantage". Associated with the above are proper strategies of business.

These are the four important corner-stones of international business on which edifice... looking like a diamond... is or can be erected. Porter's theory was micro-economic as against the macro-economic theories of all other authors.

We can "construct this diamond which can be of any size.

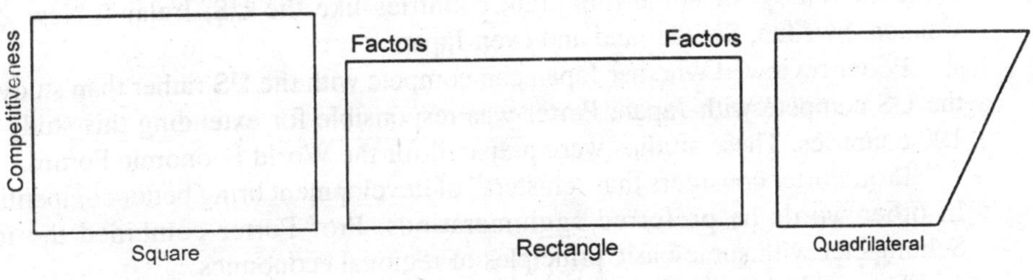

The foreigners (West) have their own "mutual appreciation society" and make a mountain of a mole hill. [The west did not award Nobel Peace Prize to Mahatma Gandhiji who started the demoliation of imperialism in the world without violence.]

Suppose we construct a "real" diamond with six still more important, determinants of international business:

(i) resources, technology and adequacy of production of quality,
(ii) demand—high and perpetual
(iii) fair prices, competitive prices
(iv) non-restrictive markets,
(v) global facilitation of all types-linkage and monetary, and,
(vi) government and all external elements.

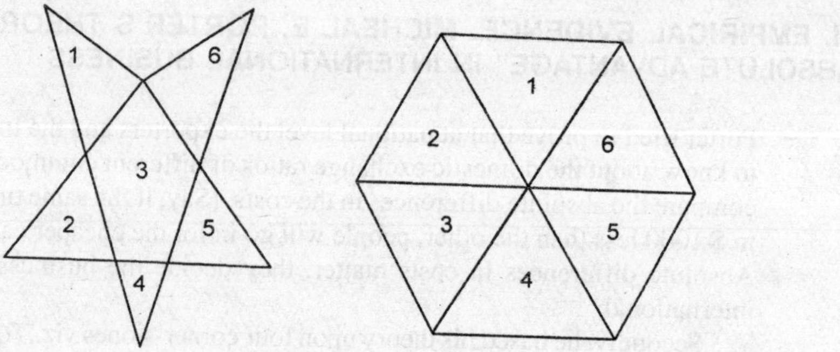

Fig.

Diamonds can be proportional and non-proportional. These factors are more important and these diamonds are more realistic but the Western World will not bother about such presentations.

Prof. Porter, a philanthropist, MBA of 1971 batch of Harvard School of Business, wrote about innovations. He studied the "comparative national innovative capacities". Prof. Porter advocated competition and control on monopolies and oligopolies for domestic as well as international business. His important works are in the post 2000 period starting from 1980s.

Porter advocated competitiveness and environmental improvements to be complementary. Porter's book (1990), "The Competitive Advantage of Nations" was motivated by his appointment in 1983 by the late US President Ronald Reagan to the "Commission on Competitiveness". Porter was of the view that if a nation can beat others in competitions, then all sectors, regions and groups of persons develop.

His main works relate to judging the competitiveness (or the relative competitiveness) of some important countries like the US, Ireland, New Zealand, Canada, Sweden, Switzerland and even Japan.

Porter reviewed whether Japan can compete with the US rather than studying can the US compete with Japan. Porter was responsible for extending this study to over 100 countries. These studies were prepared for the World Economic Forum.

Prof. Porter considers that "clusters" of development bring better competitiveness. In other words he preferred agglomerations. Prof Porter combined the ideas of Schumpeter with some basic principles of regional economics.

The world is aware of the territorial division of labour from the times of Adam Smith. Adam Smith wrote about the advantages of the localization of industries. Thereafter Marshall studied the same topic with reference to internal and external economies.

Regional economists want clustering of economic activities. However, they want many clusters spread over the entire space according to the regional comparative advantages. The regional economists prefer "punctiform" economic and industrial development.

Schumpeter wrote about innovations. If new products are brought into the market they are "innovations". However, discovery of cheaper raw materials and/or cheaper but effective new processes of production are the next two important types innovations.

Finding the new markets and reorganizing the business to form a viable and then a strong economic entity were fourth and fifth most important innovations.

Porter simply wanted the clustering of innovations at competitive points of the space.

Porter published many books. One book was "Green and Competitive Relationship", (1955). Then was another book "Toward a New Conception of the Environment Competitiveness Relationship", (1955), and "National Environment Performance Measurement and Determinants". The last book had 63rd printing by 2006!. It was translated many languages. Some of this books have seen upto 38 printings Michael E. Porter enjoyed this privilege of getting his book printed several times because he belongs to Harvard Business School. Porter was MBA of 1971 batch and became author of 17 books (2006). His book micro-economics of competitiveness is taught in the graduation programme at Harvard.

His studies devise competitiveness strategies for various clients. Porter made studies how Japan competitiveness stands in various goods in various countries.

More than the principles, Porter provides case studies. Porter proves that absolute advantage if substantial can be the basis of international trade even if the comparative advantage does not exist. The wide gaps in absolute advantage are enough.

The author of the present book would like to present Porter's views with an example. If Indians see Sony TVs of various sizes, types and prices as also the Samsung TVs of different sizes, functions and prices they do not compare the comparative relationships of these prices with wheat and rice prices. In Ricardo's theory the domestic exchange ratios of two goods were compared with the external exchange ratios between the same two commodities.

What actually happens that people take into account the absolute prices and the absolute capacity to purchase various models. Some models are not purchased because the purchasers may not have sufficient purchasing power to spare on that product. Big cars and luxury cars costing several lakhs to several crores of rupees are not purchased by persons because they do not have the absolute purchasing power. (The present author is one who cannot change his car with a newer and bigger on due to lack of "means". Means are those resources which are at the command of the persons. There is hell lot of money in India but not with the author.)

The conventional wisdom of Factor Endowment Theories H.O. or Comparative Cost Theories of Ricardo and Haberler are challenged by Porter.

Porter said "comparative cost theory is no divine inheritance" Four things are important in determining the international business:

1. Factor conditions.
2. Demand Conditions.
3. Related and supporting industries
4. Strategies of the rivals.

Porter wanted each country to study its own export pattern. The directions and volumes of exports should be studied. It should be studied why and how a country could export to another country and why it could not.

Absolute advantage is more important. If the same or almost more or less the same type of thing is available at considerably cheaper rate, people will buy the same.

The assumptions of the comparative advantage theory about two countries and two factors are too unrealistic to be a base for a theory. In other words exporters of the two countries will not bother to calculate the domestic rates of transformation between two commodities or goods in the home country and in the foreign country.

$ 5000 and $ 40000 a-piece make all the difference. To capture the market the lower absolute cost will stand out as the most important factor

Porter studied these four factors with reference to case studies from Ireland.

Factors: Those factors are important which are created and not which are found. Only natural resources are passively inherited. However, they became "active" only when discovered. A country may be having a lot of coal, iron, gold, silver, crude oil … reserves but unless they are discovered and exploited in the most economical manner, they do not matter as much. Inside the earth they can be regarded as unknown wealth; outside and in use, they become factors and resources.

Unskilled labour is "generalised factor". Skilled and educated labourers with motivation and urge to have higher productivity become specialised labour. Unless the generalised factors are made specialised, there cannot be international business. Considerable investment is necessary in making the generalised factors the specialisd factors. Only the presence of specialised and advanced factors enables the country to have a competitive edge over its rivals in the international business. A country or an industry becomes "high tech" only due to the graduation of general factor into specialised factors. This one important determinant should be reinforced with the presence of the other three requirements, mentioned hereafter.

DEMAND CONDITIONS

There is the domestic market. Many industries develop inside the country to support domestic market. Then they become competent to export in the international market. Not only domestic demand but international demand should be there for high international business.

Import replacing imports are part of international business. They strengthen the domestic industries first and then the export industries.

International competitiveness depends upon catering to the needs/demand of various markets. Both quantitative and qualitative aspects of demand are to be taken into account.

RELATED SUPPORTING INDUSTRIES

Porter preferred industrial clusters. Agglomeration of industries generated internal economies to the producers. If the industries are mutually supportive, they can provide better opportunities for competition with the outsiders. In other words strong supporting industries can be better bet for higher exports. Clusters create linkages and linkages create economies. Economies create advantages in costs… both relative and absolute.

Innovations develop better in clusters. The firms acquire competitive edge over the foreign firms in the domestic market and in the international market against other competing firms.

STRUCTURE OF THE FIRM: STRATEGIES OF THE FIRMS: RIVALRY

There should be domestic rivalries between the firms even when complementary or supplementary. Firm in the competitive market alone can develop abilities to compete. Protective policies harm the competitive spirit and in the long run that becomes unsuitable for competition. Porter also states that countries will succeed where the goal and motivation fit the source of competitive advantage and these goals are strongly determined by ownership structure. MNCs have high goals. There are spin-of effects on the national prestige of not only the industries but also of the countries of these industries/MNCs. MNCs have even the mobile specialised management and labour personnel.

Porter does not conceive a big role for the government in international business.

Firms should have the real competitive edge over the rivals to sustain In the market. Government can help some firms achieve artificial efficiency. in the long run this will be counter productive. Porter states that these policies of the government will fall because they create a competitive advantage which is unsustainable In the long run due to the pressures of the market and continuous innovations. Government reinforces determinants but cannot create competitive advantage.

FDI and FII in the world move according to the future opportunities. Foreign direct investment will be where the investors hope to have competitive advantage. Porter uses the word competitive rather than comparative for advantages.

Grants and subsidies do not make firms competitive.

Critical Appraisal

1. Porter does not disprove the validity of any theory. Do we not see that Japan used to manufacture car engines in Japan and used to get the entire car manufacturered in other countries. Now even the engines can be manufactured abroad, as in India. If at all, Japan concentrates for the most vital parts only. Everyone and every country in the world is adhering to the comparative specialisation. Ricardo stands.
2. We still agree with Haberler that if a country leaves the production and export of something it should be that product in which the opportunity cost (gain) was the least.
3. Haberler's theory that abundant factor should be used intensively to have competitive or comparative advantage also stands its grounds.
   Porter revival of the theory of absolute advantage of Adam smith is at a micro level. One can agree that when an individual buys a car or a tv or whatever, he simply compares the absolute prices
4. Porter's model is ex post model. It is not predictive. If he wanted to draw attention to absolute advantage also, he was partially successful. He was totally unsuccessful to oust other theories from international economics. Poter's theory is micro through and through.
5. Porter called his theory "diamond theory" based upon four cornerd diamond. We can construct a real diamond if we take six factors that determine international business.

ME PORTER, 1994 "comparative Advantage of Nations", Harvard Business Review, Central Statistical office, Trade Statistics, Dublin, Ireland.

3 Mill's Theory of Reciprocal Demand or Demand Theory of International Trade

(1) Introduction
(2) Mill's Theory
(3) Evaluation of the Theory. (H-O Theory is also partly a demand theory).

1. INTRODUCTION

John Stuart Mill was apogee of classicism. He enjoyed a reputation in his generation superior even to that enjoyed by Adam Smith in his time. J.S. Mill was a precocious child. He was an author of economics by the age of 13. Mill brought the writings of Adam Smith up-to-date; confirmed the doctrines of Malthus and wrote a 'readable' Ricardo. The classicism reached its culmination at his hands. But later on as Mill became socialist in thinking, classicism suffered some loss of prestige. Mill was of the opinion that laws of production are ordained by nature but there is nothing so sacrosanct about the laws of distribution which should be changed.

The classical theory of value and trade was essentially one sided. It was a cost theory. Mill regarded it as incomplete. He introduced the demand elements in both. Later on Marshall synthesised the demand and supply elements to near perfection. Mill never rejected the Ricardian theory of comparative advantage. He developed it by expressing the costs in terms of money. He, however, regarded the Ricardian theory as one sided and hence incomplete and blended it with the demand elements.

Mill recognized that international trade can take place only when the domestic terms of trade (barter terms of trade) are lower than the international terms of trade. Mill included the elements of intensity of demand for exports and imports into the theory of international trade. He wanted that the international trade theory should not be separated from the value theory. He was interested in knowing not only how gains emerged in international trade but also is knowing as to how they were shared.

2. MILL'S THEORY

Mill expressed his theory thus:

"The actual ratio at which goods are traded will depend upon the strength and elasticity of each country's demand for the other country's product, or upon reciprocal demand. The ratio will be stable when the value of each country's exports is just enough to pay for its imports."

Ricardo's formulations explained more the qualitative aspects of international trade, while Mill wanted more to know the quantitative aspects of the same. If Portugal exports wine and England cloth, upto what limits they will trade? A point will come when they will not find it possible to trade. Naturally, one such element which will decide the limits of trading will be the total demand. The other, and the more important, will be the "international terms of trade." If 'A' country earns more from its exports, it can import more from the 'B' country. To earn more from exports, either the prices should be high or more goods shculd be sold; if possible, best of the both worlds will be better if elasticities favour.

The prices of the two goods arrange themselves in such a fashion that the quantities demanded by the respective countries exactly balance. If there is greater demand for coal in France than there is for wine in England, then England will obtain a greater quantity of wine in exchange for her coal and will consequently find herself in a very advantageous position. Mill gave us a demand and supply theory of international trade. "Import prices multiplied by import quantities will equal to the total of export prices multiplied by the export quantities."

Mill made some interesting observations, with which we may not agree. The first related to his observation that the poor countries are like retail traders while the rich countries are like wholesalers. The latter gain by large *turnover* (but a small profit margin) while the former gain more by high profit *margin* (though lower turnover). Thus both gain. Empirical evidence suggests that the rich countries can gain in both ways while the poor countries may lose both ways—that is the reason they are indebted.

He makes another observation. The rich countries have a large demand for foreign goods while the less developed countries do not have means for such a large demand. Therefore, the rich countries will tend to have adverse balance of payment. This too is not vindicated by facts. The rich countries are practising protectionism against the poor countries now. Mill was essentially a 'free trader' but is more known for his infant industry argument and Mill's test.

Mill's theory can be explained with the help of the following example:

Table. 3.1:

Country		Production with given money costs in a certain time period	
		Iron	Jute
1.	India	20 tons	20 tons
2.	Bangladesh	10 tons	15 tons

From the above table it is clear that India has absolute advantage in both the commodities. However, the relative advantage is more in iron. India can produce iron at half the cost of production of Bangladesh, while the jute can be produced at three-fourth cost of Bangladesh. Thus, it would be profitable for India to specialise in the production of iron and let Bangladesh specialise in the production of jute.

The terms of trade will have to be determined. Bangladesh would like to have more than 10 tons of iron for its 15 tons of jute. India, on the other hand, would like to have more than 1 ton of jute for 1 ton of iron. (20: 20) *"The limits to the possible barter terms of trade (the international exchange ratio) are set by the domestic exchange ratios established by the relative efficiency of labour in each country"*, in terms of Mill's analysis. Thus India's DER =1:1 and Bangladesh's 1: 1.5.

Now the range of ITT (international terms of trade) will be (with respect of India) between 1 to 1 tons of jute. Demand and supply elasticities have to be studied.

(a) If the demand in India for Bangladesh jute is very strong (inelastic), then the maximum limit of exchange will be 1: 1, *i.e.,* India's DER. It means all gain will go to Bangladesh. Bangladesh is trading at India's domestic exchange ratio, and, thus, India gains nothing.

(b) If on the contrary, Bangladesh's demand for India's iron is very strong (inelastic)—at present not taking into consideration the demand aspect of jute in India—then India will be in strong position. The ITT can be 1 ton if iron to be exchanged for 1½ tons of jute. Since India is trading at Bangladesh's domestic exchange ratio, all gain comes to India and none to Bangladesh.

(c) If India cannot sell its iron to any other country, or if it has to sell it at whatever price (this is scarcely possible for iron is not a perishable good), then the ITT will go against India because of its supply inelasticity.

(d) If Bangladesh cannot sell its jute to any other country, or if it has to sell it at whatever price, then the ITT will go against Bangladesh, because of its supply inelasticities.

Inelastic demand for foreign goods and inelastic supply of export goods makes a c6untry very weak in bargaining and this country can be pushed to accept the ITT which may be nearly equal to DER (domestic exchange ratio). This will happen if the other country has similar situation.

If both countries are in strong position or both in weak position, then the ITT may settle somewhere between the two extreme limits. In case only one is strong/weak then the ITT will be pushed to the extreme.

Mill perceived that the equilibrium exchange ratio would be determined by the condition that the quantity of each of the two products that importing country is willing to take at this ratio be equal to the quantity that. the exporting country is willing to give at this ratio This is the equation of international demand:

$$P_a \times Q_a = P_b \times Q_b$$

$$\text{Then} \quad \frac{P_a \times Q_a}{P_b Q_b} = \frac{Value of\ exports}{Value\ of\ imports}$$

P for price: Q for quantities, 'a' for export good and 'b' for import good.

Thus if the price of export good is Rs. 5, and Rs. 10 for the import good and if 100 units are exported, then the income will be Rs. 500. It means only 50 units can the imported. The actual ratio of exchange will fluctuate till the demand and supply are in equilibrium to find the purchasing power for import purchases, both ways.

In the model of Mill *"comparative costs do not determine the exchange ratio. They determine the limits of exchange. The actual ratio will be determined by the demand and supply."*

The theory of Mill tells us that the greater the divergence of international exchange ratio from the domestic barter ratio, the greater will be gain from the international trade. Actually, the international terms of trade cannot be equal to the domestic terms of trade. Then the country will not be interested in trade. India will not be interested at 1:1 trading and Bangladesh will not be interested in 10: 15 or 1: 1½ trading. Bangladesh should get 10 tons of iron for less than 15 tons of jute, and India should get more than 10 tons of jute for 10 tons of iron.

3. EVALUATION OF THE THEORY

J.S. Mill's theory is very important It is not only an improvement over the Ricardian explanation, but a separate theory in itself. Mill combined the supply and demand aspects of international trade into one theory, though he laid more emphasis on the demand aspect. Marshall developed this aspect into the "offer curves" analysis. The supply aspect was developed subsequently into (i) opportunity costs theory; and (ii) Heckscher-Ohlin theorem of international trade.

Kindleberger interprets the Mill's doctrine in the following words:

"If the two countries are of unequal size, the reciprocal aspect of demand may not come into play at all. The price ratio of the larger country will prevail, and the smaller country can sell as much cloth or wheat to the other as it chooses at the established given price. *This is the importance of being unimportant.* In theory at least, the small country can reap large gains from trade... The case of trading at the price ratio existing in the larger country before trade, which is one limit of profitable trade, may be more frequent than the classical economists have suspected. But where demand and supply in one country of the other are not so large as to overwhelm demand and supply In the other, the law of reciprocal demand comes into play to settle price."

Ellsworth summarizes Mill's Theory:

"In summary, (i) the possible range of barter terms is given by the respective domestic terms of trade as set by comparative efficiency In each country; (ii) within this range, the actual terms depend on each country's demand for the other country's produce; and *(iii)* finally, only those barter terms will be stable at which the exports offered by each country just suffice to pay for the imports it desires."

Joseph Schumpeter acknowledges the important contribution made by Mill in the theory of International trade. He regards Mill's theory not merely extension or refinement of the Ricardian theory, but a new theory. He writes:

"The demand-supply schedules, whose intersection gives geometrical picture of the equation of reciprocal demand, represent an approach that Ricardo always rejected except for temporary fluctuations and for monopolized commodities. They introduce a new and more general principle.

The greatest drawback of the theory is that changes in as $P_a \times Q_a = P_b \times Q_b$ are *not* realized.

That is the reason why balance of payment remains in disequilibrium.

4 Haberler's "Opportunity Cost" Theory or Neo-Classical Comparative Costs Theory of International Trade

(1) Introduction
(2) Trade Under Linear Production Possibility Curves or Trade Under Constant Rate of Transformation Expressed in Opportunity Cost Terms
(3) Trade under non-linear Production Possibility Curves—Increasing O.C.
(4) Trade Under Decreasing Opportunity Costs
(5) Evaluation of the Theory

1. INTRODUCTION

Gottfried von Haberler, a famous name in international economics, first used the term "opportunity cost". He rejected the Ricardian concept of cost, but accepted the comparative cost theory. Real or labour costs are immeasurable and involve cardinal measurement. There are serious handicaps in reducing all costs in labour terms. Costs and advantages should be calculated in terms of "opportunity cost or gain".

This was an important advance in the comparative cost theory of Ricardo. It is also a supply side theory. It also emphasises that international trade takes place when ITT are higher than DTT. This theory is superior to the comparative cost theory of Ricardo because here PPCs (production possibility curves) under increasing and decreasing returns are also drawn. Whereas the comparative cost theory used to emphasise the complete specialisation, the opportunity cost theory admits possibility of complete specialisation only under constant or decreasing costs. Under increasing costs or diminishing returns, it will be partial specialisation that will be possible and desirable.

In the words of Wells:

"Haberler's approach to international trade theory lifts it out of a real cost strait-Jacket in which it had been held so for many generations… It demonstrates that where production possibilities differ countries will gain from freer trade. But it does not take us very far along the road towards explaining why production possibilities differ between countries."

In practice when a country wants to produce more of one commodity, it may have to produce less of some other commodity. When scale of production is changed there is usually reshuffling of various units of factors. Capital and/or labour intensity in production is changed. When capital and labour (or for that matter, natural resources) are scarce, more of a commodity can be produced by sacrificing the production of some other commodity. *The opportunity cost of anything is the alternative that has to be sacrificed in order to have it.*

The neo-classical theory of international trade tells us:

"A country has a comparative advantage vis-a-vis a second country in the production of the commodity in which it has a lower opportunity cost".

This is how the comparative advantage is measured.

2. (A) Trade under Linear Production Possibility 'Curves or Trade under Constant Rate of Transformation-Expressed in Opportunity Cost Terms

Before we proceed to examine the theory of comparative costs based on opportunity costs analysis, let us first understand the rate of transformation between two commodities—(on which the production possibilities curve is based)—based on the concept of opportunity costs.

Suppose there are two countries: India and Bangladesh. India produces maunds of wheat and Bangladesh yards of jute cloth. The domestic rates of production are as under:

	India	*Bangladesh*
Maunds of wheat per day	50	20
Yards of jute cloth per day	30	60

We take in our example that India, with all resources at its command, can produce 50 maunds of wheat or 30 yards per jute cloth, and Bangladesh with all resources at its command can produce 20 maunds of wheat or 60 yards of jute cloth. With the given amount of resources, India can produce more of wheat and Bangladesh more of jute cloth, because of the differences in the endowments. We can draw India's production possibility curve:

The line AB is the production possibility curve of India. At each point of this curve we get different combination of two goods that can be produced with the given endowments of India. For example, if India wants to produce 25 maunds of wheat it can produce only 15 yards of jute cloth. With 20 maunds of wheat, the corresponding coordinate of cloth will be 18 yards. This production possibility curve is downward sloping to the right, showing that more of one can be produced at less of another. However, the sacrifice is *at constant rate.*

The straight line connotates constant rate of sacrifice. India will have to give up 5 maunds of wheat for every 3 yards of jute cloth. Thus, we can say *(i)* the opportunity cost of producing 5 maunds of wheat is 3 yards of jute cloth or *(ii)* the opportunity cost of producing 3 yards of jute cloth is 5 maunds of wheat.

The ratio 5:3 can be called the rate at which transformation is possible. It is in geometric terms, the slope of India's production possibilities curve.

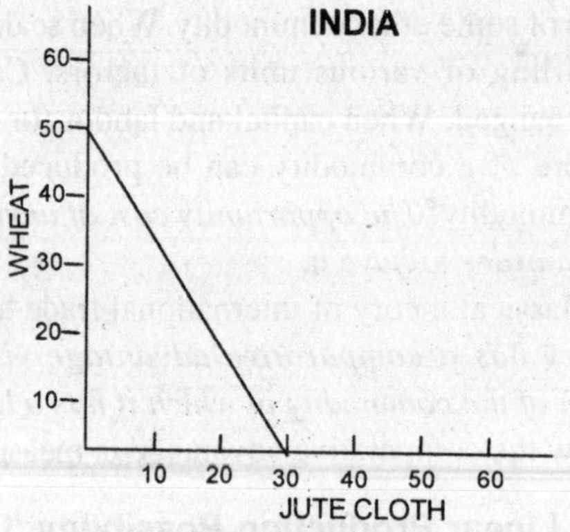

Diagram 4.1

The production possibility curve of Bangladesh will be as under:

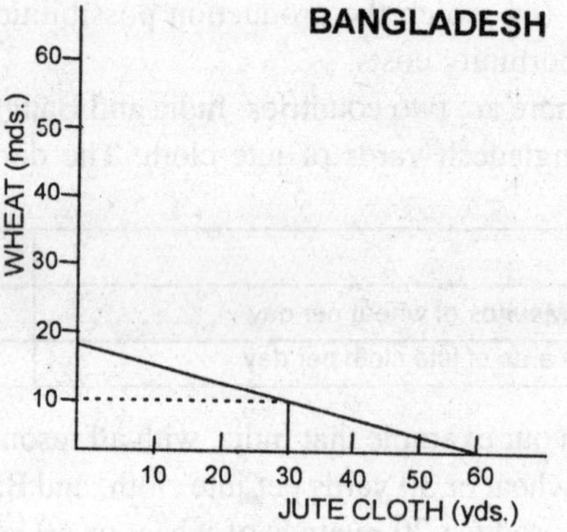

Diagram 4.2

This is also a straight line. It shows rate of the transformation in Bangladesh. It is on ratio 2/6 or 1/3. (We have reduced it to 1/3 so that the denominator of India and Bangladesh becomes common.). This constant curve shows the constant rate of transformation or opportunity costs. This shows that at all levels of additional wheat (jute cloth) production, jute cloth (wheat) will have to be at the constant rate. Thus the straight line production possibility curve is called a constant cost production possibility curve also. Like the production possibility curve of India, the PPC of Bangladesh also shows on its each point the co-ordinates of two goods that can be produced within given endowments.

Suppose these countries choose point 'A' on their respective transformation curves as autarky (no trade or self-sufficiency) point. These points are arrived at with the help of the community's indifference curves.[1]

These indifference curves are convex to the origin showing diminishing marginal rate of substitution. As one person prefers more of one good, he will be prepared to sacrifice some of the second for the same amount of marginal gain.

A country will choose it autarky point where its production possibility curve and the highest possible indifference curve are tangent.

Following diagrams illustrate how the autarky points will be located on different production possibility curves

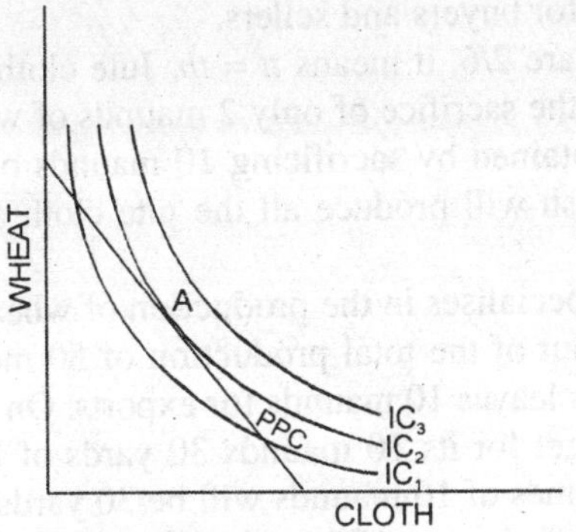

AUTARKY POINT ON A CONSTANT PPC (CONSTANT COSTS)

Diagram 4.3

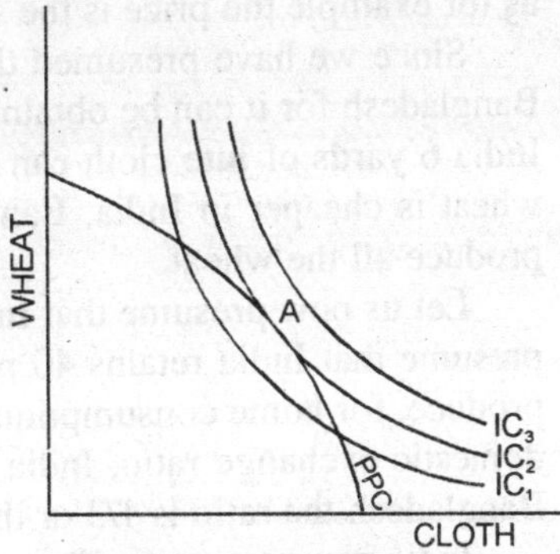

AUTARKY POINT ON A CONCAVE PPC (INEREASING COSTS)

Diagram 4.4

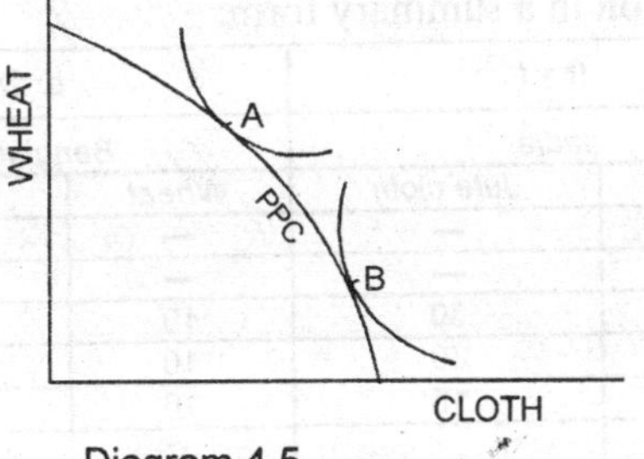

Diagram 4.5

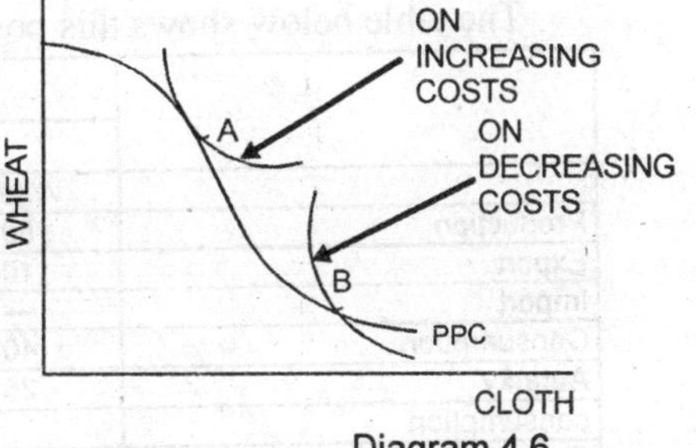

Diagram 4.6

Autarky Point at Different Tastes in Difference Curve a Point Shows Wheat Preference and B Point Cloth Preference

The autarky points chosen here in our examples are mid-points of 25/15 for India and 10/30 for Bangladesh.

2. (B) Can there be Trading at Bangladesh's Domestic Rate of Transformation?

The international trade theory demonstrates that no country will trade on the same terms of trade as are obtained in the country. It is thus clear that if there is international trade at Bangladesh's terms of trade, only India will gain. Bangladesh will not be interested in trade, in this case. This can be demonstrated with the help of following example and illustrations.

We have seen that the DER (domestic exchange rate or domestic rate of transformation) in India and Bangladesh are 50/30 and 20/60 respectively. We can reduce these production figures to a common denominator, say, 10/6 and 2/6 or 5/3 and 1/3. Let us use the terms *tt* for international terms of trade; *ti* for terms of trade at India's DER; and *tb* for terms of trade at Bangladesh DER.

International terms of trade are the ratio at which country's imports exchange for a country's exports. The international terms of trade are the same for both the countries as for example the price is the same for buyers and sellers.

Since we have presumed that *tt* are 2/6, it means *tt* = *tb.* Jute cloth is cheaper in Bangladesh for it can be obtained at the sacrifice of only 2 maunds of wheat, while in India 6 yards of jute cloth can be obtained by sacrificing 10 maunds of wheat. Thus wheat is cheaper in India, Bangladesh will produce all the jute cloth and India will produce all the wheat.

Let us now presume that India specialises in the production of wheat. Let us also presume that India retains 40 mds. out of the total production of 50 mds. that it can produce, for home consumption. This leaves 10 maunds for exports. On Bangladesh's domestic exchange ratio, India will get for its 10 maunds 30 yards of jute cloth. (In Bangladesh the ratio is 1/3 or three times of 10 maunds will be 30 yards.)

India now consumes 40 maunds of wheat and 30 yards of jute cloth. Without trade it was consuming 25 maunds and 15 yards respectively. India gains 15 maunds of wheat and 15 yards of jute cloth, after trade. However, Bangladesh gets nothing. Its post-trade points remain the same. Out of the total production of 60 yards of cloth, it gives 30 yards in exchange for 10 maunds of wheat. Thus its consumption is the same 10 maunds and 30 yards—the autarky point consumption. Obviously, Bangladesh will not be interested in international trade.

The table below shows this position in a summary form:

	tt = t		*b: 2/6*	
	India		*Bangladesh*	
	Wheat	*Jute cloth*	*Wheat*	*Jute cloth*
Production	50	—	—	60
Export	10	—	—	30
Import	—	30	10	—
Consumption	40	30	10	30
Autarky consumption	25	15	10	30
Gain (post-trade)	15	15	—	

Diagrammatically this can be illustrated as under:

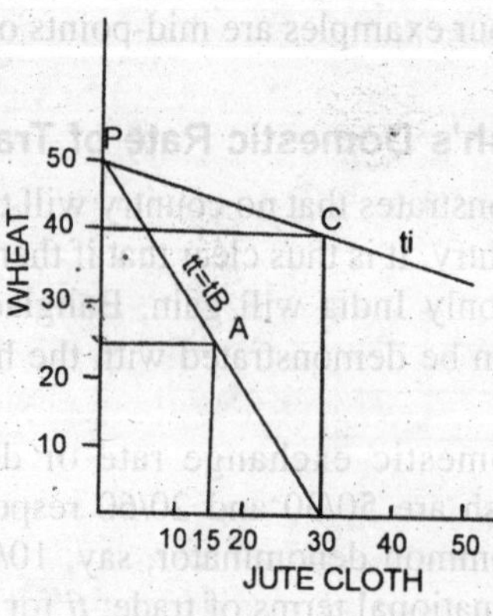

Diagram 4.7

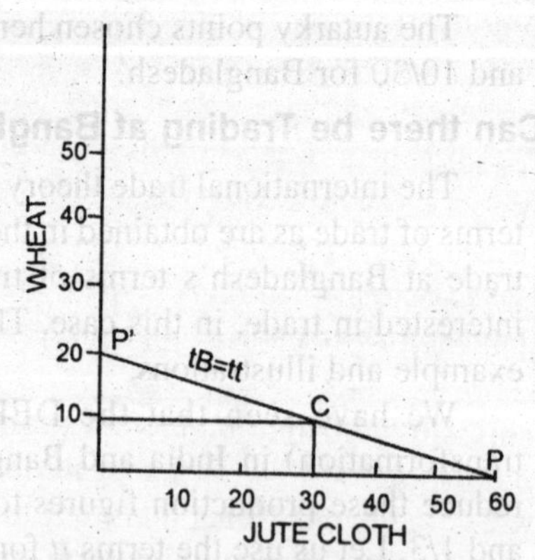

Diagram 4.8

(i) P is the specialisation point of India, whereby 50 maunds of wheat are being produced.

(ii) India now trades with Bangladesh. She will now move along the line PC. The slope of PC has the same angle to point P' as Bangladesh's PPC to point P'. Another way of drawing this line is to extend the line PC towards 150 yards of cloth. (If for 20 maunds, jute cloth production is 60, then three times of 50 will be 150.)

(iii) In our example, we have taken India's consumption at 40 maunds of wheat and exports of 10 maunds. Thus India will travel along the line PC until point C, where the consumption point of 40 maunds and 30-yards of jute cloth are obtained.

(iv) It can clearly be seen that post-trade point *'C* gives higher co-ordinates of wheat and jute cloth in comparison to the pre-trade or autarky point of 'A'.

(v) Bangladesh's autarky and post-trade points converge at the same point" 'A'. Since Bangladesh does not gain anything, she will not be interested in trading.

2. (C) Can There be Trading at India's Domestic Rate of Transformation? the Answer is Again, No

If it is proved that Bangladesh will not be interested in trading with India if it can secure the same *tt* as is the DER of that country, the same can be proved in case of India as well. India will be interested in trading only when the *tt* are higher than the DER. Trading at India's DER will be highly profitable to Bangladesh.

We proceed with the same assumption that India specialises in the production of wheat and Bangladesh in the production of jute cloth. Suppose out of the total production of 60 yards of jute cloth, Bangladesh retains as much as was being consumed at pre-trade point *i.e.,* 45 yards. She will thus export 15 yards which at India's DER of 10/6 will get 15 maunds of wheat. (15 is 2½ times of 6 and 2½ times of 10 will be 25.).

In the form of a table, this can be illustrated as under:

	tt = ti: 10/6			
	India		*Bangladesh*	
	Wheat	*Jute cloth*	*Wheat*	*Jute cloth*
Production	50		—	60
Export	25			15
Import	—	15	25	—
Consumption	25	15	25	45
Pre-trade consumption	25	15	10	30
Gain	—	—	15	15

We see that all gain goes to Bangladesh and none to India—a position, India will certainly not like

Diagrammatically his can be illustrated as under:

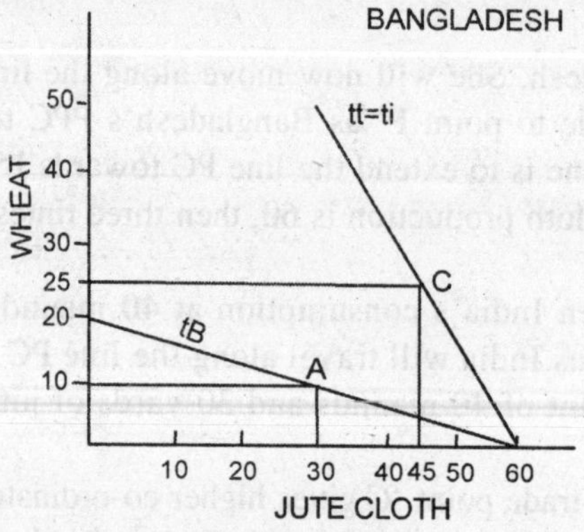

Diagram 4.9

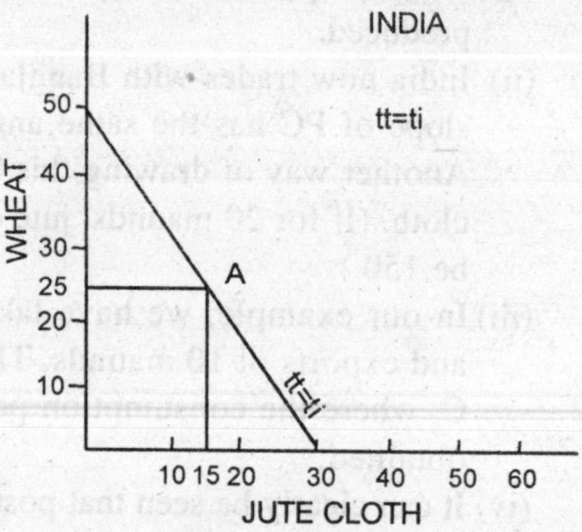

Diagram 4.10

(i) Here we can see that Bangladesh moves to specialisation point P from his original autarky point A. B.D. retains 45 yards of jute cloth, and sells 15 yards of the same. At the trading terms are 10/6 (India's DER) she will get 25 maunds. B.D. moves along the line PC until C point is reached. The basis of drawing the curve is the same as in previous case *i.e.,* the angle of PC is the same as that of India's PPC at the corresponding points on x-axis. (The line moves from 30 towards 50 in India's case; with 60 it will move towards 100.)

(ii) At point C, 45 yards of jute cloth are retained. Co-ordinates of wheat and jute cloth at this point are 45 yards and 25 maunds. Post-trade point is higher than pre-trade point.

(iii) India, on the other hand gets the same post-trade point as the pre-trade point.

(iv) This too is not realistic.

2.(D) Trade Will be at Intermediate Terms, Though not Necessarily Just Middle Terms

It is thus clearly demonstrated that international trade cannot take place either at 10/6 or at 2/6. Trade can be at terms which are in between these terms *i.e.,* on terms 9/6 or 3/6. For the sake of simplicity we presume that the terms of trade are 6/6. This supposition is made simply to make the examples easier.

If India specialises in the production of wheat and Bangladesh specialises in the production of jute cloth, they will produce 50 maunds and 60 yards of wheat and jute cloth respectively. We suppose that if India exports 20 maunds of wheat it will gain 20 yards of jute cloth because, we have presumed that the terms of trade will be intermediate *i.e.* 6:6.

In this case the total consumption in India will be 30 maunds of wheat and 20 yards of cloth. This will give India gain of 5 maunds and 5 yards over the autarky point, of 25 maunds and 15 yards.

In this case the total consumption in Bangladesh will be 20 maunds of wheat and 40 yards of jute cloth. This will give Bangladesh consumption advantage of 10 maunds of wheat and 10 yards of jute cloth over the autarky point of 10 maunds of wheat and 30 yards of jute cloth.

It can also be seen that if there is no trade between the two countries, the total production of wheat in two countries would have been 25 maunds of wheat in India. and 10 maunds of wheat in Bangladesh *i.e.,* total 35 maunds, The total of jute cloth in both countries will be 15 plus 30 *i.e.,* 45 yards. When both countries specialise the production figures become 50 maunds and 60 yards. Thus, there is production gain of 15 maunds and 15 yards, which is shared by India (5 and 5) and Bangladesh (10 and 10).

At India's DER, India gains nothing on 10/6 and at Bangladesh DER (2/6) Bangladesh gains nothing. At intermediate terms, both the countries gain. Diagrammatically this can be shown as under:

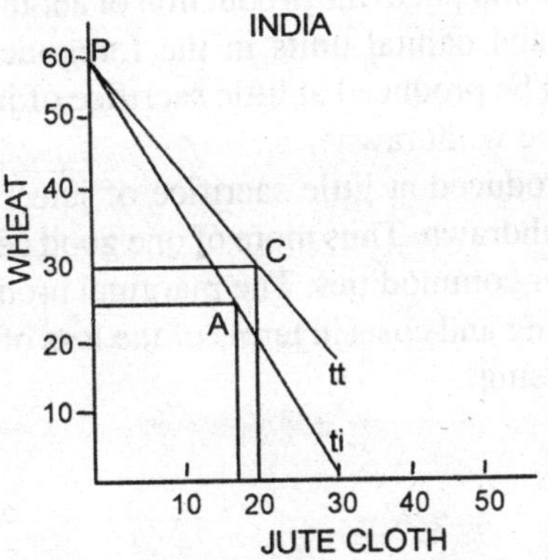

Diagram 4.11

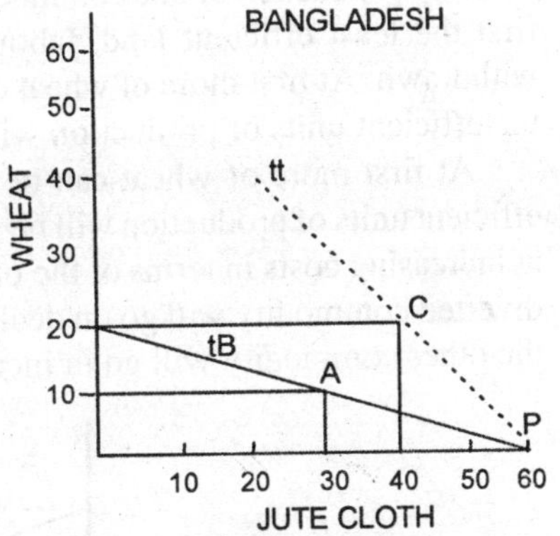

Diagram 4.12

As we have seen above there are two extremes of the terms of trade: 10/6 and 2/6. At 10/6 India gains nothing; at 11/6 or above India loses. At 2/6 Bangladesh gains nothing; at less than 2 or 6 yards, of cloth, it loses. In between 10/6 and 2/6 there is a zone of gain for both. At 6/6, as we have seen both countries gain—though not equally. The following diagram shows this position.

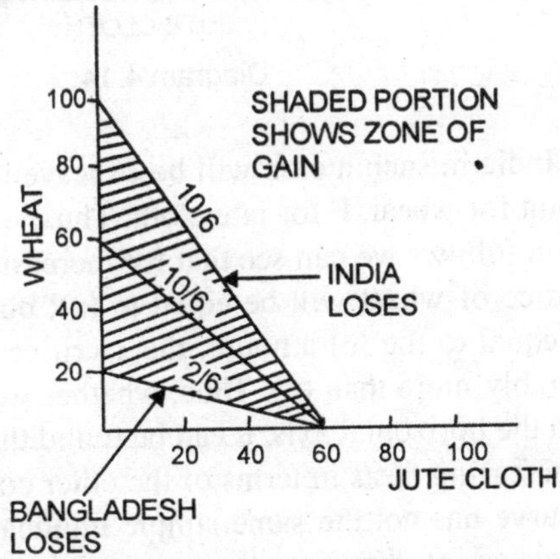

Diagram 4.13

3. (A) TRADE UNDER NON-LINEAR PRODUCTION POSSIBILITY CURVES

Increasing Costs

Constant rate of transformation between two commodities is not a very distinct possibility. Therefore, the assumption of linear production possibility curve can be considered to be unrealistic. Non-linear production possibility curves are distinct possibility, the increasing cost function is even more so.

If India wants to move from its autarky point towards the production of more wheat and less jute cloth, there will be diversion of land, labour and capital from the production of jute to the production of wheat. When land and labour are withdrawn from the production of one commodity and put to the production of another commodity, first the least efficient land, labour and capital units in the foregone good will be withdrawn. At first more of wheat can be produced at little sacrifice of jute. Then even the efficient units of production will be withdrawn.

At first more of wheat can be produced at little sacrifice of jute. Then even the efficient units of production will be withdrawn. Thus more of one good can be produced at increasing costs in terms of the other commodities. The marginal productivity in the diverted commodity will go on declining and costs in terms of the loss of production of the other commodity will go in increasing.

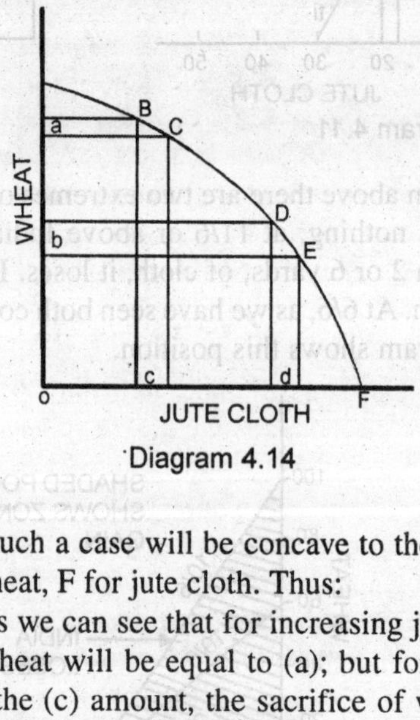

Diagram 4.14

The PPC of India in such a case will be concave to the origin. A is the complete specialisation point for wheat, F for jute cloth. Thus:

In the diagram follows we can see that for increasing jute cloth production by (c) amount the sacrifice of wheat will be equal to (a); but for producing (d) amount of cloth—which is equal to the (c) amount, the sacrifice of wheat will be equal to (b), which is considerably more than (a). Thus, whether we move from O on the vertical axis or from O on the horizontal axis, it can be found that more of one commodity can be produced at increasing costs in terms of the other commodity. O to A or 0 to F.

A concave curve has not the same simple implications as the linear PPC curve. The A and F points are at different places and have different implications. Since the domestic rate of transformation is equal to the slope of the PPC, the rate will be different for each point on the curve.

3. (B) Trade and Increasing Costs One Country Example

Here also the principle of international trade is the same. Two countries will trade only when the international terms of trade are different from the DRT. In the figure follows we presume that India wishes to consume Oe wheat. Given PPC, it is easy to find the corresponding amount of cloth 0b. At point A, it is autarky point at which amount produced is equal to the amount consumed.

Ta line is drawn which is tangent to the PPC at A. Its slope represents the DRT at point A. Ta is domestic terms of trade line, TT is international terms of trade line.

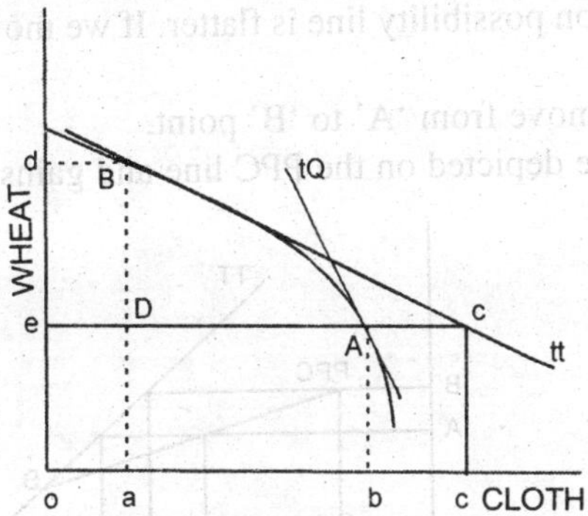

Diagram 4.15

TT line reflects the terms of trade available to India. The line *tt* is flatter than Ta It indicates that less wheat exchanges for more jute cloth abroad than in India. That is the reason why India finds it profitable to export wheat and import jute cloth. A question that is to be settled is how much wheat should India produce and how much she should export. India moves from her autarky point towards the specialization point towards P. As India moves upwards along her PPC, she finds her export good wheat, which at A was relatively cheap, becomes more and more expensive in terms of cloth. Eventually, at point B, the DRT or opportunity cost has reached the level indicated by the line TT. If India continues specializing in wheat beyond point B, she will produce her wheat more expensively in terms of cloth, than she will be able to sell wheat according to her terms of trade *tt*.

Increasing costs, therefore, preclude complete specialisation in this case. At any point between A and B production costs of wheat (in terms of cloth) are lower than revenues (in terms of cloth) from exporting wheat. India, should, therefore, continue specialising as long as this cost advantage exists, *i.e.*, she should move no further than point B.

If she moves further than point B, her costs (in terms of jute cloth) will be higher than her revenue (in terms of jute cloth). If she remains somewhere between A and B, she will lose the opportunity of selling more wheat at a revenue (in terms of cloth which is higher than their cost (in terms of jute cloth).

India can now choose her consumption point along the line TT, after having shifted her production point from A to B. If we assume that India would consume as much wheat as she was consuming before the trade, then point C will be her consumption point after trade. Her gains from trade will be of jute cloth, where *be* simply measures the horizontal distance between the pre-trade consumption point A and the post-trade consumption point C.

After the trade, India produces at B and consumes at C; her experts are the amount by which wheat production exceeds wheat consumption, or *ed* in the diagram above. Her imports are, naturally, the excess of cloth consumption over her production or *ac*.

Let us blow up the portion of diagram beyond the point 'B'.

In the above diagram the terms of trade line is steeper. If we move up on this line the gains are shown.

The production possibility line is flatter. If we move further along this line we can know the costs.

Suppose we move from 'A' to 'B' point.

Now costs are depicted on the PPC line and gains are depicted on the TT line.

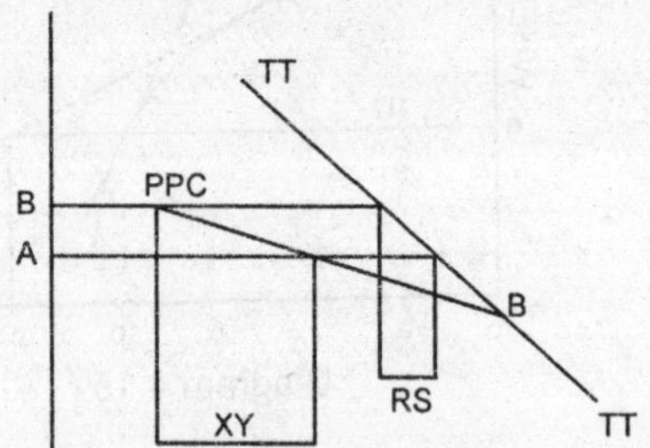

Diagram 4.16

For the same movement AB, the corresponding co-ordinates of sacrifice and gains can be seen on the horizontal line.

The sacrifice is XY taken from the PPC and AB points.

The gains is RS taken from the TT and AB points.

It can be seen that XY is greater than RS. Hence, specialization beyond this point will not be desirable. It will be costlier.

The position can be summarized.

Indication	Commodity	Before Trade	After Trade
1. Production	Wheat	Oe	Od
	Jute cloth	Ob	Oe
2. Consumption	Wheat	Oe	Oe
	Jute cloth	Ob	Oc
3. Exports	Jute cloth		ed
4. Imports	Wheat		
	Jute Cloth		ac
5. Gains	Wheat		
	Jute cloth		be

The triangle BCD, showing exports, imports and the terms of trade called the trading triangle.

3. (C) Increasing Opportunity Costs Two Countries Example

We can show the same results with the help of the PPCs of two countries, shown on a single case. In this case also the principle of comparative advantage is vindicated. We shall reach the same conclusion *viz.*, there cannot be complete specialisation under increasing opportunity costs.

In the diagram below, the PPCs of two countries are drawn on the same base.

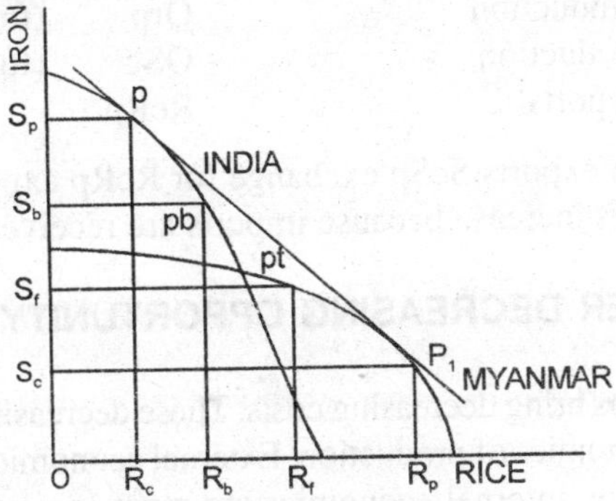

Diagram 4.17

In this example, we show the PPCs of India and Myanmar. It is presumed that factor endowment of India favour greater attention to the production of iron and factor endowments of Myanmar favour cultivation. The slope of PPC of India shows that it can produce more iron and less rice with a given amount of factors. The slope of PPC of Myanmar shows that she can produce more rice and less iron with a given amount of factors. The DERs of the two countries clearly show that rice will be cheaper in Myanmar (in terms of iron) and iron will be cheaper in India (in terms of rice).

In the diagram above, Pb is the autarky point for India and *Pf* is the autarky point for Myanmar. (These points are arrived at with the help of the community indifference curves.) It is obvious that since comparative advantage exists with India and Myanmar for iron and rice respectively, both of them will be profited by trade. It is clear that India will export iron and Myanmar will export rice.

As both countries will have increased demand for the product of their specialisation, they will produce more. As more is produced, the opportunity cost of both iron and rice will increase in the respective countries.

Trade between two countries will establish a new cost structure. *Trade will go on till opportunity cost are equal to the international exchange ratio.* This is the point of specialisation. When 1:1 ratio between the rice and iron is established, there shall remain no profit in trade beyond that.

A tangent on PPC of both countries cuts both curves at P and P' points. These are the points of specialisation for India and Myanmar. India will increase the production of iron and reduce that of rice (Myanmar doing the opposite) till the ratio 1: 1 is read ed.

In the diagram on previous page:

Taking the Case of India

(1) Iron production Sp (formerly Sb—now more).
(2) Iron consumption OSc
(3) Iron exports ScSp
(4) Rice production ORc (formerly ORb—now reduced).

Taking the Case of Myanmar

(1) Rice production Orp (formerly ORf—now increased).
(2) Iron production OSc (formerly OSf—now decreased).
(3) Rice exports RcRp.

India's Iron exports ScSp exchange for RcRp exports of Myanmar. Thus welfare of both countries increase because imports are received at cheaper rates.

4. TRADE UNDER DECREASING OPPORTUNITY COSTS

Increasing returns bring decreasing costs. These decreasing costs are the result of external and internal economies of production. External economies, though important, are equally shared. Therefore, internal economies are more important for a firm. They may even help a firm take over an industry or the firm may get monopolistic control in a country or even in the world. External economies help maintain competition perfect; only internal economies will help in the emergence of oligopolies or monopolies. Indivisibilities play an important part in decreasing costs. In the words of Kindleberger:

"In some cases, the increasing returns have resulted from imperfection of competition, such as inadequate knowledge or barriers to entry, such as unavailability of technology or capital. Many of these cases increasing returns are irreversible, and the economic theorist may call them historical downward shifts of supply curve rather than increasing returns."

The production possibility curve under decreasing costs will be convex to origin. If the production function changes from increasing returns to decreasing returns then the PPC will take the convex shape from a point of inflection (inflexion). Thus:

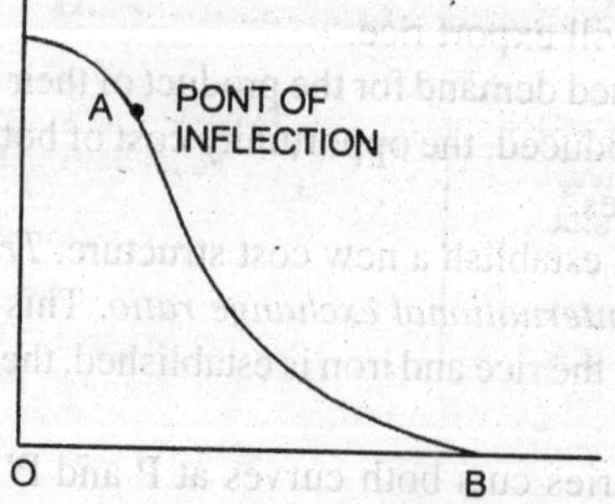

Diagram 4.18

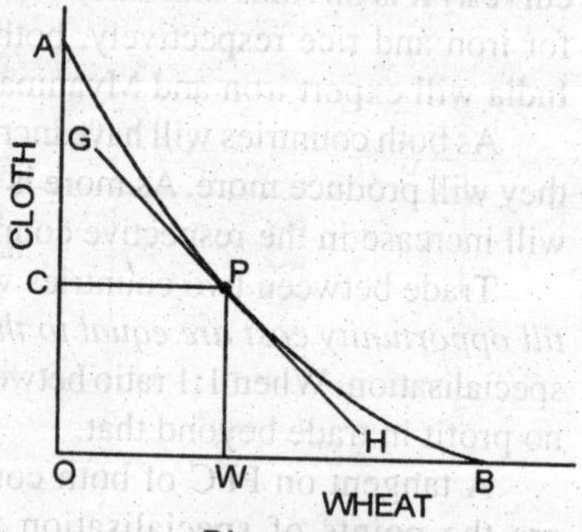

Diagram 4.19

We proceed from a single convex curve. In the diagram below we can show the trade pattern under decreasing costs. In this situation a movement away from autarky point to the point of specialisation will carry the country to the. point of complete specialization. If the country is producing say wheat and cloth and if the demand from wheat rises *first* then the country will produce more wheat and since the opportunity cost of production will go on declining, the country will stop at nothing short of complete specialisation. The country could have specialised in the production of cloth if only the price of cloth had risen first due to changes in demand.

In the diagram 4.19, AB is the concave PPC curve and P is the autarky point. Line GH shows the DER line corresponding to this point. Co-ordinate OC and OW show the amounts of cloth and wheat produced at autarky point. A will be specialisation point for cloth and B for wheat, if all resources are devoted to any one of them (due to availability of internal economies).

Trade pattern between two countries can be shown if we draw two increasing production function PPCs on one base, as in diagram shown

In the diagram above AB is the PPC curve of India and XY the PPC of Pakistan. P and P' are the autarky points of two countries respectively. The lines that are tangent on these points show the DER ratios of two countries with respect to autarky points (ab and xy lines). The slopes of these lines show that India has advantage in the production of cloth and Pakistan in the production of wheat.

International terms of trade line is represented by RT. India specialises in cloth because cloth is costly in international market (RT is flatter in comparison to *ab,* showing favourable term of trade in international market).

For Pakistan wheat is costlier in international market and cloth cheaper *(xy* is flatter than RT). The equilibrium point can be anywhere between RT, depending on the total demand requirements of the two countries.

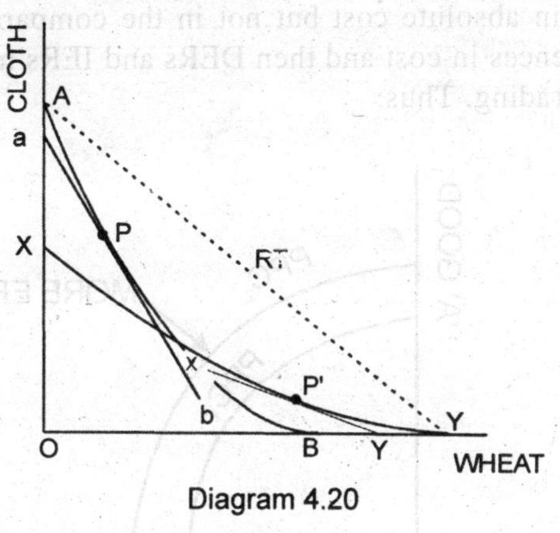

Diagram 4.20

5. EVALUATION OF THE THEORY

While the Ricardian theory was 'real cost' theory of comparative advantage, the Haberler theory is 'opportunity' cost theory of comparative advantage. Opinions may differ whether costs should be expressed in labour terms, or opportunity terms or simply in money terms. Labour costs are nearly immeasurable. If we are to measure the irksomeness of production, or the disutility of production, or the amount of leisure foregone all these things will be very difficult. Lot of subjective elements enter.

Compared to the real costs, the opportunity costs are not difficult to measure. We can always measure how much wheat or cotton can be grown on a plot of land or how much iron or jute can be produced with a given amount of capital or how much cloth or wine can be produced by labour.

While the Ricardian theory may be said to facilitate better "welfare analysis", the opportunity cost theory enables us to have better "position of pedagogic analysis".

The opportunity cost theory not only tells us why trade takes place or when should it take place; but also gives us the zone of trading. It also explains how the gains are shared by different countries on different international terms of trade.

Opportunity cost theory does not explain trade conditions under the strait jacket of constant production possibility curve. It can demonstrate them under conditions of increasing and decreasing returns. It is also capable of explaining when complete specialization is possible and when it is not (*i.e.*, when only partial specialization is possible). In the words of Samuelson:

"The opportunity cost approach is more fertile because it can be readily extended into a general equilibrium system. It is, therefore, not surprising that the opportunity-cost approach had gained more and more popularity and It is used even by those who, in principle, attack it."

Opportunity cost theory suffers from drawback that it fails to take into account the differences in the factor endowments as the causative factor in differences in costs. It gives more importance to differences in the efficiency of factors of production. It should be noted that differences in efficiency will certainly make differences in absolute cost but not in the comparative costs. This may lead to equal differences in cost and then DERs and IERs may not differ and hence there may be no trading. Thus:

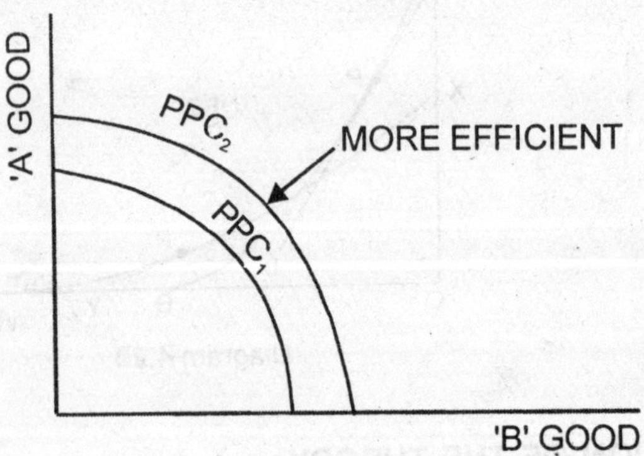

Diagram 4.21

Conclusions: There will be

A. *Complete Specialisation* Under constant and increasing returns (or constant and decreasing costs).

B. Partial specialization decreasing returns or increasing costs.

NOTES

1. An indifference curve, as the readers of this volume will see chapter 8, shows different combinations of two goods that give the consumers (or a country if we are talking about preference mix of two goods in a country) equal satisfaction. The consumer is neutral or indifferent between different combinations. An indifference curve is like a contour line on a map, which shows all planes a the same height above sea-level. Instead of representing height, each indifference curve represents a level of satisfaction. It is, however, quite impossible to measure levels of satisfaction in the way that one can measure height above sea level.

5 Heckscher-Ohlin's (*) Theory of International Trade: Also Known as Factor Endowment Theory/"Modern" Theory of International Trade.

I Salient points: factor abundance defined.
II Assumptions of the theory.
III Factor intensity diagrams; diagram that proves that partial specialization leads to full employment of factors; full specialization leads to partial unemployment of factors.
IV Deductions from the theory.
(*) to be pronounced as Oleen.

Heckscher-Ohlin theory is both a supply side theory and a demand side theory. The theory emphasises that international trade between two countries will take place and should take place on the principle of comparative advantage in prices and not merely in costs. That can be secured by utilising the abundant factor intensively to reach a point of such partial specialisation in the two commodities/goods that full employment of both the factors of production is secured.

S.M. Surakovicik (his modificiation 2006) using quasi-linear production function, instead of assuming constant returns in the theorem and using a lot of algebra and geometric diagrams proved that

"those goods will be exported which are produced with the help of relatively abundant factors."

The only change was the use of the word "relatively" abundant. instead of assuming perfect competition, condition of monopoly and oligopoly were also admitted. (Wikipedia, 2008).

H-O theory is a supply side theory because it talks of comparative advantage in the costs of production as the first essential point. It is a demand theory because it talks of comparative advantage in costs translating into prices also. Prices are never determined without demand.

The H-O theory is a cost theory explicitly.

It is a demand theory implicitly.

The theory is macro-dynamic. First, it recommends for the benefit of all countries of the world that they should produce such outputs which use their abundant factor intensively. The theory, therefore, makes recommendation that all countries should provide full employment to labour and full utilization of the capital. Relevant technologies should be used. It is not a ploy to make the developing economies to import capital goods from the rich countries. It, at the same time, recommends that the rich countries should import labour intensive goods from the developing economies.

The salient points of the theory and factor abundance are discussed hereafter.

I. SALIENT POINTS OF HECKSCHER-OHLIN THEOREM/THEORY[1]

Eli Heckscher was the teacher of Bertil Ohlin (to be pronounced as OLEEN). Their theory is known as Factor Endowment Theory or Modern Theory of International Trade. This theory was a little bit different from the other theories i.e., it was a theory which incorporated all previous theories plus added may new elements.

There are 5 important points that should be remembered about this theory.

1. International trade takes place or should take place on the basis of comparative advantage in prices and not merely in costs. Prices can differ from costs due to several factors like different types of taxes in different countries, conversion into different currencies, subsidies and supernormal profit. Though perfect competition is assumed in the theory (normal profits are conceived in this,)', there are ground realities of super normal profits affecting prices.
2. The prices taken in the theory/theorem are general equilibrium prices.
3. Differences in costs/prices are not merely due to differences in efficiencies of production in different countries but due to differences in the quantities of factors of production. Theory explains in words. Theorem explain in geometry and algebra. The theory takes into account both quality and quantities of factors of production.
4. Abundant factor of production should be used more intensively and scarce factor less intensively to obtain comparative advantage in costs.[2]
5. Specialisation should be partial. It was proved that complete specialisation leads to partial unemployment of factors. Partial specialisation leads to full employment of the factors.

If due to pressure of trade unions wages are higher then that country will be treated as labour scarce. If I/W is higher than the I/W in the other country, we will treat the first county to the capital poor and labour rich. ***H-O theory/theorem proves that in all definitions that may be taken of factor abundance and scarcity, the rule that abundant factor should be utilised intensively will stand.***

It is not said in H-O theory/theorem that a labour-surplus economy should not produce any capital-intensive good. It can and should but only in exceptional cases. Labour intensive productions also require capital. Hence first as many labour intensive goods that require less capital should be produced.

The least profitable labour intensive goods can be left so that capital is spared for the most essential capital-intensive goods.

II. ASSUMPTIONS OF THE H-O THEORY

1. It is a 2 + 2 + 2 model i.e., it is assumed that there are two countries, two commodities and two factors of production.
2. There is perfect competition in factor and product markets.

3. Mobility is "perfect" inside the country but not between the countries.
4. Constant production function is assumed.
5. There are no transport and storage costs.
6. Countries differ not only in the quality of endowments but importantly in quantities of factors and resources.
7. Capital abundant country uses capital intensive technology and labour abundant country uses labour intensive technologies. Capital intensive technologies use less labour; labour intensive technologies use less capital.
8. Government is neutral i.e., does not favour or punish any type of producers.
9. Factors of production are homogeneous inside the country. Technologies used continue and no reversal is there.
10. Demand conditions are the same. Supply function is the same.
11. The theory is for exports and imports of **commodities and goods on** and not for services.
12. Partial specialisation is the assumption and proof of the theorem.

Important: Factor abundance or scarcity is relative. It can be in three senses. First the absolute quantities, second the l/K or K/L ratios and the third I/W or W/I ratios in two countries. H-O theorem proves the same thing as the theory.

These are the points that are taken into account in finding out the general equilibrium prices:

(A) Purchasing power of the people and its distribution amongst various categories of persons determine demand for commodities, goods and services. There are a host of other factors like tastes and fashion that determine the demand.
(B) Demand for commodities, goods and services determine the demand of factors of production.
(C) Demand for factors of production also depends upon technology-mix.
(D) Demand for factors of production (land or natural resources, labour, capital, organizers and technology) determine the factor prices as rent, wages, salaries, interest and critical minimum normal profits.
(E) Factor prices determine the prices of the commodities, goods and services.

It is a round-about world. Prices of factors determine prices of commodities, goods and services: and, prices of commodities, goods and services determine the factor prices.

If price of one thing determines price of every other thing, then the process makes the price determination indeterminate. ***H-O take a film of the all prices. A film keeps on rolling. There are changed situations in every frame. So which prices are to be taken ? They are "snap shot" prices, relevant for the moment.***

This analysis of Walras (to be pronounched as WALRA) is used in the theorem.

Examining the H-O Theory with reference to India.

H-O theory proves itself with all countries. It is to be remembered that H-O theory explains what it also recommends what should be.

India can export capital goods to Bangladesh because India is capital rich vis-a-vis Bangladesh. Bangladesh can export rice, jute and fish to India because Bangladesh is relatively rich in labour and the production of these three commodities requires greater labour intensity.

India capital rich proved: or India labour poor proved:

$$\frac{K}{K_I} > \frac{K}{L_B} or \frac{L}{K_B} > \frac{L}{K_I} or \frac{I}{K_I} < \frac{L}{K_B}$$

Bangladesh labour rich proved:
Bangladesh capital poor proved:

$$\frac{L}{K_B} > \frac{L}{K_I} or \frac{K}{L_B} < \frac{K}{L_I} ...$$

On the other hand. India's exports to the USA will be utilising labour intensively while the imports will be of such products which employ capital and technology intensively.

HERE IT SHOULD BE NOTED THAT IN TAKING JUST TWO FACTORS OF PRODUCTION; THIS HAS BEEN DONE:

Land is lumped with capital, even though land is a free gift of nature; but for the nation as a whole and not for individual production firms.

Organisers/managers, entrepreneurs. technocrats and technovators are all included in "labour" because they are humanbeings after all.

III. FACTOR INTENSITY LINES: (TO BE USED IN ILLUSTRATING PPCS)

The factor intensity lines determine the production path. One commodity may require (say) 4K + 1L and we can say that it uses capital more intensively. Another commodity may use (say) IK + 4L and hence is more labour intensive. We can have a third commodity which uses 2K + 2L and we can say it is equal-factor-proportionate. These quantities will go on increasing in the same way e.g., first case 8L + 2L; second case 8L + 2K; and third case 4K + 4L and so on. Thus we will have expansion path lines.

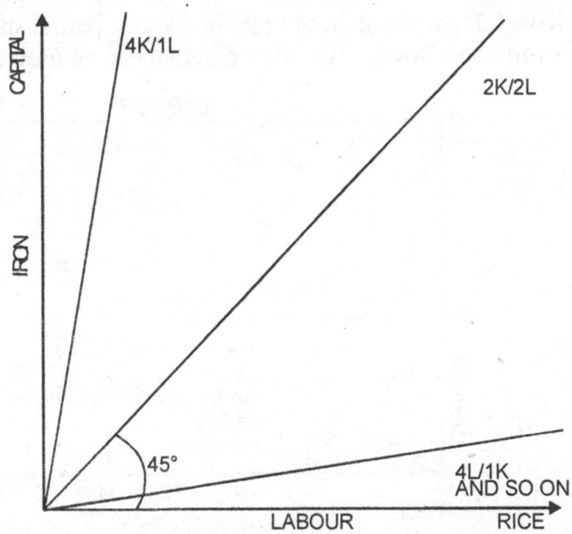

Fig. 5.1

We can also derive the expansion path lines with the help of isoquants and price lines. The isoquants for the capital intensive goods will be akin to the vertical line of capital, steeper for capital. The isoquants for the labour intensive goods will be flatter—akin but not parallel to the horizontal base line. At the points of tangency with the price lines we will get points of equilibrium at each isoquant and all these points, when brought in a straight line will give us the expansion path lines. We can illustrate them thus:

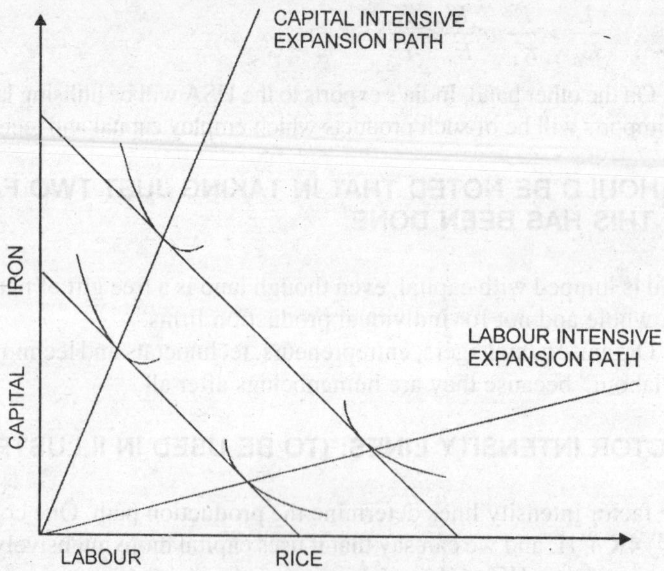

Fig. 5.2

H.O. Theorem proves that there can be no complete specialisation. This is true on noneconomic considerations also. It is also a fact of life. The theory proves that (a) partial specialisation will leave some of one or both factors unutilised, and that (b) in order to have full employment of both the factors, partial specialisation is necessary.

Edgeworth and Bowley type Box diagram can be used to illustrate the position.

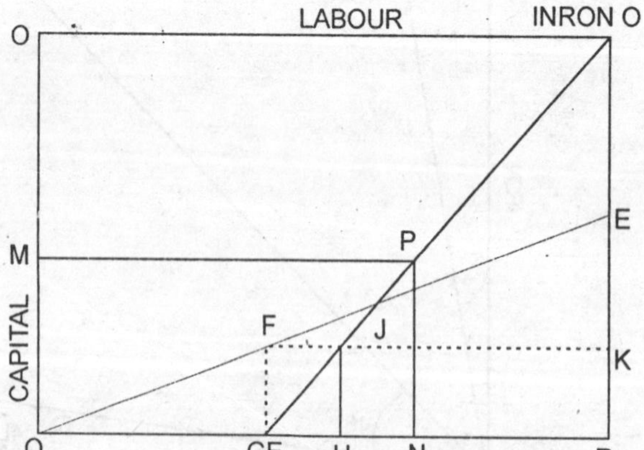

Fig. 5.3

It can be seen in the above diagram that:

(a) OE and O'E' the production paths of two commodities. OE is drawn from O while O'E' is drawn from O'.

(b) The co-ordinates are OR and OQ for the first commodity—rice, and O'Q and O'R for the second commodity—Iron.

(c) If any country goes in for complete specialisation, then it will not be able to use both the factors of production completely. Complete specialisation means partial employment; partial specialisation will secure full employment.

(d) If the country produces only rice, then it will use OR labour but RE capital only. O'E capital will remain unused. If, on the contrary, the country produces only iron, then it will use O'R capital and RE' labour only. OE' labour will remain unused.

(e) It is necessary that for maximising national income all factors of production be used fully. For this purpose the expansion path for the country will be O'PO (If we invert this curve we can see that is a concave production possibility curve with a kink at P.)

(f) At point P, production expansion path lines of rice and iron intersect each other. Accordingly, production of rice will be upto OP point and of iron upto O'P point.

(g) If rice is produced upto OP point we use OM capital and ON labour. For O'P iron, we use MQ capital and NR labour. Thus complete quantities of both factors will be used.

(h) On any other point some of the labour and/or capital will be left out of utilisation. Any other point on either expansion path, say, F on OE, capital and labour will be able to produce at J on the expansion path for iron; OG of labour will be employed in rice and HR in iron. RK of capital will be utilised in iron and O'K' in rice. But GH if labour will be unemployed.

IV. OTHER IMPORTANT POINTS OF THE THEORY

1. Capital rich countries produce capital goods more than other goods. Labour abundant countries make and should make labour intensive commodities and goods more than the other goods.
2. Capital rich countries can also produce for domestic consumption labour intensive goods. Labour abundant countries can produce capital intensive goods for domestic consumption. The HO theorem/theory proves that for international trade the rule remains: "export those goods which utilise the abundant factor intensively."
3. Even the straight line PPCs will differ for different commodities and countries. Then the relative price? will differ. Trading will be on the principle of comparative advantage in prices for ***all commodities, goods and countries***.
4. Heckscher-Ohlin theory proves that free trade and partial specialisation can create conditions of full employment provided production and exports are ***maximum maximorum***.
5. Free and multi-lateral trade help the abundant factor get higher incomes. Such trade reduces the "rent" elements in factor prices. [If normal salary of Sanskrit teachers in the schools, colleges and Universities is the same as of others but there is scarcity of Sanskrit teachers, then the employer can offer two or four advance increments. This is rent element].

6. If the high incomes of the factor are to the scarce factor are to be continued, the protection will be necessary. But this will keep the factor prices of the abundant factor down.
7. The fundamental of the theory between many countries and involving many goods can be on the same "beads in the string" basis.

Wrong political policies have made Indian scenario "contaminated". India is labour rich and capital poor. Then why are the interest rates are also down even as wage rates are down in real terms. Abundance of labour has made Indian labour market casualised in most segments. Even regular jobs are not permanent. The hire and fire policy for labour under reforms also proves India is labour surplus. **It is an economic contamination that both wages and interest should go down at the same time.**

How did this happen. India allowed $ 120 billion dollars to come mostly in foreign institutional investment and not direct investment. Government of India prints new money to acquire dollars from the open market. The exporters and other receivers of dollars sell them to the authorised dealers. The money supply is increasing by leaps and not by bounds. Money supply was Rs. 2700 crore only in 1969. It was Rs. 51,00,000 crore in November 2009. ! Unemployment of labour is actually shortage of capital, so observed Ricardo. Why increasing capital is not reducing unemployment ? Most of the FII is in speculation. It is spoiling the stock markets and the bulls and bears are looting the asses (common men). Now daily fluctuations in stock market dictate terms to the chief executives of India. India is paying 4 times more interest to foreigners while interest to the Indians was reduced by 60 p.c. Capital intensity is in papers and not in the production of real goods and it is not ending abundance of labour through employment generation.

NOTES

1. Theory explains in words. Theorem explains with geometry and algebra.
2. Factor abundance; is relative. India is capital rich and labour poor vis-a-vis Bangladesh, while the position is reverse with reference to the USA. The USA is capital poor vis-a-vis Canada and labour rich. Canada has small population and capital per unit of labour is more. K/L. ratio is higher in Canada. L/K ratio is higher in the USA. In other words. USA has less capital per unit of labour and Canada has less labour per unit of capital. Suppose two countries have the same ratios: K/L. L/K in one country and K/L. L/K in another country. Then I/W interest wage ratio will decide.

   Ray and Kundu wrote a 550_page book on this theory.

6 | Factor Price Equalisation and Factor Price Reversal Hypotheses: Leontief Paradox

FACTOR PRICE EQUALISATION HYPOTHESIS

THIS WAS DEVELOPED BY NOBLE PRIZE WINNER IN ECONOMICS, PROF. PAUL SAMUELSON. THUS THIS IS ALSO KNOWN AS H-O-S THEORY.

An *intuitive* proof of the theorem is provided. If the trading continues between the two countries on the basis of the H-O theory, then both the *absolute and relative* prices of the factors will become equal: relative prices mean the W/I ratios. Here the trade ceases, unless the comparative advantage re-emerges due to reversal of the factor intensity and then factor prices. Step by step there are three statements:

(a) International trade on H-O principle will reduce the factor price differences.
(b) International trade on H-O principle will equalise the factor price ratios.
(c) International trade on H-O principle will reverse the factor price ratios, if some inequalities re-emerge.

Theoretically this should happen stage by stage. However, it has not happened. Thus what we observe is that only (a) can happen.

It can also be demonstrated (and this has been done with many obfuscating diagrams) that because of the differences in currencies and several other things, the absolute prices may not get equalized but the relative prices may get equalized.

The entire discussion may be intellectually interesting but in the absence of complete freedom of the movement of labour and capital between the countries, factor prices are difficult to get equalised. Transport barriers also pose problems: so do several other types of restrictions.

Above all, there are restrictions on free flow of goods and services between the countries. The old exporters of the theory of free trade have become great protectionists now !

Factor Proportion Reversal: Factor Price Reversal Hypotheses

Factor prices reversal hypothesis is the extension of the hypothesis of the 'factor price equalisation'. If the latter is not ever realised, then the first hypothesis is a non-starter. Not much ink need be wasted on this !

The formulation of the hypothesis is simple. Suppose India exports iron to Bangladesh and Bangladesh exports jute to India. In due course of time there will be so much demand for the labour in the production of jute that the wage-interest ratio in Bangladesh will become higher than the wage-interest ratio in India. The wages in Bangladesh rise because of the continued demand for labour in jute production. A time comes when there is not only full employment of labour but 'over-full' i.e., shortage of labour relative to its demand !

Meanwhile the same process for iron is repeated in India. India exports so much of iron that capital becomes short and interest- wage ratio becomes higher in India relative to Bangladesh.

In such case India will find itself suitable for growing jute and Bangladesh for iron, if nature permits. Specialisation, factor intensity and factor prices will be opposite of what they used to be. H-O theorem will continue to be valid. Only the factor abundance and scarcity change. The principle remains the same "export that commodity in which the comparative advantage in prices is the highest, based on the principle of intensive use of the abundant factor and less-intensive use of the scarce factor."

We can say that there can be a tendency towards factor price equalisation. But equalisation does not take place. Reversal also does not take place.

USA once used to export cars to (say) Japan. Now Japan can export and is exporting cars to USA. This trade reversal should be traced to changes in the demand rather than in the cost or price ratios. Car users found the small cars of Japan an answer to traffic congestion at that time. They were not noisy as well. The fuel efficient cars were demanded not because of the differences in the purchasing prices but because of the costs of running and maintaining them.

2. (b) How Far is The Above Analysis Realistic?

Many economists are of the opinion that it may not be so unrealistic to assume that commodity prices can get equalized due to international trade, but some caution should be exercised in asserting that interest and wage rates in all countries will get equalized. It is true that it will pay to trade only when commodity prices are different and if they are not different or if equal differentiation in cost emerges, further trade should cease. In the words of Ingo Walter:

> "It is much more difficult to believe that a complete equalization of relative factor prices will occur more or less automatically as this model suggests."

All we can say is that trade will likely to equalize the relative prices of factors of production internationally. This too will happen under certain conditions:

(a) only two commodities are produced in two countries;
(b) identical productive techniques prevail in both countries i.e., in both countries a capital intensive good is produced with the same type of capital intensity;
(c) one product is capital intensive and the other product is labour intensive;
(d) capital in two countries or the labour in two countries is identical;
(e) both factors are used in the production of both goods;
(J) supply of factors remains the same;
(g) there are no transport costs;
(h) perfect competition prevails in both the markets and there are no artificial restrictions of any type.

Here the assumption of identical technological conditions is crucial and since it cannot be found, the entire exercise is unrealistic. There is always a lag between inventions and innovations on the one·hand, and world-wide application on the other hand. The technology of not only developed and less developed countries differs but also between one developed and the other developed country.

2. (c) Factors That Come in the Way of Factor-price Equalisation

The tariff and quota restrictions, the presence of transport costs and the absence of perfect competition either in the product or in the factor market come in the way of factor-price equalisation in different countries. The monopolies, the transnational companies, and international oligopolies introduce all sorts of distortions in the imaginary world of those who wrote about factor price equalisation.

In a dynamic world, constant returns to scale and identical factors of production to be used in production cannot be imagined. Iron cannot be produced in China and USA or India and Japan or Bangladesh and Germany with the same type, level and quantum of technology.

Interestingly, one of the reasons given by some economists that hinders the factor-price equalisation is "factor price reversal" ! If there is a high wage-interest ratio in USA compared to (say) India, it will not become equal to the ratio in India, because over a period of time it will have a higher interest-wage ratio; it is a case of confusion getting worst confounded. A non-operational thesis is proved to be non- operational because of something else which itself is non- operational. Thus factor-prices will differ: either they will be of high wages-interest variety or high interest-wage variety in the same country.

Factor price equalisation theorem is highly static in nature. There is no reason why a capital rich country should remain capital rich. If a capital rich country exports capital intensive goods, it earns foreign exchange; foreign trade multiplier works (see chapter on the same) and income and employment rise in the country. Out of the increased incomes, there will be extra-savings and hence greater capital formation.

How can we prove that a labour abundant country will remain labour abundant ? Will not increased income from exporting labour intensive good, increase the employment and income of labour ? Will they not save and become capital rich ? Or, something different can happen ? It can be (and has been) argued that international trade may lead to high degree of immiserisation due to deteriorating terms of trade. Thus poverty may increase ! If that is so the attitude of people towards family planning may remain as irrational as ever. So population may increase !

In this section again, it will be more realistic to conclude that international trade everywhere should increase the share of labour in absolute terms. Whether a country remains labour abundant or not will depend upon a myriad of circumstances and causes, in which international trade will have very little role to play. However, the role of international trade in increasing capital accumulation will be more direct and substantial.

2. (d) Conclusion

There are always leads and lags in technological applications. Then the character of the people, the climate, topographical conditions and the role of government differ. The productive factors are not qualitatively identical. Differences in nutrition, education, discipline, socio-cultural-economic- political environment, work habits, and rectitude of character also determine the qualitative aspects of workers. Therefore, there may be some tendency towards equalisation —or to put it more precisely—towards reduction in differences, there will be no tendency towards complete equalisation. Walter wrote:

"Some of the assumptions (of factor equalisation theory), are not always essential for factor-price equalisation to occur in each and every circumstance. But, in the main, their restrictiveness is sufficient to render the notion of complete factor-price equalisation non-operational for all practical purposes.

LEONTIEF PARADOX
(CRITICISM OF THE H-O MODEL: THEN CRITICISM OF THE PARADOX)

Wassily Leontief, Nobel Prize winner in Economics, disturbed the serenity of the H-O theorem. Leontief also worked on input- output tables. Leontief test was very famous and controversial test of the H-O factor endowments theory of comparative advantage. The Harward economists' theory was first published in 1953.

As we have seen, according to the factor-endowments theory, a given country should be importing commodities which would have used its scarce factor intensively and should be exporting those commodities which use abundant factor intensively. USA, as everybody would readily acknowledge, has a very high capital- labour ratio and can be regarded as capital rich and labour 'poor'. Its exports are expected to be capital-intensive and imports labour-intensive. Leontief, using data for the year 1947, gave a startling finding that USA exports were more labour intensive.

Leontief came to this conclusion by adding 'human capital elements' to labour. He considered the U.S. labour three times more efficient than the U.K. labour Hence he multiplied the number of U.S. hours expended by a factor 3 to show higher labour intensity. He drew opposite inferences from American data and explained that this was due to the fact that real world conditions differed markedly from those presupposed to exist according to H.O. theory. For example, full employment had never been attained by any capitalist economy; production functions are not everywhere the same; costs are not the only deciding factors and demand conditions play an important part and finally, which is more important, trade restrictions and discriminations of various sorts are the order of the day.

W.W. Leontief : "Domestic Production and Foreign Trade: The American Capital Position Re-examined" *Proceedings of the American philosophical, Society.* Vol. 97 Sept. 1953.

Leontief : Factor Proportions and the Structure of American Trade: Further Theoretical and Empirical Analysis. Review of Economics and Statistics. Nov. 1956.

N.S. Buchanan : "Lines on the Leontief Paradox." Economia International. Nov. 1955.

B.C. Swerling : "Capital Shortage and Labour Surplus in the United States." Review of Economics and Statistics. Aug. 1954.

Stefan Valavanis-Vail : "Leontief's Scarce Factor Paradox." *Journal of Political Economy.* Dec. 1954.

Leontief : "Domestic Production and Foreign Trade: The American Position Re-examined".

Wassily Leontief wanted to find out input-output relations for various American (USA) industries. It is generally believed that full employment or near full employment in USA could be largely due to armament production and if war industries reduce their production, the economy will be engulfed in a severe slump. Leontief sought to find out the input-output relation of USA's armament industries with other industries. He found that armament industries are more input consuming than output supplying with respect to other industries. (This means a curtailment in armament production will not bring widespread slump.)

Leontief also found that if exports worth one million dollars were to be reduced, they would save more labour than capital. Thus, to his surprise and to the surprise of all, it was found by him that exports of USA were more labour using than capital using. This went against the H-O theorem. Marginal reduction in exports, averred Leontief, would release more labour than capital.

By common observation or consent USA is capital rich i.e., has more capital per labour. Its exports "should have been", in the light of the H-O theory, of goods which are manufactured with capital-intensive technology. Its imports should consist of labour-intensive goods. If this is so then H-O theorem holds good. If not, it does not. Or, it will be proved that USA is not so capital rich.

Leontief himself acknowledges the H-O position that America has more capital per worker than in other countries. He goes on to explain the paradox:

"American labour was getting three times more wages in comparison to (say) British worker. Still it was able to export goods to that country. What was the reason ? Apparently, this was due to the fact that American worker's productivity was more than three times higher. Thus, American worker was three times more efficient than the workers of other countries."

Leontief, therefore, wanted that labour-efficiency ratios be compared. He wanted American worker to be explained in terms of labour efficiency units. Actual labour is a certain multiple of apparent labour supply there. This is how Leonticf finds that American exports are more labour intensive. Superior organisation of American industry makes American labour more efficient.

Leontief used the inter-industry matrix that had been developed for the United States to test the validity of H-O propositions. He took representative baskets of exports and imports goods worth $ 1 million each. The capital and labour intensities of different goods were included in the composite index in the same proportion in which the goods figured in the exports/imports. If a particular good constituted 6% of the exports, its c/l ratio was calculated for an amount of $ 60000 i.e., 6% of the million.

Leontief calculated four numbers: (i) capital required for $ 1 million exports; (ii) capital required in $ 1 million imports; (iii) labour required for $ 1 million exports, and (iv) labour required in $ 1 million of imports.

For the year 1947 he found this:

Inputs required	*Exports*	*Imports replacing imports*
Capital	$ 25,50,000	$ 30,91,000
Labour man-years	182	170
C/L ratio	$ 14,011	$18,182
(S per man-year)		

For the year 1951 he found this:

Inputs required	*Exports*	*Imports replacing imports*
Capital	$ 22,56,800	$ 23,03,400
Labour man-years JC/L	174	168
ratio	$ 12,970	$ 13,710

Thus, he found exports to be less capital intensive and imports to be more capital intensive. In opposite terms he found USA's exports to be more labour intensive thean the imports.

The capital co-efficint for imports was highr:

$$1947: \frac{\text{Capital/labour ratio of imports}}{\text{capital/labour ratio of exports}} = 1.3$$

$$1951: \frac{\text{Capital/labour ratio of imports}}{\text{capital/labour ratio of exports}} = 1.106$$

In both the years he found high capital intensity in imports than in exports.

His refutation of H-O model was also based on imports analysis. American imports were capital intensive. This conclusion was arrived at by him by comparing American exports with those imports that were import replacements.

Critical estimate of the Leontief Paradox

(1) Leontief paradox itself has been criticised by many writers of international economics. It is pointed out that Leontief paradox was based on American trade data of 1937-47. At that time the American trade policies were highly protective. The exports of American goods were also influenced by protective policies of other countries. Trade flows at that time were not free (they never are). American industries were not so capital intensive in those years as they are now, nor was America producing so many capital goods. Then most of the imports into America were from American firms.

(2) Secondly, it is pointed out that Leontief should have compared capital or labour intensity of imported goods with respect to the country of origin. He committed the mistake of comparing capital intensity of American exports with those imports that were to become import replacement goods. Such goods arc naturally produced with capital intensive technology. Actual exports and imports should have been compared with respect to the countries in which they were produced. Leontief compared capital intensity of both types of goods with respect to American production function.

(3) Such comparisons were irrelevant to the H-O theory. Capital-labour and labour-capital ratios of two countries should have been compared. Leontief made no input-output study of foreign countries. Instead he fell back on the capital intensity of import replacement in America. Since America is a capital rich country and employs capital intensive production methods, import replacement would naturally use

relatively more capital to produce similar goods than the foreign countries supplying them to America.

(4) It was also a mistake to put the H-O theorem into reverse viz., on the basis of his analysis Leontief should have inferred that America was capital-poor country. This means that one cannot infer from trade pattern what relative factor endowments are.

(5) Leontief paradox can also be explained by the fact that the author failed to include investment in human capital formation (health, education and training) in capital. Labour productivity is a function of investment in human capital which enhances skill, knowledge, performance and motivation. Leontief himself alludes to the fact that the labour productivity in America's exports sectors is considerably higher than in the import competing sectors. Such doubts were expressed by *Arrow, Chenery, Minhas* and *Solow*. It is pointed out that this might well be the result of a high rate of investment in human capital in the export sector. Hence, if capital is defined as physical plus human capital, America may still be found to be exporting capital intensive goods. This interpretation would have resolved the paradox even with respect to the time Leontief demonstrated it.[1]

(6) Samuelson has pointed out that many imports in USA are of those things in which the third factor (land or natural resources, which are abundant, say, in Africa or Latin America) play an important part. Those natural resource factors were arbitrarily apportioned by Leontief to capital and labour. Thus "Lcontief definition of factors of production" was different from H.O. Hoffmeyer also finds that many resource-factor rich imports were taken by Leontief in his classification as capital rich.

(7) *Swerling* argued that the inclusion of certain industries with low capital labour ratios excessively influenced Leontief's results. W.P. Travis has pointed out that Leontief paradox is the result of US and foreign tariffs which distort the pattern of trade which would reflect relative factor endowments.

(8) *Romney Robinson* has suggested that demand conditions within a country might be so biased towards consumption of a product embodying a relatively abundant factor of production that its relative abundance is neutralized by a high level of domestic demand. Likewise, a country well endowed with capital may import the capital-intensive commodity if it has reached the level of real income at which its income elasticity of demand for such goods is high. Similarly a labour endowed country may export a capital-intensive product if its income level at the margin is such that it chooses to use the labour-intensive product at home.

(9) *Bharadwaj's study of India's* export to USA shows that India's exports were capital intensive while the imports from USA were labour-intensive. His study accords with the Leontief paradox.

(10) *Bo Sodersten* is of the opinion that Leontiefs explanations are too good to be true. The subsequent studies and 'proofs' provided by Leontief have been regarded by Sodersten as quite unconvincing. "They were more theoretical curiosum than a very likely empirical possibility." Sodersten says "it is not easy to swallow the multiplicative constant 3 without further ado." There are certain contradictions also in Leontiefs contentions; at one time he assumes homogeneous factors of production and at other times he talks of differences in productivity.

(11) *Stolper* studied the trade and factor intensity data for East Germany and Tatemote and *Ichimura* made similar study for Japan. They made disaggregative study and found that exports to less developed countries from these countries are capital intensive. Their results accord with the H-O theorem. In trade with the US, Japanese exports were more labour intensive and imports capital intensive. However, exports from Japan to other less developed countries were more capital intensive.

Surprisingly, Wahl found that for Canada, whose trade is mostly with the USA, exports to US were mostly capital intensive.

Wells concluded: "Clearly much more research remains to be done in this very intricate field; so far we really know very little about the precise relationship between any country's pattern of trade and its factor endowment."

When Leontief made his study, the main items of imports were crude oil, paper pulp, primary copper and lead, and metallic ores. These products were imported because the US was not in a position to produce them. They were Capital intensive.

Sodersten concludes:

"Nothing has established or refuted the H-O theorem. It might seem strange that so much theoretical speculation has been built on such fairly limited empirical investigations. This has not only to do with the fact that many economists prefer theoretical inventiveness to painstaking emprirical research. It has also, probably, to do with the fact that the pure theory of trade is quite abstract by nature. Static theories such as the factorce-equalisation theorem or the H-O theory of comparative advantage should perhaps not, primarily be viewed as geared onward empirical testing. They are first and foremost means of studying the general equilibrium characteristics of open economies." (107)

OTHER POINTS OF CRITICISM OF H-O THEOREM

The Factor Reversal and Factor Equalisation theses have been presented as 'criticisms' of H-O theorem. Similarly, the Leontief paradox is also a very important point of criticism of H-O theory. We have already examined how far they are true and valid criticisms. Here some 'other' criticisms of the H-O theorem are presented.

(1) H-O theorem tells us that trade between two countries can take place only when factor proportions differ. Differences in the quality of factors do not matter. These propositions have not been found acceptable by many critics. They point out that the overwhelming proportion of trade in manufactures takes place between different countries of EEC which have more or less similar factor endowments or between the countries of Africa.

(2) Not merely differences in prices and costs but also differences in the quality of products, innovations and other technological considerations (inventions for example) play an important part in determining trade pattern. Demonstration effect transcends costs and prices considerations. The desire to have "phoren" (as the word foreign is sarcastically put) ignores cost and price considerations and is responsible for regular and non-regular (smuggling) trade.

(3) It has also been pointed out that many economists who have tried to prove or disprove the theory have twisted the data to suit their observations. Empirical data can be used for both purposes.

(4) H-O theorem assumes constant production function, which is far from correct in any time period. Perfectly competitive prices were assumed while in practice we

find international prices are now monopolistically or oligopolistically determined.

(5) To prove the factor price equalisation theorem, one will have to know the pre-trade prices. For knowing this the trade will have to be stopped ! Obviously, this cannot be done. This is the crux of the problem. Some critics, on the other hand say, "product prices are already equalised except for the differences due to tariff, transport costs and the like."

(6) It is also argued that two countries can have identical factor endowments and identical tastes and still can trade because, the use of different technologies leads to differences in domestic rates of transformation.

In conclusion it may be said that H-O theorem has great pedagogic value. It is, a central theory of international trade for reasons that are not directly connected with its realism. The theory emphasies the international trade flows depend on factor proportions and prices of factors. It proves that complete specialisation is not beneficial.

A theory will, however, remain a theory. The theory too does not provide with a complete explanation of the international trade flows. Identify of production functions eliminates differences in knowledge and techniques, and the constant returns to scale eliminate differences in size, so that only one difference remains —a difference in proportions between qualitatively identical factors. Now-a-days there is so much trade in "intermediate goods". These goods are 'final goods' for one producer but become 'inputs' to another producer. Apportioning of the factors congealed in these types of goods between 'A' and 'B' countries — both of which participated in the production of that commodity—becomes very difficult.

All said, the consensus of economists supports more the H-O hypotheses and conclusions that of those who have advanced the factor equalisation, factor reversal and factor-embodiment paradox.

Kravis, Keesing, Kenen, Baldwin, Bowen, Leemer etc. on Leontief Paradox

Leontief himself used new data rather than the data close to World War II to find out the validity of his observations. He confirmed the paradox, though admitted that the labour intensity to the tune of just 6 p.c. extra.

Kravis wrote about Leontief paradox and his observations were incorporated in some books as 'separate theory'. He found that the USA exports were labour intensive because of *better human capital of USA* which made goods of better quality not made in other countries. *Better technology was the result of better human capital.* Highly protected industries of the USA and this feature even more prominently. Kravis wrote about the "availability" and "non-availability" determining international trade. Availability is marketable surplus due to better "supply responses" i.e., the ease with the additional resources can be marshalled to produce additional supplies according to the actual or projected demand. Non-availability is, naturally, the opposite.

Kravis, however, did not write about the absolute and relative availability and non-availability. The de Beers company of South Africa exports diamonds to those countries also which produce diamonds e.g., India. Some have total unavailability and the exports of diamonds from South Africa will be due to "absolute unavailability" and some have limited availability for domestic consumption and entre-pot trade (imports for exports) as in India. Sometimes the non- availability and availability may relate to better goods. A country may be producing cars but not of the better qualities availability elsewhere.

Kravis conducted empirical research and found that the productivity of the USA workers was precisely 15 p.c. higher than elsewhere for the same wage per hour. Kravis wrote that "production base" (volume and quality) is more important for the trade, which the USA had. *It is the quality of human resource that uses the natural resources better and fully and that develops technology*. Government policies and price differences will come next. Kravis also used several diagrams which were of the same nature as in the previous theories.

Kennen (*1965*) also argued that the comparative advantage in international trade emerged due to differences in *human capital* and defined capital as result of "waiting". [This was nothing new, Ricardo had defined capital as "stored up labour" and there is naturally waiting for future use if one stores] Human capital is the mother of technology and then later on technology helps in the improvement of human capital. It is the quality of labour and not merely the quantity that is important (criticism of H-O theory). The capital element in humans is their tradable skill and their capacity to develop and use technology. Quality element in land and machines was also taken into account by Kennen. Vast barren land of Australia is of no comparison to fertile land elsewhere. Then there are good, better and best machines producing the same thing. According to Kennen, it was the better human capital of the USA which was responsible for better use/change in land use and for better technological developments getting embodied in machines.

Kravis, Keesing, Kenen and Baldwin were the supporters of the thesis of higher productivity of the USA labour due to better capital-contents-in-labour. The US labour was skill- intensive, and hence the goods were skill- intensive. Kenen with this empirical data and his formulations about human capital elements "succeeded" in eliminating the Leontief paradox i.e., he found it correct.

Baldwin, Branson and Monoyios while accepting the concept of human capital found it difficult to separate the human and physical capital elements. Learner argued that in a multi-factor world we should comparc the capital ratio in production versus consumption rather than exports versus imports. He found that this was higher in US production in comparison to consumption but could not enlighten how to resolve the paradox that production goods enter consumption. Bowen and Sveikauskas found with data from 27 countries and 12 resources that in half the cases H-O theorem stood good and in the other half the paradox ! We are left no where.

1. IB Kravis: "Availability and Other Influences on the Commodity Composition of Trade" Journal of Pol. Eco. April 1956
2. P. Kenen: Nature, capital and Trade: Journal of Pol. Eco. Oct. 1965.
3. RE: Baldwin: Determinants of the Commodity Structure of US Trade: A.E.R. March, 1971
4. WH Branson and N Monoyios. Factor Inputs in US Trade Journal of International Econ.
5. EE Learner: The Leontief Paradox Reconsidered Journal of Pol. Eco. June, 1980.
6. SB Linder: An Essay on Trade and Transformation NY, Wiley 1961
7. MV Posner: International Trade and Technical Change, Oxford papers 1961
8. R. Vernon: International Investment and International Trade in the Product Cycle. Quarterly Journal of Economics, May 1966.
9. Dominic Salvatore: International Economics Ch. 7 Opt Op. cit. Ibid.

NOTE

1. In 1951, Sir Donald MacDougall tested various hypotheses on international trade advanced by the classical and neo-classical economists. He tried to discover whether exports of USA were relatively more capital intensive than those of the U.K. MacDougall's criterion for capital intensiveness was the amount of horse-power used in the various industries. His results showed that the U.K. did not have a relatively smaller, and the US a relatively larger share in the market in capital intensive commodities. To this extent his conclusions shed some doubt on the validity of the H-O approach.

7 Some Important Post H-O Theories of International Trade

(1) LINDER's ECONOMIES OF SCALE THEORY AND 'PREFERENCE SIMILARITY' HYPOTHESIS (1961)
(2) POSNER's "LAGS/GAPS AND LEADS" MODEL (1961)
(3) VERNON'S PRODUCT CYCLE MODEL (1966)

Many writers wrote about many topics of international trade but not all contributions were related to the "pure theory of international trade" which tells us "when shall two countries trade and to what extent they shall trade". Theories which prove "gains of international trade through changing terms of trade" also come under the pure theories. Many contributions were to the '*applied*' international economics rather than to the pure economics and hence they are not included in this chapter.

Economists who wrote about the theories of protection vs. free trade or about tariffs, quotas, custom unions, trade blocs, exchange rate determination, exchange rate management, flows of labour, capital and technology, bilateral and multilateral trade arrangements, terms of trade **problems**, interface between economic growth and international trade, interface between transport costs and international trade, dumping, devaluation etc. *find place in other chapters of applied international economics.*

The entire pure international economics is the extension of the comparative cost theory of Ricardo just as the entire pure monetary economics is the confirmation or refutation of the quantity theory of money.

Some contributions were presented as empirical evidences on the validity of H-O theorems or of Leonlief paradox and do not deserve the place of being regarded as separate theories. *Many theories had very little to offer as something new. They were just "one-point theory" either of the demand side or of the supply side.* Naturally, despite being worded in the modern jargon and elaborately illustrated with algebra and geometry they cannot fall in the categories of the contributions of the great masters. Hence in this chapter only three important post H-O theories of international contributions have been included; but once again *it is emphasised that even these theories are eclectic in nature and are not of the same class as the theories discussed earlier.*

1. LINDER's ECONOMIES OF SCALE THEORY AND PREFERENCE SIMILARITY HYPOTHESIS (1961)

This theory tells a very simple thing that for any producer or group of producers to be able to export it is necessary that the good in question should be produced at the lowest possible cost. This lowest possible cost will be achieved when the internal economies exceed the internal diseconomies to their maximum extent. At this stage the good in question will become fit enough to be exported on the comparative cost basis.

Infact a curious extension of this model was that economies of scope come in the way of economies of scale. It was argued on the basis of some case studies that there were many firms of Europe and the USA producing similar products but the USA had comparative advantage because the firms there were not enmessed in the production many other items of the same type and genre in the same plant.

This is a curious observation in the sense that most frequently economics of scope further the economies of-scale. **The comparative advantage to the USA could be due to its exchange rate and dollar being the "vehicle" currency of the world.**

So far as the empirical evidence about economies of scope and scale being (i) complementary or (ii) competitive or (iii) neutral is concerned all types of results were obtained. Somewhere widening of the scope helped and somewhere the narrowing of the scope (division of labour) helped. Economists who adduced "proofs" used the case of one country producing under **decreasing opportunity costs (increasing returns) and the other under constant returns/costs.** It was easy to prove that economies of scale helped. There is nothing magical about it. We have seen in the Haberler's theory that if the production is subject to increasing returns, then complete specialisation will be profitable. **It will all depend upon the "accident" of which country receives the first order for which thing.** As soon as this order is received more production is made and the cost of production goes down further. The switch will continue i.e., less of the other commodity will be produced progressively till (in the two commodity model) there is complete specialisation in the first thing. The second thing will be imported more and more progressively till the entire quantity needed is imported.

Linder's theory is not new. Besides take the case of Japan: it now exports many things to India of which there is no use in Japan e.g., greetings cards of Indian festivals. It just penetrates Indian market and people buy for the novelty of it with Japanese paintings in the card. China is also doing the same.

Staffan B. Linder's starting point, as was seen, was that unless domestic market is assured, the country will not develop a new product. There is greater surety of achieving economies of scale in the home market than in the alien lands. Then the exports can be made to those countries which have similar levels of income (or atleast income levels to suit the sale of that good) and tastes. *This is meant by "preference similarity".* Tastes and incomes are highly correlated. As such the theory ipso facto implies that countries of the same per capita income levels will be easier to trade with. Similar tastes and dissimilar factor endowments give rise to price differences and hence international trade takes place. Thus the theory of Linder applies to manufactured goods.

If the exports are of "commodities" i.e., from the primary sector then "*scale*" means abundance of the good quality raw materials. If the exports are of goods *of manufacturing* (factory sector), then the *economies of scale* (*i.e.,* internal economies exceeding diseconomies in technical aspects, financial aspects, personnel management, production and marketing processing, transportation and storage process) will all count.

Linder was of the opinion that the economics of scale are to be obtained in the domestic market first and then they will automatically extend to the external market. *Domestic market is not regarded as "risky" by Linder and here he was in error because there may be presence of foreigners who will be exporting to this country. Then the domestic competition is also not to be disregarded.*

Critical evaluation of Linder's views:

Linder was of the opinion that since domestic surpluses are exported the innovations come first for the domestic market. However, if we take the case of Japan, most of their innovations are for exports. There are firms which produce for the foreign market. Their domestic market is quite "saturated" in the sense that most Japanese have everything they may need. Ever since the USA has forced inroads in Japan for its exports, the Japanese domestic market is not without risk. Infact it cannot be said for any country. India had bulging stocks of foodgrains in the year 2000 to the tune of 40 m.t. yet it was under an obligation to import 3 p.c. of its domestic consumption from outside. Low import prices were putting Indian farmers to risk.

Assumptions of similarity in the "preferences hierarchy" for "different quality of goods for different classes" are some after-thoughts that were incorporated to save the theory in the event of the main thrust point not being accepted by economists.

Linder was at pains to explain how two countries with similar factor endowments can trade (a criticism of H-O model) with the advantages of economies of scale. However, in carrying that argument to its logical conclusion with valid arguments, Linder introduced unconvincing elements.

2. POSNER's "LAGS/GAPS AND LEADS" MODEL (1961)

These authors have argued that differences in comparative costs emerge now due to technological differences. It is not necessary that one country may be having all the technological development and the other may not be having any technological change. Other countries can also innovate or imitate the technology of others or can take the right of the use of technology from the parent company on payment of royalty. The ultimate difference will be on the *type and extent* of the use of technology. Thus even with the same technology there can be technological gaps. Not the factor endowments alone but technological gaps determine the cost of production. *Then cost of production is comparable for the same type of the product.* The countries do not import the cheapest cars; they may be made inside the country and the most advanced cars may be imported at high prices from outside. If the other production bases are sound (*e.g., in India*) *then they can be manufactured in the country itself.*

Viewed in this light the *H-O model was made to appear static and placid* ! Technological gap model was developed by Posner in 1961. Similar things were happening in "Growth Economics", where models after models were pouring in as cars come out of the assembly lines. Solow went in so far as to *quantify that now eighty percent of growth is due to technology* and the rest twenty percent due to natural resources, labour and capital. Capital is now embodiment of technology. The latest railway engine which can haul lot of goods at top speeds is far superior to steam engine and though the N, L and K component may be equal it is difference in technology that makes it a separate product. *This model is extension of the views of Schumpeter and Solow from growth economics to international trade.* All innovations (which are of five types listed below) give temporary monopolies to the innovator or "technovator". The five types of innovations are:

(1) bringing a new product;
(2) producing it with new technology or production process;
(3) producing it with new raw material;
(4) finding a new market and
(5) reorganisation of the firm to have commanding position.

Now a days the innovations and new products are protected with patent rights. After GATT-8 and WTO (World Trade Organisation—see chapters elsewhere in this book), the imitators face stiff action. Most of the basic inventions came from the USA. This was due to several factors and one of which was that many innovators could not get appreciation or price for their innovations in their home economies. The USA grabs them. Besides the USA imports not only the innovations but innovators. The investment in research and development in USA is unmatched by any other country or even bloc. Thus USA became keen to protect its IPR (intellectual property rights). Imitators are taken to "the international court for trade matters" i.e., WTO. Their persons posing as tourists and buyers find out where the counterfeits are being sold. The USA gets them destroyed and this happens in computer software to other things of high value and low bulk e.g. Film and music c.ds. Only this enables it to export to full potential. (WTO sided with India in the case of patents relating to *neem, haldi and basmati). Those countries get comparative advantage in trade introduce new technology and before it is copied it brings still newer technology and their products.*

Critivaluation

Posner too makes certain assumptions as go with the theories. However, it was probably all right for earlier economists to make some simple assumptions but they sound hallow for modern theories. He makes the assumption of there being two countries while his observations will hold good for all countries taken together in order of relative comparative advantage.

Assumption of similar demand and supply conditions (factor endowments) in two countries was unnecessary as it was wrong. Posner was in error when he emphasised that the initial advantage is absolute; this may be true but the fundamental principle that for international trade to take place the advantage should be absolute *plus* comparative should have been made. The assertion that first the product is sold in the domestic market and then after saturation point is reached it is sold in the international market is also not true; this can be done simultaneously.

Posner was, however, right in pointing out that it is absolutely possible for an importing country to so imitate the production that it can have the comparative advantage *vis-a-vis* the original country. Everyone in the decades of 60s till the end of the 20th Century had the Japanese, Taiwanese, Korean, Singaporean, Hong Kong experience in mind. *These economies which were practising "export-led growth model" and were known as "Asian Tiger economies"* were doing that. Posner and most of the post H-O theories were based on these type "empirical evidences".

Posner's analysis of some "lags" and "leads" was also based on empirical evidences. He was right in noting that as soon as the product comes in the market, it takes time for its demand to emerge and pickup, (*domestic demand lag*). There will then be lag in the producer deciding that the product is to be exported and then create demand abroad.

The entire network of agents or channels of trade are to be built up. This will be "*demand lag" in international market.* The "imitation lag" will also emerge. This will again be of three types: imitation for domestic market and/or international market by the domestic producer and the third imitation by foreign producers in different countries for their own market. The third type of imitation can become so important that the imitator may pick up the foreign market of the original producer and not only that may export to the first exporting country ! Everything will depend upon the degree and nature of imitation and comparative cost advantage.

Posner talks of "demand lags", (domestic and foreign) and "learning period lags". Instead, he should have discussed in a comprehensive way the "supply lags" (anything less than what is needed and demanded in the domestic and international markets; and, to be more precise, about the all 'response' lags whether of "supply elasticities" or of "demand elasticities" relating to prices and incomes. Infact the 'cross elasticities with competitive firms and products' should have been discussed in greater details as to what shall happen and to what extent.

The less complicated the technology of the composition and process of manufacturing and the less the period of adjustment of finding inputs, factors, resources and means the easier it will be to fulfill the supply lags whether of the "original type" or of the "imitation type". Posner was in error in calling the "quick imitation" as "dynamism". Authorised and unauthorised imitation now determine the international trade. If imitation replications are found, they are destroyed.

What was 'dynamism' of 1960s is now subject to IPR in the 21st century. International trade is not allowed in such imitations which violate the intellectual property right (see relevant chapter on GATT and WTO in this book elsewhere). *Were Posner to revise the theory today he would be advised to use the word "adaptation" rather* than imitation.

Another problem with this theory is that the "balance of payment surplus" is made a function of high degree of imitation. The role of innovations and *high quality combined with comparative advantage for the goods by various income groups should have been emphasised.*

Had that been done that Posner would have sounded no different from Schumpeter. While it cannot be denied that countries made fortunes with imitations but imitations are now frowned upon. Imitations are common in the domestic market. There are 'counterfeit goods'. For example, many small time washing soap manufacturers use someone else's brand name or logo to sell goods. [There was a company manufacturing almirah under the name "PODREJ" but the word was so written in the style that it looked like "GODREJ". The almirah was an almirah, though not of the same finish and finis as Godrej. The manufacturer could have used some other name and tried to build goodwill for his product. The urban and educated persons cannot be taken for ride. On railway platforms of India several toothpastes are sold under the name colgate and the tube and packing looks almost the same as of Colgate except for the words G/C. The illiterate or those who could not observe the deception get cheated]. Such things can continue in the domestic market but counterfeiting or imitating big products is now closely monitored. *Firms now have their "economic spies"*.

It is true that imitators in international trade do not imitate or replicate the brand name and the logo. They imitate the process and the outer designs but the "basics and fundamentals" of the goods remain the same. *But the big companies which innovate are ever prepared to introduce new elements and they do so deliberately one after the another.*

The USA used to export radios based on vacuum tubes technology. Japan copied and captured big chunk of market due to the cheapness of its products (the labour is cheap in Japan in money terms and much more in terms of productivity). US introduced transistors and the Japanese again imitated. US then introduced printed circuits.

Take the case of computers; in India they were introduced as 386, 486, pentium... and so on gradually. This was done to first sell something which was out of the market in western countries. The foreign firms did not dump but sold the 386 computer at two times the price of the high-tech computer just in a period of five years of 1995-2000.

In international trade apart from imitation, there are several other healthy and unhealthy practices. For good political relations, the "less developed countries have to accept the old technology land even hazardous wastes in their country. Imitation is not enough.

3. VERNON'S PRODUCT CYCLE MODEL (1966)

Vernon presented these views in the form of "*product cycle model*". This again was an extension of the Schumpeter's growth economics in which he had pointed out that "innovations take place in clusters or in bunching". There is a sudden outburst of innovations and then lull and then again an outburst. The views of Schumpcter were lateron criticised that now-a-days the innovations are "daily affairs" and they are taken in strides. *But it cannot be denied that innovations of far reaching importance come rarely and not regularly. This gives rise to "product cycles" on the same pattern as the cycle of inflation, disinflation, deflation and reflation as discussed by Schumpeter.*

The first phase is characterised by the emergence of innovation for which credit is taken to be converted into capital. There is whole reorganisation of production process. There is money lead and goods lag because the new goods appear after the gestation lag. The prices rise and this is encouraging for the producers of new products which face no problem of not being sold at higher prices.

As demand is met and as production increases (as imitative investments are also made) the products are not sold in the same quantity, much less at the old prices. The recession starts; gets converted into deflation. Then the profits are low and everything is down. This shall continue till new innovation brings new products and then first the deflation is ended and then there is once again boom. *Some call it price cycle, others call it income cycle and still others call it product cycle.*

As the new product comes, there are limited number of machines and there are a limited number of workers who can produce that. There may be just one firm producing that product. Soon the technology becomes transparent. There can be movement of highly skilled labour to another firm. A rival-firm will hire such an expert at a very high package of Ps (pay, perks, power, promotion, pelf, position) and start production. Soon there will be many more persons who can produce that item as there will be many more machines to produce the same or similar product.

The product cycles depend upon the *war of attrition between the original producer and/or innovator of the new process and the imitators. The imitator has the advantage of not having spent anything on the research and development.* Japan had the bad reputation of just dismantling the products made by others and then deciphering the contents/process. Their imitations were cheap due to their cheap labour. Japanese labour proved cheap because they were, and still are, "workoholics". This was true of all types of electronic goods. '

The USA brought about most of the improvements in automobiles; the Japanese and the Koreans became world-famous by putting those things in small cars.

Posner-Verner Model is different from H-O model in one respect. The comparative advantage in costs and prices is with one country for ever in H-O model; in P-V model it can shift from one country to another; back to the same country and when this is happening the product and more precisely the product differentiation for different categories of the buyers will change in favour of or against a country. *This is the cycle.*

Most of the new theories were developed *with reference to the US economy* and the product cycle theory also related to that economy. After the initial innovative production comes in the market, the four product cycles were envisaged for the US only and they were:

1. The USA produces for the domestic market;
2. The USA then starts exporting;
3. The USA can export less as other countries start producing; and
4. The USA becomes net importer as foreign prices fall.

This happened in the US for certain products as radio, television, synthetic fibres, transisters and calculators. There were cases in the US when it found itself in the fourth stage bypassing the second and third stages. This put it under tremendous loss. The following diagram shows the four stages:

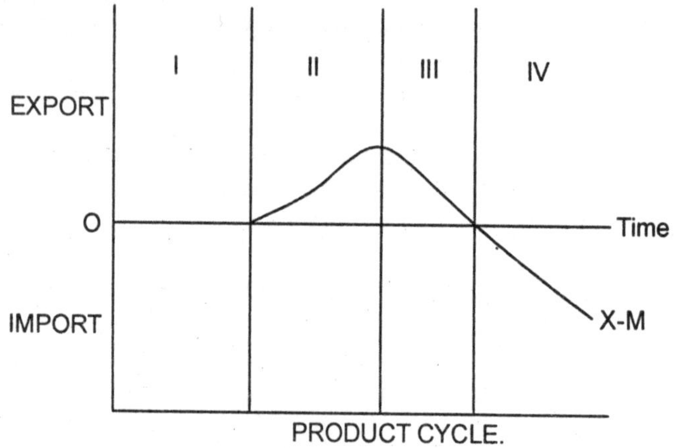

Diagram 7.1

The innovating country gets the lead but it can be temporary and hence new innovations in the same product will have to come to make it become a little more different. The comparative advantage is also temporary and it can go to the country which imitates. The high allocations of funds and high devotion of the persons to innovate and develop made the USA a leader in new product only to suffer at the hands of the imitators. If the imitators achieve the economy of scale fast and their imitations look like and function like the "real'/origional ones, the innovating country loses even more.

The USA had comparative advantage in innovation but later it was snatched away by the imitators in production. The factor proportion and the comparative advantage theory is vindicated but imitators snatched away that advantage illegitimately. The imitators adjusted factor endowment availability to the imitated product to gain comparative advantage.

The imitating countries had cheap labour. Economies in money term in the use of that were utilised to be diverted to capital accumulation for the imitated product. That was the lament of the US economists.

Critivaluation

Vernon *makes assumptions of ignorance on the part of others*! In his theory, the domestic produces do not know what is happening in foreign markets nor the foreign producers know what is happening elsewhere. The products are solely designed or redesigned on the basis of the knowledge of the domestic market. *Assumptions are part of theory but for dynamic theories, as they claim to be, the assumptions of the type which assume 'isolation and insulation from outside world' are self- contradictory. Objection is not to making assumptions; objection is to making self-contradictory assumption. The assumptions of theory which are not realistic to the time in which the theory was set cannot be accepted. If the assumptions become wrong in time to come, we cannot blame the author.*

Another assumption of the type of neo-classical growth models (such growth models assume that workers consume all and capitalists save all) that all innovations take place in capital rich countries is also not correct.

The assumptions of the new models that the entire production of the innovating company is *first* solely for the domestic market is not correct. It is not correct to assume that only 'genuine marketable surpluses' are sold in the international market. Many countries produce different things for the domestic and international market separately right from the start. It is common to find the firms advertising that a product being of "export quality" in the domestic market itself. India prepares costly rugs (*Qaaleen*) or aromatic tea for foreign markets. It is also common to find that desire to earn foreign exchange forces the government to export things which are highly demanded/needed in the domestic market. The result of the exports of such goods is that their domestic price goes up and then everyone has to either curtail some demand or some have to forgo the consumption of it altogether, (onions in the past for example in India).

Vernon lumped the countries into three groups about domestic consumption vis-a-vis exports.

(1) Countries which produce the new product both for the national and international market right from the very beginning e.g., the rich capitalist countries.
(2) Countries which start exporting only after domestic demand is met and then export; as middle range countries; and
(3) Countries which always remain importers for the product.

The problem is not with classification but with a neat division into three categories. There are a few poor countries which may start a particular production for exports only. India had many HPEU (hundred percent export units) and they were established by foreign countries to avail the advantage of cheap labour in India. Some industrial estates were designed for such industries only.

Long long back Waber had talked about raw materials being of two types — ubiquitous and specific. Ubiquitous raw materials are found everywhere while the specific raw materials are tied. The last one are those which carry low value in high bulk. Their processing is to be done near the source of raw materials. *Similarly the new product, when it is produced by many and can be produced by any, becomes "standardised". The product is raw in the initial stages and "mature" when the original producer can export it. New nomenclature does not impress.*

NOTE

1. It is rare to find mention of the important contributions made by the non-Europeans in international Economics. However, even a casual use of a word by a western economist becomes a "hypothesis", "theory", "policy proposition" or 'paradigm".

8 International Trade and Demand and Supply Curves Theory'—The Offer Curves ("Gains analysis included")

I. OFFER CURVES AND TERMS OF TRADE LINES

Ordinary partial (or particular) equilibrium of price determination of a commodity is shown with the help of a demand curve and a supply curve. In international trade, however, there are two goods — and hence two supply curves and two demand curves. Price can be expressed in money terms but it is also a fact that the commodities offered in export are in fact prices of the commodities imported. The problem of showing two demand and two supply curves in one diagram is solved by offer curves.

Offer curve is an important tool of analysis in international economics which shows how gains from trade can be illustrated with the use of this tool. With the help of offer curves analysis, we can show the inter-action of the demand and supply forces of international trade. Offer curves were used by Edgeworth and Marshall and since then are being used in the diagrammatic representations of the theories.

An offer curve of the country is both a supply curve and a demand curve. As a supply curve it shows the various amounts of exports that a country will be willing to exchange against specific amounts of imports. As a demand curve it indicates the amounts of imports that a country will be willing to acquire for specific amounts of exports. The offer curve is, however, different from ordinary demand and supply curves. They show the various quantities demanded or supplied at different money prices. The offer curve expresses the demand for one good (import) in terms of the supply of another good (export). If we treat the second good as money, the offer curve could be construed, as a demand curve in terms of the quantities of goods against total amount of money. It would, however, be a total revenue curve, as opposed to an ordinary demand curve which relates quantities of a good to price or average revenue per unit.

At the intersection point of two offer curves of two countries we get the 'terms of trade line', which is the same thing as 'equilibrium price line' in an ordinary demand and supply diagram.

An offer curve can be defined as the locus of all two-commodity combinations (wheat-cloth) which a country (say Pakistan) finds acceptable in trade. Its shape is derived from both supply and demand conditions in a country. The offer curves of two countries determine the terms of trade at the points of intersection. Volume of trade will then be a function of these terms of trade available.

Offer curves determine the ITT (international terms of trade) on which exports are traded for imports. These ITT have to be higher than the DTT. The difference will determine the zone of trading. Zone of trade gives an idea about the quantum of gains from the trade. The ITT and DTT lines will show how these gains are shared.

These offer curves can be drawn. Suppose India and Pakistan are two countries which are specialising in wheat and cloth respectively. The offer curve of Pakistan can be drawn:

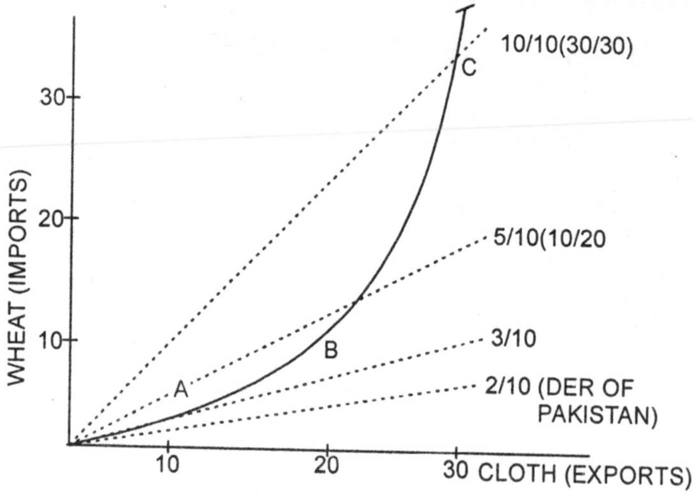

Diagram 8.1

In the above diagram we see that at point 'A' Pakistan offers 10 metres of cloth for only 3 maunds of wheat. As more cloth is demanded, Pakistan will demand higher price (wheat). Thus for 20 metres it demands (say) 10 maunds of wheat; for 30 metres it demands as much as 30 maunds of wheat. As Pakistan offers more cloth to India, the importance of cloth in Pakistan increases because less of it will be left there. The importance of wheat will decrease (because of the declining marginal utility of wheat there). Pakistan will accept increasing wheat imports (offer cloth) only in exchange for decreasing amounts of cloth per maund of wheat.

Pakistan's offer curve is cloth supply curve and wheat demand curve. It is presumed that PPC of Pakistan is under increasing costs so that it has to demand higher price for higher supply.

The lines drawn from the point of origin 'O' arc the terms of trade lines.

2/10	or	2/10
3/10	or	3/10
10/20	or	5/10
30/30	or	10/10

It is presumed that 2/10 is the DTT of Pakistan and hence on these terms of trade Pakistan offers nothing. Pakistan starts offering above these terms (say) at 3/10. As Pakistan moves from 3/10 to 10/10, the terms of trade of Pakistan improve. An offer curve shows (*i*) for higher supplies more will be demanded, (*ii*) at low prices more will be demanded and at higher prices, less will be demanded.

Offer curve of India

Offer curve of India is shown here on vertical axis. It could be shown on the horizontal axis also but we have already earmarked cloth for horizontal axis.

This curve is also based on the fundamental principle that more will be offered at higher price (expressed in terms of metres of cloth). More and more cloth will be required as more and more wheat is to be exported. In other words, offer of wheat for the same amount of cloth will decline.

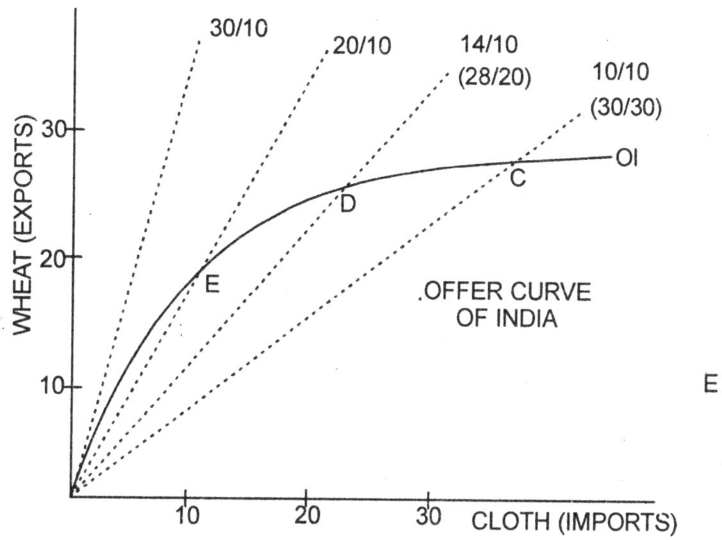

Diagram 8.2

In the above diagram, 30/10 line represents the domestic terms of trade in India. India will offer nothing on these terms to Pakistan. When it offers (or Pakistan is willing to take) less than 30 maunds for 10 metres of cloth, India will start offering wheat (say 28/10). The points 20/10 and then 14/10 (28 maunds for 20 metres) and 10/10 (30 maunds for 30 metres) represent improvements in the terms of trade available to India. India will offer more when for the same amount of wheat, it gets more cloth; or, put it another way, she has to offer less wheat for the same amount of cloth.

II. EQUILIBRIUM TERMS OF TRADE

Equilibrium point: is arrived at the intersection of the demand and supply curves. As we have seen, each offer curve is the demand curve and supply curve. For example, the offer curve of India is the supply curve of wheat as also the demand curve of wheat for Pakistan. Thus at the intersection of the two offer curves two supply and two demand curves intersect in effect. No other point except the point of equilibrium equates the demand and supply. If the price is higher than the equilibrium price, supply will become in excess of demand both due to increase in supply effect and fall in the demand effect. If on the other hand, price is less than the equilibrium price there will be unfulfilled demand.

The equilibrium terms of trade, with the help of offer curves of the two countries, will be determined as under:

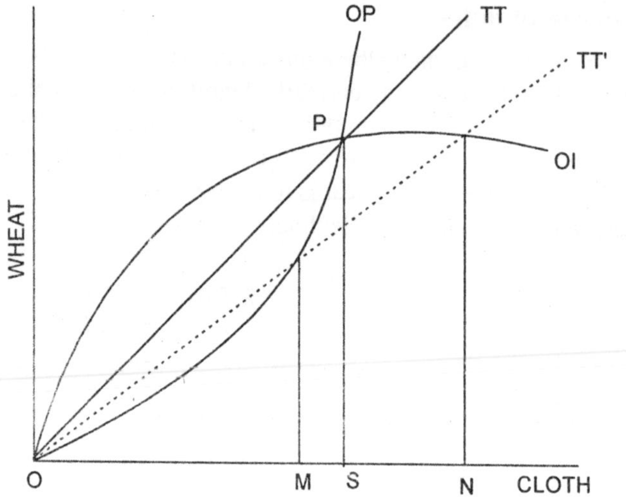

Diagram 8.3

In the diagram above, the equilibrium terms of trade are determined at point P, represented by TT. No other point gives equilibrium terms of trade. If the TT should have been term of trade line, then Pakistan will offer less cloth (OM) (formerly OS) while India would requires more (ON), MN shall then be unfulfilled excess demand for cloth.

This excess demand will tend to drive the price of cloth (in terms of wheat) upward until the quantity supplied is equal to the quantity demanded. The TT' line will consequently rotate to the left until it reaches the position TT If TT are to the left (steeper), there will be excess supply till the TT' rotate to the right on the equilibrium point.

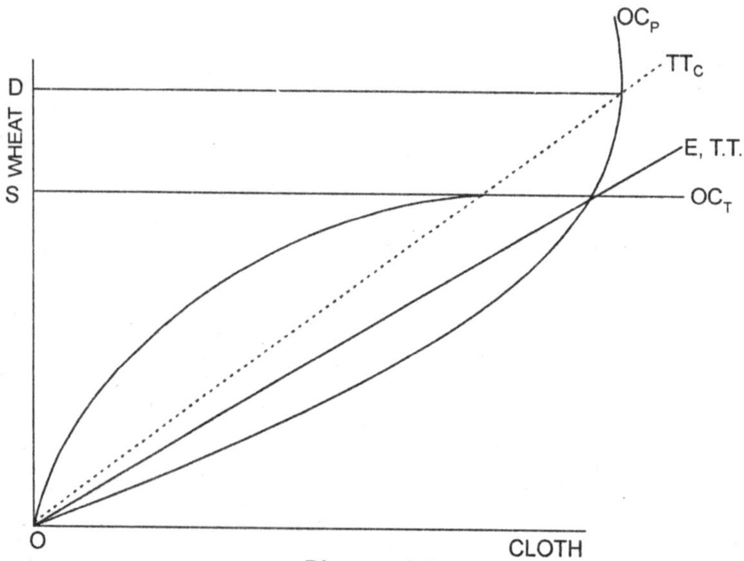

Diagram 8.4

In the above diagram we show OQ and OQ and equilibrium terms of trade.

If the TT line is changed to TTc, then India will offer OS wheat while Pakistan will demand OD wheat (on the points of intersections of OQ and OCP with new TT line TTC).

DS will be unfulfilled demand of wheat. The it line will have to rotate back to TT, if OQ and OCp remain the same and equilibrium is sought.

III. THE OFFER CURVE AND CHANGES IN DEMAND

If Pakistan demands more cloth for its own consumption, then its offer curve OP will becomes OF i.e., it will shift leftwards. Now it will require more wheat to part with its cloth. Or, in other words, will offer less cloth for a given amount of wheat.

The effect of this increase in demand for cloth in Pakistan will be that less of both wheat and cloth will be traded, because if it exports less, it will be able to import less.

In this case the terms of trade of Pakistan improve. There is a logical explanation for this: cloth is being valued highly and more wheat is demanded for. Thus:

The co-ordinates of D and C points show that (*a*) less trading of both, and (*b*) that Pakistan loses less of wheat and saves more of cloth. The TT of Pakistan improve as it demands more cloth for itself and sells/offers less. Price of cloth in lines of wheat goes up. The slopes of the two TT lines differ.

It, is however, not possible to say *a priori* whether improvement in terms of trade will also increase the welfare, for new positions of consumption, exports and imports will result. In the words of Klaus Friedrich:

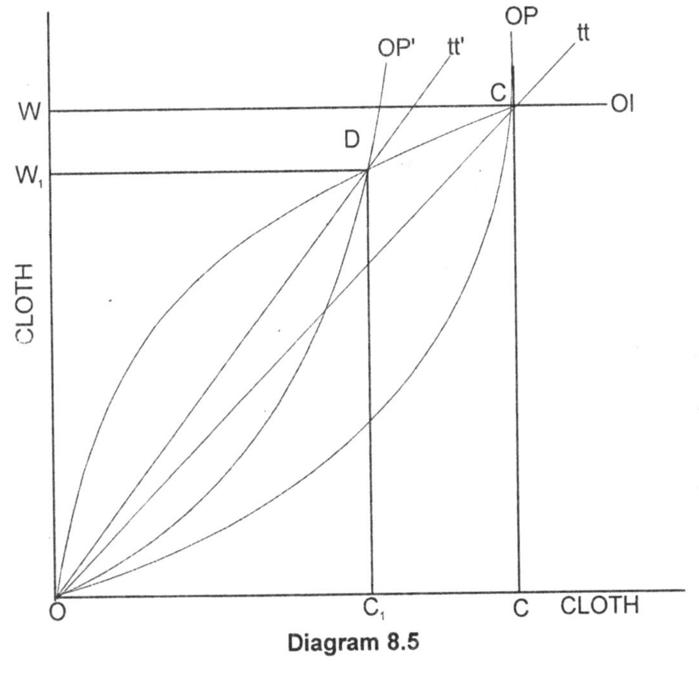

Diagram 8.5

"It is impossible to judge the effects of a change in terms of trade on the welfare of a country whenever such a change is caused by a shift in its demand structure... To know the welfare position we have to compare autarky and other post-trade points.... We cannot tell which of these points indicates the higher level of welfare, because each point lies on an indifference map of its own.... The logic of this difficulty is easy to see. Each demand structure serves as one measuring rod in comparing levels of welfare. To compare two levels by using two different measuring rods amounts to measuring one level in inches and the other in centimetres, while lacking the formula for converting inches into centimetres." (pp. 53-54)

If Pakistan demands less cloth for its consumption i.e., it offers more cloth, then the TTc line will show deterioration in the terms of trade for Pakistan. In the above diagram OCp shifts to the right. Pakistan offers more cloth CQ. (See the movement of Q... this time it is to the right; in the previous diagram Q was to the left of C. This is to be interpreted that Pakistan offers more cloth and gets relatively less extra wheat. In the previous case it was the case of Pakistan saving more cloth. In this case it is Pakistan offering more cloth. In the previous case it was the case of Pakistan losing relatively less wheat. In the present case is Pakistan gaining relatively less wheat in exchange of greater cloth.

In diagram 8.7, it has been shown that India now demands more wheat for itself. This will change its offer curve from OQ to OQ'. The terms of trade of India will improve from TT to TTc. The result is that India now offers less wheat WWi. In return it gets less cloth also CQ. However, the loss of cloth is less than the saving on the wheat.

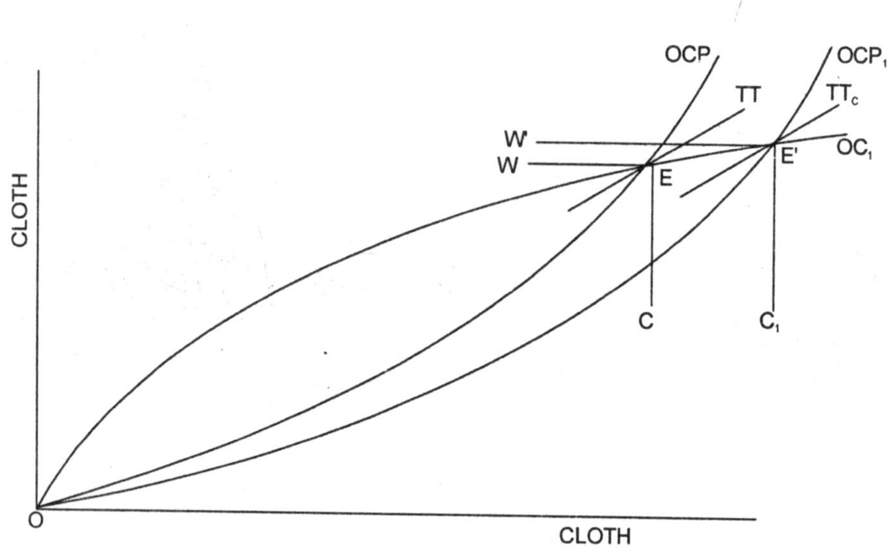

Diagram 8.6

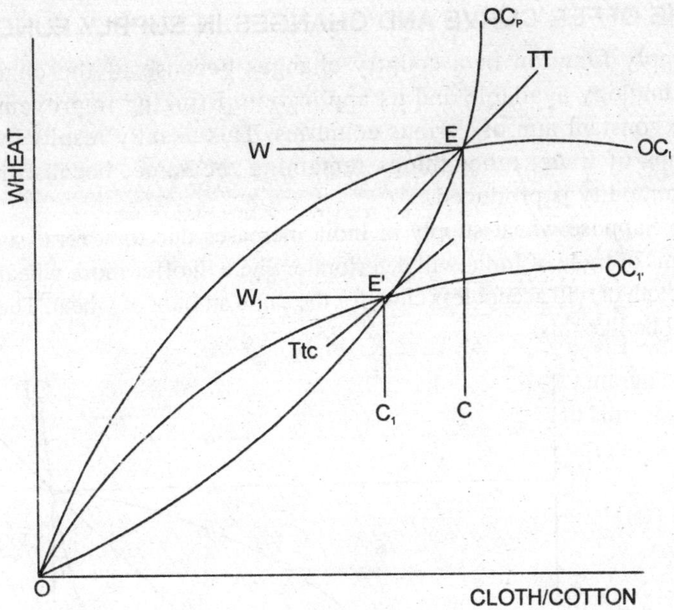

Diagram 8.7

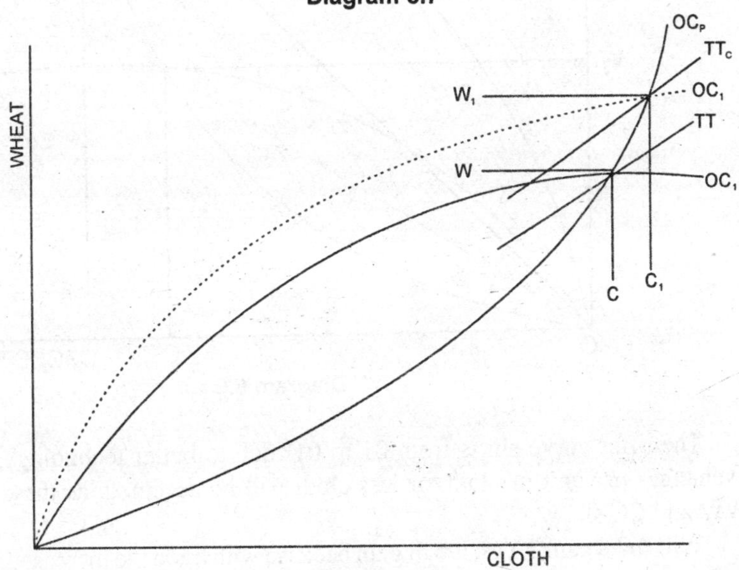

Diagram 8.8

In diagram 9.8, it is shown that India now demands less wheat for itself. It offers more wheat to Pakistan. As a result of this the terms of trade move nearer to the DRT of India or in favour of Pakistan. Now the OQ changes to OQ\ India has to give more wheat. It gets more cloth also but the gain in cloth is relatively less.

In diagrams 9.7 and 9.8 the WW" are towards/away from O' respectively. In same is true of cloth CC

IV. THE OFFER CURVE AND CHANGES IN SUPPLY FUNCTIONS

Supply function in a country changes because of the changes in the level of technology available and its application. Bringing improvement in technology is the constant aim of various countries. This usually results in deterioration of the terms of trade, other things remaining the same, because more of a particular commodity is produced.

Suppose wheat supply in India increases due to several such reasons. Then the terms of trade of India will deteriorate. She will offer more wheat for the same amount of cloth or will accept less cloth for the same amount of wheat. The offer curves position will be like this:

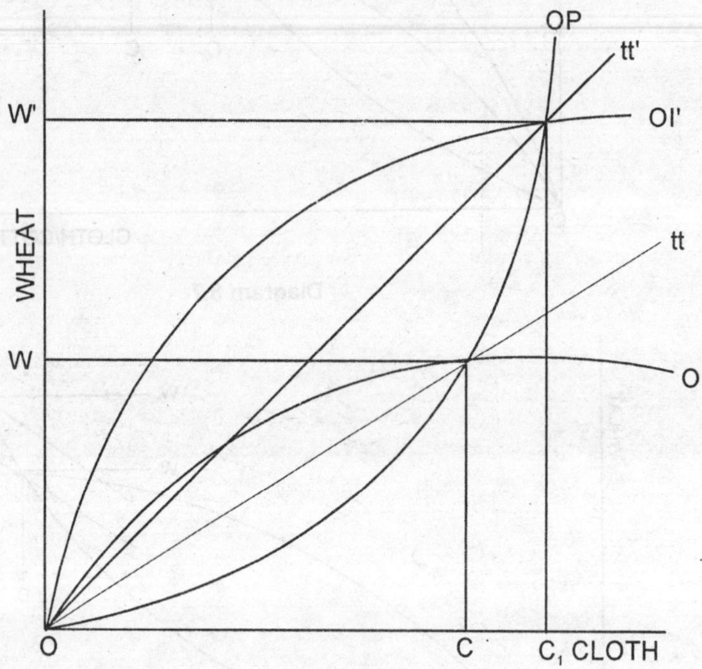

Diagram 8.9

The offer curve shifts from 01 to 01' due to better technology, for more wheat exchanges per unit of cloth, or less cloth will be accepted, as the distances between WW and CC show.

Will India gain ? Yes, it will gain because with trade the increased wheat is obtained without the sacrifice of cloth (in terms of the production possibility curve analysis). India's autarky point will increase as more wheat can be consumed. Higher wheat production can now be used to buy more cloth. *So even if the terms of trade decline, more of both commodities will be consumed.*

If, however, demand for wheat in foreign country increases, then India will gain from increased wheat supply for, then it can be sold at the same terms of trade (or, might be, at better terms of trade). The ability of a country to affect its terms of trade depends on the share of its exports and imports in the world trade.

If the new terms of trade curve is flatter and takes on a higher indifference curve, than India will gain. In case of a steeper term of trade, curve, India will lose. The supply curve will shift to the right if India's supply of wheat decreases.

Pakistan's offer curve will shift to the right of Pakistan's supply of cloth increases or if Pakistan's supply of wheat decreases. It will shift to the left if Pakistan supply of cloth decreases or if Pakistan's supply of wheat increases.

When the supply from India gets reduced:

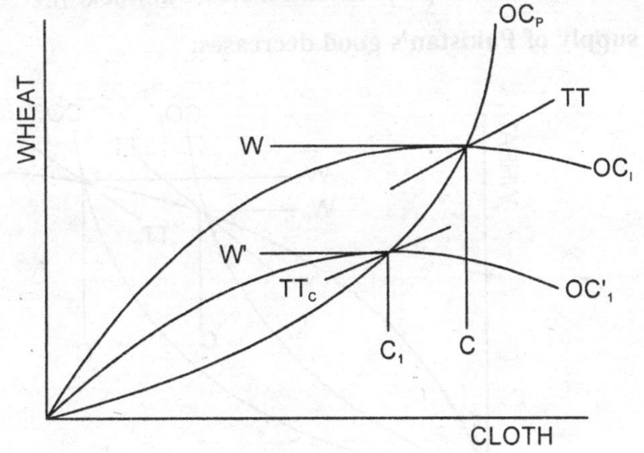

Diagram 8.10

When supply of Pakistan's good increases:

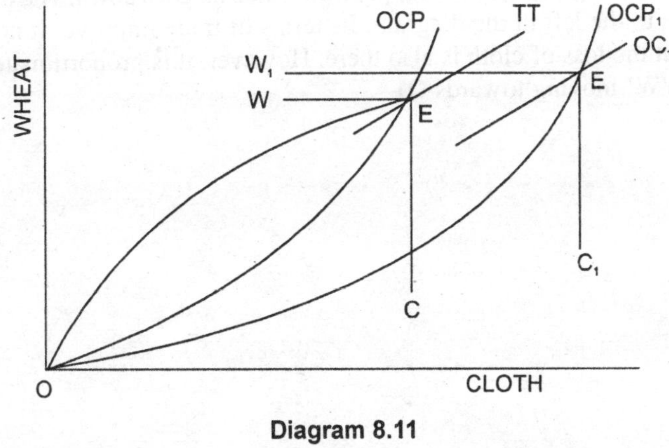

Diagram 8.11

In diagram 8.10 we have shown that if the supply of the exportable commodity from India becomes less, and the demand for the same good from Pakistan is inelastic, than the term of trade of India will improve. India will give less wheat and will get less cloth, but the loss of cloth will be comparatively less. (See change from W to W' and of C to C.) The saving of wheat is more than the loss of cloth. Since less of both the commodities is trade, the welfare goes down in both the countries. The offer curve of India moves to the right.

In the diagram 8.11 we show what happens when Pakistan's supply function improves. The offer curve of Pakistan moves to the right. Pakistan supplies more cloth and gets more wheat but proportionately less than what is offered in the form of cloth. Terms of trade of Pakistan deteriorate. However, since more of both the commodities is traded, we can say that the consumption welfare in both the countries improves. CC sacrifice brings less than proportionate increase in wheat WW. See from O to outwards.

When supply of Pakistan's good decreases:

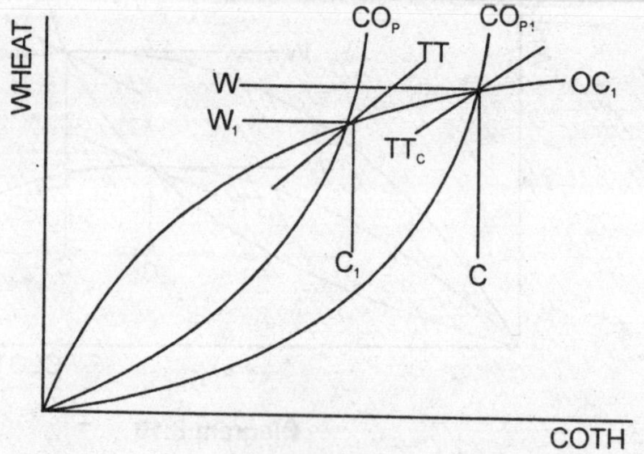

Diagram 8.12

In the diagram 8,12 the supply from Pakistan goes down. The offer curve of Pakistan moves to the left in the diagram. Its terms of trade improve. It now exports less cloth CC but the loss of cloth is also there. However, it is proportionately less. (We see CC and WW' moving towards O)

9 | Terms of Trade

I. INTRODUCTORY ANALYSIS: MEANING AND IMPORTANCE

As we have seen in the preceding chapters, terms of trade decide the gains that will accrue to a country. Domestic terms of trade mean the ratio at which one commodity will exchange for another commodity. International terms of trade measure the ratio between the domestic terms of trade of two countries at which goods are cleared. There are ambiguities in the interpretation of the meaning of various types of terms of trade and the ambiguities obscure their use. Changes in the terms of trade between various nations bring changes in the monetary and real incomes, employment and other economic variables. They have far reaching welfare implications also. Representatives of the less developed countries have been pleading in UNCTAD (United Nations Conference on Trade and Development) that something should be done to improve the deteriorating terms of trade of the less developed countries. The developed countries also complain that in cases where trade conditions favour them, less developed countries do not hesitate to exploit conditions to their (less developed countries') advantage.

Study of the terms of trade became important after the World War II. Gains from international trade depend on terms of trade also. Similarly the balance of payment disequilibrium also depends on the terms of trade. Terms of trade affect the volume of national income and even its distribution. Changing pattern of the terms of trade brings changes in the pattern of gains. The division of gains between the exporting and importing countries depends upon the terms of trade which prevail. The more favourable are a country's terms of trade, the greater will be its share of the total gains from trade.

Terms of trade determine the net effect of economic forces which affect international economic relations. They are important from the welfare point of view also. They tell us about the net effect of all economic variables and forces on balance of payment. Their use is very frequent yet not necessarily always clear.

Countries against which terms of trade move, lose in millions or even billions of (say) dollars. Though less developed countries complain more about the adverse changes in their terms of trade, even the developed countries can face the problem of terms of trade going against them. The oil price hikes by the oil producing countries have adversely affected the developed countries. A country which experiences a favourable shift in the terms of trade available to it, will find it possible to develop at low costs. Other things remaining the same, improvement in terms of trade increases production and employment.

Economists from Adam Smith to Keynes paid considerable attention to the study of terms of trade. Smith, Ricardo and Mill were of the opinion that though improvement in terms of trade should be welcome in any country, they should not be improved artificially. Protective tariffs were not liked by the classical economists even if they could improve the terms of trade available to a country because protection involves sacrifices that free trade brings to a country. Ricardo was against artificially improving the terms of trade because it meant foregoing comparative advantage. Mill and Edgeworth considered changes in "consumers surplus" rather than changes in the "terms of trade" as a better index of changes in the amount of gain from trade. Most economists agree that if only there are no offsetting factors, changes in commodity terms of trade will benefit the country.

II. A. (1) NET BARTER TERMS OF TRADE

They are also known as "COMMODITY TERMS OF TRADE". They can be expressed as

$$N = \frac{P_x}{P_m} = \frac{\dfrac{cP'}{eP^i}}{\dfrac{iP^\circ}{Ip^\circ}}$$

Here e and *i* express exports and imports respectively. P' and P° express the current and base year prices respectively.

Alternatively, P_x and P_m are price index numbers of exports and imports.

A rise in the terms of trade indicates that a larger volume of imports could be received, on the basis of price relations only, in exchange for a given volume of exports. Net barter terms of trade (according to Taussig) are relevant only when only commodities (and not services) are traded.

Terms of trade will deteriorate when opposite effects are there.

Net barter terms of trade, however, give no indication about the change in the income and welfare in any country. A country can earn more, even when its export prices fall. Increase in the volume of exports will compensate fall in export prices, if the foreign demand for exports is elastic. Then, unless an account is also taken of the factor-contents of imports and exports, the real position regarding the gains to 'A' country or 'B' country will not be revealed.

Measurement of the 'improvement' in terms of trade presents certain difficulties. There are several difficulties in preparing index number of changes in prices of export and import commodities. As we know, two countries trade in more than two commodities. Many problems arise: *(i)* which year should be taken as the appropriate base year ? *(ii)* which time period should be chosen to measure the change in the terms of trade ? (For example, it will not be meaningful to measure changes in India's terms of trade between 1919 and 1979); *(iii)* changes in the prices of commodities may be due to changes in the quality (if the import prices change because import commodities have now better quality, it will be incorrect to say that terms of trade have 'deteriorated'). A composite index for a country becomes difficult. Now-a-days there are exercises about the changes in the terms of trade of developed versus less developed countries. It will be very incorrect to read too much in the aggregates of such indices and interpret the data too casually. Countrywise or regions-of-the worldwise indices should be interpreted even more cautiously. Then, the problem of assigning weights also presents difficulties.

Changes in prices can be due to changes in *(i)* foreign demand or *(ii)* costs of production or changes in production function (productivity). Thus, to understand the things better, it will be necessary to take into account the -factoral terms of trade'.

II. A. (2) GROSS BARTER TERMS OF TRADE

Gross barter terms of trade take into account other exchanges than merely trade in merchandise. Gifts, tourist income and unilateral transfers are also included. Gross barter terms of trade measure the "proportion of real price of export to the real price of imports." Gross barter terms of trade will improve if the physical quantities of exports are the same and the volume of imports increases. The Gross barter terms of trade can be measured thus:

$$G = \frac{Qm}{Qx} \text{ or } \frac{\frac{Qx'}{Qm'} \cdot \frac{Pm'}{Px'}}{\frac{Q_{mo}}{Qxo} \cdot \frac{P_{xo}}{P_{mo}}}$$

Here Qm and Qx are volume index numbers for imports and exports, respectively, and

Px'	:	current year price of exports;
Qx'	:	current year quantity of exports;
Pm'	:	current year price of imports;
Qm'	:	current year quantity of imports;
Pxo	:	Base year price of exports;
Qxo	:	Base year quantity of exports;
Pmo	:	Base year price of imports;
Qmo	:	Base year quantity of imports.

Gross barter terms of trade do not measure the gains from trade in satisfactory way. Countrymen may get more satisfaction from a reduced bundle of imports because of changes in quality and tastes. As written earlier, it will also be necessary to take into account the changes in tastes, income and productivity.

II. A. (3) INCOME TERMS OF TRADE

Income terms of trade can be calculated by converting barter terms of trade by multiplying them with exports quantity ratio. According to Dorrance, we can get income terms of trade by calculating the ratio of the value of exports divided by the price index of imports. The income terms of trade can be expressed as

$T_i = N.\ Q_x$ Net terms of trade multiplied by the volume index.

Income terms of trade improvement means that country's capacity to import has increased. Capacity to import, as we know, is the function of capacity to export. Capacity to import increases not only when volume of exports increases but income from exports increases and income car increase with increase in capital inflow and other invisible exchange receipts.

Income terms of trade cannot be interpreted as a measure of the gain from trade or an indicator of welfare. It is simply a measure of the quantity of imports bought by exports.

The changes in I (income terms of trade) and N can be in opposite directions according to the direction and magnitude of the changes in Px and Qx. Fall in export prices when leading to increased exports, increase income. Income terms of trade can improve despite a deterioration in the commodity terms of trade.

Income terms of trade can be calculated thus also:

$$I = \frac{Px.Qx}{Pm}$$

The terms Px, Qx, and Pm denote the price of exports, the price of imports and the quantity of exports. To know the correct position about a country, it will be always better to understand changes both in the commodity terms of trade and income terms of trade.

II. B. (1) SINGLE FACTORAL TERMS OF TRADE

Factoral terms of trade consider the changes in productivity in the production of export goods of two countries. When factoral terms of trade are considered, they may be 'single factoral' or 'double factoral'. Single factoral terms of trade measure "how much quantity of imports can be obtained per unit of factor-input used in the production of exportables". Single factoral terms of trade improve when more can be obtained in this sense. The single factoral terms of trade can be measured:

$$S = N.Z_x$$

Here S refers to the single factoral terms of trade; N for commodity terms of trade and Z_x for export productivity index.

This means that if the export prices fall (say by 15%) relative to import prices, but export costs fall by greater (say 25%), then the country gains. The concept of factoral terms of trade was developed by Marshall and Jacob Viner. In the above case the improvement in the terms of trade is equal to:

$$\frac{85}{100}.\ 125 \textit{ i.e.}, \text{ by } 6\tfrac{1}{4}\%$$

The use of commodity terms of trade is thus less precise than the use of single factor terms of trade. In the words of Viner himself:

> "If it were possible to construct an index of the cost of production in terms of the average technical co-efficients of production of the export commodities and if the commodity terms of trade index was multiplied by the reciprocal of the export commodity technical co-efficient index, the resultant index would provide a better guide to the trend of gains from trade than the net barter terms of trade or the commodity terms of trade index by itself."

II. B. (2) DOUBLE FACTORAL TERMS OF TRADE

If barter terms of trade are corrected for changes in productivity in producing imports as well as exports, the result is the double-factoral terms of trade. Thus,

$$D = N.\frac{Z_x}{Z_m}$$

Here Z_m is an import productivity index. When one unit of home factors embodied in exports now exchanges for more units of the foreign factors embodied in imports, the double factoral terms of trade will be said to have improved. We can thus measure how much labour is congealed in 'A' bales of exports and 'B' units of import goods. Double factoral terms of trade assume importance when production in two countries is carried on under non-constant returns to scale and there are transport costs also. In a world of changing technology, their study is of great importance.

However, single factoral terms of trade—though less refined theoretically—are more relevant than the double factoral terms of trade. A country is more interested in what its factors can earn in goods and not what its factor services can command in the services of foreign factors. In other words, what matters to the importing country is whether it receives more goods per unit of its "exported factor-input" (an improvement in S)—not whether these imports contain more or less foreign inputs than before. Double factoral terms of trade are also known as "Bilateral factoral terms of trade." The same point has been emphasized by Wells thus:

> "In practice, an index of the double factoral terms of trade is almost impossible to calculate since it involves measuring and comparing productivity changes in the export industries of a large number of countries. Moreover, even if it were possible to produce, such an index would be of less value as a guide to policy making than the simple factoral index. After all, the citizens of a country are interested in the real effort, not in the relative efficiency or otherwise of other countries. The single factoral terms of trade index focuses attention on something which is susceptible to policy—namely domestic efficiency. Adjusting for productivity changes in other countries is only likely to obscure its message." (p. 63, *Op. cif).*

II. C. (I) REAL COST TERMS OF TRADE

This concept measures the welfare implications of the terms of trade. The real cost terms of trade can be calculated by multiplying single-factoral terms of trade index by the reciprocal of an index of the amount of disutility per unit of productive resources used in producing exports. A country is interested to have more imports for a given amount of real costs. Real costs measure sacrifice or irksomeness of production.

II. C. (2) UTILITY TERMS OF TRADE

Exports involve sacrifices of utility. The countrymen have to forego consumption of goods exported. Without exports they would have consumed more at cheaper prices. However, imports enable them to consume goods that they would not have consumed. Thus we have to compare the utilities gained and foregone.

Utility terms of trade (U) equal real terms of trade (R) multiplied by an index of the relative utility of imports and foregone commodities. Measurement of utility or real costs will always pose problems.

Thus of all the concepts of terms of trade, the net barter terms of trade, the single factoral terms of trade and the income terms of trade have greater relevance.

III. TERMS OF TRADE AND LESS DEVELOPED COUNTRIES. THE TERMS OF TRADE AND THE NATIONAL INCOME IN THE GROWTH PROCESS

Concern with the domestic and international terms of trade can be found in the writings of the classical economists even. Smith, Malthus and Ricardo had recognized the possibilities of deteriorating terms of trade for working class (due to rising population) and agricultural class (due to Law of Diminishing Returns and recourse to inferior lands). They also saw the possibilities of deteriorating terms of trade for countries producing raw materials only. Manufacturing nations' terms of trade improve with development. Increasing population was considered to be the main cause of deterioration in the terms of trade because it meant greater demand for foreign goods. Technical progress was not taken into account by the classical writers as having even greater impact on the changing terms of trade.

There is another world of thought in Singer-Prebisch Theory of Development. The Theory of Development developed by Singer and Prebisch, with particular reference to the less developed countries, deals with the influence of the business cycle on the terms of trade, the inter-relationship between factor rewards and the terms of trade, the effects of different market forms on the terms of trade and so on They point out that as less developed countries (actually they were writing with reference to South American countries) increase their primary production, they meet falling terms of trade, because the income and demand elasticities facing them in their export markets are so low, but they need rising export incomes in the development process, because their own marginal propensities to import are so high.

The core of the Singer-Prebisch case is:

> If the income elasticity facing the exports of the less developed countries is low and if, furthermore, the demand and supply are inelastic with regard to price, little is to be gained from pushing these exports. However, high the domestic growth rate within the export industry may be, most of the productivity gains within the export sector will be exported away through falling terms of trade.

Singer and Prebisch argue that while the developed countries sell their manufactured goods through monopolistic or oligopolistic market arrangements, the less developed countries export their goods under competitive conditions. Developed countries secure better terms of trade, therefore.

Baumol, Galbraith, Sylos-Labini and others have also gone into this question. They argue that the competitive firms are of smaller size than the oligopolistic or monopolistic firms. Possibilities of technological progress are great in the latter. The fruits of technical progress are not translated in the form of lower prices but are reaped in the form of higher profits. The firms of developed countries are well organized. The organized labour does not permit downward flexible wages and this is one more reason why the prices of industrial goods do not go down. Technical progress is used in developed countries for increasing profits; it is used in less developed countries for expanding output, which has the effect of lowering of prices. Decreasing prices do not increase foreign demand in the developed countries. The result is *that growth under these circumstances might even become impoverishing.* Those who produced more now suffer the prospect of becoming unemployed. They will have to seek employment in other occupations and industries. Both home production conditions (weak trade unions, supply inelasticities) and strong conditions of importers (oligopolistic buyers and elastic demand) conspire to keep the terms of trade of·less developed countries down and fluctuating. Increase in the labour force of less developed countries down and deterioration in the terms of trade of these countries. As the import propensity of these countries increases, the terms of trade go down. Less developed countries need more capital goods and technical raw material, while the developed countries are succeeding in finding the substitutes for the raw materials of the less developed countries. The tragedy of the export sector of less developed countries is that technical progress brings deterioration in the export goods sector because of the demand conditions abroad.

How the real national income is affected by technical progress, depends to a large extent on the course of the terms of trade. If the terms of trade deteriorate heavily for the progressing country, the increments to the real income will be small. This will be the case especially if the country has a large export share. If the adaptability of the country is low, and if it is so dependent on trade that the export sector is the only progressive part of the economy, the risk is great that the country will export away most of its productivity gain. Growth in these circumstances easily becomes self-defeating.

If the real income of a country increases, then changes in terms of trade have positive welfare implications. As terms of trade rise during the growth process, its real income can rise faster than output. This happens because the purchasing power of a unit of its exports rises. An improvement in the commodity terms of trade might facilitate an expansion in domestic output by permitting the release of resources from export production to domestic production. If the improvement is due to a rise in export prices, this may contribute to an increase in public savings is through tariffs and state trading.

NOTE

1. If you want, prepare your own brief notes from the write-up of the chapter.
2. Terms of trade will improve when: Suppose both are index 100

	x	m
(a) Export prices remain *same:* import prices fall.	100	90
(b) Export prices rise: import prices remain same.	110	100
(c) Export prices rise: import prices fall.	115	80
(d) Export prices rise: import prices rise. but export prices rise more than proportionately).	120	115
(e) Export prices fall: import prices fall. (but import prices fall more than proportionately).	90	80

9B Importance of the Study of the Terms of Trade. Necessary Policies About the Terms of Trade

(WITH REFERENCE TO DEVELOPING COUNTRIES LIKE INDIA)

INTRODUCTION:

(A) Theoretically speaking all countries would like to ensure that all types of their terms of trade improve. That is impossible because if some countries have favourable terms of trade others must have adverse.
From 1971 to 2008, the terms of trade of oil producing countries-are jumped as "leap frog' effect, the upward trend went down in 2009, but started rising in 2010.

(B) The most important terms of trade are "income terms of trade", which can go up even when other terms of trade are adverse.

(C) Raul Prebisch, HW Singer and Gunnar Myrdal were the first influential economists of the ""world who wrote about the tragedy of the deteriorating terms of trade of the poor countries and wanted that they should improve.

We are presenting herewith the top ten catch points about the *(a)* retrospective positions, (b)current state of affairs, (c) prospective policies that will be needed about the terms of trade. These points were/are raised In the UNCTAD, (United Nations Conferences on Trade and Development). So far the position is that what the developing - economies demand/request falls on the deaf ears of the powerful nations. The terms of trade of the poor countries are not allowed to improve. That is why we can call UNCTAD as

"Until Next Conference Talk and Delay". OR

" Under No Circumstance Take a Decision".

The top 10 points about the policies of terms of trade can be presented as under

(1) Barter terms of trade of poor countries deteriorate through the deterioration _ of the "net barter" terms of trade or "commodity terms of trade".

The commodities (which come from the primary sector) terms of trade lag behind. If the prices of industrial goods rise by (say) 15 p.c. but of agricultural commodities by 10 p.c. we say TT have gone against commodities, for rural activities and for the poor countries, because they export these commodities most. The terms of trade (in the above example) are 33.33 p.c. down. 10/15 - 0.66661=0.6666-1 -0.3333 x 100 - 33.33 P.C.

Net barter terms of trade for agricultural products do not improve in international trade due to inelasticties of supply. This means that the crops come at a certain time and they require immediate sale otherwise the agricultural products can rot. Hence the farmers/exporters accept whatever price is" offered to them. The international buyers are oligopsonies (big and only "a few")

There is need for improving the net barter terns of trade of not only agriculture but of agriculturists also.

One way of improving them is to establish many agro-processing and agro-industries. Then there will not be glut of agricultural goods.

Commodity funds were sought to be established by the developing economies. The intention was to enable the farmers to hold back stocks and receive payment for waiting. But the rich countries did not allow. "Do you think we are fools to give to funds so that you can charge higher prices for the commodities you sell to" us", said the rich countries in international meetings.

Net barter terms can at best be checked from falling much. Secondly, they can be made to improve only if there is massive movement of "ruralisation of industries" and not merely "rural industrialisation". Rural industrialisation means establishing industries in rural areas. Not all industries will employ rural persons or take raw materials from the rural areas. "Ruralisation of industries" (which Gandhi ji wanted) means such industries (i) which take raw materials from the rural areas, (ii) of which output is used in rural areas and (iii) which employ rural people.

Net barter terms of trade can improve if, "rural industrialisation is near the rural people, is for the rural people and is managed/run by the rural people."

(2) Gross barter terms of trade should be protected with all possible measures otherwise there will be drain of the economy.

We can take the example of oil prices. Crude oil (petroleum) prices were $ 1.2 a barrel in 1972. Then the Arab countries decided to hike the prices so that they could earn enough to annihilate Israel. There were 'leap frog' hikes in the prices always going, up and up. In 2006, they reached $ 74 a barrel. In 2007-08, they reached $ 154 a barrel. In 2009 they were down to $ 74 a barrel. India is exporting more real goods to get the same oil. No country of the world could raise the prices of their goods as much as the petroleum exporting countries could do.

What ran the developing economies do ?

(A) The world as a whole will have to find alternative sources of automobile fuel a e.g./ hydrogen or atomic capsules so that the power of the oil exporting countries to charge higher and higher prices is reduced.

(B) The USA and other western countries should stop war mongering due to which they keep extra stocks for six months to one year.

(C) In case of other goods/ alternative sources of supplies (countries) or alternative goods should be purchased so that a poor country will not have to part with larger exports.

(3) Income terms of trade should be tried to be Improved. Elasticties should be kept in mind.

Note the following:

(A) If terms of trade deteriorate, it is still possible to have improvement in income terms of trade.

(B) Improvement in terms of trade should at the same time improve balance of payment. See the following example.

EXAMPLE I;

Suppose India was importing 10 tanks Rs. 10 crore each. Then import bill was Rs. 100 crore.

Suppose India was exporting @ Rs. 1 crore (per standard quantity measure) and was exporting 100 such quantity unite. The income from exports was Rs. 100 crore. Both import and export bills were equal.

Suppose India raises the price of tea it was exporting by 10 p.c. and since tea is an essential commodity its demand abroad should be inelastic. Hence if the foreign country keeps on importing the same quantity/ India will get income from exports equal to Rs. 110 crores.

Suppose the foreign country raises its prices by 10 p.c. but India imports then only 9 tanks (demand is elastic) then the import bill will be Re. 99 crore. The second country has weak power.

India gains Rs. 110-99= Rs. 11 crore

India will be strong when:

1. Demand for tea abroad is inelastic.
2. Supply of tea is elastic i.e., can be sold to other countries which pay more.
3. Demand for the tank should be elastic i.e., demand can be reduced.
4. Supply of tank should be inelastic i.e., the tank producing country cannot sell to any other country

If India is strong on all the points, the elasticity coefficient can start from 4. It can be higher or lower than 4 also. It is to be remembered that if two countries are advantageous position, then the degree of strongness and weakness will determine the income terms of trade,

(4) Uti1ity terms of trade should Improve for the masses and not for the classes only.

If a country exports those commodities and goods which are needed by the common people (the masses), and imports things which are needed by the upper classes (the rich), then utility terms of trade will go down. Hence the following rules are necessary to be followed to improve utility terms of trade.

1. Import essential commodities, goods and services.
2. Luxury goods and services should either be not imported or imported in limited quantities only.

3. Essential commodities and goods should not exported if the domestic prices rise high and poor and middle classes suffer from inflation.
4. Only genuine surpluses should be exported.
5. The productivity in export goods industries should be high.
6. Capital goods, heavy goods and wage goods should be given preference in imports.

IT is NECESSARY THAT THE TERMS OF TRADE OF COMMODITIES, GOODS AND SERVICES SHOULD IMPROVE IN SUCH A MANNER THAT THE ULTIMATE IMPROVEMENT IN INCOME TRADE IS THERE.

(5) Developing economies face the problem of the developed countries usurping all benefits In the factoral terms of trade for themselves.

The developed countries are constantly inventing and innovating. The ultimate result of these things is that they can produce their products cheaper. When the productivities of capital and labour rise and when the cost of production go down the developed countries increase the wages of their workers and the producers reap higher profits.

Gains in productivity are not translated in the form of lower prices of their export goods (which become the import goods for the poor countries).

What can be done about this ? The answer lies that in the long run the poor countries should devote more resources for innovations.

In the short period/ the developing countries should do some "hard bargaining" to get lower prices.

(6) If developing economies want to keep the terms of trade higher they have to impose tariffs and use other methods of control of trade. they may not devalue their currency even when there is inflation in other words, the exchange rate may not be reduced.

These are "artificial methods of improving the terns of trade". In the present time of liberalisation, privatisation and globalisation/ these methods will not be permitted. Yet it is to be kept in mind that if to some extent the above methods or one or the other method is resorted to, there can be temporary improvement in the balance of payment. The burden of foreign debt may become less. In the long run these methods will be harmful.

(7) If the country is getting better technology from abroad, It should not bother about adverse terms of trade.

When the new technology comes, there will be economies of large scale production. The width of production (many types of goods) or "broad-banding" will improve. In the long run this will be helpful for improvement in terms of trade.

Modern technology will first Improve the domestic production base. This will then make greater exports from the country possible. If domestic products are good, the imports will go down. Indians now use India made foreign cars rather than import foreign cars.

(8) Inflation should be controlled If terms of trade in international business are to be saved from worsening.

Inflation makes exportable goods costlier. That is not an advantage. The foreigners reduce the demand. Exchange rate falls due to low exports. That further makes the export goods costly. There is double drag on the exports.

Recession (which is not to be preferred because it causes unemployment), however improves the balance of payment. Prices of home produced goods go down. So demand for import goods goes down. Foreigners import from "us".

(9) Unilateral inflows of capital improves terms of trade.

This is via effect on exchange rate. Exchange rate does not fall. The country need not export more goods to get the same imported goods. Gross barter terms of trade do not deteriorate.

This will be beneficial only when all the four elasticties favour. In other cases this will not be possible.

(10) Demonstration effect in foreign trade makes the terms of trade adverse.

If the imports are of luxury goods (cosmetics/ fast food, costly cars/ exotic whiskies/ soft drinks that are fizzy but harmful....etc), then the terms of trade of the country will go down.

Import of only those things which are needed for the development of the economy will improve the terms of trade in the long run.

Increasing population brings down terms of trade as more imports nay be needed if the domestic production base is not good.

High tariffs by foreigners and/or non-tariff barriers will reduce the terms of trade of the poor countries if they have inelasticities.

Overcoming indivisibilities, immobilties and inelasticities in production is required to improve the terms of trade of the developing economies.

10 Gains From International Trade

PART-A

"Gains" from international trade are discussed in international economics in a different way than the "advantages" or "merits" of free trade. "Gains" are usually discussed with the help of algebra and geometry. For example:

(1) The gains can be shown with the PPC lines of different slopes as in the Ricardian theory.

(2) The gains can be shown if we compare the post-trade point with the pre-trade point as in the Haberler's theory. The diagram which illustrates the zone of gain and its division between two countries is also a way of showing the gains of the trade.

(3) Offer-curves analysis is a very good way of showing the gains of free trade.

(4) In Heckscher-Ohlin theorem the gain is shown at that unique point where the partial specialisation in two goods is such that both factors are used fully.

(5) International terms of trade have got to be different from the domestic terms of trade for gains to accrue to both the countries.

(6) Rybczynski theorem is like- H-O theorem. It also demonstrates that abundant factor should be used intensively. If productivity of capital increases, more of capital should be used and that will be labour saving. If productivity of 1abour increases, more of labour will be used and that will be capital saving.

(7) Dynamic gains are more important than static gains. Same gains in the same quantities are static. New gains and in increasing quantities are dynamic gains.

(8) Dynamic gains are gains in efficiencies.

(9) Resource discovery and larger factor endowments are gains. The factors with increasing productivity/efficiency bring such gains which are akin to the increase in factor endowments.

(10)General equilibrium gains (as were discussed in H-O theorem, are more important. and international trade can deplete them and at the same time encourage resource discovery and better use. (Net effect will, therefore, differ)

Diagrams in the chapters on tariffs, quotas, customs unions etc. all show gains in the form of post trade or post-event situations.

As international trade increases, there can be greater use of (i) both the factors in balanced way, (ii) relatively greater use of capital and (iii) relatively greater use of labour. Whichever be the case there will be greater capital accumulation and greater improvement in the supply of labour. (Population need not increase; it may simply mean that 'stock' of unemployed and under-employed persons gets converted into 'supply' i.e., into active labour. The skill and motivation also improve.)

The production possibilities curves will move up due to growth of factors. The production frontiers improve, bringing all round developments. There will be more output, more employment, more productivity, more income of the nation, more revenue to the government, more domestic consumption yet more to export and hence more to import etc.

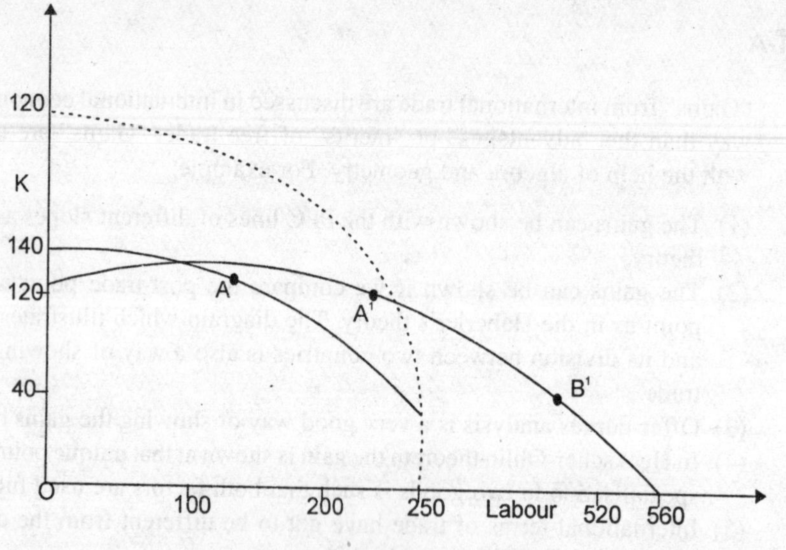

Fig. 10.1

Production frontiers improve as a result of better/higher capital and/or labour endowments.

Improvement in productivity or Technical Progress

Technical progress means that (a) in order to produce the same quantities of output, less inputs are required and this is true *at incremental level also;* and, (b) *same inputs or increments thereof, produce more than proportionate outputs* and *hence both capital and labour are released.* These released quantities of capital and labour can be used for reaping the economies of the scale as well as economies of the scope. In other words, the labour and capital need not become unemployed/unutilised but can be used to produce other goods or more goods.

International economists have demonstrated this with (a) constant returns to scale (b) same K/L ratio and (c) same W/i ratio.

It can be demonstrated that the labour saving technical progress increases the productivity of *capital* proportionately more than the productivity of labour. As a result, more capital is substituted for labour in production so that K/L rises at unchanged w/i ratio. Capital saving technical progress is the opposite of labour saving technical progress.

The above explanation can be put in a much simpler way thus:

(A) If the productivity of capital increases, more of capital will be used and it will displace labour: hence this becomes labour-saving.

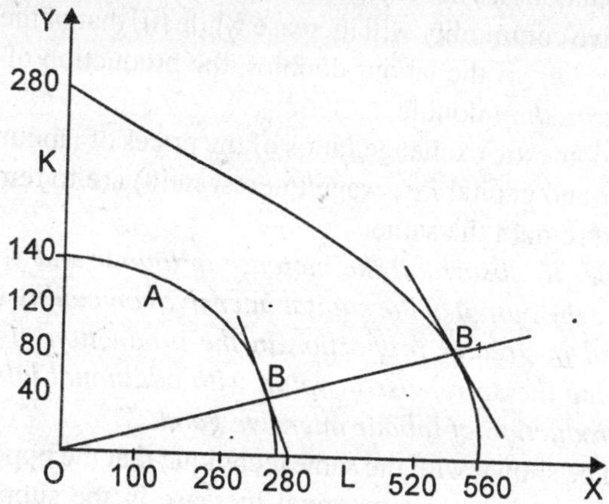

Fig. 10.2

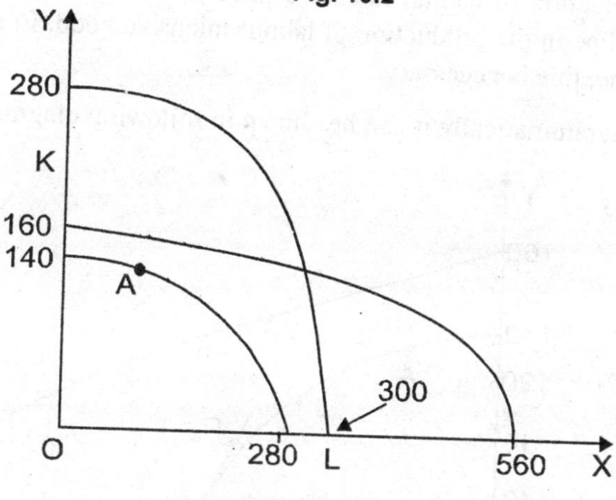

Fig. 10.3

(B) If the productivity of labour increases, more of labour will be used: hence it becomes capital-saving.

(C) All technical progress shifts the PPC outwards. As was seen earlier, the new PPCs can be parallel to the old PPC or their shapes may change in favour of one commodity or the other. Thus three simple PPCs can be drawn.

In 10.2 and 10.3 as both K and L double, the outputs of X and Y goods also double from B to B' diagram we show higher outputs PPCs when one factor increases more than proportionately.

The Rybczynski Theorem

International trade will alter the *output combinations* as a result of the changes in *factor proportions,* with factor price ratios remaining the same. (The geometric proof is elaborate: here a simple version is presented.)

(A) If labour doubles but capital increases only marginally, then *(i)* production of labour intensive commodity will increase while *(ii)* that of the capital intensive commodity will *decline.* If the labour doubles, the production of labour intensive commodity will *more than* double.

(B) If the domestic exchange ratios of the prices of labour and capital PL/PK (prices of labour and capital *i.e.,* wage/interest ratio) are to remain the same, then K/L ratio should remain the same.

(C) *In order to absorb all the increase in labour and yet to keep the K/L same, is to reduce the output of the capital intensive commodity so as to release capital (which is used in greater proportion in the production of capital intensive good), and combine the so-released capital with additional labour at the lower K/L used in the production of labour intensive good.*

(D) It can be shown with the same technique that the opposite will happen when capital doubles and there is marginal increase in the supply of labour. In this case the production of capital intensive good will more than double and there will be a decline in the production of labour intensive good. In order to keep the L/K ratio same, this is necessary.

Diagrammatically it can be shown in following diagraml (10.4.

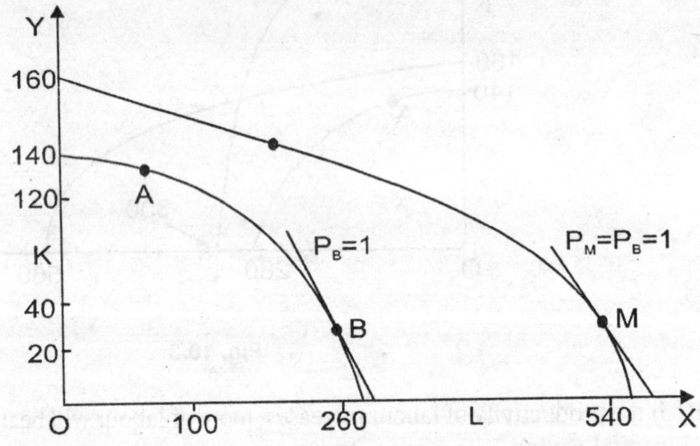

Fig. 10.4

At point B the outputs are 260 and 40 of commodities X and Y. At point M the outputs are 540 and 20 of commodities X and Y. With the price ratios P_x/P_y and $P_B = P_M = 1$ remaining the same (the *tt* lines are parallel) more of labour intensive good and less of capital intensive good is produced with expanded labour supply.

Theoretically speaking, international trade benefits both the small and big countries. If international trade were to benefit only the big countries, small countries would not have participated in international trade. Trade could not be forced upon on them.

There is clear benefit if the output of the nation's exportable commodity increases proportionately more than the output of its importable commodity.

However, sometimes it may be more necessary to increase the production of the import-replacing outputs. For this import- replacing-imports may be necessary. This will be beneficial in the long run.

Balance of payment deficit today means we are consuming more or using capital goods more than what we are legitimately acquiring through our exports. In due course of time this will increase the balance of 'indebtedness'. Ultimately all deficits are to be paid back. In that case, someday the exports have to increase more than the imports. Today's deficits will be financed by tomorrow's surpluses. No nation can hope to keep on incurring deficits and taking loans for ever. Such a country will have to mortgage its economic and political sovereignty. Either exports promotion has to improve, and/or imports replacement programme has to improve or we have to learn to practise austerity. Austerity is to be practised today or in future, if we cannot increase exports and reduce imports.

Beneficial effects will also be reaped if the *consumption of importable commodity (but provided by domestic production), increases proportionately more than the consumption of its exportable commodity (which will leave more exportable surpluses to the nation).*

If the volume of trade increases, national welfare may increase but the terms of trade may go down.

It is also possible (See chapter on terms of trade), that while the terms of trade improve, the nation's welfare may be adversely affected. The terms of trade and welfare combinations can be both positive also. If both the terms to trade and the 'wealth effect' of international trade/economic growth are favourable, the welfare of the nation will definitely improve. Otherwise, it will remain the same or decline.

PART 'B' OF THE CHAPTER

[If there is a question on gains of international trade which is very general like "explain the gains of international trade", the students can write thus:

Gains are the same as advantages of free international trade, the rules for which have now been formulated by WTO. Conventionally, however, there is use of diagrams In explaining these gains. Gains are positive when there are spread effects and negative when the backwash effects exceed the spread effects.

CHOOSE THE ZONE OF GAINS DIAGRAMS, ONE DIAGRAM FROM THE RYBCZYNSKI and any one showing changes in terms of trade one from the Offer Curve Analysis.

No student has ever reproduced all the diagrams that are in the text books about the '"gains" nor can ever do. They are far too many.]

POSITIVE GAINS FROM INTERNATIONAL TRADE: SPREAD EFFECTS

Higher and higher exports do not mean more and more gains particularly when domestic consumption of the masses is adversely affected. Imports, if they are of luxury goods at the cost of imports of the essential consumption goods, inputs, intermediate goods, heavy capital goods do not bring gains. Favourable balance of payment may not translate into "gains" if the forex is used for the benefit of the microscopic minority of high powered persons and vested interest groups.

Gains: Spread Effects	*"Negative gains": Backwash Effects*
1. Entire world can become a vast market for exports and imports. Consumers can buy at the least costs. The producers too can obtain all inputs needed for improving scale and scope of operations. Producers maximise exchange values, even at competitive prices. Consumers maximise use values and hence their welfare.	1. If national resources get drained out due to activities of the multinationals, there can be effects of "immiserisation" of the nation. **Unequal exchanges** favour the rich more than the poor and middle class persons. Elitist consumption, production and trade may harm interests of the common people. Politicians loot the country.
2. Production increases and imports get reduced if the country can import imports-replacing capital goods and technology along with the necessary raw materials. That will increase employment and there will be multiplier effects. (See **chapter on foreign trade multiplier**).	2. **Trade can replace production** when due to foreign competition small scale industrial units close down and the village and cottage industries are wiped off. Fewer persons get employment in trade than what they were having in village and cottage industries or in small scale and medium scale industries.
3. **Consumer really becomes** supreme. It used to take upto 10 years to get a telephone connection in India upto 1980s; now mobile phones with international connectivity can be had in a jiffy. It used to take 15 years to get a Vespa scooter in 1970s in India. Now a telephone call can make the car seller knock at your door within half an hour accompanied by the financier.	3. It is said that, the consumers are the "kings" and "queens"; but **the "king" or "queen" in the free international trade,** are in reality the haves. Consumers are led to buy unnecessary and superfluous things after they are bombarded with advertisements and publicity. The sales on credit finance can make a person indebted for life. Not only individual but even national indebtedness can increase.
4. New technologies bring efficiency in production lines, first economic dualism and then social dualism can get reduced. Even the masons and truck	4. International trade can promote non-egalitarianism. The multinational companies dominate and the domestic producers and traders play a second

drivers now have mobile phones.	fiddle to them. India, for example, cannot compete with the top two MNCS of the world because their sales exceed the total national income of India!
5. Usually the regimes of exchange control and fixed exchange rate systems go. Due to demonstration effects in production, distribution and promotion, entire development scenario becomes modem.	5. Exchange rate may fall. The country may have to export more real goods to get the same real imports. Imports prices may rise relatively more (controlled by the MNCs) than the export prices.
6. Germany was war ravaged and divided into two after 1939-45 War. Hitler killed 60 lakh Jews and had attacked many countries. Japan too was having its policy of expansion in the Asia. Both were defeated in wars. Japan was in the list of backward countries after the II World War. It was international interface that made them develop. East Germany (socialist) got united with the free economy of the West Germany. Free international interface gives a high level of living that the socialists failed to provide.	6. Social consequences of economic transformation are ignored in the paradigm of capitalism and free international trade. Colonising the poor country was the result of the desire of the rich countries to have control over the raw materials of the poor nations. That economic imperialism continues. Prebisch and Singer two great economists from Latin America pointed out that the free international trade exploits the poor countries in two ways. First, they pay low prices for the commodities of the poor countries and secondly, they charge very high prices for the exports to these countries. This is double exploitation.
7. Diminishing returns in production lines can be postponed with the application of modern technology. That is true of agriculture, mining, industry etc. Now even developing countries can hope for reaping the economies of scale and economies of scope.	7. Free movement of capital in the world has modernised the production sectors, sub-sectors, functions and activities in the developing economies also. However, the direct investment in industries is usually first in "useless' types of industries *e.g.,* soft drinks, cosmetics, junk food etc. Billions of dollars earned by less developed countries by exporting essential goods are frittered away in the production and consumption of the "superfluous" goods. Foreigners bring capital for investment in bonds and other papers. They withdraw these investments suddenly after making phantom piles of money and that creates a downward spiral in the exchange rates of the poor-countries.

UNIT II

Balance of Payment Study.

Applied Commercial Policies for the Management of Balance of Payment.

11. Balance of Trade and Balance of Payment. Defined and various accounts.
12. Disequilibrium in balance of payment.
    * Causes and types of disequilibrium.
    * Various theories of disequilibrium.

    Encapsulated top ten measures for correcting b.o.p. disequilibrium of deficit/surplus types.
13. Methods of Controlling Adverse B.O.P.—I. Tariffs. Tariff effects: Optimum Tariff.
14. Methods of controlling adverse B.O.P.—II. Quotas. Partial Equilibrium Analysis. Types and effects. Subsidies.
15. Methods of controlling adverse B.Q.P.—III. Exchange- Controls. Types and their functionalities.
16. Methods of Controlling Adverse B.O.P.—IV. Devaluation. Meaning and effects. Indian case.
17. Foreign trade multiplier. Effect of the methods of correcting BOP deficits as also of export promotion/imports compression.
18. International trade as the engine of economic growth. [As a result of the effects discussed in chapter 17 above]
19. Interface between international trade and economic development

11 | Balance of Trade and Balance of Payment

0. Introduction

I. Balance of Trade and Balance of Payment.

II. Components of Balance of Payment Account.
   Current Account Items.
   Capital Account Items.
   Unilateral Transfer items.
   Official Reserve Account or Loan Adjustment Account.

III. "Balance of Payment always balances". In what sense?
   OTHER ITEMS.
   Basic Balance of Payment.
   Balance of International indebtedness.
   Accounting Balance.
   Programme Balance of Payment.
   Market balance of payment.

IV. Balance of Payment as an index of the economic conditions of the country.

0. Introduction

"Balance of Trade", as this chapter explains is the balance of exports and imports of commodities and goods. Commodities are those which come from the primary sector *e.g.,* wheat, rice, fruits, vegetables, animals, food, mineral ores, forest products. Goods are those which come from factory sector and village industries. [These products are known as 'industrial products" or, products of the manufacturing sector. A new word has been coined recently and that is "manufactoring" goods which come from the factory sector. This word has not become common as yet]. Goods include "bads" also. Goods as those which have utility and are scarce. Hence they command a price because there is demand on one side and matching or non-matching supply *on* the other side. There is nothing good in tobacco products. They are killers. One can question the utility of the war goods or of narcotic intoxicants. However, all goods that command price are known as "goods".

Since the commodities and goods can be seen their trade is known as the trade of the "visibles". Commodities and goods go: foreign money comes. Commodities and goods come; money goes in foreign exchange (now the reference money is dollar).

It is to be remembered that:

Exports of commodities and goods are losses in real terms **but** are **gains in monetary terms.**

If a country exports fruits, the countrymen (consumers) will have lesser quantities to consume and hence the prices will rise. It is possible that low income group persons may not be able to consume as much as they want due to higher prices.

Hence "genuine" exportable surpluses should be exported; **but this is seldom done.** Without exports the domestic market may not give higher prices. So the producers export. If the exports are real surpluses, then the producers gain but the consumers do not suffer consumption losses.

Balance of payment is calculated in money terms. Hence exports are always regarded as gains. It is in the "welfare analysis" that we can take into account the "real" side of the exports.

Imports of commodities and goods are gains in real terms; but **are losses in money terms.**

A country imports those commodities and goods which it cannot grow/produce in sufficient quantities. Some may not be produced at all. Hence when they come they increase the consumption base and the production base. Subsequently the exchange and distribution bases also increase. Imports can be of heavy goods, capital goods, wage goods, white goods (goods of comforts in households *e.g.*, washing machines), and luxury goods. These imports ward off hunger, improve standard of living, standard of production because capital goods embody higher technology.

However, as commodities and goods come, the money goes. The money can be in the form of accumulated past balances of foreign currencies. Foreign currencies *are* usually converted into dollars or dollar values. **Imports are gains in real terms but "leakages" in money terms.**

* Money values of exports—(minus) money values of imports of commodities and goods are balance of trade.
* If export values exceed import values, it is balance of trade surplus.
* If money values of imports exceed the money values of exports of commodities and goods, it is balance of payment deficit.

Many developed countries have deficits on balance of trade account. Even England has it: almost as a rule. See the last page of the chapter.

Developed countries gain more by exports of "invisibles". These invisibles are exporting insurance services, banking services, educational and medical facilities for the rich of the poor countries, tourism, and most important of them, income from the capital "exported" earlier. Capital is "exported" in the form of FDI *i.e.*. foreign direct investment and FII, foreign institutional investment.

It is a very profitable business of the rich countries to take their capital to foreign countries, buy shares and other bonds and make hefty profits. Then they can take their profits and money away.

Balance of Payment has three accounts mainly: current, capital and unilateral transfer. There are two sides: payment side and receipt side. Suppose: (in billion dollars).

Account	Receipt	Payment	Balance
Current	100	150	— 50
Capital	100	20	+ 80
Unilateral transfer	50	5	+ 45
Balance of payment surplus ± =			+ 75
Another example			
Current account	100	200	— 100
Capital Account	40	30	+ 10
Unilateral transfers	20	5	+ 15
Deficit			— 75

A question arises that how can a country pay more than it has received. This is possible if the country had past balances of dollars. If that is not the case than these $ 75 b. will be a loan. The receipt of loan will be recorded in a loan account on the receipt side. Then the receipts and payment side both will show the total of 235 b. dollars. The fourth account is the adjustment account.

A country which has BoP surplus is a loan giver having assets in foreign exchange. A country with BoP deficits is a loan receiver with liabilities.

CONCEPTS

The meaning of *(i)* balance of trade, *(ii)* real and monetary balances of trade, and *(iii)* balance of payment deficits and surplus have been understood.

The politicians are interested in balance of power; the military men are concerned with the "balance of terror"; the economists are concerned with the "balance of payment". The BoP can be calculated for the two States also. However, the smaller the region, the more difficult it is to calculate the balance of payment. No one records the balances of payment between two districts. It is easy to calculate balance of payment between two countries as accounts as maintained. However, illegal trade is not taken into account. Smuggling of goods, commodities and monies are not included in the BoP.

We have noted and shall see hereafter that outflows and inflows on account of commodities and goods come under the balance of trade account. This is one component of the current account. The other components are the inflows and outflows on services account.

In the capital account only inflows and outflows of capital are recorded. Interest and or dividend payments will go to the current account—both outflows and inflows. Unilateral transfer account will record the one-sided gifts, grants, subsidies etc. A country can receive them as well as pay them to other countries. India can receive grant from the USA and can give grant to Bhutan. When relatives send money from foreign countries, it is unilateral transfer. Loan adjustment account is the last account.

It is seldom, if ever, that the three accounts balance. They usually remain unbalanced. It is after the inclusion of the fourth account that the balance of payment always balances.

Short period balance of payment is for a year or a few years. Basic balance of payment or structural BoP is for long period. Balance of indebtedness is an open account which starts from a hoary past. It is the sum total of ± "plus and minus" balances of foreign exchange as it stands today. Market balance of payment is what we get without government interference. Programme balance of payment is what is planned. One can plan an adverse balance of payment. For example, India planned in early planning years imports of imports-replacing-imports. Heavy electrical goods come under the category of "heavy capital goods". If instead of importing them, Government of India imported (1954) BHEL machines, these imports become imports-replacing-imports. They avoid future deficits.

All countries cannot have favourable balance of payment. If balance of payment surplus is too large, the exchange rate will rise and then experts will be discouraged and imports will be encouraged. (See chapter on rates of exchange, and the next chapter)

Adverse balance of payment accumulates into foreign debt.

BALANCE OF PAYMENT

(I) Balance of Trade and Balance of Payment
(2) Components of Balance of Payment Account
(3) Balancing of the Balance of Payment
(4) Balance of Payment as an Index of the Economic Conditions of the Country

1. BALANCE OF TRADE AND BALANCE OF PAYMENT

Balance of trade, which is just one part of the balance of payment, is the net balance of imports and exports of commodities or of 'visibles'. Balance of payment includes all credits and debits in foreign exchange, visibles and invisibles.

Balance of payment is a summary statement of all the transactions between the residents of one country and the rest of the world. It covers a given time period, usually a year. It includes all payments made during the period by foreigners to residents, all such payments are called 'credits' and all payments known as 'debits' made during the period by residents to foreigners. It consists of a record of all the transactions undertaken on the international trade account. Like the national income and expenditure account, it also consists of exports and imports which are indicated in the form of two convenient accounts: the current and capital accounts. It is a summary of the money value of all exchanges and transfer of goods, services and evidences of debtor ownership appropriately classified between the residence, business and government and other institutions of one country and the rest of the world for a given period of time. It is a statement that takes into account the values of all goods, all gifts and foreign aid, all capital loans, or I.O.Us ('I Owe You' documents) and all gold coming in and going out and the inter-relation among all these items.

What the periodic table of elements is to the chemist, the balance of payments is to the international trade economist. Balance of payment is a systematic and complete record of a county's monetary payments to foreigners and its receipts from foreigners; included are payments for goods and services, gifts, investments, loans, and all other transactions that call for international money flows. However, despite all efforts, there will be manifold statistical problems connected with measuring and recording international payments and receipts. These, render a complete record of international monetary transactions.

2. COMPONENTS OF BALANCE OF PAYMENT ACCOUNT

There are four components of the balance of payment account *viz., (i)* the current account, *(ii)* the capital account, *(iii)* the unilateral transfer (unrequited receipts and unrequited payments) account, and *(iv)* the official adjustment account.

2. (a) The current account

There are two sides of the account: one the debit side which records the payments and the other the credit side which records the receipts. They can be presented as under:

Transactions giving rise to money claims on foreigners (credits) receipts	*Transactions giving rise to money claims on home country (debits) payments*
1. Exports of goods.	1. Imports of goods.
2. Use of domestic transport services by foreigners.	2. Use of foreign transport services by domestic users.
3. Expenditure by foreign embassies in the country.	3. Expenditure by the embassies of the country abroad.
4. Insurance policies sold to foreigners.	4. Insurance policies taken by domestic users from foreigners.
5. Tourist expenditure in the country.	5. Domestic tourists spending money abroad.
6. Interest receipts on capital lent abroad.	6. Interest payment on capital borrowed from abroad.
7. Dividend receipts on the capital invested abroad.	7. Dividends payments on the capital invested by foreigners in the country.
8. Agency commission and brokerage received for the services rendered to foreigners.	8. Agency commission and brokerage paid for the services rendered (underwriting services) rendered by foreigners.
9. Payments received by national working abroad or rendering services abroad	9. Payments made to foreign experts or workers for their technical and other services.
10. Other items.	10. Other items.

The current account includes payments and receipts on account or imports and exports of visibles and invisibles. Visibles mean exports and imports of goods. Invisibles mean exports and imports of services. Visibles constitute a very high percentage of the receipts and payments in the balance of payment account of less developed countries. In these visibles and invisibles only 'legal' transactions are included for the simple reason that the 'illegal' (smuggling) transactions are not known.

The entries in the account can be made on the basis of the actual arrival or dispatch of goods or on the basis of the 'advices' sent. Usually, they are made on the basis of the receipt or dispatch of invoices or day to day and monthly accounts are prepared by the concerned departments but only annual accounts are published. Port and bank accounts will differ, for mercandise exports because the former relate to the arrival and dispatch of goods while the latter relate to the payment figures. There will be time differences in the two accounts. One discripancy that can arise in the merchandise account will be due to the practice that exports are entered in different way from imports. Exports are entered as f.o.b. (free on board cost) basis and the imports are entered as c.i.f. (cost insurance and freight cost) basis. In the balance of payment account these payments appear separately as invisible transactions. Among the invisibles of the "other types' category there can be several other items, *e.g.*, payment of royalties, patent fees, rental for films or television reels.

2. (b) The capital account

The main items of capital account are as under:

Credit side	Debit side
1. Foreign long-term investment in home country less redemptions and repayments. (Direct investment, Investment in securities, Loans taken etc.).	1. Long-term investment abroad less redemptions and repayments made.- (Direct investment, Investment in securities, Loans given etc.).
2. Short-term capital inflows (portfolio transfers) including bank deposits. Increase in short-term liabilities to foreigners	2. Short-term capital outflows (portfolio transfers) including bank deposits. Decrease in short-term liabilities of nationals (or increase in short-term liabilities of foreigners)

Capital account records all short-term and long-term international movements of capital. If a country is investing abroad, it is a payment and will be recorded on the debit side. This will have adverse impact on the balance of payment account. However, in the long run these investments will bring revenue by way of interest and dividends and will be recorded on the credit side of the current account. Receipt of the principal back, is revenue but will reduce the future revenue of the current account. Similarly, when loans are received the balance of payment position improves via capital account entries, but debt servicing entails responsibilities on the current account.

The balances of the debit and credit sides of the current and capital accounts are known as *(i)* net balance of current account and *(ii)* net balance of capital outflows and inflows. Alternatively, redemptions and repayments can be directly deducted on the credit and debit side. Direct investments mean investment in 'brick-mortar and steel', while portfolio investment means purchase of stocks and bonds. Government loans are usually official loans given/taken to or from foreign countries. When these receipts and payments are for periods of less than one year they are regarded as short- term credits and debits. Bank deposits can be sent by the countrymen to foreign banks for short and long period and similarly residents (persons, firms, institutions and governments) of other countries can send deposits in the banks of the country for the short and long period. Sometimes, the current account balances are also recorded within the capital account, but are shown separately.

The changes in the capital accounts are due to autonomous transactions that involve the exchange of money capital for various kinds of real or financial assets. Portfolio asset re-shuffling in the expectation of earning more interest and/or dividend becomes the cause of capital account changes in credits and debits. What is an asset to the holder becomes a liability to its issuer. If the credit side is increasing in one country then the debit side must be increasing in the other country. Less developed countries which import consumers' and capital goods, therefore, show net excess of debit side of the capital account.

2. (c) Unilateral transfer account

Unilateral transfer means gifts and grants by individuals, organisations or governments to persons, institutions, organisation or governments of foreign countries. When such gifts are given they are entered on the debit side and when they are received by a country they are entered on the credit side. Big and advanced countries virtually receive no such gifts and grants. In case of less developed countries, such gifts and grants may constitute an important item of balance of payment account. In some cases, even pensions are included in the unilateral transfer account. Indemnities and compensation amounts are also included in the unilateral transfer account. Nations may sometimes pay compensation and indemnities on the losses incurred by a country due to certain actions or policies of the other country. Such amounts do not involve *quid pro quo.* Thus if a country sent machines worth \$ 25 m. to another country out of which machines worth \$ 2 m. were gifted, then on the credit side only \$ 23 m. will be recorded as payment received and \$ 2 m. as donation. Donations are thus shown as substituting for an entry recording payment received. These receipts and payments are also known as 'unrequited receipts'. When Indians go abroad and send money to their relatives, such receipts are recorded in the balance of payment accounts of India under the head 'unrequited receipts' *i.e.,* receipts which the residents of a country receive 'for free', without having to make any provision for future payments in returns.

2. (d) Official reserves account

The ultimate deficits or surpluses of the first three accounts are settled through the Official Reserves Account. Suppose the position of the first three accounts are as under:

1.	Current Account	(—) \$ 100 b.
2.	Capital Account	\$ 50 b.
3.	Unilateral Transfer Account	(—) \$ 20 b.

It is clear from the above that the country has spent a total of \$ 70 b. more abroad than it has earned. To that extent the monetary claims on the country by foreigners exceed similar claims on the country the balance of payment shows 'deficit'.

This amount is to be paid ultimately in gold or in any other acceptable form. These are classified as official reserves and constitute the holdings, by offical government agencies, of gold and other means of payment that, are readily available to meet balance of payment deficits.

Ultimately in the official reserves account either a country is indebted to others or others are indebted to it. A compensating entry is made on the side where the amount is short. Deficit requires loan from abroad, Surplus means others are indebted to us.

On othe credit side	On the debit side
1. Official sales of gold abroad.	1. Official purchase of gold from abroad.
2. Official sales of foreign currencies abroad.	2. . Official purchases of foreign currencies.

Thus, if the three accounts show a deficit of $ 70 b. for debit therefore, then on the credit side $ 70 b. are to be written. The foreign countries must have granted credit to the country or must have taken gold or our foreign exchange reserves.

If the three accounts show a surplus of the same amount of $ 70 b. the official reserves account will show a debit balance of the amount via purchases (imports) of gold, foreign currencies or balance of indebtedness of others towards us.

Thus balance of payment always balances and when we say in loose sense that there is 'deficit' or 'surplus', we refer to the net balance of the first three accounts only. When there is 'deficit', the country will draw on reserves and when there is 'surplus' the country will add to the surplus. These transactions they undertake are *"induced" and "accommodating". In the first three categories we will include transactions that are ordinary or autonomous.* Autonomous transactions cannot balance unless these are induced and accommodating transactions.

3. BALANCING OF THE BALANCE OF PAYMENT

Thus it is said "balance of payment always balances". If this is true, then it is not correct to talk about deficits or surpluses or about disequilibrium. The fact is that when we talk about' deficits' or' surpluses', we are referring to the net balance of the three accounts only. It is not in the strict accounting sense. When we take into account the 'Official Reserves Account', the balance of trade always balances.

Balance versus Equilibrium

It is clear from the above analysis that only when all the four accounts are combined, the accounts will be in balance and in equilibrium. Next year also they will be in balance and in equilibrium, but with higher or lower figures in the four account?.

However, there is little chance of the first three accounts being in balance and in equilibrium. There will be deficits or surpluses and thus disequilibrium.

Sometimes the countries try to meet the deficits of current account with surpluses of capital account. Thus a balance of payment deficit will mean an *ex post* excess of autonomous payments over autonomous receipts while a balance of payment surplus will mean an *ex post* excess of autonomous receipts over autonomous payments. When induced and accommodating payments and receipts are also included, then balance of payment will balance.

Other Terms

(a) The Basic balance of payment

This is prepared to give long-term position. Tastes, changing fashion at home and abroad, development of technology at home and abroad, changes in resources, inflationary and deflationary trends all determine of country's export and imports of goods and services in the long-run. Relative scarcity of capital is also taken into account as it gives rise to national differences in long-term interest rates and thus determines the flow of long-term capital.

However in practice it becomes difficult in statistics to separate the short-term and long-term capital movements. The concept of 'basic balance of payment' is essentially a theoretical concept. From practical point of view, short-period balance of payment gets more attention.

(b) Balance of international indebtedness

The balance of payment is a 'flow' concept. It gives a picture for the year. The balance of indebtedness is a 'stock' concept. It gives the position of investment of a country or in a country over the entire "life" period or a very long period. It gives the international investment position. If in a country foreign investments are of the order of Rs. 1,800 crores and its investments in other countries are to the order of Rs. 1,000 crores, it is a debtor in the net sense.

When a country registers a net capital outflow (private or government), its balance of international indebtedness improves. Its net creditor position is enhanced and its net debtor position is reduced. Grants, however, do not enter into this account. Settlement of balance of payment accounts (the first three accounts) influences the balance of indebtedness. When deficits are settled by reducing reserves in foreign countries or by increasing the reserves of other countries in the country, the effect, is that net investment credit side is reduced. It also means the net investment side of foreign countries is increased.. (It can also mean that the country's debtor position will increase and the foreign country's debtor position will be reduced.) Thus, to put. the same thing in other words, a deficit in the balance of payments will reduce, the net creditor position or increase the net debtor position. However, only if a net capital outflow is accompanied by an equal, combined positive balance on current, unilateral transfer and gold accounts will it serve to improve a country's balance of international indebtedness. Only if the payment deficit is settled wholly or in part by an export of gold will the balance of international indebtedness be changed in its favour.

To know the latest position of investment, the present market, values can be token into account, but then in this case the figures will not tally if the balance of indebtedness is prepared from the past accounts of balance of payments.

When deficit, are financed by loss of reserves, the balance of indebtedness remains unchanged. Exchange rates changes show different amounts of delats in rupees.

Balance of indebtedness can also be prepared for a short period of time or for a long period of time. The long-term investment position is of less immediate importance. Long-term investments are unlikely to be withdrawn on short notice and tend to respond more to long-range, basic economic considerations. The long-term investment position is of significance in determining the international flows of interest and dividend payment which appear in the current account of the balance of payments.

Gaps in data and uncertainties over the claims-value many a times make the problems of data collection difficult.

(c) Accounting balance

The four accounts we studied give us accounting balance. It is an *export* concept. If only three accounts are taken into account then we can talk about 'deficits' or 'surpluses' but if all the four accounts are taken into account then, as we have seen, the balance of payment always balances. Corrective actions become necessary for tackling the deficits' and 'surpluses' of the first three accounts.

(d) The programme balance of payment

This is an *ex-ante* concept. A developing economy or a planned economy can plan about the future incomes and payments on account of all the four accounts of the balance of payments. It may find that on the first three accounts there will be deficits. These deficits of the three accounts are not symptoms of mismanagement but of deliberate planning. Deficits now show that the planning is aimed at developing a country through import of capital, technical know-how, and vital inputs.

(e) The market balance of payment

There is always a foreign exchange rate that will equate the demand and supply of foreign exchange. On a particular rate, the demand may exceed the supply and then the market balance of payment will show deficit. On a certain foreign exchange rate, the demand may be less than the supply and then the market balance of payment will show surplus. Deficits in market balance of payment show that the demand for imports is more inelastic than the demand for exports. Corrective fiscal, monetary, income and other policies may become necessary to effect the elasticities of demand and supply for exports and imports.

4. BALANCE OF PAYMENT AS AN INDEX OF THE ECONOMIC CONDITIONS OF THE COUNTRY

Balance of payment and balance of indebtedness can show the summary positions of the trends of balance of liquidity and balance of long period assets and liabilities. The deficits and surpluses of various accounts give an idea about the economic conditions of a country. However, not all deficits are to be frowned upon and considered something which are not in the interest of the economy. Present deficits may enable a country to earn furture surpluses if import of capital leads to the economic development of the country. Import substitution, export promotion and industrialisation programmes require large deficits to be incurred on the first three accounts of the balance of payment. Balance of payment study reveals whether the country is self-sufficient to the extent that it can finance its current imports from the current exports.

The balance of payment balances in the 'trivial sense' only. The three accounts show the direction of disequilibrium. Depletion of reserves or accumulation of reserves are indicated by the study of various types of balance of payments. They show the weakness or strongness of the economy. The composition of the items also throws light on the nature of goods and capital imported or exported.

Outflow of capital brings interest and dividends lateron, but may create short-period problems. Inflow of capital brings instruments of development and finances the deficits but creates interest and dividend liabilities for the future. Few countries bother about surpluses; it is the deficit that merits attention and countervailing actions.

Even when the deficits and accommodating capital inflows may be the same, two countries may have very different general economic situations. To understand fully one has to take into account the causes of deficits and the policy measures that are being taken and can be taken. The more the restrictions and controls, the less scope a country has for getting rid of a deficit. If a country is already pursuing tight, monetary and fiscal policies and has high tariffs and import controls, yet. still has a deficit, it may be very difficult to get rid of the deficit, The more restrictive the greater the requirements of "management of balance of payment disequilibrium". Only totally controlled communist countries could have that "freedom". In free economies highly restrictive wage/salary policies or monetary and fiscal policies have their own limits. Inflow of capital [See chapters on "theory of capital movement", FDI and FII] can help in the short period. In the long period the use of that capital in increasing production for export promotion and import replacement/curtailment will be important.

2009					
BOP Defict Countries $ b.			*BOP Surplus Countries $ b.*		
1.	USA	524	1.	China	218
2.	Britain	127	2.	S. Arabia	212
3.	India	77	3.	Germany	168
4.	Spain	76	4.	Russia	101
5.	France	55	5.	Norway	51
6.	Greece	45	6.	Netherland (Holland)	47
7.	Turkey	36	7.	S. Korea	38
8.	Hong Hong	26	8.	Malaysia	34
9.	Egypt	25	9.	Japan	28
10.	Pakistan	14	10	Brazil	26
11.	Poland	08	11.	Singapore	22
12.	Mexico	07	12.	Thailand	20
13.	Italy	06	13.	Taiwan	20
14.	Austria	06	14.	Swilzerland	18
15.	Israel	05	15.	Indonesia	17
16.	Australia	03	16.	Argentina	16
17.	Canada	03	17.	Belgium	16
18.	S. Africa	03	18.	Chile	12
			19.	Sweden	12
			20.	Venezueta	07

Economist, London, Janvary 2,2010.

12 Disequilibrium in Balance of Payment: Methods Of Correcting

I. Introduction: Meaning of Equilibrium in external BoP.
II. Causes and Types of External Disequilibrium.
Short term: Cyclical: Long term (secular): structural, disequilibrium of flows and other causes.
III. Theories of Disequilibrium.
Price theory of classical writers.
Income theory of Keynes.
Demonstration effect disequilibrium of Duessenberry.
Backwash effect theory of disequilibrium of Myrdal.
Productivity differential theory of disequilibrium.
IV. Problems associated with disequilibrium of surplus BoP. Top ten consequences of adverse B.O.P.
V. Top ten measures to tackle adverse/deficit BoP disequilibrium.

I. Meaning of BOP Disequilibrium

Balance of payment disequilibrium is generally taken in countries like India as balance of payment being adverse. Indians think so because it is reality of economic life of India. ***Balance of payment disequilibrium is always with reference to the first three accounts of the BoP.*** The fourth account balances with loans taken or outstandings of receipts of foreign exchange.

Surplus balance of payment is as much a disequilibrium as deficit. Anything other than equilibrium of perfect balancing of the first three accounts is disequilibrium.

BoP disequilibrium is there when the demand and supply of the foreign exchange are not equal or in balance.

A country can have BoP surplus with some countries and BoP deficits with other countries. All that matters is the net balance: whether it is deficit or surplus. BoP deficits and surpluses can differ from year to year...commodity, goods and service-wise and country-wise. Once again the ultimate total matters. However, if BoP disequilibrium is to be corrected, then the correctives are to be applied country-wise as well as itemwise for exports and imports.

If Japan has balance of payment surplus in total, it means it has large foreign exchange reserves and other countries owe to Japan. Japan may also be owing a lot of foreign exchange to some countries as some countries owe to Japan. It is ultimate total that counts.

Balance of payment deficit means the country will be indebted to the extent of deficits for the current year. Balance of indebtedness is the sum total of net debts of the past till date.

Foreign exchange or foreign currencies are sum total of different currencies of the world that a country has in its reserves. All currencies. except the national currency, *are* foreign.

However, there *are* some '.'key currencies". Dollar is the most important key currency. EURO is currency of European Union. (See relevant chapter). In practice countries accept and keep only a few key currencies.

Ultimately all currencies are converted into dollars in actual or in accounting. Even if India is having £ or EURO in the currency reserves, its dollar equivalent will be taken into account.

Forex reserves are different from foreign currency reserves. Forex reserves *are* equal to *(I)* Gold reserves valued at international prices or a fixed price considered right by the Central bank + *(II)* Reserves of different currencies converted into dollar equivalent + *(III)* IMF tranches/reserves.

If payments on all the three accounts exceed the receipts on all the three accounts in total, it is adverse or deficit BoP. If receipts exceed payments on all the three accounts in total it is BoP surplus. Balance of payment cannot be in balance on each day, week or month. We take a year. If the BoP deficit or surplus is carried over and over different years, it is known as secular or long term of chronic BoP disequilibrium of one type or the other. Short period imbalances cannot be avoided.

Balance of payment disequilibrium changes the rates of foreign exchange. Changing rates of foreign exchange bring new disequilibrium. ***Economy moves from one disequilibrium to another disequilibrium. It is seldom in equilibrium.*** Problem is not of the type but of the amounts.

II. TYPES AND CAUSES OF VARIOUS TYPES OF DISEQUILIBRIUM IN BOP

BOP DEFICIT DISEQUILIBRIUM

2 (a) Short term disequilibrium.

This is usually associated with ups and downs in the agricultural and allied activities in poor countries. A shortfall in production lines in agriculture will mean less exports and less earnings. Prices rise due to low production but the poor countries have inelastic supplies and hence cannot take advantage of higher prices. BoP goes in deficit. In case of bumper crops, the fall in the prices may not bring high revenues. Even this can be problematic. For a few months after the crops arrive, the exports of less developed countries may exceed the imports and there may be surplus foreign exchange earnings. These short period deficits or surpluses may balance in some countries but not in most of the less developed countries.

2 (b) Cyclical disequilibrium

Cyclical fluctuations in prices, production, employment and incomes are endemic in the developed capitalist economies. These changes bring periodic fluctuations in the exports and imports, thereby causing cyclical disequilibrium in balance of payments.

If a country has a higher rate of inflation than other countries, its exports will fall and imports will rise and a balance of payment deficit may result. The deficit and surplus of balance of payment in periods of non-stable prices will depend on the respective elasticities of demand and supply of different countries.

2 (c) Secular (Long-period) disequilibrium

Long-period disequilibrium in balance of payment can be due to several reasons. A poor country will in most cases have less foreign exchange receipts and more foreign exchange payment obligations. This state of affairs can be due to supply inelasticities and excess of demand over supply. Or, it can be due to massive imports of capital goods, vital inputs, essential commodities and technology during the initial period of planning. It can also be due to mismanagement of the economy. In all such cases the long-period deficits in balance of payment will increase balance of indebtedness. These deficits must have been financed by large debt-inflow. A planned economy cannot avoid such balance of payment deficits but should do well to see that within five decades no deficits are incurred.

2 (d) Structural disequilibrium

Depletion of certain vital resources in the country, structural disequilibrium at factor level (shortage of labour or shortage of capital or shortage of trained personnel, resulting in the unemployment of other cooperant factors of production), and various types of supply inelasticities can be responsible for massive deficits in the balance of payment. A foreign innovation that competes very adversely with the export commodity can also cause such disequilibrium. These very factors can be responsible for surplus in other countries.

2(e) Disequilibrium due to changes in the money incomes and changes in the capital flows

A fall in the money incomes during deflation reduces the balance of payment deficits or may even convert it into a surplus, if exports pick up and more output is produced. Such inflow of income will ultimately end deflation. Rise in money incomes during inflation, particularly if the country is at full employment level and when the marginal propensity to import is very high, will make imports exceed exports. A balance of payment deficit will result.

III. THEORIES OF DISEQUILIBRIUM

Balance of payment surplus and deficits are both disequilibrium. Less developed countries are saddled with huge balance of payment deficits and in countries like India. We discuss problems of adverse balance of payment.

No country can have in all the years a balanced balance of payment on first three accounts. Short term disequilibrium will always be there. The long term trend will show whether the country is moving towards higher 'balance of indebtedness' due to deficits or is moving with bulging forex stocks due to balance of payment surpluses. ***India's $ 256 b. forex reserves in Dec. 2008 and of $ 286 b in 2009 were not genuine but in the form of debts. India's external indebtedness ($ 256 b.) was almost equal to***

***the forex** reserves.* Developing countries have adverse balance of trade due to structural backwardness of their economies and due to low productivity per person or per lump of inputs.

1. **Price theory or Cost theory or Classical theory** emphasises that if the costs of productions are high due to low productivities, the countries will experience BoP deficits. Their remedy was to leave everything to the market. In the long run everything **will be all right!** ***While we can agree with the cost theorists that high costs of production or low productivities are the causes of deficits, we cannot agree that market will automatically reduce balance of payment deficit.*** Government cannot sit on the fence and watch unequal fight between big business of the Western countries and much smaller companies of their countries.
2. **Income theory of Keynes** emphasises that as the incomes of the people/firms of the countries increase, the incremental income is increasingly used in buying foreign goods. In other words, the "marginal propensity to import" rises at a faster rate than the "marginal propensity to consume". Import of capital and heavy goods of technology are the prime causes of deficits in the early stages of development....and such conditions can last one century !

   The first is the supply side explanation; the second is the demand side explanation. Both are partially correct. Taken together they provide acceptable explanations.
3. Duessenberry wrote that the firms and people of developing economies ape and imitate the ' consumption, production, distribution and furnishing systems of the West. That is premature. Because of this the developing economies lose precious foreign exchange in huge amounts. ***Vanity of a few is satisfied before the basic needs of the majority.***
4. Gunnar Myrdal was of the opinion that the developed capitalist countries earlier colonized the poor countries and exploited their resources. Exploitation continues under "economic imperialism". Spread effects (good) are less than the backwash effects (bad) and there are cases of *immiserisation" of the poor countries through more exports for the same imports.*

Modern Theory of BoP Disequilibrium. The current explanations of BoP deficits are taken as modern. They include all the previous explanations, but add two more explanations of importance. They are: (i) modern goods bring new types of disequilibrium in balances of payment (both types) and (ii) differences in productivities help in bringing the BoP towards equilibrium and the same factors can create further disequilibrium.

1. If productivity increases in the export industries, the cost of production will become low. Lower prices of exportable goods can be charged. If the foreign demand is inelastic, then no gain will accrue for BoP deficits. If new bushes of tea are planted and they have better and more tea leaves, the prices can be reduced (say) by 30 p.c. However, if the foreign tea consumers consume the same amount of tea, no orders for extra tea will come. In this case the profit margin of the tea producers can increase if they keep the prices at the same level. If the domestic demand picks up for the extra tea, there will be no need to reduce the price equal to the reduction in the cost of production. ***Productivity gains help the country most when the goods are luxury goods or comfort goods.*** Their demand is elastic.
2. Increase in productivity does not, in any case, lead to the deterioration of BoP deficits.

3. If the productivity increases in those lines of manufacture which are lines of import also, then BoP deficit will be reduced. If a country was meeting the domestic demand both with domestic production and with imports, the domestic production will be meeting larger percentage of demand as costs go down and then prices are reduced. Less will be spent on imports.
4. When the productivity rises and more real outputs are available, there should be no crash in prices due to demand remaining static. Demand increases due to increase in population and purchasing power. Hence, in practice, no producer will increase productivity in such a manner that only prices crash down and no additional demand comes from anywhere. Hitherto poor consumers outside the market can enter into the market as things become cheaper.
5. If the gains of productivity are not shared equitably there will be no help in BoP. If the benefits of increased productivity are reaped by the industrialists and traders only, their real incomes will increase. If they demand more foreign goods than the national goods, the BoP will deteriorate. However, in practice workers will also share the benefits of productivity. They usually demand domestically produced goods. The benefits of higher productivity have to be passed on to the domestic consumers. Hence full leakage of benefits of productivity to foreign countries is seldom possible. ***Productivity should increase in export promoting industries and import replacing industries for reducing the BoP deficits. The linkages effects should be high for economic development of the country in all sectors, regions, functions, facilities and for groups of people.***

IV. PROBLEMS ASSOCIATED WITH SURPLUS BALANCE OF PAYMENT

It is seldom realised that balance of payment surpluses can also bring problems. The countries which have BOP surpluses find that the exchange rate of their currency appreciates: (like if $ 1 becomes Rs. 44, from Rs. 47.5) it is appreciation of Indian rupee and depreciation of dollar. Indian rupee can appreciate vis-a-vis dollar not because Indian economy has become strong but can also appreciate if the US economy has become weak ***or availability of dollar increases in India.*** Exchange rate of Indian rupee in 1947 was $ 1 = Rs. 4.5). Surpus BOP is one reason of the exchange rate improving. Japan does not want its exchange rate to improve because it sells mostly luxury goods and they become dear to foreigners. BOP surplus and rise in exchange rate can bring these situations:

(1) Imports become cheaper and more goods can be imported. (2) Exports become dearer and less goods can be exported. (3) If the imports are of essential things, they may not increase. (4) If exports are of essential things, they may not go down. (5) Rising exchange rate will make the exporter of the country to request the foreign importers to hurry up payment because if the payments are received late, the countrymen (say Indians) will receive lesser money (rupee). (6) If the exchange rate is rising (say in India), the Indian importers would like to delay payment because in future dollar can be had in lesser rupees.

TOP 10 CAUSES AND CONSEQUENCES OF ADVERSE BALANCE OF PAYMENT

1. Adverse balance of payment becomes "balance of indebtedness" in the long run. If year after year there is BOP deficit, the country is living beyond its means and will be indebted. Interest obligations on debts will go up. Credit ratings will go down. BOP deficit creates conditions for higher BOP in future.
2. BOP deficit can also be due to crop failures if the country is primarily exporting agricultural raw materials. The international oligopsonies (a few buyers) may not allow the prices to rise in case of shortage of exportables from the developing economies.
3. In case of bumper crops, the international oligopsonies may delay the purchases to make the prices crash down. Hence it is seen that BOP deficits can be inflicted upon the poor countries by the developed countries in both partial crop failure and bumper crops situations. Developed countries do the same thing in the case of mineral ores and other exportables of the primary sector.
4. Fall in demand for exports of a country due to international depression can be one reason. If the resources get depleted or if they exhaust, exports will go down. Middle East countries fear that one day their oil reserves may exhaust.
5. If the incomes of people in a developing country rise fast and become high in due course of time, the rising incomes will be used for importing foreign things rather than buying domestic products. Rich persons prefer foreign wines, cars, cosmetics, fast food or travel to outside country rather than buy domestic things. This is known as ***rising marginal propensity to import.***
6. If a country keeps its exchange rate artificially high (which is known as "high peg") then foreign imports will become cheaper and our exports will become dearer to the foreigners, particularly when there is high rate of inflation in the country. This will create and/or aggravate BOP deficit.
7. The same thing will happen when the government imposes high export duties and keeps the exports price high. Then also the exports will be discouraged. Whatever discourages exports creates BOP deficits. Whatever promotes imports (for example fall in domestic production) will also create BOP deficit.
8. If a country receives large grants from foregn countries because the country grants military bases or cooperation to the super power (as Pakistan did and does), then its BOP deficit will be brought down. It can even experience BOP surplus.

   If a developing country does not sell its freedom, it can face BOP deficits. However, such BOP deficits are preferable than selling country's dignity. In such cases the imports should be brought down and should be confined to very essential things only.
9. A very good way to tackle BOP deficit is to increase domestic production. Good governance and production efficiency will be helpful. ***The well managed TATA company of India, did India proud when in 2004 it purchased the parent Daewoo Company of Korea, promising Koreans that it will be run by the Koreans.*** TATAs bring glory to India. Many other Indians have become super rich in foreign countries. ***Unrequitted remittances or unilateral transfers*** (as money sent by the sons employed in a rich country to the parents in a poor country) will improve BOP.

Absence of or reduction in such unilateral flows will create BOP deficits. Exploitation (known as backwash effects) by the rich foreign countries, low productivity and high costs of production in the poor countries, and "demonstration effect" (the habit of imitating the consumption/production pattern of the rich) create BOP deficits. ***High expenditure** on war **goods is a great cause of BOP** deficit just as the imports **of** luxury goods **for the benefit of the** microscopic minority **of** the super rich in small and poor countries*

TOP 10 MEASURES TO REDUCE ADVERSE BALANCE OF PAYMENT: IF POSSIBLE TO CONVERT IT INTO A SURPLUS

It is easy to make suggestions on paper than to implement them. There are simple suggestions for removing the adverse balance of payment and they are correct also. The problem is that the simple suggestions are difficult to implement. The importers and exporters may not cooperate with the national government. The first and the foremost (and the only) suggestion that can be made is to "remove the causes, remove the problem".

1. High Tariffs. Tariffs or customs duties or taxes on imports are the first measures to control adverse balance of payment. India used to impose very high customs duties (even 500 p.c. of the value on foreign costly wines) yet continued to have adverse balance of payment because the super-rich continued to import. ***High customs duties promote smuggling.***

Now a days the World Trade Organisation does not allow high duties on imports. "Caps" (maximum limits) have been fixed for the average tariffs. Now a days the belief of the world is that let there be maximum international business with all countries of the world. By 2015 the cap of import duty will be 3.5 p.c. of value.

If high customs duties or tariffs or import taxes are imposed, others will also impose such taxes on the exports of the tax levying country. Nothing positive will come out. Double taxation will become multiple taxation. Trade will be reduced. There will be lower production, lesser employment and fall in the incomes.

WTO allows raising of tariffs if the** balance **of** payment problem **is very serious. The governments should** make use **of** the permissible **taxes to the upper limit wherever possible. That is all that can be done.

Tariffs bring imports compression. High import duties increase the prices of imported goods. It is expected that the total import bill will fall.

If the demand for imported goods is inelastic, there will be no reduction in imports. The government will earn revenue from import duties.

If the supply of the foreign exporter is elastic, *i.e.*. the exporter can take the supplies to other countries, then the foreign exporter will not reduce the international prices. Here again tariffs will not be of any benefit.

2. Quota restrictions. Quota restriction is fixing quantities to be imported from foreign countries. [See chapters on Tariffs and Quotas also for details]. The Government can fix the number of cars to be imported...say, 1,00,000. The quotas can be allocated thus:

USA	25,000
Japan	30,000
Korea	30,000
Germany	5,000
UK	10,000

Quotas are discriminatory and are resented by the countries on which quota restrictions are imposed. India does not like the USA imposing quota restrictions on the exports of ready-made garments from India.

Quota restrictions can be higher against that country with which the country has large balance of payment deficits. Cars cannot be smuggled but many other items which are not numbered can be smuggled due to restrictions of quotas and tariffs.

The same conditionalities which were mentioned for tariffs apply to quotas also. If India wants import compression, the following conditions are necessary for quota restrictions.

1. Demand for the products should be elastic.
2. Foreigners' supply should be inelastic.
3. Goods should be such which cannot be smuggled, like number bearing goods.

3. Export duties to be reduced. Balance of payment deficit can be reduced through (i) imports compression and *(ii)* exports promotion. If the exportable goods have inelastic demand abroad, the government can impose export dutites to earn tax revenue.

If the exportable goods have elastic demand abroad, then export duties are to be reduced. If the co-efficient of elasticity is more than one, then exports will rise and the export earnings will rise. Luxury goods have high elasticity of demand. Suppose a 50 p.c. reduction in export duties increases the exports to double, the co-efficient of elasticity will be 2. Higher export earnings thus reduce balance of payment deficit by bringing more foreign exchange.

4. Devaluation. It is also helpful. This is deliberate reduction of the exchange rate vis-a-vis key currency or currencies. If suppose exchange rate is $1 = Rs. 4.5 (this was the exchange rate at the time of independence of India), and the Government of India announces the exchange rate to be $ 1 = Rs. 5.5, this is devaluation. If the exchange rate changes due to market forces, it is a case of fluctuating exchange rate. Devaluation is relevant in the case of fixed exchange rate. We take another example. If the exchange rate is $ 1 = Rs. 45 and the government gives 10 p.c. more *i.e.,* Rs. 4.5 more the exchange rate will become Rs. 49.5 and will encourage exports because the foreigner was earlier getting goods worth Rs. 45 in one dollar. Now the foreginer will get goods of Rs. 49.5 in the same price one dollar, there is no inflation.

If there is 20 p.c. accumulated inflation differential (supose inflation was 10 p.c. in three years in the USA and 30 p.c. in India during the same period, the inflation differential is 30-10 i.e., 20 p.c.) then a reduction by 20 p.c. in the exchange rate will be "clearing the backlog of inflation". It is not devaluation in the real sense. **Devaluation should be more than 20 p.c. to be effective.**

The IMF does not allow devaluation by **a** high percentage to compete with the foreigners. Competitive devaluations are not allowed. Devaluation makes imports costly and exports cheaper to foreigners. Hence it can reduce the adverse balance of payment. This happens when the country gets more revenue from exports and spends less on imports. The sum of four elasticities should be high (say 4) to give substantial advantage. [See chapter on Devaluation].

5. **Subsidies.** The government can give subsidies to those producers who produce goods which the country was largely importing. Hence domestic production will reduce imports. The outflow of foreign exchange will be reduced.

Subsidies can also be given to the exporters. India's export of sugar used to be subsidised because international prices were lower. The subsidy is given in rupee terms but the higher exports bring foreign currencies or **dollar which is the vehicle currency" of the world.** All currencies have dollar as 'reference variable" for exchange rate.

The first three accounts of BoP are known as "autonomous" accounts. The fourth account is known as "induced account". All *measures of **imports compression** and export promotion should ensure **balance In the first three** accounts.*

Subsidies can reduce BoP through exports promotion. But these subsidies put a burden on the domestic "balance of public finance".

6. **Increasing productivity** per person, per machine, or per "package of inputs for production" help in reducing balance of payment deficit in the most efficient way. Goods of good quality sold at low price (higher productivity brings lower cost of production) increase exports. Domestic consumers also will find domestic goods to be cheaper and of the same quality. Hence they can switch over from imports to domestic production.

Higher productivity reduces the cost of production.
Then there is reduction in prices.
Then imports can get reduced as people prefer domestic goods.
Then exports will pickup.
Now a days subsidies are subject to WTO regulations.

.For higher productivity the country requires modern technology embodied in capital goods. They have to be imported first. This will increase the BoP deficit. In the long run higher productivity will translate into *(i)* higher exports, *(ii)* higher domestic consumption and *(iii)* lesser imports. ***Payments are reduced** and receipts increase.*

7. **Exchange controls.** Exchange control requires that all foreign exchange should be taken by the government and the exporters should get the domestic currency equivalent. This discourages the exporters.

One simple measure is that there can be bilateral arrangements. Imports are paid for with the exports. Two countries can agree that both of them will have equal amount of trade. This becomes international barter. If Bangladesh imports coal from India for Rs. 400 crore. Bangladesh can sell gas to India for Rs. 400 crore.

If this can be done country-by-country (which is very difficult), the balance of payment will balance.

8. **Control on oligopsonies and monopsonies of foreign countries.** In India exports quality fruits abroad, the sellers are many but there can be a few buyers only in foreign countries (oligopsonies) and they may not pay proper prices. Government can provide support so that the farmers do rot make distress sales. Foreign monopsony

(one buyer, several sellers) has to be controlled with diplomatic pressure of the government on the government of the country of monopsony or digopsonier. Oligopsonies if they connive can be treated like monopsony. Monopsonies and oligopsonies of different products pay less to the growers. Governments alone can fight with the multinational monopsonies and oligospsonies.

9. Control on foreign monopolies and oligopolies as they trade with a country. The foreign monopolies charge high prices and many a time sell junk goods. Government will have to stand up.

Take the case of 386 computer. They were sold In India first for Rs. 65000 or so with stabiliser etc. Then after the sellers had sold their Junk 386 models, they brought 486 model. That too is now out of date. The present most modern Pentium series computers were sold very late. **Billions of rupees wore taken away by the foreign sellers with whom the Indian traders connived.** Such monopolies and oligopolies are responsible for BoP deficits. Keeping them under control is not easy because the governments of such multinationals come openly to their side. Monopolies, multinational companies and oligopolies dictate terms even to their own governments what to say to the governments of the developing economies.-

10. Anti-dumping measures and ban on certain imports. These things can be done. If a foreigner sells below his cost of production this is dumping. It can be in large quantities. Government can impose countervailing duty to take away all advantages of dumping. Dumping means a lot of money goes out even at lower prices. Adverse BoP can be controlled.

13 Methods of Correcting Adverse Balance of Payment—I Methods of Exchange Control —Tariffs.

Under the new regime of the World Trade Organisation all countries are to have minimum possible rates of tariff so as to promote multilateral trading. Hence tariff as a tool of exchange control and or of securing favourable balance of payment has become less important. However, the system of tariff has not been abolished. The minimum tariff will be atleast so much that the expenses of customs department are recovered. From the theoretical point of view the entire discussion about the effects of tariff remains the same as during the regime of high tariffs.

Tariff is a charge levied on goods as they enter a country, crossing the national customs frontiers. A tariff is a schedule of duties levied upon the importation of commodities into a given nation from abroad.

VARIOUS TYPES OF TARIFFS:

Specific tariff is a fixed amount per different goods e.g., Rs. 20000 per car. *Ad Valorem* tariff is according to the price of a good e.g., 10 p.c. on "A'" and 16 p.c. on B and so on. Luxury goods are taxed at higher rates. *Combined tariff* means a fixed rate upto a certain price, then ad valorem on good of higher price after a limit. *Single column tariff* means same rate on same type of good irrespective of wherefrom it is coming. *Double column or multiple column or discriminatory tariff* means low tariff from certain countries as from a bloc and high from others. Such tariffs can differ countrywise. For a change, further negotiations will be necessary. *Maximum tariff* rate is known as "caps" tariff. [on a body cap is over the head]. *Minimum tariff* is what the name suggests the lowest rate. *Optimum tariff* is one which brings best of the combined effects [see later in this chapter].

Thus there are many effects of tariff, and the four main effects are:

1. Protective effect

A tariff will have protective effect for domestic industries only when the demand for imports in highly elastic. Rise in the price of the imported commodity as a result of the increase in tariff will force consumers to consume less. The tariff can in such cases be borne by the foreign exporters, but if their supply is also elastic *i.e.,* they can sell the commodity elsewhere or can withhold its sale, then they will also not bear the burden of tariff. The result will be that imports will fall considerably and the domestic industries can take up the production.

The following diagram shows not only protective effect of tariff but also other effects of tariff that will be discussed in the following pages.

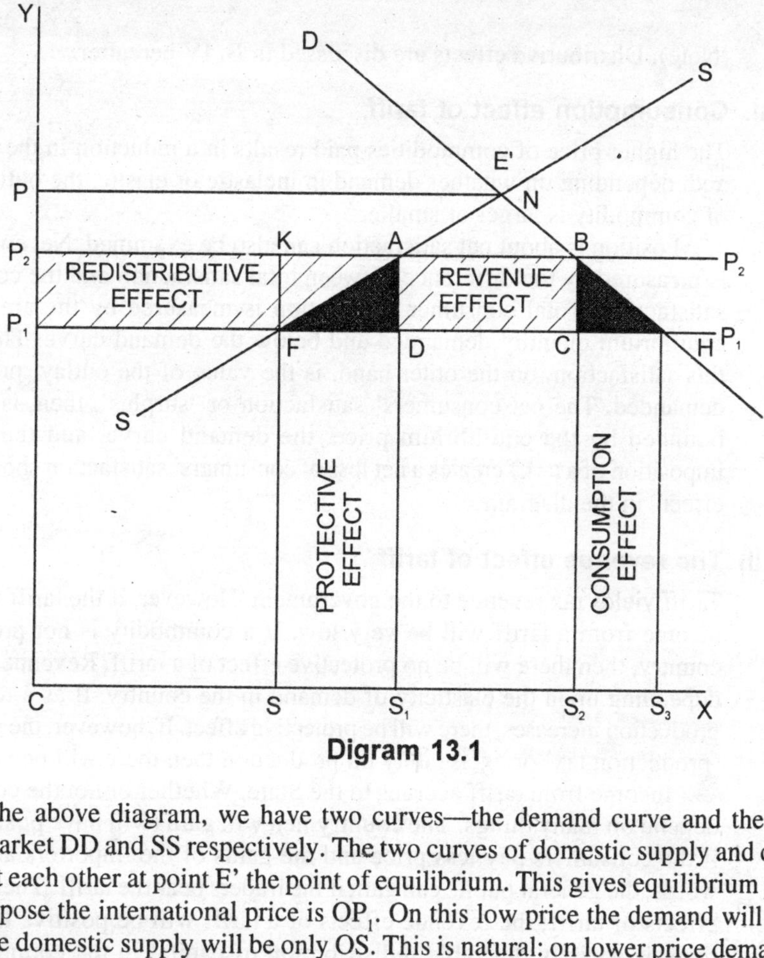

Digram 13.1

In the above diagram, we have two curves—the demand curve and the supply curve market DD and SS respectively. The two curves of domestic supply and demand intersect each other at point E' the point of equilibrium. This gives equilibrium price P.

Suppose the international price is OP_1. On this low price the demand will be OS_3 while the domestic supply will be only OS. This is natural: on lower price demand will increase and supply will fall.

Now if the Government imposes a tariff equal to the amount P_1P_2 to give protection to home industries, the price will rise to OP_2. Now the domestic as well as import price of the commodity will be OP_2. At higher price, naturally the demand will decrease (as compared to free import price) and supply will increase. Imports will be reduced. Imports will not be reduced by the amount S_2S_3. Home production will increase by SS_1. Total domestic production will now be OS_1. Total imports will now be S_1S_2.

(a) Revenue effects: abcd (Gain): This we get by multiplying the imports S_1S_2 by tariff amount P_1P_2.

(b) Consumption effect: S_1S_2 (Loss): Old consumption was OS_3 but the new consumption is only OS_2 Consumption is thus reduced as a result of imposition of the tariff.

(c) Protective effect (Gain): — Protective effect of tariff is equal to SS_1. Formerly production was OS, now it increases to OS_1 after production.

(Note): Distributive effects are discussed in B. IV hereafter.

II. Consumption effect of tariff

The higher price of commodities paid results in a reduction in the quantity consumed and, depending on whether demand in inelastic or elastic, the outlay on consumption of commodity is larger or smaller.

Position is about net satisfaction can also bc examined. Net consumer satisfaction is measured by the difference between total satisfaction and the cost of obtaining that satisfaction. Total consumer satisfaction is measured by the area to the left of the equilibrium quantity demanded and below the demand curve. The cost of obtaining this satisfaction, on the other hand, is the value of the outlay: prince times quantity demanded. The net consumers' satisfaction or 'surplus', then, is the triangular area bounded by the equilibrium price, the demand curve, and the vertical axis. The imposition of a tariff creates a net loss of consumers' satisfaction shown as "consumption effect" in the diagram.

(III) The revenue effect of tariff

Tariff yields tax revenue to the government. However, if the tariff is highly protective, income from a tariff will be very low. If a commodity is not produced at all in the country, then there will be no protective effect of a tariff. Revenue effects can be high, depending upon the elasticity of demand in the country. If as a result of tariff, home production increases, there will be protective effect. If, however, the government imposes 'production tax' or excise duty on production then there will be no protective effect.

Income from tariff accrues to the State. Whether or not the countrymen gain will depend on many things. The countrymen will gain (will have positive revenue effect) if the consumers pay less price and the gains of the importers are reduced. In other words, the general public can gain if the traders bear the tariff. There are re-distributive effects of tariff; the revenue effects of a tariff will be positive to the countrymen if there is socially desirable redistribution of capital in the country. Revenue effects will also depend on how far the import replacement effects succeed in export promotion.

It should be noted that there is a maximum limit of the revenue effect of the tariff. This will depend on the relative elasticities in the country and abroad. The maximum revenue tariff is equal to the product of the two elasticities of reciprocal demand for exports minus unity.

The revenue effect of tariff is realised through savings in foreign exchange that result from reduced imports (increased home production).

(IV) Redistributive effects of tariff

The redistribution effect is realised through the higher price and higher profits for the existing producers. The redistribution effect usually means transfer of consumers' surplus to producers in a single commodity.

We have studied earlier that *(i)* free trade raises the price of the abundant factor and lowers the price of the scarce factor; and *(u)* protection. does the oppositive *i.e.,* raises the price of the scarce factor and lowers the price of the abundant factor. If a tariff provides producers protection, the factor incomes will undergo redistribution.

Scarce factors therefore, want protection so that their monopolistic or quasi-monopolistic position is maintained. Abundant factors, on the other hand, want greater and freer trade so that market is widened and they get greater employment. Whatever increases the intensive use of the factor brings redistribution advantage. Thus redistribution effects of a tariff can be explained in the same way as the "high wages (or factor prices) effects" of protection. Thus both the "cheap labour" and "dear labour" arguments can be advanced by the 'vested interest' groups. Redistributive effects of tariff will depend whether the trade policies are benefitting the abundant factor or the scarce factor. Government policy may deliberately strive to alter the distribution of income in the 'general interest'.

The redistribution effect is the transfer of income from consumers in the form of an economic rent accruing to the producers. This arises due to higher prices paid by the consumers to the domestic producers on each unit of their *total* output and not only the additional output. If the diagram, the redistribution effect of the tariff is shown by the quadrilateral P1P2 AF. Of this total area, the area covered by the shaded rectangle P1P2 K.F is due to the additional economic rent paid to the pre-existing domestic producers and the area measured by the triangle KAF is the rent (extra price) paid to the new producers on additional production taken up by the old producers.

In the diagram the total loss of consumers' surplus due to tariff levy is equal to the area of the quadilateral P1P2 BH. Of this total loss suffered by the consumers, PjP_2 AF amount is transferred to the domestic producers and ABCD amount is taken away by the government from the tariff revenue.

The loss of the consumers is represented by the shaded triangles AFD and BCH and it is neither transferred to the domestic producers nor does it accrue to the government. Nevertheless, the consumers suffer this loss.

Consequently, the triangles AFD and BCH represent the net loss suffered by the society. The loss of shaded triangle AFD is due to the inefficient use of resources *i.e.,* due to rising cost of production under decreasing returns. The resources drawn in the new production due to higher domestic price were earning returns equal to SS_1 (x) OP_1 or (SS DF) in some other industry. But due to protection the expenditure on SS_1 is SS_1 AF.

Consequently, the net loss to the community on the production side is AFD. Similarly the expenditure diverted by the consumers to other products brings satisfaction equal to HCS_2S_3.

As a result of this, the net loss suffered on account of cut in consumption is shown by the shared triangle BCH. The total loss of AFD suffered on production and of BCH suffered on consumption is called the real loss of tariff **to** the society.

It is to **be** noted at the end of this discussion that:

Free traders and those who do not worry about balance of payment deficit	Protectionists who worry a lot about BoP deficit.
They regard tariffs being harmful to the people and the country. They bring net loss.	They regard tariffs as important tools to save money on imports to keep the BoP deficit down

As we noted earlier and shall see in the chapter on WTO, the world is moving towards low tariff regime. Hence it seems difficult now a days to tackle BoP deficits with the help of tariffs only.

(V) Terms of trade effects of tariffs

"Terms of trade" are the ratios of change in export prices to changes in import prices." These are known as net barter terms of trade. Suppose the index of export prices changes from 100 to 120 and the import prices index changes from 120 to 140. Then the percentage changes are:

20 p.c. for exports and 16.66 for imports: 120/100 versus 140/120 respectively. Hence 20: 16,66 means 20 p.c. improvement.

Suppose these changes are shown as being opposite, then terms of trade will deteriorate to the same extent. The essential point is that the price terms of trade or net barter terms of trade should rise, other things remain the same.

Gross barter terms of trade mean ratio of imported goods obtained for the exported goods. If India exports 1000 cars to get a battle tank in one year but in the next year the same battle tank can be obtained by sending 1050 cars, it is clear that gross barter terms of trade have deteriorated. If the same battle tank can be obtained by selling 950 cars the gross barters terms of trade have improved, quality of both products remaining the same.

Income terms of trade are more important. On lower prices of exports our income should fall. But if the fall in prices induces high foreign demand and we sell more, the income terms of trade improve: 100 cars @ 3 lakh rupees give us income of Rs. 300 lakhs. However, if the price is reduced to Rs. 2 lakhs and we can export 200 cars, then total export income will become Rs. 400 lakhs. So the country earns more even at lower prices.

Tariffs can have the following effects:

- Imports will be reduced if the demand is elastic in the import levying country. This will save foreign exchange.
- If the demand is inelastic in the tariff levying country, the consumers will bear the tax and the same imports may continue.
- If the supply of foreigner is inelastic (he cannot sell to any other country), the foreign country will bear the cost by way of charging lower prices. In other words tariff levied in country "A" will be absored by the producers of the country "B". BoP deficit will go down. If the supply is elastic in foreign country, the foreigner will not bear the tax. If the demand in tariff levying country is also elastic, volume of trade will go down. Employment and income generation will go down.

Tariffs provide great benefits when the tariff imposing country is strong and the foreign country or countries are weak.

When we are strong, the foreigners become weak. When we are weak, the foreigners become strong. A country cannot and should not impose tariffs if it is very weak. If India is imposing tariffs, it should not be weak and the following conditions should not apply.

1. India's imports should not have inelastic demand in India.

2. The foreigners supply should not be elastic. It should be inelastic. In other words the foreigners must be having large supplies which that country wants to sell even at lower prices because it cannot take it to other places.

Finally, the income earned or expenditure saved due to tariffs should be used well. The additional income should be used for increasing such production as is expert promoting and/or imports substituting.

Internal and external cost-price effects.

(vi) These should be carefully understood.

1. If the production is under the constant returns/costs, the burden of tariff will be equal to the amount of tariff. It can be shared between the domestic buyers and sellers (either domestic or external or partially by both) in the proportions of the strength of their elasticities of demand and supplies.
2. **Suppose tariff eliminates imports. Then all production will have to be made by the domestic producers.** We presume the law of increasing costs or diminishing returns. As the domestic producers produce more their per unit cost of production increases. Hence the burden of tariff on the domestic consumer will be equal to the amount of tariff + increase in the per unit cost of production due to increasing costs, if the demand remains the same.
3. Suppose imports cease. Suppose the tariff is 50 p.c. extra. As this is imposed, the price will go up. At higher prices, demand goes down. **If the demand goes down,** then the producer will produce less. Suppose the cost of production in "A", 'B'', arid "C" cases are as under:

Units	*Constant costs*	*Decreasing costs*	*Increasing costs*
100	10	10	10
150	10	9	11
200	10	8	12

If 200 units were being sold from imports and domestic production. Suppose a tariff of 50 p.c. is imposed. The price will go up by 50 p.c. Then the demand will go down. If the demand goes down to 150, the burden of tax in constant costs will be equal to 50 p.c. over the price (suppose) of Rs. 10/-.

Under decreasing costs, when the production is reduced to 150 units, the cost of production will become 9. Earlier it was Rs. 8. [It is assumed that price is always equal to cost of production, which includes normal profits). The price was Rs. 8. Tariff will be Rs. 4 @ 50 p.c. Now the price becomes Rs. 8 + 4 = 12. Due to reduction in demand the costs will become 9 and when the tariff of Rs. 4 is added the total burden will be Re. 1 more = 9 + 4 = 13. Now if the price is fixed at 9, the tariff will become 4½ @ 50 p.c. Cumulatively the demand for foreign goods can keep on going down. The thrust point is that under decreasing costs or increasing returns or efficient production, tariffs increase the burden on the consumers which is more than the burden of tariff. This will happen immediately after impact of tariff.

Under increasing costs, the initial price will be Rs. 12 t= to the cost of production). Burden of tariff is Rs. 6. The new price will become 18. The demand (suppose) falls to 150 units. Now the cost of production will also go down to Rs. 11 hence the burden of tariff on price will be equal to Rs. 11 + 6 = 17.

These things will hold true for domestic price when all imports cease. Since the long term condition is that of decreasing returns or increasing costs, the tariff burden will be lower than the amount of tariff.

It should be remembered that if the tariff reduces the imports to a great extent or completely, and the domestic producers take up production for meeting the demand, then these will become domestic price effects. If the imports continue almost as usual then for the imported goods, these effects will become international price effects also if the foreigner continues to export.

(viii) Income effects

Income effect is different from the 'revenue effect". Revenue is the tax income of the government. Income effect means impact on the national income.

If the domestic production increase as a result of tariff, there will be more investment, employment generation and income propagation. There will be multiplier effect also i.e., the chain effect. More capital and more inputs will be required. There will be higher production in the upstream as well as downstream activities. (For cotton textile industries, growing of cotton is a upstream or backward activity. All those things which are required for growing cotton will be further upstream activities. After cotton textiles are produced from the mill, there will be downstream activities e.g., more sewing machines, packing products etc. There are several direct and indirect upstream and downstream, (forward linkages) activities. Savings, capital formation, investment, employment. income, demand and then supplies will have a healthy circle. If foreigners retaliate by imposing tariffs on our exports, then all good effects of tariffs cannot be realised. Retaliations there will be.

(ix) Factor incomes will not have a tendency to get equalised

If India imposed tariffs, domestic industrialists gain but consumers will suffer. Capital will continue to get high rate of interests. International trade promotes export of those products which utilise our abundant factor intensively. Hence wages in India cannot rise.

(X) Competition will be eliminated/reduced and hence domestic monopolies can exploit more

Technological developments will not be there. They are there in competition.

Balance of Payment effect. Initially BoP deficit may be reduced. If there is retaliation, then exports will go down. BoP will again go into the old deficit. If tariffs reduce BoP deficits, if they increase the national income through higher domestic production, after some time the marginal propensity to import will go up.

Conclusion on this point is that market mechanism is better. Controls are anti-production. In 1971 Vespa had a waiting/booking period of 15 years ! Now one can get it in a moment. Free trade is better. Tariffs should be used as a tool to improve BoP rarely and in selected cases.

OPTIMUM TARIFFS

We saw in the text of this chapter that there is always optimum rate of taxation. This optimum is that point below or above which we do not get the best. India can have a high "maximum" population but there will be deaths of the crores of persons. Hence an optimum population is to be conceived to which India can provide a reasonable level of living.

Optimum tariff is one which takes the interest of the consumers and the domestic producers in balance. A very high rate of tariff cut down imports so much both domestic consumers and investors will suffer. Besides, It will antagonise the foreign exporters/ countries who will not import from India. Then it should also take care of the domestic producers so that the foreigners do not indulge in dumping.

Tariffs can increase the domestic production, domestic employment, domestic prices of scarce factors of production and domestic incomes. They can even improve terms of trade and balance of payment positions.

Tariffs, however force domestic consumers to pay higher prices. Domestic consumers may have to purchases inferior domestic goods even if the foreign goods are of better quality and technology. The welfare of the people of the tariff levying country may be adversely affected. Hence an optimum tariff is to be imposed.

Now a days the WTO is insisting in lowering the average rate of tariffs. These average rates are lower than the optimum tariff. The concept of "optimum tariff' is not so relevant now. It was very relevent in the case of high tariff regime and exchange controls. Now maximum rate after 2010 may become 3.5 p.c.

Too high tariffs may mean no revenue to the government because foreign exporters may divert their exports to other countries where tariffs are low. This is possible when the supplies of the foreign exporters are elastic.

Complete protection with the help of very high tariffs may deprive consumers with the required amount of consumption. The domestic producers may not be able to produce as much as the foreign exporters were exporting to the tariff levying country. In other words, the domestic-producers may not be able to produce as much as was being imported. The country may be lacking the necessary capital, technology and high grade skills.

If the tariffs are too low then the domestic producers may not get protection against dumping by foreigners.

If the domestic demand for the imports is inelastic, the previous imports may continue and the adverse balance of payment will not improve.

- Optimum tariffs help only when there is no retaliation from the foreigners.
- If the foreign supply is inelastic the optimum tariff can be high.
- If the foreign supply is elastic the optimum tariff has got to be low.
- If the foreign supply is perfectly elastic, no tariff will yield the home country improved terms of trade and the concept of optimum tariff will become irrelevant.

- The greatest difficulty about levying an optimum tariff is that the country will have to engage itself in many exercises of upward and downward adjustments. Then only the optimum tariff may be found. Problem arises when the optimum tariff has to satisfy both domestic producers and consumers.
- Optimum tariff once found may become irrelevant for the next time period. It remains elusive concept.
- We can conclude that greater the inelsticity of supply of the foreign exporter, the higher the pagging of the optimum tariff. Contrariwise the higher the elasticity of supply, the lower the level of optimum tariff.

There are four elasticities in international trade. Suppose India is exporting ready-made garments and the USA is suplying high grade electrical locomotives. The four elasticities would relate to two supply elasticities of two goods of two countries and two demand elasticities of two goods of two countries.

14 Methods of Controlling Adverse Balance of Payment—II Methods of Exchange Control –Quotas and Subsidies

(UNDER PARTIAL EQUILIBRIUM ANALYSIS)

Quota regime is minimum, if at all, now a days under the World Trade Organization. The system and therefore the theory are still studied,

MEANING AND TYPES-OF QUOTAS

UOTAS are maximum limits of exports and imports that can be expressed in specific quantities. There can be export quotas also like not more than so many lakh tonnes of baasmati rice can be exported. Or it can be quota of not more than so many cars of different types (allocated car-wise and/or country-wise) can be imported.

Tarrif-quota. This is expressed this way that upto first 2000 cars, there will be low rates of tarrif and if more cars than that are imported then punitive tariffs will be imposed. **Unilateral quotas** are imposed without consulting other countries. **Global or non-discriminatory quota** means the total number cannot exceed the quota and there are no restrictions about the country wherefrom imports can be made. **Allocated, selective or discriminatory quotas** those where not only the maximum limit is fixed but it is also decided how much will be imported from different countries. More may be imported from countries with which we have favorable balance of payment and less from the "hard currency" countries i.e., those countries of which currency we do not have much in reserve. **Licence quotas** mean that not only the country limits are fixed but the importers are issued licences to import. In order to avoid corruption, it is desirable that the **quotas may be auctioned** and it should not be mock auction. **Bilateral quotas** are fixed after consolation with all countries and then other countries do not feel aggreived. **Mixed quotas** mean that various quotas listed above may be combined. Additionally the producers may be asked not to use 100 p.c. inputs from outside. Domestic inputs are also to be used. If cars are to be imported, the prospective domestic car producers may be encouraged to produce cars so that not all cars required are imported.

PARTIAL EQUILIBRIUM ANALYSIS

Partial equilibrium analysis is done under various assumptions. Many other things are assumed "to be the same". Transport costs are ignored. Many other types of costs *e.g.,* selling costs are ignored. It can also be assumed that other countries are not taking countervailing actions. In other words, other countries are not retaliating, much less more than retaliating.

We are talking about import tariffs and import quotas. They become export tariffs for a foreigner and quota restrictions for the foreigners. Partial equilibrium analysis means that a small country is being taken into account. The 'smallness' of the country is in terms of its economic size and not geographical size. It can be for a big country also for one commodity or good taken at a time is isolation.

Diagrams showing the four effects of tariff or quota namely the protection effect, the consumption effect, the revenue effect and the redistribution effect are the best illustrations of the partial equilibrium analysis.

If should be noted that the partial equilibrium analysis can be done for the big nation also. It can be for the short period. Partial equilibrium ignores the effect of tariff and/or quota on "A" commodity as it affects the production, trading and subsequent production effects of other commodities.

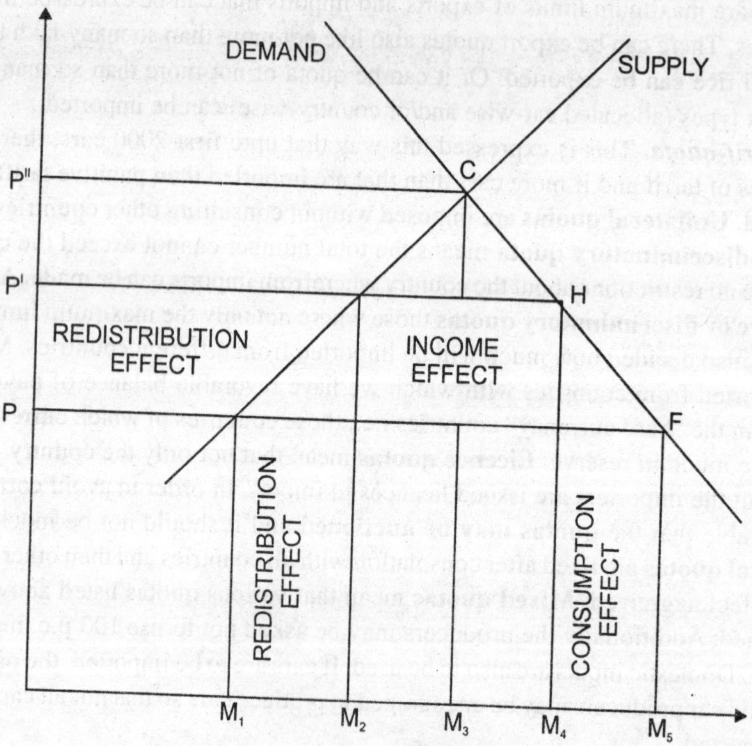

Fig. 14.1

If quota is fixed on ready-made garments, we will not trace the effects on what happens to those who are engaged in packaging, manufacturing sewing machines, extracting iron for machines, pesticide sprinklers on cotton, tractors used in cotton fields, threshers, winnowers or machines in ginning mills etc.

General equilibrium analysis will take into account all big and small nations, all commodities and goods, all services, all factor prices, all prices of all commodities and goods.

With so many variables to be handled at the same time, even computers cannot give the results of direct and indirect effect. General equilibrium analysis is intellectually fascinating but is an impossible task to handle. **Alfred Marshall, the master economist who gave us the complete binder on pure theory (managerial economics, or advanced economic theory, or International economics or whatever relating to pedagogic analysis) advocated partial equilibrium analysis. The price theory that all students (of all subjects related to it in the faculties of Commerce, Economics and Management) study Marshall's partial equilibrium analysis.**

Elaborate algebra and geometry are used in GE analysis. The analysis is totally archaic, abstract and pedagogic. Partial equilibrium analysis with simple diagrams is practical and pragmatic for drawing direct inferences. There are theorems and theorems in the GE analysis. (*)[1]

Quotas and their effects. 1–4 Protection, consumption, income and redistribution effects

In the diagram the world market price of the good is shown by P. At this price, the country demands Om_5 of the good and produces OM_1. Thus, imports amount to m_1 m_5. When authorities decide to provide protection to local producers through quota system, the imports will be reduced to M_2 M_4.[2]

The import price rises to P. In the above diagram the effects of quota are shown in the same way as that of tariff. The effect on domestic production, consumption, domestic price, international terms of trade and imports are the same. The only difference between the effects of tariff and effects of quota lies in the fact that while the revenue effects of tariff accrue to the government, the quota holders get benefits because they enjoy the position of oligopolists.

A question arises that when quota deprives the government of revenue (which goes to the quota holder) why should government prefer quota to tariff. The answer lies in the fact that when the supply of export goods is inelastic and the demand is also inelastic raising of tariff will not provide protection. In such cases only quota can provide protection. Tariffs are useful in perfectly competitive conditions.

Tariff may not provide protection in all those cases where imports continue to be made freely at the tariff-inclusive price. In case of quota, a domestic producer can benefit from the quantitative restrictions to establish a domestic monopoly, whereas if tariffs had been used, he would have had to accept full international competition.

Besides limiting competition in domestic markets, quotas attach a scarcity value to imports and it (scarcity value) gives rise to an economic rent (higher price in the short period is called rent').

If the government merely introduces a quota and if domestic producers are organised, and foreign producers are not, the domestic producers will capture the "rent" *i.e.*, *(i)* the extra price that the sellers obtain in the short period due to shortage of supplies and *(ii)* the extra-normal or super-normal profits that the domestic producers can earn in the short period till the supplies become equal to the demand.

If the foreign producers are organised and domestic ones are not, then the foreign producers can get a substantial part of the "rent" by increasing their prices and turning the terms of trade against the country.

The government can capture the rent by auctioning the quota where by there has to be bidding and the higher bidder wins. High "rents" are now obtained by the government. Government of India had many systems of quota:

OGL Any one can import certain commodities in any quantity from anywhere. No quota infact.

EI The quota permissions are given to 'established importers'. Consumption goods can figure in such quotas. Since they are to be imported in large quantities by a large number of importers, the quotas are/were allocated.

AU Under such a system the quotas are given to the actual users. If the imports are of capital goods quotas become AU-CG.

WTO does not like quotas but has not banned the quota system.

5. Terms of Trade Effects of Quotas:

They can improve if the USA imposes quota restrictions *on* Indian ready-made garments, the Indians may reduce the export prices of garments so that they get more share in the quota. In other words, the USA can increase the quotas of India. It comes to the same thing as saying that the quota restrictions against India may be reduced.

6. Government Revenue Effect:

If quotas are auctioned, the government gets the "economic rent" as discussed above. If certain countries exceed quotas and the goods come to the shores of the country, instead of sending back the consignments, the government can collect fines. Thus government revenue effect will be there.

7. Internal Price Effect of Quota:

Imposition of a quota will raise the domestic price of goods because supplies will be reduced, it is not possible immediately that the domestic producers can fill the gap of the previous total supplies. In case of the quota restrictions, the domestic prices can rise sharply if the quotas are strict. In case of the tariff, normally the burden on price is equal to the amount of tariff (constant costs assumed). In case of the increasing costs, the effect of tariff on domestic price can be less by the amount the cost of production is reduced due to reduction in demand. Only in case of the decreasing costs or increasing returns the total burden of tariff will be higher than the amount of tariff. However, in case the foreign producer has increasing returns or declining costs per unit, the government should do well to allow imports for the benefit of the consumers. But it can impose tariff for the benefit of the domestic producers. In quotas, the foreigners cannot continue to sell the same amounts as in tariff. A ban can raise prices sharply.

8. Balance of Payment Effect of Quotas:

Quotas restrict imports and if exports remain the same *i.e.,* other countries do not impose quotas for our exports, the import bill can get reduced. There will be favourable BoP effects. Whether quotas alone convert a deficit balance of payment into a surplus balance of payment cannot be said a priori. That will depend upon on how many commodities and goods the quotas have been imposed. Other things remaining the same, the greater chances of a favourable effect of quota, will depend upon picking up luxury goods which involve high amounts of imports.

It is asserted by the free traders that efficiency (higher productivity) and novelty of exports (innovations) are better ways of improving Bop through export promotion because quotas certainly evoke relaxation.

In the following conditions quotas will not help the BoP situation.

1. When the foreign countries also impose quotas on our exports.
2. When quotas increase the price of imported raw materials which are used in the manufacture of commodities/goods that are exported from the quota fixing country. It is presumed that no country will be silly to impose quotas in such cases.

9. Monopoly Effects of Quotas:

Quotas can lead to emergence of domestic monopolies. This monopoly may emerge in the hands of those importers who corner all quotas. For this purpose the importer can float many firms which will be proxy of the main importer. There may be many firms belonging to the same business interest that corner all quotas from the government.

It is a fact of life that under the quota-permit raj there is widespread bribery of the politicians, administrators and others for cornering the quota. If quotas for cars are fixed, cars from different countries and of the different models may be imported by cartel of firms. Many firms may connive. They may agree to compete in a sham way. There will be a tacit agreement of not competing. When a monopoly is formed the consumers will be exploited even more. They get double disadvantage. They cannot get all the goods at internationally competitive prices in the quantities they want and then they are made to pay much higher prices to the domestic quota holders. Conversion of quota to tariff eliminates the chances of a monopoly or a cartel emerging.[3]

TARIFFS VERSUS QUOTA: A STUDY OF THEIR RELATIVE EFFECTIVENESS: ECONOMIC ARGUMENTS IN FAVOUR OF QUOTAS

Quota system was first introduced by France in 1931 and since then it has become a practice with all countries of the world to impose some sort of quota restrictions on certain imports in some period of their economic history. Quota restrictions are naturally preferred in those cases where tariffs will not provide protection. When the foreign supply of an import good is nearly inelastic, a tariff cannot increase the domestic price of the imported good for the exporter will bear it. Tariff thus will improve terms of trade and will yield more revenue to the government but its protective effect will be almost zero. Income redistribution in favour of domestic producers cannot be achieved with the help of tariff. In all such cases quota restrictions will achieve the desired results.

Quotas eliminate uncertainty and have direct effect on such imports as are having elastic supply curves. Another advantage that quotas possess over tariffs is that quotas can be changed and altered easily to suit the trading changes with certain countries. Imports can be excluded surely and quickly through quotas than through tariffs. Greater administrative flexibility thus makes quotas more popular.

In all those situations where the domestic users and foreign exporters cannot be controlled in such a manner that there be no imports above a certain amount or above a certain physical quantity, quotas prove very effective. Countries facing acute foreign exchanges problem (more so with a few selected countries) find quota restrictions to be more effective. During a period of economic distress at home, quotas can prove highly effective in checking the income leakages abroad. Similarly when there is deflation abroad and the foreign exporters want to 'export deflation' quotas can prove helpful. Of course the consumers of the country benefit when foreign exporters are forced to sell at cheap rates but the impact on domestic producers may prove disastrous. The domestic suppliers can market all of their output at current prices without fear of "ruinous" import competition.

Uncertainty with regard to foreign supply conditions constitutes a strong reason for the use of quotas as opposed to tariffs as an instrument of protection. Quotas are not only effective in all those cases where foreign supply is inelastic but they are equally effective if domestic demand for a particular imported commodity is particularly inelastic. In such cases imports may continue at the same level even at high prices. Quotas alone can offer an effective alternative to tariffs. Tariffs are often regarded as relatively permanent measures and rapidly build powerful vested interests which make them all the more difficult to remove. Quotas have many characteristics of a more temporary measure, are designed to deal only with a current problem and are removable as soon as circumstances warrant. Quotas can be imposed and withdrawn in a flexible manner.

Quotas are easily implemented as emergency measures and are usually unencumbered by reciprocal trade agreements and other institutional forces making for rigidity. Other countries may be less apt to view quotas as permanent trade barriers and as threats to their exports, and thus are perhaps less likely to retaliate swiftly with new trade impediments of their own. Thus quotas can help a country insulate itself from the economic misfortunes of other countries easily. A nation can invoke quotas as the most administratively feasible way of cutting back the potentially damaging waves of imports (or exports by other countries). In all such cases, quotas prove superior to the tariff as an instrument of commercial policy.

Limitations

As we have seen, quotas can be misused by importers and shady officials. They may be obtained at a bribe price and may be sold at black-market prices. If quotas are granted on a selective or discriminatory basis with political, military, social and other considerations interferring in the operation of trade between nations, they are likely to give rise a very distorted pattern of trade. They will then do much damage to the international trade mechanism by removing it from the operation of the price system and market forces.

Then quotas give rise to monopolies of the importers and exporters. All quotas tend to support concentration among importers and exporters. The administrative allocation of quotas to importers reduces competition and fosters the development of import monopolies. Quotas tend to promote concentration among the foreign exporters also. They can then bargain effectively with the home country's importers. In the words Kindleberger:

> "Quotas introduce a wholly arbitrary new dimension into international trade. The use of quotas is a step backward towards the economics of the Middle Ages...quotas pour fuel on the inflationary flames, while tariffs bring in revenue which removes inflammable desirable than alternative lines of action is never more in point than in the case of quotas imposed to reduce the balance of payments effects of uncontrolled inflation at home."

Quotas when they become too restrictive can invoke retaliation also. Quotas discriminate most severely against those importers who are not corrupt and have no strings to pull with the officials and politicians.

Precisely these objections have led to a general rejection of quotas as a legitimate policy tool under the General Agreement on Tariffs and Trade (GATT) to which virtually all major trading nations subscribe under the WTO.

PART II—SUBSIDIES

Subsidies do not impede import competition. If the domestic suppliers cannot produce at costs cheaper than foreign suppliers then the national government can help the domestic producers with subsidies to render national suppliers more competitive in both the domestic and international markets. Subsidies can be given overtly or covertly. A government may take a very low charge on goods hauled by its transportation system. Higher rates of depreciation on machines may be allowed so that the firms can switch over to new technology. Tax concessions may be given to firms in the form of tax holiday for an initial period of say, five or seven years. Reduced profits tax, sales tax, or turnover tax may be charged. Subsidies are usually given to exporters and it is quite possible for the government to refund taxes in full on the exported goods. Yet another comprehensive system of giving subsidies can be that government will make up any loss a firm may have on its books at the end of the year if it has to sell below costs either to compete with a foreign seller in the home market or in the international market. The government may also provide 'sort of insurance' against non-payment loss or a political risk of expropriation.

Now-a-days most of the governments promote their trade interests in foreign countries by organizing exhibitions, trade fairs or by providing information through their commercial attaches. In the absence of such expenditure being borne by the government the private, investors would have incurred it.

When the foreign supplier is selling goods at cheaper rates in domestic market, the government may allow the countrymen to reap and advantages arising out of cheap price. Domestic producers can be helped with subsidies. Subsidies will not invoke retaliation from the foreign governments. The effects of subsidies on imports and to import competing industries and naturally different from those of tariff. As subsidies are provided, the domestic producers are enabled to lower the prices. Domestic consumers can consume more at lower prices and they may consume greater quantities of domestic goods. Imports may thus be reduced and the terms of trade may improve. There will be a redistribution of income as domestic producers are enabled to produce more and meet foreign competition. There will be beneficial impact on domestic income and employment.

The economic impact of subsidies on export industries are not easy to generalize. As export prices are lowered the terms of trade deteriorate, but domestic prices and consumption remain the same. Increase in exports will, however, have multiplier effects even more so when exports increase substantially. A transfer of real income occurs as tax revenues are used to lower prices charged foreign consumers and perhaps also certain groups of domestic consumers.

Subsidies to both import competing and export industries necessarily distort the structure of both the domestic and foreign economies. Domestically resources allocation departs from the optimum dictated by market forces as labour and capital are drawn into the subsidized industries. In foreign countries, the artificial increase in competitiveness of subsidized imports drives resources out of import competiting industries into other less productive employment. In other countries, whose exports become less competitive in the world market, competition from a country which subsidies exports also drives resources out of the export industries and into less productive tasks.

In distorting the pattern of international trade based on comparative advantage principles, subsidies are not different from tariffs and quotas. However, once the foreigners realise that their exports are facing competition due to the system of subsidies, countervailing actions can be taken by them. Pure theory tells us that subsidies will also reduce world welfare. However, the free trade model has given place to the system of second best' and in those situations where protection becomes desirable, subsidies cannot be condemned.

Subsidies are likely to be misused by powerful and inefficient domestic producers. Producers who have control over the political system of the country and are corrupt may use the system of subsidies to further their interests. The entire system of subsides may become thoroughly misused and vested interest groups may obtain these subsidies for their own personal good through manipulation. Now industrialists and inter national businessmen get fiscal packages to the tune of several lakh-crore each year.

Export subsidies are helpful only when the demand for the subsidized product is elastic in foreign countries. Then only loss in terms of domestic currency can be made up with gains in foreign currency. If the external demand is inelastic, subsidies will neither be necessary nor helpful.

NOTE

1. For example we have studied that if trade is carried on according to H—O theory, the export
2. 1. Protection effect 2. Consumption effect 3. Revenue/Income effect. 4. Redistribution effect
3. Cartel is a sellers' monopoly. OPEC (Organisation of Petroleum Exporting Countries) is a cartel. Different countries own their own oil fields. There is no joint ownership in production but only in selling. That is the reason why petroleum prices are being hiked. Instead of reducing the prices, the OPEC cuts down production.

15 Methods of Controlling Balance of Payment Disequilibrium III: Exchange Controls

1. Meaning and objectives.
2. Direct Methods.
3. Indirect Methods
4. Overall efficacy of exchange controls.

We saw in the previous chapters that (1) high tariffs on imports, (ii) fixing quotas on the goods of the foreign exporters, (iii) giving subsidies to domestic producers on various functions, (vi) devaluation of currency vis–a–vis dollar, (v) taking anti–dumping measures, (vi) control on big foreign operators etc. are methods of correcting adverse balance of payment, which type of disequilibrium is tried to be controlled, more

Now rigorous exchange control measures are not allowed to be implemented by the WTO. If at all they are to be there, they have to be in minimum.

Exchange control is superceding the market determined prices, exchange rates and all international transactions. Foreign currency reserves are used by the central Bank. Imports are sought to be restricted. Exports of essentials are sought to be restricted. Exports are sought to be promoted through "artificial" means. Exchange rates are controlled. Discriminating exchange rates may be there for the importers and exporters. Consignments of foreign trade can be checked. Invoicing can be checked so that there is no under-invoicing of exports and over–invoicing of imports to build up reserves abroad. Those who earn foreign exchange cannot retain the same. The reserves are impounded by the government and equivalent domestic currency is given to them. Tourists going out maybe given paltry amounts And they will get foreign currencies from the black market. Capital inflows and outflows are controlled. Foreign exchange is given as a matter of favour and expediency. Black market naturally emerges under exchange control system.

Objectives

The top 10 objectives can be listed as under:

1. Market mechanism can give a country huge adverse balance of payment. Under exchange control system it can be reduced to the minimum. That means denial of the use of many imports or in the required quantities.
2. Under–invoicing of exports is checked. If exports are of $ 100 b. but the bill is of $ 85 b. $ 15 b. may be are retained abroad with mutual connivance between the

parties. If the imports are_over–invoiced then also the illegal reserves of foreign exchange are built up abroad. Suppose the imports are of $ 150 b. but the bill that comes is of $ 165 b., then $ 165 will be sent and the foreign exporter will take $ 150 b. and keep $ 15 b. for the (say Indian) importer. The foreigners do these works for their commission. In these two transactions $ 30 b. of reserves have been built up abroad. Suppose there is exchange control and the official rate of exchange is $ 1 = Rs. 40, the buyer of dollar will be given dollars $ (say) 1 = Rs. 45 by Hawala operators If suppose an Indian wants dollars abroad. He will pay the rupees in India and carry a coded letter or slip to the US (or wherever he is going) to the agent and he will deliver the dollars.

3. Hot money (money invested in papers) flows will be controlled. Foreign money which is brought for speculative buying and selling of shares may not be allowed or only some selective inflows may be permitted. Similarly, hot money may not be allowed to be taken out to cause reserves crisis. Flight of capital is not permitted.
4. Rising prices given natural inducement to domestic buyers to prefer imports; but are not allowed under exchange control when the currency of a country becomes over–valued at official per due to rising prices in the country, the exports of the country have inelastic demand abroad and (ii) imports into the country have elastic demand.
5. Exchange control becomes necessary when scarce foreign exchange reserves are to be rationed. In such cases socially necessary imports are allowed. Socially necessary goods are not allowed to be exported. Capital goods are preferred for imports. Protection to domestic industries is also provided this way. Necessary inputs of industrialisation are imported. If certain exporters earned huge amounts of foreign exchange they can be given "bonus vouchers of foreign exchange" to import what they want, subject to certain limitations. Foreign exchange is auctioned also so as to get high prices. High rates of exchange rates can be charged from importers; high demestic currency equivalent may be given to big exporters. Cyclical fluctuations can be controlled.
6. Governments recover the cost of administering the foreign exchange control administration but may even earn huge profits from differential prices of foreign exchange.
7. It is easy to repay foreign debts under exchange control because the government can retain as much foreign exchange as it wants.
8. If foreigners dump it can be checked by imposing higher import duties on the dumped goods. Exchange controls become necessary during the war period and for many years after the war. If imports far exceed exports, then balance of payment becomes adverse and exchange control may become necessary. The foreign exchange can be rationed.
9. Exchange controls insulate the economy from foreign economic onslaughts. The country can expand its money supply to provide full employment through many economic activities yet the exchange rate may not be allowed to go down.
10. Exchange controls permit national economic policy makers broad freedom of action in all times.

Disadvantages

Exchange controls leave the way open for a serious inflation of costs and prices. The official rate of exchange becomes over–valued. Imports become costly and many types of consumption may be disallowed. Industrialisation too may suffer if necessary plants, machinery and inputs are denied to be imported. Exchange controls are further required to maintain an over–valued exchange rate. Administration has many types of power and corruption becomes rampant. Competitiveness of the economy may go.

DIRECT METHODS OF EXCHANGE CONTROL

1. Bilateral trade Agreements

If two countries are short of foreign exchange, they can export and import commodities/ goods of equal values. 'A' can export "coal" of the same value as the 'B' country exports cotton. Similar deals can be there but of equal value. Imports are thus paid by exports. This method is useful for those countries which do not have vehicle currency (as dollar) also known as the hard currency) in adequate quantities.

2. Private Compensation Agreement

This is also a barter deal. Suppose (A) India imports jute from Bangladesh, and (B) exports coal to Bangladesh., and they are all of equal amounts. Then money need not cross the country. The payments can be settled thus.

(I) Importer of coal in Bangladesh will pay to exporter of jute from Bangladesh.
(II) Importer of jute from Bangladesh in India will pay to the exporter of coal from India.

Indian will pay to the Indian. Bangladeshi will pay to Bangladeshi.

If there are brokers their payment can also be adjusted the same pay but the parties have to keep their brokerage charges of the same amount. The rates of exchange will differ and the equal amounts will be according to the exchange rate.

3. Clearing Agreement

In this case the two countries will open accounts with the Central Bank of their different countries. For each country there will be a separate account. If the Indian imports jute from Bangladesh, the Indian will put the amount with the Central Bank. When an Indian exports to Bangladesh, the Indian exporter will draw the amount from this account. Other traders will do likewise. If however less amount is put than is to be withdrawn, then the exporter from India wll have to wait. This is the drawback. The amounts will be put/withdrawn according to the deals and according to the exchange rates of the two countries. If the amount in the account is less and the exporter wants the money immediately, then the Central Bank will have to make "swing credit" arrangements.. The Central Bank will take back its credit when there is excess balance. Such arrangement makes the uses of the dollar, (or Euro or the vehicle currency or the hard currency or the key currency) unnecessary. If there is excess balance in the account then the money will "retire" temporarily i.e., will become blocked. In case of shortage and no "swing credit" the exporter will have to bear the loss of interest. Capital flows are excluded from such arrangements.

4. Payment Agreements

When capital flows, interest charges, tourism monies, insurance payment, shipping charges etc. are included in the above agreement, this becomes "payment agreement". This is like bank "clearing" system. After an agreed time, the, transaction balances can be settled in gold/dollars. Payment\Union will have to monitor the functioning for periodical settlements.

5. Multiple Exchange Rate System

Now a days, the exchange rates are decided by the market forces and they can fluctuate several times a day. Under the exchange control system, the exchange rate is fixed by the government. Even if there is inflation there will be no devaluation. Even if the economy is strong, the exchange rate will not be revised upwards. However, multiple exchange rates can be there. There can be higher exchange rate in domestic currency for the exportes, who will got higher amounts of rupees than the exchange rate warrants. The importers will pay more rupees to get dollars for importing. The exchange rates can be different for different commodities and goods. Undesirable imports will be costly in terms of domestic currency. The Government will decide what is desirable and what is not. Importers can get the dollars at the official rata for necessary imports. They can get the foreign exchange for very essential goods at less amount of rupees than the official rate. That rates are discriminatory and may involve administrative work. If the multiple exchange rates are announced beforehand, there can be consignment checking. Black marketing will be greater under such a system, however.

6. Blocked accounts and restrictions

If there are serious shortages of foreign exchange reserves the accounts may be blocked i.e. no payments outside may be allowed for some time. The accounts of those who defaulted on one point or the other may also be blocked. Gold and jewellery will not be allowed to be taken out. There will be strict checks of the invoices and consignments.

7. Transfer moratoria-and standstill agreements

If the country cannot pay the foreign dues due to shortage of foreign exchange, old loans may be converted into new ones but at higher rates of interest. Restrictions are for short period and the foreigners are interned about the same.

Infact the permission of the other countries will have to be taken if the repayment of the loans or payments are to be delayed.

8. Pegging action intervention

Pegging means fixing. The exchange rate can be pegged up to discourage exports or it can be pegged down to encourage exports.

If for the same amount of rupees less dollars are given, this is pegging to discourage imports. If less dollars enable the exporter to get more rupees this is pegging for the benefit of the exporter. Both the things can be done at the same time.

If domestic currency is to be made cheaper, more of it is to be printed/issued. If the foreign currency it to be made cheaper it should be sold from the reserves. This means buying of the domestic currency to make it less in supply and to raise its rate. A lot of intervention become necessary for pegging.

9. Disorderly crossed rates

If "A" currency is 10 units for "B" and "C" currency is 5 units for "B", then one unit of C should be equal to 2 units of A. Suppose this is C 1 = A 1.97, then this is disorderly. Market brings orderly rates. Intervention bring disorderly rates. The buying and selling rates are different and disorderly. There will be more administrative work for the same.

INDIRECT METHODS OF EXCHANGE CONTROL

1. "Buy Swadeshi" type of appeal.

   Gandhiji had issued a call for buying swadeshi clothes and not "Videshi" (foreign) clothes. The Indians then burnt the "holi" of the foreign clothes. Buying domestic products naturally saves foreign exchange on imports.
2. More subsidies and tax concessions in the production of export goods.
3. Higher taxes and procedural restrictions on imports.
4. Tariffs and quotas.
5. High rates of interest so that foreign money comes and domestic money does not go out.
6. Provision of land, water, electricity and transport facilities at confessional rates to export promotion units.
7. Imposing extra duties to check dumping.

All measures of promoting exports and restricting imports are resented by the foreigners. They will do unto such country what this country is doing unto them. There will be retaliation. Now a days the emphasis is on free trade on the principle of comparative advantage. Competitiveness is sought to be encouraged. Production efficiency alone can bring export efficiency. This will bring the efficiency for "imports replacement", "imports compression", "imports restrictions" and "reduction of imports by a certain planned percentage." The balance of payment cannot be made favourable by restrictions but by achieving competitiveness over a long period. Free trade makes it possible to import things that are needed for export promotion e.g., new technology. Exchange controls bring inflation. When they are removed, it is like bursting of an irrigation dam—trouble and deluge all around. Protection is neither possible nor desirable.

16 Methods of Correcting Bop-IV: Changes in the Value of Indian Rupee. Devaluation of Indian Rupee.

[POST-INDEPENDENCE PERIOD]

I. Meaning of Devaluation and Allied Terms

Devaluation is deliberate reduction in the par value of currency vis-a-vis another currency usually the US Dollar and is done under the fixed exchange rate system.

Before Independence, Indian rupee was tagged to the Pound Sterling. All currencies of the countries which were under the rule of Great Britain were tagged to Pound Sterling. The Pound Sterling commanded higher value and international prestige than the US Dollar. If the value of the Sterling used to go up or down, the value of the Indian rupee also used to go up or down by the same percentage.

WHY AND WHEN IS THE RUPEE OR ANY OTHER CURRENCY DEVALUED ?

At the time of Independence the rate of exchange of Indian rupee in the US dollar (adjusted afterwards) was \$ 1 = Rs. 4.50 (more or less).

The rate of exchange is officially expressed upto 5 or even 6 decimal points. It is like this (example only) \$ 1 = Rs. 45.987654. Actually when there are exchanges of millions and billions of rupees, even the decimal points mean quite a lot of money.

Devaluation is done deliberately to clear the inflation backlog.

Devaluation is done to clear the inflation differential. Suppose the exchange rate is \$ 1 = Rs. 46 and there is 10 p.c. inflation in India and 1 p.c. inflation in the US, the inflation differential is 10—1 = 9 p.c.

If the Government of India does not change the rate of exchange, then two rates will emerge. One will be the official rate, known as official par value. The other will be the market rate. Market rate will certainly be 9 p.c. less. Less means 9 p.c. more rupees will have to be paid. Nine p.c. of 46 will be Rs. 4.14 and hence the market rate will become 46 + 4.14 = Rs. 50.14.

This will be done only when the government fixes the rate. Now a days the rate of exchange changes or can change several times during one day. Hence the adjustment is automatic. In fluctuating exchange rate system, there is no question of deliberate devaluation. Devaluation is done when the countries are on fixed exchange rate system. Fixed exchange rate system has been left or jettisoned.

Why should the USA force India to devalue its currency when there is inflation differential higher than in the US ?

When **the** official rate of Indian rupee is (say) Rs. 46 per dollar and the market rate is Rs. 50 dollars (example only), then the US will get goods of Rs. 46 per dollar only if there is trading on the official per value. if the US trades in the black market, it will get goods of Rs. 50 for the same one dollar.

Hence the USA will force India to devalue. **Why should not the USA revalue its currency instead ?**

Revaluation means raising the par value. Raising means paying less. If the USA raises its exchange rate by 9 p.c. In this case the USA will pay \$ 0.91 for Rs. 46.

It is to be remembered that there are serious changes in the international business due to devaluation and revaluation.

Devaluation makes the exports cheaper and imports dearer.

Revaluation makes the exports dearer and imports cheaper.

The USA will not revalue its currency because this will make its exports dearer. It requires devaluation of the Indian rupee. If it revalues its currency it will be raised against all countries. The exports of the USA will suffer.

Devaluation is always done at 12 O'clock in the night!

It is announced by the Finance Minister.

The Finance Minister may call a mid-night meeting of the media. However, if the media asks "Mr. Finance Minister, are you announcing the devaluation ?" The Finance Minister will say "certainly not". He will instead keep the media busy with announcements about how the Government will take certain measures to defend the rupee.

Then at 12 O'clock in the night i.e., at 00.00 hours, devaluation will be announced !

The economic world gets the inkling of the impending devaluation. The Governments usually put a ban on the transfer of money a few days before the devaluation. If that is not done, then people can earn millions of rupees. If someone is knowing about the devaluation and he sends \$ 10 crore out to a foreign country by purchasing dollars for Rs. 460 crores at the official rate of \$ 1 = Rs. 46, after devaluation he will get those \$ 10 crore back and now he will get Rs. 500 crore in return at the new rate of \$ 1 = Rs. 50. He earns Rs. 40 crore in just (say) four days.

Government try to check such things.

Before we study further, let us understand certain terms:

2. Debasement of the currency

If a coin wears off or chips off a bit, it is debasement. Similarly, if a currency note (Americans call it a "bill"), becomes soiled due to oil, ink or gets mutilated or torn, it is debased.

The entire currency remains as valuable as earlier. Only a few units of the same become bad. They can be changed at the bank, if the numbers are intact.

3. Depreciation of the currency

If the purchasing power of the currency goes down due to inflation, it is known as the depreciation of the currency.

See how the prices rose and the currency depreciated over time: In 1939, one quintal of wheat of the best quality used to come in Rs. 3 only for two persons for one year!

In 1944, 4 "samosas" used to come in one paisa, which was l/64th part of a rupee. One rupee could buy 100 oranges. A rupee used to have 64 paise and not 100 till 1960.

There were 192 parts of a rupee in the form of 'pie'. People used to buy with the help of pies. (very old persons still surviving may say to their grand-children, I will not give you a pie even.)

In 1960, one kg. of sugar used to come In 0.6 rupee. In 2009-2010, It was costlier by 58 times or by 5800 p.c. Best quality food made of pure ghee (even vegetables) and with 8 courses in the lunch/dinner, used to cost Rs. 35 a month in 1959. Pure milk, unadulterated even with a drop of water used to come @½ a rupee per kg.

Now in 2010 it is Rs. 28 a kg.... again 56 times In price. The monthly rent of many government bungalows used to be Rs. 7 or so with water and electricity free. Pulses in 2009 were 350 times or 35000 per cent higher. However salaries around 1947-48 were also low. An IAS officer in 1948 used to get Rs. 300 per month.

Why do the prices rise and the value of money falls ?

Population increases and everything becomes short in supply. Meanwhile the government issues new money. Money supply in December 1969 was just Rs. 2669 crore. In January 2010, it was nearly Rs. 52,00,000 crore ! i.e., 1948 times. India's population increased between 1947 and 2010 (estimated) by 3.58 times. As much population as it increased between the years 0001 and 1800 now increases in 14 years ! Every night is a nightmare !

Devaluation (already studied)

Depreciated currency is a bad currency. It needs devaluation under fixed exchange rate system.

4. Down Valuation

If a currency has depreciated by some percentage, and if there is fluctuating or floating exchange rate system, then the exchange rate of the currency will go down automatically.

If the exchange rate was $ 1 = Rs. 45 and there was 5 p.c. inflation then the exchange rate will automatically become Rs. 47.25 rupees per dollar.

If on a particular day, there was inflation differential against India by 0.75 p.c, the depreciation in the exchange rate will by 0.3375. Now the exchange rate will become Rs. 45.3375 automatically due to market forces. Down-valuations are automatic, enforced by the market; This work is not done by the Finance Minister.

5. Devaluation under fluctuating exchange rate: Competitive devaluation

Now a days India is not on fixed exchange rate system. The exchange rate goes up and down according to the demand for the dollar supply of the dollar differential rates of inflation speculative conditions about future.

Now a days the economy is not adjusted to a "stupid" foreign exchange rate (as remarked by Milton Friedman, the great monetarist and the champion of floating exchange rate who won Nobel prize in Economics and who died in November 2006). The exchange rates keep on getting adjusted according to the changes in the economy.

But the Government of India can devalue its currency by a percentage more than warranted by the above four and other conditions.

This will make India's exports cheaper and imports dearer. This is known as competitive devaluation. This is not permitted by the IMF beyond a marginal adjustment upto 10 p.c. to meet BoP deficits.

Other countries resent both competitive devaluation as well as non-adjustments in the downward direction if the conditions require. The old freedom of "artificial pegging" (fixing at a high rate) is now gone.

6. Revaluation

If a country is having persistent balance of payment surpluses it will have huge reserves of foreign currencies. Then the value of its currency will rise. In other words the exchange rate will rise. China is one such country which is not revaluing its currency.

In the fixed exchange rate system, this will have to be done by the government. It is to be announced the same way as devaluation is to be announced.

For example Japan, which was devastated after the Second *World War.* has now become the second most powerful nation in the world in terms of the national income. It captured the world market with its cars and electronic goods, not to speak or many other types of goods from cloth to toys.

The rate of Yen is rising vis-a-vis the dollar. The rate rises automatically. In the days of fixed exchange rate system, the USA used to exert pressure on Japan to revalue its exchange rate.

Without revaluation Japan's exports were proving cheaper. It was outselling the USA. Its foreign exchange reserves were bulging. China's forex reserves by Dec. 2008 were $ 1946 b. while of India were $ 256 b. only.

Japan had to invest a lot of foreign exchange in foreign countries to avoid revaluating the Yen by a big margin. A high rate of revaluation makes Japanese goods dearer. But Japan cannot and could not avoid revaluation.

A currency of which purchasing power is rising or a country which is accumulating foreign exchange becomes strong country. Its currency becomes a good currency. Good currency needs revaluation.

7. Upvaluation

Like "down valuation", the upvaluation is also automatic handiwork of the market. If the value of Yen is rising in the market while the Japan government is not changing its parity officially, in the market it will command dollar in lesser Yens. This is upvaluation for Yen.

8-9. Lowly valued and highly valued

If under fixed exchange rate system the value of Indian rupee falls due to inflation or due to shortage of supply of the dollar, then more rupees will be required to get a dollar. Rupee is lowly valued is in the market.

If (for example) the Yen is appreciating and requires revaluation, but the Japanese government is not revaluating it, then in the market it will be highly valued. Less yens will command a dollar in the market. More Yen will be required to get a dollar at the officially parity.

10-11. Under-valued currency and over-valued currency

Under-valued currency is a good currency.

Over-valued currency is a bad currency.

The terms refer for the par values, or official exchange rates.

A currency which requires devaluation but is not devalued is over-valued at par *i.e.*, officially. In the market it will be lowly valued.

A currency which requires revaluation but its not revalued is under-valued at par *i.e.*, officially. In the market it will be highly valued.

DEVALUATION AFTER 1947

When India became free in 1947, it put the final "death nail in the coffin of British Imperialism." The Second World War had left Britain quite devastated. Germany was defeated but Russia, France and Britain suffered much. Smaller countries lost their freedom. Hitler killed 60 lakh Jews. Only the USA remained unscathed by war in the sense that war was not fought on its soil.

The British pound sterling was devalued by 30.5% in 1949.

Common wealth Countries all based on £ devalued their currency by the same percentage.

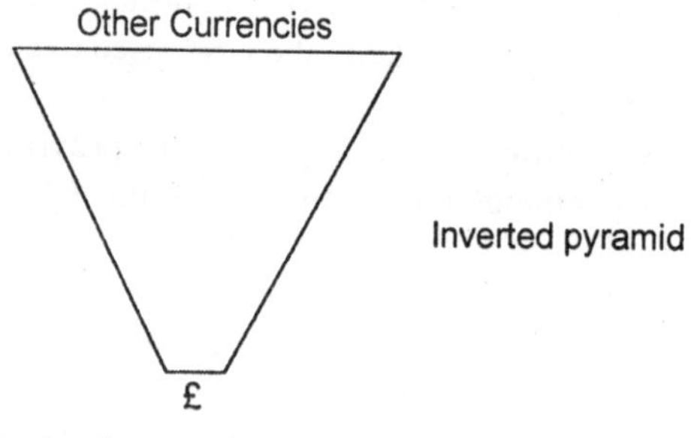

The erstwhile colonized countries had the relationship of inverted pyramid. The base was just one currency. All other countries were having their currency based on it. Hence when the £ was devalued by 30.5% vis-a-vis $, India's rupee was also devalued by the same percentage. The rates after devaluation were

Re 1 = 18 Pence before and after devaluation, as both were devalued by the same percentage.

Re 1 = Sept. 1949 $.3025

= after Devaluation $.2100

$$\frac{2100}{3025} = 0.6941 - 1 = -0.3058 \times 100 /$$

$$= 30.58\%$$

1949: Pakistan's Folly of not Devaluing its Rupee that Ultimately Resulted in East Pakistan Getting Liberated as Bangladesh

Pakistan did not devalue its currency. This was to harm India. It was the only commonwealth country that did not devalue its currency after the Great Britain did.

After the partition of India 99% jute mills were in India and almost 90% jute growing areas were in East Pakistan, now Bangladesh. Pakistan thought that India will pay them 30.58% extra price for jute. India had to take important decision.

India started growing jute in its rice growing area. Then India started importing rice from Thailand, Cambodia (Kampuchia), Burma (Mynmar). Laos or Vietnam—from anywhere it would get. The golden fibre of East Pakistan rotted. East Pakistan's economy was adversely affected. They could not open so many; jute mills. Nearly 90% of the foreign exchange used *to* be earned by East Pakistan but all was spent in West Pakistan (The present Pakistan).

The West Pakistan did not allow the East Pakistani to become P.M. even when the election was won by an East Pakistani.

The East Pakistanies were hated by fair coloured West Pakistanies *for* their speaking sanskritised Bangla, and for being dark coloured and short statured, (as the west Pakistanies used to refer item.)

Destruction of the jute economy was not forgotten by Bangladeshies. In 1971 they got freedom, thanks to the help by Mrs. Indira Gandhi who managed influx of 1 crore Bangladeshies in India. Sheikh Mujibur Rehman became the father of the nation of Bangladesh, but was killed lateron Pakistani elements.

1966 DEVALUATON

This was done on 6th June. 1966. At that time the parity was fixed in terms of grams of gold. Earlier

Re 1 = 0.186621 gm. of gold

Then Re 1 = 0.118516 gm of gold

$$\text{Devaluation} = \frac{0118516}{0.186621} = 0.635 - 1 = 0.36494\text{x}100$$

$$= 36.494\%$$

Or nearly 36.5%....

In terms of dollar

$1 = Rs. 4.76

Then $1 = Rs. 7.50

$$\text{Devaluation} = \frac{7.50}{4.75} = 1.5756\text{x}100 = 157.56 - 100$$

$$= 57.56\%$$

In terms of £ 1 = Rs. 13.33

Then £1 = Rs. 21.00

$$= \frac{21.00}{13.33} = 1.5754 \text{ x } 100 = 157.54 - 100$$

$$= 57.54$$

Actually with 6 digit adjustments, both were more or less the same *i.e.* 57.55%

Why the devaluation of 1966 ?

India started planning *w.e.f.* 1st April 1951. The first five year plan saw price stability. In the second five year plan, there was investment in big projects and a lot of purchasing power was released. During the third five year plan (1961-66) two wars were imposed on India. In 1962, China attacked India. The first Prime Minister of India died in 1964 (Nehruji). There were two severe drought years and two serious flood years. In 1965, Pakistan attacked India, thinking that the short-height P.M. of India could be subdued by Pakistan. Shastriji (Lal Bahadur) allowed India Army to attack any weak point on Indo-Pak border and not remain confined to Kashmir, Lahore was "captured" from three sides...a road was allowed to remain open to supply things to Lahorc. Pakistan surrendered. Shastriji was invited to Tashkent for peace talks then in the then USSR where he reportedly died of heart attack. Some say he was poisoned.[1]

These created double digit inflation and India had to devalue its rupee.

The arithmetic of devaluation should be understood. Suppose $1 = Rs. 10

Then Re 1 = $ 01.0

Suppose then $1 = Rs. 12, then

Re 1 = $0,083

$$\frac{0.083}{0.100} = .83 - 1 = -0.167 \times 100 = -16.7\%$$

The appreciation of $ = $\frac{12}{10}$ = 1.2 x 100 = 20%

Hence up and down percentages differ.

1991 Devaluation

In 1991 India was on fixed exchange rate system as also on non-convertibility. There were two exchange rates. Official rate was $1 = Rs. 26.5 (or so) and the market rate (known as black market rate or smugglers' market rate) was $1 = Rs. 36.50. There were pressures to allow the fluctuating exchange rate. India's adverse balance of payment was very high. The name rupee is used in India, Pakistan, Nepal, Seychelles, Sri Lanka, Mauritius, Indonesia and Maldives.

Two quick devaluations were done one after the other in two days, moving towards Rs. 36.5.

- Ultimately the rupee was allowed to float.
- The rate become $ 1 = Rs. 31.5.
- In 1999 the rupee was equal to 1.6 Pence.
- In 1947 the rupee was equal to 25 pence.
- The $1 reached to maximum (minimum for the rupee @ Rs. 47.5).
- In 2006 the rate was around Rs. 46.5 or so. Between 1991-2006; Dec 2009, $ 1 = Rs. 46.40.

  India first allowed forex earners 60% of the dollars earned by them...first in the form of import licence and then in $ India allowed full convertibility on trade account; and, then on current account. The government India resolved to have full convertibility in SEZ, Mumbai. (Special Economic

Zone). Many SEZs are coming up, unfortunately on agricultural lands. India did not yet have full convertibility on capital account.

TOP TEN EFFECTS OF DEVALUATION.

1. Foreign importers will find they can get more goods for the same dollars.

Suppose the old rate was $ 1 = Rs. 45 and the new rate after devaluation is Rs. $ 1 = 49.5, the foreigners can get goods of Rs. 49.5 in the same $ 1 instead of the earlier amount of Rs. 45. However, it is to be remembered that if the rate of inflation differential was itself 10 p.c, this is no gain.

Devaluation will make the exports of devaluing country cheaper to foreign importers only if the rate of devaluation is higher than the differential rate of inflation. Otherwise It will be illusionary gain.

For example earlier if we used to walk 5 miles and now walk 8 kilometres, there is no change. We do not walk more. It is illusionary to think in this case that 8 km. is bigger than 5 miles.

Another condition that is necessary is that, the exports of the country that devalues should have elastic demand abroad. If India's exports (suppose) are of tea only, the foreign importer will not be able to sell a lot more tea to the people of that country because the demand for essential goods/commodities does not increase in the same percentage as the percentage decline in price. On the contrary if India is exporting luxury goods, the cheapening in foreign currency increases the demand more than proportionately to the reduction in supply.

2. Devaluation makes the imports dearer in the domestic currency after devaluation.

India will pay Rs. 49.5 for the same $ 1 for which earlier it was paying Rs. 45. In case the imports are luxury goods there will be reduction in imports. In case the imports are of essential goods, the same imports will continue to be bought even at the higher prices in rupee terms.

Thus:

1. Devaluation helps when the demand for imports abroad is elastic. 2. Secondly it helps when the demand for foreign imports in India is elastic.

If India, devalues, but the exports of India have inelastic demand abroad, India will not gain. Similarly, if the demand for imports by India is inelastic, Indians will pay higher prices for the same things.

3. If after devaluation, exports do not pick up, then imports should go down.

If after devaluation, imports do not go down, then exports should pick up.

Usually there should be double effect that exports should pick up and imports should be down. A mix of both effects is necessary. Total and absolute change in one only is scarcely possible: it should be mix of both. BoP should change for the better.

4. Expenditure Switching effect:

Devaluation, as we have seen, makes the foreign goods costlier in the currency of the country that devalues its currency. Therefore, the domestic production is preferred over the foreign imports. This is expenditure switching.

This reduces the balance of payment deficits, commodity by commodity and goods by goods. When there is import replacement, then there will be greater investment in domestic production. That increases domestic production and employment. There is greater income propagation as production replace trade.

5. Expenditure reduction effect.

Reduction in imports is reduction in expenditure. Not all imports of goods and services get reduced by the same amount. In extreme cases, some imports may stop altogether. Imports of different commodities and goods may get reduced by different margins. The imports of very essential things may not get reduced at all.

It is necessary that while different imports get reduced by different percentages and by different amounts, it is necessary that the total savings on imports should be lower than earlier. The expenditure on essential items increases but in total there should be reduction in imports.

What is more important is that when competitive devaluation is done the exports of other countries go down. The other countries resent. They may adopt one or several countervailing or compensatory measures. It is vital that after taking these effects into account, there should be net reduction in the amount spent on imports.

There will be two adverse effects immediately. As we have seen, there will be increase in the amounts spent on the Import of essential commodities and goods. The second effect will be that other countries may impose restrictions on the exports of the country that devaluates.

Against these adverse effects the favourable effects should be more. That will help the countries that devalue.

The country can impose **"across the counter cuts also".** That means that all imports may be reduced by (say) 10 p.c. These across the counter cuts are difficult and irrational. Hence cuts in imports will be in different percentage terms on different commodities and goods. There may be no cuts on the imports of certain commodities. **Quotas and tariffs** may also **be imposed. Exports may be subsidised.**

There can be such cuts as reduction in expenditure in all the emabassies of the country abroad. Travelling abroad may be permitted in essential cases. Interest rates may be raised to check the outflow of capital. Amounts due to be taken out may be permitted after some delay (known as transfer moratoria). Unilateral transfers may be reduced. Lower brokerage and commission charges may be negotiated.

Foreign countries may pulverize with counter measures the countries that indulges in "competitive" devaluation.

7. Elasticities of imports and exports should be more than 1 each *i.e.,* as a result of devaluation imports should get reduced more than proportionately and exports should increase more than proportionately.

If these things happen, we will say that the things are happening according to the thinking of the "elasticity optimists". There are many economists (all free traders) who argue that "elasticity pessimism" will work. Things will not change due to devaluation so much and if they do they will change only for a short period.

8. Devaluation with deflationary measures

Exports can be promoted when the prices go down. But creating deflation will adversely affect the profits of the producers. They will invest less and employment will suffer.

It will be like cutting one's nose to spite the face or to cure a cold ! It will be like burning one's house to roast the toast.

9. Reversal effects of devaluation:

Suppose a country devalues by **a** hefty margin. Suppose there is substantial reduction is imports and substantial increase in exports. That will bring balance of payment surplus or atleast reduce the balance of payment deficit substantially.

The national income of the country will increase. It will then increases through multiplier effect—success leading to more success.

With the increase in the national income, the marginal propensity to import will go up. Hence there will be leakages in the national income by way of imports.

10. Devaluation helps in the short period.

It is necessary that in between there should be structural changes in the production. Production should be made efficient for export promotion and import replacement.

Devaluation is a palliative measure. It tackles short term problem. It is not a development measure, Devaluation cannot bring such structural changes that the production becomes efficient permanently for export promotion and imports replacement.

Control on population, better exploitation of natural resources, improvement in technology, better use of the factors of production, improvement in the internal structure relating to all aspects of production.

Rupee rate over the years

We have noted in the earlier chapters of the book that now we are in the era of fluctuating exchange rates. Exchange rates fluctuate several times during the day by a few decimal points. The exchange rate can be quoted upto 5 or 6 decimal points. Hence a snap shot view of exchange rates at 4 p.m. is taken.

- In 1947 the rupee was linked to pound sterling and not to the US \$. Even then the indirect conversion came to \$ 1 = Rs. 4.5 in that year.
- In 1966, the exchange rate was \$ 1 = Rs. 7.50.
- In 1991, before, convertibility was allowed (see next chapter, the exchange rate was on average \$ 1 = Rs. 26 or so while the unofficial and black-market rate was \$ 1 = Rs. 36 and on abolishing the dichotomy, the rate became \$ 1 = Rs. 31.5.
- We have given the table of exchange rates for September 2003 and Sept. 2004. \$ 1 = Rs. 47.52 and \$ 1 = Rs. 46.13 respectively: Dec. 2009 = \$ 1 = Rs. 46.40. On 2nd April 2010, the rate was \$ 1 = Rs. 45.05.

EXCHANGE RATES

Indicative direct rates in rupees a unit except yen at 4 p.m on January 03, at 4 p.m. on Dec. 4,' 09

Currencies	*TT Buying*	*Dec. 4,' 09*	*TT Selling*	*Dec. 4,' 09*
US Dollar	44.17	46.08	44.48	46.40
Euro	58.45	69.41	58.87	69.90
Sterling Pound	86.71	76.70	87.34	77.24
Japanese Yen	37.02	52.16	37.29	52.54
Swiss Franc	36.20	46.07	36.46	46.51
Singapore Dollar	28.82	33.35	29.04	33.60
Australian Dollar	35.07	42.64	35.33	42.95
Canadian Dollar	37.76	43.70	38.04	44.02
Swedish Kroner	6.48	6.70	6.53	6.75
Danish Kroner	7.84	9.33	7.90	9.39
New Zealand Dollar	31.11	33.36	31.35	33.62
Hongkong Dollar	5.67	5.95	5.71	5.99
Malaysian Ringitt	12.57	13.62	12.67	13.74
Kuwati Dinar	152.00	164.84	154.66	163.67
UAE Dirham	12.02	12.54	12.11	12.64
Bahraini Dinar	116.93	122.01	118.23	123.31
Qatari Riyal	12.12	12.64	12.22	12.75
Saudi Riyal	11.77	12.28	11.86	12.37
Omani Riyal	114.43	119.26	115.84	120.92

DEVALUATION OF INDIAN RUPEE

The commentary can be as under for these days. "The rupee on Wednesday turned weak against the US currency due to fresh dollar demand along with covering up of short positions by traders and closed at..................In the active trading at the interbank foreign exchange market the Indian currency started on a steady note at................Later, it went down to a low of Rs before closing at lower than the previous close of........Good dollar buying by State run banks also dampened rupee sentiment."

In Oct. 2008, in the aftermath of US crisis financial banks, The exchange rate of Indan rupee fell to Rs. 48 per dollar. Betmen 2003 and 2009, Indian rupee declined against all the above currencies. In early 2010, rupee improved to $ 1 Rs. = 45.

NOTE

1. When someone asked Shastriji "You are short in height and General Ayub Khan is a giant. You must be having a lot of difficulty in talking." Shastriji replied, "Yes, I was talking with my head high and he was talking with his head down."

17 Foreign Trade Multiplier [with Impact and Reversal Effects]

MACRO ECONOMIC IDENTITIES

INTRODUCTION.

Multiplier means how something changes in a certain multiple as a result of change in something else.

If as a result of 10 p.c. *increase in consumption, there is increase in investment of 10 p.c, as a result of which there is increase in employment in other lines and "subsequent lines of linkages", to the extent of 40 p.c, then the value of multiplier will be 4. This is Employment Multiplier.*

A. CLOSED AND OPEN MULTIPLIERS:

Open K is Foreign trade multiplier. (Notation 'K' is used to depict it).

Closed multiplier does not take into account the exports and imports. It is *presumed* (though it never happens) that there are no exports and imports. And, the national income is divided into three parts Y = C+S+I *i.e.* national income (Y: we use notation Y because I is reserved for investment and "i" for Interest): Y is equal to the total of consumption + savings + investment.

Now if the national income of a country is $ 100 billion, and consumption is $ 60 b. it means the savings are $ 40 b. If all the savings are invested, then Y will be equal to C+I. That is what it should be. One person's expenditure is another person's income. Saving is individual virtue but creates a macro problem, if they are not invested. If out of $ 100 b., the consumption is $ 60 billion and investment $ 20 billion, the total of both *(known as* 'absorption') will be $ 80 b. and $ 20 b. will be the savings taken as "hoarding". The multiplier will be high if "a" absorption is high and will be low if savings are high. As incomes increase savings also increase. Increasing saving in Keynesian economics reduce the national income in the next time period if they are not invested. If savings gap is of $ 20 b. and multiplier will be 5 and if the gap of $ 200b. is to be filled up only $ 40 b, be invested more. Then 40x5= 200 and gap will be filled up. We illustrate the formulae and give examples.

$K = \frac{1}{(1-MPC)}$ or $\frac{1}{MPS}$. If savngs are 20% and 40% respectively in two cases then

$$K=\frac{1}{\frac{1}{\frac{20}{100}}} \text{ or } \frac{1}{1}\div\frac{20}{100} \text{ or } \frac{1}{1}\times\frac{100}{20}=5$$

$$K=\frac{1}{\frac{1}{\frac{40}{100}}} \text{ or } \frac{1}{1}\div\frac{40}{100} \text{ or } \frac{1}{1}\times\frac{100}{40}=2.5$$

Multiplier goes up with C+1 or A for "absorption".

B. FOREIGN TRADE MULTIPLIER

B.I. Multiplier

Multiplier can be discussed with reference to a closed economy, but its discussion will be more realistic if we study it with reference to an open economy. An economy is 'open' if it imports and exports. As we understand, imports bring' leakages' in the working of the multiplier and exports reinforce the multiplier. Imports have the same effect on the working of the multiplier as savings have on the working of the multiplier in a closed economy. Exports means the same thing as increase in consumption. When a foreign country imports (making it possible for another country to export), a fall in home demand, if any, is compensated by an increase in the demand for the home goods in foreign countries.

Changes in the consumption and saving pattern and changes in the imports and export pattern bring changes in prices and income. Changes in income and prices bring further changes in the consumption, savings, investment, imports and exports pattern. The multiplier changes and in turn brings changes in other economic variables; we are studying a highly volatile and dynamic world.

At constant prices, the net national product (NNP) and the national income (NY) are the same. They are same in closed economy. In an open economy, however, changes of trade (TT) bring unequal changes in the NNP and the real NY. If the TT change in favour of the country, then the net national income (NNY) will be higher than the GNP, if they change against the country then the NNY will be lower than the GNP, for some part of the income will leak out.

In this discussion of the effects of the TT on the NNY, we assume the prices to be constant. We can presume that changes in money income will bring changes in the real income also. This assumption in necessary because consumption and imports will depend more on changes in real income. We shall study changes between two periods but not the changes in the periods in between, that is the process of change will not be studied. The foreign trade multiplier is studied as "Simultaneous Multiplier". Simultaneous multiplier study is simple and easy to comprehend. Innumerable other economic variables (government expenditure, taxation, "expectations", production function, rate of interest, money supply etc.) are also assumed to be constant.

Before we understand the working of the foreign multiplier, it will be necessary to understand the "Import Function" and "Export Function".

B. II. Import Function

A country may follow the policy of complete autarky and then it will not have any 'import capacity'. China, in past years, did not import many commodities even though they were needed in that country. It still follows the policy of austere consumption. It does not want to import much from foreign contries to impress upon the countries of the world that its policy of economic self-sufficiency is working.

In terms of Keynesian economics, we can say that poor countries will have high need to import and the rich low need to import. A poor country may not be producing all what it needs and demands and thus will have to make heavy imports, particularly of capital goods. The volume of imports of a rich country may be larger than of a less developed country, but in terms of percentage of NNP, the less developed country will have higher propensity to import as it will have higher propensity to consume. A country may however, have less actual imports because government has put restrictions on imports.

The import propensity or import capacity can be expressed by M/Y. where M represents total imports and Y the total national income. Marginal propensity to import can be depicted by dM/dY. If the national income rises by 10% and imports rise by 2% as a consequence, the marginal elasticity of imports will be said to be 0.2; *i.e.,* if the national income increases by Rs. 100 crores and imports increase by 20 crores of rupees then the marginal propensity to imports is 0.2. If the entire increase in income in utilized for imports, the dM will be said to be one (1).

Nothing definite can be said about the nature of imports that increase as a result of increase in income. However, other things remaining the same, luxury goods have high income elasticity of imports than ordinary goods. A less developed country, trying to develop at a rapid pace, may utilize a large part of its increased income in importing capital goods and essential raw materials and may put severe restrictions on the imports of non-essential (luxury) goods. The propensity to import can have a cyclical tendency rather than secular tendency. The marginal propensity to import brings changes in the average propensity to imports and hence is more important.

The relation between the average propensity to import and the marginal propensity is expressed by the ratio called "income elasticity". It is percentage change in imports associated with a given percentage change in national income. Expressed in algebraic terms, income elasticity can be measured by:

$$\frac{dM}{M} / \frac{dY}{Y}$$

This is percentage change in imports that can be co-related with a given percentage in national income. This can be calculated by dividing the marginal propensity to imports by the average propensity. If these are the same values, the income elasticity of imports is unitary, or in other words, a given percentage change in national income will produce a change of equal percentage in imports.

A curve (line) of marginal propensity to imports can be drawn. It can be a curve of declining imports propensity also when imports decline with the increase in the level of development (autarky may be preferred and may be possible) and increase in income. However, a rising imports propensity curve at uniform rate can be preferred under simplifying assumptions. Thus:

Fig. 17.1

Import propensity increases when there is depletion of raw materials in the country and reliance on imports increases. Import propensity of different countries even at the same level of income and economic development (per capita basis) can be different. Much will depend on **the** trade policies pursued and type of exchange controls and tariffs imposed. The average propensity to imports of USSR in 1971 was 3%, of USA 8% and of such highly specialized countries as Norway, Belgium or New Zealand between 20 to 40%.

B.III. Export Function

Exports increase the national income of the country. (Here we are talking about money incomes, not real incomes when a country exports, its goods go out and so income, if it is to be calculated in commodity terms decreases; national income in commodity terms increases when we import goods. This is not the view that can be taken for studying the foreign trade multiplier because income is measured in money terms. Then, services are also **imported and** exported. Therefore, multiplier is always studied with reference to the money income and monetary value of imports and exports.) For the sake of simple exposition of the foreign trade multiplier, the export function is assumed to be constant. It can be presumed that a country exports those goods which it cannot consume and which have income inelastic demand. However, it is not intended here to prove that exports can never be declining or increasing function of income. Thus the export function can be depicted as:

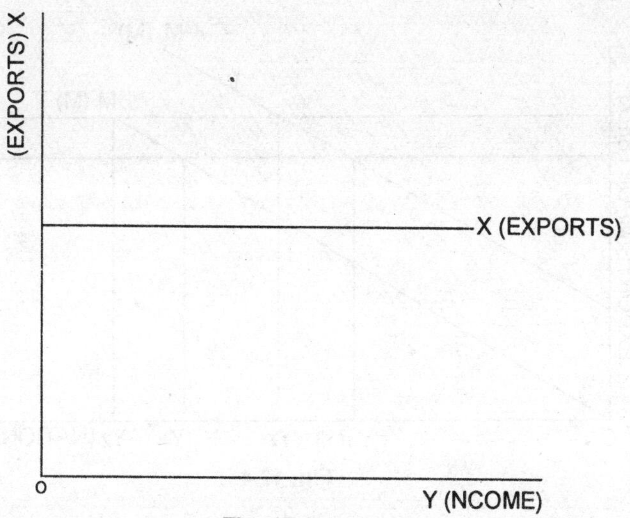

Fig 17.2

B. IV. Foreign trade multiplier

If for the time being we ignore C, S and I, then it is clear that multiplier effect on Y will be due to increase in exports and/or fall in imports. In the two diagrams appended below, it has been shown that with import function remaining the same, an increase in exports leads to multiplier effect on income. In the second diagram it has been shown that with export function remaining the same, increase in income is brought about by a decline in imports and decrease in income is brought about by an increase in imports in a multiplier way. In the second diagram, the notations in the parentheses show the increased effect on Y of a decline in M. In such a case when C, S and I are not taken into account, the foreign trade multiplier will be:

$$K_f \frac{1}{MPM}$$

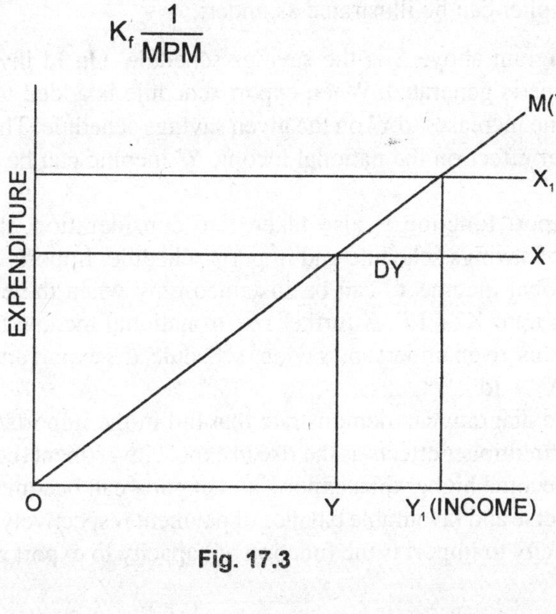

Fig. 17.3

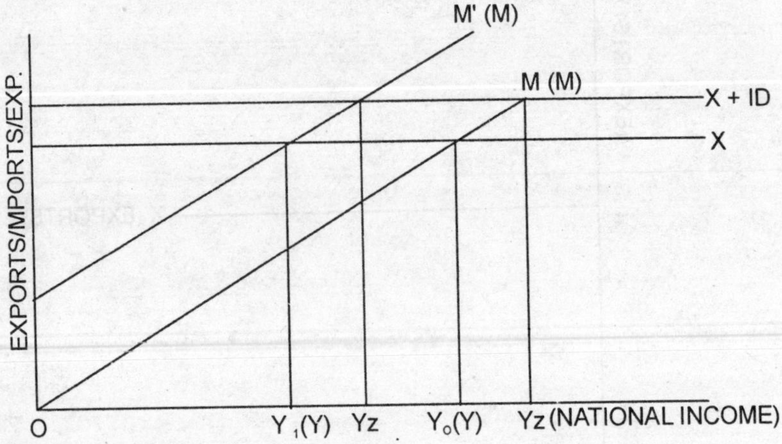

Fig. 17.4

B.V. Foreign trade multiplier with savings taken into consideration

The export multiplier (foreign trade multiplier) in an open economy where there are savings also (in net additional terms) will be combination of the closed economy multiplier and the multiplier in an open economy without savings. Now there will be two, instead of one, leakages *viz.*, the savings and imports. High value of consumption, investment and exports will increase the value of the multiplier. The multiplier is now the reciprocal of the slope of the sum of the two functions M(Y) and S(Y), and will be the same for an increase in exports or an increase in investment. Thus the foreign trade multiplier in this case will be:

$$K_f \frac{1}{MPS + MPM}$$

The multiplier can be illustrated as under:

In the diagram above S is the savings schedule. On Id investment schedule, Y_0 national income is generated. When export schedule is added to the Id schedule, the national income increases to Y' on the given savings schedule. Thus increase in exports have multiplier effect on the national income Y' income can be sustained on reduced savings also.

When import function is also taken into consideration, the M + S line is the combination of savings schedule and imports schedule. Imports are leakages and now the same national income Y' can be sustained only when the export and investment schedule goes upto X' + I*d'*. A further rise of national income to Y" will be possible only when on this given import and savings schedule, the export and investment schedule goes upto to X" + Id".

The above diagram can demonstrate that fall in the imports/savings function will have the same multiplier effects as the rise in export/investment (consumption) function. Imports can become higher than exports and exports can become higher than imports, leading to adverse and favourable balance of payment respectively. However, ultimately, since the capacity to import is the function of capacity to export and capacity to export is the function of capacity to import, exports should be equal to imports and savings should equal to investment.

C. INTERACTION WITH FOREIQN TRADE MULTIPLIER: FEEDBACK EFFECTS ON PRICES AND INCOME

There are feedback effects of international trade. When one country imports from another country, the goods supply in the other country goes down and money supply goes up. Income goes up. All these things exert pressure on prices in the other country. In due course of time, the increase in MPM in the other country will induce the other country to import from the first one. (Only two countries are assumed). Here also the income, factor prices and commodity prices will go up.

However, much will depend upon the sizes of the countries and their incomes. For example, if the national income of Mauritius doubles because of the greater exports from that country, this increased income, even if spent completely on imports from USA will make almost no difference on the national income of the USA. But if the national income of USA increases and there are import-leakages, a country where these leakages go will experience substantial increase in the national income. If, likewise, USA reduces its imports from any country, the economy of the adversely affected country will have drastically reduced income propagation. That is the reason it is said; "When USA sneezes, the rest of the world gets pneumonia".

In an open economy (with exports and imports): C for consumption, I for investment, G for government investment, X for exports and M for imports.

$$Y + M = C + 1 + G + X$$

$$\text{or} \quad Y = C + 1\,G + (X—M)$$

In the above equation (X—M) represents the balance of the trade which can be either positive or negative. In an open economy there are two leakages *viz.*, savings and imports. Imports can increase due to changes in tariffs, tastes, income, prices and levels of production. A rise in import function will mean that fewer home produced goods will be consumed in relative percentage terms. Domestic industries may get reduced orders, production may go down and workers are laid off. The income of home goods producers and factors will decrease. In this case the multiplier will work in downward direction. Equilibrium will then be at lower level. A net favourable balance will do the opposite—the same way as increase in C, I or G will do. In this case the foreign trade multiplier can be put as under:

$$K_f \frac{1}{\text{MPS}+\text{MPM}} \text{ or } \frac{1}{\frac{dS}{dY}+\frac{dM}{dY}}$$

Calculation. NY goes up when these are high. NY = C + X + I. In the open economy 'A' absorption becomes equal to C + I + X (exports). The remaining part is S +M or savings + imports **or**

Suppose				
C	=	50%	45	p.c.
X	=	15%	25	p.c.
I	=	15%	15	p.c.

M = 15% 10 p.c.

S = 5% 2

Then

$$FTM \frac{1}{1\text{-}(MPC+MPI+MPX} \quad \text{or} \quad \frac{1}{MPS+MPM}$$

Here I is investment.

First case $\frac{1}{1}+\frac{20}{100}$ Second case $\frac{1}{1}+\frac{15}{100}$

$$\frac{1}{1}+\frac{20}{100}\ \frac{1}{1}+\frac{15}{100}$$

$$\frac{1}{1}+\frac{100}{20}=5 \quad \frac{1}{1}\times\frac{100}{15}=6.67$$

Lower value of exports + C + 1
and higher imports + S will
Keep the **FTM relatively** lower

Higher Exports and
ower imports
Iincrease value of FTM.

We have seen what MPX as also what MPM is. MPX should be high. MPM should be lower for higher FTM, other things remaining the same.

The foreign trade multiplier, when applied to real conditions, can be as valid as our estimates of MPC, MPS, MPX and MPM are and as these are stable.

Small countries with small national incomes are virtually unimportant in the foreign multiplier study, unless a small country is unique from the point of view of a very scarce raw material.

In case of the foreign multiplier also, if the economy is operating at less than full employment level, the change will be on the real income. An injection into the income stream of an economy already operating at full employment shall raise nominal incomes only without changing real or physical outputs. It should also be kept in view that multiplier operates with a time lag. In the words of Kindelberger:

> *"If the effect of the change in imports on income abroad is significant and if the effect of income changes abroad on a country's exports is again appreciable, there is a foreign repercussion. More complex formulae are now necessary to express the relationships among savings and import propensities in the countries involved. If an accelerator is at work so that an increase in income due to a rise in exports leads to an increase in investment, the increase in exports may produce a larger increase in imports and turn the balance of trade unfavourably,"* (p. 355-6). (IE)

There are many economists who regard the entire concept of multiplier as fuzzy or even worthless, but probably they are too harsh.

Three important points to be remembered:

1. High marginal propensity to consume and high marginal propensity to export increase domestic employment and income in a multiplier way.
2. The multiplier operates over a period of time and hence there is a period of favourable impact.
3. When national income rises, people have a tendency to prefer foreign goods to domestic goods. Hence marginal propensity to import rises. The multiplier effects leak out. Now there is reversed effect. Multiplier is not deterministic in precise mathematical way.

Later on multiplier will leak out to the foreign country. Once again domestic production, exports, employment and income will rise.

OPEN ECONOMY IDENTITIES
[That Affect the Open Economy Multiplier)

As we have seen open economy multiplier is more popularly known as the Foreign Trade Multiplier. There is over-emphasis on the word "open';... for the simple reason that "closed" economy does not exist. It is a "theoretical construct" *i.e.,* exists only in the book. "Closed economy" means *autarky.* It is that economy which exports and imports nothing. It is totally insulated. Not even the most regimented communist economies of the past were totally insulated. The extreme cases of insulation were of North Korea, Albania and China. Now China is more open than India!

We take the following 'open economy identities" but which affect the FTM or foreign trade or open economy multiplier.

(1) The Macro Identities

Y = C + Sp + Ip + Ig

This simply means that the national income of a country is equal to consumption + savings. In the first instance, National income is a flow and not a fund. It is generated and consumed simultaneously. As we have seen, everyone saves something. Savings are withdrawals from the national income stream, if they are hoarded. If the national Income is $ 200 b. and consumptions and savings are $ 180 b + $ 20 b. It is obvious that in the next time period the national income will fall to $ 180 b. because the savings are held back or withdrawn.

Hence savings should be invested. Then the national income shall remain the same. But not all savings can be invested. Savings for *precautionary motives i.e.,* for contingencies and emergencies will always be there. Hence the remaining savings alone can be invested, that will still keep the national income down. Investment private should be supplemented with the investment from the government. *It cannot only till the gap but even be more than the gap, with the result that the total national income shall be higher in the next year.'*

Open Economy Identities.

Y = C + S + I+X — M±U

This means that the national income of a country is equal to consumption + savings + Investment + exports — Imports ± unilateral transfers.

Consumption should be optimum possible.

Savings should be minimum necessary.

Investment, both government and private, should exceed savings so that the national income of the succeeding years is higher.

Exports should be as high as possible.

Imports are leakages from the multiplier Oust like savings) and should be only which are very necessary.

(2) Exports, Imports, FDI and FII.

- Exports should not be of the necessary, i.e. genuine surplus be exported.
- Imports should not be of the unnecessary.
- Imports should better be of the nature of "imports replacing imports" that which make domestic production of hitherto imported thing possible in the country.
- Imports should better be of capital goods, heavy production goods, essential consumption goods.
- Imports of luxury goods—which are very usual in the international trade... are great leakages of income and they bring the reversal of the application of the multiplier of the open economy in the country.
- Foreign direct investment should be directly productive activities which add to the material component of the national income.
- FDI should be in increasing the production capacities and capabilities.
- If necessary infrastructure facilities do not exist in the developing economies, then FDI in infrastructure facilities will be welcome as without it the product-increase will be a non- starter.
- FDI in taking over of the domestic companies ***can*** be welcome if that brings modernisation, rationalisation and technological upgradation of the production system.
- FDI in mergers and acquisitions is also important in the way listed just above.
- FII (Foreign Institutional Investment or Portfolio Investment) in bonds and debt papers is important provided it is not all of speculative nature.
- FDI or indirect FII in real estates is also welcome if the strong ordering is followed *i.e.,* the most essential things (as habitat improvement) are taken up first. FII is very dangerous if the rogue punters of other countries create bullish tendencies and then when the prices are taken artificially high, they sell the "papers" and take out hell lot of money. The "Asian Tiger" countries which were/are following export-led growth models nearly collapsed in the later 1990s when their exchange rates fell to half or more *i.e.,* when the dollar rate increased from two to three times in a short span of time. They started getting one-half to one-third of the imports for the same exports. Their "fundamentals" were not correct. They were not only not self-sufficient in food but were importing blood also for transfusion !

(3) Exchange Rates:

Exchanged rates of the countries should be flexible, if not totally, then within the narrow band. Now a days countries follow "Snake in the tunnel" policy. The ± limits if fluctuations are fixed at about 2.5 p.c. only in case of serious structural problems, these rates go beyond that. The economy has to produce more and well. The "fundamentals" of self-sufficiency in most of the requirements should be all right. Not all countries can maintain the fluctuations within the bandwidth. Weak countries will helplessly see their exchange rates going down steadily.

- Low exchange rates increase exports and increase the size of the FTM but at a cost. Lot of real goods are to be exported to get the same imports.
- Falling exchange rates and increasing exports are possible when the exports have elastic demand abroad. Falling exchange rates will make imports costly and the leakages of imports can be reduced only when the imports have inelastic demand in the country. The foreign supplies, on the other hand, should be inelastic. In other words, these supplies cannot be taken elsewhere and if the demand falls, the foreigners will reduce their export prices.

Convertibility of the currency in different currencies is necessary for high exports and adequate necessary imports. Then only the value of the FTM will be high.

(4) Exchange Controls, Anti-dumping Measures: Some Protective Measures.

The present era is the era of LPG—liberalisation, privatisation and globalisation. The value of FTM or open multiplier will be higher if LPG is practised. Controlled economies of the communist countries failed. They could not take the production and consumption up. What was worse they could not remove poverty. The second most powerful nation of the world, the then USSR, had the same 40 p.c. people below the poverty line in 1991 as many as India had.

- Under the WTO (World Trade Organisation) regime, the tariffs are to be reduced to around 6 p.c. on an average. Only in exceptional cases and high balance of payment deficits, the tariffs can be high. This will maximise exports but imports also. Less developed countries are in the danger of high leakages for keeping the FTM high.
- The protective measures of various types like quotas are also going to be abolished. There are dozens of measures of protection. They all go. This will also be an opportunity and a challenge. All said and done, the developing economies will find that there are higher leakages in the FTM. The developed countries will have high open economy multiplier effect in their countries.
- Exchange control measures (which too run into dozens) are not possible now a days. This will also reduce the FTM for the developing economies; will increase the FTM of the developed economies and of the world as a whole. But a country like China or India will in due course of time find FTM value rising.
- Anti-dumping measures are very necessary.

What is dumping ?

(A) Dumping is not when the foreigner sells below our price.
(B) Dumping is not when the foreigner sells below its own domestic price.
(C) Dumping is not when the foreigner sells below our cost of production.
(D) Dumping is when the foreigner sells below its own cost of production.

Three p.c. clumping is allowed. The FTM of the dumper rises. The FTM of the country where dumping is resorted to goes down.

(5) Acquisitions and mergers

By the foreigner in the country will increase FTM when the exports increase. However, the natives will lose ownership. If the Indians (for example) take over companies abroad, the net income will come to India. It will have the same effect as that of exports from the country. The FTM will go up. Investments abroad first result in the outgoings but they bring income later on.

(6) Franchising, licensing and similar arrangements.

They can have two way effects. If the foreigners do that (say) in India, there will be more sales of the foreigners. FTM will become lower for India. If the foreigners produce here and sell here then the production will go up. Domestic income will rise. Only profits will be taken out. The net result is likely to be favourable on the multiplier due to higher C+I in India. If a foreigner outsources some production to India, India's FTM will go up.

(7) Monetary and Fiscal Policy Tools and FTM

Shortage of money hinders economic growth. A plethora of it cannot ensure it. Money supply should never be excessive otherwise it will cause inflation and this will bring down exports. Even the falling exchange rate will not improve the FTM.

"Creditflation" is also harmful for the high FTM or OEM (Open economy multiplier).

Fiscal policy should be ***pro-to-type.*** It should tax the rich at higher rate without harming production. The public expenditure should create infrastructure facilities. It should ensure healthy interface between SOC and DPA *I.e.* social overhead capital (socio-economic Infrastructure) and directly productive activities.

The debt burden should be kept low. International debt should be taken only to increase production capacities and capabilities. Regressive fiscal policies will harm the nation and lower the FTM.

Inequlities promote imports ! FTM goes down. Bad monetary and fiscal policies can ruin the country or can catapult them.

(8) Labour laws and Wage income policies.

The LPG model requires that the producers should have the freedom to "hire and fire" the labour. They want that if old laws cannot be changed for the old workers, new laws should be there for the new workers. Social security system should go. Labour should seek personal security with the insurance firms. Wages of the workers should not increase the cost of production, otherwise the exports will go down. Social and ethical norms require that development should not be at the cost of the workers but for them also. Hence what is necessary is a positive productivity-wage-productivity wage link. Both should keep on rising. Then exports will enjoy comparative advantage. FTM will go up.

(9) Interest rate and inflation rates management.

Management of inflation differentials (that having a lower rate of inflation) helps in increasing exports and keeping the imports down. It also helps in keeping the exchange rate stable. These are the right ways of keeping the FTM high.

Giving high rates of interest to foreign depositors should be done only when the forex reserve position is very down. Otherwise it will entail a high burden of payment of interest. Having foreign money this way is no way to improve the forex reserves because external debt also goes up. One can have high FTM at one's own strength.

(10) Setting public sectors right.

Public sectors had a great role in developing the poor countries. Infected they created (*i*) external economies for the private sector, (*ii*) large employment for the populace, and (*iii*) a lot of income in the national income. Their output was both import-saving and export-promoting. Then the politicians, ministers, bureaucrats, labour leaders (trade unions), work shirkers, contractor mafia made them inefficient and non-competitive in most of the developing economies.

Most public sector projects In the developing economies cesspool because of corruption and reduced FTM.

They should either be privatised or run jointly with the known business houses of the country. Then only the positive impact on the FTM will be there.

(11) Developing economies should form Economic Unions

Wherever possible which will reduce the expenses of currency conversion and make economies complementary. They will export more also and FTM value will rise.

(12) Population control

In India, for example, every night is a nightmare. India adds one Australia +20 p.c. more now every year. India is adding nearly 2.5 crore persons every year. Imagine growing extra food for nearly 69,000 persons each day. Each day planning a small city of 69,000 with 44 p.c. non-adults, with nearly 8p.c. aged and with 12 p.c. unemployment, only 36p.c. remain. If we deduct from them the housewives, students and "other" as in jails or hospitals nearly 20 p.c. population of India produces for the rest 80 p.c. Such things keep the exports down and FTM value remains low.

Though written as the last item, population control is the first pre-requisite if macro identities of high FTM. In recent years there were massive leakages due to import of foodgrains.

18 International Trade as Engine of Economic Growth

(1) INTRODUCTION

"Engine" of economic growth is one which is the "prime mover". Engine pulls at the top of the train. The "engine" of economic growth is actually "domestic investment from domestic savings,"[1]

International trade can be said to be the "second engine".

It can be regarded an the second engine but not the engine. International trade can be engine of growth for island counties like Seychelles or Maturities. It cannot be "engine of growth" for a country like India.

(2) INTERNATIONAL TRADE AS THE ENGINE OF ECONOMIC GROWTH WAS A REALITY IN COUNTRIES WHERE "EXPORT-LED GROWTH MODEL" IS FOLLOWED

Exported growth model (ELGM) was followed by Singapore, Malaysia, Hong Kong, Thailand, S.Korea, Japan, Indonesia and Taiwan (earlier) know as formosa – (which China claims its own, as it was in the past where capitalism is the system). These countries developed export industries and promoted tourism. They earned foreign exchange and then imported what they needed. A lot of FDI and FII used to come to these countries. (Japan and Korea invest outside). These countries started being known as the "tiger economies"— economic tigers. They had a near collapse in the late 1990 the foreign investors who had invested in shares and bonds bought at lower prices and then sold them at very high prices. They earned huge profits and then withdrew their money. Malaysia called them "Rogue punters" i.e. criminal type speculators. Exchange rates of domestic. In other words the exchanges rate of dollar became 2½ times, while in Indonesia it became 6 times or more than 600 p.c. Imports become very dear. These countries were not self sufficient even in food production. Here the cost of living went up. Their "fundamentals were not correct. India did not suffer because India's "fundamentals were right,"

ELGM has "bubble effect," i.e. bubble can burst in short period. ELGM is, however, relevant for Seychelles,[2] Mauritius, or Singapore. Small countries can have "export of tourism" and of high-value-low-bulk goods (as watches) as the "prime activities." The rule is:

"bigger the country less the chance of international trade being engine of economic. It is "engine" of economic growth for small island type "countries."

The Asian Tiger countries had to after their production system. Domestic production for domestic consumption is more important.

IMPORTANT EFFECTS OF INTERNATIONAL TRADE ON DOMESTIC ECOMOMIC GROWTH

Our contention is that I.T. is the "second engine" of economic growth. The favorable effects of I.T. on production, business, employment and national income can be listed as under. We can list the favorable effect of international trade (I.T.) in the following 10 catch points.

(1) International trade takes away what is surplus and brings in what is necessary, increasing both "price gains" and "utility gains" respectively

Countries have production which are surplus to their requirement. Bangladesh has excessive jute products and hence they are exported abroad. Had they remained in Bangladesh they would have remained unsold. Jute will rot in Bangladesh without exports. Its prices without exports would have crashed. Bangladesh imports (with its export earnings) capital and industrial goods that it cannot produce. Without international trade, Bangladesh would have remained without them. India has the largest number of cattle in the world and largest production of hides and skins and then of shoes. (The largest number of barefooted persons walk in India). India is the largest exporter of shoes in the world.

Countries import what

(i) they cannot produce at all

(ii) they cannot produce in the required quantifies, and

(iii) they cannot produce of the required quality.

Countries export and get foreign exchange. It is used for importing. Actually we pay for imports with exports. Money or foreign exchange is only a medium, The world is now a village. All international trade is barter now between all continents. One country's imports are another country's exports.

The world now follows LPG model.

L stands for liberalization which means no restrictions from the government of private enterprise.

P stands for privatization which means denationalization of public sector enterprises.

G stands for globalization, which means international trade with all continents. International trade widens markets.

(2) International trade brings foreign direct investment technology goods and technical know-how

According to solow, now 85% economic growth is due to technology. New technology is factor capital. A sickle, and axe, or a wooden plough are capital. But they are not modern capital goods. Modern capital goods embody technology. Earlier a road-roller used to be used for paving asphalt roads. New there are advanced road- laying machines which do efficient work very fast. We need modern technology. Modern technology came and still comes from western capitalist countries.

Free IT and IB (international business) bring in capital or foreign exchange for investment. Foreigners can bring direct capital goods also for production plants. Foreigner can bring their experts (known as technical" Know-how" also) who can install plants and machinery and can promote industrialisation.

The capitalist world invents and innovates. These inventions and innovations are transformed into modern capital and other goods. In other words, technology gets embodied in goods. Then goods are exported. This is the way of diffusion of technology. Developing economies can never become modern without western technology.

Hence if we want to say "IT is engine of growth" we should say " international trade in technology is the engine of growth."

IT in technology reduces the time of production and per unit cost of production. Fixed costs become high, but due to large scale production, the per unit cost of production becomes low. Then prices become lower. Market widens. Employment generation becomes high. Higher incomes are propagated.

Technological development of the poor economies bring three way circular relationships.

(A) There will be higher domestic production.

(B) There will be higher exports, and monetary inflows.

(C) There will be more imports for (A) and for consumption. Again these effects will get strengthened.

(3) I.T. and I.B. bring systems of "outsourcing" and "in-sourcing

This is a new system. 'Honda' company of Japan has technical outsourcing with 'Hero' company of India for the production of motor cycles and bi-cycles. Hyundai company of Korea and Suzuki company of Japan produce their cars in India with collaborations. Same is true for L.G. Samsung....etc. What is outsourcing for Korea is insourcing for India. India reportedly gets its watches manufactures in Japan, though Indian logos are displayed. Outsourcing of one country is insourcing for the other. Insourcing of one country is outsourcing for the other. There are resorted to for ensuring the lowest cost of production per unit. Japan and Korea off-load their work to India because labour is cheap in India. The four corner-stones of the edifice are: (They come to poor countiries).

- Technology or capital goods,
- Technical experts financial experts marketing experts,
- Necessary raw materials,
- Necessary finance.

Hyundai and Suzuki now export cars from India. In the long run there are (i) import replacements, (ii) higher domestic production and (iii) export promotion.

(4) International business helps a poor country develop its primary sector

International business brought to India GM seeds (genetically mutaed or modified seeds). Foreign trade in India brought capital goods and technology for the production of the following:

Tractors	Harvesters	Tillers	Threshers
Irrigation pump	Tube wells	Fertilisers	pesticide
GM seeds	Bio-manures	Tools	Implements
Storage *systems*	Transport *systems*	Levelers	Weed-weaners.

International business and international trade help both agri-industries and agro-industries. Agri-industries are those which supply inputs to agriculture. The industries which produce goods of the above 16 categories are agri-industries.

Agro-industries are those which use outputs of the primary sectors as inputs. There are hundreds of such industries. Jute mills, cotton textle mills, edible oil extraction industries, food processing industries, wood industries etc. are agri-industries.

If international trade is there commodity prices will not fall in case of bumper crops. The agriculturists are saved from ruin. In case of shortage of agricultural products, imports can be made. The consumers are saved. They get commodities; and, prices also do not rise much. Horticulture, plantation, silviculture, pisciculture, acqaculture, floriculture, animal husbandry, poultry farming, food forestry etc. all develop due to international trade and business. Netherlands (Holland) is the exporter of the longest flowers of the highest value in the world.

Rural employment and incomes increase due to international trade.

(5) International trade promotes industrialization

What were luxuries to princes are now essential things for lower income group persons.[3] International trade helps industrialisation in the following six ways:

A IT and IB bring capital and finance for investment.
B IT and IB bring advanced technologies for production.
C IT and IB bring necessary natural raw materials.
D IT and IB bring modern and synthetic raw materials.
E IT and IB bring technical know-how.
F IT and IB bring investments in shares and bonds also.

Industrialistion become deep and wide—i.e. scale of production and scope of production improve for all categories of goods:

K Goods i.e.capital goods. (K for capital).
C goods i.e. consumption goods.
U goods i.e. luxury goods.
W goods i.e. white goods (like frig or to or washing machine…….)
H goods i.e. heavy industry goods.
W goods i.e. heavy industry goods.

Industrialisation become "punctiform" i.e. gets spread over the wider space after international trade widens and becomes large. @

(6) International trade helps in the upgradation of infrastructure facilities.

A president of the USA once said (Abraham Lincoln)

"USA roads are not goods because the USA is developed. Actually, the USA is developed because its roads are goods".

Hence there is two-way relationship here also. (A) Developed infrastructure facilities promote international trade and (B) IT brings development in infrastructure facilities. Good roads, road transport, railway (container service), good ports and harbours and modern shipping and air cargo facilities promote international trade.

A Now India is getting to modern airports and port facilities upgraded with the help of foreign experts and capital.

B India is now promoting medi-tourism. Foreigners are finding Indian doctors efficient and hospital facilities relatively cheaper. (Prime Minister of Fiji was getting himself treated in India in 2006).

C As foreign capital is coming and as India's national and international trades are enlarging, India's banking, telecommunications, medical educational, financial, insurance, and transport facilities are improving.

(7) IT and IB bring in FDI (foreign) direct investment) and FII (foreign institutional investment) in the country.

FDI is in production and is for long period.

FII in shares and bonds and is for short period.

FDI improves production base. Production on large scale is facilitated. Many types of goods are produced. There are improvements in the "scale" and "scope" (broad-banding is also the word that is used) of production. These things bring down the cost of production and then the prices. Market widens. Wide market enlarges production further.

India receives much less FDI than China. In the year 2005-06 India received only $ 3.25.6. (i.e. $ 325 crore) but China received *26 times* more (including) Hong Kong). Foreign FDI investors prefer China because it has reserved one region with full facilities and freedom. India is a free country, but not a free economy because the administration is "bribe-seeker". India received 26 marks out of 100 for no-corruption. In honesty India ranks at number 88 in about 100 *major* counties. Total of FDI received reached $ 100 b. between 1947 and 2009.

FII investments are in shares and bonds. Such investments improve capital and money markets. However, there is a lot of swindling in stock markets. When FII comes in, exchange rate improves. When there are outflows. Exchange rate falls.

FDI and FII make I>S i.e. a country can invest more than it saves. Such investments increase employment and income.

(8) IT promotes all types of investments. It promotes autonomous investments.

There are many types of investments that are promoted. *Autonomous:* these investments are in the production of "sunrise" industries based on new inventions and innovations..

Imitative investments are made by "duplicators", which business is of sub-standard goods as NKAI TV instead of AKAI TV. Cars cannot be duplicated but radios can be.

Complementary investments are in packaging and manufacturing of spare parts.

Supplementary investments are in the production of goods which are based on the by-products as cut-pieces of the industry of readymade clothes can be used for producing/stuffing cushions, pillows, seats, dolls etc.

Multiplicity of investments promotes employment generations. It brings in innovations. They are brought in by the FD investors. Or, the foreign innovators allow others to produce new goods on payment of royalty. There are five types of innovations.

(A) New product is invented like colour TV was invented.

(B) New type of raw material is found, as they are finding plants for bio-diesel. Synthetic raw materials are invented.

(C) New processes of manufacturing are introduced.

(D) New markets are created abroad.

(E) New business organizations are forged/developed to have a commanding position in the market

(9) IT increases employment generation in a multiplier way

- Higher international trade means more exports and imports.
- Imports can be for consumption or for use in domestic production.
- Higher domestic production increases domestic consumption.
- Higher domestic production increases exports.
- Higher IT involves more trade, transport and finance also.
- There is demand for persons in many types of employment,
- When people become richer they demand better food, clothes, houses and goods of comforts and luxuries.
- More and more persons are employed all around.
- If employment increases in international trade for 1,00,000 persons and the total employment increases for 4,00,000 persons, the employment multiplier will be 4.
- For multiplier of foreign trade is equal to

$$K \frac{1}{1-(MPC+MPX)} \text{ or } \frac{1}{MPS+MPM}$$

- It is to be noted that multiplier increases due to consumption and export. It goes down due to savings and imports. Hence we write 1-(MPC+MPX).

Foreign trade multiplier will be high if (i) domestic consumption is high, (ii) if exports are high. It will be very high if both are high. We take three examples. The following tables show percentages out of national income

	1_A &	1B	2nd	3rd
Consumption	60	40	40	45
Exports	20	40	45	15
Savings+Imports	20	20	15	40
	100	100	100	100

In 1A and 1B, The S+M are the same in percentage terms. Hence the multiplier will remain the same. If 'C' is low 'X' (exports) should be high.

FTM

	A	B	C
	$\frac{1}{20/100}$	$\frac{1}{15/100}$	$\frac{1}{40/100}$
	$\frac{1}{1} \div \frac{20}{100}$	$\frac{1}{1} \div \frac{15}{100}$	$\frac{1}{1} \div \frac{40}{100}$
or	$\frac{1}{1} \times \frac{100}{20}$	$\frac{1}{1} \times \frac{100}{15}$	$\frac{1}{1} \times \frac{100}{40}$
	5	6.66	2.5

Hence the great favorable effect of it on economic growth is through multiplier effect of the exports.

(10) IT increases national income and standard of living

One thing can be said with certainly that the *living standards of the masses of poor may take decades or even centuries to improve.*

National income may go up but the benefits may not percolate to the poorest of the poor.[4]

- It increases investment, and production.
- Then employment and national income also increase.
- Then personal incomes and savings also increase
- Then again the investments increase.
- Government incomes (revenues) from various types of taxes also increase.

Living standards improve because of the following four effects.

A There is increase in personal incomes.
B There are cheaper domestic goods and services available in large number at competitive prices.
C Imported goods are available for consumption at competitive prices.
D Employment is higher and rewarding.

PART B

DRAG IMPACT OF INTERNATIONAL TRADE on Economic Growth

There are two earlier theses (Plural of thesis) about negative effects of international trade. One is of *Gunnar Myrdal.* He wrote about two types of effects:

(A) Spread effects
(B) Backwash effects.

Spread effects are *more or less* the same as the have discussed above. Myrdal had two types of such effects in mind.

A. Forward or down stream effects.
B. Backward or upstream effects.

Suppose the foreigners develop a cotton textile mill. Then cotton will be grown, cotton seeds, manure, irrigation systems, pesticides, herbicides, fertilisers, machines etc. will be needed. *Agri-industries will develop. These are backward Linkages or upstream effects.*

Forward linkages or downstream effects are those which will be in the form of establishment of agro-industries. If Cotton is grown, there will be Cotton textile mill. If cloth is produced sewing machines will be produced. The readymade garment industries will be there. There will be exports also.

Growth promotion	:	If SE>BE i.e., ie spread effects are greater than backwash effects.
Resource drain	:	If BE > SE.

The following are the possible drag effects on economic growth. *It should be remembered that the growth effects are always greater than the drag effects. No country will continue international trade and business if there is deceleration due to IT and IB.*

Top ten drag effects.

(1) *Drain on natural resources*

The imperialist countries took away the raw materials of the "Colony countries" at cheap rates. The export of iron are from Bastar in Chhatisgarh and from kudremukh in Karnataka will have drag effect on India's growth. Instead, there should be steel plants in India.

(2) *Drain of human resources*

At present the I.I.T. pass outs migrate outside the country. The foreign countries pay them much more than they can ever get in India. This is "export of cream of human resources." India's MBBS, doctors, engineers and top technical persons leave for foreign countries. This is a great loss of *"potential"* economic growth.

(3) Mounting Indebtedness

If a poor country imports more than it exports, there will be a foreign loan. If balance of payment is deficit, foreign loans increase, India's foreign exchange reserves of about $ 286 b. are "fake" because the foreign indebtedness is also as much. Real reserves are those which are due to X>M exports being higher than imports.

(4) Domestic S and I can be crowded out

Government of India pays foreigners higher rate of interest. In USA the depositors used to get nearly 1%rate of interest. In India they got 8 to 12 times more. Government of India reduced the rate of interest to Indian depositors to half. India savers are being penalised.

(5) Foreigners dump

Dumping means that the foreigners are selling their products below *their* cost of production to destroy foreign industries. Chinese are selling their power saver bulbs at Rs. 25/- a piece while Indians sell that at Rs. 150/- Suppose the cost of production in China was Rs. 35 per unit. Then selling at Rs. 25 a piece will be dumping. Dumping ruins domestic market. Foreign dumping harms our industries. The country can, however, impose high taxes or countervailing duties.

(6) Unnecessary goods are imported

Luxury goods are generally imported for the rich. The rich control the economy. They are the beneficiaries of public expenditure. They are tax dodgers and corrupt persons. Imports are for their benefit. Exports are of such goods which are used by the lower income groups.

(7) *Exchange rate falls in poor countries*

(A) ER falls because poor countries get adverse balance of payment.

(B) Domestic rate falls; dollar rate goes up. Suppose \$ 1= Rs. 50. Then Re 1 will be equal to $\$\frac{1}{50}$ or 0.02 dollars. Fall means \$ 1 Rs. 51.

(C) Falling exchange rates makes imports costlier in rupee terms, even if the dollar prices remain the same.

(D) A poor country will have to export more goods to get the same amount of dollars.

(8) Terms of trade go against

Less developed economies frequently find that they are paying more and more for the imported goods, while at the same time the prices of their exports are either falling or not rising as much.

(9) Trade may replace production

Local producers cannot compete with the producers of developed countries. One can see that the Koreans have displaced Indian producers of Refrigerators, TVs, Washing machines and many electronic goods. Most of the Indian producers are gone. The soft drink inustry of India was destroyed by the multinational companies like Pepsi and Coca Cola.

(10) Village crafts die: artisans get immiserized: rural Industries die: Employment goes down

Chinese are selling in India cheap goods. They have displaced hand-made "bindi" makers even. The Chinese and Japanese sell their cheap variety saries in India and have made the life of handloom weaver miserable. The village crafts are dying. Many rural artisans have become laborers. Hand-made ropes from the local plants and grasses cannot be marketed by the villagers as plastic ropes are available at cheaper rates. Instances can be multiplied.

NOTE

1. It is not play of words. The description is for the first determinant—always. Hence our designation of second engine is right in academics.
2. Author's son lived in Seychelles for 1½ years and he calls is "paradise on earth". Tourists flock there. The main island has population of just 50000. Every spec of sand is beautiful. It is the best island in the world.
3. Emperor Akbar did not have on electric fan, a bicycle, a scooter, a car, a refrigerator, an air-conditioner (or even) an electric heater), a TV set (with VCP, VCR, CVD, DVD….), a radio, a three-in-one, spec, a watch, ……. @ India used to import paper pins from abroad. The thorns of babool used to be used in government officer as pins! India used import even railway lines from abroad. Progress of industries was slow before liberalisation. Liberalisation and globalization pushed up both national and international business.
4. The author conducted a detailed survey (in 500 pages) on behalf of DFID of the U.K. and found many families in many villages who did not have even a rupee in the form of saving.

19 Interface Between International Trade and Economic Development of Sectors and Functions

Interface means mutual interdependence and interaction. Free trade brings inputs and technology for the development of agriculture for example and, agricultural development both in qualitative and quantitative terms increases international trade. Chapter on "international trade as engine of economic development" can also be consulted for the topics discussed hereafter.

1. Interface between size and structure of national income and international trade

The process of economic growth and development is non-conformist in nature and it cannot be predicated ex ante.

Just as we cannot predict *ex ante* how many children will a girl bear in her reproductive years, we cannot predict the exact relationship between international trade and economic development. Both can be understood *ex post*. The analysis gives better insight about the qualitative aspects than about the precise quantitative relationships. Free international trade brings inputs of development of various sectors, capital, technology, technical know-how etc. These increase both domestic production for imports compression and exports promotion. A lot of imports can be "imports-replacing-imports". National income will rise. Rising national income means favourable effects on all sectors, functions, sectors, sub-sectors and regions. More output will be released for higher exports. Since exports pay for imports, there will be a healthy circuit of higher imports and imports. Competitiveness will have to be ensured otherwise the rising national income may go for imports. Economic development in the initial stages means (i) falling death rates, (ii) slowly falling birth rates and (iii) net increase in population. That increases domestic consumption. In the initial stages some " tightening of the belt" (austerity) may be necessary for increasing the exports. Multiplier effect of international trade on national income will apply. So will apply the reversal effects. Economy will progress "from crises to crises", just as a child becomes young and then old through various illnesses.

2. Interface between higher international trade and agricultural development

Higher yielding variety seeds, machines and implements, fertilizers, pesticides, herbicides, irrigation systems, tractors, levelers, harvesters, etc. can be imported or produced at home with the imported machines and technology. These are related to agri-businesses and higher outputs from agriculture will provide inputs for agro-industries like sugar mills, cotton textile mills, oil extraction mills, food processing units and so many others.

India was living from " hand to mouth" or rather from "the ship to mouth" after independence. Now India is food secure, though all the Indians are not food secure. Growth has to be "inclusive" (it was earlier known as "deep percolating growth" also "growth with justice"). The percentage contribution of agriculture should go down (goes down) but the contribution in total increases. In India this is now 18 p.c. of the GDP whereas at the time of independence it was 80 p.c. However, the employment contribution of agriculture is still high in India (two third of total employment) and this is a trap of backwardness. Not only production but output (production in money terms of all the three seasonal crops), physical productivity per acre, physical productivity per unit of time, physical productivity per package of investment, and value productivity should also go up. Rising international trade helps in these processes. However, nations will have to stand up to the developed countries to get fair prices for their products. USA and India produce the same amount of wheat. Since the USA has much smaller population (less than one third of India), they use a lot of their foodgrains as 'feedgrains" (to be fed to animals so that their meat becomes succulent).

It is necessary that all the three sectors — primary, secondary and tertiary (service) sectors — should develop but in the initial stages the material component of the GDP should be high. The big nations should not be allowed to dump their cheap agricultural products in the developing economies because their agricultural products are highly subsidised ($.1 b. a day) and will ruin the agriculture of the developing economies. Judiciously, the developing economies can import toward off hunger in their countries. Developed countries should not be allowed to introduce "self-destructing seeds" (outputs of which cannot be used as seeds in the next sowing season). International trade in "hunger" should not be allowed to be perpetuated.

3. Interface between industrial development and industrial development

The international trade in industrial items is even more strictly on the principle of comparative advantage. In the case of agriculture, if there are conditions of starvation, imports can be at higher prices even but from the nearest possible countries. The rich countries outsource their products or parts thereof to the developing countries if the latter can produce them cheaper. Countries with poor resource base (as Japan and Korea) can import all the inputs from abroad and with the help of their innovative technology can become (as they have become) leading industrial nations. Research and development have won the day for them. Industrial development is such now a days (thanks to rising international cooperation) that what were luxuries to the princesses are now essentials for the housemaids. There can be some initial adverse effects in the form of further adverse balance of payment but in the long run, there will be improvements. However, all countries of the world cannot have favorable balance of payment at same time. At best they can have balanced balance of payment. *Adverse balance of payment increases balance of indebtedness hence it is necessary that the balance of utilities foregone in exports should be less than the utilities gained from imports.* Complementarities between various nations increase with greater trade. The USA agreed to have agreement for supplying nuclear fuel to India because it expected orders worth hundreds of billion dollars from India. International trade should be in this order: K goods (capital goods), H goods (heavy engineering goods)/ w (small w) goods (wage goods necessary for the common people) W goods (white goods i.e./ goods of comforts necessary for the middle classees) and U goods (luxury) goods.

4. Interface between service sector and international trade

Higher international trade will require A +++ grade "hospitality" services e.g., of hotels, transport, banking and other facilities which the foreign visitors want. However, dichotomy is bad i.e., if around a five star hotel there are filthy slums, the facility of five star hotel will not count. *The best policy is that first of all a country should end hunger (that will require creation of sustainable employment facilities), and then remove ugliness from the scene.* Queen Elizabeth once remarked that Delhi is the dirtiest capital is Asia and Islamabad the best in Asia. Transport facilities and cost divide the goods into tradable and non-tradable e.g., gold bricks are internationally traded and house bricks are not. The ratio of transport costs to the total value should be small: costs of offloading-unloading, freight charges, insurance and interest etc. included. *Infrastructure facilities develop international trade and developing international trade can even bring investment in infrastructure from abroad.*

If the inputs of production are ubiquitous in nature, the plant should be nearer the markets or at the ports. If the products are specific e.g., iron are, the plants should be nearer that bulky material that is cheap also. A steel plant should be near the mines of coal rather than of steel. Consumption goods should be produced nearer the market. There should be coalescence of market areas for most of the commodities and goods.

There should be nodal points of excellent medical facilities at par with the developed countries of the world to promote international business and trade. Afterall persons visit to negotiate about the trade. *International business has the indirect impact on the emergence of the quarternary sector of superior e.g., AIIMs at Delhi or Apollo at Chennai/ Hyderabad, Breach Candy at Mumbai etc.* Other hospitals belong to the tertiary sector.

It was due to international trade that Indian transport scene has changed so much. The roads are full of cars and other four wheelers so much so that there is clogging. Aerodromes have queues of aircrafts waiting to take off or land. Steam engines are gone; diesel and electric engines are far better; and imported ABB electric locomotives are driving fast trains. Indian trains are lavatories in motion ! This state of affair can end if foreigners invest in infrastructure because government investment had been inadequate, inefficient, and full of corruption leakages. *International trade will increase much more only when infrastructure facilities become world class.*

5. International trade and consumption

[Impact on production is the same as on GDP] The depth (scale) and the width (types) of production improve with international trade. There is technological revolution everywhere. Technical experts are exported and imported with ease ! International trade may force a country to close down certain lines of production. Here "trade replaces production", but many new lines get opened. There are always newer and better products.

Without international trade people of a country consume what is produced inside a country. This is autarky. However, if we think how international trade has improved the medical scenario new instruments, new medicines, new diagonistic techniques, new procedures etc. then one can realise the importance of international business. The super-rich people of middle-east come to India for "medical tourism". The total costs are very low. And, India is still a country where over 50 p.c. of the poor of the world abound. Consumption improves because the domestic base improves and the people can consume imported goods. Satiation levels improve.

6. Interface between international trade on one side and savings, capital formation/flows, and investment on the other side

If national income rises, the propensity to save rises and the total quantum of savings will be high in a country. These savings will be both financial (in the form of money and several proxies of the same) and real savings (more seeds with the farmers). Naturally there will be higher capital formation in the real and monetary forms. Capital for direct investment (FDI) and institutional investment (shares, bonds, derivatives) will be higher. Outflow and inflow of capital, (if not altogether speculative), will increase investment and will provide broad-banding (increasing the scope) of the same.

Autonomous (innovation-induced)/ imitative (of autonomous investment), complementary (as packaging for the main product), supplementary (based on the by-products of the main product) induced (in sun-rise and other sectors) defensive (in sun-set industries to keep them afloat as far as possible) all increase due to international trade. Profits increase for all participants and functionary and this explains a lot about every positive effct.

There is a lot of "capital consumption" due to international trade. Many types of mopeds and scooters are no longer produced in India now because they cannot be sold. The capital invested in them is of no value except scrap value. This is now known as "constructive destruction." Scams assume international dimensions. Ill effects of money market collapse become world-wide. Countries may be caught in debt trap as imports increase at a faster rate than the exports.

7. Interface between international trade and terms of trade

One is not sure whether the developing countries will get adequate prices for their exports. The foreign monopsonies and oligopsonies (buyers' side) are too powerful to allow the exporters of developing economies to gain much advantage. It is also seen that the developing countries export more real goods to get the same real imports. It is generally found that the income terms of trade improve for almost all countries. Most important of all, the "utility terms of trade" which are not measurable improve for all countries.

8. Interface between international trade and human development and welfare

Employment displacement and emergence of new employment opportunities happens at the same time. In the long run more persons are employed and they all get higher incomes. A collector used to get Rs. 300 in 1947, he gets 100 times more at the start of the career in 2008 Only the unfortunate ones continue to have immiserisation due to "non-inclusive" development and increasing international trade. The rich have become richer.

9. Factor use and International Trade

Infact the capital and labour may be used in different proportions that they were being used earlier. Domestic factoral terms of trade will undergo a change. *Production frontiers expand with either capital intensity or labour intensity or neutral intensity i.e., at the same mix of K-L ratio as was earlier.* Greater factor use will improve the factor-income terms of trade or if this is not so the depressed terms of trade of factor-income will improve. Factor mobilities increase and that will increase their incomes if they were earlier depressed. In case some factors were having higher factor-income ratios they will come down. The following diagram shows four types of change in production frontiers and factor-use intensity which will bring changes in factor-income ratios of capital and labour.

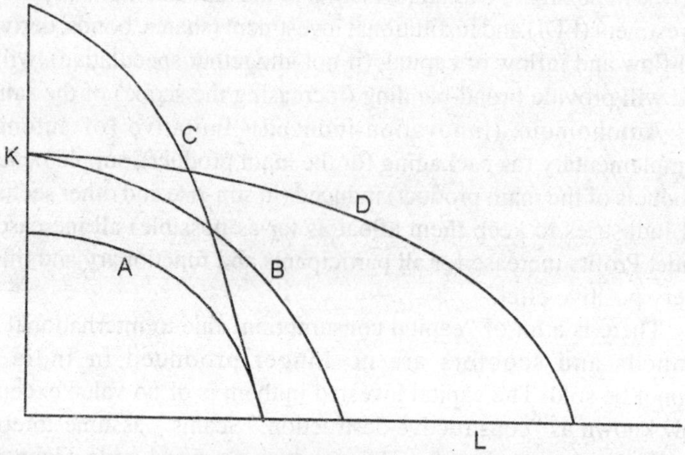

Diagram 19.2

(A) is earlier production frontier. (B) is higher production frontier of neutral type; (C) is higher production frontier with greater use of capital and (D) is higher production frontiers with greater labour-use.

10. International Trade and Employment

Employment and international trade

If there is under-employment it is certain that the country is not producing to its maximum capacity. Full employment should go along with fullest possible *(maximum maximrum)* production. Full employment without realising the full production potential will cause inflation as there will be money lead (due to payment to factors) and goods lag due to the economy not realising its full capacity utilisation and full production. "Full production" with factors remaining unemployed is actually sub-optimal position. In this case there can be dearth of matching entitlements or purchasing power. The money lag and goods lead will also create problems. Full employment should ensure proper loading of factors and their maximum physical and revenue productivities. The USSR provided full employment as a right and duty but full production potentials were not realised. They diverted a lot of funds for military hardware and productivities in farms and factories were neglected. Everybody's business was nobody's business. Erstwhile USSR's exports had to be managed through State Trading Organisation. They entered into trade deals on the negotiated prices which they said were real prices. They considered the prices set by the market as artificial prices fixed by the multinational and transnational companies, monopolies and oligopolies. They could export to their satellite countries on the basis of their political hegemony. In the free economies *full* potentials of employment, capacity utilisation or productivities are seldom realised. Increasing employment will have beneficial effects on international trade if employment increases in traded goods.

UNIT III
Exchange Rates of Currencies

20. Theories of Exchange Rates—I
    Mint Par of Exchange. Purchasing Power Parity (PPP) theory.
21. Theories of Exchange Rates—II
    Demand and Supply theory.
    Equilibrium Exchange Rate Theory.
22. Other leading exchange rate theories.

    (1) Mundell Fleming model.
    (2) Monetary model
    (3) Sticky vs. flexible exchange rate model
    (4) Random walk model
    (5) Portfolio banking model
    (6) Current Account model.
    (7) Capital Account monetary model.
    (8) Asset market model
    (9) Direct and indirect Exchange rate (determining factors)

23. Fixed Vs. fluctuating exchange Rates. Pros and cons. Managed floating *or* alternative Exchange Rate system or multiple exchange rates.
24. Convertibility of Indian Rupee.
    Prospects of full convertibility on capital account.

20 Theories of Exchange Rates—I (Mint Par Theory: Purchasing Power Parity Theory). Modified PPT.

(1) INTRODUCTORY
(2) FOREIGN EXCHANGE RATE UNDER METALLIC STANDARD (THE THEORY OF MINT PAR OF EXCHANGE AND SPECIE POINTS)
(3) THE PURCHASING POWER PARITY THEORY OF EXCHANGE RATE

1. INTRODUCTORY

The foreign exchange market

International trade involves not only exchange of goods and services of two countries but also of two currencies. Dollars are to be exchanged with Rupees or Japanese Yen or EURO. Broadly defined, the foreign exchange market is a vehicle that makes possible the exchange of different national currencies. In metallic standard all international transactions were settled in gold, which used to have a free flow. Now different countries have different currencies which are backed by the fiat of the state and have different purchasing power: that too changing. But all countries keep some gold in reserve.

Foreign exchange market is not an organised market. There is no membership system nor the financial institutions dealing in foreign exchange operate under a unified code or rules. The foreign exchange market itself is a broad, somewhat nebulous institutional arrangement. Most banks dealing internationally maintain balances in a number of foreign currencies with correspondent banks or affiliates abroad. Foreign exchange market involves the change of different currencies at a certain rate of exchange. This rate of exchange itself keeps on changing—sometimes marginally and sometimes quite substantially in either direction. When a buyer wants the currency of a foreign country he deposits the currency in a bank to take other country's currency. The bank provides it directly or itself buys it from another country's banks. The foreign- exchange market thus consists of an unorganized group of banks throughout the world that simply maintain foreign currency balances with one another, and transactions of which are generally made by cable transfer.

Transactions in the foreign exchange market are generally made by net-cable-telegraphic transfer. If a bank finds itself with excess foreign-currency balances, it can sell these balances to other banks, foreign currency brokers or to the Central banks of the concerned countries themselves. They are the buying sources as well.

The foreign exchange markets can supply currencies of the foreign countries now or on an agreed date in future. In case certain countries maintain fixed exchange parities with other currencies and their central banks buy and sell on that rate only, while in the open market their currencies command less value (due to inflation in the country) then black market in exchange currency will develop. Thus there emerge 'grey' or 'black' foreign exchange markets.

The foreign exchange market (or the banks dealing with foreign exchange) provides credit for international trade and thus acts as a vehicle for the financing of exports and imports. It also makes contribution as a way of hedging against exchange risks. Even if the importers default, the banks pay. Banker's acceptance of the exporters bill is a promise or a guarantee by a bank. This market remains open 24 hours a days.

The foreign exchange rate

The exchange rate is the price of one currency in terms of another currency. The rate is vital for international trade. Even Ricardo was aware of the importance of the exchange rate when he wrote:

> "In speaking of the exchange and the comparative value of money in different countries, we must not in the least refer to the value of money estimated in commodities, in either country. The exchange is never ascertained by estimating the comparative value of money in corn, cloth, or any commodity whatever, but by estimating the value of the currency of one country, in the currency of another." (p. 128 *op. cit.*).

An exchange rate can be expressed in terms of a better known currency or in terms of a common currency. It is customary to express the exchange rate of different currencies of the world in terms of USA dollar. However, there are always two rates for two currencies, expressed in terms of each other *e.g.*, if $ 1 is equal to say, Rs. 8 then Re. 1 will be equal to $ 0.125. The first expression *viz.*, $ 1 = Rs. 8 is easily understood. This is an example only. (In Dec. 2009 $ 1= 46.75 rupees and in April 2010 the rate was $ 1 = Rs. 45). The question of foreign exchange and exchange rate assumes importance in international trade. It is quite possible that imports from country 'A' may be preferred to imports from country 'B' because the necessary foreign exchange of country 'B' may not be easily available or may be available at higher exchange rate, relatively speaking. International trade involves comparison not only of prices of commodity and services of two countries but also of the prices of their currencies.

The exchange rate of two currencies is also determined, like the price of any commodity, on the respective elasticities of demand and supply. If the supply is easily available (elastic) then the value of that currency will depreciate. This currency will become 'soft' currency. If, on the other hand, the supply of a currency is relatively less (compared to its demand) then its value (price) will appreciate. A country which has an unfavorable balance of trade will find the value (price) of its currency going down in international market, and *vice versa.* Thus, both the demand for, and supply of, foreign exchange are derived from the underlying demand for domestic and foreign goods, services and investment opportunities.

Unilateral transfers (compensation paid or donations), credit transactions and delayed payments make it difficult to identify the total foreign exchange transactions with the balance of payment. Thus, this imbalance brings change in the exchange rates.

Since demand and supply conditions of goods, services, investment transactions (as also unilateral transfer) will differ, the supply and demand conditions of currencies will also differ from time to time. If such markets are free from arbitrary controls, and if governments refrain from influencing market forces in any way, the exchange rates will be *freely fluctuating*. Fluctuating exchange rates will ensure equalisation of supply and demand of foreign exchange over a time period and a country cannot have a balance of payments problem, though some other problems may emerge.

Various countries of the world can define their exchange rate in terms of gold and then the exchange rates of different currencies will remain fixed. The demand and supply will be regulated to maintain the rate rather than the rate being allowed to float according to the demand and supply. This method was practised between 1945 and 1971, when under the arrangements that established the IMF the dollar was defined in terms of gold ($ 35 per ounce) while other leading currencies were given par value in terms of the dollar and pegged to that currency within a range of plus or minus 1 per cent. (In Dec. 2009 this rate was $ 1214 per ounce of gold.) When the rate of exchange on the dollar of a given currency, say the German Mark, approached the upper limit, the German monetary authorities used to sell Mark against dollars to hold the exchange rate down. As the exchange rate approached the lower limit, they bought Mark with dollars to support the rate. (In 2002 EURO replaced Mark and many European currencies)

The entire system was based on the principle of "changing lock to suit the key". It had its own advantages but they were overwhelmed by the disadvantages. Fixed exchange rates produce deficits or surpluses in balance of payment and are responsible for giving rise to non-official rates of exchange.

(The question of fixed versus floating exchange rates is discussed in this section of the book elsewhere).

Type of rates

First, there is the *spot rate of exchange*. It is rate at which foreign exchange is available now and here. It is the rate at which cable or telegraphic transfer (purchase and sale) can be arranged immediately. It is determined at the current demand and supply conditions, the speculation tendencies and other relevant conditions. However, the spot rate can be quoted at different rates between two countries. If in England the spot rate is £ = $ 2.8, in USA it may be quoted at $ 2.84 = £ 1 or $ 1 = £ .3521. This difference is due to differences in insurance charges, dealers' commission and transport rates.

When a buyer of foreign currency pays to the bank, price for foreign currency in domestic currency, the account is credited with foreign currency on the spot at this rate. A spot rate of foreign exchange is higher than the rate applicable for drafts etc., because the money will be actually delivered after a few days.

The Long Period exchange rate

The basis of the long rate of exchange is the rate of interest. Thus as the number of days are extended from a zero time horizon, the exchange rate turns into a long rate. The essence of the transactions is that the purchaser pays one currency now in return for the right to receive another currency at a fixed future date.

When premium is added or discount is deducted from the spot rate of exchange, we get the time exchange rate. If the spot rate is £ 1 = 2.80 and the rate of interest be 6%, then on a 30 days bill (credit sale) $ 0.014 will be deducted per pound. On two and three months bill $ 0.028 and $ 0.042 will be deducted. Thus the exchange rates for one, two and three months will become $ 2.786, $ 2.772 and $ 2.758 respectively, per pound.

When a buyer buys on credit from a foreign country and accepts the bill (to be paid not on 'sight' but after a time period), then the creditor will have to pay in future interest on the delayed payment and the exchange rate will be calculated after the addition of the interest rate per pound. *This is also known as the Usance rate of exchange.*

Third, there is *forward rate of exchange.* Importers and exporters are interested in getting fixed amounts of foreign exchange at a particular future date on rates known to them before hand. Then they can plan their imports and exports. The importers and exporters are not interested in earning profits arising out of changes in exchange rate but only in profits arising out of purchase and sale deals. The risk of changing exchange rates is borne by the speculators who trade in changing prices of currencies. When a buyer of foreign exchange enters into a deal to buy a particular currency after a certain time period, say, three months, he settles the price *now.* Even if the actual price of foreign currency becomes higher, the forward buyer will get the currency at the agreed price. However, if the price becomes lower than the agreed price, even then the buyer will have to buy it at the agreed price. The buyers attach more importance to certainty about the rate of exchange.

The foreign exchange banks and firms are traders in exchange prices. They carry on their transactions of buying and selling in the hope of earning profits. However, many of them can incur losses when the exchange rates they had anticipated do not materialise due to changes in demand and supply conditions. These speculators, however, enter into hedging deals or countervailing transactions with other parties. Ultimately, however, some one incurs a loss or makes a net gain.

The rate of interest has also an important bearing on the rate of foreign exchange in forward exchange market. If a country pays a high rate of interest on securities (if the central bank pays a high interest rate) then the forward exchange rate of its currency will be low. The longer the time period of forward buying, the higher will be the discount rate or price of foreign exchange. The higher the difference in the rate of interest between two centres of foreign exchange buying and selling, the higher will be the rate of discount or the price of foreign exchange. These differences in the rates of selling/buying foreign exchange at different times under different circumstances are termed as 'forward margin', 'swap margin', or 'swap rate'.

If the supply of a foreign currency abundant in comparison to its demand the forward exchange rate may be near about the spot rate and if the supply is likely to increase in future (relative to demand) the forward rate can be lower than the spot rate. Such a currency will not command premium or, in other words will not be sold at discount rate now. If a currency is in great demand it commands premium in future. The sellers receive premium.

The demand for foreign exchange is made by the importers of goods, services and capital goods, by brokers and by those speculators who are 'bulls' *i.e.,* who buy now in order to sell later when the expected rise in price comes. The supply of foreign exchange is provided by the exporters of goods, services and capital goods, by brokers and by these speculators who are 'bears' *i.e.,* who expect forward rate to fall in future (therefore, they sell now and buy in future). The speculators and the brokers or arbitragers take their foreign exchange reserves from one country to another to trade in changing prices.

These institutions and firms which deal in foreign exchange enter into buying and selling transactions simultaneously. They buy foreign exchange from exporters and sell to importers. Banks usually so buy and sell foreign exchange that they do not suffer losses due to changes in the prices of currencies and can earn their profits from commission. Actually every dealer in foreign exchange tries to insure against loss by entering into countervailing deal with others. However, someone ultimately may suffer loss; he will be the one who could not enter into such deal or who thoroughly miscalculated the future trend in the rate. Countervailing transaction is known as 'dealer's cover' also.

The supply and demand for foreign exchange becomes equated through changes in the interest rate. If, for example, the rate of interest is 8% in London and 7% in (Mumbai) then foreign exchange will move out of India, and when the rates at two places become equal then the movement will stop. Movement of rupee out of India to earn higher rate of interest will *(i)* increase the future supply of Indian rupee and *(ii)* the spot rate of Indian rupee will fall, provided transfer is permitted.

The exchange rates can be orderly or disorderly. For example, if one unit of currency of A country is equal to 20 units of B country and 40 units of C country, then one unit of the currency of B country is equal to 2 units of the currency of C country. This is orderly cross rate. If these equations are not maintained then the rates will be said to be disorderly cross rates. Once disorder enters then it may lead to further disorder. Free market of currencies usually creates disorderly cross rates.

2. FOREIGN EXCHANGE RATE UNDER METALLIC STANDARD (THE THEORY OF MINT PAR OF EXCHANGE AND SPECIE POINTS)

Though gold standard is no longer world monetary standard, still it will be useful to study how the exchange rate will be determined between two countries which are on gold standard. Present exchange systems take their roots in the gold coin standards and are modifications or developments of these older systems. Study of the determination of the exchange rate under gold coin standard (which no longer prevails anywhere), puts the subject into historical perspective. IMF had gold of $ 4000 b. in 2009 and will sell 80 p.c. of it in the next five years upto 2013. Countries buy and sell gold.

When two countries are on gold standard, then the exchange rate of two currencies (ignoring the cost of minting) will depend on the gold contents of the two currencies, provided there are no restrictions on import and export of goods and gold. This exchange rate is known as 'mint par of exchange'.

The mint par depends not on the coin itself but on the legal definition of it; not on the sovereign *de facto, but on the sovereign de jure... unless and until the law* (regarding the gold content) is altered the mint-par cannot alter. Mint par is thus an expression of the ratio between the statutory bullion equivalents of the standard monetary units of two countries on the same monetary units of two countries on the same monetary standards.

The mint-par rate of exchange is based on the ratio of pure gold contents of two currencies. For example, if the coin of A country is of 10 grains and its purity is 9.5/10 and the coin of the B country is of 100 grains and its purity is 9.6/10, then the mint-par of exchange will be determined as under:

∴ Pure gold contents in the coin of $= \frac{9.6}{10}$ or $\frac{96}{100}$ grains.

B country:

∴ Pure gold contents in the coin of $= \frac{9.5}{10}$ or 9.5 grains.

A country:

∴ *In terms of B country's coin.*

$\frac{9.5}{10}$ grains are equal tosd 1 coin.

1 grains will be equal to $\frac{10}{95}$ coin.

96 grain will be equal to $\frac{10}{95} \times 96 = 10.1053$ coins.

∴ *In terms of A country's coin:*

96 grains are equal to 1 coin.

1 grains will be equal to $\frac{1}{96}$ coin.

9.5 grains will be equal to $\frac{1}{96} \times \frac{95}{10} = 0.09896$ coins.

Thus:

1. Rate of national currency in terms of 1 unit of foreign currency

$$= \frac{\text{Gold in 1 unit of foreign coin}}{\text{Gold in 1 unit of national coin}}$$

2. Rate of foreign currency in terms of 1 unit of national currency

$$= \frac{\text{Gold in 1 unit of national coin}}{\text{Gold in 1 unit of foreign coin}}$$

If the currencies of two countries are on "gold bullion standard" (the governments issue paper currency which is convertible in a certain minimum amount of gold bullion) then also the mint-parity theory will determine the rate of exchange between such countries.

Mint parity can be calculated in this way also: If America gives 350 dollars in exchange for 1 ounce of gold and Britain gives 145.83 pounds in exchange of 1 ounce of gold, then:

145.83 pounds are equal to 350 dollars or
1 pound is equal to 2.4 dollars (app.).

The mint rate becomes the basis of trade for those countries also which are on silver standard. In contrast to flexible exchange rates, the value of each national currency under the gold standard is fixed in terms of gold. Each currency is defined as so many fine ounces of gold standard purity; whether the currency itself is of gold, or whether it is merely fully or partially backed by gold is immaterial. The government must be willing to buy and sell gold for the national currency freely to everyone and in unlimited quantity. Thus, the exchange ratio between two metallic standard countries' currencies will be determined on the weight-to-weight basis of the metallic contents.

Limits of fluctuations: The gold points or specie points

When the currencies are on metallic standard the exchange rates in theory should be orderly crossed rates. In other words, the exchange rate equations between various currencies should be in mutual order. However, although exchange rates cannot diverge far from these cross rates determined by metallic purities, there is likely to be some divergence. This is because it costs money to ship gold from one country to another and there are packing, interest and insurance charges also. The rate of exchange differs from the par in that the rate is determined, not by relative amounts of gold in the respective monetary units but by the demand for, and the supply of, means of payment *i.e.*, bills, bank drafts and sometimes the currency itself. Shifts in the relative demand and supply for relative demand and supply for means of payment brought the actual rate of exchange to fluctuate above below par. David Hume was the first economist who gave the theory of "price-specific-flow mechanism" in 1752.

The mint par upper and lower limits point are determined by the demand and supply conditions of the external currency. The foreign currency is supplied by the exporters and is demanded by the importers. The importers provide the domestic currency in exchange for the foreign currency. If more dollars are demanded and their supply is relatively scarce, then the value of dollar in terms of, say, pound will go up. In other words, this will result in a pound commanding less than the mint par rate of $ 2.4 per pound. On the contrary, if dollars are relatively in excess supply then a pound will command more than $ 2.4 per pound. However, there are upper and lower limits to fluctuations in the rate.

If Americans demand a very high price of dollar, the British importer would rather dispatch gold if the cost of dispatching gold (inclusive of all expenses) is less. When gold is dispatched there are expenses to be incurred on packing, office expenses, transport expenses, insurance, loss of interest, telephone etc. In all probability the expenses will be same from either direction. Suppose such expenses per 1 dollar equivalent of gold come to 0.05 dollar, then this amount will set the upper and lower limits.

The upper and lower limits will thus be had by adding and deducting these amounts to and from $ 2.4, *i.e.*, they will be $ 2.45 and $ 2.35. In other words, the importers of Britain will not pay more than 0.05 dollars per dollar nor accept more than 0.05 dollars less than the parity rate. If the market rate fluctuates within the limit set by $ 0.05 dollars the British people will prefer to buy and sell currencies; if not, then they will prefer to handle gold.

If the trader in Britain prefers to export gold $ 2.45 becomes the gold export point or upper gold/specie point. If the trader in Britain prefers to receive gold then $ 2.35 becomes the gold import point or lower gold/specie point. However, these upper and lower limits will also change if there are changes in the expenses of sending gold from either (actually both then) direction. However, till these expenses do not change the upper and lower limits will remain firmly set. The actual mint-par will fluctuate within these limits. Diagrammatically, these can be shown as follows:

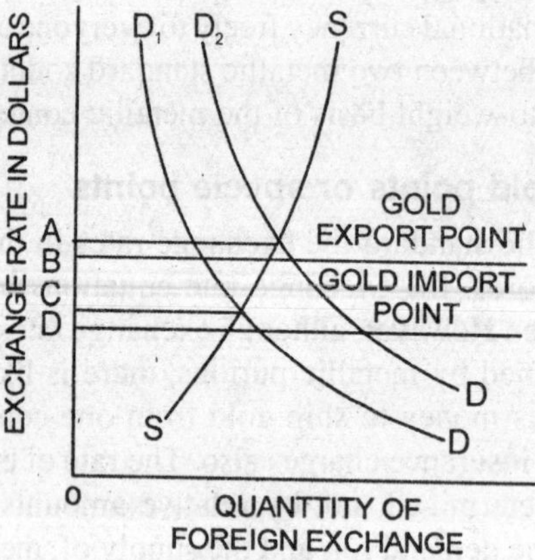

Diagram 20.1

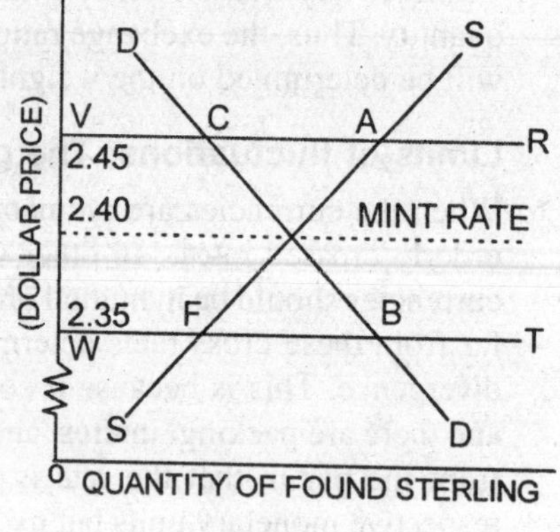

Diagram 20.2

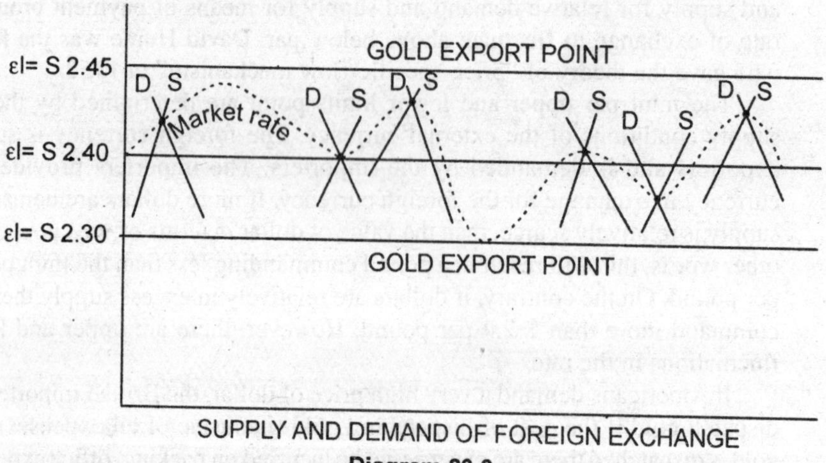

Diagram 20.3

In diagram 20.1, SS is the supply curve of foreign exchange and D'D' is the first demand curve of foreign exchange. E is the equilibrium point. OC will be the exch nge rate. When demand increases to D"D", the equilibrium point becomes E". OA now becomes the exchange rate. However, since the OB is the upper specie point the equilibrium rate will not be paid. The market rate cannot exceed OB nor it can go lower than OD.

The diagram 20.2 shows the same effect with the help of just one supply curve and one demand curve. It is static equilibrium analysis.

In diagram 20.3 the moving zig-zag line is the actual market rate of exchange which moves within the upper and lower specie points. At certain points of the market rate, the corresponding demand and supply curves are shown.

Thus is gold standard there will be a fixed exchange rate in this sense that the limits of fluctuations will be very narrow indeed. The exchange rate has certainty element. There is no such things as destablizing speculation, because, as everyone knows including the speculators, the exchange rate cannot possibly vary above or below the gold export and import points. Moreover, because under the gold standard international gold flows tend to have a direct bearing on the domestic money supply, short-term capital flows will tend to move in the opposite direction from prevailing gold flows.

Mint par when one country is on gold standard and the other on the silver standard

Bimetallism was prevalent during the middle ages and continued during the entire 19th century in many countries. In order to find the mint par of exchange between two countries where one is on gold standard and the other on silver standard, we will have to find out first the pure gold and silver contents of the two currencies or their equivalent in exchange. Then on the basis of the ratio of prices of gold and silver in the market, the mint par of exchange can be found out.

The same can be explained with the following exercise. The mint par of exchange between India and Britain (between rupee and pound sterling) upto 1898 used to be determined between silver and gold standard. The Indian rupee had 165 grains of pure silver in it. At that time 165 grains of pure silver used to buy 7.53344 grains of pure gold. At that time the pound sterling of Britain used to contain 113.0016 of pure gold in it. Thus, the exchange rate used to be Rs. 15 for £ 1. This was worked out as under:

Re. 1 = 165 grains of silver

165 grains of silver = 7.53344 grains of gold.

£ 1 = 113.0016 grains of gold.

$$\text{£ } 1 = \frac{113.0016}{7.53344} = \text{Rs. } 15.$$

Thus

In such a system also there will be gold import point and the gold export point. However, there is an important difference in such a situation: In such a situation the country on gold standard would like to pay in gold while the country on silver standard would like to pay in silver.

Therefore, (£) if a country which is on silver standard then the exchange rate will not exceed the mint par *plus* the cost of sending the gold abroad and *(ii)* in a country which is on gold standard the exchange rate will not be less than the mint par value *minus* the expenses of sending the silver abroad.

Since the cost of transporting silver will be greater than of transporting gold, the specie points will be higher than under gold standard countries.

Exchange rate between countries when one is on gold or silver standard and the other is on paper currency standard

The exchange rate of the currency which is not on gold standard will depend on the purchasing power of the paper currency in terms of gold. If the purchasing power of the paper currency falls/rises (in terms of gold) during the period of inflation/deflation, then the exchange rate will also fall/rise. Since paper standard cannot be so managed as to maintain the same stability as in the gold standard, the exchange rate will not be stable but unstable. The rate of exchange can fluctuate to any extent and there will be no upper or lower limits. A country which is on gold standard can check fluctuations in exchange rate by importing or exporting the gold. A country on paper standard will not be having much gold and will have very limited capacity to check fluctuations in exchange rate. If a paper standard country exports gold to maintain the exchange rate of its currency, people's confidence in the currency falls and its value falls further due to this reason.

Comments

The Mint-Par theory of exchange rate determination cannot be 'criticised' for the simple reason that it is a mathematical truism. The mint-par of exchange rate can be compared with the 'normal price' of perfect competition, which is the long period price. The actual rate of market rate of exchange fluctuates around this rate within the limits set by the specie points. The supply and demand conditions (or the balance of payment disequilibrium) bring fluctuations in the market rate.

The modern disequilibrium in balance of payment theory would tell us that disequilibrium can be to any extent in either direction. However, this could not be under gold standard. Hume demonstrated that price-specie-flow mechanism will automatically bring equilibrium back to the same level. Hume and later other classical economists (Adam Smith, Malthus, Ricardo and Mill) demonstrated that the mercantilist system "was clotted economic non-sense" under the gold standard. Mercantilists wanted countries to amass gold and silver through restrictive imports policy. The classical economists demonstrated that gold inflows would itself give rise to tendencies for gold outflow. Gold inflow will raise the internal price level which will encourage imports and discourage exports. This will increase the outflow of gold. Similarly outflow of gold will reduce the internal price level which will discourage imports and encourage exports. Gold will flow back. There cannot be permanent gold-losing or gold-gaining under free trade and price-specie-flow-mechanism. Gold inflow gives rise to inflation and gold outflow to recession; they cannot reach the extremes but a chain of causation and counter- causation will bring equilibrium conditions back to old equilibrium level. Only the net increase or decrease in gold supply can change the level of equilibrium, as for example when a country discovers gold mines in the country.

Thus, in the opinion and analysis of the classical economists, the market rate of exchange between the currencies of the countries on metallic standard is anchored to the mint parity and the factors underlying the balance of payments adjust themselves to the mint parity exchange rate. (The classical system took into account the changing income effects on international trade also as incomes are related to prices.)[1].

3. THE PURCHASING POWER PARITY THEORY OF EXCHANGE RATE

Gustav Cassel is credited for 'developing' this theory; the theory was, however, first propounded pobably by Henry Thornton in 1802 (An Inquiry into the Nature and Effects of the Paper Credit of Great Britain, London) David Ricardo also expounded this theory. Ultimately it was developed in 1916 by Cassel.

The theory concludes that the equilibrium rate of exchange between two national currencies not on metallic standard must equalize the "purchasing power" of the two currencies. If the purchasing power of the US dollar is five times that of the X currency for a representative "basket of goods and services", then the equilibrium-exchange rate should be $ 1 = 5X. If it is only two times then the exchange rate should be $ 1 = 2X (Example only).

The PPP theory has been presented in two forms: *(i)* in absolute form and in *(ii)* comparative or relative form.

In absolute terms the PPP (Purchasing Power Parity) will change in the proportion of the changes in the purchasing power reflected in the index numbers of the two countries. For example, if the index number of two countries in a certain year were 100 each and then after 5 years the index number in A country becomes 400 while in the B country it becomes 200, then obviously the rate of exchange will become half of the previous rate for A country. Suppose the base year rate was 2 units of A country equal to 1 unit of the currency of B country, then after five years the rate of exchange will be 4: 1. The PPP in absolute terms can be found.

$$Ri = R_o \frac{\text{A country's new Index of prices}}{\text{B country's new Index of prices}}$$

The exchange rate of two currencies on paper standard will be determined by the respective purchasing power of the two countries and it will become normal rate of exchange; only in certain special circumstances the market rate will differ from the rate set by purchasing power parity.

This was explained by Gustav Cassel in the following words:

"Given a normal freedom of trade between two countries, A and B, a rate of exchange will establish itself between them and this rate will, smaller fluctuations apart, remain unaltered as no alteration. In the purchasing power of either currency is made and no special hinderances are imposed upon the trade. But as soon as an inflation takes place in the money of A. and the purchasing power of this money is therefore, diminished, the value of the A-money in B must necessarily be reduced in the same proportion. Hence the following rule:

When two currencies have been inflated, the new normal rate of exchange will be equal to the old rate multipled by the quotient between the degrees of inflation of both countries. There will, of course, always be fluctuations from this normal rate, and in the period of transition these fluctuations are apt to be rather wide. But the rate calculated in the way indicated must be regarded as the new parity between the currencies. This parity may be called the *purchasing power parity,* as it is determined by the quotients of the purchasing powers of the different currencies."

Purchasing power parity in relative terms

In relative, terms, if the purchasing power of one currency declines compared to that of another, this decline should be reflected in the exchange rate. We can know this by multiplying the old purchasing power parity by the ratio of the changes in the internal purchasing power of the currencies. This was Cassel's revised version of PPP theory given in 1920. This can be formulated as under:

$$Ri = \frac{Pa_i}{Pa_o} / \frac{Pb_i}{Pb_o} \times R_o$$

Here Pi means the present rate of exchange;
R_0 means the old rate of exchange;
Pa_0 means the price level of A country in base year;
Pai means the present price level in A country;
Pb_0 means the price level of B country in base year;
Pbi means the present price level in B country.

The new parity on the basis of old parity can be calculated with the help of an example. Suppose the base year is 1970. In that year the base year Index in India was 100 and in USA 90. Suppose the same was 225 and 135 respectively in 1980. Then the exchange rate if it was \$ 1: Rs. 5 in 1970 will become \$ 1: Rs. 7.5 in 1980, thus:

$$Ri = 5 \times \frac{225}{100} / \frac{135}{90}$$

$$= 5 \times \frac{225}{100} \times \frac{90}{135} = \frac{15}{2}$$

$$= 7.5$$

The index numbers prepared in two countries can serve us. Index numbers naturally include a representative basket of goods and services. Index numbers can be comprehensive but cannot be based on all commodities produced in a country.

The purchasing power parity therefore becomes time and space relative. Free market rates of exchange reflect the composite character of the commodities which underlie demand and supply for exchange and demand and supply curves take their shape from the relative elasticities of these two factors. The strict purchasing power parity doctrine not only stated that the exchange rate *should* reflect relative currency values; it also stated that it *would* do so if no interferences prevented it.

Critical estimate of the theory of PPP

The PPP theory was critically evaluated by many economists notable amongst them Wasserman and Hultman, Aftalion, Hawtrey, Taussig, Pigou and S.E. Harris.

Wasserman and *Hultman* have pointed out that in the absence of common standard commodities that form the basis of index numbers of two countries, it becomes erroneous to compare the purchasing power of the two countries' currencies on the basis of the index numbers. Commodities that materially affect the index number of a country may not be produced at all in the other country.

Aftalion has rightly pointed out that while the PPP theory emphasizes that a change in the price level (say inflation) brings change in the rate of exchange (it falls), the opposite can also be true. Any cause may first bring a fall in the rate of exchange and this may raise the price level or bring inflation.

Hawtrey has suggested that while comparing the purchasing power of the currencies of the two countries the prices of services should also be included in the index numbers of the countries. He has rightly pointed out that since the price of' services' is usually higher in developed countries, their non- inclusion shows higher purchasing power of the developed countries. The inclusion of the prices of the services which are cheap in less developed countries will show a lower rate of inflation in comparison to developed countries.

Taussig, Neisser and *Pigou* suggested that if the exchange rate determination theory is to be linked to the purchasing power (as it is) then the index numbers that are to be used to compare the relative rates of inflation (or deflation) must be prepared on the basis of those commodities only that enter into international trade. Goods and services that used domestically should not be used to prepare the index numbers to be used to compare the international purchasing power of two currencies.

Harris also points out that internal prices of only those commodities and services that enter into international trade should be compared. Even *Gustav Cassel* later acknowledged that the exchange rate under paper standard is not determined solely in the ratio of relative change in purchasing power of two currencies; international movement of capital also affects it profoundly.

Heckscher has also criticised the theory on the same grounds as Harris, Pigou, Taussig or Neiser have criticised. He is also of the opinion that the theory is not valid when applied to the general price levels. He writes:

> "The conception that the exchanges represent relative price levels; or what is the same thing, that the monetary unit of a country has the same purchasing power both within the country and outside it is correct only upon the never existing assumption that all goods and services can be transferred from one country to another without cost. In this case, the agreement between the prices of different countries is even greater than that which is covered by the conception of an identical purchasing power of the monetary unit, for not only average price levels but also the price of each particular commodity or service will then be the same in both countries if computed on the basis of the exchanges."[2]

J.M. Keynes had similarly written:

"Only internationally traded goods will influence the demand for and the supply of foreign currency and consequently, the rate of exchange. Commodities which are only domestically traded, on the other hand, have no direct bearing on the exchange value of the currency and their prices may, therefore, fluctuate without affecting directly and immediately the exchange rate. Confined to internationally traded commodities, the purchasing power parity theory becomes an empty truism.[3]

Halm also believes that the domestic prices follow rather than precede the movement of exchange rates. He writes:

> "A process of equalisation through arbitrage takes place so automatically that the national prices of commodities seem to follow rather than to determine the movement of the exchange rates.""[4]

Ragner- Nurkse considered the theory of limited value because it takes into consideration only the price movements as the main causative factor. There are innumerable other factors that affect foreign exchange rate and they are not taken into consideration by Cassel. He writes:

"The theory treats demand simply as a function of price, leaving out of account the wide shifts in the aggregate income and expenditure which occur in the business cycle (as a result of market forces or government policies), and which lead to wide fluctuations in the volume and hence the value of foreign trade even if prices or price relationships remain the same.[4]

Pointwise there criticisms can be put as under:

(1) A satisfactory measure of purchasing power of two currencies is generally lacking. Index numbers published by different countries are based on different base years and are not strictly comparable. The number of commodities that are included in different countries not only may differ in number but also in nature and quality. There are innumerable commodities and services that are not produced and consumed in other countries. Index numbers may be based on different weights assigned to different commodities. As such even index numbers do not give true picture of the relative purchasing power of the two countries.

(2) This theory does not analyse the demand aspects of foreign exchange fully. This theory is based on the assumption that foreign exchange is demanded for imports only. Foreign exchange is demanded as loans for the repayment of foreign loans, for making gifts, for unilateral transfers, for payment of royalties or for payment of compensation and indemnities also. Foreign exchange is also demanded for making use of such invisible import services as shipping, insurance and banking. Interest and profits dividends to foreign creditors and investors (dividends) are also to be paid in foreign exchange. The foreign exchange is thus the result of the working of a myriad forces summarized by the balance of payments and not simply by the balance of trade.

(3) The exchange rate according to this doctrine should reflect the prices of all goods and services in an economy. Yet *the true comparisons of purchasing power can be made on the basis of the relative price changes in the internationally trade commodities only.* Construction, the majority of services, as well as a host of commodities (typical for domestic consumption only *e.g., dhoties* in India) effect the domestic price level only and have no bearing at all on international trade or the market for foreign exchange. Changes in prices of all such goods and services should be reflected in the PPP exchange rate only insofar as they affect the costs and prices of traded goods and services, which is necessarily only partially.

(4) *The transport costs are ignored by the PPP theory.* Just as the cost of sending gold (insurance, interest, packing and freight charges) do not allow the market rate of exchange to become equal to the mint par rate of exchange in gold standard, similarly the transport costs do not allow the actual market rate of exchange to become equal to the rate determined by the purchasing power parity in paper standard. Differences in transport cost will not permit international trade, even when there are differences in purchasing power; if the former are greater.

(5) *The PPP theory ignores changes in incomes, tastes and balance of payment.* Even if the purchasing power of one currency deteriorates, the balance of trade of that country may actually improve and the exchange rate shift in its favour as a result of factors other than price changes. Price changes correspond to income changes only during periods of full employment and even then only in an upward direction. Only at such times a rise in monetary incomes is likely to be reflected rather fully

in the form of a general rise is prices and an equivalent decline in the purchasing power of the national currency.

(6) *It can also found that the changing purchasing power of the currency does not always act as a causative factor of exchange rate change;* opposite can also happen. Changing exchange rate also brings changes in the price level of the country, hence in the purchasing power of the currency. If the exchange rate of a currency is deliberately reduced and kept low, exports will be encouraged and imports will be discouraged. Money supply will increase and commodity supply for domestic consumption will go down. This will bring inflation in the country. PPP theory described the relation between purchasing power and exchange rate as being one-sided.

(7) *PPP theory is based on the assumptions of perfect competition and free trade, and hence is not realistic.* In the real world, myriad restrictions to international-trade variously separate the price structure prevailing in one country from those obtaining in others. Hence, the PPP theory in practice is even further limited as a guide to equilibrium-exchange rates. In practice, we can find that tariffs, quotas, exchange control measures, discriminatory practices can enable a country to maintain a higher than parity value of its currency. Restrictions on equalization of commodity and factor prices will not reflect the true purchasing power of the currency.

(8) *Wider aspects of changing economic relations between various countries are not taken into consideration by the PPP theory.* The exchange rate between two currencies can change with the entry of third country in trade or when the trade with a third country so changes that the trade with the second country is substantially changed. As the flow of trade will undergo changes, the demand and supply conditions of the foreign currency will change and hence the exchange rate will also change. The greater the share of foreign trade in national income accounting, the greater will be the change in internal price level as a result of change in exchange rate. It can never be said that the change in exchange rate is always the consequence of the change in domestic prices.

In the words of *Walter:*

> "The PFP theory might be considered a rough indicator of long-term, secular shifts In the equilibrium-exchange rate. Yet, in an age of large-scale, long-term capital flows in varying directions, variable unilateral transfers of large magnitude, and military commitments involving substantial, rigid flows of international payments, even this use of the PPP theory may be lost. in fact, the theory may even prove to be highly misleading about the equilibrium rate of exchange under such conditions."

Conclusion

Exchange rate is determined by several factors. Exchange rate is both a determined and a determining factor. Structural or real changes as well as monetary policy are relevant to the determination of an equilibrium exchange rate. The relative importance of various factors will differ. However, the relative rate of inflation (or deflation) dominate the rate determination in rough measure, if not in exact measure. The PPP theory gives a good approximation of an equilibrium rate.

Yeager has advanced the argument that any departure of the equilibrium rate from the purchasing power par caused by other than monetary forces is held within limits. These are termed as "commodity points", akin to gold points. He draws upon the well-known fact that, as a free exchange rate is driven up or down (as by long-term capital movements), more and more commodities will enter or leave the export list and more and more will depart from or enter the import list. This provides a defense measure against the departure of the equilibrium exchange rate from the purchasing power par. (However, commodity points will differ from commodity to commodity according to transport costs). PPP and fluctuating exchange rates go together.

Modified PPPT

This can be seen in computer sites. There is nothing special in this so-called theory. We can summarize the same in seven points:

(1) If we have lower inflation, our ER will improve.
(2) If we have favourable terms of trade, our ER will improve.
(3) If rate of interest rises and funds flow in, our ER will improve.
(4) If FDI and FII inflows are high in *net* terms, our ER will improve.
(5) If money supply remains as necessary, our ER will improve.
(6) If there is no creditflation, our ER will improve.
(7) If our fiscal deficits are not used in a massive way for public expenditure, our ER will improve.

NOTE

1. For merits of fixed exchange rates see elsewhere in this section of the book
2. See: "Sweden, Norway, Denmark and Iceland in the World War, 1930", *p.* 151.
3. See: "A Tract on Monetary Reform", p. 101.
4. See: "Monetary Theory", p. 524.
5. See: "International Currency Experience.", p. 126

21 Demand and Supply Theory of Exchange Rate Equilibrium

(1) INTRODUCTION
(2) DEMAND OF FOREIGN EXCHANGE
(3) THE SUPPLY OF FOREIGN EXCHANGE
(4) EQUILIBRIUM CONDITIONS AND FLUCTUATIONS IN EQUILIBRIUM
(5) EVALUATION OF THE THEORY

THE BALANCE OF PAYMENT OR DEMAND AND SUPPLY THEORY OF FOREIGN EXCHANGE RATE DETERMINATION

1. INTRODUCTION

Exchange rate is a price. It is the price of one currency in terms of another currency. Like any other price, its determination has also to be explained ultimately in terms of demand and supply. All other theories provide only partial explanation of the determining factors. Myriad factors that affect the price can be included in the demand and supply explanations. Ultimately the good old theory of demand and supply comes to the rescue of economists out to explain comprehensively the price determination of any commodity or service, money and foreign exchange included. (This probably led someone to remark that even if a parrot learns to speak 'demand' and 'supply' he can very well be called an 'economist'.)[1]

The determination of the foreign exchange rate can be explained with the help of elasticities of demand and supply. Haberler, therefore, wrote:

> "The exchange rate between the means of payment of two countries is determined, like all other prices, by supply and demand."

Ellsworth wrote:

> "There is a symmetry in the forces determining the demand and supply of foreign exchange. This symmetry helps one remember them. Four elasticities are involved on each side of the market, and of these, two are domestic in origin and two foreign."[2]

Mrs. Joan Robinson similarly writes:

> "The exchange rate is determined from day to day by supply and demand of home currency in terms of foreign currency. Such transaction is two sided and sales are equal to purchase, any change in the conditions of demand or of supply reflects itself in a change in the exchange rate, and at the ruling rate, the balance of payments balances from day to day, or from moment to moment."

Mchlup wrote:

"The study of the elasticities of supply and demand, its. thus, the core of the theory of foreign exchange rates."

Ellsworth writes:

"The two exchange rate systems (fixed and fluctuating) contrast. Under fixed rates, a balance-of-payments deficit or surplus actually develops and is measured (on the official settlements criterion) by the amount of official. compensatory financing undertaken by the monetary authorities. Under flexible rates, however. If market forces are allowed to work unimpeded, the demand and supply of foreign exchange establish a rate of exchange that automatically clears the market, so.that no actual or ex *post* payments deficit or surplus can appear."[3]

Sidney J. Wells writes:

"If a country is in external equilibrium at any given rate of exchange and the demand for its currency falls, we can speak of a deficit in its balance of payments, using the terms "balance of payments' In the sense of a market balance, as opposed to the concept of a classification of accounts. On the other hand, if demand for the currency rises, at any given rate of exchange, we can speak of a surplus on the balance of payment."[4]

2. DEMAND OF FOREIGN EXCHANGE

Before we study the equilibrium- foreign exchange rate of two currencies, we should first understand the nature of demand and supply of foreign exchange.

Foreign exchange is demanded by those who want to import commodities and services from abroad or who want to borrow equity/debenture money or foreign exchange for speculative transactions. The demand for foreign exchange is *derived* demand; dollar is not demanded for the sake of just having a dollar but because it can buy goods from USA and also from any other country. Foreign exchange is demanded for so many commodities and services and its demand is thus 'composite demand'.[5]

The elasticity of demand for foreign exchange reflects the responsiveness of buyers to a change in its price (rate of exchange). Thus demand is the function of rate of exchange; and rate of exchange is the function of its demand (also supply). There is thus two-way relationship between demand and the rate of exchange. The elasticity of demand is percentage change in quantity demanded divided by percentage change in price.[6]

If the demand for foreign exchange changes in the same proportion in which the rate of exchange changes, then the demand will be said to have unit elasticity. If, it changes in greater proportion it will be said to have elasticity greater than unity and if it changes in less than the same proportion in which the rate of exchange, then it will be said to be having elasticity less than unity.

For example:

(a) If the rate of exchange falls or rises by 10% (in other words the foreign currency becomes cheaper/costlier by 10%) and the demand for foreign currency increases/decreases by 10% then the demand is elastic.

(b) If the rate of exchange falls by 10% but the demand increases by more than 10% (say'20%), or when the rate of exchange rises by 10% but the demand decreases by more than 10% (say 18%) then the demand will be said to be highly elastic.

(c) If the rate of exchange falls by 10% but the demand increases by 8% only, then the demand for foreign exchange is inelastic or less elastic. Similarly when the rate of exchange rises by 10% but the demand falls only by say 7% then the demand for foreign exchange is less elastic.

Thus when the rate of exchange falls [7] (or when the value of domestic currency In terms of foreign currency increases):

(1) In case of the elastic demand the total foreign exchange payment will remain the same;

(2) In case of the highly elastic demand, the total foreign exchange payment will increase;

(3) In case of inelastic demand, the total foreign exchange payment will decrease.

When the rate of exchange increases[8] (or when the value of domestic currency in terms of foreign currency decreases):

(1) In case of the elastic demand, the total foreign exchange payment will remain the same.

(2) In case of the highly elastic demand, the total foreign exchange payment will decrease;

(3) In case of the inelastic demand, the total foreign exchange payment will increase.

Thus the demand for foreign exchange reflects infact the demand for foreign goods, services and capital. Demand for goods is the function of its price, the demand for foreign exchange is the function of the exchange rate.

***According to* Machlup:**

(*a*) The elasticity of demand for foreign exchange will be higher, the higher is the elasticity of the domestic demand for the articles which we import;

(b) The elasticity of demand for foreign exchange will be higher, the higher is the elasticity of supply of domestic products which compete in the domestic market with our imports.

(c) The elasticity of demand for foreign exchange will be higher, the higher is the elasticity of supply by foreign producers of the articles which we import.

(d) The elasticity of demand for foreign exchange will be higher, the higher is the elasticity of the foreign demand for their own products.

The elasticity of demand is the total of various types of demand for different commodities and services. Different importers will have different elasticities for the same commodities and services. The demand for certain commodities and services will be elastic, highly elastic and inelastic with different persons. The aggregate demand for foreign exchange will be the composite demand of various types of demand and the relative share will be important.

The demand for foreign exchange will also depend on the relation between imported and domestic commodities. But whatever be the elasticity of demand for a particular consumption article, its import demand will be having higher elasticity in comparison to its domestic demand. If domestic commodities are highly competitive to imported commodities in quality and price and can be produced in required quantities then the demand for imported commodities will be highly elastic indeed.

The demand for imported commodities will be highly elastic (hence for the foreign exchange also) if the commodity is luxury commodity, or when imported commodity has close substitutes in the country and when domestic substitutes supply is highly responsive to price changes.

As opposed to the above situations, the demand for foreign exchange will be less elastic or inelastic if the commodities to be imported are essential commodities and have no close substitutes in the country and when the supply of domestic goods is inelastic.

The demand for foreign exchange will mirror the demand for imports. The only difference is that the demand for foreign exchange is expressed in rates of exchange and amounts of foreign exchange, whereas the demand for imports is stated in terms of import prices and quantities of the goods (or services) demanded.

Most of the import commodities can be expected to have elastic demand. (Here we are taking into cosideration only the changes in the exchange rates and not in the export prices of the imported commodities.)

The demand for imports is not static. When the exchange rate goes up, the import prices go up. This enables many domestic producers to compete with foreign goods suppliers. The imported commodity may no longer be imported as. it becomes costly. Thus the import demand is always more elastic than the domestic demand.

Demand for foreign exchange for import of services, expenses in foreign countries and for transfer of capital

Foreign exchange is demanded by all these persons who want to go to foreign countries. Nations have to incur expenses on their diplomatic missions abroad. Nations have to spend money in exhibitions in foreign countries to bolster up their trade.

Foreign exchange speculators demand foreign currency if they expect that their price will rise in future (or their exchange rate will appreciate). If the interest rate of any Central Bank of foreign country rises, and is expected to rise further, the currency of that country will be demanded more by other countries. Foreign currency is also demanded by those investors who want the foreign capital goods. These investors will invite debenture credit or equity participation by foreigners. However, the equity participation will depend on the expected rate of profits on investment. In the words of Ellsworth.

> "International transfers of capital with the aim of profiting from an increase in the value of the principal, rather than to earn an income, may be like rifle shots, directed at specific long-term assets, or like the scattered discharge of a shot-gun directed at foreign assets in general. Purchase for appreciation of a particular long-term foreign asset, such as the stock of a corporation, would not be undertaken unless the buyers were reasonably certain that the foreign currency purchased would remain stable, or that it would appreciate, for currency depreciation could wipe out any gain from the appreciation of asset." (pp. 353-54).

Foreign exchange is demanded by all those who want to gift money abroad, who want to avail of the insurance services, services of the transporters, services of the brokers etc.

The demand curve of foreign exchange will be of the same type as the demand curve of any commodity. It will have negative slope downward towards the right.

However, the slope will be steep or flat according as the demand is inelastic or highly elastic. Thus:

The elasticity of demand for foreign exchange will depend not only on the elasticity of demand for foreign goods, services and capital but also on the elasticity of supply of import-competitive goods and services. The elasticity of demand for foreign exchange will also depend on the elasticity of supply of imported goods and the elasticity of demand for imported goods in the country of their origin. If the exchange rate of a currency of any country falls then these elasticities decide whether or not the foreign price of the imported good will fall or not. If the foreign price of the imports remains the same then the price of the imported good will change in the importing country solely due to change in the exchange rate. Then the elasticity of demand, for imports will determine the demand for foreign exchange.

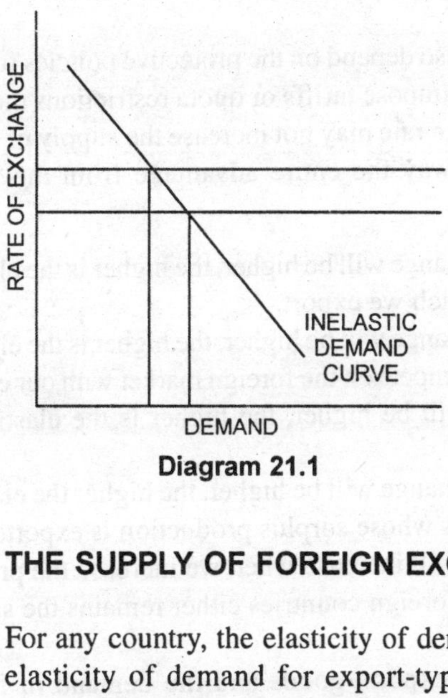

Diagram 21.1

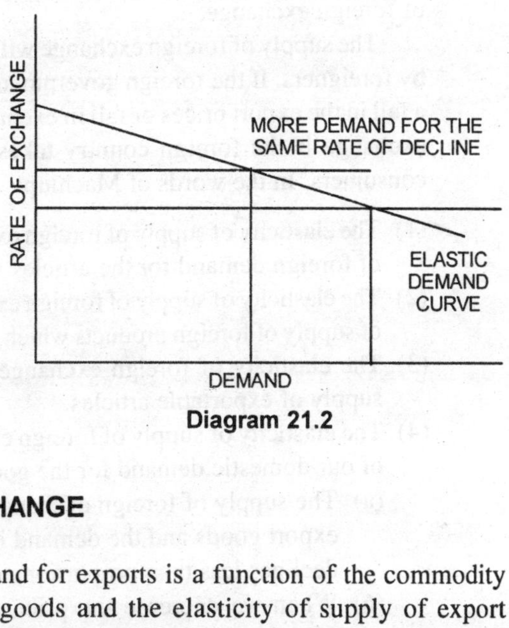

Diagram 21.2

3. THE SUPPLY OF FOREIGN EXCHANGE

For any country, the elasticity of demand for exports is a function of the commodity elasticity of demand for export-type goods and the elasticity of supply of export competing goods. The elasticity of supply of foreign currency will depend on the elasticity of supply of our exported goods and services.

The supply of foreign exchange comes from the exports of goods and services by a country and the amount spent by foreigners in the country as by tourists and embassies (which, in fact, means supplying goods and services to these tourists and embassies). The supply of foreign exchange will depend on *(i)* the supply elasticities of exportable goods and services and *(ii)* elasticity of domestic demand for these goods and services.

These elasticities determine how much increase will be there in the domestic prices of the exportable goods as a result of the rise in the exchange rate. If the domestic prices remain stable, then the international price of the exported goods will change according to the change in the exchange rate.

If as a result of the cheapening of the price, and elastic foreign demand, foreigners buy more and the supply of foreign exchange will increase. If as a result of the cheapening of the price, the demand of the foreigners does not increase in the same proportion, then supply of foreign exchange will not increase proportionately. The supply of foreign exchange in a country will increase when foreigners have great demand for goods and services of that country and when they are keen to bring capital, or are keen to visit the country as tourists and spend more and more money through their embassies. In other words, more receipts on account of the items of credit of the current and capital accounts of the balance of payment, increase the supply of foreign exchange.

If the commodity exported is a necessity then the foreigners will spend more even if the price is raised and the supply of foreign exchange will increase. In case the commodities exported are luxuries then an increase in price will not increase the supply of foreign exchange.

The supply of foreign exchange will also depend on the protective policies followed by foreigners. If the foreign governments impose tariffs or quota restrictions then even a fall in the export prices or fall in exchange rate may not increase the supply of foreign exchange if the foreign country takes away the entire advantage from the foreign consumers. In the words of Machlup:

(1) The elasticity of supply of foreign exchange will be higher, the higher is the elasticity of foreign demand for the articles which we export.
(2) The elasticity of supply of foreign exchange will be higher, the higher is the elasticity of supply of foreign products which compete on the foreign market with our exports.
(3) The elasticity of foreign exchange will be higher, the higher is the elasticity of supply of exportable articles.
(4) The elasticity of supply of foreign exchange will be higher, the higher the elasticity of our domestic demand for the goods whose surplus production is exported:
   (a) The supply of foreign exchange will increase when we increase the prices of export goods and the demand in foreign countries either remains the same or declines less than proportionately;
   (6) When we decrease the price of exports goods and the demand in foreign countries increase more than proportionately;
   (c) When the foreigners demand more of our goods, the domestic producers can respond and increase the supply;
   (d) When we increase production a large part of it can be exported and the marginal rate of exportable surplus increase is higher than the average rate; and
   (e) When we increase price of export goods the foreigners may not be able to increase the supply of those goods in their countries.

The supply curve of foreign exchange will be

(i) positively sloping from left to the right if the elasticity of foreign demand for the country's exports and, therefore, for its curency is greater than unity;
(ii) it will be vertical if the elasticity of demand for the country's exports is unity; and
(iii) it will be backward sloping if the elasticity of foreign demand

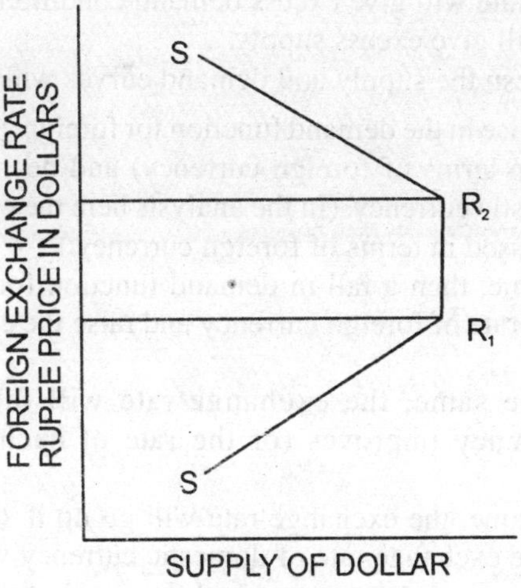

Diagram 21.3

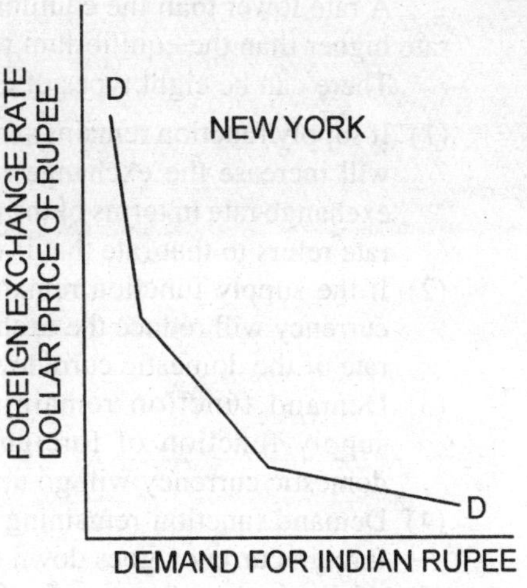

Diagram 21.4

The supply curve shows that while it is positively sloping even a rise in exchange rate increases the supply of foreign exchange; when the supply curve becomes vertical, then rising exchange rate keeps the supply of foreign exchange at the same level and when the supply curve becomes backward sloping, it shows that a rise in the exchange rate of domestic currency will decrease the supply of the foreign currency.

The demand curve has also been shown to have three segments. From D to A a fall in the foreign exchange rate increases the demand for domestic currency abroad in less than proportion; between A and B in the same proportion and between B to D' in more than proportion.

4. EQUIUBRIUM CONDITIONS AND FLUCTUATIONS IN EQUILIBRIUM

Like any other price, the exchange rate is determined at the intersection of the demand and supply curves. This gives equilibrium rate of exchange. It shall remain unchanged till the supply and demand curves remain the same or so change that the change in one is exactly counteracted by the other. Thus:

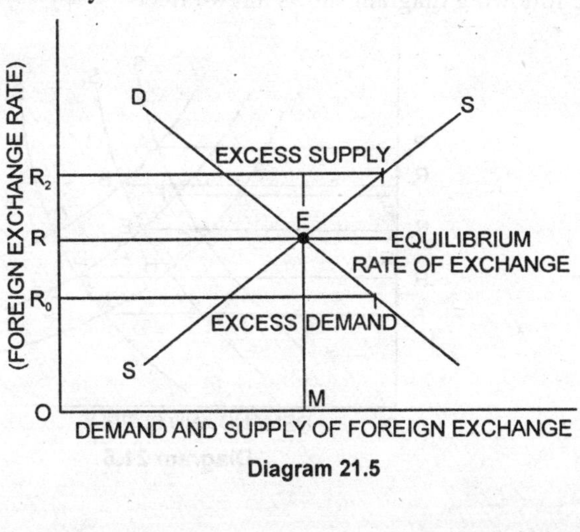

Diagram 21.5

A rate lower than the equilibrium rate will give excess demand condition while a rate higher than the equilibrium rate will give excess supply.

There can be eight types of changesn the supply and demand curves which are:

(1) If supply function remains same, a rise in the demand function for foreign exchange will increase the exchange rate (in terms of foreign currency) and decrease the exchange rate in terms of the domestic currency. (In the analysis here the exchange rate refers to that rate that is expressed in terms of foreign currency.)

(2) If the supply function remains same, then a fall in demand function for foreign currency will reduce the exchange rate of foreign currency and raise the exchange rate of the domestic currency.

(3) Demand function remaining the same, the exchange rate will fall if the supply function of foreign currency improves (or the rate of exchange of domestic currency will go up).

(4) Demand function remaining the same, the exchange rate will go up if supply of foreign currency goes down (or the exchange rate of domestic currency will fall).

(5) If the demand function for foreign exchange goes up and the supply function of the same goes down, then the exchange rate will rise considerably (or the rate of exchange of domestic currency will go down considerably).

(6) If the demand function for foreign exchange falls and the supply function of foreign exchange increases then the rate of exchange of foreign currency will go down considerably (*i.e.*, less domestic currency will exchange for foreign currency or the rate of exchange of domestic currency will go up).

(7) If the demand function for foreign currency goes up and the supply function also goes up, then the effect on foreign exchange rate will depend on the ratio of change between D and S. If the demand function increases relatively more than the effect of exchange rate will be the same as listed at (1) above; and if the supply function increases relatively more than the effect will be the same on exchange rate as listed as (2) above

(8) If the supply function of foreign exchange decreases and demand function also decreases, then the effect on rate of exchange will depend on the ratio of change between D and S. If the demand function decreases relatively more than the effect on the exchange rate will be same as listed at (3) above and if the supply function decreases relatively more than the effect on exchange rate will be same as listed at (4) above.

The following diagram shows a few effects:

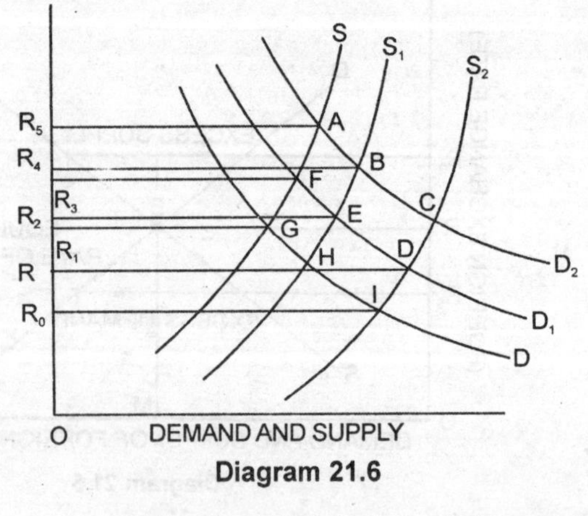

Diagram 21.6

In the above diagram it can be seen:

(1) Exchange rate OR rules at equilibrium point H and D. In these cases changes in the demand and supply function in the same direction (rise: if we move from H to D fall; if we move from D to H) cancel out each other and there is no change in the exchange

(2) On demand curve D as the supply function shifts from S to S_1 and S_2, the exchange rate falls from R_l to R and R_0. If we take into account the shift from equilibrium points I to H and then to G, it can be shown that falling supply function will increase the exchange rate.

(3) Movement from F to E to D and from D to E to F repeat the same thing as in the point (2) above. The same is true about the movement from A to B to C or from C to B to A.

(4) A movement from G to F to A shows that on the same supply function when the demand function)for foreign exchange rises, exchange rate also rises from R_1 to R_3 to R_5. If we study the movement from A to F to G we can show the effect of fall in demand function for foreign exchange, when the supply function is the same.

(5) If we study movement from H to E to B/I to D to C or the reverse movement from B to E to H/C to D to I, we get the same result as in (4) above.

(6) The above diagram also shows that changes in exchange rates from R_0 to R_5 are not uniform. These are due to changes in demand and supply functions different directions/ratios.

The supply and demand conditions change dut to exchange rate and the exchange rate changes due to changes in demand and supply. *When we study the changes in exchange rate as a result of the changes in the demand and supply we study the theory of price / exchange rate; but, if we study the changes in demand and supply as a result of the changes in the exchange rate, we are studying the laws of demand and supply of the foreign exchange. The theory of exchange rate determination studies change in the exchange rate us determined factor and not as determining factor.*

5. EVALUATION OF THE THEORY

The theory is regarded as comprehensive. However, it is a perfect competition theory and since the perfect competition in international trade/money movement does not exit. It is not considered to be adequate to explain many types of changes in the exchange rate. As a balance of payment theory it poses a problem: how to explain changes in exchange rate when strictly speaking, "balance of payment always balances". If payments must necessarily balance, there can be no meaning to a decline in the exchange rate during an unfavorable trade balance; an uncovered balance simply does not exist. So we take into account the supply and demand conditions of the first three accounts of balance of payment. In other words the reserve adjustment account of loans taken and loans given for b.o.p. is not taken into accounts. changing equilibrium makes the theory indeterminate. However, despite imperfections the theory is nearer to truth. Probably the PPP theory and BOP theory combined can give us better insight into the theory of exchange rate determination.

NOTE

1. Fritz Matchlum: Ch.. 5 "Readings in (he Theory of International Trade". 1949, I.E.A.
2. Mrs. Joan robiason: Ch. 5: "The Foreign Exchange", I.E.A's *op. cit.* Ellasworth: *op cit.*
3. Mrs. Joan Robinson: I.E.A's *op. cit.*, p. 83
4. Machlup: I.E.A.'s *op. cit.*, p. 111.
5. Ellsworth: *op. tit.*, p. 336.
6. Wells: *op. cit.*, p. 177.
7. Say, becomes \$ 1 = Rs. 19 from J 1 = Rs. 28. We can write 48 also.
8. Say, becomes \$ 1 = Rs. 27 from \$ 1 = Rs. 28 or we can write 47 to 48.

22 Some Other Theories of Determination of Exchange Rate

1. Mundell Fleming Model.
2. Monetary Model.
3. Sticky Price Model *Vs.* Flexible Exchange Model.
4. Random Walk Model.
5. Portfolio Balancing Model.
6. Current Account Model.
7. Capital Account Monetary Model.
8. Asset Market Model.
9. Direct and Indirect Exchange Rate.

At the very outset the author would like to comment that

If these models are *important,* they were *not original.*
If these models were *original* they were *not important.*

The writers had something to say but all they could manage was to rehash the words and points of the components of the demand and supply theory. Words changed but substance was the same.

1. MUNDELL FLEMING MODEL

Actually this model was a writeup about devaluation. The economists of the developed countries wanted that the developing economies should not protect their exchange rate during inflation. They were of the opinion that if the developing economies were having adverse inflation differential (higher), then they should devalue their currencies forthwith.

The less developed countries were advised that if they keep on devaluing their currencies periodically (bringing down the exchange rate of their currencies and allow the rate of exchange of dollar to rise *vis-a-vis* their own currency), then their exports will increase.

Devaluation helps only when the four elasticities favour:

(1) The demand for our exports abroad should be elastic so that when the international prices go down, there is higher demand from abroad after devaluation.

(2) The demand for the imports from foreign countries should also be elastic so that when the foreign goods become costlier, less of them are purchased.

(3) The supply of the foreigners should be inelastic. In other words, when the demand for their goods in the country which is devaluing the currency, imports less they have to reduce their export prices. Then the devaluing country will not pay more. Infact they can keep on paying the same price in domestic currency as well. The foreigner should not be able to sell elsewhere.

(4) The supply responses of the devaluing country should be positive. Devaluation makes the exports cheaper and if the demand picks up from abroad, the devaluing country should be able to produce more.

2. MONETARY MODEL OF EXCHANGE RATE

(1) Monetary model emphasises that the impact of the change in money supply on the exchange rate is indirect via its impact on the rate of interest. (Excess credit is also included in excess money supply).

(2) A plethora of money supply reduces the rate of interest and on this count only, there will be adverse effect on the rate of interest it will go down. Less funds will flow in. ER will be down.

(3) At the same time there will be higher inflation which will reinforce the downward drop in the exchange rate.

(4) If money supply is less, then the rate of interest will rise and this will attract the foreign funds. ER will improve. Besides absence of inflation or lower inflation also help in ER going up. **But the monetary model does not make a recommendation that in order to improve the rate of exchange money supply should be reduced. Monetary model suggests the linking of money supply to the requirements of economic development of the country.** Money is to act as a facilitator or a catalytic agent of development.

3. STICKY PRICE MODEL VERSUS FLUCTUATING EXCHANGE RATE MODEL

This is nothing except the discussion on fixed versus fluctuating/floating exchange rate. The fixed rate is called "sticky".

- PPP theory accepts that there will be changes in the international purchasing power and hence there will be changes in the exchange rates. The flexibilities in the exchange rate will be subject to the PPP.
- Exchange rate can be sticky due to government intervention. It has tendency to remain sticky as much as possible. PPP may change but many prices may not change. Prices may change but PPP may not change. PPP may change but the exchange rate may not change.

Sticky exchange rate is that when the PPP falls, the currency should be devalued; but it is not devalued, and the ER remains more or less the same.

(See chapter on Devaluation).

This is not something that deserves to be called a new theory of exchange rate.

4. RANDOM WALK MODEL

This is no model but a play of words.

1. Exchange rate does not "stand still."
2. It cannot and should not be allowed to "run down" or "run up"
3. It will have a "random walk"; and it should have it.

"Random walk" is unsteady and unpredictable, Just like that of a drunkard. He can take a step forward or backward even when trying to go forward. He may go forward while trying to go backward. **Moose** and Rogoff (1983) had two things to say: First, exchange rate can depend upon any factor. Secondly, the change in the exchange rate as a result of some other change is not instantaneous but after a time lag. To have a favourable exchange rate, following things are necessary:

1. Self-sufficiency in food.
2. Strong defence.
3. Subdued inflation.
4. Low external loan.
5. Right structure of the sectors of the economy.
6. Changes in the sectoral growth to be of right dimension.
7. Changes in the ER to be in the right direction.
8. Balance between exports and imports.

5. PORTFOLIO INVESTMENT MANAGEMENT AND PORTFOLIO THEORY (From Which the Exchange Rate Economics Can Also be Deduced)

This theory was propounded by HM Markowitz. He demonstrated how the risks can be "calculated". Returns can be calculated easily because they are a much certain position.... atleast in interest calculation.

More the changes of high returns, higher the risks.

Least risk assets are likely to be less profitable as well. Hence it is necessary that the asset portfolios should be divergent. Nothing was new because there was a very old saying "do not put all of your eggs in one basket".

- Diversified portfolio is Active portfolio.
- Non-diversified portfolio is Passive portfolio strategy.
- Patient portfolio is one where fixed returns are received.
- "Aggressive" portfolio is one where those which have promise of high returns and high risks also.
- Conservative portfolio is one where the past trend of returns is examined first. The growth rate in returns is studied. Then with an eye on the prospective yields, the investment is made.

"There is play of words in these five points." Markowitz got Nobel Prize in Economics for this in 1990, for writing on balancing the risks and profits.

There were exercises about the coefficient of corelation between various types of portfolio risks and returns.

Exchange Rate

If a country receives a lot of foreign exchange from abroad because its investment portfolios attract foreign inflows, then the rate of domestic currency will rise and vice-versa.

Massive inflow will mean greater reserves of foreign currencies and hence higher rate of domestic currency.

If foreign portfolios are desired by the "natives" and there are outflows of investment in them, then the rate of foreign currencies will rise and of the domestic currency will fall.

A portfolio is actually a bag with many pockets/folds. One can keep many currencies/papers in those pockets. If two pockets hold the US $ and EURO respectively, buying EURO and selling dollars is portfolio reshuffling. The dollar is sold if its value or exchange rate is expected to fall. The holder will be a loser. Buying EURO is safe because its value is rising. Then who buys the dollars when its value is falling ? Naturally those countries which need dollar reserves and were not having them in sufficient quantities.

Expectations play an important role in reshuffling. **Two persons may take different actions under the same circumstances and at** the same **time to different perceptions or expectations about** the future. There is a circuit of changes.

- Demand and supply factors change the exchange rates.
- Exchange rates change the demand and supplies of goods.
- Changes in the demand and supply of goods change demand and supplies of the factors of production and hence their prices.
- These changes bring changes in the supplies and prices of goods. Then demand also changes.
- These changes bring further changes in exports, imports and rate of exchange.

There is constant reshuffling of the "positions" which relate to not merely commodities, goods, services, prices, demand supplies, but also in the rate of exchange. Causes bring consequence and consequences become the causes. The reshuffling goes on and there are interventions also. Financial assets are perfect substitutes of each other and their rates (exchange rate is a price/rate) of reshuffling bring constant changes.

It goes without saying that the rate of exchange of that currency will go up of which demand is more and supply is relatively less. The rate of exchange of that currency will go down of which supplies are relatively more.

Important currencies matter to all, but domestic currency is relevant to the country concerned. The currencies of Urundi and Brundi (which are constantly having tribal warfare) are unimportant to India and to the USA but these countries will have to have a rate of exchange with dollar. They want dollar to import with the help of their money, the imports are paid for with exports. Money is a medium. Balance of trade matters in the exchange rate economics. Higher rate of inflation brings down the exchange rate. Higher rate of interest can raise the rate of exchange if funds are attracted from abroad.

6. CURRENT ACCOUNT THEORY

Some new theories like *(I)* Current account theory, *(II)* Capital account monetary theory. *(III)* Asset theory, (/v) Portfolio theory are at best partial theories of exchange rate. Too much importance has been given to too little.

The theory tells us that if the current account balance is adverse the rate of exchange will go down. If it is surplus the rate of exchange of the domestic currency will go up or of the foreign currency/currencies will go down.

This is not vindicated always. Take the example of 2006 only for India. The curent account was adverse to the tune of $ 7 b. during the year. That came to $ 700 crore and translated at the terminal exchange rate on 31st December, it came to Rs. 31325 crore. Yet during the entire year of 2006, India's exchange rate improved.

There are many items of the currernt account and not the individual item but the balance of all items would affect the rate of exchange. These items are:

Inflows and outflows due to exports and imports.

Net flows due to tourism.

Net flows on embassy expenses (of other countries in any country and of that country in all other countries.

Net flows due to interest payments. Net flows due to brokerage, commission and all types of charges of the middlemen.

Net flows on insurance.

Net flows on international transport and communications.

As, was seen elsewhere **also, there are four accounts of the balance of payment. BALANCE OF PAYMENT ALWAYS BALANCES. IT IS NEVER IN DEFICIT OR IN SURPLUS:** But this is only when all the four accounts are taken into account. **Balance of payment will** be **in deficit or surplus on the first three accounts.** Hence not the current account for the "reserve adjustment account" will decide the rate of exchange. **If loans are taken, exchange rate falls. If loans** are **given the rate of exchange rises.**

See: $ b. + is loan given, (—) is loan taken

	Case 1:			Case 2:
	Payments	*Receipts*	*Payments*	*Receipts*
Current	1500	1400	1400	1500
Capital	100	300	300	100
Unilateral	60	450	450	60
Transfer	1660	2150	2150	1660
Reserve Adj.	+490			—490
	2150	2150	2150	2150
ER Rises			**ER will fall**	

7. CAPITAL ACCOUNT MONETARY MODEL OF DETERMINATION OF EXCHANGE RATE

(l) This model emphasises that if money supply is greater than the demand for money, the prices will be higher and the exchange rate will fall. This will not be instantaneous but via effect on production and purchasing power. Infact it will depend upon the interface between the last two variables.

(2) If the money supply is less than the demand for money, this will be deflationary. This is no way to increase the exchange rate. There will be low production. Then higher prices can result. One does not burn one's own house to roast the toast free! No country can and should, follow a deliberate deflationary policy. The Nirwana of exchange rare management does not lie in keeping the money supply low.

(3) **CAPM (Capital Asset Pricing Model) is also related** to **ER.** This **model** emphasises that if returns are imperfectly correlated, then diversify the assets. There should be unequal distribution. If foreign assets are also involved, exchange rate will be affected.

(4) If the returns on capital are perfectly correlated, **which is not a fact of life,** then equal distribution is possible.

(5) Impact of capital account flows (inflows and outflows) are obvious. If net inflows are in favour of the country, then ER will rise and vice versa.

(6) Capital risk diversification affects ER via hedging and arbitrage operations. International trade in derivatives, options, futures and forwards profoundly affects the ER.

(7) The higher the size of the national income the higher the ER, provided inflation is managed: and, vice-versa.

(8) The rate of increase in national income is also important. The country with high benchmark GDP as well as high growth rate will see that its ER is rising.

(9) If money supply in a country increases at a faster rate than the other country, then ER may go down via inflation effect.

(10)Capital account of the balance of payment, if favourable, will increase the ER and vice versa.

8. "ASSET APPROACH" TO DETERMINATION/MANAGEMENT OF FOREIGN EXCHANGE RATES.

It is to be noted that 'asset approach" is proxy of the "current account monetary model" because assets, particularly, foreign assets have an impact on current account.

(Hence *when a question is on any one theory or model, the students can include other models either as improvements or as complementary theories/models. Then their answer will become of a proper size also).*

(1) Asset model is related to exchange rate. In the first instance we purchase two assets only after comparing the price. Suppose a car made in the US comes in $ 10,000 and a similar car comes from Italy in comes in 9,500 EURO. Then (at the rate of 1 Euro =$ 1.2, it will come in $ 11,400, though it looks as if 9500 are lower

than 10,000. This comparison will be valid only if the two cars are of the same quality.

(2) Assets are purchased more from that country of which currency is depreciating because fewer units of the foreign currency will be needed. In case the value of the foreign currency appreciates, less will be purchased as more units of the foreign currency will be needed.

[Once upon a time a Rouble (currency of Russia) used to command higher market price $, under the communist regime. Then in 2000, its exchange rate was $ 1= 6 Roubles 6. In 2001 if rose to 26 roubles I if price of vodka in Roubles was the same 100, then in dollar terms it was coming in $ 16.7 and in 2001 if was coming in just $ 3.88; hence the asset preference will be for Russian goods, if the quality is the same.

(3) We can discuss something more about certain assets. It is to be remembered that all assets have degree of moneyness in them. A car purchased earlier has also moneyness in it. It can be sold as a secondhand car. Its moneyness is not as liquid as of the rupee proper. It will take time to convert it into money. If instantaneous conversion is required, the buyer of the secondhand car will pay very little taking advantage of the dire need of the seller.

We can list the following national and International assets for the purpose of exempllifying the impact on exchange rate. The list of the assets can be endless indeed. Here we are listing any a few.

NATIONAL Assets	**INTERNATIONAL Assets**
Money	Key Currencies
Commodities	Commodities
Goods	Goods
"Human capital"	"Human capital"
Domestic debt papers	International bonds
Bills of exchange	Bills of exchange (Int.).

(A) Explanation of Interfaced between International assets and Exchange rates.

Key Currencies. They are inter-changed in the business of making money with money. Banks, financial institutions, non- banking financial institutions, multinational corporations, other companies **of which value is high and is expected to become higher.** The sellers in this case are those who do not wait for further rise in that currency. Each transaction requires two parties to get completed. They sell those currencies of which **value is feared to become lower** and they find buyers who would like to buy at a lower rate.

Expectations and actual rates. If the value of Yen is expected to rise and of the dollar is expected to fad, then the professional operators in the finance market will buy Yen and sell dollars. **What was expected will happen.** The dollar rate was expected to fall and it will fall due to its selling., the Yen rate was expected to rise and it rises due to higher demand.

Then as the rate of dollar becomes lower and lower, speculators expect it to rise. They start buying to take advantage of the market situation. Then the dollar rate starts rising. **Expectations can play havoc with the currency of which is expected to fall and can catapult the currency of which the rate was expected to rise.**

Commodities are asset with the seller. Their selling brings foreign exchange. The more one can sell (provided the prices of commodities do not crash due to excess supply), the more one earns the foreign exchange. Better balance of payment position will raise the rate of exchange of the domestic currency.

It is the net balance of buying and selling commodities. If the commodities bought involve greater payment, then the exchange rate **will fall.**

Goods and services. They are assets with the holder. Their buying means paying foreign currencies and selling means getting foreign currencies. **Balance of the net flows will decide the impact on the change rate on the good old principle of demand and supply.**

The **rules are simple. In the** case of domestic economy, higher demand for commodities, goods and services (supply function remaining the same) will **push up** prices. Similarly in international business **the impact on exchange rate will be earlier than on the intenational prices or on the prices where from commodities, goods and services emanate.**

"Human Capital". If a family prefers giving high education to the children and wards. It means that the preference for money is nor there. Preference is for future human capital. In simple words, money will be spent it will not be hoarded. If Indians go abroad in large numbers for getting higher education then the exchange rate of Indian rupee will be adversely affected (come down). If the Indians settle abroad and earn huge incomes in comparison to what they would have earned in their "native" countries, then the inflow will improve the exchange rate.

Bonds. If foreigners invest in Indian bonds, the inflow of money will improve India's ER. If indians are investing abroad, the ER of rupee will go down. The impact will be on the net flow. Bonds are preferred to money if the future yields are expected to be high. Past yield curves are a good guide in this regard.

Bills of exchange are assets. They temporarily "lock-in" the money. If Indians export and prepare bills (invoices) money will come from abroad. Exports improve ER. Large number of bills receivables also do the same. if they are discounted. If not (which is not done), then the impact will be after a time lag. Bills payable are for imports and they depress the country's ER or improve the ER of the vehicle currency.

Asset theory emphasises that the fixed ER avoid shocks but they become shackles. The fluctuating exchange rate give shocks as well as absorb shocks, provided hedging and insulation facilities are therein the **developed** countries, the asset markets are similar in size. In less developed countries, **the** asset markets are dissimilar in size. Some centres have somewhat bigger market and some smaller. In all cases the asset markets **of** the developing economies are smaller in economic size than those of the developed countries.

Segmentation of the asset markets

Surprising it may seem, this does not relate to any spatial or temporal segmentation. Those who wrote about this theory wrote that there are two segments of the exchange rates:

(*i*) Fixed ER markets
(ii) Fluctuating ER markets.

We are once again at the same topic of fixed, fluctuating and managed float rates. Earlier words had elegance of simplicity. These new fangled words give us nothing new but some "bombastic" words.

Changes in exchange rates are now designated as "shocks". Since **the changes are by different percentage points, these are known as "asymmetric".** As the impact various changes are always different even if the percentage change is the same, in the asset theory of exchange rated these differences are known as "differences in the "velocity of shocks".

Ultimately, the theory emphasises that there should be "optimum exchange rate." Markets bring random changes. Interventions can bring the optimum. The concept of optimum, however, remains elusive in the theory.
Some other points mentioned in the theory are:

- Choose the assets which give high interest.
- Choose the assets which give high returns/profits.
- Choose assets which are least costly for the same quality.
- Choose assets which promise high liquidity *i.e.,* easy convertibility to cash.
- Choose assets with least risks.
- Calculate the returns with care and proper mathematics. Have hedging and careful arbitrage.

DIRECT VERSUS INDIRECT QUOTING OF EXCHANGE RATE

It is **wrong** to say that if $ 1 = Rs. 45, then Re. 1 = $ 0.022 recurring. **Both are direct rates.** Those who say that the second quoted is indirect^ are wrong.

Indirect quotation of exchange is that if $ 1 = 5 rupees of Seychelles, then Re. 1 of Seychelles is equal to Rs. 9 of India.. Here the direct demand and supply conditions of Indian rupee versus Seychelles rupee have not been studied.

23 Theory of Exchange Rates: Fixed/Pegged Vs. Fluctuating/ Floating Exchange Rates: Multiple Exchange Rates: Discriminating Exchange Rates: Managed Float or Alternative Exchange Rate System.

SUMMARY POINTS.

PART A: FIXED EXCHANGE RATE SYSTEM:

Features and advantages that were conceived of this system that has been left.

1. Was in force between 1945-1971.
2. Exchange rates were fixed between currencies. Only the governments could change them up or down.
3. Exchange rates were changed on inflation differentials.
4. IMF used to force 'devaluation' on currencies that lost purchasing power, as much as it fell.
5. Fixed exchange rates discouraged exports if there was inflation and no devaluation.
6. Fixed exchange rates made imports costly after devaluation and there used to be smuggling due to non-devaluation.
7. IMF could force revaluation also on countries which kept currencies pegged even when they had massive balance of payment surpluses.
8. Fixed exchange rates enabled countries to know to how much they would have got for their exports and what were their liabilities for imports all fixed.
9. The interface between the economy and exchange rate was "certain".
10. Fixed exchange rates were associated with exchange controls and non-convertibility. Smuggling was common and imperative.
11. Fixed exchange rate system, if a devaluation in the rate was expected made importers hurrying payments and exporters delaying the receipt of payment. This was because

after the fall, importers would have paid more and exporters would have received more rupees.

12. Under the fixed exchange rate system and associated exchange control and non-convertibility, the exporters did not get dollars but rupees only and that too at official rate. The importers could be denied foreign exchange or were given dollars at very high rates.
13. Most of the dollars were used by the government for intervention to keep the rate stable. If the rate started falling in rupee terms, dollars were sold.
14. Government could not change the rate without the permission of the IMF, except in cases of change being less than 10 p.c.
15. Public sector planning used to be on assured costs.

Features and advantages of the "flexible" or "fluctuating" or "floating" or " volatile" exchange rate system GENERALLY THIS IS BEING FOLLOWED NOW A DAYS

1. Fixed exchange rate was a fetter on production. Now free availability of foreign exchange promotes production.
2. If all prices change, exchange rate cannot be kept stable and it is also changed according to demand and supply. Market changes the exchange rate.
3. Flexible exchange rates abolished two rates of exchange - one official and the other open market rate, and established one that was based on d' and s'.
4. Fluctuating exchange rates do not require smuggling.
5. Fluctuating exchange rates promote liberalisation and globalisation and massive international investment.
6. Fluctuating exchange rates help in creating greater employment. Inflation, if created, is auto-liquidating.
7. Fluctuating exchange rates do promote speculation. But excessive speculation itself kills excessive speculation.
8. Fluctuating exchange rate system gives true cost price relationship. Fixed exchange rate system was the system of "tail wagging the dog?. Economy had to be adjusted to the rate. Now rate is adjusted to the economy. This is the system of "tog wagging the tail". Right one also.

MULTIPLE EXCHANGE RATES SYSTEM OR DISCRIMINATORY EXCHANGE RATE SYSTEM

1. This was under fixed exchange rates.
   Different exporters could get rupees for dollars at different rates. Different importers could be given dollars at higher or lower rates. Tourists could be given more rupees for dollars.
2. Luxury exports could be made cheaper by giving more rupees per dollar. Essential goods could be imported at cheaper rate.
3. Dollars could be sold at higher rates for imports of luxury goods.
4. Balance of payment difficulties could be handled.
5. Capital goods could be imported cheaper for production.

Discrimination was practised against countries, importers, exporters/ investors or everything/everyone.

ALTERNATIVE EXCHANGE RATE SYSTEM, OR THE "MANAGED FLOAT" SYSTEM, OR" THE SNAKE IN THE TUNNEL SYSTEM", OR " MIDDLE SYSTEM", or the system of "CRAWLING BANDS" OR "TRAGETED BANDS". All countries follow this one system which has so many (as above) names

1. Upper and lower limits of fluctuations are fixed.
2. If domestic exchange rate falls, dollars are sold.
3. If the domestic exchange rates rises, dollars are bought.
4. Government purchases dollars, when its rate is down.
5. Government sells dollars when its rates are up.
6. Excessive fall in exchange rate ("dirty float") not allowed; Interventions (4 and 5 above) are made.
7. Governments purchase dollars by printing additional domestic currency and can buy dollars from the authorised dealers.

THEORY OF EXCHANGE RATES III

FIXED (PEGGED) VS. FLUCTUATING (FLOATING) EXCHANGE RATES MULTIPLE EXCHANGE RATES: DISCRIMINATING EXCHANGE RATES

THE TEXT

FIXED OR PEGGED EXCHANGE RATES. THEIR ADVANTAGES

The disadvantages of the fixed rates can be studied in the form of the advantages of the fluctuating exchange rates. They are one and the same.

(1) Fixed exchange rate system was forced by the IMF in the post Second World War period and it continued till 1971 so far as the vehicle currency dollar was concerned. Between the 1944-45 and 1971, the fixed exchange rate was $ 35 for one ounce of gold. All other currencies used to have their parities fixed in dollar. For example, in 1947, $ 1 was equal to Rs. 4.5 (or nearabout). In 2009, Dec. the rate was $ 1214 per ounce of gold.

(2) Under the fixed exchange rate system only the government used to change the rate even if the market rate of exchange used to become different. Market rate of exchange becomes lower if there is higher inflation differential in the country vis-a-vis the US dollar. For example, if the exchange rate is suppose $ 1 = Rs. 45 and inflation in India is 10 p.c. while in the US it is 1 p.c., the inflation differential becomes 9 (10 - 1). Now 9 p.c. extra rupees will have to be given in the market, i.e., $ 1 = Rs. 49.05. 9% of 45= 4.05+45=49.

(3) The official rate (known as parity rate) will remain the same under fixed exchange rate. It will change only when the government changes. The IMF used to force that. If the rate of the domestic currency is brought down to Rs. 49.05 or say Rs. 52, it used to be known as devaluation.

(4) Under the fixed exchange rate system the rate used to be changed once in several years. Devaluations and revaluations were resisted by the governments. There used to be open or black market rates and the official rates.

(5) Devaluation of the currency makes the exports cheaper and imports dearer. It has one advantage that it will encourage exports and discourage imports. But it had disadvantage also. It meant exporting more goods to get the same number/amount of goods in imports. If the demand for our exports is inelastic abroad, cheapening did not help. If India exports rice, lower prices of various types of rice will not increase demand from abroad. If India is exporting luxury goods (say cars), then only the devaluation will help as more cheaper cars will be demanded.

(6) Devaluation makes imports costly. If their demand is inelastic (way for wheat and pulses), we cannot reduce the imports. We will only be paying more.

(7) Revaluation used to be forced on the country of which the balance of payment was very favourable. Countries resisted revaluation because it made their exports dearer and imports cheaper. Japan has favourable balance of payment. It exports luxury goods. If the value of Yen was fixed higher, then exports were discouraged.

(8) *Fixed exchange rates meant that the country knew always what will the exports bring and how much the imports would cost.* In fluctuating exchange rate system the figures can change unless there was an agreement about the fixed payments.

(9) Fluctuating exchange rates keep on changing. They bring changes in the economy. These changes in the economy bring changes in the exchange rate. The world becomes ever-changing. The world of the fixed exchange rates was certain.

(10) Under the fixed exchange rate system ***there used to be (i) exchange controls and (ii) non convertibilities also*** Suppose under the fixed exchange rate system, the rate was \$ 1 = Rs. 26 while in the market the rate was \$ 1 = 36. Suppose a firm exported goods of \$ 100 crore. The draft of \$ 100 crore used to be given to the Government. The government used to give Rs. 2600 crore in exchange. Had that been sold in the market, the firm would have got Rs. 3600 crore. Fixed exchange rates promoted smuggling of goods and currency therefore.

(11) Under fluctuating rate if \$ 1 = Rs. 45 but is expected to become \$ 1 = Rs. 47, then the importers will hurry making payments because less will be paid now. The exporters will delay receiving the payment because more will be received in future. *In fixed exchange rate system speculative actions were not taken. Payments used to be orderly.*

(12) The exporters had no right over the dollars they earned. The government used to sell dollars to the importers at higher and lower prices (in rupees) at its sweet will. It also could deny selling of dollars. For example, if an importer wanted to import Scotch Whiskies, the foreign exchange could be denied to him.

(13) The national government of a country used to keep all the dollars or other foreign currencies. The government used to have *"sterilisation"* operations. This meant that if the dollar rate went up or the rupee rate went down, then the government used to supply/sell dollars. It came to the same thing as buying back the rupees. That way it used to prevent the rate of dollar from rising or the rate of the domestic currency from falling. *This is known as intervention.* It was not always successful because poor countries did not have enough dollars to intervene.

(14) The Government of the Centre had the power to change the official parity by less than 10 p.c. The IMF had the power to force the change higher than that.

(15) The project planning and the planning of the public sector development were easy under the fixed exchange rate system. Our liabilities towards others and the liabilities of others towards us were known.

FLEXIBLE. OR FLOATING EXCHANGE RATE SYSTEM

Economists realised that *economies should not be changed according to the exchange rate. The exchange rate should change according to the changes in the economy.*

The dog (economy) should wag the tail (exchange rate).The tail should not wag the dog.

(1) The market equates the demand and supply. If market mechanism is suppressed/ black markets emerge. Under fixed exchange rate system, there were no freedoms for the producers. Market functions blindly but not arbitrarily. If we leave everything to the market/ the demand and supply get equated or atleast adjusted. There is no need to control exports or imports.

(2) Dual exchange rates go. In other words, the "dichotomy" goes. Fluctuating exchange rates promote full production and full employment easily in the long run. That is economic neutrality. Just as the prices of various commodities, goods and services change as the incomes change, the exchange rate should also be allowed to change. People and the economy adjust. Price of wheat was Rs. 3 per quintal in 1938. Now it was Rs. 1800 per quintal. Incomes also change.

(3) Price stability is a myth. If all prices change, why and how can the exchange rates remain the same, except by chance. Over valuation and under valuation *of official rates* go away under flexible exchange rate system. *Up valuation and down valuation of the exchange rates in the markets also go.*

(4) The entire administration used to remain busy in checking the exchange rate fluctuations and "smuggling". The fact was that smuggling of goods and currencies used to be there *not despite government administration but because of them.*

(5) Balance of payment disequilibrium used to be there under the fixed exchange rate system also. Then the balance could be obtained by denying imports for industrial development and for consumption. Levels of living used to be low. Under the flexible exchange rate system, *exchange controls are removed and convertibilities of currencies are allowed.* These things promote liberalisation and globalisation. Trade and industry increase. Investment and employment increase atleast in the long run. The levels of living rise. Cheaper and better goods are available.

(6) Fixed exchange rates were deflationary. Flexible exchange rates are inflationary. But they can auto-liquidate the inflation. Flexible exchange rates encourage exports and imports on the basis of comparative advantage. Production increases in the long run. Hence inflation gets controlled.

(7) Government can acquire the foreign exchange from the market. The Central Bank of a country can have the dollar reserves. The Government can control violent fluctuations in exchange rate. Market can also be controlled. But rigorous controls as were needed under the fixed exchange rate systems are not necessary.

Uncertainties cancel uncertainties. People become used to them. Speculations are there in fluctuating exchange rates. But speculative activities keep wild speculation under auto-controls. There are bulls and there are bears. They check each other.

(8) Fluctuating exchange rates reflect the true cost-price relationships between various currencies.

MULTIPLE AND DISCRIMINATORY EXCHANGE RATES

They were under the fixed exchange rate systems. Under the multiple exchange rate system:

- Dollars for importing essential goods could be given at cheap rate in rupees.
- Dollars for importing luxury goods could be given at higher rupee (or domestic currency) rates.
- Those who earned huge amounts of dollars from abroad by exporting could be given the right to have higher amounts of dollars at higher rupee rates. In other words if all exporters were given Rs. 26 for a dollar/ the efficient ones could be given more than Rs. 26 per dollar.
- If more tourists were to be attracted, they could be given more rupees (or domestic currency if we are studying all countries in general) per dollar. This rate could be as near as market rate as was possible.

Multiple exchange rates are also known as discriminatory exchange rates. All are not treated equal, If that is so, it is discrimination

These advantages were *advantages of multiple/discriminatory rates.* They were so numerous that ultimately it was decided practising officially fluctuating exchange rates.

(1) Multiple exchange rates could promote exports on the basis of the elasticities of demand abroad. All goods need not be made cheap. Luxury goods could be made cheap. Incentives were there for exports in the form of higher rupee rates.

(2) Essential goods could be imported at cheaper rates. For example a dollar could be given at less than Rs. 26. (Here the example of 26 is an example but it was the official exchange rate in 1991, when flexibility in exchange rate was allowed in India for the first time).

(3) Imports of non-essential things could be made costlier. To import such things dollars could be given at higher rate say at Rs. 36 (this was the actual market rate in 1991) or even higher.

(4) With multiple exchange rates, exports could be promoted and imports could be discouraged. Thus balance of payment deficits could be tackled, if not fully atleast substantially. Multiple exchange rates are *best suited to tackle adverse balance of payment with selected countries,*

(5) Capital goods can be imported cheaper and this helps in capital formation, investment and higher production.

(6) Sun-set industries can be revived if foreign exchange is made available at lower rate. Higher production, employment and government revenue are generated by multiple exchange rates.

Multiple exchange rates are discriminatory some are favoured others are not. There can be corruption. They are resented by foreign countries. Exports are best promoted under competition and free exchange rate. Multiple exchange rates are sort of "instruments of protection". They are disallowed by two now. Even multiple exchange rates cannot check unnecessary imports if there are purchasers for them in the country. Now they are gone. They were also known as disorderly cross exchange rates.

ALTERNATIVE EXCHANGE RATE SYSTEMS

This is the modern expression for the "managed float", which is a system between the fixed exchange rate and the fluctuating exchange rate.

Once the economic literature used to have a word "snake in the tunnel system". A snake in a drain pipe or a big water pipe can slither and move ahead in a zigzag way. But the upper and lower limits of the movement are there in the form of the ceiling and the floor of the pipe, or the sideways of the pipe if the pipe is standing erect.

Now we use the words "crawling bands" or "target bands", for the "snake in the tunnel", or for "limited fluctuations.

How can a country manage the float? First, how can a country manage that the rate of domestic currency does not fall below a certain point?

Suppose India's exchange rate on is $ 1 = Rs. 45. Suppose the Government of India decides that it will not allow the rate to fall by a percentage higher than 5. This means that the Government of India will intervene if the exchange rate falls below Rs. 47.25 (2.25 being 5 p.c. of 45 rupees.)

This is fall in the rupee rate or the rise in the rate of dollar. The intervention that is necessary is to sell the dollars so that the shortage of dollars is ended. *This is the same thing as saying that the GOI will buy back the excess rupees from the market.*

Wherefrom the GOI have the dollars?

The Government of India can have dollars on its own trading and exports from the public sector. *The Government of India has a greats advantage. It can print new (additional)rupees and buy the dollars from the open market.* This is in a way a costless way, though done in excess this will create inflation and there will be further fall in the exchange rate. Hence domestic production, exports and dollar earnings better ways to acquire dollars. This intervention will be better.

The GoI will not allow the rupee rate to fall because it is akin to the fall in prestige of the rupee. However, if inflation differential is against India and if Indians demand too many dollars, a fall cannot be checked *fully.*

A fall in the exchange rate means more can be exported if the demand for Indian goods abroad is elastic. If not, then there will be loss. *Besides in all conditions a fall in the exchange rate of the rupee will mean that India will export more to get the same imports.* Hence lower limit of the float is managed.

Why, when and how can a country intervene to check the rate of domestic currency from rising or the rate of foreign currency form falling?

Suppose the rupee rate rises from $ 1 = Rs. 45 to Rs. 43 per dollar. (As is well understood rising rate means paying less of our currency.) Earier $ 1 used to come in 45 rupees; now $ 1.045561 come in 45 rupees. It is this way that the rise can be understood better.

Rising rupee rate means exports become costlier and can go down. It also means that the imports become cheaper and may go up. This will create balance of payment problems. The BoP will be less favourable or may become adverse.

Japan has this problem. Its balance of payment is favourable. Hence the value of Yes is constantly rising. Japan is, therefore, buying dollars. It is in other words, supplying Yen. It increases the supply of Yen so that the value of Yen may not go up as much. *Japan buys properties in foreign countries and Japan buys foreign companies. The two top film production units of the USA, for example, have been bought by Sony.*

India can also buy dollars when the value of rupees is rising. *The value (exchange rate) of rupee vis-à-vis dollar can rise without Indian economy becoming much stronger. Actually the exchange rate of rupee is rising because of the massive expenditure by the USA in Iraq War. In 2006–07, the USA wanted $ 150 b. more from its "Congress" for Iraq war.*" Dollar rate went down for plentiful supply. Hence the rupee rate rose. Rupee rate rises due to fall in dollar rate.

Raising of rate of interest is another way of attracting foreign money into the country. This will add to the supply of foreign currencies. The exchange rate of the domestic currency will rise. However, when interest is paid, it will fall. Hence there should be use of the foreign money to earn foreign money. If this is not done then it will be suicidal to increase the rate of exchange for the foreign countries and reduce it for the domestic savers.

Both the NDA and NPA governments did this. They increased the rate of interest to the foreign depositors to 10 p.c. minimum. They were getting l to 3p.c. in their own countries. The peak or 'cap' savings rates for the Indians were reduced from 14.5 to 5.5p.c p.a. The foreigners got 1000 p.c. to 350 p.c. more. Indians got 62 p.c. less. The rates were slashed down by nearly 2/3rd. In other words, the rate of interest was brought down to one third l/3rd level!

Banks were NOT giving cheap credit to the borrower. Depositors were giving. The banks were/are financial intermediaries. They had no business to do that without taking the consent of the depositors. On average, in 10 years time ending 2006-07, the banks transferred nearly Rs.1 crore-crore rupees each year from the depositors to the borrowers. Between 2007-2010, banks Thus "nationally" and indirectly transferred three crore-crore rupees from the depositors. The depositors were mostly small and middle income group savers (in the banks) the borrowers were well to do persons. In post 2007 years transfers from the middle class to the upper classes are continuing.

The "prosperity" that India is seeing is also because the borrowers did not return 1,50,000 crore rupees of the banks once again.

Under the ASFER (alternative system of foreign exchange rates) *there is US, dollarisation.* Countries may trade in two currencies which are say Yen and Won of Japan and Korea but Japan will convert the Won into US dollars as Korea will convert Yen into US dollars.

Thus the economies of various important economic countries are getting *integrated, with the-US. economy.* This is not to say that countries cannot keep other important currencies in their kitty. Many countries keep EURO, Yen and some of those currencies which are Gulf currencies.

ASFER is intermediate regime of the exchange rates. It is not fully fixed exchange rate system through intervention. It is not fully floating system which is also called "dirty float". The upper and lower limits of fluctuations *are tried* to be maintained.

When India resorted to (i) fluctuating exchange rate system, (ii) partial convertibility and (iii) no exchange control, there were two exchange rates \$ 1 = Rs. 26 (nearly) official, and \$ 1 = Rs. 36 (nearly) market rate or black/grey market rate, the rate came to \$ 1 = 31.5 (nearly) in 1991.

Thereafter with intervention the rate was kept for many years at this rate. This raised the real rate versus the nominal rate of exchange. In simple words, even though the economy was experiencing inflation, had high unemployment, had the weaknesses of adverse balance of payment, and had tremendous demand for dollar, the rate of exchange remained unchanged. *India printed new additional money and bought dollars and then sold dollars.* Indian economy became flushed with rupees.

If there is inflation differential against a country but the exchange rate is kept at the same level, the REER or the real effective exchange rate is said to be rising. That discourages exports. India had to leave that type of intervention.

Then the exchange rate of India started falling. It came to Rs. 47.5 and a little bit more. Then the Indians were fearing that the rate would become Rs. 50 or so. But then came the Iraq war and dollars were plentiful supply hence the rate of exchange of Indian rupee improved. It was nearly Rs. 46 per dollar in Dec. 2009, and Rs. 45 in April 2010.

Now a days ecomomists say that "ad hoc managed float" is like "fighting guerrilla warfare". Managing partial float or "alternative system of exchange rate" is difficult as countering guerrilla war.

Three ways:

First way is the *fixed exchange rate.* It has been left. Second way is floating exchange rate. It is there. *Third, way is "managed float" It is everywhere NOW.*

It has been noted that the fixed exchange rate system that prevailed in the world between 1944-45 to 1971 failed. In its place all countries are on floating or fluctuating exchange rate systems.

Dirty float is not wanted. Hence there is the middle path for which meddling is necessary. Dirty float means that the rate of exchange can go down to any extent. The rogue punters of the west can do that. That can bring down the exchange rate to half in one day ! That is the reason why the Central Banks and the Central Governments of the countries have to be cautious.

They have to intervene. *Managed float/partial float/ alternative exchan~e rate system, or middle path in exchange rates emerges.*

All countries of the world intervene now. The degree can differ. There are the same two methods of intervention. Either buy dollars and sell your currency. Or, sell dollars and buy your currency. The second is done when the exchange rate of the domestic currency is falling. The first type of intervention is done when the rate is rising.

Good times and bad times and exchange rate

On the basis of favourable balance of payment, India never had a good time. Except in one year, when the b.o.p. surplus was nominal (just like Rs. 1 crore or so), in all the years, the b.o.p. was deficit.

Yet when the deficit is less, and when the inflation is less, *and when the domestic exchange rate improves or the dollar rates become cheaper, the GoI or the RBI or the central bank of various countries buy dollars.*

It is like storing water in desert when there is rain for a short time. These dollars are sold, when the exchange rate of domestic currency falls.

Anti-cyclical interventions

Interventions are made in the exchange rate regimes for three purposes, (i) high inflation, high recession or high deflation (whichever) is brought under control; (ii) exports are promoted and (iii) unnecessary imports are restricted.

Managing the exchange rate fluctuations is a two edged sword ! The finance ministers or the governors of the central banks of various countries require luck. With luck immense gain can come. Or there can be serious losses. For example if the rate of exchange is checked from falling/ it may do immense good to the economy or may bring down the exports substantially.

Managed float is better than the free float. Free float is better than fixed exchange rate. But one thing is better than managed float even. *It is having a common currency.* The EU (European Union) has EURO and now there is no problem in EU about the costs of exchange rates.

Indian rupee used to circulate in Pakistan also after 15th August; 1947, till Pakistan printed their own currency. Then within a few years, the official parities differeed. Pakistan was in trouble. Rs. 100 of India became equal to Rs. 144 of Pakistan in the open market. *There was once shortage of paper and students were given promotion because the universities had no paper for answerbook,* as was reported then. Pak rupee is nearly Rs. 2 for Indian rupee. Without free money from the USA, China and Saudi Arabia it would have become P. Rs. 10 equal to I Rs. 1 (one). Then Pakistan got free money from China also. It gets money from Saudi Arabia free for protecting (reportedly) the high powered persons. It got money from the USA to create Talibans to fight the USSR. Now it gets money to keep the Talibans under control. *If SAARC becomes one union, then there will be one rupee only that will circulate in India, Pakistan, Bangladesh Nepal, Bhutan and Sri Lanka. It is a dream at present.* Besides there is not much trade as there should be. Afghani cannot be included in the rupee because there is anarchy in Afghanistan because *Pakistan still wants strategic in Afghanistan so that it can keep its aircrafts or tanks there.*

If there is need for balancing the free float or market mechanism there is need for balancing the interventions also. If interventions are too many and too substantial, the country goes back to the fixed exchane rate system. It will be bad now in the era of liberalisation and globalisation. Besides WTO will not permit that.

Full fluctuations lead to wild speculations in the financial market, Managed float smothers the extreme fluctuations. The rate cannot go up or down much. It will remain within limits set earlier These limits should be reasonable. They will change with time.

24 Convertibility of Indian Rupee: Transition from 'No-convertibility Regime' to Virtual Convertibility': Convertibility on Capital Account

Part A—'Partial Convertibility Regime' of Indian Rupee

There was a time when different countries of the world used to adjust their economies to a "stupid" (Milton Friedman) fixed exchange rate. That period is gone. Even command economies which used to insist on fixed exchange parities are gone. The IMF jettisoned the system when USA by 1971 failed to keep the price of gold from rising (or failed to keep the dollar 'price' from falling even after liquidating over three fourth of its gold reserves of Fort Knox). Non-convertibility and fixed exchange rate systems are things of past and cannot be defended. Besides, with whom is a country going to follow the non-convertibility and fixed exchange rate system when other countries are veering round the regime of convertibility?

We take the scenario as it started from the 1990s. The slogan 'export or perish' was gaining currency. It was found that all previous efforts including promoting "hundred-per cent export oriented units', developing 'export promotion zones', giving all sorts of conceivable assistance at the pre-production and post- production stages to exporting industries, two-times devaluation (between 17.21 and 18.75 percent against various important currencies), and such schemes as "advance licensing system", "cash compensatory scheme", "import replacement scheme (REP)", failed to increase the exports in such a way that the balance of payment position could improve.

Exporters were being given the IPR (international price reimbursement) and the EPCG (export promotion capital goods) scheme was further liberalised to reduce import compression for the exporters. It related to the leasing of capital goods; import of components and goods in SKD (semi-knocked down) and CKD (completely knocked down) condition and furnishing of legal undertaking instead of bank guarantee by export houses as well as trading and 'star' trading houses. These categories of exporters were being "pampered" at the State cost yet they were not achieving the targeted results. Even exporters of 'deemed exports' were being given many concessions at the cost of the State. Before 1991 there was "no convertibility" system. Market rate of \$ 1 was Rs. 36 or so and the official rate was \$1 = Rs. 26 or so.

Since the sum of exports and imports elasticities of India does not exceed one in a substantial manner, the 'elasticity pessimists' proved right over the 'elasticity optimists' after the devaluation of the 1990s.

1. The Exim Scrips system was introduced (1991).

Under this system the exporters could retain 60 percent of the foreign currencies earned by them and the government impounded 40 percent of the export earnings. These 40 per cent foreign currency reserves were pre-empted by the government for "socially necessary imports" like defence goods, petroleum products and several other categories of imports, particularly those needed by the public sector and the governments, at official rate of exchange.

The exporters could dispose of their 60 percent reserves at premium in the open market/stock exchange as 'scrips'. *For this purpose, the forex holdings of the exporters were first converted into import licences which were to be traded as 'scrips' in the stock exchanges. Exchange rate emerged $ 1 = Rs. 31.5 or so (Six digits) in the market.*

The Exim scrips were issued as tradable import licences issued to exporters. They could be used to import a wide range of items which were earlier importable against supplementary licences. With the introduction of Exim scrips, supplementary licences were abolished. Exim scrips could be traded in stock exchanges at a premium which accrued to exporters of goods and services as well as to those making remittances to India.

However, Exim scrips also had to be issued case-by-case like other import licences and required physical handling, and needed surveillance as they could be forged, (like the first prize winning lottery tickets). There used to be complaints that shady persons could produce the forged first prize winning tickets and EXIMSCRIPS by printing the exact replica).

A big problem that arose was that the speculators used to corner the Exim- scrips for their gains. These speculators were neither importers nor the exporters yet the major gains accrued to them. This went against promoting the exports market imports compression still was in operation for the exporters, producers and consumers because the speculators made the free market foreign currency costlier than it otherwise would have been. On decentralised basis there would have been several suppliers of foreign currencies, competing amongst themselves. After the cornering of the Exim- scrips there were oligopolistic suppliers of foreign exchange.

2. The Liberalised Exchange Rate Management System

From March 1, 1992 the Liberalised Exchange Rate Management System (LERMS) was introduced. The arrangement was still the same 60 percent to exporters and 40 percent to the government of all the foreign exchange earned by the exporters.

Under LERMS the exporters could sell their foreign exchange holdings to anyone at the market rate of exchange, which meant in all cases getting higher than official rate of exchange. This was to be done by the authorised dealers only once the foreign currencies are sold by the original exporters.

Those who needed foreign exchange for importing goods and services or wanted to undertake travel abroad were able to buy forex at market determined rates from the authorised dealers (ADs). The only stipulation was (and continues presently and shall continue under any future regime also) that banned goods were not to be exported and imported. Under liberalised system no national-heritage goods could be or can be exported nor 'drugs' norcotic could be or can be imported.

All foreign exchange receipts on current account transactions (exports, remittances etc.) were required to be surrendered to ADs in full. The ADs in turn used to surrender to RBI the 40 percent of their purchases of foreign currencies representing current account receipts (including the foreign currency equivalent at the official rate of receipts in convertible rupees) at the official rate announced by the RBI.

The *RBI also participated in foreign exchange operations at market rate.* This actually was its 'intervention' to keep the rate from fluctuating too much. Theoretically, this meant that if the rupee rate was falling vis-a-vis other currencies, those currencies used to be sold in the open market by the RBI and rupee taken in lieu of them. In other case if the rupee rate rose, the foreign currencies could be bought.

The RBI used to sell foreign exchange at the official rate to ADs only for *(i)* imports of specified goods covering government departmental needs, crude oil, diesel, kerosene and fertilisers, as authorised by the Department of Economic Affairs, Ministry of Finance, Government of India, *(ii)* imports under Exim Scrips unutilised as on February 29, 1992, and *(iii)* imports of life saving drugs and equipment under licences. Forex was also available at the official rate for imports under Advance Licences and Special Imprest Licences and imports for replenishment of raw materials for gem and jewellery exports *but* for 40 percent of the value. The remaining requirement had to be met through purchases in the free market.

In case of some foreign currencies, there was 'full convertibility'. In those cases, 15% could be retained in the form of the then non-convertible currencies also, provided the amount was kept in Indian banks (out of the total amount that was to be surrendered to the ADs at market-rates).

The facility of providing forex at official rate to the unutilised Exim scrips holders was granted for the remaining period of the maturity of the scrips. No new scrip was issued thereafter as LERMS arrangement came into operation.

RBI used to buy (spot transaction and forward transaction) US $, Pound" Sterling, Deutsche Mark and Japanese Yen in the open market also. The dollar was currency of invoicing as also the currency of intervention. *The official rates used to be announced on each business day for the currencies mentioned above.*

It was stipulated that *"money changers"* could sell their collections of foreign currency notes etc. to ADs who purchased 40 percent forex at the official rate and the 60 percent at the market rates. Full-fledged money changers *had to* sell daily to ADs 40 percent of their gross collections which could be purchased by the latter at rates based on the official rate. Accordingly, money changers could buy foreign currency travellers' cheques and notes and sell currency notes (from/to members of public) at suitable rates.

Part B—Regime of 'Full' Convertibility for Goods Trading on Current Account, then Full Convertibility on Current Account

Indian rupee was declared as being 'fully' convertible on current account trading of goods. It meant that services could not be imported after free conversion. The exporters/ ADs were under no obligation to surrender any part of the foreign exchange acquired by them through exports/purchase. The government itself used forex in the open market. The end-use of forex was not permitted for services (holders of forex could not invite foreign engineers to build their houses), nor the forex could be used for transactions with plastic money (credit card) abroad and capital goods could also not be imported freely (this is subject to export import policies).

Two quick devaluations with a gap of one day only after 1st July, 1991 (17.21 and 18.75 per cent) were not adequate and the international money dealers were knowing after the first devaluation that further devaluation would/ought to follow. Hence there was the danger of capital, flight to avoid the incurring of the opportunity cost of not taking the money out. Reverse outflows were in the offing and second devaluation was done. Ultimately the devaluations meant reductions in the then par values by 17.21 percent against DM, 17.38 percent against pound sterling, 18.5 per cent against dollar, and 18.75 percent against yen.

These two devaluations proved symbolic only. By making our imports dearers to ourselves and exports cheaper to foreigners, a chain reaction did not emerge which could take care of adverse internal and external disequilibrium conditions. Portfolio investment was not coming from abroad in the desired way and massive direct investment inflows were a far cry. (*Yet,* there was no economising in the use of petroleum product by the government sector and its sinecures.)

India was not getting as much IDA assistance as China was getting even with its higher per capita income (an important criterion in dispensation of aid from IDA) was higher. It was considered then that the debt-equity buy-back arrangements were a good escape way for 'debt-swap'. *These things would not have been possible without full convertibility of Indian rupee on goods trading of the current account.*

Indian rupee was made fully convertible on current account in the budget of 1993-94. When the rupee was made fully convertible on current account for goods, it virtually eliminated the smuggling of normal economic goods. Only banned goods could not be exported and imported. Thus for getting normal goods one need not have taken the help *of' 'havala'* traders who provided money to the importers.

The official and market rates of foreign exchange were different by about 15%. At official rates, imports were being *subsidised and exports taxed* implicitly. After declaring the rupee 'fully' convertible, both of these were withdrawn. The arrangement was thought to be a bold step towards "export-led growth" strategy.

Earlier to this system India was having partial convertibility *with profound restrictions on the "end-use" of forex by Indians.* Now that restriction was abolished but for banned goods and capital imports (unless permitted by other policies of the Government). *India has not as yet given up the right to ask the money changer the question "where from you got the rupee/forex balances ?"*

As India moves from partial to virtual' convertibility in future, it will be imperative that the economy of India is put well on road to 'self-sustaining growth'.

It could be argued that the regime of partial convertibility of the rupee could have been continued for some more time. Exporters could have been allowed to convert 80 percent of their forex earned in open market. The Government of India could have retained 20 percent forex earned by the exporters for socially necessary imports. The imports of defence goods, unless financed by exports from public sector units, will become costly. Petroleum imports' will also become costly and once again the burden of higher prices will be borne by the over-burdened middle class, who cannot travel/ commute on government or company account.

Part C—Towards the Regime of 'Virtual Convertibility'

There is one advantage in the convertible exchange system with flexibility in the rates that the government can acquire the forex reserves in a painless way—through the newly created money and *then use these balances* for stabilisation operations. It has been found that somehow *there is* a built-in tendency towards balance of payments adjustments via price effect. *The most crucial thing necessary in such an economy is the capacity of the producers for positive supply responses.* Japan has shown what miracles can an entrepreneurial class achieve (even with imported raw materials) in a regime of liberalisation and flexible (with intervention for management of exchange rate) exchange rates.

India can move towards 'virtual convertibility' only and not the 'true full convertibility'. Indian rupee has no prospect of becoming universal vehicle currency. Rupee cannot be used as "currency of intervention" in the world nor it has any chance of being used as the "currency of billing".

Most importantly, there is no prospect of India producing so many real goods that whatsoever is the amount of Indian currency held by the foreigners, it can be honoured with (when tendered back to the RBI or India's ADs) the export of real goods..The rupee cannot have a solid backing with gold reserves, forex reserves, and goods reserves for ready supply. Thus the chances of India making use of the printing press to print new money and then to purchase goods and services produced anywhere in the world (using rupee as vehicle currency) are non-existent.

USA can do so; its massive b.o.p. deficits or fiscal deficits have not ousted the dollar from being used as vehicle currency. Everyone wants to have dollars; it is a different matter that few want to keep them.

The 1993 convertibility *was not for the consumers* but for the *traders* and end-use of forex for *investors* will be subject to industrial policy of India.

Convertibility at this stage is like "blind bid" in the "card game of flash". If the results come out good, and India does not lend itself in serious trouble (which hopefully it may not), then further convertibility on capital account can be introduced. At present the Indian psyche is apprehensive of "foreigners draining out our resources"; doing an 'East India Company' on India again: and "repatriating massive profits". In this connection it may be said that it is wrong to expect foreigners to swap equity for debt and yet not repatriate profits. It is a wrong notion that profits repatriated are a drain. Besides if these profits are allowed to be retained in the country, then the foreigners will buy Indian properties which may not be liked by the country.

When there is 'virtual convertibility' of the rupee then the course of exchange rate in the capital account will be governed by interest rate differentials, as distinct from the inflation differentials that bear upon the current account.

A high *'real rate of interest'* (higher than in a competing country) will be necessary. This will encourage the foreign investors but will discourage domestic investors. A precarious balancing act will be necessary. Credit to superfluous investors will then have to be curtailed. India then would not be able to afford a fiscal and monetary system that can tolerate high rate of inflation. Inflation containment will be a big job. This could be achieved only at the cost of curtailing expenditures of the government sector. *In India while 'regulations' have been reduced, the 'regulators' remain.* Would they be happy to see that their most favoured job (spending someone else's money) is curtailed ? Private sector will have to be trusted more.

How soon the Government of India make the rupee 'virtually convertible' will depend upon full convertibility on trade account proving 'problem-solving rather than 'problem-aggravating'. It will also depend upon their approach about how soon they want to jettison most functions related to economic *growth* to the private sector and retain with them the functions which promote economic *development* with themselves.

The IMF used to classify Indian rupee as "managed floating currency" and not among *"basket-linked" currency.* Now Indian rupee has moved towards the second category. The immediate scenario will be to keep the 'management' going on for travel and consumption accounts and to liberalise the system for capital account. *It will be necessary that the government acquires sufficient forex reserves to intervene with the floating exchange rate within the limits of "snake in the tunnel".*

Crities in India have always argued that full convertibility can be had only after budgetary deficits are reduced to almost nothing and exports pick up so much that they exceed the imports on current account. Obviously, this was putting the cart before the horse. They expected avalanche of' outflows' while the government expected torrents of 'inflows'. The crities were apprehensive that exports of India will not pick up while the government was expecting that India could have fair share of their imports needs for consumer goods. The crities that Indian rupee will always have a "dirty float" (downwards). The government now has greater faith in Indian and NRI entrepreneurs who are expected to rise to the occasion. It is surprising how critics of full convertibility expected capital/funds outflows *for all time to come.* High exports and rising forex balances were perceived by the government *not as the precondition* but as a *consequence* of convertibility.

SUMMARY

EFFECT ON INDIA'S INTERNATIONAL TRADE AND CONVERTIBILITY OF INDIAN RUPEE

Non-convertibility and fixed exchange rate regime existed upto the end of the decade of 1980s. Those who exported had to no right to use the dollars they earned. They had to be given to the Government at the official rate of exchange. Thus the exporters required import licences and foreign exchange to import capital goods and essential raw materials. Infact even to go abroad for exploring market, foreign exchange could be denied. The politicians and the top officers, however, made merry in foreign countries. Then came the era of convertibility.

1991 **EXIM SCRIPS** replaced the CCS i.e., the cash compensatory, system under which some subsidies and entitlements were given but on *ad hoc* basis, depending upon the mercies of the regulators. Under the EXIM SCRIPS system, an exporter could retain 60 p.c. of the foreign exchange earned in the form of import licence; the balance 40 p.c. had to be given to the government on the official rate of exchange. If the exporter did not want to import, the EXIM SCRIPS could be sold to others at premium or market rate of exchange. This scheme was abandoned after one year because *(i)* counterfeit EXIM SCRIPS were printed and *(ii)* speculators purchased them from the exporters and made huge profits in selling them to the importers.

1992 **LERMS:** Liberalised Exchange Rate Management System was introduced under which the 60: 40 p.c. retention: surrender to the government were retained but the 60 p.c. could be sold in the open market at the market rate of exchange. (At that time the offical exchange rate was nearly 26 rupees per dollar **and** the market rate was 36 rupees per dollar, here decimal points are ignored).

1993 Full convertibility on trade account was allowed. Now the exporter could retain 100 p.c. and could sell all export earnings in the open market. However, the end use was restricted to imports of goods for selling purposes. In other words, a car could be imported for selling it to others but not for self- use. Obviously, everyone found loopholes.

1994 **Full convertibility on current account was allowed.** As soon as this was done, one rate of exchange was established at $ 1 = Rs. 31.5 and it remained so for considerable period of time. The Government too had to buy dollars from the open market. *[Actually, this job is done in India by 6 leading authorised dealers (Though there are nearly 1000 ADs in India) and the government buys from them.]* The dollar became dear to GOI even for buying things for defence purposes or importing anything from petrolto fertilisers. If the exchange rate showed tendency towards ecline, the government intervened with the sale of dollars. This as known as "sterilisation operation". The government acquired ollars with the newly printed money. Money supply started increasing in India. By 2000, the market rate was Rs. 47 for one dollar after Iraq war it improved from Rs 48 to Rs. 46.79 in May 2003 and came to $.1 = Rs. 45 or so in 2004. in January 2010 it no nearly $1 = Rs. 46. Increasing prices, continued balance of payment difficulties, high demand for dollars to cover future fall in the exchange rate of rupee and a host of other factors brought a decline in ER.

Indian Monetary System Did Not Have "Full Convertibility On Capital Account" even in January 2010. It was proposed to introduce it in SEZ, i.e. special export zones. All things, except the banned ones and the capital goods, could be imported freely subject to importers' ability to purchase dollars from the open market. Indians could even engage services of the foreign experts and pay in foreign currency. An Indian can pay another Indian in dollar now.

Full convertibility on current account depends upon the ability of the country to manage the inflation differential. If the inflation in the USA is 10 p.c. and 20 p.c. in India, the exchange rate of India will fall by 10 p.c. If there is no inflation in the USA, the exchange rate of India will fall by the same rate as the rate of inflation in things that enter into foreign trade.

Full convertibility on capital account is the function of the ability of a country to maintain the 'interest rate differential'. If India raises the rate of interest by 1 p.c. above the maximum global rate, then *(theoretically speaking)* all the portfolio capital will come to India. But wherefrom does India pay the interest to the Investors Hence India cannot make Indian rupee convertible on capital account easily.

Capital account convertibility was already there in 2000 for foreign Institutional investors, the NRIs but not to ordinary Indians.

Indian rupee was "virtually convertible but not fully convertible on capital account in January 2010. TARAPORE COMMITTEE had recommended that (1) inflation rate not be above 3.5 p.c. (2) fiscal deficit to be around 3.5 p.c. of the GDP, and (3) recovery of bank dues which in 2009 must be equal to Rs. 1,60,000 crore.

FULL CONVERTIBILITY OF INDIAN RUPEE ON CAPITAL ACCOUNT IN PHASES BY THE YEAR 2011–2015

Full convertibility on capital account will **mean that there** will be full freedom to exchange foreign currencies **for** all purposes, except those banned *e.g.*, private parties cannot import war goods or banned drugs.

Tarapore Committee had earlier set certain conditions. These were not fulfilled. In the 2006, the Prime Minister informed the nation about the policy of the GoI that it will be permitted from SEZ of Mumbai on experimental basis. On that basis the industrialists started clamouring for many SEZs. Despite a commitment to the nation from the Finance Minister that agricultural land will not be taken, the communist government in West Bengal allocated agricultural land for the small car project of the TATAs. Later Tata had to move away to Gujarat. Industrialists were choosing agriculture lands for SEZs and the farmers were beaten blue and black to get the villages vacated. Compensations were @ 1/25 of the market rate.

Tarapore Committee had asked for certain conditions to be fulfilled (known as "signposts") but there were wide divergences from them in 2006.

Signposts	*2010 Status Jan.*
Fiscal consolidation	
Reduction in gross fiscal from 4.5 p.c. of GDP in 1197-98 to 3.5 p.c. in 1999-2000.	Gross fiscal deficit at 6.8%
Mandated Inflation Rate It was to be 3 to 5 p.c. p.a. Not achieved. It went up to 12 p.c. in 2008.	Inflation shown to be averaging at 12 to 18 p.c.p.a. That too with the "cheating" method of ignoring doulding of prices of many food items. Food inflation was 300 p.c. between 2007-2010
Strengthening of financial system. Interest rates to be fully deregulated.	Saving bank interest rates still regulated at a low of 3 p.c.p.a.
CRR was to be reduced to 3 p.c. by 2000 from 8 p.c. that it was in 1997-98	It was 5 p.c. in jan. 2007
Gross NPAs (non-performing) assests [actually bad and doubtful debts of the banks] to be brought down to 5 p.c. from the 12 p.c. by 2002	Banks now "show" them to be 5.25 p.c. Independent observations are for Rs. 1,80,000 crore for the commercial and cooperative banks.
Forex reserves should not be less than 6 months import cover.	Forex reserves cover 13 months imports, unnecessarily excessive and 90 p.c. of them were debts.

Full convertibility on capital account is the function of the management of interest rate differentials. We have seen that, full convertibility on current account is the function of the management of inflation rate differentials. India will find the following things very difficult if full convertibility on capital account is allowed.

(A) If interest rate is raised to attract inflow and/or to discourage the outflow of capital, wherefrom will India pay interest on the funds it gets. Government of India is not very famous for earning forex from public sector exports on huge scale.

(B) Since the rates of interest in foreign capitalist countries are lower, it will not be possible to park the funds in western capitalist countries to pay the obligations of interest.

India had in April 2010 "virtual convertibility" and was moving towards "fuller" convertibility and not towards "full convertibility". Full convertibility on capital account means that restrictions on foreigners buying real estates in India will be lifted. Foreigners will be able to buy shares also of the Indian companies.

There are worries about the US using its printing press for printing new/additional dollars and US people purchasing Indian companies, hotels, palaces and buildings etc. in India (except heritage monuments). It is such a big risk.

If Indian Government reduces the fiscal deficit to 3.5 p.c. of the GDP (once it contemplated to reduce it to zero by the year 2008, but in that year it was 6.8 p.c. Where will the common Indians invest ? When the people of India purchase NSC or Indira Vikas Patra or deposit money in post offices, it becomes fiscal deficit. Where will the common people of India find safe portfolio of saving?

Full convertibility on capital account means Indians can open accounts abroad and keep money there or transfer money there.

Such full convertibility on capital account is not permitted even in the USA. Hence FCOCA (full convertibility on capital account) will carry several restrictions.

India has introduced KYCR (know your customer rule). The banks have to find out who is sending dollars abroad or who is receiving dollars from abroad. Money laundering **will** not be **permitted** even under FCOCA.

FOCA will require that there should be *(i)* rupee debt market abroad *(ii)* a bond market in rupees abroad and *(iii)* hedging in rupees abroad. All the three are absent. India will have to leave managed floating or "alternative middle system of exchange rate". India will not be able to do that.

If there is small pond near the sea; both separate. If suddenly they are, connected, the pond will not takeover the sea. It will be the other way round.

The exchange rate market will become too volatile. The rate of exchange will fluctuate so widely and wildly that the entire economy will rock due to shocks.

It is true that India is a strong ccuntry. According to the reports 8 countries of the world viz., Japan, China, Hongkong, Taiwan, South Korea, Singapore, Russia and India collectively hold two-third of the world's external resources. (These external resources of reserves of dollars and key currencies. The USA is not in them because it does not hold others' currencies in reserves. Others hold its currency in reserves. Yet India comes after Singapore and Hong Kong mere dots on the map of the world. India is behind S.Korea and Taiwan the district like countries for India. India has to go slow over this.

The policy of full convertibility in one SEZ of Mumbai can be tried. Additionally there should be restrictions here also. It should not be fully convertible for all purposes here also. Otherwise it will become conduit for the entire country and for all operations. Our biggest bank is a pigmy in comparison to the biggest of the world. The total banking system of India is not equal to the top half a dozen banks of the world in resources. This could not happen in 2009-2010 even.

Capital account convertibility

Risks

Partial capital account convertibility already exists in India. Capital can be brought in; it can be invested; investment can be liquidated and capital can be taken out Now CAC actually means "liberal" CAC.

The risk of capital account convertibility is that it may lead to sudden outflow of capital. It will depress the exchange rate and can even have contagion effect on the currencies of the region. There had never been a proof that freer CAC had led to the robust growth of the economy both rural and urban segments. Growth can be enclave growth in a few regions, in a few activities and for the benefit of a numerically small number of the people.

Benefits.

Fuller CAC will ensure massive inflow of capital for investment in diversified fields leading to great gains in_productivity. Governments will have be careful about their fiscal deficits and about the inflation. High rates of inflation will distort the structure of the interest rates and that shall make the CAC not very manageable. Managed exchange rates will be necessary. For the benefits we can see how the automobile industries, telecommunications industries/services or computer industry/services improved in India giving rise to massive employment in these sectors. CAC will ensure that there is relatively more FDI than FII.

Nachane *(EPW, Sept. 8 2007),* views CAC more beneficial to the developed countries. Nachane finds *no* empirical evidence to prove the following:

(A) That there will be optimum global distribution of investible resources.
(B) That the marginal productivity of capital will become more or less equal in all countries.
(C) That technology transfers and transfers of technical know-how will follow.
(D) That free mobility of capital will absorb shocks.
(E) That governments of developing economies will become more disciplined in the fiscal areas.

CAC is a model of IMF and in practice it has been seen that it traps the less developed countries in huge debts and economic enslavement.

Many economists think:

Rising forex balances ($ 286 b. in Dec. 2009) is strong indicator that India can have capital account convertibility. But this is not enough.

First, investment in real estate should be confined to persons of Indian origin only. Secondly, gold stocks should be used to provide a buffer against exchange crises, if they arise.

India is not fit for full convertibility on all accounts.

UNIT IV

Theory of Customs Union: Economic Blocs (*) Regional Trade Agreements. International Financial Institutions Like IMF, World Bank, Asian Development Bank, International Organisation Like UNCTAD, WTO......Multilateralism

25. Theory of Customs Union; Economic Integration: Free Trade Blocs; Regional Trade Agreements; Regional Integration Agreements.
26. India and European Union. Indian and SARRC: INDIA AND ASEAN. INDIA AND BIMSET.
27. THEORY OF CAPITAL MOVEMENT IN INTERNATIONAL TRADE. Foreign Direct Investment (FDI): Portfolio Investment (FII), *with particular reference to India.*
28. UNITED NATIONS CONFERENCE ON TRADE AND DEVELOPMENT. UNCTAD.
29. General Agreement on Tariff and Trade. GATT.
30. World Trade Organisation.
31. WTO and Multilateralism. Globalisation and International Business.
32. Structure of the National and International Monetary Systems before IMF. (Brief History).
33. International Monetary Fund IMF
34. European Monetary System and EURO in European Monetary Union.
35. World Bank and Other International Financial Institutions. International Finance Corporation. International Development Agency. *Asian Development Bank.*

* Not to be written as "block".

25 Theory of Customs Union: Free Trade Blocs; Regional Trade Agreements (RTA): Regional Integration Agreements (RIA)

INTRODUCTION

Customs unions have now become economic unions as the EU or the European Economic Union. However, many unions of the world still remain the customs unions. Hence the theory is important. This theory was developed with the help of a lot of algebra and geometry. It is in a very difficult form in the western text books. Here it has been presented in succinct form.

DEFINITION

Customs union is an union of member countries which do not impose tariffs or taxes or duties on the imports and exports from and to the member countries but the same are imposed on the non–member countries.

Jacob Viner and Richard Lipsey have made important contributions to the theory of Customs Union.

Jacob Viner has defined all the effects of Customs Union. They are broadly speaking (a) positive and (b) negative. POSITIVE EFFECTS ARE KNOWN AS 'TRADE CREATION EFFECTS' WHILE THE NEGATIVE EFFECTS ARE KNOWN AS 'TRADE DIVERSION EFFECTS".

Positive effects are on two aspects: (a) production and (b) consumption. Negative effects are also on two aspects: (a) production and (b) consumption.

POSITIVE OR "TRADE CREATION" EFFECTS OF CUSTOMS UNION

* When new industries are located within the union at the point of least cost per unit, this is positive effect on production. At higher cost of production per unit, there is no competitiveness. Gaining competitiveness is positive effect or trade creation effect.
* When the goods are produced at the lowest possible per unit cost of production, the price is also low. In economics, price is always taken as equal to the cost of

production, which includes normal profits. The consumers pay less and gain. They gain satisfaction. This is also positive effect or trade creation effect.
Both of them together make the total "trade creation" effect.

NEGATIVE OR 'TRADE DIVERSION' EFFECTS OF CUSTOMS UNION

* Because of the formation of the CU, the businessmen cannot buy things from outside if they are available within the customs union, even if the foreign goods are cheaper. The producers of the customs union will produce goods at costs higher than the costs outside the union. This is known as the inefficient allocation of resources or inefficient production., For this the CU will have to impose taxes on the imports, otherwise the businessmen will buy from outside the union. This is negative production effect. This is part of the "trade diversion effect".
* The consumers from within the union will be purchasing high cost goods from within the union while the cheaper goods were available from outside. The domestic goods may be of poor quality also. This is negative effect on consumption. This is part of the trade diversion effect.
* Both of them together make the total "trade diversion" effect.

Positive effects are gains. Negative effects are losses. Hence it is necessary that *trade creation effects should exceed the trade diversion effects.*

It is to be remembered that if there are no customs unions, there will be free trade in the world. The entire world will become a "custom union". Then there will be no negative effects or diversion effects.

In simple words this means there will be advantages of free trade if there is multilateral globalization.

There are differences whether the same type of countries should form customs union e.g., countries which are primarily agricultural or which are industrial and industrial. Customs unions can be formed between competitive countries and this will reduce or end competition. –Customs unions can be formed between complementary countries for the obvious reason that they will complement each other. All depends upon those who manage the customs union. The politicians, administrators, bankers and the economists should work for the success of the same. Before a customs union is formed it should be calculated whether the "creation" effects will be more than the "diversion" effects. Detailed exercises should be there about what results can be expected from its functioning on a certain pattern in future. Revenues and costs can be simulated. Gains versus losses can be "gueestimated". Then only the union should be formed.

One thing is clear that customs union cannot be formed between countries far off from each other. If the countries are contiguous, the customs union can be formed very easily. If not then there should not be much distance. A land–locked country in between will pose problems.

There is nothing wrong in forming a customs union between a few rich countries and a few not so rich countries. *If later on it is found that the gains from the formation of the union have become less and the losses are becoming higher because the outside world is developing better, the customs union can be dismantled also.*

STATIC VERSUS DYNAMIC EFFECTS OF CUSTOMS UNION

Static Effects are at a Point of Time, Best Illustrated with a Diasram. The Dynamic Effects are Expressed in Words for a lons Period

First the dynamic effects are summarized below:

1. Customs unions help the union countries to get lower and lower cost of production per unit in various lines of production. The consumers get goods at cheaper prices.
2. The producers have assured market. They do not fear fierce competition from abroad. They expect to get their "exchange values" (prices) give them higher revenue.
3. Higher revenue on one side and lower cost of production on the other side means higher profit per unit. And when the volumes of production and sales are also high, there will be higher total profit.
4. There will be competition. It is not necessary that inside the customs union, monopolies or oligopolies are bound to develop. They need not. There can be firms of bigger sizes but need not be monopolies or oligopolies. Efficiency will remain.
5. External economies are provided by the government and the internal economies will be developed by the firms. Firms will be encouraged to do so in the protected atmosphere. Input–output relations develop as they should due to protected atmosphere in the union.
6. Infrastructure facilities will be developed by the economy itself to suit its needs. The SOC–DPA balance will be there. (SOC mean social overhead capital or infrastructure facilities; DPA mean directly productive activities). A healthy circle of more savings, higher capital formation and higher and diversified investment will be there.
7. There will be import compression and import substitution. There can be export promotion and improvement in the income terms of trade.
8. Mobility of labour as well as of capital increases. Inside European Union, there are millions of workers who move from one country to another for work and return home for the night. That gives a political will to be friendly. Sometimes the same issues can lead to problems but the economic necessity soon ends the opposition.
9. What used to be external debts become internal debts. The debt which the German owed to France and France to Germany got converted into EURO debt with no fluctuations in the exchange rates. Exchange rates become one rate and there are no costs of exchange. Harmonization of fiscal policies makes the tax, public expenditure and public revenue policies more or less the same over the entire region. Regional differences over the space get reduced.
10. Customs unions provide better safeguards against deflation. Deep depression is not possible. Inflation too can be controlled. Balance of payment deficits with the outside world become lesser and lesser. They may end also. They can get converted into surpluses.

The Effects of the Customs Union Shown with the Help of a Diagram; the Effects of the 'Second Best Position

Customs union is known as the "second best" position. The best is free trade. The founder of Economics, Adam Smith, had written "free trade like honesty is the best policy". The worst policy, according to Adam Smith is protection. Protection was favoured by the German economists. Free trade was favoured by the British economists. List was the most important name amongst the protectionists. The Americans were under the influence of the German thinkers.

Jacob Viner, Richard Lipsey, Jaroslav Vanek, Namesw Meade, Kelvin Lancaster, Tibor Scitovsky, Harry Johnson and Jan Tinbergen were the important economists who preferred the position of the "second best" i.e., of customs union.

The Regional Trade Agreements are also like customs union arrangements.

Custom union is not a state but a process. It means there can be constant changes in the arrangements of the customs union. The theory of customs union, which got a lot of fame, is actually the second of the four stages.

Stage One: The Free Trade Area. In this all member countries abolish import duties and other taxes against each other. They keep them against the non–members of the FTA i.e., the free trade area.

Stage Two: The Customs Union. There is what is there in the FTA plus there is free movement of commodities and goods inside the CU area. Capital also moves freely. The decisions are taken collectively on wide ranging issues. Labour movement is also there.

Stage Three. The Common Market. There is greater economic integration like the producer of one country can open the plant in another country. Other factors of production like entrepreneurs, skilled managers, technology "think–banks" also move freely. No impediments remain on trade of commodities, goods, services and factors inside the CM area.

Stage Four. The Economic Union. (Next chapter is on European Economic Union).

Here the economic integration is complete. There can be common currency. There is in EU. All nations remain. They retain their political identity. But there can be a Union Parliament and even an army. Taxes and interest rates policies are the same. Most other economic policies are also more or less the same.

The "trade creation effects" and the "trade diversion effects" were studied earlier in words. Now we can study them with the help of a diagram. As was noted earlier the trade creation effects are positive effects. The positive effects are also two—the positive effects on production and consumption. The trade diversion effects are negative effects. They are also two —on production and consumption. *The essence of the customs union theory is that the positive effects should exceed the negative effects. In other words the "trade creation effects" should exceed the "trade diversion effects".*

In cases when consumers of the customs union buy at higher cost from member countries of the union (though at lower costs/price in comparison to the pre–customs union period) when goods at cheaper price are available from countries outside the customs union, this can be termed as *the negative consumption effect.* For adopting the unified tariff, some members may have to impose new tariffs on some imports which may have been allowed to enter the country freely before the formation of the customs union. Consumer purchases will thereby be diverted from low–cost outside producers to high–cost producers inside the customs union. This is *the negative consumption effect* of a customs union. *Combination of negative production effect and negative consumption effect is known as trade diversion effect of a customs union.*

Trade creation increases the gains while the trade diversion reduces the gains from trade. The net effect will depend on the relative strength of each of the effects. Trade creation increases the volume of trade and improves the allocation of resources. This increase in efficiency benefits customs union countries as also the outside world. Trade diversion brings misallocation of resources, which harms customs union countries and the outside world also.

In a world which is not divided into various customs unions and follows the free trade pattern, there will be no trade diversion effects. The entire world becomes a customs union. Thus the wider the customs union, the greater will be the trade creation effects of customs union. If the tariff walls were very high before the formation of the customs union, the trade creation advantages will be greater even. Trade diversion, on the other hand, will be relatively unimportant, since high tariffs have already restricted the volume of outside trade before the customs union was formed, and there is consequently little trade to divert. It implies that a low pre–union level of trade restriction will narrow the scope for trade creation and increase the possibility of trade diversion.

Customs union brings greater benefits to competitive economies than to complementary economies. In complementary economies there is little overlapping in the assortment of goods that are produced. In competitive economies, customs union increases the resource allocation efficiency and hence provides great trade effects. Competitive economies must be having high tariff walls and their removal naturally will have greater creation effect. Complementary economies would have little reason to construct tariff walls between themselves, since there is little to protect.

Diagrammatic Illustration of Trade Creation and Trade Diversion

Fig. 25.1 shows the trade creation and trade diversion effects of customs union

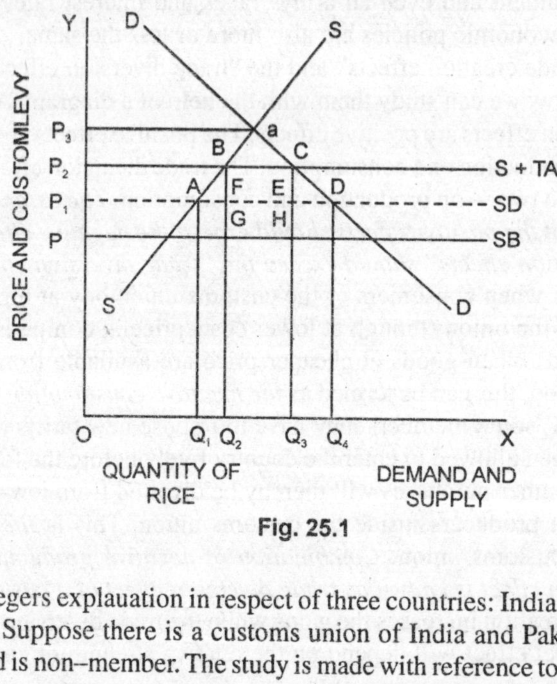

Fig. 25.1

Fig. 25.1 regers explauation in respect of three countries: India, Pakistan and Rest–of–the–World. Suppose there is a customs union of India and Pakistan: naturally, the rest of the world is non–member. The study is made with reference to India. The domestic supply and demand curves for rice in India are SS and DD respectively. The supply curves of Pakistan and ROTW (Rest–of– the–World) are shown by *Sd* and *Sb* respectively. These horizontal supply curves indicate perfect elasticity of these curves of products produced under the constant production function.

Suppose there were no imports in India before the formation of customs union (complete autarky or protective policy). Then at the equilibrium point of domestic demand and domestic supply, the price of rice in India will be OP_3. The price in ROTW is OP on which PP_2 tariff is levied. Therefore, Indians can buy all the rice at this price of OP_2 and, therefore, domestic price can never be as high as determined by the equilibrium of domestic demand and supply, unless import is not premissible.

Since OP_2 price is lower than the OP_3 price the aggregate demand will now be higher at OQ_3. Of this quantity only OQ_2 will reproduce in India. The balance Q_2Q_3 will be imported from ROTW P_3S, therefore becomes the effective supply curve of rice after the imposition of the tariff.

Trade Creation

After the formation of the customs union, the tariff will be abolished on imports from Pakistan. Thus the price will come down to OP_1. On this lower price, there will be less production in India and more will be imported from Pakistan (QQ_1 and Q_1Q_4 respectively). The increase in imports (equal to the Q_1Q_2 and Q_3Q_4) isthg trade creation effect. Thus trade creation effect is due to both decrease in domestic production as well as increase in domestic supply. Imports are equal to these amounts. Since Pakistan is a low–cost country, there is advantage to the consumers is greater imports from Pakistan.

The difference between the total domestic resource cost and the total import cost in India constitutes a net saving of ABF. This saving represents a net increase in welfare due to the trade creating effect of the union. There is increase in the consumption by Q_3Q_4 because of the lower price. After the formation of the union Indian consumers pay only Q_3EDQ_4 amount of money in the purchase of Q_3Q_4 quantity of commodity. Before the formation of the customs union they were paying Q_3CDQ_4 amount of money for the same quantity of rice. Thus, there is a net saving of ECD amount of expenditure which shows increase in the community welfare on the consumption.

The gain from trade creation will be higher if the elasticities of demand and supply are more than one (or are not inelastic) and the pre–customs union tariffs were very high.

Trade Diversion

Before the formation of the union, India's imports were Q_2 Q_3 of rice. Formation of customs union makes the ROTW non– member. Pakistan now becomes a member counry. Diversion of trade from ROTW to Pakistan is trade diversion. If there was a country which was producing rice at cheaper cost than Pakistan, trade preference to Pakistan is a loss to India and is trade diversion.

Formerly India was importing Q_2Q_3 quantity of rice from ROTW for which an amount of money equal to Q_2Q_3 (x) OP_2 was paid for imports, represented by the

Rectangle Q2BCQ3 in the figure. Of this total money payment made for imports GBCH amount goes to the customs authorities in India. This represents income redistribution within India. After the formation of the customs union, India pays for the same amount of imports of rice from Pakistan an amount of money equal to Q2FEQ3. Earlier only G2GHQ3 amount was paid for imports from the rest of the world ROTW. Now an extra amount GFEH is paid. This is the trade diversion loss. The net welfare effect will depend upon if the TC > TD or positive effects > negative effects.

Economic Size of the Customs Union

Smaller nations form customs union to become bigger in economic size i.e., increase their national income or the GDP. If the nations are already big in economic size they can achieve very good results. The potential for specialization and expanded internal market in the union becomes higher. Then PE > than NE or TC > TD will be there.

Economic Distance Between Member Countries Should be Less

Economic distance becomes less if the cost of transport is low. Bad roads within the union will increase the cost of transport as the speed of the trucks will be less and more fuel will be burnt. There will be stalled trucks and losses of goods transported. There will be a lot of reshuffling of production points within the union after the formation of the customs union. There will be shifting of production units from some places (if this is possible) to the most efficient points. This will be possible only if there is transport efficiency. Reshuffling will be done only when very necessary.

Some "Static" Gains from Administrative Economies

It is not clear why the propounders of the theory of customs union called these gains as "static". Nevertheless they are to be so explained here. Trade barriers will be eliminated. The collective costs of administration will be lower. Lesser staff will be there for customs department. There will be savings on their salaries. The staff can be put or re–deployed to other jobs so that they do not become unemployed. Patrolling will be less. There will be no checking of invoices and consignments within the union. {However, illegal things can be checked any time any where like consignments of narcotic drugs or arms or banned things}. Nothing will be done which will deprive the union population of the goods and the goods are sent to the buyers outside the union.

Inter–country and Inter–commodity Substitution will Also be There

After the formation of the customs union, many hitherto imported things will be produced within the union, if there are no technical difficulties for the same. The consumers will get those things cheaper. They will be without the import duties and hence the prices will be lower. There will be substitution in consumption and this will lead to higher welfare.

There will be substitution within the customs union and substitution between the customs union and non–union countries. More production and better production will be there. Consumers will also gain, therefore.

Those who advocate free trade argue that customs union has a protection side (with outsiders) and it has a free trade side (within the union). Hence the free traders call the gains of the customs union as static only. There cannot be dynamic gains because future gains outside the union will not be available to the consumers of the customs union.

REGIONAL TRADE AGREEMENTS (RTA)
RECIONAL TRADE INTEGRATION (RTI)

There can be regional trade agreements without forming the union. There can be regional trade integration, which will be higher than the "agreement" status but less than the "union" status.

RTAs and RTIs can be formed between the countries. There are three things that are important: (A) Agreement is reached and all conditions are pre–agreed. (B) No tariffs are levied on the trade between these countries and cooperation is ensured wherever possible and (C) High tariffs are levied on non –agreement and non–integration countries. *In integration countries there is better cooperation in production and other economic activities.*

Regional trade agreements are entered into between countries which are mutually complementary. If one country has resources but not capital while the other country is rich in capital and technology but not in resources, then there can be regional agreements.

Regional agreements and regional integration will not be called "regional" if they are not between countries adjoining each other.

It will *not* be correct to say that there was an agreement between the Latin American region and African region. *RTIs make GATT, a RATT (Regional agreement on trade and tariff). WTO does not like RATT.*

It is easier to have a RTA than RTI. RTI is a theoretical possibility under the regime of WTO now. SAARC is a regional agreement but there is no "integration" in/ of the member countries India, Pakistan, Afghanistan, Bangladesh, Nepal, Bhutan, Sri Lanka and Maldives. The brotherhood of "integration" is lacking. Theoretically it is possible to have an agreement about the integration! But in practice it is very difficult (rather impossible) to have a real integration. For that a union is necessary.

It is to be noted that the RTAs or RTIs can be bilateral or trilateral. RTA can be between say India and Bangladesh. It can be between India and Pakistan. However, the political relations should be good otherwise there can be neither RTA nor RTI. Both RTA and RTI can be between more than three countries also. SAARC is between 8 countries. ASEAN is tried to be extended to over a dozen countries. There can be multilateral RTAs and RTIs. As written earlier, RTIs are difficult.

The world also has GSP (generalized system of preferences) and MFN (most favoured nation) status. They can fit with the RTA and RTI. Under the GSP preference is given to the member countries. This is spelled with reference to various commodities and goods e.g., if India gets fish from abroad it will get Hilsa or Ilsa fish first from Bangladesh. MFN is also about things. It is expressed this way that if India wants to have cotton it will give first preference to Pakistan. Thus these are expressed with reference to commodities/goods and nations respectively. But these distinctions are not rules. They are ways of explaining.

It may be noted that in many cases the writers treat RTAs and the RTIs as the same. They do not highlight the differences as noted above. But there are differences as were noted.

Effects of RTAs, RTIs and Regional Economic Blocs

(In some syllabi "blocs" is written as "blocks". Unfortunately the wrong spelling is there in even UGC syllabus. Hence this is written.)

We discuss only the beneficial effects, Disadvantages of regional trade agreements, or regional trade integration, or of regional economic blocs are the same as are the advantages of free trade. In other words if these RTAs, RTIs and EBs are not there, there will be greater advantages of the globalization. Still RTA, RTIs and EBs exist.

The advantages of the RTAs, RTIs and EBs can be put as under:

1. Competition from the outsiders is reduced. The producers of the agreement/integration/bloc area can produce under protection. The producers can emulate the producers of the outside the union. It will not be correct to say that all competition will end. There will be healthy competition between the producers of the area. Production units will be located at the sight of the least costs.
2. The quality of the products will also be good. After all there is competition within the RT area. The prices will also be competitive. The producers cannot form a monopoly. That can be checked by the governments. Hence the consumers will also be benefited.
3. There can be free movement of labour and capital inside the bloc or area. That will equalize the wages and the rate of interest. Labour will move from the low wage areas to high wage areas till the wages become more or less equal. Interest rates will be within a lower band of differences. Interest on various types of the deposits and loans will differ but the range will become lower.
4. There will still be "punctiform locations" (at several places) but the overall transport costs will be lower. Efficiency will be tried to be achieved in transport costs between various places. Cross transport costs will be reduced. Deliveries will be from the nearest production site.
5. The firms inside the area will get cheap raw material. Raw material will not be exported abroad. Power, communications and transport network will develop. As the scale of domestic production will increase, the economies of production will also increase. Both external and internal economies will be higher. Therefore, the cost of production per unit will be low. This will enable the producers to charge less. That will widen the market. Wide market will yield higher revenue. Higher revenue – (minus) lower costs will increase profits.
6. Competitiveness will go up. Comparative advantage will emerge for more exports. *The (i) product mix, (ii) price mix, (iii) placement mix or distribution mix and (iv) the promotion mix will develop.* This is known as all round development.
7. There will be higher savings, then higher capital formation, then higher and diversified investment and then more production. GDP will increase and that will increase employment. All factors, producers and consumers can be better off.
8. FDI (foreign direct investment in physical production) and FII (foreign institutional investment or "portfolio investment" or investment in shares and bonds) will flow more. Capital base will improve. There will be innovations as technology develops. The entrepreneurs will develop.

9. The input–output relations will be better and as required. Cooperation and coordination will develop. There will be modernization. *Terms of trade will develop with the outside world. This is a great advantage.* But economic blocs of very poor countries cannot achieve all advantages, least of all this one about the terms of trade.
10. Danger of nationalization goes. Tax policies become uniform. There can be more public expenditure in the regional area. Banking policies become uniform. No administrative barriers are placed. This is known as the "harmonization of the fiscal and monetary policies". External debt can go down. Inflation and deflation will be subdued. Political decisions will be uniform. The political hostilities will end. Development will be at faster pace. Developing countries can become developed. Public and private sectors can develop in coordination. Balance of payment position can improve. It will be easier to take loans from abroad, e.g., from the World Bank.

26 Important Regional Blocs

I.. European Union and Euro
II. ASEAN
III. BIMSET-EC
IV. SAARC "BLOCS: SEM

EUROPEAN UNION [SOME OLD IMPORTANT LANDMARKS]

1. It was in **1957** that an agreement was reached about the **ECM. (EUROPEAN COMMON MARKET)** for coal and steel trade between the original six " countries West Germany (East Germany was then communist country and hostile to the West Germany). France, Italy, Belgium, Netherlands (Holland, whose people are known as Dutch), and Luxembourg.
2. **Nine more countries** joined between 1973-1993 and they were UK, Ireland and Denmark (1973), Greece (1981), Portugal and Spain (1986), Sweden, Finland and Austria (1993). **They are known as the original 15, (6 + 9).**
3. **Ten** more countries joined between 1993 and 2007. They were Cyprus, Czech Republic, Estonia, Hungary, Latvia, Malta, Poland, Lithuania, Slovak Republic and Slovenia.
4. In January 2008, Romania and Bulgaria also joined. In April 2008 there were 27 countries. Turkey's application is still pending (2010).
5. The last 15 countries account for nearly one-fifth of the area and 15 p.c. of the population of the EU. **They account for just 5 p.c. of the GDP of the EU.** There are poor and rich countries amongst the EU. **India's trade with the last 15 countries is of 0.5 billion dollars per year only.**
6. EU members impose (import and export) duties on the average of 3.6 p.c. of the total value but the adjoining countries impose on average 9 p.c. tax.
7. EURO was introduced on 1st January, 1999 but national currencies were abolished on 1st January 2000. The UK, Denmark and Sweden did not become part of the EURO system.
8. There used to be **"SNAKE IN THE TUNNEL SYSTEM".** The countries were supposed to allow their exchange rate to be plus/minus 2.25 p.c. **If the rate fell down by more than 2.25 p.c. then the country used to be supplied dollars i.e., its currency was purchased by other countries. That checked the domestic rate from falling.** If the rate of exchange rose higher than 2.25 p.c, then the country was made to liquidate a part of the dollar reserves. **[A snake in a big pipe cannot move higher than the ceiling and lower than the bottom limit !]**

EEU'S 27 MEMBERS

Now also referred as EU only (European Union) Position 2007-08 (2010 Approximant also)

Romania and Bulgaria were the last two countries admitted, though Turkey was expected to be admitted. The total number of EU countries in April 2008 was 27.

They are listed below in alphabetical order:

1. Austria
2. Belgium
3 Bulgaria
4 Cyprus
5 Czech Republics
6 Denmark
7 Estonia
8 Finland
9 France
10 Germany
11 Greece
12 Hungary
13 Ireland
14 Italy
15 Latvia
16 Lithuania
17 Luxembourg
18 Malta
19 Netherlands (Holland)
20 Poland
21 Portugal
22 Romania
23 Slovakia
24 Slovenia
25 Spain
26 Sweden
27 United Kingdom

There are certain other countries with whom certain islands are associated and they are also members of the EU. Between 2010 and 2012, Malta, Poland, Slovakia, Czech and Turkey may be admitted.

France: Guadalope Martinique Reunion.

Spain: Canary Islands.

Portugal: Azores Medeiru

Turkey could not be admitted because it has no contiguity with the present members. **COPENHAGEN CRITERIA** is to be satisfied. These relate to certain socio-economic conditions e.g., freedom for market access and everything that is there is GATT rounds for the developed countries. Human rights issues also figure.

SOME OTHER IMPORTANT POINTS

The USA was the most powerful country in economic terms and even more so in military terms. **It is the God of small nations, at least it thinks so.**

Within next five years, the US may lose its first position in economic terms. In 2009, it was a 13 trillion dollar economy while India was just 1 trillion dollar economy. EU will become economic power number one, unless the USA can defend its position. The USA's military involvement, (here-there-everywhere) is causing a serious drain on its economy.

EU, JAPAN, CHINA. INDIA AND KOREA (if two koreas become one) ARE COUNTRIES THAT CAN BE IN THE NEXT FIVE POSITIONS. RUSSIA AND BRAZIL CAN SPRING SURPRISES

EU is moving from having 40 p.c. share in international business to 50 p.c. share. The position of the USA is threatened. Even Ford sold its Jaguar and Land Rover to the Tatas of India. The Fiat is struggling in Asia. The top two world film making units of the USA are in Japanese hand. The USA remains supreme because it sells war goods and super aeroplanes. Reader's Digest filed for bankrupt in USA.

Meetings of EU are held in Brussels or Luxembourg. There is a bank, **European Investment Bank,** that lends to the relatively poorer members of the EU. It raises funds from the financial markets and can lend funds to other banks also. It is a no-profit and no-loss bank.

EUROPEAN MONETARY COOPERATION FUND (EMCF) is an institution where the members could deposit 20 p.c. of their reserves in gold and their own currencies to get others to cope with the fluctuations In the exchange rate. EURO has made these transactions unimportant. **Germany is the leader in decision making in EU. Along with France, UK and Italy, Germany is the leader of the "Gang of Four".**

EU is important to India. India is unimportant to the EU. India's imports and exports with these 27 countries are equal to 0.5 (just half percent) of the **total trade of EU.** EU has a very low investment profile in India. **Russia will not become part of EU because it is the biggest country of the world.** Now its GDP is less than that of India.

There are "problem" countries inside the EU where the rate of inflation is around 6 to 9 p.c. p.a. on average. New entrants are problem countries. Amongst the old countries Italy, Spain, Portugal and Greece can be mentioned.

As Keynes had highlighted, people always prefer full employment with somewhat higher inflation to "steady prices but high unemployment". **France voted out a government in 2004 on the issue of high unemployment but with price stability.** There are ups and downs in the EU also.

EU follows the norm that the national public debt should not exceed 60 p.c. of the GDP. There are countries where the public debt is above this limit; sometimes equal to the GDP and sometimes exceeding the GDP. Luxembourg, Belgium, Ireland, Italy, Portugal, Greece and recently admitted countries have this position. The best position is that of Germany.

EU maintains a separate EU army, Another than under NATO. It decides the fate of other countries. **The EU pulverised Yugoslavakia, which was once a very important country as a member of NAM i.e., the Non-Aligned Movement.** It has been "balkanised" i.e., broken into many countries. In 2008, Kosovo was allowed to declare itself as a separate country. EU was very harsh on Slovaks. Their President was captured and he died under mysterious circumstances. **EUU is also practising economic imperialism just like the US.**

Yet both are at loggerheads.

The US is losing economic battle: (i) US never wanted EURO to achieve 1:1 parity. By Dec. 2009 the US is 66 p.c. of the value of EURO. EU wants the entire Europe to be zone of EURO. After this target is achieved EU wants EURO to become reserve currency in the world. In 2010, Euro could not displace $ but 15 per cent of world reserves were in Euro.

However, for defence purposes, EU still depends upon the USA. If there is a war (a hypothetical situation as at present), the EU cannot withstand the US.

Both US and EU are protectionists. **They advocate in the world that "the cat be protected against mouse"!** They are highly discriminatory and protective against India. Germany, France, the UK and Italy **enjoy veto power in decision-making.** One main business of the US and EU is to destroy a country and then "fighty amongst themselves to have a share in the rebuilding programmes. That is how they get business and investment opportunities.

THE EURO

1. The Euro become the single currency of the European Monetary Union which was adopted initially by 11 out of the 15 EU members.

   Greece was not allowed to join and the UK, Sweden and Denmark did not join.

   From January 1, 2002 the Euro notes (Americans call them "bills") started replacing the old currencies. Coins were also changed. EURO also has 100 cents. Conversions can continue but many persons have retained old currency and coins in pursuance of the hobby of coin/currency collectors. **The whole continent will have atleast 12 billion bank notes and around 80 billion coins. France alone (for example) was estimated to be requiring 7.6 billion EURO coins. Euro coins required two acres equivalent space for storage.**

THE EU SAVED $ 85 BILLION IN CURRENCY CONVERSIONS IN EXCHANGE FEES, IN THE YEAR IT WAS INTRODUCED

2. National currencies of those countries which started having EUROs, were abolished. **CEU (Council of European Union), EUP, (European Union Parliament), ECECJ (European Commission and European Court of Justice)were established.**
3. There are five conditions of convergence for issues relating to EU and EURO. **First**[1] inflation should be around 1.5. p.c.p.a. and maximum 2 p.c.p.c. for middle level countries but the average of three years should become 1.5 p.c.p.a. Secondly long term interest rates should not be more than 2 p.c. points above the average yield in the three lowest inflation countries. Thirdly, fiscal deficit should not be more than 3 p.c. of the GDP in any year. Fourthly, national debt should not exceed 60 p.c. of the GDP. Fifthly, exchange rates are to be maintained (vis. others) with the ERM band.
4. The USA and the EU are such that just as there are sun flares that affect the seasons, climates and production on earth, the above normal changes [1]" in the corporations of the US or EU (Microsoft is $ 5 trillion ($ 5,000 company billion, the recessions or upswings there bring economic earthquakes in the rest of the world. From Paris alone there are daily $ 3 trillion remittances under arbitrage. **Imagine then EU negotiating with India about $ 3.3 million worth of exports of textiles EU is so miserly.**

On January 1, 2002, EU started having EURO @ =$ 0.85 and all countries except the UK, Sweden and Denmark are locked In the system. In Sept. 2004 one EURO was equal to 1.23 dollars. **Dollar lost a lot of its market value after the Iraq War. In Sept. 2009 Euro 1 = $ 1.46, but in Dec. 2009 it was Euro = $ 1.52. Even the Taj Hotel in**

Mumbay insists upon the tourists to pay in rupees after getting their dollars converted into rupees. This is so because $ was losing exchange rate on dally basis.

WHEN THE EURO WAS BORN ON FIRST JANUARY 1999 (Printing notes/ bills and minting coins took time), THE RATE OF EURO WAS 0.85 dollar or 85 cents. On fourth April 2008, the EURO commanded 155 cents, that meant 70 cents more. EURO got up valued to the Index number 182.4 and the dollar was down to the Index down by 45.16p.c. In other words, its value was down to 100—45.16 = 54.84.[2] In Dec. 2009 Euro I was equal to 152 cents or $ I was nearly equal to 0.657 Euro.

2. **There are now EURO bonds and not bonds in the currencies of member countries. Even when the twin towers of the New York, USA, were revaged, the average pattern of reserves of different countries was:**

Kept in US dollars	68 p.c.	1971 $34	=	1 ounce gold
Kept in EURO	13 p.c.			
Kept in gold and IMF reserves	19 p.c.	2009 $ 1214	=	1 ounce gold. (Dec.)

There is great possibility of countries keeping more and more reserves in gold, EURO, US $ and IMP reserves in that order. Values of gold and EURO are rising Gold was 36.35 times dearer between 1971 and 2009 (Dec). That indirectly meant devaluation or rather down-valuation of dollar. (Devaluation is announced and down-valuation happens due to market forces). **A day may come when not more than 20 to 25 p.c. reserves of various countries may be in dollars, unless dollar stabilises.**

3. Not all members of the EU can automatically become part of EURO. They will have to keep the inflation below 1.5 p.c. before being admitted. ERM (exchange rate management) is managed in EU by the German Central Bank. There is a trade off between inflation and unemployment. EU countries are having a lot of unemployment (even upto 12 p.c. of the work force that wants work at the prevailing wages/salaries).

These countries pay social security benefits rather than risk higher inflation due to efforts to generate employment. Instead cheap labour is imported from Turkey.

ASEAN
(ASSOCIATION OF SOUTH-EAST ASIAN NATIONS)

ASEAN is known as 10 + 3 association. The original 10 members are:

1. Indonesia	2. Singapore
3. Malaysia	4 Brunei
5. Myanmar	6. Thailand
7. Laos	8. Vietnam
9. Cambodia	10. Philippines

These countries pronounce it as AZIAN / AH - See - Ahn / AA - ZEE - Ahn.

The "Plus three" members are

CHINA, JAPAN AND KOREA

India wants to be a member of ASEAN but China is opposed to it. China does not probably want ASEAN to be known as 10 + 4 bloc. **Another reason why India could**

not become member of ASEAN is lobbying of Pakistan. If India goes forward can Pakistan be far behind? If Pakistan cannot be admitted, it lobbies through China not to take India as member. If India becomes a member, **Pakistan would plead for admission of SAARC in ASEAN.** Pakistan infact wants to make China a member of SAARC.

India is a free country but it is still not a free economy. Foreigners say that the "babus", the bureaucrats and the politicians are great bribe seekers for business deals.

India is recording a "high growth" rate in recent years (8 to 9 p.c.p.a.) but was recording inflation at the rate of 6 to 7 p.c. and the residual rate came to hardly 2 p.c. real growth rate.

India trade with ASEAN was

1991-92	$ 1.0 b
2000-02	$ 3.4 b
2007-08	$ 30.0 b

The FII (investors in stocks and bonds) brought near collapse of the ASIAN TIGER countries i.e., most growing countries of Asia, including in the ASEAN. Thereafter the FDI investors came in and the USA alone invested $ 250 b. in manufacturing and services on equal basis.

In the Conference of the Prime Ministers of the ASEAN countries, India also participated as non-member. The Charter of the Summit highlighted the following points:

1. Poverty be alleviated.
2. Inter-sectoral and inter-sectoral gaps be reduced.
3. Environment be protected through sustainable use of natural resources.
4. All types of transport linkages be promoted. There is proposal for railway line from India to Vietnam.
5. ASEAN to become free trade bloc by 2015.
6. Goods, commodities, services and investment to have free flows, including labour and capital.
7. There be no proposal for common currency.
8. ASEAN to negotiate unitedly in WTO.
9. There be democracy and peace in the region.
10. There be no interference in the internal affairs of other countries.

A common currency can reduce the dependence on the US dollar in a common market. But, the systems of governance and differing sizes of the economies will make common currency mechanism difficult. India-ASEAN trade which was 2.4 b. dollars in 1992, rose to $ 23 b in 2005 and to $ 30 b in 2007. Like NAFTA, SAFTA, AND PAFTA, India wants a free trade zone.

India wanted (2007 Conference) to create an arc of advantage. India could not achieve anything substantial, much less the entry in ASEAN. Some inane things were mentioned. Between 1976 and 2009, is conferences were held.

* There be about one million tourists from ASEAN to India.
* Trade of India with ASEAN be taken to $ 5 b. early. and
* There be open sky and rail linkages policies.

* Ninety seven (97) projects were listed for cooperation with ASEAN.
* In the field of Asian traditional medicines, there be greater cooperation.
* India cannot give further concessions to make India a free zone in all respects.

The meetings were held in these years

1976,	Indonesia,
1977,	Malaysia,
1987,	Philippines,
1992,	Singapore
1995,	Thailand,
1998,	Vietnam,
200,	Brunei
2002,	Cambodia
2003,	Indonesia,
2004,	Laos,
2005,	Malaysia,
2007,	Malaysia,
2009,	Thailand
2009,	Thailand
2009,	Thailand

ASEAN countries pointed out that the free trade system that was to be introduced by India from 1st January, 2006, was not started. These related to crude edible oil, refined edible oil, tea and pepper. Duties were to be 40 p.c. according to the value. On edible oil it was reduced by India to 29 p.c but on pepper and tea, it was 100 p.c. **In 2007, there were still 489 items that were on negative list of imports. Earlier the is it included 1414 items in the rounds.**

Horizontal expansion of cities, eating away agricultural land in the farm houses of the VIPs has reduced the land under cultivation by one-fifth during the last 25 years. The Bhopal round was 18th informal round and 74 delegates participated in it on 8th Jan. 2008. Instead of the countries having lists of expanding free trade in many more lines, the countries had negative lists of trade and reciprocal concessions were to be negotiated. **ASEAN demand for reduction in duties was right. The leftists and even the other political parties were harping on the interests of the small and medium farmers. If India can import edible oil, pulses, tea, coffee, then the land can be used for other crops. Wheat and rice could be grown on the land.** The crisis in India is due to rising population and falling acreage under agriculture and forests due to the activities of the realtors.

BIMSET-EC

1 It is an acronym that baffles !
2. It stands for Bay of Bengal initiatives for multi-sectoral technical and economic cooperation between India, Nepal, Bhutan on one side and seeking greater cooperations with Thailand, Singapore, Bangladesh, Sri-Lanka (once known as Ceylon) and Myanmar (earlier known as Burma).

Nothing substantial has happened on ground.

SAARC 1985-2008-2010 [SOUTH ASIAN ASSOCIATION OF REGIONAL COOPERATION]

SAARC has 8 countries India, Pakistan, Bangladesh, Nepal, Bhutan, Sri Lanka, Maldives and now Afghanistan also. Its meetings were held earlier as under:

1985	Dhaka (Deca in 1947), Bangladesh Till 1971 Bangladesh was known as East Pakistan and was liberated with the assistance of India from the socio-political-economic yoke of Pakistan.
1986	Bangalore, India.
1987	Kathmandu, Nepal
1988	Islamabad, Pakistan
1989	Male, Maldives
1991	Colombo, Sri Lanka
1992	Dhaka, Bangladesh
1993] 1995	New Delhi, India
1997	Male, Maldives
1998	Colombo
2002	Kathmandu
2003	Islamabad
2005	Dhaka
2007	New Delhi

SAARC COULD HAVE ACHIEVED MUCH BUT FOR PAKISTAN. INDIA GRANTED MFN (Most favoured nation) status to Pakistan decades back but the same has not been given to India.

Pakistan harps on Kashmir in every forum. In 2008, while it was talking on reaching a compromise on Kashmir (acceptable to India, Pakistan and the Kashmiries), it raised the issue in Organization of Islamic Countries. **Late JN Dixit, India's ex-Ambassador (i.e. High Commissioner) in Pakistan once observed that "even if you ask for a glass of water in Pakistan, they say solve the Kashmir issue" first. Years 2009-2010 were impressing *Afpak* issues.**

2007 SARC summit was held on 3rd April in New Delhi. We cannot do better than quote some important points raised by the then beloved President of India, Dr. APJ Abdul Kalam:

1. SAARC had 147 crore population which came to nearly 25 p.c. of the global population. It had the largest population of the youth in the world. The region has the highest biodiversity regions of the world. The actual and potential purchasing power of the region are very high. The region is known was its civilization even more.
2. Kalam "Sahib", as he is popularly known made the delegates aware of his vision and was sure that its realisation was possible by 2017. The dream of Dr. Kalam will remain a dream due to corruption and terrorism.

    * Poverty can be reduced from 25 p.c. to zero.
    * Per capita income can be raised to $ 10,000.

* Infant mortality can be brought down from 1,000 per one lakh births to 10.
* All countries can arrange for safe drinking water and quality health care.
* All SAARC counties can have 100 p.c. literacy for persons above or 8 + years of age.
* It is possible to empower all with quality education, and employment.

3. Each country has immense potential:

India. It can become developed country. **Under PURA** (Providing Urban Amenities in Rural Areas) countries can secure rural urban continuum. PURA cluster size can be of 30 villages and the populations can differ. Gandhian self-sufficiency can be achieved there.

Pakistan can progress further in agriculture, cotton textiles and animal husbandry.

Sri Lanka can ride to further success by itensively developing its tea growing and rubber plantations.

Afghanistan is endowed with precious stones, fruit fields, natural oil, minerals and metals, animal husbandry.

Bangladesh can achieve further development through its Grameen Bank Scheme, which can be emulated by others, **a model for its concept of "happiness index" of Bhutan.**

Maldives is known for its innovative tourism.

Nepal can prosper by utilising its hydel energy and the utilising the bio-diversity.

4. Dr. Kalam wanted "inclusive growth" which ensures that rural areas and poor persons are not by passed by the growth process and infact develop more so that the rural urban chasm is bridged.

Growth rate, infrastructure facilities joint family system can increase "prosperity and happiness" index.

ASEAN BASIC DATA

Malaysia	330,257	25,580	117,776	221,471
Myanmar0	676,577	54,745	10,463	5,034
Philippines	300,000	82,664	86,407	76,940
Singapore	697	4,240	106,884	363,431
Thailand	513,254	64,469	163,525	190,446
Viet Nam	330,363	82,022	45,277	55,261
ASEAN	4,465,502	549,852	800,735	1,047,927

Sources: Finance and Macro economic Surveillance Unit (FMSU) Database for GDP and Merchandise the (BOP basis)

ASEAN Statistical Pocket book 2005 for Total Area and Population

Notes:

2004 figures as proxies, the figures were computed based on the average rate of growth of 1995-2000, for Brunei Darussalam and Myanmar, (1996-2000 for Lao PDR), and based on of national projection for Cambodia, Indonesia, Malaysia, Philippines, Singapore and Viet Nam, Thailand based on growth rate 2000-2002

Total exports and imports of goods, BOP basis

Rough estimate using GDP real growth and inflation as a proxy to GDP deflator

Rough estimate based on the available data until Q3, using simple extrapolation method.

NOTE

1 "ly" is not added in first. First is written as first, "ly" is added from second onwards
2. ONE EURO WAS COMMANDING 1.55 US DOLLARS ON 4TH APRIL 2008, and 1.52 in Dec. 2009.
   If $1 = S 0.85, then $1 was equal to 1.1765 [1i- 0.85]
   If $1 = $1.55, Then [1 -i- 1.55 0.645]
   0.645 ± 1.1765 = —45.16 is fall in the value of $.
3. Pakistan wants to annexe Kashmir through terrorism. It lost three wars with India and hence thought that pinpricks will bleed India to death. Under the terms of accession 1946-47 only the border states could exercise the right to merge with India or Pakistan. LYALLPUR was a Hindu majority state ruled by a Nawab. The option was with the ruled by a Nawab. The option was with the ruler and not with the public. The Nawab wanted to merge with Pakistan and it happened. Lyallpur is now known as Faislabad. The US and the UK were presuading Maharaja Hari Singh, the ruler of Jammu and Kashmir to declare J & K independent and the Maharaja dilly dalied. Meanwhile assisted by the British, the tribes of Pak attached J & K. Balistan and Gilgit and a small portion of J & K were captured by them.
4. When India was deceived to take the matter to the UNO, the two resolutions were passed: (A) PAKISTAN ARMY WOULD VACATE THE AREAS HELD BY IT ILLEGALLY AND THEN (B) a PLEBISITE BE HELD TO FIND OUT THE WILL OF THE PEOPLE OF KASHMIR.
   Pakistan asked its armymen to remove their uniforms and remain their in civilian dress ! Even the UN understood the trick. The UN resolution lapsed. Mr. Bill Clinton, the president of the USA accepted this. His Secretary of the State's (Mrs. Madaline Albright's) father was the supervisor of the cease fire on LOC after ceasefire
   PAKISTAN FOLLOWED THE POLICY OF THE HITLER'S INFORMATION MINISTER THAT "A LIE REPEATED HUNDREDS OF TIME WILL BE TAKEN AS A TRUTH BY THE WORLD". Pakistan had only two things to repeat parrot like. India is neither vacating the Kashmir (army withdrawal) and has gone back on the promise of plebiscite." It was the case of thief accusing the police of loot.
5. During the tenure of the first Prime Minister of India, late Jawaharlal Nehru, (whose term lasted 17 years), the Information Minister, late Shri Satya Narain Sinha (to be pronounced as Singh), also enjoyed the same tenure.
   Once members of Parliament complained that the world believes the Pakistan version even though false and does not believe India's version, even though the UN admits it ! The minister replied "the Pakistanies speak lies'.
   Someone "advised", "why do we not match Pakistan in telling lies ? To this the Indian Minister replied, "Oh, they outwit us". Asked "how", the Indian Minister said:
   Once we tried to spread the information that in India the chicks come out of the eggs in one day and start flying" To this the Pakistanies replied" In our country the EGGS FLY !".

26B | Other Economic Blocs

I. OTHER ECONOMIC BLOCS

The ultimate aim of EC is to convert into Single European Market (SEM) *with in inclusion of EFTA* (European Free Trade Association) of once 'Outer Seven' countries of ECM. United Kingdom, Denmark, Norway, Sweden, Austria, Switzerland, Portugal and the United Kingdom (some of which are already members of EC or EU). EC + EFTA (with some countries figuring in EC from EFTA) will make up SEM.

Although the CMEA (Cooperation for Mutual Economic Assistance) covering erstwhile USSR and its East European Allies has collapsed, the probability of these countries and CIS (Commonwealth of Independent States of former USSR) either forming a new economic alliance or joining EC continues. The Czech and Slovak Republics, Hungary and Poland have concluded separate discussions on Association agreements with the EC.

NAFTA will get enlarged in future. Uruguay, Paraguay, Brazil and Argentina have signed a pact to form a free trade zone by 1995, (a name will come up) and Bolivia, Venezuela, Peru, Ecuador and Columbia are moving towards an Andean Common Market (ACM). In 1988 CUFTA was for US and Canada only.

NAFTA (North American Free Trade Association) was formed in 1993. The member countries were the USA, Canada and Mexico. More Latin American countries will join it. Its total population in 1993 was 36.2 crore with per capita income as high as of the EC.[1]

G-77: South-South bloc was a loose type of association. The term 'south' for less developed countries started from Italy of which southern part is "back ward" and northern part developed. Thus developing/less developed/ backward/under-developed countries are known as 'south' countries. 'South-South' cooperation means making the economies of these countries mutually complementary. These countries once numbered 77 and were known as G-77 countries even when their number increased. They were also known 'third world' countries—the first two worlds being (A) Developed Capitalist Economies, and (B) Socialist Countries. With the collapse of socialism, there are only two worlds now—the developed and less developed with the G-77 not receiving pampering attention. OPEC (Organisation of Petroleum Exporting Countries) got out of G-77 for all practical purposes.

ASEAN (Association of South East Asian Nations) was formed in 1967 and its member countries are Indonesia, Malaysia, Philippines, Singapore, Thailand and Brunei. With population of nearly 32 crore, its average annual per capita GNP was US $ 984 in 1993. It is now known as 11 + 3 bloc.

APEC (Asia-Pacific Economic Cooperation) was formed in 1989 and the membership is of ASEAN + USA, Japan, China, South Korea, Australia, New Zealand, Canada, Hong Kong, and Taiwan. India is not there in any bloc.

AFRICAN TRADE BLOCS

1910 South African Customs Union (SACU)
Most powerful South Africa had customs union arrangements with Botswana, Lesotho, Namibia and Swaziland.

1966 **UDEAC (Union Douaniere et Economique de L' Africa.** The French-speaking countries of Cameroon, Central African Republic, Chad, Congo, Gabon.

1989 Equatorial Guinea joined them.

1994 Name changed to "CEMAC" (Economic and Monetary Community of Central Africa.)

1967 **EAC: (East African Cooperation):** Broke up in 1977. Revived now. Kenya, Tanzania and Uganda are the members.

1973 **CEAO: Economic Community of West Africa.** Its members are Benin, Burkina Faso, Cote d' Ivoire, Mali, Mauritania, Niger and Senegal. Economic Market aspect was put on agenda of greater action in

1975 **ECOWAS Economic Community of West African States.** Benin, Burkina Faso, Cape Verde, Cote de' Ivoire (Ivory Coast), Gambia, Ghana, Guinea, Guinea-Bissau, Liberia, Mali, Mauritania, Niger, Nigeria, Senegal, Sierra Leone, and Togo are its members.

1976 **CEPGL Economic Community of the Countries of the Great Lakes.** Burundi, Rwanda, Democratic Republic of the Congo.

1980 **SADC South African Development Community.** Angola, Botswana, Lesotho, Malawi, Mozambique, Swaziland, Tanzania, Zambia, Zimbabwe, Namibia, South Africa, Mauritius, Democratic Republic of the Congo and Seychelles. First Nine members were there in 1980. Others joined between 1990 and 1998.

1984 **IOC Indian Ocean Commission: Comoros,** Madagaskar, Seychelles (*) and Mauritius.

1992 **CBI Cross-Border Initiative.** Burundi, Comoros, Kenya, Madagascar, Malawi, Mauritius, Rwanda, Namibia, Seychelles, Swaziland, Tanzania, Uganda, Zambia and Zimbabwe.

1993 **COMESA: Common Market for Eastern and Southern Africa.** Angola, Burundi, Comoros, Djibouti, Egypt, Ethiopia, Kenya, Lesotho, Malawi, Mauritius, Mozambique, Rwanda, Somalia, Sudan, Swaziland, Uganda, Sambia, Simbabe. **Most wide.**

1994 **WAEMU: West African Economic and Monetary Union:** Benin, Burkina Faso, ivory cost, Mali Niger, Senegal, Togo and Guinea-Bissau.

EUROPE
[OTHER THAN EU]
(EU SEPARATITY DISCUSSED)

EEA (European Economic Area) includes the EU + Iceland, Leichtenstein and Norway.

EU & Bilateral Agreements. They are with Hungary, Poland, Bulgaria, Czech Republic, Estonia, Latvia, Lithunia, Slovak Republic and Slovenia. These were erstwhile socialist countries of Europe.

LATIN AMERICA

I960 **CACM** Central American Common Market was formed by El Salvador, Guatemala, Honduras, Nicaragua and Costa Rica. Panama was not there.

LAFTA was also formed in 1960 but had to be infused with new blood in 1980. **Now this functions as LAIA i.e., Latin American Integration Association.**

1973: CAR/COM. [Caribbean Community and Common Market) covers Antigua, Barbuda, Barbados, Jamaica, St. Kitts and Nevis, Trinidad and Tobago. **These are "West Indies" countries. As it known to all, there is no country of the name "West Indies". They are known as such for cricket only.**

[It may be of interest to know that the present Indonesia was known as **"EAST INDIES"** under Dutch its occupation till 1949].

After 1974 Belize, Dominica, Grenada, Montserrat, St. Lucia, St. Vincent and the Grenadines, the Bahamas also joined. The last one has certain conditional reservations.

MIDDLE EAST AND ASIA

ASEAN AND APEC: (discussed in details hereafter), have (i) 10 + 3 countries and (ii) Australia, Brunei, Canada, Indonesia, S. Korea, Malaysia, New Zealand, Philippines, Singapore, Thailand, the US, China, Hong Kong (China), Mexico, Papua New Guinea, Chile, peru, Russa and Vietnam. **INDIA HAS NO PLACE ANYWHERE EXCEPT IN THE NON-FUNCTIONAL "SAARC".**

1981: GCC (Gulf Cooperation' Council) was formed by Bahrain, Kuwait, Oman, Qatar, Saudi Arabia and United Arab Emirates.

GAFTA: Greater Arab Free Trade Area (1998) had Bahrain, Eqypt, Iraq, Jordan, Kuwait, Lebanon, Libya, Morocco, Oman, Qatar, Saudi Arabia, Sudan, Syria, Tunisia, UAE and Yamen.

India wanted 'SAPTA" on the pattern of NAPTA for South Asian preferential trading agreement but it could not take off (1994).

USA is keen to develop economic cooperation between NAFTA and APEC. Europeans have their own common market, North America their own and so do have the East Asians. India has been left in the cold because the US still considers India a less open economy. It is prepared to cooperate with the 'socialist' China but not with free India ! The reasons are best known to them though India is almost as big a market as China is.[2]

APEC, however, will witness clashes of interest between USA, Japan and China who would like to dominate and most certainly would not like to be not earning as much in this group. India is not a member of EC but has good access. It can have similar access with NAFTA or APEC if US 'permits'. IOEG (Indian Ocean Economic

Grouping) with South Africa, Kenya, Saudi Arabia, the UAE, Oman, Iran, Thailand and Indonesia and of course with SAARC can be tried. If only India and Pakistan could cooperate things would have been quite different. If they cannot then India has to further its interest facing opposition from Pakistan. In this connection USA and Pakistan were strange partners against India. *"The US let loose NAFTA and APEC also force Europe to make peace with GATT on Washington ' terms"*. It is uni-polar word that makes USA invoke its 'Super 301' to punish any country which it feels is not allowing USA to have favorable balance of payment with it —irrespective of the fact whether the country is big or small. The USA is so annoyed and jittery about some countries coming up in the word notable Japan and Germany, that it is in foul mood with those who do not accept its terms over GATT *even !*.

The world had seen limited economic bloc within a block like Benelux of Belgium, Netherlands and Luxembourg within EC. India could have forged on such. COMECON, which is a cartel. It would cut down production of oil rather than allow prices to fall. Can India have G-3 of China India and Iran? Might be if USA twist the arms of these countries to much.

L.A.F.T.A. (Latin American Free Trade Association). Negotiations for this started in 1954 and agreement was reached in 1960 and the Association came into being from July 1, 1961. (Treaty of Montevideo). Argentina, Brazil, Chile, Paraguay, Peru and Uruguay were the members from South America and Mexico was the lone country from North America. These seven countries were later joined by Colombia, Bolivia and Equator.

Throughout these years this Association has been more of less non-functional. A common market could not be frothed much less a union of these countries even in a limited way.

LAFTA was superseded by the Latin American Integration Association (LAIA. This too is ineffective.[3]

II. INDIA AND THE EU

EU is important for India, but India is not important for EU. As seen earlier, India's share in the EU trade was 0.5 p.c. i.e., nearly one-fourth of the imports came from that bloc.

Out of the total exports of Rs. 141604 crore exports to EU countries were 26 p.c. UK (5.7 p.c), Germany (5.6), Netherlands (2.3), Belgium (3.9), France (2.5) were the main countries out of them in exports. The rest of the 10 countries of EU accounted for just 5.8 p.c. of the exports of India.

Similarly the shares in imports of different countries were: UK (6.1), Belgium (6.0), Germany (5.1), France (1.7), Netherlands (1.1) and the rest of the 10 countries of EU accounted for 3.6 p.c. of the total imports of India.

India cannot send to them what they want. Besides, the EU countries are highly restrictive in their imports from India. These countries are keen to export but if they do not import much from India, India has the problem of funding the imports. EU was not increasing the quota of imports of textiles from India, which it is supposed to increase by the year 2005..India's exports of textiles to EU were 3.3 billion EUROs. Now the EU countries have started exporting their jeans and other types of clothes (one country calls their shirt as "honest shirt") to India. Infact, it is repotted that rejected pieces and used pieces are being imported under "rags" from there and the Indian sellers sell them as high quality products.

EU recorded lower rates of growth in output in recent years. The following figures show the relative positions.

Years	**EU**	**US p.c. growth**
1999-2000	3.8	4.7
2000-2001	0.8	2.2
2001-2002	1.7	2.8
2002-2003	2.5	3.7
	GOI	**Econ. Survey 2003**

EU investment in India in some years had been as under:

	US $ in millions
1990-1991	6
1995-1996	652
1996-1997	1386
1997-1998	849
1998-1999	322
1999-2000	889
2000-2001	913
2001-2002	515

Exports to EU are increasing at a very tardy pace. If exports to one EU member country go up, they go down with others.

In 2001-2002, for example, exports were down by the following percentages to some important EU counties:

	P.C.
UK	**—6.0**
Germany	—6.2
France	—7.4
Belgium	—5.4
Non-EU	

Exports to EU	**Rs. Cr.**	**Imports**
1960-61	232	417
1970-71	282	320
1980-81	1447	2639
1990-91	8951	12680

NOTE

1. Entire chapter prepared with bits and pieces appearing in learned economic journals, IMF and WB publication about such organisation. See Wikipedia also.
2. See Times of India, November 28, 1993. Details of population and GNP PC etc. from the write ups of A.N. Das, Sanjay Bara and L.K. Sharma
3. C.A.C.M. was established in 1960 and dissolved in 1969. It was 'common market' for Central American States. Members were Costa Rica El Salvador, Guatemala,, Honduras, and transformed into a common market in 1973 *(CARICOM).*

   EAEC (East African Economic Community) was established in 1967 by Kenya, Tanzania, and Uganda and it collapsed in 1977.

   ECWA Economic Community of West Africa was established in 1974 but never assumed powerful significance.

27 A. Theory of Capital Movement in International Trade. B. FDI and FII in India

International capital moves for earning higher profits. The same is the reason for the movement of national capital.

There are two parties involved —the "donor" nation/company and the recipient nation/party. Both seek benefits from the capital movement. The donor country is interested in higher returns and safety. The receiving country is interested in adequacy/ low costs and high benefits. Imperial governments and their capitalists (at present multinationals) were/are no paragons of benevolence. They cannot exploit the developing economies the same way they used to do earlier. They still seek high profits and that is also taken as the form of exploitation.

The countries which receive capital, expect the following benefits:

(a) import of technology-goods and know-how;
(b) funds for importing necessary raw materials;
(c) funds for importing experts for transformation of antiquated production system into a modern one.
(d) reduction in the costs of production so that competitive (and lower) prices can be charged;
(e) expansion of markets globally;
(f) more exports and ability to import for higher domestic production and exports;
(g) higher production, higher employment and higher per capita income;
(h) higher levels of living and diversified livelihoods; reduction in balance of payment deficits and if possible conversion to surplus;
(i) higher national income, higher welfare and
(j) freedom from indebtedness.

The beneficial effects are known as the "spread or favourable linkage effects". These linkages can be "backward or upstream" (higher production of cloth will stimulate production of cotton and pesticides for cotton and of many more things. The second type of linkages are "forward or downstream" i.e., if there is cotton cloth there will be many more tailors or manufacturers of sewing machines who would be in business. Backwash effects are adverse effects. Naturally it should be SE> BE.

Initials effect of inflow is that the country which receives capital will find its balance of payment position improving. Its exchange rate will go up. Or, if it was falling, it will not fall at the same high rate. Much will depend upon the amount of capital. There will be beneficial effects on different variables.

Long-term effects of inflows can be and should be beneficial. There will be import of better machinery, raw materials and technology. Production base will improve. The scale and scope of operations will improve. There will be several types of economies both internal and external. These economies will reduce cost of production and then prices. Then more can be sold/exported. There will be higher incomes. Employment, investment, savings, capital formation etc. will all go up. National and per capita income will improve. Total welfare will improve provided corruption, inequalities and other evil things are not there.

Initial effect of outflow will be adverse on balance of payment. However, it is to be kept in mind that no country exports or sends capital out unless they are in surplus. Hence the adverse impact may not be felt.

Long term impact of outflow will be that there will be inflows of profits and interest in the donor countries. The impact will not be opposite of the long term impact of inflows.

Both donor and recipient countries gain. If that were not to be so, then there would not have been capital movement.

Capital movements promote real movements, India will not borrow dollars just for the sake of keeping them. They will be utilized for importing commodities, goods, machines, technology and technical know-how. Thus real thing are imported. If our capital moves out to another country that country will import real things from our country. Long term effects of capital movement are (i) thicker base of domestic production (ii) higher exports, (iii) higher imports despite import substitution and import compression.

Capital movements are FDI (foreign direct investment) and FII (foreign institutional investment).

(See pages on FDI and FII elsewhere in the Chapter particularly in the context of India.)

It is to be noted that the outflows of capital have an adverse impact on balance of payment. However, if surplus capital is exported, the net and long term result will be productive.

Indian industrial houses are purchasing companies of the European and even American countries. This outflow now brings inflows later on. However, the tasks of investment in India were not complete. There are several sectors e.g., infrastructure sectors (power generation, irrigation, roads, improvement in railways to many others) development, modernization of agriculture and investing a little bit more in "wage goods" industries.

In such cases the outflows provide benefits to the industrialists and not to the "general public."

Capital movements improve both the scale of operation an scale of operation. Kindle berger and Gerald Meier are of the opinion that

(A) Less developed countries should welcome capital movement from outside if scale and scope of operations improve and if economies of production are realised.
(B) The capital inflows are welcome in public or private or cooperative sectors so long as their spread effects are high.
(C) The capital inflows should improve both technical and economic aspects of the economy.

Capital movements are now a days for mergers, acquisitions, franchises' takeovers and starting new ventures. The ultimate test is the same. There should not be high-adverse short term effects and there should be massive favourable long term effects.

Capital movement is welcome if capital goods sectors improve. They are equally welcome if supplementary and complementary investments go up. They are welcome if the "H" (heavy industries), W. (white goods), 'w'{wage goods), Cd (consumer-durable goods) sectors develop. Diversification and concentration both are welcome so long as the long term effects are positive as necessary.

"Funds follow flag". Capital movements depend upon good political relations.

Outflows of funds mean outflows of real resources. Inflows of funds mean inflows of real resources. Outflows can be deflationary. Inflows can be inflationary. These aspects need careful management.

Short term capital movements are of credits, investment in demand deposits and investments in securities and the reserve flows thereof. These can be inflows and outflows. What are inflows for the recipient country will be outflows for the "donor" country.

Inflows of today will involve the/outflows of future and vice versa. Inflows of capital can strengthen the production base and will bring inflows from exports. Exports many a times require imports of raw materials and technology first and cause outflows. Outflows and inflows per se are of less significance in comparison to the ultimate effects on national income, its spatial and inter-personal/distribution, its sectoral distribution, employment generation and income propagation.

Capital flows are coveted as well as feared. Socialists/communists always speak against "imperialistic flows" but they themselves get them for their countries. Communists debate; debate more. They were engaged in their ideological debates, when the communist systems collapsed in 1991. They do not participate in democratic governance but act as scare crows to others. If it is found that the capital inflows/outflows in some present communist/socialist countries are greater than in, the similarly placed democratic countries, it is due to the fact that the socialists have secret negotiations for the capital movement.

On its own, the capital moves to those lines of investments which involve less risks and promise high security and profits.

If the investors get positions of monopolies or oligopolies they prefer to take their capital there. Foreign-investors value the stream of-flows of returns" more.

HYMER suggested that the capital movement will depend upon I/r. "I" is the stream of income the capital produces and "r" is the market rate of interest. Stream of flow should be in higher multiples of the "r". \$ 200b/8 is better than \$ 200b/10 : \$ 300b./7 is better than both.

Capital of MNCs "moves" first to the extraction of valuable minerals—oil, gold, silver, iron ore copper to nuclear energy raw materials. Then they prefer the plantations. Capital movement depends upon (i) high returns and (ii) easy terms. Countries that invite capital argue that it will increase welfare. Countries that send capital out argue about high expected returns in future.

All capital movements thus involve transfer problems and there are feedback and counter feedback effects of them. Inflow of capital will bring inflow of raw materials, machines, technology, and even expert manpower. Thereafter, the production base improves. That will promote exports. Exports are outflows in real terms. A country will lose its raw materials, goods, commodities etc. Since the balance of payments accounts are prepared in money terms, exports become inflows, of money. Imports become outflows, of money. Flows are important as much as they affect the total economic growth and development and ultimately the welfare of all more importantly of the common people.

Capital movement can be for mergers, acquisitions, franchise, branches and participations. Outsourcing and in sourcing can be involved. Capital movement seeks a minimum oligopolistic position by those who invest. Employment of the abundant factor increases. The pressure of the shortage of a scarce factor is eased. Scarce factor gets lower prices that it would have commanded. Surplus factor gets higher factor remunerations that it would have got otherwise.

Immediate and initial effects are known as "feedback effects". Long term and reversal effects are known as 'counter-feedback effects.'They-emanate from the direct investment. Portfolio investment flows bring these effects indirectly.

Capital flows between governments are now less important. The erstwhile socialist countries used to give loans/grants for public sector projects. Khrushchev promised financing of the Aswan Dam of Egypt on the river Nile but had to lose his job because he committed too much. The public sector projects used to be show pieces of efficiency of public welfare. Later on they were deeply in losses. The losses of the public sector were due to the politicians, bureaucrats and other rank officers and officials milching them dry.

Movement of capital for/private sector is for achieving optimalities of all types, wherever required. Technical, commercial, linkage, financial marketing, and other types of the internal economies were ensued. Income, savings, capital formation, investment, production, output, profits, employment etc. all increase. There will be higher exports and imports. Then there will again be higher flows of capital movement. Developing economies get what they they lacked (capital); the rich economies get what they wanted, (avenues for investment for higher interest/profits). The world as a whole is better off due to multiplier effects of the capital flows.

When the multinational companies are involved in capital movements they do everything to earn super profits for themselves.

Foreign economic powers that move the capital demand several concessions from the governments of the host country and get them. India is giving water use rights to the MNCs manufacturing soft drinks, These soft drinks are hell lot costly for the common people. They water tables have gone down in the areas of their operations. They local residents are getting poor quality water, if at all. There are cases when the local population had to move out as water for them.

Raw materials are taken away. Local units of production are ousted or merged. Unemployment may result in the old lines of production of the natives. The palms of the high powered persons are "greased" with bribes to get undue advantage. International capital movement can be a source of massive exploitation or massive boost to the domestic/host economies.

Foreign capital movement depends upon making fiscal tools blunt. They cannot be used. Big capitalists, whether domestic or-foreign, usually take away the land of native peasants, The same is happening in the SSZs (special economic zones) in India, The farmers who lose land get peanuts as compensation, if they survive the bullets of the governments that is. This is true to many other government projects. Towns are obliterated from the maps (Harsud in Madhya Pradesh) and the people are asked to disperse anywhere. (A few shanties were erected for "Harsud"). India lost lakhs of hectares of agricultural land (even as population is increasing to realtors.

Portfolio investments or capital movements

Direct investment capital movement depends upon the profit differentials. Portfolio investment in bonds, debt papers, shares, options and derivatives etc. depend upon the interest rate differentials. Foreign investors are bringing money in India. They invest in the stock market create bullish sentiments; send the prices to dizzy heights; then make phantom pile of money by selling at high prices and then take the capital out.

When the first part of the drama is being enacted, foreign exchange reserves rise and the exchange rate goes up. There is no guarantee that b.o.p. will become favourable. When the second part of the drama is enacted, there is a drain on foreign exchange reserves and the exchange rate of the domestic currency goes up.

Money is now fungible in shares etc. and can be carried to different countries. (In 1930 in Hiteler's Germany any irregularity was punishable with death). Foreign capital is invested but it need not remain invested for long. Business of trillions of dollars is done in one stock exchange alone in one day in western countries. International capital movement has its positive and negative sides. Market returns do not reflect the social returns do not reflect the social returns due to distortions. Now foreign capital is capturing "native" companies by buying shares.

External capital movement is discouraged by infrastructural and institutional bottlenecks. However, the foreign capital movement/investment can remove such difficulties and improve the infrastructure and even superstructure. (Capital movements can be in the tied projects (e.g., money, for the project for steels will be used in the same project) or "untied" project (the can use it for any purpose). Those capital investments are best which do not involve long gestation periods i.e., where the projects start production early. Early production, early sales, early incomes/profits etc. will mean early repayment of loans. Soft loans/capital investments are at a low/concessional rate of interest. Loans at market/high rates of interest are "hard".

INDIA'S IMPORTANT FACTS

- By 2009 the sunk foreign capital FDI was estimated to be of $ 100 billion.
- India's share in FDI inflow is 0.23 p.c. of the world. China's share is 3.70 p.c. of the world
- By the end of 2008, India's forex reserves were — $ 250 b.
  India's external debt was — $ 164 b.
  (See chapter on IMF also)
- Between 1991-92 and 2001-02 Total FDI in flows — $ 35.0 b.
  Outflows .... amortization — $ - 19.8 b.
  Interest — $ - 13.2 b.
  Net inflow — $ 2.0 b.
- 2001-02 to 2008-09 net inflows averaged — $ 4.0 b. per year.
- Averages inflows net of FII were around — $ 15 b.
- In 2009, India purchased 200 tonnes of gold from the IMF. When V.P. Singh became P.M. of India, India's forex reserve was less than $ 1 b. only and RBI's gold had to be mortgaged abroad.

27 B Foreign Direct and Portfolio Investment: Pros and Cons: FDI and FII in India

- Foreign direct investment is in production or/and infrastructure rather than in shares and bonds. It directly increases the national income of the country. It increases employment while FII may not increase employment at all.
- Most of the FDI is between developed and developed countries. Nearly 37 p.c. of the FDI is from the developed to developing economies. Only 1 p.c. is between poor and poor countries. The rest is between the developed economies. 62 p.c.
- FDI brings technology with it. Even some top key technical persons may also come. When Suzuki came to India they came with capital, technology and technical know-how. Labour, land and raw materials were taken from India. Technology and FDI improve everything in which they come e.g., construction, power, transport, telecommunications, medical services, insurance, banking, plantations even contract agriculture.
- FDI investments are "autonomous". Thereafter supplementary and complementary investments follow. The total production profile of the country improves.
- There can be three bad effects. First, the domestic producers become the second fiddle to the multinationals through which or of which FDI comes. Secondly, employment generation is poor as the capital-labour ratios are high in FDI. Thirdly, rural development, employment generation, poverty eradication, control of population etc. take a back seat.
- FDIs are capital flows. There are outflows from one country which become inflows in other countries. They become part of the balance of payment.
- Outflows bring adverse effects on the balance of payment. Inflows bring favourable effects. When the inflows of yesteryears are taken away they become outflows. When outflows of yesteryears are brought back they become inflows. Hence net effect on balance of payment is important. Global flows are not double–counted.

For foreign direct investment (FDI) took several steps to push it up. China is getting about 12 to 15 times more FD than India despite it being a socialist economy and India a free enterprise economy.

Capitalists should shun communist economy and should prefer free/capitalist economy. This is because the foreigners acknowledge that India is a free democracy but not a free economy. The law and order situation in certain States is horrible. Certain other States keep themselves shut from any "outside" investment. In certain States infrastructure facilities are woefully bad. China opened a certain region for any type of investment to any extent and with full freedom. India, on the other hand, has kept the entire country open but with a lot of restrictions on ground. Whichever functionary is involved in file pushing asks for "departmental dowries"(Words of the Ex-president R. Venkataraman).

The following table gives the figures of FDI given by UNCTAD, World Investment Report 2005, taken from Economic Survey GoI 2006) about FDI in some countries of Asia and comparison with India. If China and Hong Kong are taken as one then the FDI there is 20 times as high as in India.

S.No.	Country	Foreign Direct Investment Inflows. $ USb.			Shares in World Inflows		
		2002	2003	2004	2002	2003	2004
1	China	52.74	53.51	60.63	7.36	8.45	9.35
2	HongKong	9.68	13.62	34.04	1.35	2.15	5.55
3	India	3.45	4.27	5.34	0.48	0.67	0.82
4	Indonesia	0.15	(—)	1.02	0.02	(—)	0.16
5	Korea South	2.98	3.79	7.69	0.42	0.60	1.19
6	Malaysia	3.20	2.47	4.62	0.45	0.39	0.71
7	Philippines	1.79	0.34	0.47	0.25	0.05	0.07
8	Singapore	5.82	9.33	16.06	0.81	1.47	2.48
9	Sri Lanka	0.20	0.23	0.23	0.03	0.04	0.04
10	Thailand	0.95	1.95	1.06	0.13	0.31	0.16

By 2009, world FDI flows increased to 2000 b. dollars. (See last page of this chapter)

FDI is permitted upto 100 p.c. but subject to the regulations. These regulations deter the foreign investors.

1. Where industrial licence is required 100 p.c. FDI cannot be there.
2. Where the foreigner has joint venture, trade mark agreement and or technical collaboration there also 100 p.c. FDI is not permitted because this will mean ouster of the Indians.
3. Where SEBI does not permit transfer of shares to foreigners. In April 2010, SEBI stopped India's private insurance-investment companies to linking with units", i.e. ULIPs, i.e. ULIPs were banned.
4. In those sectors where FDI is not permitted (Atomic energy for example).

Some Recent Measures about the FDI in India

1. In the domestic airlines the FDI cap (upper limit) can be 40 p.c. But, a NRI (non-resident Indian) can invest upto 100 p.c.
2. FDI upto 100 p.c. under the automatic route is now permitted for development of townships, housing, building up infrastructure and construction projects. The minimum area requirement has been reduced to 10 hectares for serviced housing plots and 50000 square metres for built up construction/development projects.
3. FDI "cap" has been raised from 49 p.c. to 74 p.c. in basic and cellular telecom services. The revised cap includes both FDI and portfolio investment.
4. In FM radio the FDI limit is 20 p.c.
5. Transfer of shares between NRIs and Indians in both ways are permitted liberally by SEBI.
6. Debts can be converted into equities but subject to the maximum limits for each sector.

7. Provisions, for repatriation of FDI funds have been liberalised a bit.

It is alleged that VIPs have some of their companies in Mauritius. It is not merely the tax concession that makes the Mauritius route important. Even the USA sends money via Mauritius. The share of Mauritius is 37.2 p.c. and of the USA nearly 16 p.c.

* Capital flows can be for ever. They can get sunk. However, the company or the industrial unit can be sold to the natives (Indians will be called "natives" in India). Then the foreign exchange equivalent is taken out.
* FDI improves the profile of industries and industrial units. Wherever FDI is put, the efficiency and productivity increase. National income and employment go up. The foreign investors make good payments to the employees. There is increase in the demand. There is chain effect in other activities—agriculture, construction to services (hotels, hospitals, educational institutions). The chain effects or the linkages effects of FDI are high.
* FDI is desired as well as feared. The fear is that the MNCs may subjugate the economy of the country of investment. MNCs act like monopolies though they are oligopolies. They are more concerned with profits.
* Investment in extracting mineral ores and taking produces of plantations had been favourite direct investments of the capitalist/imperialist direct investors in the past. Now they prefer high-tech industries also.
* Direct investors get best terms if the host countries are desperate for industrial and related developments. Take the case of India. Almost all the raw materials needed for the development of infrastructure in India is available in the country still foreign direct investment in infrastructure is desired for two reasons: (a) first, the corruption of Indian contractors and officers/officials cannot be checked as it has become institutionalized and (6) second the quality of work is far inferior to what is in the foreign countries, shoddy work being the concomitant of corruption.
* Such direct investment which brings capital goods along with technology, managerial skill and finance and which stimulates the native private investment becomes most welcome. Direct investment is needed for enlarging the scale of operations and widening the scope of operations (broad-band of the products). It is now a proven fact that almost 85 p.c. development is due to technology rather than capital. Labour and natural resources come next. There are a few countries where one can stumble upon rubies and precious rocks yet cannibals may be living there. The direct investment has both linkage effects and multiplier effects. The chain of feedback effects should be kept such that there are favourable effects on domestic production and balance of payment. Adverse feedback effects on both will be injurious to national dividend. Infact FDI can have beneficent effects on each and every productive activity of the country if it is not in enclave sectors.

Pros and Cons: Controls

* Foreigners may demand multiple concessions—permission to repatriate high profits and package of concessions at the time of establishing the projects e.g., free land and water and low taxes or power charges. The foreigners may produce luxury goods and thus cater to the needs of the upper classes of the economy. The welfare implications may be low.

* To attract foreign investors it is necessary to ensure that they do not face red tapism. The foreign direct investors may require tax concessions, concessions on exchange controls, suitable labour law, (of allowing hiring and firing at will), guarantees against expropriation, inflation adjustments, and no restrictions on repatriation of profits.
* FD investors should not be allowed to harm the owners of agricultural land, peasants, the domestic producers, domestic traders, domestic consumers, infant industries etc. They should not bribe the politicians and the administration and should not influence the internal democracy. However, it is necessary that we should not have xenophobia or fear of the outsider instinctively. There should be power in the hands of the governments to ensure that the FD investors indulge in fair play; if not there should be regulatory machinery for them.

PORTFOLIO INVESTMENTS

* Portfolio investors bring money for taking advantage in safe interest rate differentials. The funds are non-debt funds. Portfolio investors bring money for the short period and seek no- risk investments. Portfolio investments can come from outside in government bonds or in banks. Wherever there are chances of inviting foreign capital in shares, debentures and other "papers" there are chances of portfolio investments, which can be for medium and long period also. Generally they are for the short period. Savings get optimally distributed over the world if all destinations are good. Portfolio investments improve international liquidity to help in balance of payment difficulties of the needy country. They can help in the production also indirectly. Developing economies should have capital/share/money markets. When the developing economies borrow in geometric progressions their woes can also increase in the same proportion if the FII investors are interested in nothing else but speculation. India was averaging equal to Rs. One Lakh-crore annually in FII flows by 2010.

FDI and FII should increase production base and not trade base. Besides the loans should be utilised for "real productivity" than for monetary gains. There should be a balance between what the host country and the donor countries want.

FOREIGN INSTITUTIONAL INVESTMENT SCENARIO UPTO 2009

* Of the $ 286 b. forex reserves in India, nearly one-third were FIIs funds that were brought into India by the investors to buy and sell shares and similar papers on which speculation could be done. The foreign institutional investors are not interested in investing in productive capacities which we call investment in "brick, mortar and steel" (Keynes) but are interested in making quick money. FDIs (foreign direct investments) get sunk. What comes in the form of FDI is first converted into rupee balances for all things of investment that are purchased in India from the Indian production. If foreign machines are imported, then that much will leak out. Whichever gets sunk becomes a permanent part of the India's forex balances. Such balances are not debts. FII balances are also not debts.
* The usual modus operandi of the FII investors is to bring foreign exchange convert the same in the rupee balances....purchase the shares and derivatives through their

buying and other means create bullish sentiments in the share markets....sell when Indians are willing to buy them at higher prices make hefty profits in rupees....convert the rupee balances back to dollar and take them away.

[Derivatives are "options". "Options" are rights to participate in future trading. Derivatives are "futures" also. "Futures" are financial instruments or can be in commodities even. They are sold at the presently decided prices and are delivered in future. In future, however, only the differences are paid/received as one is a loser/ gainer".

Derivatives are contracts, tradeable cash instruments. Derivatives derive their value from underlying securities.]

* FII balances when they come improve the balance of payment position but when they are taken out bring a serious fall in them. **If FII investment remains permanent i.e., in the primary market and is not traded in the secondary market, then there is no problem of foreign exchange being taken out.** If the FII investors operate in the secondary market for the purpose of siphoning off the cream of the share markets, they loot the country and can leave it in a position of foreign exchange crunch.

* **If India incurs balance of payment deficits, then India becomes indebted due to some country selling us on loans. There can be direct loan taking also.** However, if there are unilateral inflows like money sent by Indians to their parents, other grants, gifts, subsidies etc. **and FDI and FII, these become non-debt flows**

* It is to be kept in mind that just as something cannot be taken out of nothing by human beings, so also the share market bullish tendencies cannot continue for ever. What goes up should fall, if not to the starting point, then to a fairly lower point for the "market corrections". Two things are happening now a days: (a) the bullish tendencies are being pushed up by foreign FII punters (assisted by the Indian bulls) and (b) secondly, when the market takes a down turn the bulls do not lose as much or the bears do not gain as much as the common men (whom we call "asses") because the bulls and bears ensure that when the bad days come they somehow put the dud papers in the hands of the gullible common men.

* In recent years around $ 10 b. per year came to India on average for FII. (post-2000).

* **The process of accumulation of forex reserves (= balances of foreign currencies IMF tranches + gold reserves) is somewhat as under:**

1. there is addition of direct net balance of exports over imports by the government sectors.
2. There come the direct grants, subsidies, gifts and unilateral transfers to the government.
3. Exporters earn foreign exchange and can surrender it to the authorized dealers (6 of them most important out of nearly now 1000, counting the sub-dealer also who really are important) at the market rate of exchange. The authorized dealers give "instant" market prices i.e. exchange rates and keep the exporters/ importers free from the official hassles. Importers who want to import surrender rupee balances and take dollars from the authorized dealers at the market rate. The ADs, keep a difference between the buying prices and that gives them their profits. Now under the full convertibility on current account the

Government of India itself purchases dollars from the ADs. In doing so it can print new money also. Hence rupee supplies in the market increase. Money supply number 3 i.e. (i) currency with the public (ii) all the deposits of cooperative and commercial banks increased from Rs. 2670 crore in Dec. 1969 to Rs. 52,00,000 crore in Dec. 2009 and nearly 55 lakh-Crore by April 2010. (rounded off). Government of India/RBI purchases dollars from the market to meet the needs for importing goods and services that they want e.g., defence goods, petroleum products. RBI can also buy dollar on behalf of the public sector projects and State governments, subject to the approval of the Government of India.

* FII inflows were $ 377 m. in 2002-03 but shot upto $ 8 b. in 2005, $ 10b in 2008.
* After 1971, the RBI indulged in sterilisation operations and is still engaged in the same. RBI purchased dollars from the open market and used the same when the dollar rate showed signs of increasing. In 1971, when dichotomous exchange rates used to rule 1 $ - Rs. 36 in the open market and $ 1 = Rs. 26 at the official parity (decimal points ignored here), and when EXIMSCRIPS system was introduced (*), the two rates emerged as one at $ 1 = Rs. 31.5 (rounded off).
  It became a puzzle while despite ups and downs In the economy, the balance of payment position, and despite some times high and sometimes a little subdued inflation, the exchange rate did not change for months and months together. It was due to countervailing interventions by the RBI with the dollar reserves. RBI sold dollars If rupee rate was to fall or the dollar rate was expected to go up.
* FIIs are "money on wings" or hot money balances ready to be transferred from one country to another. There is a lot of speculation involved in this. If (suppose) rupee rate is $ 1 = Rs. 45 and is expected to fall to Rs. 46 per dollar, then if anyone takes $ 1 billion out for a day and brings the same back after the fall, the person earns Re. 1 extra per dollar Le., 1 billion rupees or Rs. 100 crore through mail transfers in one day. The speculators are doing that. The rogue punters will put India in great trouble if they suddenly take away a lot of hot money after making hefty profits in the bull market.
* It is reported that India is dominated by six leviathan authorized dealers. They are at the top. Others may be independent but their fortunes are not. They are somehow hitched to them. Now independent outfits are emerging. In January 2006, there were 823 registered ADs. They are known as Portfolio Managers for FIIs. They do the work of sub-contracting for the outsiders who are their clients. There are "papers" for the business and they are known as "participatory notes". These 'participatory notes" are "derivatives". The Indian ADs buy these PNs on behalf of the ineligible investors with the money of the investors. It is to be noted that illegal and irregular work if done by two parties, they remain "honest" with each other but not with the public, government and the Indian nation. Indian agents buy and sell to the outsiders. When there is increase in the prices of derivatives/shares the foreigners sell to their buyers: make hefty profits; and then take away balances in dollars.
* **The best situation** about flow of funds is that the country should have a favourable balance of payment on current, capital and unilateral transfers account. It should

be able to find investible funds for buying foreign capital, raw materials, technology and technical know-how from these genuine reserves. No external debt is involved in this.

* **The worst situation** is when the FII is brought to buy shares and derivatives and bullish sentiments are created. After the prices rise artificially, the foreign institutional investors sell back the shares to the natives and then take away their huge profits. In this process they leave the foreign exchange reserve position in a critical state and the exchange rates tumble down.
* **The second best situation** is that bulk of the capital that comes is in FDI (foreign direct investment) or DFI (direct foreign investment).Such capital gets sunk. Part of the FDI is used in bringing capital goods and essential raw materials from abroad and part is used for running the plants. What is used in the country becomes permanently absorbed. FII should be for genuine investment purposes and not for short term bringing in and taking out after earning speculative profits.

FII flows should not be allowed to come in such a manner that they bring down the rate of interest on deposits down so much that the domestic savers do not get fair returns. In India, for example, roughly the domestic savers lost 1,80,000 crore as "lower interest received compared with the once peak rate (15.5- 5.5 p.a)] The foreign investors in India were getting 8 to 10 p.c. while in their own countries they were getting 1 to 2 p.c. only. Loss to Indian depositors became gain to (i) foreign depositors, (ii) domestic borrowers and (iii) banks.

There is the danger that if the household sector, which provides 85 p.c. savings to India, is thus mulcted, India will find savings base eroded if the FII investors suddenly run away with their money. In 2009, the rate was raised by 0.25 percentage point. This was cumin seed in the mouth of camel. Indian depositors should receive inflation + 2 p.c. as the RBI wants the banks to receive. The minimum fixed deposit rate should be 7 p.c.p.a. with 8 p.a.p.a. for the senior citizens. The minimum rates of interest on loans should be 9 to 10 p.c.

There is more than meets the eye that even the US FIIs come via Mauritius. Some VIPs are probably involved. There are fake sub- accounts, fake PNs and fake ADs. SEBI is toothless tiger. It sides with the rich. It sides with the cat in catching the mouse.

FDI and FII flows are not only from the developed countries to the developing countries but "emerging economies" were sending the "reverse flows" also. Indian tycoons had purchased quite a few big firms in the European and American countries.

The USA was the greatest borrower of the savings of the emerging nations. Japan and Korea (South only) had given 35 p.c. of the capital flows to the USA. Accumulation of foreign exchange reserves were enabling emerging countries to send capital in many directions. Reserves-with the- emerging countries, were $ 0.5 trillion in 1999. They went up to $ 2-trill ion in-March 2006.

It is to be noted that if the exchange rates of the currencies appreciate vis-a-vis dollar, then the real rates of returns decline on FDI and FII in terms of the domestic currencies.

The US domestic deficits in 2009 were 13 p.c. of the GDP. Fast emerging nations like China, India and Taiwan (claimed by China), and a few others should, invest their foreign exchange reserves in developing infrastructure and they can earn returns on them. If reserves are kept as reserves, there is no return. If the value of dollar goes down the returns become negative. Hence this issue requires being addressed. India keeps 35 p.c. of its forex reserves in the U.s. to earn interest. Other countries decide their own percentages.

ACCORDING TO THE UDOTTI GREENSPAN RULE RESERVES SHOULD EQUAL TO ONE YEAR'S SHORT TERM DEBT. On this criterion, the excess reserves of some countries were as under:

Country	*excess-reserves 2003-05 $ million*	*Excess reserves as of GDP-2004*
1. China	724080	41
2. Taiwan	210134	69
3. Korea	136711	18
4. Russia	118154	20
5. INDIA	107703	15
6. Malaysia	58613	30
7. Algeria	50518	60
8. Mexico	47083	7
9. Thailand	35486	21
10. Saudi Arabia	73897	29

Mexico has largest short term debt in the above 10 countries relative to its GDP. India is in the next worse position. Then comes Korea. China had the largest absolute forex reserves. From percentage wise excess Taiwan and Algeria stood at top positions. Forex reserves of India are higher than that of the oil rich Saudi Arabia. (See ch. on IMF also.

The following table shows the non-resident flows (for India they are known as NRI for China NRC).

Country	$- billions,.
1. India	25.7
2. Mexico	24.7
3. China	22.5
4. Philippines	14.5
5. France	12.6
6. Spain	8.9
7. UK	7.3
8. Belgium	7.2
9. Germany	6.7
10. Bangladesh	5.5

Indians remittances constitute 3 p.c. of the GDP of India. The smaller the country in size and in the GDP/ the higher will be the percentage of remittances to the GDP. Many small countries receive as much as 40 p.c. of their GDP from their non-residents (Moldova for instance). Nepal receives 15 p.c. of its GDP from NRNs.

High profitability in the Indian stock markets is attracting a lot of funds of NRI account, though there is a loss to them on account of appreciation of the exchange rate of the India rupee. It proves that the gains due to bullish tendencies are greater.

Inflows in India-exceeded $ 55 b. between 1st April 2007-and-December-2007,

Indians are resenting the FDI in the retail sectors vehemently. They are infact opposing the entry of the big industrial houses in the retail trade as of the Reliance in stores selling fresh vegetables and fruits. McDonalds and Wal-Marts are despised by the retail traders of India.

FDI in India is not permitted in certain fields e.g, manufacturing of arms and ammunition, atomic energy, railways, coal and lignite mining, mining of iron, manganese, chromium, gypsum, sulpher, gold, diamonds, copper zinc and other items reserved still for the public sector. The FDI in some recent years, camc, from (CF K Muthalagu and K vijayrani), Yojna, July 2006.

	Countries	*% of FDI of total*
1.	Mauritius	35.34
2.	USA	20.21
3.	UK	3.62
4.	Germany	6.16
5.	Netherlands	8.45
6.	Japan	5.23
7.	France	1.90
8.	Singapore	2.76
9.	Switzerland	2.76
10.	South Korea	0.560
11.	Other	12.94

As written elsewhere also in this book, it is alleged that some high powered persons in the government have their firms in Mauritius. It is not the love of that island country in the hearts of the Indian Government but allegedly broker firms established in that country by the high powered persons of India that Mauritius is the biggest source of inflow in India. Even the investors of rich country route their funds from there. There are some tax concessions also.

NOTE : FACTS

1. After US meltdown in Sept. Oct. 2008, $ 406 billion were taken away. see a note at the end of this section. Decadal average of FDI in India was $ 46 billions a year and of FII about $ 10 billions per year.
2. If an exporter earned $ 1 billion, he was given Rs. 2600 crore at official rate. All dollars were impouned. Under EXIMSCRIPS system 60 p.c. was given in dollars but in the form of import licences and the rest 40 p.c. was taken over at the official rate. The system was left in one year as fake EXIMSCRIPS were printed just like fake lottery tickets. Besides, the speculators used to buy import licences from the exporters for selling at higher rates.
3. Of the total movement of FDI in the world

   62 p.c. was between rich and rich countries.

   37. p.c. was from rich to poor countries.

   1 p.c. was between poor and poor countries.

4. FDI figures in the world were

1996	385	billion	u.s. dollars.
1997	478	"	" "
1998	695	"	" "
1999	1090	"	" "
2001	1492	"	" "
2009	735	"	" "

1090 b are 1.09 trillion. The drop was after 2008 u.s. financial melt-down, By 2009, the global FDI flows were estimated at 2 trillion us dollars or $ 2000 b.

28 United Nations Conference on Trade and Development [UNCTAD]

UNCTAD Secretariate exists but the WTO almost replaces the conferences

1. UNCTAD I TO IX
2. UNCTAD X and XII

1. Switzerland	1964	UNCTAD Secretariat now-a-days publishers each year or in a year, reports on sundry aspects of global economic trends. These reports are even topic-wise, continent-wise and country-wise
2. India	1968	
3. Chile	1972	
4. Kenya	1976	
5. Philippines	1979	
6. Yugoslavakia	1983	
7. Switzerland	1987	
8. Colombia	1992	
9. S. Africa	1996	
10. Thailand	2000	
11. Brazil	2004	
12. Ghana	2007	

United Nations Conferences on Trade and Development were held between years 1964 and 2000. *Late Prof. Raul Prebisch of Argentina was the "father" of UNCTAD.* It was because of his efforts that such meetings were held and the problems regarding trade and development were discussed there. The main concern of the developing economies used to be about "commodities". Earlier there were three groups of countries which were known as

(a) group "A" countries *i.e.,* the rich capitalist countries; or developed countries;

(b) group "B" socialist countries; and

(c) 'group of 77' *i.e.,* third world countries or the poor countries of the world. *Though there are now more than 77 countries in this group, they continue to be known as that.* Now the nomenclature is not popular. Nor are they known as the third world countries because socialist world has collapsed. They are now known as "developing economies".

There are now two groups only i.e., the developed capitalist countries and the developing countries. Earlier all developed countries (including of the Southern hemisphere of the world like Australia or New Zealand) were known as "group of north"; developing economies were known as "group of south". The nomenclature was an extension of Italian position where northern Italy was developed and southern was not developed. These nomenclatures have also been dropped.

Developed and developing economies in the past as in the **present mostly "agree to disagree".** There are lots of speeches but the rich countries do not grant concessions to the poor countries. UNCTAD can stand for

"Under No Circumstance Take a Decision" or "Until the Next Conference Talk and Delay".

This is the type of language that is used in such meetings:

> "Economic downturns provided occasions for a flourishing bazar of ideas...UNCTAD was a vigorous debating society...various ideas floated were blurred and got submerged in the final proposed plan of action...the session had to reach for the pill of concensus...the global economy continues to lurch through the ongoing crises there is little doubt that the ideas raised in the UNCTAD will be resurrected, perhaps in still more bold formulations....there was a crisis of legitimacy and...that spirit of generosity was sorely lacking...in future there will be indefinite prolongation of the mood of confrontation that has now beset the organisation

We discuss the *top 10* problems that are always discussed in UNCTAD with varying emphasis: (We are not discussing conferences—wise points.)

1. Increase drawing rights from IMF and increase total SDRs.

IMF quotas in 1947 were $ 7.4 b. and because of the persistent demand from the less developed economies they were $ 400 b. (SDR 294 b.) in 2000. The less developed countries demanded that the condition of putting 25 p.c. IMF quota in gold another 25 p.c. in hard currencies be abolished. That was done. However, IMF quotas or SDR requirements were not linked to the needs for development. In 2009, IMF had SDRs equal to $600 billion.

2. Transfer of 1 p.c. GDP of the rich countries to developing economies by way of soft loans, if not as grants:

Raul Prebisch, eminent economist of Argentina and the father of UNCTAD, once advocated greater ODA (official development assistance) to less developed countries. U. Thant (late Secretary General of UNO) and Robert McNamara (once Defence Secretary of the USA and lateron President of the World Bank) pleaded that 1 p.c. of the GDP be transferred to less developed economies by way of soft loans, if not grants. The percentages went down; then they pleaded for 0.75 p.c.; then for 0.5 p.c. and when it came down to 0.25 p.c. the issue was dropped in UNCTAD. There was no point in pleading before the deaf ears.

The USA consumes more electricity in neon lighting and air-conditioning that India and China use for all purposes. The money which the USA spends on tinned dog-food and cat-food is more than the total amount of "assistance" (loans, actually) which they give to less developed countries. *There had been very earnest requests that let the USA and NATO countries reduce their military expenditure by 5 p.c. then hunger, illiteracy and high morbidity of the poor countries can be eradicated.* These countries did not reduce that expenditure even by 1 p.c. UNCTAD members from the developing economies became too tired about that and now virtually there is no talk in the world about disarmament, except that the USA and the Russian Federation do sometimes discuss about reducing their nuclear arms.

In 1999, the total GDP of USA was $ 6.95 trillion, of EU $ 6.SI trillion and of Japan $ 5.22 trillion. The US economy in 2008-09 was of $13 trillion and of India $1 trillion.

These countries are worried more for a low rate of inflation than about unemployment. The USA had 5 p.c. unemployment; Japan 3.4 p.c. and the EU about 12 p.c. They want more exports and can afford to provide unemployment insurance benefits to their people. If EU does not care about its own unemployment (surprisingly it has to import semi-skilled labour from outside) it cannot be expected to care for unemployment, poverty and development issues of the developing economies.

3. Easing the burden of the debt

By 2008, the poor countries owed the rich countries nearly $ 3 trillion i.e., nearly $ 3000 billion. Most of the less developed countries, particularly of Africa, were unable to repay the loans. They wanted cancellation of the loans "across the counter" in total or by (say) 80 p.c. of the loans of all countries. However, that would have led to collapse of many European Banks from which money might have been taken by the WB, IDA, IMF and others indirectly. The developed countries agreed to review the distress cases. Case-by-case approach was accepted but not the "across the counter approach". India never demanded that its debts be written off.

Two-third of the countries of the world had per capita income of less than $ 500 even in the year 2000. Out of the population of over 6 billion or 600 crore. nearly one fourth was suffering from acute/chronic hunger. They were subject to every misery of life, *living in economic hell on earth: victims of inflation and unemployment.* These persons were illiterate and suffering from high morbidity, including millions from AIDS.

Eighty percent of the increase in the GDP of the world is taking place in the countries which are already rich. In those countries where 60 p.c. of the population of the world resides, not more than 10 p.c. increase in the global GDP is taking place. The countries with less than $ 300 per capita income, did not have even 6 p.c. increases in the global GDP.

In some of the countries, nearly 60 p.c. export earnings go in debt-servicing. Some have been caught in debt-trap; their export earnings fall short of debt-servicing and then all the imports have to be on loan. To some of such countries, sops were offered in reducing the debt burden.

4. "Take more exports", demand of developing economies.

Less developed countries face a stone-wall of protection from the developed countries. There are quotas, though under WTO arrangements the tariffs rates have to be low. The developed countries now talk about *standards.* They either find fault with quality (sometimes saying your textiles catch fire or your agricultural products have microorganisms on them—as if they can be eliminated in the developed countries) or say that the products sold by less developed countries cannot be accepted as they were produced by child labour or "exploited labour". The definition of "exploitation" was that the less developed countries were not paying wages equal to what are paid in the developed countries ! They say all these things with the use of words "voilating labour standards".

Developed countries take mostly raw materials and mineral ores from the developing countries. Even semi-processed goods are not accepted in the quantities that would help the developing economies. *Exports are well taken if the exporting firms in the developing economies belong to the developed countries.*

5. Do not dump your goods or force higher imports on us, say developing economies to the developed world.

The developed countries invoke the principle of "comparative advantage" and push down the throats of the developing economies such exports which the developing economies can ill-afford. The developed economies export luxury or semi-luxury goods to poor countries which are purchased by the rich people of less developed countries, causing a severe strain and drain on the forex reserves. Dumping was a big problem mostly faced by the poor economies but anti-dumping measures were mostly taken by the developed countries ! The following table shows anti-dumping duty measures in force and major "culprits" and major "victims" as of December, 31, 1999:

Measures maintained by parties			*Affected Parties*		
Country	*No. of measures*	*Percentage of total*	*Country*	*No. of measures*	*Percentage of total*
1. US	315	29.2	1. China	198	18.3
2. EU	189	17.5	2. EU	167	15.4
3. S. Africa	86	8.0	3. Japan	82	7.6
4. Mexico	80	7.4	4. Taiwan	59	5.5
5. Canada	79	7.3	5. US	56	5.2
6. India	64	6.0	6. Korea	52	5.0
7. Argentina	45	4.0	7. Brazil	43	4.0
8. Australia	44	4.0	8. India	33	3.1
9. Turkey	36	3.3	9. Russian Fed	33	3.1
10. Turkey	36	3.3	10. Thailand	29	2.7
11. R. Korea	26	2.4	11. Romania	20	2.0
12. Others	78	7.4	12. Others	308	28.0

WTO and UNCTAD arrangements allow anti-dumping measures but only if they are *"legitimate"*. The dumper country always says that its cost of production is low and that the prices charged are not below the cost of production. The dumped country always refutes that.

In the above list *no country could dump in* China, Japan, Taiwan, Russia, Thailand, and Romania. They had the status of "dumper" only. *Countries which were "dumper" and had "affected party status" were:* the US. the EU, India and Brazil but the category of "others" includes 308 cases, from a few other countries.

There are either anti-dumping duties thereafter or "price undertåking by the exporter". *India faces a lot of dumping via Nepal.* Nepal is a land-locked country. It is entitled for passage rights via India and Bangladesh. It imports from China, Taiwan, Hong Kong and other far eastern countries things of high value in much larger quantities than its GDP or per capita income would warrant. It sells them to India. [Take the case of pen-cell; it is sold at 0.5 rupee while others are sold at Rs. 5 to 7 per piece]. Dumping provides great benefits to the consumers but the producers and their workers are very adversely affected. *UNCTAD reports record the concerns of the countries which were adversely affected by dumping as also of the dumpers which complain about protective measures. India records its displeasures in UNCTAD if duties are imposed on its exports to EU or USA and gets the similar sentiments recorded in UNCTAD or WTO when China dumps in India.* The problem is ticklish as trying to please God without offending the Satan.

6. Terms of trade Question: Do not bring them down, say developing economies

Developing countries are exporters of agricultural commodities, crude mineral ores and semi finished goods mostly. The income elasticity of demand in western countries is low for such goods. The price inelasticies should be there but since there are supply inelasticities also, the less developed countries cannot take advantage of that. The goods and *particularly the services (invisibles)* that the developed countries supply are sold each year at higher prices. There is thus gradual deterioration in the gross barter terms of trade of the poor countries. For the same *real* exports, they get less *real* imports, even if the technology of the imported goods is the same. In other words, to get the same *real* imports of the same technology, the poor countries have to part with higher *real exports. Less developed cou:.tries demanded strongly not to develop substitutes of their products, say jute and hessian.* The developed countries did not care and now the world is littered with harmful polythene things.

UNCTAD had agreed to watch the multinational companies but the multinationals watch the UNCTAD, WTO, IMF, WB and everything of importance in the less developed countries. They are beyond the control of anyone.

7. Developed countries should be soft on royalties

The less developed countries were always very vocal in arguing that the wc:tern countries supply goods of higher technology at exhorbitant prices. *The 386 computer was introduced at Rs. 45000 a piece. The Pentium III is now cheaper than that. The cause of complaint is that while the advanced computers were already the western countries these countries first sold their old models and the result was that the Indians had to lose money everytime they went in for the advanced model.*

The developed countries did not concede this point. Infact they had a great victory in GATT VIII where the developing economies had to concede everything that they demanded about TRIPS (trade related intellectual property rights). The less developed countries can neither copy the process (which is illegal) nor the product. They have to pay hefty royalties for years to come. It is true that the developed countries require compensation for investing heavily in research and development but they extract too high prices. China and Japan produce those very things cheap, of course after imitation. The western countries are suppliers of war goods, ultimately supply and vital spare parts as dear as the main products.

8. Developed countries are forcing exchange rates of the currencies of poor countries down vis-a-vis dollar.

We present 10 points:

(1) It is true that foreign exchange rate (FER) falls due to higher rate of inflation in comparison to the USA and adverse balance of payment. But the poor countries point out that the developed countries take more goods at cheap prices and hence inflation results. They thrust upon their exports (*i.e.*, make the poor countries import even on loan), and hence the exchange rate falls.

(2) Developed countries bring portfolio capital for investment in shares and debentures. When they suddenly withdraw these balances, the FER falls. The rich countries gain more because then they pay less for their imports from developing economies. The exports of the poor countries become cheap. They cannot earn more because they sell at lower FER.

(3) The rich countries take high charges for all services like shipping, insurance, air transport, and many other services.

(4) The developed countries take away high profits and high interest earnings and cause balance of payment disequilibrium.

(5) Developed countries force upon the poor countries war conditions and sell their military equipment. All the earnings of poor countries are largely recycled (*i.e.*, taken back by the rich countries) in this way.

(6) The rich countries do not allow what they call "double compensatory system". If the less developed countries borrow from the World Bank. International Development Agency, and International Monetary Fund, the rich countries do not permit UNCTAD/GATT to extend concessions.

(7) Developed countries do not permit the poor countries to impose high import duties or to fix quotas of imports. Thus the poor countries cannot even reduce their unnecessary imports. The poor countries have to import according to the dictates of the rich countries.

(8) The poor countries cannot give subsidies to their exports or to export industries.

(9) Developed countries policy is "what is good for their multinationals (MNCs) is good for the poor countries also". The poor countries should do what their MNCs want and MNCs will not do what the poor countries want.

(10) If the FER of the poor countries is falling, the rich countries impose more economic reforms. They do not help but ruin the economies. Argentina is ruined. Mexico is highly indebted. Brazil is in trouble.

9. Poor countries demand/require rationalisation of GSP and MFN.

See about them in the chapters that follows GATT.

10. Developing countries request the developed countries to reach an agreement about "commodities and compensatory finance for them".

This point is also discussed in chapter on GATT.

OTHER IMPORTANT ISSUES RAISED IN UNCTAD

(1) For land-locked countries, either free ports be constructed by international agencies for them or they should receive compensatory assistance for extra transport expenses.

(2) Less developed countries be helped to have some share in international shipping. Another matter concerning transport was the concern of the developing economies about the sky-rocketing oil prices [They rose from $ 1.2 a barrel in 1972 to $ 42 a barrel spot prices in one year. In post - 2000 period, they rose even upto $ 154 a barrel. By the end of 2009. The price was $ 74 per barrel. In 1972, Oil Facility (special loans from IMF) but of $ 1b. only was secured. There is no long term solution from this exploitation. The costs of Israel-Arab battles/wars are to be financed by the developing economies, which is beyond their capacity.

(3) Mining rights of deep sea bed of less developed economies should be recognized. Infact there should be some arrangement from WB to help less developed countries in this. International aid should come in the form of exploring the resources of the poor countries and then developing them in such a way that the host countries gain substantial advantages.

(4) There is a lot of brain-drain from the poor countries. (India loses most of the engineering graduates of the IITs and MBAs of IIMs to the west.) *There should be a long term compensation for such manpower.* It should not depend merely on such persons sending some money to their parents for some time and then severing all relations. *Intellectual property rights in the reverse should also be acknowledged by the developed economies.*

(5) The developed countries should (as Smt. Indira Gandhi once demanded) jettison the policy of "arm today and disarm tomorrow". Developed countries have their own political aims for which they create cold and hot war conditions. (The USA armed Pakistan and Afghanistan on unprecedented scale to topple a government which talked of land reforms, education and employment to all because it was USSR-friendly. The arms which the USA supplied to Pakistan to be used against the communists, were *always* used against India).

(6) Developed countries should not insist on the developing economies adjusting their economies to the needs of ending recession in the developed countries. The anti-recession policies of the developed countries should be changed to suit the development needs for the poor countries. This will be in the interest of all in the long run.

(7) Developed countries minced no words about the "quality of leadership and governance in the poor countries". They wanted LPG model directly; which indirectly implied that *development of the poor countries cannot be entrusted to the leaders of the poor countries only.* The developed countries know how much bribes the leaders had demanded and got and then put them in the banks of the developed countries.

(8) Less developed countries wanted the developed countries to include developing economies in some economic blocs or help them form their own ones. They wanted level-playing ground for the benefit of the big and small nations and the globe as a whole.

2. UNCTAD 10

This conference was held at Bangkok in 2000 in the backdrop of the fiasco of the Ministerial Meeting of the WTO at Seattle, USA in 1999. In this conference Asia was granted half a term of the Presidentship of WTO. Asia was complaining about the crisis of 1997 which was triggered up by the rogue punters of the west. They suddenly withdrew their portfolio capital, which brought great crash in the exchange rates of the ASEAN countries. The liberalisation, privatisation and globalisation meant free movement of capital but not; free movement of goods from the poor countries to the rich countries. *The rich countries say the surplus capital of the west can be utilised by the poor countries but not agree that the surplus labour of the poor countries can be utilised by the capitalist countries.*

ASEAN countries were lured into accepting "export-led growth model". They were made to neglect their food sector. There was free flow of capital in these countries. Their foreign exchange reserves swelled. These countries experienced high rates *of* growth in income and employment. Then suddenly the capital was withdrawn and foreign exchange shortages brought exchange rates tumbling down. The ASEAN countries had to import even food at high prices because of the fall in exchange rate. Their fundamentals were exposed as wrong. These economies known as '"Asian Tiger" economies experienced an 'economic melt-down'. The USA, the EU, IMF and World Bank did nothing, intact they were the roof causes, as was exposed in the crisis.

The "gang of four", as the ASEAN called them wanted further inroads of western capital in ASEAN. Infact in UNCTAD X (10) the less developed countries became aware that LPG was another ploy to take over the economies *of* the poor countries once again. The western countries were more worried about the *"yield famine in their profits"* than the actual food famine conditions that they created, particularly in Indonesia.

The western world gave long term loans to the white- coloured countries where erstwhile imperialist countries ruled but gave loans of short term maturities to Asian countries which brought all the destabilisation after their sudden withdrawal.

The lending programme to the Russian Federation was also scandal ridden. Not caring about the ground reality of low purchasing power with the masses of the poor countries, all that the rich countries wanted was that they should buy more cokes, jeans, ice- creams, fast-food, junk-food, cosmetics, electronic goods, cars, and discarded clothes sold as new. If they remained unsold, the capitalist countries complained that the poor countries were not sufficiently reformed or liberalised and were not integrating their markets with global markets. *Developed countries virtually want that most production lines in less developed countries should stop and people become distributors of their goods produced in developed countries. Then they become highly indebted and "economic colonies" once again.*

The IMF twins (IMF+ WB, IDA) harp on "second generation" and "third generation" reforms always being dissatisfied with the pace of "reforms" of *all* poor countries. They find fault with others; never with themselves and the economic blocs of the rich. Rich countries say that their money is not the water that can be thrown to extinguish the economic fires that the poor countries generate themselves. The rich countries never criticised the sudden withdrawal *of* portfolio funds by currency speculators of their country. *The rogue punters of the west converted Asian countries as "casino countries", while the economists of the rich countries argue that all problems of the poor countries are because the politicians practise "crony capitalism"*. They do not say it so bluntly but in indirect ways.

As soon as the developing countries agree to more conditionalities, new conditions are imposed. More exports are tried to be thrust upon; more restrictive policies are followed for imports from developing countries; more stringent loan conditions are introduced; lesser grants are available and more lessons given on the LPG model.

UNCTAD emphasises the "private-investment led growth" and the private investment should preferably from the developed countries, the rich countries argue. *The voice of the poor countries in UNCTAD to help them in poverty eradication falls on the deaf cars of the rich countries.* Two problems which the poor countries face were raised in the UNCTAD X also, but they were cold-shouldered:

First, the rich countries talk about "standards" i.e., they always find fault with the quality of goods sent from the poor countries. They said that the blackpeppers of India have microbes on them!

Secondly, the rich countries once again raised the question of "labour standards" i.e., the child labour is used or old labour is used or the young labour is not paid as much as in the west. Hence the exports of poor countries are not admissible.

The rich countries showed once again in UNCTAD X that the rich countries would always prefer to act like the wolf who will kill the lamb drinking water down stream as an accused for having spoiled the water for the wolf !

In UNCTAD X the same old practice was repeated; rich nations rejecting the "requests" of the poor countries, countering them with new "demands" for changing the developing economies on the prescriptions provided by them. UNCTAD establishment is known for not taking up the issues raised by the developing economies at all until the next UNCTAD.

3. COMMODITY MARKETS AND COMMODITY FUNDS

Right from UNCTAD II, the less developed countries have been demanding that since they are the producers of "commodities" ("goods" are from industries; commodities are from agriculture and mining etc.), the developed countries should pay the right prices. *The developing economics find that the buyers for the commodities that they sell act in unison.* They are conniving oligopsonies. They do not buy at the right time, knowing full well that since the commodities of less developed countries are perishable, their prices will crash. Developed countries talk of "market mechanism" but themselves do not buy in the perfectly competitive market. They want perfect competition amongst the firms/countries which sell to them.

If there is bumper crop the prices crash down and if there is shortfall in cops the prices are not allowed to rise as the western buyers act as oligopsonies. The rich buyers of the west purchase them at the prices they fix. Export shortfalls are not compensated even by the market forces. That was the reason that the developing economies wanted buffer stock financing.

An increase in exports of the less developed countries at the rate of 10 p.c. p.a. was suggested by the well-meaning development economists of the world. That was not facilitated by the west. The west came in the way of the poor countries increasing the growth rate in manufacture by 15 p.c. p.a.. Instead they brought their own industries and took up even domestic market. (If Lever Brothers come to India they do not contribute to exports from India or any other country.)

Developed countries rejected "Agreement on Commodities". Instead wanted "Comprehensive Programme of Commodities". If the less developed countries wanted to discuss about their exports, the developed countries wantd to discuss about their own, as if they were facing a crisis. *A $ 6 billion fund was demanded in 1976,* OPEC promised $ 400 million: Philippines $ 50 m. and India $ 25 m. The fund remained a non-starter.

The developed countries say that prices of commodities which are set after agreements or after establishing any fund would be "government prices" at which they will never buy. A *Common Fund for Commodities* for $ 3 b. was once agreed upon but that was for "integrated cases" i.e., for commodities/goods of the developed countries also. Developed countries suggested *'programme'* for the *'fund'* which meant a programme of how to increase the exports of developing and developed economies.

If the less developed countries wanted a growth rate of exports of 10 p.c. the developed countries also wanted that. A 10 p.c. growth rate on say $ 1000 m. would bring an increase of $ 100 in. while if the volume of exports of a developed country was $ 10000 m. then, even 1 p.c. was equal to $ 100 m. The developed countries never bothered about the low benchmark of the developing countries.

INTERNATIONAL COMMODITIES AGREEMENTS

Just as in India there is Food Corporation of India which procures surplus foodgrains from the farmers at support price or market price, whichever is more, so that the farmers/consumers do not suffer from severe fall/rise in prices (FCI releases foodgrains through PDS), at international level the countries demand similar operations for the agricultural commodities that they sell.

Less developed countries demand international assistance to setup Boards for individual commodities which could even out the effects of wide fluctuations for the farmers. In times of bumper crops the Board can buy and stock and save the prices from crashing and *vice* versa. *The response of the developed countries had been "you must be joking: you want us to give you funds so that you can charge higher prices from us"*! The developed countries argue "find the funds yourselves, then we will see if you can make use of it to fleece us".

There are three types of international commodity agreements: *buffer-stock, export controls and purchase contracts.*

Buffer stock. Such agreements were for cocoa, rubber and tin. Even for tin which can be stored, the agreement could not be a success. Cocoa and rubber had high storage costs. The essence of the arrangement was that in times of falling prices or low prices, the commodities could be stocked so that further fall can be avoided. As the prices rise, the stocks can be released. The developed countries allowed the stocks to rot to teach the developing economies a lesson. The developed countries would in such cases like to take over the processing or buy the stocks themselves and sell them dear in the world— never allowing the advantage to be reaped by the producers of the poor countries.

Export controls. Petroleum producers, sugar producers and coffee producers in the past reached such agreements. These agreements relate to exporting less (and if necessary producing less as in the case of OPEC —Organisation of Petroleum Exporting Countries) so that the prices do not fall. Such agreements could also not succeed because the exporters could not act as agreed upon. In case of the OPEC, the USA and other car producing countries do not allow OPEC to fleece the world much. They threaten to release their own stocks for emergency and/or sell them dear what they were importing from the rich countries. Besides if the USA hints at lifting the umbrella of protection to Saudi Arabia or to Kuwait, for how many days their royal families can survive.

Purchase contracts. They stipulate *(a)* a minimum price at which importing nations agree to purchase a specified quantity of the commodity and (b) a maximum price at which exporting nations agree to sell specified amounts of the commodity. Then both buffer stock operations and export controls become unnecessary. *The two-price system did not allow such agreement to succeed.*

The Compensatory finance scheme of IMF was for these agreements. It was inadequate. There was modest success for coffee only. All others failed.

UNCTAD is now not of much importance. GATT (General Agreement of Tariff and Trade) implemented by the countries under the monitoring of the W.T.O.—The World Trade Organisation are more important. (See chapters that follow).

UNCTAD XI

It was held in Sao Paolo, Brazil in June 2004.

After four decades, UNCTAD approach is changed beyond recognition. Now we are back at the "golden era of capitalism". Now the old socialist Group is gone. China practices "market socialism." It is single party capitalism. The group of poor countries, once known as group of 77, was backed by group B of socialist countries. Now they themselves are following the capitalist path. In old days and even now they could not give substantial aid to the developing economies. The "revolutionary" rhetorics are gone from UNCTAD. The poor countries have to collaborate with the developed countries.

UNCTAD XI found developing economies virtually cringing before the developed countries. The USA and EU now ensure that they will give only when the developing countries cringe and beg. There were bilateral negotiations. The representatives of the developing economies were busy negotiating with the developed countries commodity-by-commodity and country-by-country. Developing economies used to ask for many things as a right, citing the past imperialistic exploitation by the rich countries. These words were not heard in UNCTAD—XI. It was pointed out that there were 300 crore persons engaged in agriculture in developing economies. Their survival was at stake due to the present policies of WTO. The developed countries dump agricultural goods in developing economies at highly subsidised rates. That destroys the market for the farmers of the poor countries.

If was pointed out that the US and the EU cannot feed the rest of the world with their agricultural surpluses at the same time. Hence they will succeed In selling their own products but at the cost of destroying the agriculture and allied activities of the developing nations.

Negotiations were on the pattern of W.T.O. *UNCTAD* pointed out that 50 poorest countries of the world had 5.9% share in the global GDP. UNCTAD pleads for more aid (loans) to LDCs so that they can develop enough to end proverty: 70% of the FDI to LDCs was in oil and minerals.

UNCTAD –XII

21st May – 22nd June 2007

The conference was held on a few days during the period never for more than half-a-day per session. Following things were emphasized by the developing economies.

1. Globalisation poses challenges even if there are opportunities.
2. Accelerated growth brought financial crises.
3. Monopolies were promoting mono–production.
4. Commodity producers needed profits to invest.
5. Environmental hazards were looming large and poor countries may lose all.
6. Long term real and monetary solution were necessary. Monetary solutions should be beyond devaluation.
7. Multilateral cooperation was necessary.
8. National resources of the poor countries where being exploited ruthlessly. Globalisation is integrating for the winners but was even more marginalizing the losers. The rich nations had greedy level of living.
9. Developed countries are becoming even more deaf ! MNCs are ruling the world.
10. Bilateralism is resorted to by DCs, while they advocate poor countries to follow multilateralism.
11. Globalisation is not ensuring qualitative development for the poor.
12. IMF and world Bank are doing nothing for the poor.
13. Poor countries should be saved from decline in the value of $ reserves.
14. Material comforts should be available to poor countries also. Employment should increase here.
15. WTO should help developing countries also. Everything fell on deal ears. Then there was " please help" appled.

In the after math of 4.5. financial crisis in 2008-09, the USA sucked $ 1.9 trillion from Africa above.

29 General Agreement on Tariff and Trade [GATT]

In all probability there will be no GATT now only W.T.O. Conferences. There aspects are discussed in chs. 29 and 30.

I. A. First Seven GATT Rounds.
B. THE URUGUAY ROUND or the VIII ROUND. Dunkel Proposals. Final Agreement.
C. Evaluation of the GATT VIII Agreement.

II. GSP Vs. MFN
[Generalised System of Preferences Versus
Most Favoured Nation Status]
TRIMS, TRIPS, Agriculture, Industries, Services etc.

Prolegomenon

It was in 1947 that the world thought of having an organisation to promote multilateral trading and to monitor it. *ITO* [International Trade Organisation] was established in 1947 but was changed into GATT in 1947 itself.

There are many objectives of the GATT but can be summarized in four points.

First, to promote multilateral trading by reducing/eliminating tariffs and quotas. Only in the case of *serious* adverse balance of payment difficulties, could countries have somewhat higher tariffs and some QRS or quantitative restrictions. (Developed countries surprisingly are more protectionists).

Secondly, except in the case of economic blocs which can permit some special treatments, international trade has got to be on non-discriminatory basis.

Thirdly, only with tariff measures some infant Industries could be given short-term protection.

Fourthly, all disputes are to be settled in WTO (World Trade Organisation).

WTO was established after agreement at Morocco (Marrakesh city) in April 1994 and started functioning w.e.f. January 1, 1995

It was *IWTW* (Interim World Trade Watchdog) since 1948. *GATT is temporary: WTO is permanent.* It implements decisions of GATT. WTO has quasi-judicial rights but a country can come in or get out as a member. WTO encompasses almost the entire world, China also joined it. Even by 1999 It could bring down the average tariff rate from 40 p.c. to 6 p.c.

The first five conferences were held in the following cities and countries.

1947	Geneva, Switzerland
1949	Annecy (France)

1950 Torquay, Britain 1955 Geneva
1960 Geneva

The Sixth Round was also held at Geneva but was known as Kennedy Round. The Seventh Round was held in Tokyo.

In the first five rounds *over 60000 tariff rates were reviewed and settled.* Between 1948 and 1962 the world trade became double in real terms. The average growth rate in international trade in terms of volume was 10 p.c. p.a. and in terms of value was 13 p.c. p.a. while the world output was increasing at 5.5. p.c. p.a. only.

The Kennedy round or the sixth round of GATT

This was started in 1962 and President Kennedy took the initiative of securing concessions from EEC. EEC and the USA were complaining against each other's protective measures. The tariffs of the USA were so high that 'equal percentage' cuts would have left it in still advantageous position. Ultimately tariffs were cut by different percentages on different commodities and at 1967 prices (when the round ended), the advantage to the world amounted to $ 60 billion per year at the then prices. However, the trade between *developed and underdeveloped* countries got greater boost. The highest cuts were on high-tech goods. The great disappointment with GATT-6 was that the tariff concessions were on bilateral and reciprocal basis, undermining the basic objective of GATT. *The advantage was to be in money terms.* Not the rates but the total quantum of gain from tariff reduction between two countries had to be the same. That required elaborate tariff exercises. Since multilateral concessions could not be secured by less developed countries they asked for greater concessions under GSP (generalised system of preferences) from each countries but their requests fell on deaf ears. The tariff cuts on average amounted to 35 p.c. as aginst the 50 p.c. demanded. The President of the USA wanted "across the board" (one rate for all) but the EEC wanted "harmonised" reduction so that equal advantage acrued to all. There were very elaborate arrangements for compensating the workers of the USA if they lost their jobs due to tariff cuts.

The Tokyo round or the seventh round of GATT

This round was completed between 1967 and 1973. By 1973 the oil crisis had engulfed the world. Fresh negotiations then continued till 1979. Tariff reductions on average amounted to 33 p.c. which were to be extended over next 8 years. Tariff reduction for agricultural products ranged between 7 and 12 p.c; on finished products between 24 and 39 p.c; on semi-manufactured products between 27 and 32 p.c; on raw materials between 32 and 60 p.c; and on all industrial products between 26 and 37 p.c. All trade restrictions were removed on aircraft procurement.

Agreements were reached about government and non-government trade; about subsidies and countervailing duties; about licensing procedures of imports and exports and about standards (for reasons of safety, health, consumer protection, environmental protection etc.). However, the system of 'customs valuation' was beyond the competence of the staff of the less developed countries. The developing countries made requests for tariff concessions on 5374 items valued at $ 16 billion per year but got on 850 items only valued at $ 3.3 billion only—of which $ 2.5 billion concessions came from EEC. The USA virtually did nothing to grant concessions to LDCs. Bilateral concessions were given but they were against the spirit of GATT, which emphasises multilateralism.

By 1983 the external debt of all LDCs was $ 85 billion and they were groaning under its weights. They could not obtain fair terms of trade or tariff reductions. The USA was more concerned with Japan and EEC. The USA could secure for itself tariff concessions to the tune of 31 p.c; EEC to the tune of 27 p.c. and' Japan (where only inaugural meeting was held and the rest of the negotiations were held in Geneva) 28 p.c. *GATT was caring more for the rich countries than for the poor countries: this became very clear beyond doubt.* (In 2009, the debt was $ 3000 b.)

(B) THE EIGHTH ROUND OF GATT AT PUNTA DEL ESTE (URUGUAY)

This was launched in 1986. This round was to be completed by 15th December, 1993 and the Dunkel draft was accepted with some adjustments just a day before that !

The GATT eighth round was addressed to the old problems of quotas and tariffs and promotion of multilateral trading. However, this time trade in services, emphasis on freer capital movement (TRIMS), protection of patent rights (TRIPS), trade at 'natural' prices (subsidies) became hot issues. The agreement was reached on December 14, 1993 and tariffs on thousands of manufactured products from computer chips to potato chips were slashed. Though there were 117 contracting parties, it is generally believed that ultimate will of G-7 prevailed in this unipolar world.

The agreement was formally signed in Marrakesh, Morocco in April, 1994. New GATT was variously presented by writers—some as a sound preparation for taking the world to 21st century with promise for development for the backward economies.

This agreement was signed in a peculiar world setup. While there is talk of "general agreement on tariff and trade for maximum trade with maximum number of countries" (multilateralism and through it the 'most favoured nation status MFN), there were many new trade and economic blocs coming up. They had their own 'generalised system of preference' and through these preference they seem to be granting the 'MFN' status! The first move was in pursuit of the "best theory" (*i.e.,* of the free trade) the second was the pursuit of the "theory of second best" that of economic unions !

During the one and half decade ending mix-seventies, the world trade had become 5 times as much. The world economy had doubled in size. However, the same tempo could not be maintained between the decade of mid-seventies to mid-eighties. Hence GATT addressed itself to this issue.

The issues were so controversial that it was recommended by all the critics of the Government of India that India *(i)* should not sign GATT; that *(ii)* it should better opt out of the GATT's founding membership; *(iii)* that it should forge united front against the USA and G-7 countries and not succumb to their pressure; or *(iv)* prefer to be expelled from GATT. GATT agreement was challenged in the Supreme Court as being anti-Constitution. The count rejected the plea.

However, first we should review the Dunkel proposals on the basis of which GATT-8 agreement was reached.

Dunkel draft

When the negotiations under Uruguay Round became too prolonged with no solution in sight while dead-line of the last date of agreement for approaching the Director General of GATT, Arthur Dunkel, prepared the "average" proposals for consideration.

The viewpoints of all countries were taken into account. Dunkel proposals, however, were viewed with great suspicion and hostility in country like India where they were put to democratic debate. *However, one point which proves that the debate was not open and honest but guided by political considerations was that no opposition party or personality appreciated anything of that proposals nor any person of the government expressed any misgiving.* In India opposition parties oppose everything's turn by turn.

The proposals were regarded as 'manifesto of the multi- nationals', "un-fairest trading arrangement", "exercise of the musle power of the developed countries on India and of the Government of India on the poor people of India", "colonial aggression", "weak knee policy of cringing of the Government of India before the multi-nationals at the cost of the food and health interest of the common people of India" etc. There were no takers of the Government line that India would have advantage of nearly $ 1.5 billion to $ 2 billion a year. Accepting Dunkel proposals was likened to "countdown to oblivion", as if India itself was going to be obliterated from the planet.

Dunkel drafts were the basis of GATT 1993-1994 and became irrelevant? After the agreement was reached, there were some adjustments in Dunkel draft itself when the final agreement was reached. When some Indians criticised Dunkel draft as having *'dunk'* (scorpian bite, in Hindi), or liked Dunkel with Dragon type monster, the political attitude becomes quite clear.

Mr. Arthur Dunkel submitted proposals and five aspects of those proposals were hotly debated in India *viz.,* Trade Related Investment Matters' (TRIMS), Trade Related Intellectual Property Rights' (TRIPS or just IPR or Patent Laws and Royalty Questions), 'Question of Subsidies', 'Free Trade in Services', and Textiles'. Briefly these proposals were. under:

TRIPS. There was an international convention of patents rights as far back as 110 years (1883) in Paris which sought to create monopoly for the patent holder and the interests of the consumers were not taken into account. India did not sign that convention even during the British rule. Indian Patent Act of 1970 forbade copying of the process but not of the products, generally speaking.

From mechanical goods to chemical, from engineering goods to films, from seeds to drugs, from plants, fruits to cross-breed animals/fowls etc. patents or royalty rights can be claimed by the person/firm which invented them. It was argued that the multi-national firms will claim royalty rights on almost every thing. Dunkel draft was against copying a product with minor changes in the process. This is theft, copying or counterfeiting. The process innovator has to prove originality of the process. Countries not on product patent were proposed to be given 10 years period of transition. It was feared that since new variety of seeds will be coming every now and then the entire agriculture of the less developed countries will go in the hands of the multi-nationals, unless the countries preferred to remain on their primitive or old pattern.

Many East European countries and India used to recognise the right of the patent-holder for a period of 7 years while in the USA and other West European countries this right used to be for the period 17 to 20 years. Even when technology used to become old, royalty payments were due. Dunkel proposals provided for extension of terms of patent protection to 20 years and even if the foreign companies were granted the right to produce the patented good in any less developed country, the company was not obliged to transfer the technology. It was argued by less developed countries that technology transfer would become transfer and that from farmers to scientists and from industrialists to drug manufacturers all would be under the MNCs and would be required to pay hefty sums. The consumer would be fleeced.

TRIMS. This was intended to promote FDI (foreign direct investment) in countries which signed GATT. The DCs argued that less developed countries would be profited if they allow trade and production restrictions on foreign companies. After all these countries need goods. Less developed countries used to argue for free trade in goods. DCs argued for free investment. Developed countries argued for free movement of capital; less developed countries argued for free movement of labour !

Those who opposed Dunkel proposals argued that MNCs will do "East India Company on India". Treating foreign and domestic companies alike and removing all restrictions will once again bring imperialistic draining of resources of less developed countries. India wanted that MNCs observe export obligations; that they transfer the technology to domestic producers; that they purchase the raw materials from domestic countries; they employ domestic labour/managers, and they offer equity to Indians as well. Some safeguards were desired. It was also argued that such blanket removal of all restrictions on MNCs will bring investment in 'unnecessary, luxury, or superfluous' goods and aggravate balance of payment problems of the less developed countries.

The developed countries were arguing that if free trade is good in goods it is good in capital goods/investment and in *services* as well but not free movement of labour from the developing economies. The Dunkel draft recommended that all countries should have right to operate banking, insurance, shipping, telecommunications services in other countries. In fact the less developed countries will find that they will have cheaper and better services from abroad. Less developed countries were apprehensive about their employment and income interest. FDI in goods sector and services sector was viewed with apprehension from national security and self-sufficiency points of view as well. Movement of unskilled labour was ruled out. Malhotra Committee's recommendations for insurance sector and Narsimham Committee's recommendations for the banking sector were viewed with apprehension by the employees of these sectors and there had been frequent strikes.

It was recommended that there be *rules* and *WTO* (World Trade Organisation) to monitor TRIPS and TRIMS as also to oversee agreement on 'subsidies', 'tariff cuts', 'textiles quota restrictions', etc. Liberalisation of exports, imports, capital movement and services was recommended. Substantial reductions in tariff and subsidies were recommended. Trade and investment matters were recommended to be non-discriminatory and non- reciprocal. Textile quota restrictions were recommended to be eased but in 7-9 years and above, all the patent, rights on products were recommended to be protected.

Subsidies. This issue was a bone of contention between the USA on the one side and the EEC countries on the other. France saw some of the worst riots in the post-II-W W. period over that. The European farming is less cost efficient than the USA farming but since the EU countries subsidised their farmers heavily (so that they remain attached to land and use the rural land), the US farmers could not sell their products in EU despite cost advantage. The farmers in USA were paid 'recompense' for *not* cultivating their farms so that glut in supplies and fall in prices could be avoided. The USA was arguing that if subsidies are removed/reduced the USA can sell its product and this will be beneficial to the world as a whole. Dunkel proposals were for reduction in such subsidies included on exports. Dunkel proposals provided that export subsidies be phased out if the share of the product in global trade was 3.25 p.c. within eight years or until the per capita GNP reached $ 1000 per annum. India had to abolish CCS (Cash Compensatory Scheme or bonus on exports) and had to institute the system of convertibility of rupee to ensure better market returns to foreign currency holders. Subsidies were not to exceed 10 p.c. of the cost of production in agriculture.

EEC unification in economic and political terms got threatened several times. At the time when Uruguary Round was started, the collapse of Soviet bloc was not envisaged, though its difficulties were well-known. Negotiations broke down several times. The USA was proposing to Japan that they open up their market to the USA goods and/or voluntarily restrain exports to the USA. Dunkel proposals were not very favorable to less developed countries *but they were average proposals—average of the proposals submitted by DCs and LDCs and trading blocs.*

The pressure from the USA on GATT was most severe because its current account balance of payment deficit was running to the tune of $ 90 billion a year. The USA wanted international trade at *natural* costs without subsidies, though it continued and continues to be highly protectionist on one pretext or the **other.** GATT/Dunkel proposals were hinting that through GATS (General Agreement on Trade Services), TRIMS and TRIPS there would be freer flow of capital in less developed countries and they would find it profitable where there is "equity-debt" swap. The Dunkel draft was an **attempt** to short-circuit the endless negotiations and packed all issues into **a** single text on which only minor amendments were allowed. That meant that the countries could accept them or reject them. ^Rejection meant that everything had to be bilaterally negotiated with all countries. Bilateral agreement would equal to the number of commodities multiplied by number of countries ! There was greater danger for the USA Super 301 for such countries which meant penalties. The US persuations with Japan brought no results, (though many of their Prime Ministers and Ministers had to resign) when once Premier Tanaka said to the President of the US "Mr. President, why do you insists on our importing goods from you; we have imported the theory of free trade on comparative advantage from you") meaning thereby that the USA was not having cost advantage. The USA did its best to exert pressure on GATT negotiations.

(C) GATT-8 AGREEMENT AND ITS OBJECTIVE EVALUATION

The final agreement was a 550-page document. Here only those issues are taken up which were most contentious for India.

TRIPS (trade related intellectual property rights). India has fallen in line with GATT *but its 'defeat' is in the matter of drugs* mostly.

India was already in agreement with other GATT countries about copyright, trade market, trade secret, industrial designs, integrated circuit and geographical indications. Only in product versus process patent it could not succeed. India was allowed ten years time to fall in line.

It is true that Indian drug industry became Rs. 4000 crore industry from Rs. 500 crore industry and that its exports were Rs. 1500 crores by 1991 over 1974. However, the Indian drug manufacturers were copying many products of others and had not invested much in research. *(There are sub-standard drugs and there are useless combinations.)* Indians had to be checked.

In this connection *most* of the fears were unfounded. First, *"the new GATT rules applied for those drugs which will be patented after January 1, 1995"*. This was done. Secondly, the common drugs and WHO (World Health Organisation) *essential* drugs are out of the purview of royalty payment. Thirdly, Government of India retains price control measures in the event of exorbitant pricing. Fourthly, Government can purchase high cost drugs and dispense them at low prices or distribute free if it wants and there is no bar from any quarter in the world. (In MP a few persons were found in scandals involving hundreds of crore rupees in the purchase of fake or out of date drugs but were not booked for jail) Fifthly, Indian drug manufacturers have not been able to patent drugs outside India because of lack of application in research. This will be promoted. India can gain substantially if Ayurvedic preparations are patented and sold abroad.

It is to be granted that quite a few medicines became quite costly after GATT patents. In case of these medicines, if need be, government support will be necessary. But which Government of India bothered about rising food and medicine process?

TRIMS (trade related investment measures). TRIM agreement imposes nothing on India. India was itself keen to import foreign direct investment. GATT does not force any quantity or any line of manufacture to be allowed. Indian MRTP and FERA provisions started being diluted from 1973 itself. India probably will gain a lot if equity-debt swap takes place through export promotion consequent upon FDI. It is impossible for any MNC to do East India Company on India. India itself started inviting F.D.I.

GATS (General agreement on trade in service). This is also not against Indian interests. India has opened its telecommunications sector to private sector to improve efficiency and to meet the gaps in demand. India is not *obliged* to open its life/general insurance sector to foreigners. It did so on its own. So is the case for retail banking. However, India itself can permit that India can do what it wants under *its industrial policy* but not under GATT. India can decide such things on the basis of offers/ requests received. If foreign banks are to be allowed in India, Indian banks can function abroad also. Other financial organisation/consultancy can operate everywhere, subject to certain safeguards.

Agriculture (Subsidies and seeds issues). It was decided that all subsidies (aggregate measure of support AMS) for farmers in excess of 5 p.c. of total value of production for developed countries and 10 p.c. for developing countries, had to be cut. over 10 years in case of developed countries and over 6 years in case of developing countries. That should not bother India because. Its subsidies are very meager in percentage terms.

Direct export. subsidies would be reduced by developed countries by 36 p.c. over 6 years while the developing countries have to reduce them by 24 p.c. over 10 years. Then those countries which have only insignificant imports will have to open up their markets for import of agricultural products from foreign countries subject to the minimum of 3.3 p.c. *over and above* the 1986- 87 level. India on its own imported 5.5 m.t. of whet in 2006.

India was already importing for its buffer stock operations. Besides no country can force another country to buy *at a higher than the domestic rate,* unless its aggregate demand **exceeds** the aggregate domestic supplies.

The following subsidies/supports to agriculture have also *not been reduced fully.*

(1) Public Distribution
(2) Pest Control
(3) Crop Protection Measures
(4) Extension Services to Farmers
(5) Training Services
(6) Inspection and Advisory Services
(7) Marketing Services
(8) Infrastructure Support (like irrigation, power, or credit).

In other words, the production and consumption subsidies on foodgrains were not covered in GATT. Only business subsidies were covered.

It is true that royalties will have to be paid for the seeds developed by MNCs but there are *"green box arrangements"* for the benefit of the less developed countries:

(A) No royalty will be paid by the farmers for the seeds multiplied by them for their **old stock to be** used for next year's sowing and so on.
(B) No royalty will be paid for the seeds multiplied by the farmers and informally exchanged with the neighbours.
(C) *Only if the firms or government farms multiply the seeds and sell them commercially, royalties will have to be paid.*

The problem will prove difficult if self-terminating seeds are pushed in the world by a USA firm.

These provisions appear fair enough. If a country has balance of payment problems—India always had, then importing 3.3 p.c. over and above the imports of 1986-87 is not compulsory. IMF will decide that but it cannot say India does not have balance of payment problems.

India has been permitted to club the product and non-product subsidies (non-product subsidies are on fertilisers, electricity, irrigation, pesticides and seeds) to keep them upto 10 p.c. level of the total cost of agricultural products. On the basis of the national income data India can keep subsidies equal to Rs. 30000 crore but they are equal to 10 p.c. in the case of sugarcane, rubber, oilseeds and tobacco. *The system of support prices for agricultural outputs is out of the purview of GATT.* The cheap import prices are *not* going to harm the marginal farmers of India *because they are net buyers of foodgrains and not net sellers; they simply do not have marketable surpluses in any case.* It should be remembered that those who do research in biofertilisers, herbicides or HYV seeds are not mafia group persons.

Textiles. India, as some other countries like China, Hong Kong (China), Korea, Japan, Taiwan, have great advantage in textiles because of the 'cheap' labour. The USA had all types of restrictions on the import of textiles, not following the principle of' comparative advantage in costs' which it advocates to others in hi-tech goods.

There was multi-fibre agreement (MFA) which was actually a combination of several bilaterally negotiated quotas. When textiles were brought under GATT, the discriminatory treatments become unnecessary. Under the new GATT arrangements the quotas end as under:

16 p.c. by 1997
33 p.c. cumulative (17 p.c. more) by 2001
51 p.c. (18 p.c. more) by 2004; and
100 p.c. by 2005. They were gone totally by 2010.

The beneficiaries will not be Indians only but all other countries. In fact because of better sheen and texture, better designs and colours and better marketing practices (Indian samples are better than goods supplied, as per the complaints appearing in papers) there are chances that the countries of Far East will out-compete Indians. Indians will gain from GATT provisions only if they rise to the occasion in best of the efficiency in production and marketing practices.

Tariffs. India will have to lower its tariffs from 72.2 p.c. to 32.4 p.c. *i.e.,* by nearly 40 p.c. *points* in industrial products covering capital goods, intermediate goods and raw materials. Between 2010-2015, the maximum import duties in the world will be 3.5 p.c.

However, the *actual reduction due to GATT* is much less because India was already reducing the tariffs in its liberalised budgetary policy. It is possible for any country to reduce tariffs by percentages higher than contemplated in GATT.

India need *not* reduce tariffs *as per GATT requirements* in many items like non-ferrous metals, fertilisers, petroleum, and durable and non-durable consumer goods.

Dumping. GATT has virtually permitted dumping ! If the dumping is at 98 p.c. of the cost production, it will be allowed ! Dumping is allowed if the dumped goods constitute less than 1 p.c. of the total imports in a country ! If India has cheap goods to offer abroad to earn forex, it can do so as others can do unto India.

It is expected that exports of India will increase by $ 1.5 to $ 2 billion per year due to a general expansion of the world trade following substantial lowering of tariffs. Now *member countries of GATT agreement become Most Favoured Nations: non-members are not.* India can export some of its agriculture products, *provided the supplies and marketable surpluses increase.* This will *not* be automatically possible since some of the Indian products will become cheaper in developed countries. Cheapness. is not the reasons why these essential things will be demanded more. India can export only if the "demographic consumption" is lower than the production. Production of agricultural products can increase if external technical support becomes strong. *Internal prices or international prices have not been a stimuli to boost agricultural outputs.* Had that been so, the production of pulses and oilseeds would not have been lagging behind. *The relationship that holds good in India is that "this year's output determines this year's price", but "this year's price does not provide any substantial stimulus to change the next year's cropping mix decisions".* Cob-web theorem is belied.

The higher production is sought to be increased through inputs subsidies which are lower than permitted by GATT. However, they will involve a lot of financial deficit which will be resented by IMF.

It is true that 10 years hence 'gene research in plants' will be patented and India will have to pay royally. But royalty will not be paid for naturally occurring genes and gene sequences; they will be paid if gene mutation is developed.

India fell in the line with drug patents also. However, government can exercise the right of price control, checking charging of high prices, or /and can subsidie some life saving drugs. India thus had to fall in line with the rest of the world in the matter of IPR or TRIPs or patents. But if Indians invent something they can also enjoy the fruits. Adoption of IPR is also expected to enhance flow of foreign direct investment (FDI) and technology. Those products may be produced in India itself.

Foreign direct investors cannot gatecrash in India without invitation and permission. The Government can still direct them about production lines and exports obligations. However, under GATT once the FDI unit comes into existence in India, it cannot be discriminated against.

Incorporation of explication in the revised text to the effect that PDS (FCI operations) and subsidies related to them do not come under the purview of GATT should be reassuring to Indians. These subsidies are not objected to by GATT by such organisations as IMF and IDA.

All types of service sectors cannot bulldoze into India. India has been given concession in many lines— at least in those lines where most persons are involved in employment.

The IMF, EU, OPEC, WB, IDA, WTO, the USA and Japan and other blocs of the rich countries simply ignored the plight of the developing economies. Global growth remained a myth. Poor countries did not gain. The poor of the poor countries *certainly did not gain.*

The problem, that the GATT arrangements create are equal to number of commodities *multiplied* by number of countries *multiplied* by different legal provisions"; and it has to *solve them also.* The debates in the GATT or W.T.O. have become more legal than economic only. Politics had already overshadowed economics much earlier. The foreign trade and investment regime will change drastically over the years. In particular, India will have to tighten its patents regimes, introduce products patents, grant patent protection for a much longer period. Further India will have to grant national treatment to foreign firms in matters such as government purchases and contracts. India cannot favour domestic firms and discriminate against the foreign firms. India will have to cope with the TBTs (technical barriers of trade). India has great problems with *FOGS* (an acronym for *"functioning of the GATT System")* !

3. GENERALISED SYSTEM OF PREFERENCES (GSP) AND MFN

GSP *schemes* were introduced in the EU and Japan in 1971. GSP and MFN sometimes create confusion. MFN (most favoured nation) treatment is available to all members of the WTO. If all countries of the world become members of the WTO, MFN loses its value. When all pro "most favoured" then against whom ? The GSP is more restrictive. *The case of GSP was based on the infant industry argument* and the GSP was granted by the developed countries *selectively* after bilateral and case-by-case negotiations.

GSP has not been in operation for long and its benefits were extremely "cosmetic" in nature—more apparent than real. Everything depends upon the mercy of the country which grants GSP. GSP is more relevant for those which do not enjoy MFN benefits. *They are "either or" schemes. If* one is under MFN, then the position is better. *One MFN country can enter into GSP arrangement with non-WTO country.*

GATT made GSP provision irrelevant for member countries but some old agreements continue. If a poor country wants greater concessions than under MFN they can be negotiated under GSP, till this system is allowed. More products can be included and higher tariff-cuts can be negotiated (even to zero) under GSP, if it can be reached between two countries. *The GSP of the USA was based on political considerations. If a country was friendly towards the US goals it could be granted zero tax on its exports to the USA.* The rates and commodities differed. GSP can be revised and removed and major commodities were *excluded If the exports of a country were 50 p.c. of the total exports going to the US or if they exceeded $ 30 million, the GSP was not available. Very rich countries cannot enjoy MFN or GSP.*

GSP was to continue upto 1981; it was extended to 1991 and then indefinitely", subject to the changing conditionalities.

The "generalised system of preferences is the system of preferring or not preferring the goods of foreign. countries. It is anti-thesis of MTN (multilateral trade negotiations) of GATT yet the system prevails. It would grant duty-free import (subject to certain limits *e.g.*, $ 30 million of an article) provided it helps the production and manufacture in the GSP giving country. Or else it will put trade barriers, contravening even GATT provisions. It is a selective list. The GSP is shown to those commodities which do not harm domestic producer of the country. The principle of 'comparative advantage' is ignored. It is for others to follow. ***GSP is given to that country which supplies less than 50 per cent of that commodity to the country. The GSP can be withdrawn at will by the granting country. If exports exceed $ 30, then GSP is lost on the entire amount of export. Thus exporting countries would not like to export more than $ 30 million of that commodity to get advantage of GSP. Nearly 15 per cent of the US imports are under GSP. Developing countries now feel that it is better not to have the advantage of GSP; they should rather take advantage of the GATT provisions.*** That is how the U.S. keeps its imports down.

GSP was introduced in 1971-72 was granted by EEC first. Then Japan, Norway, Denmark, Finland, Ireland, New Zealand, Sweden, Britain, Switzerland, Australia and Canada also started GSP. The USA started giving these concessions from 1975. GSP enables the less developed countries to export more because the tariff height is reduced to zero *but for limited amounts of exports per commodity per country.* The GSP creates trade and since it becomes 'discriminatory preference' it diverts trade in favour of GSP commodity from non-GSP commodity. The concessions become important for manufactured and semi-manufactured goods. GSP is a *tariff-quota system* under which zero or very low tariff is applicable if the quotas are not exceeded. The product coverage differs from country to country but the main intention of the GSP granting country is to ensure that their domestic production does not suffer. Tariff cuts, however, differ from country to country and commodity to commodity. *Safeguard measures* are all for the GSP giving country so that their national dividend/income is not injured. The country of origin is monitored by the GSP. No country can route its products through another country to get double GSP. A commodity will be considered originating from India if at least 50 per cent value- adding is done in India. In some cases this limit is just 35 per cent. However, if the goods exported from (say India) contain import components (say from USA), then the value-adding conditions are not applied.

Only less developed countries are entitled for GSP; OPEC is excluded. Countries with which there are economic disputes are excluded from GSP. [If a company of

(say) USA is nationalised without adequate compensation by any less **developed country, then that country will** not have **GSP advantage].** ***Reverse preference is not allowed.*** **Those who give GSP cannot take it from others.**

Communist countries used to give their own GSPs but their entire system went into disarray after the collapse of socialism. Oil exporting and producing countries were receiving GSP earlier; and as they became rich they started giving GSP but soon all their concessions were reduced to peanuts. *There is a lot of confusion amongst the exporters about the MFN and GSP provisions which differ from country to country* and sometimes it becomes difficult to calculate as to in what more advantage lies. Commodity inclusion/exclusion also differs. (Some types of fishes are included in the GSP and some are not; exporters, therefore, cannot believe that fish means any fish.)

There are quantitative limits on GSP rates. *After these limits are exceeded the exports from less developed countries become subject to MFN (GATT) rates.*

The effect of MFN clause is to keep a given country's tariff rates uniform and equal to all countries. In the absence of MFN imports of the same commodity from different countries will be subject to different rates of tariff. They give rise to discrimination; MFN is non-discriminatory *while GSP is discriminatory.*

The USA used to demand reciprocal concessions before giving them. *A typical system emerged: even though each agreement was bilateral, concessions contained were generalised through the MFN clause.* MFN was granted to the *main* exporter/importer countries rather than to all and sundry, termed as 'freeloaders'.

It is for the USA to exclude a country from GSP if it thinks that it has become rich even if the per capita income is low. GSP concessions were demanded by the erstwhile socialist countries as compensation for past exploitation. However, some countries like Australia, Canada and New Zealand impressed upon others in the past that they were never imperialist countries, yet granted GSP concessions.

30 | W.T.O. (World Trade Organisation) WTO and Global Trading Environment

WTO administer the agreements of GATT-8. However, now-a-days "GATT meetings" are not held. Instead the issues are discussed in WTO. meetings and negotiations. WTO itself had its "rounds" of discussion. There were held in Singapore 1996, Geneva (1998), Seattle, USA (1999), Doha (2001) and Cancun (2003)

Now "it is daily WTO meeting and Doha". (2008)

W.T.O. Meetings are still dominated by the demands of developed countries in general and of the USA in particular. These countries have greed and more greed. They are in financial crisis due to the US companies leading in papers speculation to "create gains". The developed countries demand more and more "rights", while they treat the "rights" of the developing economies as " concessions". Even in 2008 there were demands "address the Doha concern first" from the U.S.[1]

W.T.O. meetings are mostly about these issues.

1. TRIMS (trade related investment matters).
2. TRIPS (trade related intellectual property rights) or royalty questions.
3. Market access (more imports by developing economies)
4. M.F.A. (multi fiber arrangements)
5. "Standards" (developed countries find faults with The quality of the exports of developing countries) and.
7. Environment concerns.

Government of India's version of Cancun Conference was that India played a key role. It formed G-20 (group of 20) on agriculture and India played a key role. It formed G-20 (group of 20) on agriculture and G-16 on Singapore issues. India emphasized that in order to protect the high cost agriculture of their own countries, the developed countries were 8 times more protective in agriculture than in manufacturing. The developed countries were not only not importing cheap agricultural products from the developing economies but were over-producing their high cost products and dumping them in the developing economies. This was threatening the livelihood modes and incomes of rural areas of the developing economies. Developed countries, it was pointed out, were playing dirty tricks. "Zero for zero" tariff attitude was iniquitous. If suppose the USA agrees for zero tariff and non-tariff barrier on the import of cashew nuts from India and in return demands zero barriers for their cars, the outcome is heavily loaded in favour of the USA. How little will they be importing in dollar terms for cashew nuts! The tricks of the developed countries were obvious.

India forcefully emphasized that the matters of investment cannot be taken as a matter of right to be brought only under WTO. It is for the host country to invite capital where they want and when they want. This bull dozing of capital is bullying. The demand of the developed countries for "transparency": cannot be accepted because that means the government store purchases should be open to international tendering. There are many things related to national defence which will be procured by the Indians from the Indian public sector first and then from other Indians. The foreigners do not have a right in everything. "Trade facilitation" cannot be extended everywhere.

Note about environment concern. 2009

In 2007 in Bali Conference it was agreed upon that non-polluting countries will be given carbon-credits for not emitting obnoxious gases that cause green house effect or global warming causing ozone hole. World is in danger of the metting of ice at both the poles. The sea levels will rise. many island countries will be wiped off. India's part cities many go under water. Developed counties are the cause of all these looming dangers. But they can pay price to non-polluting counters for non-polluting counties for purchasing carbon credits. Polluting lights will be purchased. The poor countries will get some money, but the world will be worse off. The rich countries will continue to bring the doom nearer.

WORLD TRADE ORGANISTION
WORLD TRADING SYSTEMS UNDER WTO

World Trade Organization administers the decisions of GATT conference VIII, whereas GATT stands for "General Agreement on Tariff and Trade". After GATT VIII there are no more GATT conferences. In fact WTO is jocularly known as GATT IX.

There used to be WTO conferences as well. There were five of them between 1996 and 2003. (discussed in this chapter). Of these five conferences two stand out. One is Doha conference and the other is Cancun conference. Doha Conference is known for the rich countries arguing their view point and demanding that their demands be met by the developing countries. Cancun Conference is known as the conference in which the developing countries raised their "concerns". The world now has two terms "Doha issues" and "Cancun issues" for the demands for the developed and developing countries. There is a stalemate. Neither group of countries is accepting the demand of the other fully. On 31sl October 2009, India opined that the developed countries should accept the *Doha Lite*. What is meant by "lite"—somebody coined the term for the "second best". The developing countries argue that instead of having the best why not settle down for the second best which is just a little less than the best. There is daily WTO now.

The world trading system is now multilateral trading between all member countries of the WTO (150 of them, the rest 42 countries of the world have observer status). The WTO enjoins that soon there should be only 3 to 5 p.c. tariffs on imports, only as much as will yield the revenue for running the customs departments of the countries. The world should allow dumping to the extent of 3 p.c. of the average of the last three years.

There should be freedom to export and import and there should be no quotas. There should be exchange control that foreign exchange is denied to some. There is now free convertibility of currencies i.e., dollars and national currency are freely convertible in the market, unless some countries are not in a position to do anything orderly as Somalia. The countries can have STCs i.e., State Trading Corporations which can trade with other STCs. They were the products of socialist era. India is having one which cannot earn even 2 p.c. profit of the working capital. (Its report about profits is not related to the volume and value of of imports and exports nor to the total capital. The data about them are not published either. The STC is regarded as a white elephant. Free enterprise is considered the best for international business.

Currencies can be taken out or taken in for the direct investment or investment in the equities or debentures or other debt papers.

There is free trade in services also. The trading countries cannot infringe the patent rights of other countries nor the copy rights. If the inventions and innovations of others are to be used it can be done only after the payment of royalty agreed upon. MFN GENERAL is there automatically. All nations are "most favoured nations". If some countries want some other countries to be even more MFN, they can do so.

The most harmonious way to settle disputes in WTO is through some neutral procedure based on an agreed legal foundation. Regional trade agreements can be had even under WTO system. That is how there is EU or NAFTA or ASEAN or SAARC. "Negotiations" is the key word for everything under WTO —for trading and for settlement of disputes.

In this introduction we put all the important things about WTO in 10 catch points: First the list of five conferenc es:

1. Singapore Conference: Dec. 9–13, 1996
2. Geneva Conference, May 18–29, 1998
3. Seattle Conference, Nov. 30 – Dec. 13.1999
4. Doha Conference Nov. 9–14, 2001 and
5. Cancun Conference Sept 10–14, 2003

1. TRIMS. Trade Related Investment Matters. Developed countries ask the developing economies to provide freedom to invest there. Developing economies want direct investment. Developed countries want freedom for FII i.e., investment is shares and bonds in share markets so that they can make fabulous profits and then run away with them.
2. TRIPS: TRADE RELATED INTELLECTUAL PROPERTY RIGHTS. Developed countries want that all inventions, innovations, copyrights etc. should be used by the developing countries only after taking permission and paying royalty.
3. Market access: By this the developed countries mean that they should be allowed to have trade and business in all types of commodities, goods and services and no restrictions should be placed on the market.
4. The developed countries want that market access for agricultural products should be provided. This is opposed by the communists of developing economies. They argue that the developed countries will snatch away the self–sufficiency of the developing countries. This is partly true only. The developing economies desperately need food from the developed countr for warding off hunger and malnutrition. The USA starts their business with Coca Cola and junk food. Developing economies do not like that.

5. Developing and developed countries accuse each other of polluting the earth. For example the USA says that over 150 crore cattle and 80 prore people of India defecate and urinate in the open and India emits largest quantum of methane gas. India says that developed countries spew smoke from their chimneys and also harmful gases.
6. The developing economies say that in WTO the developed countries want to take everything and give nothing.
7. The developed countries say that in fact it is the other way round.
8. Developing economies say that the developed countries should shed the opulence and corpulence a bit. They should have less trade in arms, which they impose upon. They also keep hot or cold war alive somewhere USA uses as much electricity for neon lighting and air conditioning as India and China use for all purposes.
9. Developed countries should not cause green house effect leading to global warming. They should not buy carbon credits from the developing economies. {Those who do not pollute are given "carbon credits" which can be sold).
10. Developed countries should stop forthwith all subsidies to their production directly or indirectly.

The Text; WTO;

WTO administers the decisions which were arrived at the VIII th GATT Conference, known as Kennedy round. The first important aspect *of* WTO agreements was on TRIMS.

1. *Trims*

It means trade related investment matter. Capitalist countries say that they have enough capital and should be allowed to invest anywhere and in anything. Developing economies want their wishes to be taken into account. India received by Oct. 2009, $ 100 b. in FDI.

India's record in getting the FDI is poor, relative to China. China gets up to 10 to 11 times more! India's average had been $ 4 to 5 b. per year. China got $ 40 to 45 b. per year. India is a free country but it is not considered a free economy. There are several regulations. China has opened a region fully. India has opened the country fully but has put limitations on various aspects. The FDI comes in the large industries but not in medium and small industries.

China is pragmatic. Its "market socialism" is a peculiar combination, China says it "respects" the market and it "adheres" to socialism. China has three important features worth noting here:

1. It wants territories of others. It has made Burma another Tibet. It claims large areas of India. It once claimed up to Indonesia all countries. Indonesians killed millions of their communists in 1950s.
2. Chinese can eat anything. What they cannot eat, they use in medicines!
3. It is dichotomous economy. It hides the ugly sides of economy.

India certainly needs FDI. India is losing agricultural land very fast. Its population is likely to cross China's population by 2050. it is feared. Mothers of India are now more productive than the Mother India.\(Each city is losing agricultural area around it. Bhopal, a town of less than 1 lakh population in 1947, (where this author was born and still lives) now has population of about 18 lakhs. It has engulfed or eaten away as much as 2500 square miles of agricultural land for urban colonies). Productivity in China is two to four times higher than in India. At least that is what the Chines, India can invite foreign capital in genetically muted seeds, but with care. It is repeated that there should be pilot experiments before using.

In the name of inviting foreign capital for trade related investment matters, India should not permit dumping. The developed countries are bullies in imposing their exports. India has to be cautious without looking inhospitable, however.

2. Trade Related Intellectual Property Rights UK Tr1prs or Trips or Iprs

Innovations, inventions, research, design, and testing are involved in. production. From music systems, to computer generated films or special effects in them, to modern aircrafts, pilot less bombers, invincible tanks, atomic war ships, missiles of every type the world is witnessing newness in manufacturing almost on daily basis. No one now can replicate or duplicate the produces made by others. Reprints of the films cannot be shown in picture halls by anyone other than the authorized producer– distributor combine. The same is true of music CDs. Harry Potter books cannot be printed by unauthorized persons and sold in the market. Their translations, unless authorized, cannot be sold. For everything royalty is to be paid to the inventor or the original maker. The same is true of car or motorcycle models to all things.

Trade marks or brand names are to be taken. If someone invents something but does not take the patent, then others can replicate and can in fact charge money from the original inventor. Patents for the traditional products cannot be taken. The USA took patent for "texamati" rice and claimed rights over the "basmati" of India. WTO ruled against the USA. Many firms in the USA took patents of ayurvedic medicines or preparations from haldi. neem or karanj. They were also cancelled. The traditional folklore things are of the country without patent.

Logos, brand names, and typical packaging packing designs are patented. Non–members of WTO cannot claim the rights but there are no non–members of importance. (A) Patent is given. (B) Protection to the patent name, logo and design is given. (C) Royalties for the specific period negotiated. (D) Territories are defined. (E) All future disputes that may arise are settled.

Commodities (new seeds), goods and services çan also be protected under IPR. Authors of computer programmes to novels are all given IPRs. Those who write stories and songs for a film get IPR (copyright). Trade mark us initially for some purpose cannot be used by others for other purposes. For example, let us take it that the word "TATA" was first used for steel. No one in the world can manufacture under–wears and use the word "TATA" for the same on the argument that TATAs do not have the IPR on under–wears. They have IPR on the brand name.

As per TRIPS agreement, the period of protection of patents shall be 20 years. Marketing rights for a ¦new product patented in another country will also be ensured for 5 years, once the TRIPS is in force. The product patent system can be fully operational from January 1, 2005.

India cannot produce drugs, chemicals, wines etc. using the generic names of medicines or such names as "whisky" or "champagne".

India also has to give product patents to drugs and pharmaceuticals, agro– chemicals and processed food industries from January 1, 2005. TRIPS agreement covers seven major intellectual properties viz.,

1. Copyrights and related rights.
2. Trademarks.
3. Geographical indications.
4. Industrial Designs.
5. Innovations and Inventions.
6. Integrated circuits.
7. Information source.

These provisions are fair enough *but were unfairly used by the western capitalist world.*

India was producing hosiery items under the trademark "Murphy" which was once a great name in the production of radios. "Phillips" trade mark is used for many products which are not produced by the company. (Nepal was producing steel products under the name PODREJ instead of GODREJ but the logo was designed in such a way that it looked like GODREJ if not closely inspected, and who knows it was the handiwork of an Indian using Nepal as the fake name of the country!)

Western countries got "baasmati" patented. When protests were launched, they changed the spelling. The western producer got many herbal products patented there. *India won many cases with the WTO.*

The thing that came out was that knowing very well that patenting is required, India producers failed to get patents, trademarks and logos registered with the international authorities.

India has to grant *EMRs (exclusive marketing rights)* to the products which got patents and marketing approvals anywhere in any country where it has patent.

India had to amend its Patent Act in 2002 to come in line with the WTO. *India will have to pay royalty on patented health products for 20 years instead of 7 earlier.* [If India can get a product patented, it can receive royalty for the same period ; but either such inventions are absent or are not patented. Most of the patents are taken for ayurvedic drugs. Research and development in health sector is totally poor).

India was producing drugs synthesised in other countries by slightly altering the *process* of manufacturing and was not paying royalty. It paid royalty only when the *product was copied totally.*

Critics of the GoI and the pharmaceutical industry were highly critical of the GoI for ' 'surrendering" before the WTO.

However, in all fairness it can be said that it was not correct not to pay royalty on "product" but only on the *"same process"*. India was not on high ethical ground. India can negotiate bilaterally for production/royalty payments with the concerned firms on a little more favourable basis. India could not have claimed the right to produce "products" with alternative "processes".

India was imposing 80 p.c. import duties (on average) on the drugs to protect domestic industries. *It is to be noted that now the time of not paying the royalties on the old products is over. Hence from 2003 royalties on all new products will have to be paid as per the WTO* norms.

Multinationals and the big firms of India will capture the market. Small firms will go out of business.

But most of them were in any case producing sub–standard drugs. It is true that drugs will be costlier now. *However, under WTO arrangement there is absolutely no bar on the governments providing subsidies to the patients. In other words all Governments can buy the drugs at the market rate but order their dispensation/sale at the subsidised rates.* Life–saving drugs can remain cheap, for example, TB treatment or leprosy treatment can be free. Governments are not doing that.

* Drugs already in the market will be free from patenting. No royalty will be paid. There will be no back–dating.
* *Intellectual property rights should be recognized. If India has objections why should it not promote innovations, inventions, synthesisation and discoveries to take the same advantage.*

MARKET ACCESS:

Provisions About Agriculture:

Developed countries	Developing Countries
1. Developed countries were asked to reduce tariffs by 36% in 6 years time.	1. Developing countries were asked to reduce tariffs by 24% in 10 years time.

Developed countries	Developing Countries
2. Export subsidies were asked to be reduced by 20 p.c. in 6 years time.	2. Exports subsidies were asked to be reduced by 13.3% in 6 years.
3. Exports subsidies not to exceed 10 p.c. of the value of output.	3. Exports subsidies not to exceed 10 p.c. of the value of output.
4. To protect interests of the farmers, appropriate measures can be taken.	4. To protect interests of the farmers, appropriate measures can be taken.

Even now the developed countries were using all possible concessions for their benefits. The less developed countries were unable to provide protection to their farmers. Infact the USA was at loggerheads with the EU and Japan on this issue than with countries like India or Indonesia.

India was self–sufficient and it had to open its market to the tune of 3% of the consumption of 1993. The prices were low in India and dumping agricultural products was very difficult for the developed countries.

There are *"green box arrangements"* under which countries like India can very well protect the interests of the farmers. *If ever Indian farmers suffer, it will not be because of the developed countries but because of the GoI which may not take adequate permited actions to save the farmers.* The world protested against the "terminator seeds" i.e., those imported seeds that can be used only once. Their output cannot become seeds. The plants cannot grow or will wither away/or will not yield grains. Selling such seeds is like bombing another nation. It is hoped that such a war will not be declared on less developed countries or else all countries will be slaves of the US even for food.

"Green box arrangements" protect the interests of the developing economies. If the importers of high yielding variety seeds grow crops, a part of the crop can be used as seeds in the next sowing season. Thus, there is no royalty obligation on the food grains grown and used as seeds in the next sowing season and even further propagation of seeds is allowed. If the farmers exchange these seeds informally (i.e., give seeds of wheat and take seeds of high yielding variety rice), then also no bar is there nor is there any obligation to make payments of royalty.

Only when producers grow seeds and sell them as branded products the royalty obligation will arise. This is fair enough.

No bar on subsidising agriculture is there on India.

3. About Export Subsidies there are Sets of Requirements

Amber subsidies are those subsidies which are not prohibited by the WTO but the other country can take countervailing action i.e., it can either impose tariffs or can subsidise its own product.

Green subsidies are those which are neither prohibited nor are actionable.

Red subsidies are "partially prohibited" but the prohibition does not apply to India.

The Governments cannot give tax concessions on the profits from exports of agricultural products. Secondly, "the exporters of agricultural products cannot give bank loans at lower rates of interest than paid by others i.e., interest cannot be subsidised.

Bar on red subsidies applies to those countries only which have per capita income or more $ 1000 in a year. India does not come in that category.

IV. Multi–fibre Arrangements (MFA)

By January 1, 2005 all quota restrictions on the readymade garments were to be lifted by the developed countries against the developing countries.

But this will now be done by the end of the year 2011. This has been done by developed countries to get implementation of TRIMS at a pace that the developed countries want.

In other words, the developed countries have agreed to lift QRs (quota restrictions) and conform to the minimum permissible tariffs on the readymade garments from the less developed countries. In return the less developed countries will have to provide free access to the exports of goods from the developed countries to the developing economies. They have also to facilitate all FDI in their countries. *Now facilitation. means that the developing economies improve their infrastructure facilities —roads, railways, ports harbours, power, telecommunications or else the developed countries will insist freer entry in services. They will claim the right to build roads and operate transport services and earn profits.* India will have good roads and good transport but the net profits will be repatriated.

China, Bangladesh, Taiwan and many other countries of Far East produce better garments with good shine and sheen ; finis, and finish with finesse that Indians are not going to get much benefits. India is at disadvantage in terms of costs, colour of clothes, glaze, designs and patterns etc. India was exporting 60 p.c. of its garments to the quota–countries and not 100 p.c. and the benefits will be to that segment of export only.

Government of India fought successfully the attempts of some developed countries to block imports of garments making false accusations about "Indian clothes catch fire easily".

V. Labour Standards

WTO wants child labour not to be utilised. That is fine. However, sometimes the child labour is actually the labour of taking training. Those who are engaged in artistic manufacturing, they see no future in taking formal education to higher level ; weavers of various things, for example, Child labour should be removed from work places and put in schools and helped to play or they should receive training in a humane way. *The demand of the rich countries that the labour of the developing economies be paid like their labour is patently unfair.* This is to take away from the developing economies the advantage in costs. Child labour was banned in 2006 in India, yet it continues.

VI Environment Concerns

The USA and France are responsible for causing a big hole in the ozone layer over Antartica. Infact there can be global warming. Island countries may drown. Many countries may lose their land along the sea. *Worst, there may be such changes in climate that one does not know people of which region will die.*

The USA simply refused to agree to any "convention" or condition in changing the technology so that gases, that are emitted in their manufacturing processes which damage the ozone layer, are not allowed to get emitted. Infact the technologies have to be changed.

The main business of the USA is business. It says that if it changes the technology in question and uses the new technology it may lose cost advantage over its trade rivals. There may be production lags and gestation periods. The USA does not want to lose a penny even if it is super rich.

The problem with "environment concern" is that developed countries want to impose conditions on the developing economy", though they are great polluters.

The developed countries argue that all those goods and commodities which are to be exported to them should have the same geo–physical and bio–chemical environment as in their production in the developed countries. The developed countries want that the exports of developing economies by phyto–sanitary i.e. all eatable should conform to be standards of developed countries.

Taking this line is creating a new barrier. As the developed countries dismantled/ reduced the tariff and non–tariff barriers, *they erected this one.*

Do the developed countries want to export everything to developing economies and import nothing? How will they receive payment for their exports ? The old imperialist powers are at heart still imperialistic. They are neither fair traders nor equal traders. To expect generosity from them is a pipe dream.

B. FIRST WTO MEETING AT SINGAPORE 1996

This was held in the year 1996. What happens in the meetings of UNCTAD of GATT happened here also. Delegates from member countries speak. They present their problems but the world remains divided still between the "haves" and the "havesnot".

The position remains the. same *"East is East: West is West and the twain shall never meet"*.

Reconciliation is always there after discussions. However, once reconciliation is there new problems emerge. The rich countries say that the poor countries demand too much ; the poor countries say that the rich concede too little and are still taking away from the poor countries too much. It can be imagined that if we record what delegates of each country say, the "minutes of the meetings" will take not hours but days and weeks in writing/reading !

Singapore Round addressed the "facilitation question." The rich countries demand that TRIMS are of no consequence if the poor countries lack infrastructure facilities. No direct investment is possible. They also point out that the Government setup remains epitome of red–tapism.

In brief, the Following Seven Points were Raised/agreed Upon

1. The procedures of "valuation" by Customs Departments should be quick. Delays and unnecessary obstacles should be removed.
2. No discrimination should be against goods/commodities and services on the basis of the country of their origin.
3. There should be no delay in pre–shipment inspections.
4. Import licensing should not be made a tool for restricting trade.
5. The "sanitary and phytosanitary regulations" should not be so formulated and applied that they create unnecessary obstacles.
6. Facilitations for trade be there. [Bad roads, toll taxes every now and then, octroi duties, fees and permit fees should not create difficulties and increase costs of trading).
7. A lot of filling of forms should be avoided and there should be a single document good enough for all purposes.

Second WTO Meeting at Geneva 1998

The Issues discussed here were on more or less the same lines as in the previous GATT/ WTO meeting.

1. Both types of the countries wanted greater *"market access"*.
2. Rich countries wanted their *IPRs* protected. Less developed countries (like India) insisted that once a traditionally rich product is notified by a developing country as being in public domain, patenting of this product will not be possible. For example India has yet not taken a patent for *Chavanprash* and if a US firm takes it, things will become difficult for India. Such things are to be kept out of the mischief of the developed countries.
3. For *TRIMS* emphasis was on MIGA (Multilateral Investment Guarantee Agency) to protect foreign investors against non– commercial risks e.g., confiscation by a government.
4. There were further negotiations of *AoA* (Agreement on Agriculture) on the lines discussed earlier with some specific cases.
5. Less developed countries emphasised that their *public procurement policy cannot be disbanded* that will hurt the interests of the farmers, small scale industries and backward regions of the country.

6. Talks on *environmental standards, labour standards and "'sanitary and phyto sanitary measures"* were again dead–locked. SPS measures *are designed to protect human, animal and plant life or health. Exports and imports of food items should be safe for consumers.* These are SPS (sanitary and phytosanitary measures).
7. *GATS (GENERAL AGREEMENT ON TRADE IN SERVICES)* Issues discussed were i) cross border supplies e.g., of blue–prints, (ii) consumption abroad, (iii) tourism (iv) commercial presence like having branches of banks or hotels, (v) movement of "natural persons" *(demand for the developing countries that the developed countries should import freely but temporarily the skilled labour from the developing economies).*

Third WTO Meeting at Seattle 1999

This was held in 1999 and was a fiasco in the sense that not only the people outside the conference hall fought amongst themselves, they hurled abuses and blackened the faces of the delegates also ; and, above all the delegates themselves (reportedly) had physical skirmishes and fisticuffs !.

This happened in the US and the rich countries were accusing the poor countries of harming them !

The Poor Countries too were Accusing the rich Countries for the Same

1. *Environment concerns* were raised both by the rich and the poor countries. Developing economies insisted that the developed countries should change their technologies to stop depletion of ozone layer over the earth and check global warming. (Infact there are erratic changes in the form of warming of ice–capped regions, getting snow in deserts, getting scanty rainfalls in some high rain areas.) The rich countries accuse the poor countries for generating a lot of abnoxious gases. *[India has the largest cattle in the world and its dung is the source of largest emission of methane gas. Then about 70 p.c. population defecates in the open — another source of methane gas].*
2. *"Sovereignty question."* This actually meant that there should be freedom for the poor countries to have tariff and quota systems for protecting their industries *otherwise trade will replace industry, as is happening in India.* The loss of jobs will be a grave problem.
3. *"Standards"*. The rich countries find fault with the quality of the goods/commodities of the poor. The rich countries also want to impose *"labour standards"* i.e., not employing child labour and having the same working conditions as in the west. Concern for child labour is right but poor countries cannot have the same type of production, storage and distribution standards as the rich countries have. If they do, then their cost of production will go up.

The US and Japan control two–third of the world trade. If we add EU and other rich countries they control 90 p.c. They have social security system: the poor countries do not have. Seattle increased difficulties of the poor to further the interests of the rich.

Fourth WTO Meeting: DOHA 2001

This was held in 2001. There was review of the progress of reforms.

After long and high pressure, the developing economies could get some concessions in the area of medicines. Certain medicines as needed for treating HIV infected persons or persons suffering from AIDS were not to invoke the royalty rights. It was argued that the rich countries should not see in these medicines a source of profit.

Royalty questions was diluted in case of life–saving drugs upto the year 2016.

Developed countries, however, did not agree to the EST or environmentally sound technology questions. In other words the US did not agree to immediately change the technology which is changing the weather and climatic conditions of mother earth.

MEAs could not address the *CBD* i.e., "multilateral environmental agreements" could not be made–to conform to the "convention on bio–diversity".

It was agreed upon that all arrangements regarding 'trade questions' and TRIMS should follow the principles of (i) transparency, (ii) non– discrimination and procedural fairness, and (iii) provisions against the cartels. [Cartels are generally "selling oligopolies". ACC of India was one such cartel in the past. OPEC i.e., Organisation of Petroleum Exporting Countries, is one such now. If the petroleum prices fall due to demand becoming lesser than the supply, they curtail the supplies rather than reduce the prices.).

CANCUN (MEXICO) CONFERENCE OF THE W.T.O.
FIFTH W.T.O. CONFERENCE
10th September to 14th September 2003

It concluded in five days **without reaching an agreement.** This conference was dominated by the developing economies. India was the leader. It took along many countries like Brazil and even China. They all opposed the dictates of the US and the EU.

Nepal and Cambodia joined WTO and the total membership increased to 148 countries. A group of 21 countries opposed tooth and nail the dictates of the US. The US had even threatened certain African countries with "sanctions" (punishment). It promised that if they supported the US these small countries would be rewarded.

US wanted the same old things: import whatever the US wants to sell ; allow all sorts of capital in all sorts of investments ; and pay royalties, known as Doha issues.

One Korean committed suicide against the US policies. We are sorry for him; but have the imperialist powers ever relented even after the death of crores of persons ?] The poor developing countries were angry that these big powers were traders in (i) hunger (food) and (ii) death (arms).

The less developed countries exposed the developed countries by pointing out that the actual subsidies paid by them to their agriculture was $ 1 b. a day *i.e.,* $ 365 billion or at the then rate of exchange equal to Rs. 16,79,000 crore. India's subsidies to agriculture were 3 p.c. only in the total amount. It should be remembered that the EU and the USA combined have only half the population of India. Hence on per person basis India's subsidies were just 1– p.c. of the per capita subsidies of these countries. The US and the EU want the less developed countries to buy their agricultural products. The Japanese refuse to buy the cheap rice of the US and say that the Japanese can relish their own rice only. The US is fearful of Japan and Korea because if they spill up the dollar reserves in the market, the US dollar will go on crashing. The US and the EU are super power in military terms. They are the only super power. They are the "God of small nations".

The USA demanded (not requested/wanted/desired) that the developing countries should immediately agree for "access" *i.e.,* unlimited exports from the USA and investment from the USA and then the question of reducing the subsidies will be reviewed. The USA gave no promise ; it demanded immediate compliance.

The USA used another word **"transparency"** and by this word it meant that the governments of all developing countries should disclose to the US what the governments were purchasing for their uses. The USA wanted to submit tenders for the same. In other words if the Government of India wanted to have cloth for "bastaas" (piece of cloth in which files are taken home for disposal) it should not purchase from Khadi Bhandaars but should first invite global tenders and if the rates of Khadi Bhandaars are the cheapest, then they could supply. Even if the rates are the cheapest then the US can raise such objections (i) the US quality is better, (ii) the Khadi Bhandaars are subsidised, (iii) the "standards" are not observed in the matter of payment of wages or that child labour is employed in the product.

There seems to be no upper limit for the US and the EU for exporting and exporting more. There seems to be no upper limit for them to have higher and higher incomes. They want most of the natural resources of the wo'rld to be used there. Then the world should buy from them. Greed is the proper word for their industry and business.

There were demands for "trade facilitations" from the EU and the US. Their view points were so blatantly one–sided that even the media of their own countries criticised them. The people protested on the streets against the view points of their own governments. The Ministers of these rich countries are always on the prowl in the developing economies for finding out possibilities of selling more and more.

The objection is not about great volume of free trade. The objections are that the rich countries should then import from the developing economies and give them fair prices. The rich still import at low prices and sell at dear prices. Of course they sell technology but a lot of technological developments are by the people of the poor countries who are paid well by the US and the EU. The blame for this should be shared by the high powered persons of the poor countries. Their is crowding effect on income due to them. In simple words the national income of the poor countries is largely usurped by them. These HPPs have anti–labour and anti–employee bias. They are anti–poor in reality. They have vested interest in poverty so that poverty eradication can be used as a promise during election. This affects international trade because the cream of our manpower moves away to developed economies, who practise discrimination against ordinary labour.

The USA was exposed: its claim that its AMS (aggregate measure of support to agriculture *i.e.,* its subsidies) were \$ 60 billion a year. They were proved to be \$ 365 b. a year. The USA wanted to "address the Singapore Concerns and Doha facilitations and Standards". In these simple words a lot of meaning is hidden. As we saw, the main demand of the USA in Singapore was to allow it unlimited trade rights and unlimited capital investment rights. When the less developed countries demanded that the less developed countries should then be given unlimited rights to "export their natural factor *i.e.,* surplus labour, the USA rejected it–virtually saying that it was a silly idea. In Doha the USA had demanded even more. It demanded the rights to sell military hardware and government store purchase goods.

India and Other Members of the Group of 21 Demanded the Following:

1. Developed countries should drastically cut down subsidies to their agriculture and do it fast.
2. The USA should itself practise "transparency" ; it should disclose its hidden subsidies to its exports which the less developed countries believe is happening.
3. The USA should stop credit subsidies to its producers. The USA should have a road map (time table) for ending all subsidies in the long run—which means in not more than 15 years or so.
4. The less developed countries will reduce the import duties not at the same percentage for all goods and in all countries but at different percentages for different goods and according to the conditions in the country.
5. If the developing economies want to promote employment and protect their production system, the US should not object. The US cannot prove and insist that since it is the most efficient, no country should produce anything and import everything from it.

It was made clear to developed countries that if you do not listen to what the developing economies say, the developing economies would not listen to what the developed countries say.

At Cancun the WTO published some facts and Figures also. The figure of FDI in India (data compiled by 2003) vis–a–vis some other neighbouring countries were given as under:

Country	*FDI figures in $ bill ions*			
	FDI	Percent of the world	Exports	Percent of the exports of world
1. China	46.8	6.4	266.6	4.4
2. Hong Kong	22.8	3.1	189.6	3.1
Total [Since both are one now]	69.6	9.5	456.5	7.5
3. India	3.4	0.5	43.3	0.7
4. Indonesia	(–) 3.3	(–) 0.4	52.1	0.9
5. South Korea	3.2	0.4	150.4	2.5

Tne facts are obvious. India which is the second most populated country of the world and with 83 p.c. population of China, has only 4.9 p.c. of the FDI received in China. China has opened all sectors but in limited regions. India has opened the entire country but in limited fields.

Even Hong Kong which is a tiny island–city, just like a big metropolitan city of India receives 6.7 times more FDI. China as a whole received in 2002–03, 13.8 times more FDI. Combining the figures, China got 20.5 times more. Exports of China in total were 10.5 times; of mainland China 6.2 times ; of Hong Kong alone were 4.4 times.Position in 2008, remained the same.

South Korea which is like any big district of India received equal FDI (they do not need it in any case) and its exports were 3.5 times more than that of India. Indonesia, which has almost 15 p.c. population of India exports more than India.

Figures of some other countries were as under:

6. Malaysia	0.6	0.1	88.0	1.4
7. Philippines	1.8	0.2	32.7	0.5
8. Singapore	8.6	1.2	121.8	2.0
9. Thailand	3.8	0.5	65.1	1.1
All developing economies	204.8	27.9	2255.1	36.9
World	735.1		6121.3	

Singapore and Hong Kong are mere cities. Their economic size is vast but at best they should be equal to two of the biggest cities of India. Yet they get so much more FDI than India ! China gets more than one–third of the total FDI that the developing economies receive. India receives mere 1.66 p.c. of the total FDI that the less developed economies receive. It must have been noted from the above table that developing economies receive 28 p.c. of the total FDI while 72 p.c. FDI is between the developed and developed countries themselves.

Thailand which is less populous than even the truncated Uttar Pradesh, but receives as much FDI as India. So is the case of Korea which is like a big district of India.

Mauritius is the main source of FDI incomings. This is not because India wants to help Mauritius where persons of Indian origin reside but because the firms that facilitate the outflows to India receive funds from other developed countries of the world and there are several tax concessions.

The most important thing, reportedly, is that these Mauritius firms are owned by the HPPs (high powered persons of India.)

What India received in 12 years ending 2001–02, China received in one year of 2001–02! The shares of the inflows of FDI to India were as under:

Country	Percent	Country	Percent
1. Mauritius	38.7	6. Holland	4.5
2. The USA	17.1	7. S. Korea	3.1
3. Japan	6.8	8. France	2.8
4. The UK	5.2	9. Italy	2.4
5. Germany	5.0	10. Singapore	2.3

China does not invest in India. Of the total FDI received in recent years, the end–uses

1. Power (petrol)	30	6. Metallic industries	6
2. Telecommunications	20	7. Chemicals	5
3. Electricity	10	8. Food items	3
4. Transport	8	9. Hotel/tourism	2
5. Financial services	7	10. Textiles	1

These total up to 92 p.c. The rest 8 p.c. are invested in multifarious lines of manufacture. Oil pool account was responsible for great losses and leakages. Even the highest loss incurring constituents of the OIL POOL were squandering money on the HPPs who were at the helm of affairs. It was because of them that there were losses. The big persons of private sector drive their vehicles on company account. The big booses of the government guzzle petrol in their cars, air taxies, aircrafts on public account. The lower middle class and middle class pays for their luxuries. That is why India consumed capital and needed capital from outside in this sector.

The report on "Human Development in South Asia, 2003"* highlighted that "the WTO has failed to generate employment in the region".

Nearly 66 p.c. of the people of SAARC countries are in the working age groups. Nearly 22 p.c. of the world population lives here. Only Sri Lanka has completed the demographic transition *i.e.,* the NRR has come down to 1 or less. Other countries are still struggling, though there is some decline in the fertility. The following table gives the figures of unemployment.

Unemployment rates 1999–2001 in percent. Female and male unemployment rates in SAARC countries 1990–2000 in percent.

Country	*1999-2001*	*Female*	*Male*	*F/M Ratio IN UNEMPLOYMENT*
Bangladesh	3.3	2.3	2.7	0.9 ....
Bhutan	1.4	....	....	.....Not Available.
India	7.3	10.0	7.0	1.4
The Maldives	2.0	2.7	1.6	1.7
Nepal	1.1	0.7	1.5	0.5
Pakistan	7.8	14.9	4.2	3.5
Sri Lanka	8.2	16.2	7.1	2.3

Unemployment of the youth is the major component of unemployment. Self–employment acts as an sponge for absorbing crores of persons but incomes of all are not such that they remain above the poverty line. Unemployment of the educated is increasing. Between 1995 and 2001.–unemployment as the percentage of the work force increased by 17.5 p.c. Educated persons and " women are the worst sufferers. WTO took no action against the developed countries which practise restrictions against the imports from developing economies while they thrust down. their exports down the throats of the poor countries. All complaints to WTO about the declining unemployment go unheeded.

Developed countries are becoming ever more stingy in giving assistance (actually 'loans' and not grants) equal to the 0.7 p.c. of their GDP. Greater blame should be put on the domestic "rulers".

Government of India's version of Cancun Conference was that India played a key role. It formed G–20 (group of 20) on agriculture and G–16 on Singapore issues. India emphasised that in order to protect the high cost agriculture of their own countries, the developed countries were 8 times more protective in agriculture than in manufacturing. The developed countries were not only not importing cheap agricultural products from the developing economies but were over–producing their high costs products and dumping them in the developing economies. This was threatening the livelihood modes and incomes of rural areas of the developing economies. Developed countries, it was pointed out, were playing dirty tricks. "Zero for zero" tariff attitude was inequitous. If suppose the USA agrees for zero tariff and non–tariff barrier on the import of mangoes from India and in return demands zero barriers for their aircrafts, the outcome is heavily loaded in favour of the USA. How little will they be importing in dollar terms for cashew nuts ! The tricks of the developed countries were obvious.

India forcefully emphasised that the matters of investment cannot be taken as a matter of right to be brought only under WTO. It is for the host country to invite capital where they want and when they want. This bull dozing of capital is bullying. The demand of the developed countries for "transparency" cannot be accepted because that means that government store purchases should be open to international tendering. There are many things related to national defence which will be procured by the Indians from the Indian public sector first and then from other Indians. The foreigners do not have a right in everything. "Trade facilitation" cannot be extended everywhere.

Less developed countries acknowledge that technology–wise and product–wise the developed countries offer better choices than the old socialist countries. But the bullying by the developed countries takes away all comparative advantage. The business of the developed countries is business and that with super–normal profits and not on the exalted principle of comparative advantage and the least costs.

We have seen above how India argued about its primary sector and secondary sector business. About services India cannot agree and infact is not in a position to agree to all demands regarding services. [If the US demands that their transport services be allowed to operate in India, they will demand that roads should be handed over to them for construction and maintenance. The East India Company mentality continues.] The developed countries do not bother about the mounting loans on the developing economies. They know they will recover the loans through their oppressive ways. The argument of the less developed countries is not that they be permitted not to repay the loans. They do not want to become indebted to facilitate trade to the developed countries.

Unresolved issues of Doha round, Singapore Round and Cancun round were hot and alive even in 2008 and shall continue in future also. The WTO rounds are never–ending.

For every problems there are solutions ; for every solution there are problems. However, one thing is certain that it is a plot and not merely a story or an episode that the developed countries dictate terms to the developing countries and even bully them. The tigers are not going to change their spots.

The developed countries were rebuffed in Cancun but they are not relenting much. India gets some concessions here and there but not substantial. The position is such that even if the rich countries have hundreds of clothes per person, they are unwilling to give one to the naked.

Demands are now called "concerns." The US and the EU say "address our concerns about 'market access' to agricultural products." They are actually demanding that their highly subsidised, genetically muted and less tasty agricultural products should be allowed to be freely dumped in poor countries even if that means unemployment to those engaged in agriculture in less developed economies. They have no moral compunctions in asking for this. They call their products "sensitive" all are for them. They want us to reduce tariffs, while they go slow in reduction of quota on our exports.

Developing economies, as we saw, are stafiding up. India took the lead and was ably supported by two large countries China and Brazil. That unnerved the US and EU as their hegemony was challenged. The Arab world launched their Mecca Cola. Now they too demand access for their cola in the US for Muslims ! Whatever the threats the rich countries throw at the developing economies they have to be taken because if developing countries agree to all their demand they will take most of our production lines and make people totally unemployed.

US prefers scrapping of all tariffs by 2015. Developing economies want convergence on trade related to agricultural products not to hurt their rural people and 75 to 95 p.c. population. They want equitable negotiations on NAMA (non– agricultural products ; their market access). Those who demand market access or gate crashing should permit others also.

GATS and WTO

General Agreement on Trade in Services was developed in the 8th Round of the last GATT: (General Agreement on Trade and Tariff). It was also noted that after that WTO administers the agreements of GATT 8. Now there are no more meetings of GATT.

GATS is governed by multilateral rules. GATS is in fact in for the last 30 years by 2009. *Services represent the fastest growing sector of the global economy. They account for 66 p.c. of global output. Services account for almost one third of global employment. Services account for 20 p.c. of the global trade. In other words (66–20=46 p.c. of the services outputs that are generated are countries where they were produced).*

As usual there was opposition to GATS first. There are three parts agreement: (a) general obligations, (b) about specific sectors and (c) about specific countries. Transport, banking, telecommunications, tourism, and other professional services are covered.

WTO uses the following words (i) cross border supply, (ii) consumption abroad, and (iii) commercial presence about trade in services. *When trained and skilled persons go outside for jobs, WTO calls that as trade NATURAL PERSONS. Certain words cannot be understood because all persons are born naturally. WTO should have called* "talent capital of *persons " because the talent is not natural but acquired. But we have to use WTO words.*

The rule of GATS is also "favour one, favour all" and. "favour one to all and get favour from one to all". *and get favour from one to all".*

It should be noted that if a few countries have given MEN treatment to the_ countries of RTA or regional trade agreement or to the regional bloc countries, then they can keep that MEN status and then not grant the WTO MEN. These are known as the WTO MFN exemptions. WTO uses special words for GATS. All countries have to prepare a list of services in which there will be global trade or bloc trade. They have to specify what will be exceptions. For example, if Pakistan is not granting MFN to India. India should not limit itself to Pakistan. It can grant that status to others also Pakistan does not grant even bloc status preferences to India.

If foreign banks are allowed to operate in India, WTO will put is as *"market access commitment"*. If some or total restrictions are put by India, it will be called *"limitations" (of market access)*. If India allows one branch each to foreign banks and its own banks can have as many branches as they want. this will be called by the WTO as *"exception to the national treatment system"*.

"Bound" services agreement mean commitment is complete. *"Unbinding"* means negotiating for new status.

"Carved out" means excluded e.g., a government hospital need not be privatized. It is not necessary that government should permit under GATS foreign multinational companies to take over the government services. Government banks, railways or post offices in India cannot be asked privatized under GATS.

All GATS should be *transparent. Deregulation of government regulation is not required. WTO "RECOGNIZES" (this is the word used by them) THAT SERVICE PACTS SHOULD NOT BE DISCRIMINATORY. ALL COUNTRIES SHOULD HAVE THE SAME TYPE OF PACT FOR THE SAME TYPE OF THE SERVICE.*

The modes of payment and timings of the payment should be uniform. other words if a country is making imports of services from two countries, one should not receive early and one late payment. Only in case of serious balance of payment problem, WTO is to be informed.

If people seek temporary jobs abroad (when they are needed as per advertisement) they can do so. They have a right. However, they do not have a right to become citizens of other countries.

There are special provisions for persons operating in share market, speculation, investment in bonds, finance companies and banks giving loans. mortgaging business. The countries can regulate these services to check frauds. WTO rightly emphasizes that transport and communications require the utmost coordination and cooperation in services. The world will become moribund without them. (They have written too much on this for a book) As written earlier, WTO wants the world to have liberalization and globalization. There have to be negotiations. "NEGOTIATIONS" IS **THE** KEY WORD FOR ALL TRADES AND SETTLEMENT OF DISPUTES.

"Safeguards" are very important to be observed by the WTO. If transport services are provided, they should first be accident proof, as far as possible. "Safeguards" are to be against the risks that can be imagined. If there is a hospital service, there should be fire extinguishers and fire exit. If there medical tourism (patients come to India to avail cheap treatment relative to their countries but where the hospital rooms are like five star suite should be standards about everything—doctors, nurses, equipment, pathology.. everything is listed service-wise.

GATS came in force from 1995 and once only opportunity is granted by the WTO for exemption from the MFN. WTO mandates that countries should take *"autonomous actions" to promote international trade and business in services. They should not always be forced to do so.* WTO wants that the least developed countries should receive most concession information should be available.

It is to be kept in mind that total number of services, multiplied by their types, multiplied by number of countries, multiplied by the number of parties, give the total of the cases to be handled ! One can imagine the WTO references are.

Membership

All countries of the world are either members or observers.

The WTO divides the countries into developed and developing. From the developing countries it selects the "least developed". Nepal and Bangladesh are from the SAARC which are amongst the least developed. Afghanistan is a new entrant.

There is a list of all countries of the world, including the island countires, of which names have been given in the list. Against their names are the dates of joining WTO. The observers' names are given. From amongst them are selected the least developed countries.

The Wto Gives A List Of Disputes And The Parties Between Whom The Disputes Were. The Time Taken Is Given. Process Is Given. Essence Of All Is That There Will Have To Be 'Negotiations".

Structure and Organization of WTO

* A11 major decisions of the WTO are made by the members (150). *WTO is not like IMF or World Bank. There are no Boards of Governors. *There are no bureaucrats to take decisions. *Decisions are taken by consensus.
* The highest decision making body is Ministerial Conference.
* There is a sub–council of a few selected ministers to assist all Ministers
* There are (i) General Council, (ii) Dispute Settlement Body, and (iii) The Trade Policy Review Body. *They are one and the same. They are the three names of the same body! The same members are in the guise of being three !*
  This is known as the 'SECOND LEVEL OF WTO".
  • The THIRD LEVEL OF WTO has three more councils. These three Councils are of goods, service and trade related intellectual property rights, TRIPR or TRIP or 1PR. These Councils are known as (i) Goods Council, (ii) Services Council, and (iii) TRIPS Coubcuk. A smaller Council is there for "commodities" (products of the nature in raw and direct form).
  • They are report to the Ministerial Body. The main room of conference is known as the "Green Room*". It is no room but, naturally a hall. All decisions are known as ''green room decisions". These relate to the original new decisions or decisions about the settlement of disputes
  • The fourth level of wto. There can be 'bodies'" for different goods differently. Settlement body is there which settles complaints and its another part looks to appeals. The second "part" is of "appellate body" which settles disputes.they all, as seen, negotiate. Groups of 20 to 30 members are formed on ad hoc basis. Name a task or work or dispute or issue and there will be committees on them

There are at least 50 major issues. We will quote 10 only. (I) Market Access. (2) Agriculture, (3) Sanitary standards, (4) Dumping, (5) Customs Valuation. (6) Rules of Origin, (7) Import Licensing. (8) TRIPS. (9) Services (10) Disputes. There are conferences/committees on them. All Ad hoc for specific purpose.

Secretariat

There is a Director General of **the** *WTO who heads the WTO Secretariat.*

* There is a Council and Trade Negotiations Committee Division.
* Then there is Human Resource Division.
* Office of the Internal Audit is also there. There is Information and External Relations Division.
* There is then Accessions Division.
* There is Legal Affairs Division and Rules Division.
* There is Development Division.
* institute for Training and Technical Cooperation is also there.
* There is Technical Cooperation Audit.
* There is Trade Policies Review Division.
* Agriculture and commodities Division is there.
* There is Trade and Environment Division.
* There is a separate division for Services Division.

* Market Access Division is also there.
* intellectual Property Division is very important division.
* Division for TRIMS is also very important.
* Languages and Documentation Division is there

Main policies of these divisions

- Exports are to be promoted (thry are imports for counterparties).
- New trades are to be introduced on cooperation basis.
- Developing economies are helped from "back to top"
- If special help is necessary that is provided.
- WTO cooperates with the **IMF** and the World Bank.
- WTO keeps the public informed and keens itself also informed.
- WTO for all practical puiposes is charged with DOHA issues i.e., the issues that the developed economies are concerned.

NOTE

1. See EPW Aug 16, 2008

31 | Globalisation and International Business

GLOBALISATION AND INTERNATIONAL BUSINESS

A. Liberalisation: Current Paradigm Again.
B. Globalisation: Defining its Scope.
C: Gains of Liberalisation and Globalisation.
   1. Internationalisation of efficient division of labour.
   2. Extended Markets Globally.
   3. "Four-Cornerstone" Efficiency.
   4. Interactive Business Partnership.
   5. Efficient Non-price Competition.
   6. Higher productivities, Technological efficiencies and Competitiveness.
   7. Global Management. More FDI and FII

D. GLOBALISATION: PROBLEMS TO BE ADDRESSED

1. "Turbo", "Casino" and Crony Capitalism.
2. Predatory Globalisation.
3. High on Growth: Low on Employment.
4. Increasing Debt Burden.
5. Backwash effects exceeding spread effects
6. Tennis-like Economic '"Double-Fault".
7. Corruption.

A. LIBERALISATION

Liberalisation means "Leave it to the market" and removal of all governmental fetters on business and industry.[1] When extended to international business and industry it becomes "globalization". One important adjunct of liberalization in "privatization" i.e., denationalisation of as many business activities as possible.

Liberalisation is the new *"mantra"* of development beacuse the mixed economies/ middle-path of development (as against the extreme paths of socialism and capitalism) proved *"muddled path"* of development. Licence-permit *raj goes;* regulations go. *However, in India the "regulators" remain.*

Monetary, fiscal, income, wage, and price policies are no longer leftist. Excessive taxes and subsidies go. There are no over-riding restrictions on imports, exports, capital movement, technological collaboration, choosing lines of production, deciding how much to produce and at what prices; and, even factor-price determination is left to the market.

Economies are made market friendly; but markets can never be poor-friendly. Markets recognize the existence of those persons who have stuffed purse. The importance of the person in the market is in the direct proportion to the purchasing power the person has. Market cannot be, atleast in the present poor countries, relied upon to relieve the poor of their miseries, deprivations, unemployment and indignities. New corrupt politicians and administration siphon off funds for alleviation of poverty.

It may look surprising but the decades upto 1970s used to have policies of not allowing too much of the needed production !

Liberalisation allows free functioning of the market which functions blindly but not arbitrarily. Its rules are simple: If two persons are running after one commodity, prices will rise; if two units of commodities can be sold to one person only who needs one, prices will fall. The good old interface between demand and supply is the corner-stone of liberalisation.

There are four golden rules of liberalisation:

(A) If there is excess supply (which infact is deficit demand), then prices will fall. Falling prices will force the producers to bring down production and they will induce the buyers to buy more; equilibrium suited to both will emerge.

(B) If there is deficit supply (which infact is excess demand), the prices will rise. Rising prices will bring down demand and stimulate supply at the same time; equilibrium suited to both will emerge.

(C) *"Supply creates its own demand"* and hence *"demand creates its own supply"*. Non-interference is necessary.

(D) *In this connection there is a macro aspect of profound importance. "Over-production is a situation where all the producers in total produce "TOO LITTLE" !*

"TOO LITTLE" is infact right. If shoes remain unsold, it is because the potential buyers of shoes do not have money. If potters, carpenters, blacksmiths etc. do not have shoes they should produce more of their products and have purchasing power for buying shoes. *Over-production in one line is actually under-production in other lines.*

This is "growth economics" which is "macro" in nature. Market may see this aspect also *but the government can assist the market in achieving the fourth effect.* This is the essence of liberalisation.

Entrepreneurs marshall resources, usually with the capital taken from the savers; innovate and take decisions and swim against the current to prove themselves dynamic enough to earn profits.

Liberalisation and globalisation strengthen each other. Liberalisation does not mean that unfair, unethical, illegal and immoral practices are allowed in business and industry. Dumping, for example, is not to be condoned. Libersaliation does not mean that the governments are to be disbanded (that can never happen) nor are they required to sit at the fence and overlook all nefarious activities that may go in the name of liberalisation.

Liberalisation does not ensure full tax compliance by business and industry. All sorts of efficiencies and high productivities depend upon habit of exertion, knack of innovating and inventing, being honest and motivated and, above all, having a non-corrupt government.

Producers, consumers, exporters and importers can all gain if liberalisation is without associated anti-social trends e.g., if the precious foreign exchange is not frittered away in importing superfluous goods.

A.II. Lucas Supply Function that proves liberalisation provides net gains:

$Y = f(_{P-Pe})$

Y = is supply or increase in real outputs'

f = is the function of

p = is actual price; and

p^e = is expected price level.

This emphasises that the price "surprises" should be positive. The "price surprise" is (the difference between actual price and the expected price. Liberalisation is the spread of knowledge and that minimises the chances of wrong decisions about supplies. Expectations and realities are matched by the producers both in the national and international market. **The greater the "price surprise" i.e., the surplus about the actual price over the expected price the greater the positive response in supply.**

In 1955, the Nobel Prize Committee for Economics selected this function of Robert E. Lucas for the prize.

Liberalisation is not *laissez-faire;* total non-interference from (the government and the trade unions. In India (the foreigners used to say) the clerks, officers and the ministers still rule the roost. True liberalisation is not there, argue the industrialists and businessmen.

Liberalisation does not mean "no-tax regime". It also does not admit the possibilities of receiving subsidies from the Governments. There is no talk about "concentration of economic powers in the hands of a few". Production capacities can be created anywhere. *Liberalisation means "level-playing field" with the public sector.* When there is denationalisation of the public sector, the private sector has all the field with it. Sick, obese and inefficient public sector units cannot remain. *In the private sector also the rule is of the* "survival of the fittest". It is believed that instead of high taxes and low turn-overs, the governments should get more public revenue from the low taxes and high turn-overs.

Liberalisation has got to be there in the factor market. *The voluntary retirement schmes (known as "Golden Handshake Scheme") are proving "leaden-quake" schemes".* The labour class is subdued. Except for the highly qualified and competent, most young persons are now in contract jobs of less than or around Rs. 10000 per month. Liberalistion is pro-capitalist and anti-labour. It is, however, to be recorded here the the trade unions too had become irresponsible. They used to prove as 'scare-crows' to the industrialists and most of the trade union leaders were not working.

Liberalisation, privatisation and globalisation unless permitted at the same time will mean each one is partial.

At the same time the banking and financial institutions, the capital markets and capital movements are also to be freed from the clutches of the over-regulatory governments.

LPG model emphasizes that governments should maintain law and order; they are not supposed to produce cars. Unfortunately all the disorder is produced by the political parties in opposition whichever they may be. These things prove to be great speed-breakers of development.

LPG model in India cannot remove poverty even in a century. Hence pro-employment and pro-poor policies of the government should be strengthened as government leaves production and services in most lines to the private sector. But corruption will increase problems for non-corrupt.

B. GLOBALISATION

Globalisation is *not* a state of being but a process. It is free flow of commodities, goods, services, direct and institutional capital *but not the free flow of labour.*

Globalisation is that international business which spreads across continents—a wider term than 'international business'. Globalisation is *not* an idelogy but the inevitable natural freedom extended multilaterally. It is freedom to export, import and allow the currencies to move in the opposite direction to these flows as also to move unilaterally without there being *quid pro quo* of flows of commodities, goods and services.

There is interlinking of countries and markets inevitably under globalisation; infact globalisation gives no choice to nations not to remain so linked. In the oft-repeated cliche it is the process which converted the world to a village.

Globalisation is not a state that depends upon the level of development of countries; it now determines the levels and directions of development of countries.

Globalisation is also known as "neo-liberalism". Globalisation is anti-thesis of autarky. It disallows protectionism and is extension of national liberlisation to all other countries.

Globalisation as it is developing in recent years has no place for public sector, more or less. It requires public sectors to obey the rules of the market. (For example, if a hydro-electric project of the Government of India used to require hydro-electric generating heavy electrical machines, it used to get it earlier from its own BHEL; now global tendering is necessary).

To the socialists, globalisation is "predatory economic imperialism". To the advocates of classicism, it is "economic brotherhood of nations."

C. GAINS OF GLOBALISATION

We examine in sections C & D of this chapter the pros and cons of globalisation. Notwithstanding the facts that globalisation is creating many problems and that too for the already challenged persons, globalisation is here to stay.

The world moved from rudimentary economy of barbarism, to slavery, to feudalism, to imperialism, then to three separate paradigms viz., (a) free enterprise system, (b) non-liberalised and controlled international business and (c) a middle path.

Then socialism collapsed and the socialists all over the world got disoriented. Meanwhile the unipolar world with one centre of power, the USA, has ensured that globalisation should be the economic order of the world.

Present globalisation is unequal to the poor countries. The economies of the poor countries are unequal against the poor of their own country. Meanwhile there are blocs of the developed countries which "protect the interest of the cat against mouse."

No one can predict future. Return of feudalism and socialism seems difficult. *Probably globalisation will be between economic blocs rather than on free for all basis in the world.*

Globalisation is bringing unprecedented gains to the world as a whole but is creating problems also. The anti- views should also be studied. *At present the total perception is that globalisation is beneficient in net balance and that it should be strengthened. If that is done it will auto-liquidate the problems it creates.* It will be like Achilles lance which used to inflict wounds but which used to heal up themselves. They did not kill.

For the sake of brevity we study the points in favour and against globalisation in seven catchpoints each.

1. Internationalisation of the production process; Efficient territorial division of development efforts

Left to themselves, backward economies cannot hope to even discover the resources that they have, much less take them out or use them for high value-adding. There are international business companies whose main business is to discover precious (metallic and non-metallic) resources and then have production in which they also have economic interests.

International trade in commodities improved after globalisation. It is the run for least cost. One way of keeping the production costs low is to shed bulk at the nearest point of production. Hence processing industries are developing in the world. There is dispersal of economic efforts (in the production of primary products, in making them semi-processed and in arranging essential socio-economic infrastructure facilities.)

Without globalisation the task of processing would have been left to the developing economies themselves and since they were unable to do that in the past, the exportables were being exported at very low prices."Terms of trade" *(which mean ratios of export prices to import prices)* were going against the less developed countries. They still have not become favorable in all respects but first they stopped falling and then they improved gradually.

International trade in commodities distributes the natural resources evenly; atleast the inequalities of nature can be overcome. If jute is produced only in Bangladesh and India, the whole world can use it. Instances can be multiplied.

International business in goods is increasing by leaps and bounds due to globalisation. *Transnational companies are (i) owned by economic interests of many countries, (ii) the goods are produced by them not in one country but in many countries of the world,* and *(iii) of course they are now doing business in all countries.*

All *sub-paradigms* are optimised. "What" is to be produced "where", in "what quantities", of "what qualities", "with what technological mix" etc. are taken care of. Globalisation has seen reduction in cross-continent transport costs when rationalisation is attempted by the TNCs.

Socio-cultural aspects are taken care of. *[The UK TNC "Lever Brothers" is "Hindustan Lever" in India, "Pakistan Levers" in Pakistan or "Keynian Levers' in Kenya.]*

Production now a days is on the principle of the least cost and there are some cases of closing the units and taking them to places where this objective can be achieved. If a TNC produces cotton fabrics in Egypt it can write "made from the finest cotton of Egypt". If the production and marketing have to be in India, the logos, the brand names etc. can suit Indian ethos. Chinese are producing colour sprinklers for Holi to be used by Indians. They are producing and selling *'bindies'*. Strange are the production arrangements. Commercialisation, liberalisation and globalisation have induced persons of the religion to make things especially used by the persons of other religion.

International business in services is picking up. We have foreign banks and insurance companies in India. There is high degree of collaboration in the production of cars, automated vehicles of all sorts, electronic goods, telecommunications equipment etc. The day may not be far off when there will be participation in transport, medicare and any field for that matter.

Flows of FDI (foreign direct investment) and FII (foreign institutional investment) *[on which there is separate chapter]* are increasing in all directions with thick flows.

Earlier location used to be thus (more or less):

Communist countries	Where the projects were ordered to be located.
Capitalist countries	Where they could be produced at the least costs.
Hong Kong or Singapore	Where the projects could find space.
India	In the constituencies of the important politicians.

If *economic "goods" are now in plenty; so are also the economic "bads"*. We can have Havana cigars, wines and whiskies produced in different countries, costly cosmetics, costly soft drinks of no utility, and junk food.

Secondly globalisation helps in having an extended scenario of marketing.

One of the great principle of pricing-marketing is charging "differential prices to extend the market" and not merely to discriminate against some. There are rich and poor countries and then there are rich and poor persons in both types of the countries.

The poor countries and poor persons have low capacity to pay high prices. They have high price elasticity of demand. TNCs and MNCs can charge lower prices in one country or for one segment of population in the same country to get maximum demand from all sections *provided there is no seepage of the goods so sold under differentiated prices.* Lux soaps are produced for high, medium and low prices. Lux soaps made in Australia have better fragrance, very impressive packaging and better ingredients.

When demand peaks at a high level, the per unit burden of overheads goes down. *That leads to profits reaching the maximrum maximorum peaks,* till market dynamism wipes them. In that case the production and marketing strategies have to be redesigned; new products and innovations have to come.

Sometimes those who are doing international business suffer losses in domestic currency but that is done to earn precious foreign exchange. India used to export sugar to many countries at prices lower than the cost of production. In old days the government used to refund all taxes or used to give tax holidays or used to subsidise many inputs. Losses in rupee terms used to the "mere transfers"; earnings used to be in foreign exchange. Now such things are not permitted but competitive price differences can be there in operations in different countries. Low profits in one can be counterbalanced with high profits elsewhere.

Dumping which means selling below the cost price to oust the competitors *is not allowed* under globalisation, if more than 3 p.c. of the consumption.

International business sometimes presents strange scenarios. Daewoo's car Matiz was going strong in India till the parent company collapsed. Now the subsidiary is being revived in India by General Motors of USA. It itself is in grave trouble.

Thirdly, the "four-cornerstone efficiency" is realised

In international business there are four efficiencies required:

(A) Producers have to be more efficient than others in the domestic trade.

(B) Domestic producers have to be so efficient that the foreign exporters cannot oust them from the domestic market.

(C) International business players have to be so efficient that they can export to foreign countries thus beating the foreign producers in their own market.

(D) Fourthly the international players have to excel each other in other lands.

However, if we do these things unto others; others also do the same thing unto us.

International business *is* the survival of the fittest

Business firms are "organic entities" in one sense that they are born, they develop and then decay and die. The can get rebirths with new products or mergers and acquisitions. The firms which cannot continue to do well in international business can re-emerge in new outfits.

One cannot be there successfully in international business by merely surviving as a marginal entity. High efficiency and competitive capabilities are required. Globalisation, as the rules of the game exist at present, cannot be based upon imposing high tariff duties on imports and massive subsidies on exports. Protective regimes are anti-thesis of globalisation.

[Ultimately the will of the consumers prevails. Indian importers imported Australian apples. They were totally tasteless and no one dared to import thereafter. The same is happening for a few types of foreign garments in India.]

Imports replacing imports are good international business. India used to import heavy electrical goods. By importing plant that manufacturers them (BHEL), subsequent import of heavy electrical goods was obviated.

Fourthly, globalisation promotes interactive business partnership. How often do we see that if a TNC or MNC is doing business in several countries, it organises various programmes (as training programmes) and activities (as paid holiday to be spent in certain hotels of certain countries) in other countries. A lot of goodwill is generated.

If a TNC/MNC is producing goods in country "A" and the goods are to be sold in country "D" but before that the goods have to be transported through countries "B" and "C", then some of the production processes can be in countries "B" and "C". Levelling and packaging can be done in some other country, if nothing else. *[When the Middle East countries ordered for readymade garments from India and Japan, the Japanese could deliver them first ! What they did was to put sewing machines and stiching girls on board ship and as many processes were completed on ship as could be completed in the journey time.]* That type of efficiency is required.

Research and development should be done in the parent company, unless the subsidiary in foreign country is its own. Advantages of new innovations should naturally accrue to the innovator. *Technovators* are now necessary who translate innovations into technical products i.e., goods in which new technology gets embodied.

In the matter of international business in services, the interactive cooperation can be obtained when most of the persons required to provide services are recruited from the country. That has got to be done. Only a few persons can come. The developed countries in any case do not have enough manpower to export to do everything outside. They can depute some top persons only. *If Coa Cola does business in India it provides jobs or additional income to the millions of Indians.*

The TNC/MNC sometimes open training centres at several places in several countries to provide itemwise training e.g., accounts training in one country, training in production in another and marketing training in still another country.

This is done on the basis where facilities exist. If this proves costly, this will be done only when there is scope for business flourishing in many countries. The *employee loyalty,* however, is a rare 'commodity'; only the Japanese are famous for it. It is considered a cardinal sin for an employee to leave his/her company to join another. Company jumping is very common in India. The companies which lose employees lose all the money which they must have incurred in recruitment, training etc. However, they get the same "free" when experienced employees come from other companies.

[In Japan if a woman employee gets married, the employer instead of the father of the girl. performs the ceremony (akin to the ceremony of *Kanyadaan* in India) of giving the girl in marriage.]

Some employees are so devoted that they remain till all the tasks of liquidation of a company are completed when company goes bankrupt.

Interactive cooperation must secure employee loyalty to further the international business interests.

Fifthly, Globalisation Furthers and is Itself Strengthened with non-price Competition

Non-price competition relates to good quality of the product, good after-sales services, credit facilities, and ease of payment.

Exchange rate depreciation without there being a reduction in the price charged, proves cheaper to the foreign importer. Hence exports are promoted.

However, this makes the imports costly in rupee terms. If the imports have inelastic demand, the country will lose. If the demand for exports is inelastic abroad, then cheapening of the exported products will not raise the demand. Hence if these two conditions are obtained at the same time, exchange râte depreciation should be checked. However, a host of macro-adjustments policies of development are required for the same.

If the demand for exports is elastic abroad, then the country loses in rupee terms but gains valuable foreign exchange. If the demand for imported goods is elastic in the country, then depreciating exchange rate will mean more rupee liability and imports will go down. Then there are supply elasticities.

If foreigner has inelastic supply (cannot sell to anyone else or/and cannot reduce production), he will charge a low price and vice versa. The same applies to the supply elasticity of the other (say our) country.

Competitiveness is secured when the efficiencies in the product-mix, marketing-mix, distribution-mix, promotion-mix and research-and-development-mix are at the optimum best.

It is a well-known thing that the world over the HPPs (high powered persons) demand their "tithes" from the international businessmen. *These payments are internalised i.e., included in the cost of production with fake adjusments here and there.* It continues even under the present regime of globalisation.

The US businessmen report that the highest bribes were demanded in China and they were most attracted with offers of foreign visits and receiving gifts there. (Reports in newspapers). USA businessmen pay bribes but after some years publicly disclose the same.

Competitiveness is the function of external economies being available to all on a scale and of a quality available in foreign countries. Bad roads in India take twice the time for the same movement in developed countries. Bad roads put so much loss to the vehicle owners that in that amount all roads of India can be kept in good condition. Thus external diseconomy discourages both domestic and internation business. In 2003 WTO demanded good roads for trade facilitation. from countries like India.

Indian industrialists depended upon the crutches of the Government. For two to three decades the scooter companies used the models developed in Italy and not a screw was put extra. Non-centrally mounted engines could not be put at the centre even when millions were skidding off the roads. The industrialists wanted cheap electricity (most of them pilfer it but tampering with the meter system), cheap land, water and credit, and even cheap raw materials through various corporations formed by the Goverment. There was corruption all around and shoddy raw materials received from State Small Industries-Corporations were a problem even for the domestic users. It was the usual practice of most of the entrepreneurs to build up personal properties and assets with the money borrowed from banks for various industrial units. Many got loans for many projects but ran well one or two only. The rest were meant for diverting the funds for personal assets.

Indian business had difficulties in making a mark because they depended on all sorts of tax concessions and subsidies. Easy got easy spent policy made them inefficient.

As such some industries were born sick, some became sick and on some sickness was thrust upon. *True competitiveness comes when internal economies exceed substantially internal diseconomies.*

Sixthly, Globalisation leads to Higher productivies, Higher technological innovations and Competitiveness

It was in mid-1960s that it was asserted that two-third of all economic progress in the USA was due to technology. Technologies are what are congealed in capital goods. They provide the cutting-edge in competitiveness. New technologies have to be efficient. *[Chinese power saver lamps were available in India for Rs. 45 while the Phillips was marketing them for Rs. 250 or so; however, the Chinese bulbs can go "phut" in a week or a month; nothing is guaranteed. Others were giving guarantees for one year. Meanwhile other producers of similar bulbs brought down the price in the ratio of 3: 1 from 6: 1.* New technologies have to be cost-efficient.

Technology can be sold directly or indirectly. In indirect selling, the buyer has to buy the product also. In direct selling only royalty is to be paid and the process is disclosed and is permitted to be used.

Technologies are developed through research facilities for which there has to be adequate funding and freedom. There is need for sharing the benefits with the innovators. [In India an innovator does not share profits.]

Technology gets embodied in the products and it is through the sale of the products that there is diffusion of technology. In this case imperfect use of technology can be avoided. If the production base of the production base of the country is good, then instead of diffusions congealed in goods, there can be 'transfer rights' of technology on payment of royalties.

It is understandable that unless there are tax concessions, subsidies, cutting-down of the red rapism and sharing of honours and profits, technology transfers for globalisation of international business will not be forthcoming.

Government guarantees and counter-guarantees may be necessary — counter-guarantees that if the concerned party fails to pay, the government will. New technologies improve products for domestic use and then for exports; technological developments help countries in import substitution. *Technocrats and technovators (technical innovators) in Government Departments are discouraged in India because they cannot get status and perks higher than of the Secretary of the Government of India.* The lead is to be taken by the private sector in future. *At present the private sectors in developing economies are finding it cheaper to import technology on payment, made possible by globalisation.*

TNCs normally do not share the "generation" of technology but the "use/transfer on payment". Cooperation in generation of technology is possible only if the field of research is in the host country e.g., the US can cooperate with India and Bangladesh in developing certain technologies relating to multifarious uses of jute and jute products.

Developing economies have problems in generating technologies because the tools, equipment and machines etc. that develop technology are themselves lacking. Those equipments are themselves technology which may not be transferred. Developing economies made it impossible for their own natives to develop skills and implement them. Thus "potential" technocrats were in many cases "exported" by the developing economies. The *product mandate* that may be received might have been developed by the national of the country concerned. Diesel was innovated by a person of the same surname in Germany. "Suri effect" that is incorporated in diesel engines was developed by one Mr. Suri whose innovation was rejected in India. It was developed in Germany and then India had to pay royalty to use that.

Maruti cars, or Hyundai cars and a host of other products can be produced and marketed with new technologies under "product mandate" but if Indians can make a worthwhile innovation, the parent company will give credits for the same.

Developments in technologies are minor capital revolutions. They do not come in bunches but are now routine if the global convas is taken. Those countries can develop technologies which are prepared to do funding for taking risks and uncertainties. Technology if it is taken from outside will be "external economy"; if developed by the firm itself will become "internal economy".

The world has learnt quite a lot from the producers across the globe. The Chinese products may not be as durable as of India but the Chinese show finnese to have a good finish and finis in their products which have not only shine but sheen also.

Globalisation and technological improvements have made the enlargement of the 'scale and scope' of production and we see all around urge to have higher productivity, efficiency and competitiveness to survive and outlive others.

Seventhly, Global management issues are efficiently tackled

Global management is much more than managing it on a larger scale and know a few foreign languages. The orientation has got to be different in quality and quantum of capabilities, if capabilities could be 'quantified'.

Global management requires capabilities and strategies to keep the foreign competition inside domestic market incapable of taking all its business. Then the tasks relate to having competitive space in foreign countries. Global management cannot mean that it requires strategies to keep all foreign competitors away from the domestic market and then oust all competitors from the foreign markets. This is simply not possible now a days for even the largest TNC/MNC of the world.

There can be silent mergers, acquisitions and amalgamations. [Lakme of Tatas was taken over by Hindustan Levers without changing anything of Lakme. HL still gives the impression as if the Lakme products and other products of HL are competing products. Actually when such arrangements are made (as producing several types of toothpastes by the same company and inserting advertisements in the media as if they are competing products) the intention is that if the consumers move away from one product they choose another product of the *same* parent group. Brooke Bond and Lipton merged but the old products continue to be sold under the old brands. The merger saved the companies from top administrative infrastructure expenditure as also cut-throat marketing competition].

The essentials of global management are the same as of any other management; management of the production, purchase, sale, personnel, productivities and finance. The qualities in managers are also the same universal qualities; (i) good knowledge of the law, theories, principles and policy alternatives; (ii) abilities to interact well with the superiors, juniors (line and staff) and the public, and (iii) *inter alia* to keep the lessons of the past experiences in view, to understand the present status and profiles of business and to forecast future trends.

Risks are to be averted first rather than borne. Bold decisions are to be taken but after careful weighing of the pros and cons. To be visionary does not mean to be day-dreamer. Not to be day-dreamer does not mean to be timid and over-cautious. The leadership qualities come only when the managers learn. *It is just like a teacher and a student; a teacher is a senior student. Unless the teacher studies he cannot teach.*

The quality of global management/managers can be judged by comparing the positions in different countries but after reducing the conditions to common denominators. Performance in a poor desert country and a rich island of great tourism cannot be compared in terms of absolute figures. *Geocentric* management will be dictated by geographic and natural conditions. *Ethnocentric* by socio-cultural conditions (for example no multinational company can sell burgers with meat of boars in the Muslim country). *Region centric* adjustments are required to suit the geo-centric and ethnocentric conditions. For example, countries of European Economic Union are now just "regions" of the EU but require different management strategies relating to production and management. *Polycentric* superstructure is a sort of sum total of all the capabilities.

Broad contours/goals remain the same; ways and means can differ in different countries and for different products. There will be some differences in dealing with dealers, subsidiaries, franchises and joint-ventures. In joint-ventrures the MNCs/TNCs will not be acting in a wise way if they show bossism. Even if in economic terms MNCs/TNCs are more than equal they have to show the spirit of partnership. Maltreatment to local parties invites national hostility. Monitoring, advising and ensuring what the headquarter wants has got to be done with tact. *Global management is not government administration of imperial country over a colony.* In the process of decision making, an impression is to be created that the consultations were adequate between the partners. They were not imposed upon but mutually arrived at.

Joint ventures run well in international business when equal importance is recognized. The foreign investor may bring heavy capital, machines, technology, vital inputs, top management skills and even international finance. Yet the importance of personnel who are engaged in production and actual operation should be realised. *Even unequal real importance need not be so treated explicity.*

[*Very serious* differences had emerged between the Japanese firm Suzuki and Indian Maruti Udyog Limited over the services for should we say about way of taking decisions and management of the Managing Director. There was much acrimony of which there was only an inkling to outsiders. All that was publicised that there was a *slight* difference of opinion about *a minor issue* that will be sorted out *soon.* The compromise formula was such that it took quite a few months to implement it so that neither party could feel that it was imposed too quickly or delayed too much. Essence of management of joint ventures is that there be no bad blood.]

D. ADVERSE EFFECTS OF GLOBALISATION NEED TO KEEP THEM TO MINIMUM

Good and adverse effects of globalisation in different countries partly depend upon international factors but mostly on internal factors.

There are some basic problems of any developing economy like: (i) poverty, (ii) illiteracy and/or lack of tradeablc skill,'(iii) underemployment and unemployment, (iv) exploding population despite falling birth rates and falling death rates because birth rates are falling at a very tardy pace, (v) food insecurity despite huge food stocks, (vi) trade replacing production in village and cottage industries (vii) rural-urban chasm and villages not having their minimum needs met. (viii) depressed ethnic groups still remaining socio-economically challenged, (ix) assetelessness and houselessness of nearly one-fourth of the population, and (x) mounting corruption.

We cannot blame globalisation only for that. These problems are there despite liberalisation, privatisation and globalisation as well as because of them. The blame should first go to the domestic economic policies.

1. Globalisation is giving rise to "turbo capitalism", "casino capitalism" and "crony capitalism"

"Turbo capitalism" means that the economic reforms dictated by WTO, IMF, World Bank and the super-powers are sought to be implemented in the developing economies at the speed of "turbo jet aeroplanes". Developing economies are not permitted to set their own pace. Infact the IMF-WTO model dictates that the "second and third generation" economic reforms should be implemented at a fast pace. The developing economies cannot plan how to enable the poor to get direct benefits of the LPG.

"Casino capitalism" stands for Governments advising the savers (as was done by the Government of India) that the savers should take their money from the banks to the share markets and lose all of it to the dishonest bulls and bears. Economic progress is judged now by how the share market reacts.

"Crony capitalism" stands for high powered persons (HPPs) providing most of the benefits of LPG to their kith and kins as to their cronies. The economies go into the hands of political-economic mafia.

2. Predatory globalisation

Present globalisation is predatory. Even in the 20th century the MNCs and TNCs fought wars over mineral resources (as for copper in Congo). Oil wars still continue. *Water was tried to be privatised in Bolivia after 2000 but the efforts failed.* Modern globalisation does not have a place for the public sector. The world cannot cope with the US dictates.

> ***"America is the only country that has moved from barbarism to decadence without an intermediate period of civilisation".***

(George Clemenceau (a French) said this in 1919. Quoted from *Outlook* October 5, 1998.)

The US was not conforming to the demands of the entire world to alter its technology to save the hole in the ozone layer getting bigger. But it will have its own pace.

Globalisation has led in movement of $ 2 trillion fictitious paper transactions daily and this economy (1999 position) was 7 times larger than the economy of real goods and services".

Projected and adjusted figures for global trade in 2008 were that the trade was equal to $ 14 trillion. The poor countries were indebted almost to the extent of twice as much.

India's share in global trade is not even 0.5 p.c. EU, for example, is important for India. India is unimportant for EU.

3. Globalisation is "high on growth" and "low on employment generation"

Economic Survey of India acknowledged that even after almost two decades years of reforms, India has more unemployed persons than before. The rural urban chasm is widening.

Nearly 9 p.c. of the work force of the organised sector was employed in the public sector. There was a drop of 1 p.c. in the public sector employment in these years. The private organised sector registered an increase in employment by 0.1 p.c. only with all the effects of globalisation.

The rate of entry in work/labour force is now higher than in the population. *The Governments of all hues are employing persons on contract (university lecturers, college lecturers, school teachers and even doctors in government medical facilties)* and the payments are mere pittance. The primary school teachers get salaries of Rs. 1000 per month in government schools and around Rs. 500 in private schools in many Northern States. The result is that all members of the family— male and females '; young and old—have to seek work to have an income which can ensure food for all. This is encouraged worker effect.

It *is the rule of the market that when it is time for boom, leading companies lead and lagging companies lag even more.*

However, when it is time for reversal lagging companies lead and leading companies lag.

The same is happening to the lower classes. When distress comes it goes to them; if goods things come they go to the already rich.

The rich countries are protecting the interests of their country- persons in employment. Japanese refuse to import cheap rice. European Economic Union (EU) countries continue to subsidies agriculture much to the annoyance of the USA to protect employment interests of their people. The US too is protectionist against the developing economies to protect employment interests in its labour-intensive activities (for example, tailoring).

After globalisation became the world economic order, the developed countries are insisting that the developing economies should allow the free flow of capital in their countries from the rich countries.

It is suggested that this will bring down the rate of interest and then investment in productive and distributive activities will become easier. Besides the "natives" will not be required to forego or postpone consumption of goods for saving.

This is, the developed countries say, according to the principle of comparative advantage in international business.

However, the developed countries refuse to concede that the same thing applies to labour from developing economies to the developed economies.

Now the developing economies argue that let the "natural labour" be exported. *The term "natural labour"* is a word of which etymology is uncertain. It means *labour which is a precious resource i.e., skilled labour.*

If developing economies point out that Canada and Australia have density of just 4 persons per sq. km. and these countries should allow immigration of people/labour/ "natural labour" from developing economies, the developed countries consider this preposterous.

More than half of Australia is "ruled" by kangaroos, dingo dogs, wild camels, lemmings and ants that make all grazing animals blind by leaving a type of acid in grass. Australia requires persons for husbanding land. But Australia is selective in favour of white persons only.

The thrust point is that globalisation rules are imposed on the developing economies but the developed countries do not follow the rules of globalisation themselves.

4. Developing economies now have to say "Don't Owe; Won't Pay"

One great problem of globalisation is that a lot exports of the developed economies are thrust upon the developing economies. Normally a developing economy should buy with much foreign exchange as it can earn from its exports. Marginal excess can be taken on deferred payments (loans). However, each year the less developed countries become indebted by additional minimum 1 trillion dollars. *Globalisation is a coercive "arm-order" also.* Superpowers arm the nations; then they make them disarm ! There are hot and cold wars in various parts of the world and the developed countries get their currencies recycled from leading exporting countries of the developing group —like those which export oil or minerals.

The developed countries can send the economies of the developing economies into tail-spin. Two decades back nearly 90 p.c. of the export earnings of Malaysia used to be from the export of tin. If the developed countries were to delay import by a few months, the Malaysian economy would have got dizzy spell.

The accumulated adverse balance of payment take the shape of grindmill stone round the neck of the developing economies and then the developed countries "capture" the economy and polity of the host countries without actual occupation.

5. Backwash effects of international business are still there and in sum they exceed the spread effects

Names of Packer, Prater and Rybezynsht are frequently mentioned about their contribution to the analysis of globalization. Much profound analysis was, however, made by noble Prize winner late Prof. Gunnar Myrdal, Raul Prebisch and H.W. Singer. Myrdal pointed out how the developing economies exploited the primary resources of the developing economics that not even the hinterlands of the mining or plantations areas could develop. They received their imports at dust cheap rates and exported their goods to the developing economies at inflated rates. Thus adverse (backwash) effects exceeded the favourable (spread) effects. Economic colonization continues.

The spread effects are now more than earlier; the backwash effects are now less than they were in the days of imperialism. However, globalisation is not helping eradication of poverty, control of population, generation of employment and propagation of income in favour of the masses,*for which "native HPPs should share greater blame.*

6. Globalisation has been responsible for dichotomy in the labour payments and low rates of interest; both advantages going to the industrialists and traders

It is like "double-fault" of tennis. Now a days the MNCs/TNCs and LBHs (large business houses) take the cream of the skilled and efficient persons and pay them very well indeed but take work of two persons from one.

Rest of the labour market has now become contractual or unorganised.

Had the casualisation/contractualisation of the labour market created more employment low salaries/wages would have been welcome. The problem created by globalisation, liberalisation and privatisation is that the real incomes of the majority of work force are going down.

Surprising it may seem the US wanted India to pay high wages to all so that Indian labour-intensive goods could not compete with the labour-intensive goods of the rich countries. They wanted to impose *"labour standards"*. This happened only for the employees of the TNCs/MNCs and LBHs.

Low rates of interest in capital scare economy are anti-households. Economic theory tells us that no country can have a "low shadow rate of wage and a low shadow rate of interest at the same time."

It was under the demands of gloalisation that interest rates had to be lowered. It was said that since the capitalist world pays rates of interest, the high rates of interest were attracting foreign "parking of funds" with the Indian banks and it was not possible to bear the interest burden. The problem could have been solved by paying global rate of interest on global movement of foreign institutional investment (FII) in bank accounts and/or "commercial papers" like shares or bonds.

Policies of lowering salary structure through casualisation/contractualiation of the labour market and lowering the rates of interest *at the same time dictated by the LPG paradigm* are wrong for the following reasons:

1. The lowering of the rate of interest has hurt the households because interest rates were cut by 45 p.c. during the last 10 years on all sorts of deposits. For senior citizens the cut was about 40 p.c. It is the household sector which provides nearly 80 p.c. savings to India.
2. It was strange that when the savings-national income ratio was 22 p.c. the GoI was talking of liquidity crunch and was lamenting the fall in S/Y ratio; when it became 24 p.c, the GoI (infact a Prime Minister said this) says *"we do not need savings in post offices and banks: invest in the share markets"*. As, seen earlier this is throwing the lambs to the wolves.
3. Unemployment of labour is actually shortage of capital. Since 4 crore persons are openly unemployed in India (on person-days of employment basis), capital shortage is proved.

Industrialists cannot produce at lower costs and sell more simply because there is a low rate of interest. Keynes had said "a low rate of interest is a necessary condition but not a sufficient condition." *Full employment and high purchasing power with all economic entities alone can help in higher production and sales.* Demand side should not be neglected. At present only supply side economics is being attended to in the interest of the industries. *Producers are welcome but households should not pay the price.* All households are not of the rich.

4. The Mutual Funds managed by public sector financial institutions squeezed the savers to their bones. State Bank of India, Unit Trust of India or Industrial Development Bank of India which were supposed to give Rs. 20000 for every Rs. 10000 after 6 years lock-in period, paid Rs. 8000 or so only.
5. The vested interest economic groups have virtually looted the public sector financial institutions. All sorts of banks are fiddled with bad debts of nearly Rs. 180000 crore which the banks euphemistically call non-performing assets. The low interest rate structure is a device whereas the reverse transferences from poor to rich are

being affected. A day may come when the GoI may demand cloak room charges from the savers for keeping their money safe!

6. Governments is going back on contract. The interest rate on public provident fund was reduced to 9 p.c. for 15-year lock up. *Provident funds of the employees are not paid back in time.*
7. *"Recession" cannot be tackled by lowering the rate of interest.* The industrialists of India, for example, extracted all sorts of concessions in the form of reduced taxes but on cars, jewellery or similar super luxury things while many essential things were subjected to harsh price hike. Technological innovations will not help if people do not have purchasing power. Between Dec. 2008 and March 2009, the India Inc. controlled media got concessions of Rs. 1,00,000,crs, in the name of recession effects of U.S. financial melt-down.

The microwave ovens have been so modified by the Koreans that they can produce not only roasted non-veg items but such items as *idli, tandoories* and *kulcha.* There are linear compressors in the frost-free refrigerators which can reduce power consumption by 46 p.c. There are temperature sensors that maintain different temperatures in separate compartments off ridges. There are frostfree models as also quick-freeze features that will keep cool temperature even after 5 hours of power failure. Washing machines can handle different types of *saries.* Now the air-conditioners are available in India that can take care of temperature upto 52" Centigrade. Toys for children are now almost like live animals or live small friends. *Liberalisation, privatisation and globalisation have not generated purhasing power with the masses but with the classes.*

How did India move from the era of "liquidity crunch" to "excess liquidity syndrome" ? It was due to a few glaring reasons:

Money supply data is published by the RBI every Friday. Here is given money supply (number 3) which means (i) coins and currency with the public and (ii) all types of deposits with the commerical and cooperative banks (iii) a few other items which are of little significance here:

	Crs.
In a week in December 1969, MS 3 was in Rs. crs (nearly)	2700
In a week of January 1991	250000
On 10th Jan. 2006	2576000
In April 2010	5400000
Between 1971 and 2009 population was times	2.2
Money supply was	(times) 2000

The GoI created both primary and secondary money (credit money created by commercial banks). With this tremendous increase in money supply, a question arises why should the GoI be short of funds ? Afterall it created it. Why did it pass on its "title" to others easily that it has no funds for basic services, population control, and employment generation.

GoI and all Governments easily pass on the money to the HPPs. There is that "85% syndrome". [Late Rajiv Gandhi said that only 15 p.c. of the funds meant for the targeted groups reach them; rest are 'lost" in "programme delivery systems", not all of which in right way. Montek Singh Ahluwalia confirmed this in 2009)

[The rural India still has the usurous rates of interest which are charged @ 3 p.c. per month, or even 5 p.c. p.m. and it goes to 36 p.c. and 60 p.c. These reverse transferences from poor to the rich are going in the exalted name of "fiscal consolidation", "monetary consolidation" and "macro-economic structural adjustments". JM Keynes han said: "investors will not borrow even at zero rate of interest if effective demand is deficient".

Liberalisation, privatisation and globalisation are market friendly; but markets are not friendly to the poor. Employment generation should never be left fully to "happenstance economics" i.e., change. Or the government should control population. It itself will provide employment.

7. Globalisation involves corruption and cannot be eliminated

Corruption ruins democratic contract between citizens and their representatives. As fear of law, fear of conscience and fear of God go out of the hearts of people, corruption pervades the society and gains deep roots.

It is there in all countries more or less. Even the best country Finland got 97 out of 100 marks for being the least corrupt.

On a scale of 10, India obtained 2.7 marks and was 71st at number in terms of honesty. Corruption is there in all countries of the Indian Sub-Continent and the tragedy is that its roots can be traced to shady politicians.

It is one thing to enjoy perks of *comforts* (only) at government expenses but to amass wealth immorally and not pay taxes are just two ways of corruption. Highway robberies pale into insignificance if one learns the crores that are exchanged in mafia type activities patronised by the HPPs.

Common people now receive shocks when their top leaders are found to be not knee-deep but totally submerged in corruption.

Countries of the world do not have leaders like Mahatma Gandhi but "rulers" who are ruthless to brush aside anyone who opposes.

How much money must the corrupt persons of India be taking out of India each year ? How much must they have taken out ? Billions of dollars per year.

GLOBALISATION ENVIRONMENT

Globalisalion Environment.
Globalisation and Economic Development.
Multinational *Versus* Transaction Approach
Socio-Cultural and Political Factors.
Globalisation and Political Factors.
Globalisation and Human Resource Management.

In the previous chapter we defined liberalisation and globalisation and also examined the pros and cons of globalisation. The thrust point of the discussion in the previous chapter was that despite many limitations, globalisation will stay.

Globalisation is with us and so are the tariff and non-tariff barriers to globalisation. We have limited globalisation in the form of economic blocs. Tariff and non-tariff barriers are being lifted or are being diluted. Yet they remain.

Global economic environment is also like weather environment. [If there is snowfall in Kashmir, cold wave comes to U.P. and Madhya Pradesh]. If there is recession or slump in the economy of the US, all other economies are adversely affected. *In fact the US military ventures and movements mean expenditure of billions of dollars that roll into the balance of payment accounts of several countries. An actual war, however, can bring destruction more to some and some to all.*

There is a saying that if the US sneezes, the rest of the world gets pneumonia. Now this example can be extended to EU also.

Global business and marketing environment depends upon several factors in various countries.

1. Rate of growth in various sectors, sub-sectors, activities and functions in various countries *and* their implication in absolute figure.
2. Rate of growth in population and then in the per capita real income based upon international purchasing power parity. If a country has per capita income of $ 36000 and another $ 360 per person a very high growth rate of 10 p.c. in the second country adds $ 36 only, while only 3 p.c. increase in the p.c.r. income of the first country means addition of $ 1080. *All the running by the first country will take years and years to reach the level of country A.*
3. To what degree and with reference to what periods different commodities, goods and services can be subjected to tariffs and non-tariff restrictions. *The world has not abolished all tariffs in all countries nor all sorts of non-tariff exchange controls have been made illegal.*

Hence global marketing and business environment depend upon the mix of free trade versus *degree of regulations permitted nationwise, transaction wise and time-wise.*

This means that the same commodity may have different global environment for different countries and even if the restrictions are to be eased the time period given to different countries will be different. Certain countries may be permitted to global trade in item "z" but not in item "y".

Thus multinational and transactional aspects of global differences are temporally different.

4. *Socio-Cultural aspects* determine globalisation more profoundly than is normally realised. It is believed that if production principle, marketing principle, demand management principle, supply management principle and governmental (legal) aspects are taken care of, global marketing will be easy.

Fez (Turkish cap) used to be worn in India before Independence. Now it is seldom seen, except with the people who might have got it as gift or purchased it on personal visit. People follow social customs and have cultural practices that look weird to others. For example a big lizard in an island country is considered "incarnation of God and abode of all departed souls" and hence people kiss it and offer chickens. Sacrificial animals/birds are exported and imported for socio-cultural rituals.

People have their own code of dress which has sometimes to do with climatic conditions and sometimes because they know not other modes of dressing. Socio-cultural-religious perspectives differ and inter-mingle and determine marketing.

In Seychelles of the total population in the main Island (Out of 150) there are less than 10000 persons of Indian origin (but one-sixth of the total) and they require flour, rice, pulses, "saries", "bindies", "sindoor", sundry items for worshipping deities.

They are all available there but for a price and people pay that price generally 10 times higher than are there in India.

5. Politics is supreme in determining economic relations. India and Pakistan trade as less as possible. Officially most trade is "banned" though smuggling may be common. *When Bangladesh was East Pakistan, coal could be had from India by "just stretching the hand across the border" (so to say), however, Pakistan Government used to import it from China and it used to prove costly.*

The then West Pakistan allowed the golden fibre of East Pakistan (now Bangladesh) to rot. The economy of the Bangladeshies was ruined; they were pauperized and when they were asked not to speak and write sanskritised Bangla language, they revolted for in any case they were a colony of the West Pakistan where all freedoms except Muslim religious freedoms were denied to the Bangladeshi persons.

Good, bad and indifferent political situations determine the volume, composition and direction of global business.

6. Technological aspects of globalisation environment now a days dominate finally. Initially there can be resistance from the industries which face economic death. Indian scooter and car market continued to remain insulated behind government patronage and protection against foreign technology. Then all types of mopeds, old chain-model scooters and old cars had to go. Their industrial units were closed or they had to produce new Euro-I and then EURO-II standard motor cycles and mopeds.

Technology has two way marketing-importing and exporting. *Its marketing was being done by the foreigners into India. This is also global marketing.* India now exports the new technology cars to other countries.

Technology is now front-door gatecrasher and its entry cannot be stopped. It will come either in the form of new goods that are imported or in the form of capital goods with which new technology products are manufactured.

The erstwhile socialist countries collapsed because they improved their technology for war goods only. And, when during the regime of President Reagan of the US that "Space War" missile was invented, the then USSR virtually lost the war of attrition. *Now Russia is member of NATO which was formed to combat the then USSR.*

It used to be reported that while the socialist governments were giving figures of ever rising national income, they were not only giving exaggerated/false figures of production but were including in the production things which were non-operative and non- functional due to old technology.

7. Globalisation and Human Resource Development have a healthy interface. High quality human resources promote research; then there are discoveries, inventions and innovations. They get translated into heavy capital goods and then consumption/ investment goods. International business increases and, other things remaining the same, other countries also develop. As they develop the quality of their human resources also develops. We can say globalisation is the cause and consequence of human development.

Human resource management is a macro issue. It is a two-fold task initially. First, to manage its supply over a period of time—in case of India to control population explosion. Secondly, it means making the persons employable or self-employable i.e., to make people skilled in whatever profession they are needed or they are interested in. It is placing right.persons at the right job at right time.

Even the works of non-skilled persons can enter the international business. India exports so many agricultural products and so many things based upon mining. Millions of persons who arc producing these outputs are still totally illiterate.

For exporting goods of high order a country requires skilled human resources or manpower as it used to be known earlier. *Corporate level human resources development is for narrow specialisation.* Now the time has come when the Corporate Bodies themselves can float their own educational/human resources planning institutions which can produce the type of persons that they want.

FDI (foreign direct investment) in a country will be discouraged if the local/native manpower is not adequately trained. Only in a few exceptional cases the foreign investor can take upon himself the task of developing the required manpower in foreign country if the business relates to highly valuable things *e.g.*, diamonds, gold, silver, copper, tin, iron ore mining or any similar things.

In most cases or rather in almost all cases the country itself has to develop necessary human resources for national and international business. Affliates can, however, do for TNCs/MNCs what they would like to be done.

India, for example, is a country which is rich in total human resources in quantities first. Its creamy layer of human resources usually migrates abroad in search of "greener pastures"; and Indians have done well abroad. Infact the software industry of the USA is almost run by the Indians. *"Stand alone"* approach is giving way to *'simple integrated human resource development"* and further to *"complex integrated"* development. The Japanese and the Koreans have trained Indians in their production, management and marketing techniques—rather silently at that.

The utilisation pattern of human resources by the foreign employers has three distinct features: (i) they take the best in terms of education, skill, personality development and articulation skills; (ii) they pay very well but take two persons work from one on Indian norms, and (iii) for a very hectic schedule of work each day, they give "forced" respite from work for a week or fornight in a year. *It is only high performance and productivity that count.*

In case a company is taken over by the foreign firm, the dead wood or sub-optimum efficient persons are first laid off with compensation. They include this as the "cost" of purchasing.

The very best of human resources are engaged in international business whether the business is in the control of the "natives" or of the foreigners.

NOTE

---

1. Late Prime Minister Rajeev Gandhi wanted:
   "to take corruption out of politics; politics out of administration. and administration out of the economy."
   On ILPG see *IMF's "Finance and Development"*, March, 1996.
2. P. Balakrishan, K. Pushpangadan, M. Suresh Babu on "Trade Liberalisation and Productivity Growth in Manufacturing". *EPW.* October. 7, 2000.

3. Sec *Frontline* January 31, 2003 for opposition of globalisation by the WORLD SOCIAL FORUM, EUROPEAN SOCIAL FORUM AND THE ASIAN SOCIAL FORUS. Papers by S. Muralidharan, V. Sridhar and Samir Amin.
4. Governments are not taking into account the ""attrition factor". Posts that fall vacant due to deaths, retirement, severence (voluntarily leaving the job), dismissals and retrenchment are not filled though budget. All dues of the State employees are paid late or at lower rates. *Supreme Court threatened Government of Orissa (2002) for contempt of the Court because it had not started paying pension to a retired person who became 103 years of age* press report Schools, hospitals and many facilities are without employees (a forest guard has to look after 100 sq. kms. of forest on foot with only a cane in hand). HPPs misutilise funds.
5. On 6th March, 2003 the computers of prices ranging around *Rs.* 55,000 were sold for *Rs.* 7000 only to the MPs of Indian Parliament.
6. Methods of correcting adverse balance of payment, devaluation, anti-dumping measures, subsidies etc. also affect globalisation. See BOP section of the book.

32 Structure of the National and International Monetary Systems Before IMF (Brief History)

(1) INTRODUCTION: MONEY: DEFINITIONS: MONEY SUPPLY ANALYSIS (With Special Reference to India). NATIONAL MONETARY SYSTEMS.
(2) INDIA'S RECENT DOMESTIC AND INTERNATIONAL MONETARY REFORMS, *As they affect International Trade.*
(3) INTERNATIONAL MONETARY SYSTEM 1880-1914 INTERNATIONAL MONETARY SYSTEM 1914-1944, *including Devaluation of dollar in 1934.*
(4) INTERNATIONAL MONETARY ORDER 1944-2009*-2010.

INTRODUCTION: MONEY: DEFINITIONS: MONEY SUPPLY ANALYSIS (WITH REFERENCE TO INDIA): NATIONAL MONETARY SYSTEMS.

There is a saying that definitions do not precede a subject; they should succeed a subject. This is very true for money. Each definition is relevant for the circumstances under which it was advanced. Then the subject undergoes several changes—sometimes it becomes wider in scope and sometimes there is narrowing down of the same, known as specialisation. Hence the time makes the definitions out of date. The same is true for the definition of money also. The author can hazard this definition.

Money is a medium of exchange which is universally accepted within the national boundaries, which is a measure of value, a store **of value, a standard of deferred payment and which becomes the base for subsequent monetary advancements.**

This 'definition' has been presented on the basis of the most important functions of money. *The problem with defining money is that while it wraps the entire economy, its 'abolition', if it can be done, will not make the economy disappear.* It is important and yet economies existed without it ! There is no activity in which money is not used i.e., in buying inputs and factors, in selling outputs **and** services, in other productive activities and in redistribution of national income and wealth. It regulates and facilitates all activities concerning consumption, production, exchange, distribution, public finance and whatnot. *But real factors are more important. Money cannot be sown in the fields to take crops; but it facilitates buying of seeds.* Real efforts, real manpower, real capital, real outputs etc. are more important.

National trade is possible with national money; International trade is possible with "international money" or "components of international liquidity". Ultimately gold balances *can* be transferred. There are now many new fangled methods of international remittances but ultimately the settlement's have to be in "key currencies" or "vehicle currencies" of the world, which are most acceptable.

Two definitions stand out most important for money

"Money is what money does" (F. Walker) and "Anything is that is generally acceptable as a means of exchange, including settling of past exchange on credit (debts) and which, at the same time, acts as a measure and a store of value" (G. Crowther).

The definition of money changes every time a new component of money is included. Thus money was once coins only and now it can include currency + demand deposit balances of banks of all types and even non-banking financial intermediaries + time deposits of all types of financial institutions + titles in the form of credit cards and many new fangled devices. *Traditional definitions* have given way to *modern empirical definitions.*

There is the "primary money" which comes from the Central Bank of the country and then there is "secondary money" which comes in the form of credit money and which is facilitated by the commercial banks under the control and directives of the Central Bank. New money is printed by the Central Bank against the 'discounting of the treasury bills" (also known as accepting the treasury bills by the Central Bank which are sold in auction by the Central Government). The credit money is created against the commercial bills.*

Importance of money has been emphasised in that it removes all inconveniences of barter. It frees the economy from the fetters of barter economy. It may look surprising that *economists have always under-played the importance of money in development.* Adam Smith compared money with a road—all productive activities use road; but nothing grows on the road itself. It is also said that shortage of money hinders economic growth but a plethora of its does not ensure growth. *Money is considered unimportant by all those who have a lot of it* There are several such sayings that it can buy a house but cannot ensure a happy home; it can buy books but it can ensure that the person has imbibed knowledge, it can buy medicines but cannot ensure health; it can ensure comforts of life but cannot bring happiness; it can buy food but cannot ensure a good appetite and digestion; it can buy a bed but cannot ensure peaceful sleep etc.

Money Supply Measures: with Special Reference to India

Money supply measures are defined in different countries in different ways. For example, in the USA they are defined in 12 senses but measured in 8 senses. In India they are defined in 4 senses but money supply measures in the 3rd sense is considered "entire liquidity". In future, the money supply will be measured in the entirely new three different senses. The under-mentioned money supply measures were suggested by the RBI in 1977 and they superseded the money supply measures of 1966. Currently, *in brief,* these measures are as under: M_1 = Coins + Currency with the.public — currency returned by Pakistan;

+ demand deposits of commercial and cooperative banks;
+ some other deposits with the RBI (not significant, but are quite a few)—interbank deposits (to avoid double counting)

$M_2 = M_1$ + demand deposits with the post office.*
$M_3 = M_1$ + Time deposits of the commercial and cooperative banks.
$M_4 = M_3$ + All deposits of the post office.

From 1998 the money supply measure *were to be different but even by the end of 2009 their calculations were not started.* The old measures have become outdated due to introduction of cash cards and credit cards. The one, two and five rupee notes have been (or are being coinised). A rupee has 100 paise but there is no 1 paisa in minted state. The coins of 1, 2, 5, 10, 20 25 and even 50 paise are gone. They too are gone. The cost of minting them is higher than their face value. *Once India used to have 192 parts of a rupee, and that used to be known as "pie". It had good purchasing power.* A rupee used to have 16 annas and each anna used to be of 4 paise; thus a rupee used to have 64 paise. It was converted into metric system in 1960 i.e., each thing having 100 parts, (in 1940, 1 paisa used to buy 4 kachories!). The rupee liability of the Government of India is all but gone as notes of 1 rupee are no longer printed nor crisp ones can be found.

The inclusion of the deposits of post offices is now considered necessary and so also of the institutions like IDBI, ICICI, SIDBI, LIC and GIC not to speek of several other non-banking financial institutions. Hence the proposed future measures will be:

L_1 = M_3 + all deposits with the post offices i.e., = M_4
L_2 = L_1 + fixed deposits of financial institutions like IDBI + ICICI, SIDBI etc.,
L_3 = L_2 + deposits with non-banking financial institutions/corporations like LIC, GIC and some private organisations of the same nature.

Thus there is change from MS analysis to Liquidity analysis. M_3 shall, however, *continue to be the focus of monetary policy and data shall be published on weekly basis. The "liquidity measures" shall be published on monthly basis.*

M_3 in India increased by leaps and bounds. (Implications of the same will be examine in the next chapter).

	Rs.crs
1. In the last week of 1969 it was *(crore Rs.)* (Rounded off)	2700
2. In a week in 1991 it crossed	250000
3. In a week in 1995 it crossed	550000
4. In a week in 1996 it crossed	650000
5. In a week in 1997 it crossed	750000
6. In a week in 1998 it crossed	850000
7. In a week in June, 1999 it crossed	1000000
8. In a week in Jan, 2001, it crossed	1260000
9. In a week in Jan. 2007, it crossed	3000000
10. In a week in Sept. 2008 it crossed	4226150
11. In a week in Dec 2009 it crossed (rounded off)	5200000
12. In a week in April, 2010	5400000

Though this is not the way to calculate the rate of increase in money supply but it can be said that it was almost 2000 times in 40 years ! The current rate of increase remains between 16 to 20 p.c. per year.

MONETARY STANDARDS

Monetary standard relates to what type or types of monies a country has and what is their relative weightage in the total money supply. It is a system of small coins to the highest denominations of notes and other forms which are very near to currency—almost their proxies. Each country has its own monetary standard. The era of mono-metallism is gone and not even bi-metallism is sufficient in any country. It is a multi-money standard. There are standard coins, currencies and token coins in a monetary standard.

Monetary standard in any country keeps on changing as the type of money changes. It was once 'gold currency standard' (when gold coins used to circulate); it could have been 'silver standard' if the coins used to be of silver; it was "bi-metallic standard if coins of both metals circulated. If a country had paper currency which was fully convertible into gold bullion (i.e., not below a certain minimum limit) it was known as 'gold bullion standard'. The countries kept 100 p.c. gold reserve behind the currency issued initially but later that was considered to be unnecessary. All persons do not die on the same day; all persons do not convert their currency reserves into gold on the same day; all persons do not withdraw their money from the banks on the same day; insurance companies, monetary standards and banks depend upon this simple fact of life.

If a country cannot keep gold directly, it can keep its reserves in the form of foreign currencies which themselves are based on gold bullion standard. IMF balances and other securities can also be kept as reserve and this can be called "gold reserve standard". We can discuss them in details now:

1. Gold Currency Standard

Under this standard gold coins used to circulate and if there was paper currency also, it used to have 100 p.c. gold backing. Paper currency could be issued to save the losses of wear and tear in the coins. The purity and weight of the coins used to be specified and then fixed according to the ratios of both of them in other coin-currencies of the world. There was "free coinage" i.e., without restrictions, subject to the availability of gold, and free trade. Gold could be taken out and brought in freely under the gold currency standard, The exchange between two countries (suppose which are in the ratio of 1: 2) could not exceed the specie points. Suppose somehow the rate falls to 2.15 but all costs of sending the coins is just 0.05 per coin, then the exchange rate cannot be lower than 1.95. Similarly the exchange rate of the other currency cannot become less than 0.95 if there is a fall there. The fall there becomes appreciation of the other currency. All currencies in gold or/and silver standard (monometallism/bimetallims) were fully convertible into each other or gold, if the paper currency also circulated. Naturally the currencies were unlimited legal tender. *The standard ensured price stability but was deflationary in nature for growth. Shortage of gold hindered expansion of money and economic activities like investment. Internal and external stabilities were at the cost of growth.* The system was jettisoned during the First World War because of the shortage of gold and 100 p.c. backing of curency with gold was not possible. *The system failed because countries put restrictions on trade as well as movement of gold during the First World War.* The wear and tear losses were also great and newly minted coins used to be kept in reserve and old worn- out coins used to remain in circulation.

Gresham explained that as *"bad coins drive out good coins out of circulation"*. This was known as Gresham's Law and applies also to good. politicians being ousted by bad ones, or soiled notes remaining in circulation while crisp new notes remain in reserve.

2. Gold Bullion Standard

It had all the features of gold currency standard except that the gold coins did not circulate; they were fully convertible into gold bullion (in England the minimum lump (brick) of gold was of 400 ounces). The currency was fully convertible but only if bars of a critical minimum amount were required. There were no restrictions on the trade and export/import of bullion. Loss of gold due to wear and tear was avoided. Printing of currency was cheaper than minting of coins. National and international confidence in currency remained intact. As less than 100 p.c. gold reserves became a practice, it provided greater elasticity and the deflationary effect on the economy was reduced to that extent. It became possible for the "second ranking" countries i.e., poorer countries also to adopt this standard.

A great problem in the gold currency standard used to be hoarding of coins and that was avoidable in gold bullion standard. The conversion of currency was not in coins but in bars. This standard was also believed to be auto-correcting in practice without the regulation of the government. From the old norms, the standard was considered "less reliable" than the gold currency standard; from the present day norm it was also very restrictive.

3. Gold Reserve Standard

Gold was not standard of value much less a medium of circulation. This was non-gold standard for domestic market and a sort of gold standard for international market. The system was in vogue in a limited countries between 1936 and 1939. The leading countries used to have foreign exchange equalisation account of gold and the gold used to be transferred if exchange rate fluctuated more than agreed upon. The member-countries which were having these reserves kept everything secret. Rising price of gold in one country meant falling exchange rate of the currency of that currency and vice versa; to avoid that there used to be gold transfers from the equalisation funds.

4. Gold Exchange Standard

It was a system of "inverted pyramid". The currency of one country which itself was on gold standard used to be kept in the reserve for expansion of the domestic currency. Pound Sterling was the reserve currency for many countries under England. Java used to have in reserve the currency of Holland (the present Indonesia was earlier known as "East Indies".) India used to have sterling securities also in reserve. India had paper currency and token coins. Indian rupee was not convertible in gold but in Pound Sterling. Gold could be bought to be remitted in exchange for imports, if need be; or else, the payment could have been made in Pound Sterling which was infact regarded as better currency than dollar. In *December 2000 the exchange rate of dollar and pound via cross exchange rate of Indian rupee was in the relationship of 1 pound sterling = 1.443 dollars. On Dec. 24, 2009 one us $ was equal to Rs. 46.77 and one £ to Rs. 74.87 and one Euro equal to Rs. 67.37. Thus one Euro was equal to $ 1.44.*

Indian rupee was in the same relationship as India was vis-a-vis England—subjugated. The system was economical, less wasteful, less costly and yet sound as Pound Sterling. However, the fate was linked to England. If Pound became weak or was devalued, Indian rupee too had to be devalued as happened immediately after II World War and India's Independence.

5. Gold Parity Standard (Early IMF Standard)

The member countries of the IMF declared their "par values" in terms of gold or dollar at the time they became members. Then the par values, were changed because of the *'inflation differentials' between two countries.* If country "A" had 10% inflation and country "B" had 20% inflation in the same year, the currency of "B" country will experience depreciation in its exchange rate by 10% or will face devaluation. Since there can be (or could have been) hundreds of cross-exchange rates (inflation differentials will be different with different countries) to avoid the chaos, this was calculated with reference to gold, dollar and/or some key currencies only.

This was a new form of 'gold exchange standard'. Gold coins or convertibilities were not there but gold kept in the reserves of the Central Banks of the countries. *All monetary policies were free except that inflation had to be ultimately accounted for.* And, inflation could be due to several other non-monetary reasons. The facts of life were simple. If a currency unit cannot command "prestige" at home (because of its falling value due to inflation); it cannot command the same "prestige" outside and had got to be devalued.

The great fall of dollar and dethroning of gold from IMF order:

After 1949, the USA got involved in protecting Formosa (now known as Taiwan) from the communist government of China. It intervened China wanted to take and South Korea was saved with the intervention of the USA. USA was involved in Vietnam war and here also there were North and South Vietnam. US encircled the erstwhile USSR through NATO, CEATO and CENTO, the last two no longer exist but Pakistan was member of both. USA spent its dollars more lavishly than one would spend sea water living near sea coast. There were dollars everywhere. Everyone wanted to have dollars but after some time they wanted to convert dollars into gold. The US soldiers were spending millions of dollars on "pleasure girls" in these countries. When the countries of Europe and Asia started tendering the dollars back to US to get goods/gold, the USA preferred to give gold so that the dollar price (its exchange rate) did not fall or the gold price did not rise. The USSR and France were profoundly interested in seeing' that the gold prices rose because they had a lot of gold. Rising gold prices meant falling dollar prices. The **rate at that time was $ 35 per** ounce of gold. The **USA** lost almost more than three-fourth of Its gold stored In Fort Knox and then declared **that It** could **no longer** sustain the pressure. It allowed the gold prices to rise but tried to maintain dollar rate at official parities. It could not do that. Gold prices rose In 1973 to $ 444 an ounce. The dollar had a mighty fall. In 2009 Dec the rate was $ 1219 per ounce of gold. Then the USA got it excluded from the IMF's system. Now dollar price (exchange rate and the gold prices as do the exchange rates of all other countries) fluctuate according to the dictates of the market. In 1973, dollar was devalued by 10 p.c. only.

That ends the story of gold standard or gold standards of all types. In 2009 IMF decided to sell all its gold in a decade.

6. Paper Standard

Now the countries are on 'paper standard'. The confidence of the people in the currencies of their own currency is always shaky. They remain afraid of the money values getting further eroded. Those who receive fixed incomes e.g., pensioners are. always in jitters because of the paper standards in the countries constantly losing their real values.

In India, based on the Chakravorty Committee Report, the following increases *seem to be justified,* though not exactly the same way as the Committee had recommended:

1.	For the rising population per year (say) per cent	2.2
2.	For rising aspiration of the people, proxy of which is the maximum grow rate envisaged in five year plan to	6.5
3.	Rising rate of monetisation (rounded off for higher side)	2.8
		11.5

Add to this 4 to 5 p.c. of the Milton Friedman! Thus upto 18 or 14.0 p.c.p.c. (minimum) increase in money supply is not considered dangerous, by the Government of India.

India's paper currency standard is not based upon any reserve in fixed ratio and keeping reserves is no longer considered sacrosanct. The money supply can be increased according to the needs for development and other programmes. If there is *money lead over goods lag,* there will be inflation and the government may go slow in increasing money supply, if positive responses in goods-supplies cannot be secured. If there is *money lag over goods lead* (which is not happening), then money supply can be increased easily.

In India the government is keeping minimum gold reserves; but there is no automatic proportionate backing of the paper currency with any deposit in gold and/or foreign exchange reserve. The fixed fiduciary system is *not* followed in the sense that 100 p.c. gold and foreign exchange reserves have to be there *after* the upper limits of currency have been reached; there are no upper limits for the currency. Gold and foreign exchange reserves are *not* there is any *percentage deposit relationship.* There is no *maximum fiduciary system and there is no proportional reserve system.*

The GOI Issues new money against the "I Owe You" (lOUs) in the form of treasury bills as reserves. If the GOI becomes short of money and there is no money in its accounts, then the treasury bills passed by it should be rejected by banks for payment. *But they are not; they are discounted by banks and if the banks become short of funds, they get them redlscounted by the RBI.* If the GOI cannot pay the RBI money from its collections against those treasury bills, the TBs get monetised. There is another way of saying the same thing. The GOI becomes short of money it auctions its treasury bills. Since they are gilt-edged securities, the banks invest in them. The RBI too can take them from the commercial banks on rediscountlng. Now a days the GOI pays 12+ p.c. of rate of interest on them. These bills are safe and *now* productive also. There is now restriction on unlimited monetisation. The limit is fixed in the budget, but never followed.

EFFECT ON INDIA'S INTERNATIONAL TRADE AND CONVERTIBILITY OF INDIAN RUPEE (STUDIED IN THE PREVIOUS CHAPTER)

Non-convertibility and fixed exchange rate regime existed upto the end of the decade of 1980s. Those who exported had to no right to use the dollars they earned. They had to be given to the Government at the official rate of exchange. Thus the exporters required import licences and foreign exchange to import capital goods and essential raw materials. Infact even to go abroad for exploring market foreign exchange could be denied. The politicians and the top officers, however, made merry in foreign countries. Then came the era of convertibility. Indian rupee is slated to be *virtually fully* convertible by the year 2011.

1950-51 to 1955-56	It was between $ 1.6 billion to $ 1.9 billion
1955-56 1970-71	It was between 0.4 to 0.6 billion of US dollars—Lowest.
1975-76	It was $ 1.7 b.
1980-81 to 1995-96	It was around $ 6 billion.
1990-91	It was $ 2.2. billion.
1991-2000	It *rose steadily to be nearly $ 32 billion* in Dec. 2000.
2006	It rose to $ 176 b. Forex reserves are mandated for six months' imports. They were available for
2008 (Sept) $ 286 billion.	13 months' imports.
2009 (Dec.) $ 256 billion.	

INTERNATIONAL MONETARY SYSTEM

GOLD STANDARD 1880-1914 SPECIFICITIES

Different countries had gold coins of different gold contents and purity. If "A" country had a coin of 100 gms. with 98 p.c. purity and "B" country had a coin of 50 gms. with 99 p.c. purity, then the first had 98 gms. and the. second had 49.5 gms. and the relation of the two currencies would have been = 1 coin of "A" = 1.9798 coins of "B". Apparently it was 1 of 'A' = 2 of 'B' so long as the weights and the purities were the same the exchange rate was also the same. *[For specie points refer chapter on exchange rate under "mint par theory"].* The exchange rate was determined with the gold points by the forces of demand and supply and was prevented from moving outside the gold points by gold shipments. It was auto-correcting system. If exports exceeded imports, gold would come in. There would be excess of gold and shortage of goods. That would have sent the prices up. Imports would pick up and exports would be discouraged. Opposite would happen.

If the imports exceeded the exports, gold would flow out. However, permanent deficit could not be sustained. Import created plentiful supply of goods only to be matched with a scarce money supply. Price fell and encouraged exports. Reverse process used to become operative. There was no need to *sterilise* the balance of payment disequilibrium and *there was no need for any monetary policy.* Full production and full employment could be achieved automatically in the long run. *Necessary signals were provided and correctives facilitated by a fluctuating interest rate for the movement of international capital.*

There were either gold coins or paper currencies notes which were fully convertible. The first was "gold currency standard", and the second was "gold bullion standard". Those were the "good old days". If there was silver standard in one country and the gold standard in another, again there was no difficulty as their weights and prices could settle the things smoothly, subject to the application of the law that "bad currency used to drive out the good currency out of the market.

The origin of the standard cannot be dated as no treaties existed about the rates. The dictum of international relation was "look after the trade and the gold would look after itself. *This was the unwritten law of gold standard and when this was not fully followed i.e., when the nations tried to partially sterilise the balance of payment disequilibrium with restrictions, the gold standard collapsed.*

The people had complete faith in the standard because the coins had almost the same intrinsic and extrinsic values. The "gold points/the specie points" determined the band of fluctuations in the buying-selling "values". People used to remain "puzzled" in those days why so little gold moved between the two countries in the *net* terms. There were no permanent and big gainers and losers. A slight rise in the interest rate used to make the people unload the gold back to the country, when it was loaded to be sent abroad for settlement purposes. There was "solidarity" in monetary standards of the countries. *However, the standard was deflationary in nature. To mint coins one had to produce and export; money shortage could limit investment that limited* income propagation and employment generation. It was a 'natural order of monetary discipline' which, however, hindered growth.

Though the world in the first decade of 1900 was much less developed (if compared with the present levels of development), the early decades of 1900s were dynamic. Industrial revolution was in its initial stages. All important countries of the world were on gold standard. The countries used to follow the "rules of the game", i.e., there used to be no restrictions on the, outflow- and inflow of gold. Convertibility of various currencies in gold was free. London was the financial capital of the world and a centre which transmitted economic and technical changes to other parts of the globe.

(a) The First World War 1914-1919: Crisis in the gold standard

The First World War introduced complete chaos in the international monetary order. The influence of Britain weakened considerably in the world and gold standard started losing its automaticity as restrictions on the free movement of gold and goods were imposed. Gold standard started showining signs of strain.

(b) 1919-1930: Changes in the gold standard

After the War was over, various countries of the world geared all their energies towards the development of their economies. The statesmen and economists of developed countries were emotionally attached to their 'golden past' and wanted to revive the gold standard. They removed restrictions on the free flow of goods and services and gold standard was thus 're-established'. Trade relations started developing. League of Nations (which later developed into United Nations) was established to maintain peace and promote trade and development in the world. During the World War I, when restrictions on outflow of gold were imposed, many countries had lost a lot of their gold.

After the War, the currencies of Russia, Germany, Austria and Hungary became "worthless". The exchange rate of British Pound Sterling was $ 3.18 per pound in 1920. It was £ 1=$ 1.968. Thus $ 1= £ 0.31 14 1920 and £ 0.508 in 2007. £ was $\frac{.508}{.314}$ = 62% extra in payment in 2007 vis-à-vis the year 1920. With reference to 1925 uk was paying $\frac{.508}{.205}$ = 148% exile. [we get.205 thus 1 ÷ 4.8666). UK borrowed lot of money from abroad to strengthen the pound sterling and the old parity-of 1 pound being equal to $ 4.8666 was re-established in 1925.

Between 1927 and 1928 as many as 40 countries returned to gold standard, some after devaluing the exchange rate of their currencies. Switzerland and Holland (the Netherlands) returned on their old parities but France and Italy had to cut the gold contents of their currency by nearly 60 to 75 per cent. By the year 1928 international monetary system was re-established on gold standard. Those who were charged with the responsibility of managing the monetary systems heaved a sigh of relief for they were no longer required to administer collective measures. However, soon only USA could mint the gold coins. Countries switched over to gold bullion or exchange standard. Then in the period between the two World Wars restrictive practices (restrictions on imports, tariffs, quotas, bilateralism, and controlled capital (outflows) became more and more common.

By the year 1931 Britain went off the gold standard and the pound sterling depreciated in relation to the dollar. France too started experiencing many economic problems. Then came the 'great depression'. In April 2010, £ 1 = $ 1.

(c) The great depression

It started from USA when sales of automobiles and tyres dropped down. Since automobile industry of USA heads the list of industies in the world, the remifications becames world-wide.

There is a saying in economic world: "when USA sneezes, the rest of the world gets pneumonia". From one industry to another recessionary conditions spread at a fast pace. Share markets collapsed. In many countries of the world, the exports went down because USA could no longer import. Construction activities came to standstill. In most of the industries the average rate of capacity utilisation came to around just 25 per cent. Unemployment reached its peak figures and factor prices came tumbling down. USA reduced its imports by 75 per cent (i.e., USA imports remained at 25 per cent of the pre-depression level). UK lost so much of GDP that in shillings, The heap could "reach" the sun!

The house of economists became divided. Some thought that the depression was due to classical policies; others believed they were due to not following the classical policies faithfully. Hayek belonged to the second group.

USA erected tariff walls under the Smoot-Hawley Tariff Act of 1930. Nearly 25000 commodities were adversely affected. Exchange controls became common; 'every country to itself became the guiding mentality. Less developed countries started losing their gold.

Keynesian anti-depression tools were not available. Some countries started following even the deflationary policies in the hope that exports will pickup; Malady became ever more compounded. People started withdrawing their money; particulary those who were unemployed. Bank failure assumed epidemic proportions in so many European countries. Britain had to abandon gold standard in 1931.

Many countries continued to pursue the policy of exchange controls, tariff restrictions and bilateral trade agreements. The 'great depression' of the 1930s divided the world in several blocs like sterling bloc, dollar bloc, gold bloc etc. To preserve a modicum of financial stability, small groups of countries aligned their monetary exchange policies.

(d) 1934: Devaluation of the dollar

In the year 1934, dollar was devalued from $ 20.67 an ounce to $ 35 an ounce. USA maintained this parity till August 1971, when the value of dollar could no longer be defended by USA. The devaluation of dollar in 1934s (by 41 per cent), brought inflow of gold immediately and USA got gold worth $ 4 billion (at the then prices) between 1934 and 1936. USA economy got a new life but the economies of other countries found life-blood (gold) being sucked out of them. All other currencies became over-valued in the wake of devaluation of the dollar. Therefore, other countries also started devaluing their currencies in 1935 and 1936. France devalued its currency twice in 1938. Exchange restrictions also became common. Germany experimented with multiple exchange rate system. Germany made itself economically and militarily strong (to wage war with the neighbouring countries). Protectionist policies were pursued by almost all countries, including the USA.

(e) The Second World War and its aftermath

Second World War (1939-45) brought massive loss of productive capacity in the affected countries. Earlier preparation for war (1936-39) had brought economic recovery in many countries. Production went down during the war and sea routes became unsafe: hence, international trade was considerably reduced. The question of international liquidity went into the background. Allied powers exhibited considerable monetary cooperation and pound sterling—which was the key currency of the world then—could maintain its exchanges its exchange value at $ 4 per pound sterling.

After the War was over, international markets had to be rehabilitated. It became necessary to reconstruct the productive capacities destroyed during the War. The need was felt for such financial agencies that could provide funds and technical and economic assistance to the needy countries particularly those ravaged by War. Economists started thinking in terms of two such agencies—one for providing long-term development funds and the other for providing short-term aid to overcome balance of payment difficulties.

Since Second World War was not fought on the soil of USA, it was in a position to provide monetary and real assistance to many countries. However, most of the European countries became heavily indebted to USA. The period between 1945 and 1950 was the period of acute dollar shortage in the world. Even its allied countries (Canada, Latin America and Western Europe) were feeling shortage of dollar. While the rest of the world was reeling under inflationary trends. USA was going in top gear. It was difficult to export to U.S.

SPECIAL DRAWING RIGHTS

This paper gold is not backed either by gold or by any currency. It is an *'international fiat money of account'* which is accepted because IMF has created it or IMF has created it because some member countries have agreed that some other countries can draw on them.

SDRs cannot be used by private commercial parties or even private banks. They can be used for book entries by the Central Banks of different countries. SDRs are allocated and a balance of payment surplus or deficit over the allocated SDRs will invoke 5 per cent (earlier only 1.5 per cent) charge so that all countries try to maintain b.o.p. equilibrium or do not deviate much.

SDR allocations are put to the credit side of a country and the debtor country transfers SDRs to the creditor country. The total sum of *SDRs remains equal to that created* because only book entries are made. *SDRs have not replaced dollars or key currencies because they have not been created in adequate quantities.* The balance of payment deficit even of the USA could not be corrected. The fundamental disequilibrium of the world monetary system could not be corrected with the issuance of SDRs. Unless all gold and currency reserves are converted into SDRs, the system will not assume proper importane. Then SDRs, will compete in future with ECU.

All IMF members have 250 basic votes plus one vote each for 1 lakh SDRs and multiples thereof. The IMF failed to create SDRs to meet the demand. When a loan is taken a country purchases SDR by selling its currency; and when the loan is repaid the country 'repurchases' its own currency (we do not call its selling back SDR, because one cannot sell what does not belong to oneself). These are reverse transactions. SDRs had modest success because there are not sufficient reserves of the same. Some Central Banks deposit their SDRs in other banks to earn interest. A few bond issues in the world have been denominated in SDRs. The exchange rate pegging is also done in SDRs.

If sufficient SDRs are not created and they are not linked to the development needs of the less developed countries, they will not assume importance. In times of raging inflation the good old economies of 'barter type clearance' and bilateral transactions will be preferred. The best situation will be multilateral trading in which LDCs receive good terms of trade and they can reduce their structural internal and external balances. In the absence of such things, the daily tensions will continue. (See more in chapter on I.M.F.)

NOTE

1. Post office deposits are not-included in the *'entire liquidity' (which is equal to M_3)* because of the following four reasons:
2. Money supply data is compiled and published every Friday the RBI but the far-flung post offices cannot supply data on that basis.
3. Post office deposits partake the nature non- banking deposits; the frequency of withdrawal is less and *so* are the amounts involved. Even with chequeable accounts, they do not become chain-sequence bank transfers.

4. Post office deposits do not become to the base for creation of credit.
5. Post offices are not members of the clearing house system of banks.

   Banks may be owned partly or fully (SBI is not fully owned bank of the Government of India) and there is a move to dilute the equity of banks to 33 p.c. as government holding. Post offices are "Departmental". The net addition in the post office balances becomes the *part of the "fiscal deficit"* of GOI. It is not part of monetiseed deficit and thus is not taken as increasing or decreasing the money.

On April 12, at 4 p.m. 2010

$ 1	=	Rs. 44.58	U.S. dollar
£ 1	=	Rs. 68.70	Pound sterling
€	=	Rs. 60.51	Euro
£ 1	=	$ 1.54	Pound v. dollar
€	=	$ 1.36	Euro v. dollar.

33 | International Monetary Fund (IMF)

A. I. IMF as **provider of International Liquidity.**

II. Sixty (60) years **of IMF; Functioning and** Schemes. 1944 to 2009-2010.

India is now not borrowing from the IMF for nearly a decade. India's quota in 1958 was 4.13 p.c. In 2006-07 it was down to 1.916 p.c. as many countries joined IMF. Quota are always add up to 100; they are out of 100.

A.I. IMF AS PROVIDER OF INTERNATIONAL LIQUIDITY

International liquidity would theoretically include all the currencies of the world. It is the stock of foreign currencies, gold and **IMF** tranches etc. which are with a country. Indian rupees with the Indians are not part of the international liquidity, but their stock with Nepal will become part of the international liquidity of Nepal.

In practice, key currencies of the world constitute international liquidity to which we can add gold reserves, SDRs quotas (see lateron in this chapter) and other constituents or components.

All currencies of the world do not have universal acceptance In the sense that they are accepted freely everywhere. Nor all currencies are freely convertible everywhere. Currency of Urundi and Brundi will not be accepted In India, except in the RBI.

Dollar is the proxy of all currencies of the world. EURO and currencies of a few Gulf countries and even pound Sterling command higher exchange rate than dollar but dollar is the VEHICLE CURRENCY of the world. It is a medium of international exchange, a measure of international prices, a standard and a store of international forex reserves. Countries can keep one or many currencies in their reserves. Most of them try to keep dollars as reserves.

IL is needed because countries need imports from outside. When a country exports it gets IL but if it is not sufficient for imports, IL is necessary as loans. Loans can be taken from foreign banks, WB (World Bank) and its associates and **IMF. IMF** grants loans for balance of payment difficulties but not for development. WB gives loans for development but not for BoP difficulties. If some persons keep foreign coins and currency units for the sake of keeping them as collectors of monies, they do not become part of the IL.

For any country, its international liquidity can be measured thus:

L = $R—R_{min} + F_{0} + F_{p} \pm CR_{min}$

L = Liquid resources.

R = Gold and foreign currency reserves.

R min = Minimum level of reserves to be "stocked."

F_0 = Official financing from abroad.
F_p = Private financing from abroad.
CR_{min} = Change in the minimum reserve requirement.

Governments borrow from the IMF when forex reserves dip **down and** certain **imports (e.g., food, oil** or defence goods) are necessary. In rare cases the **IMF** borrowings can be used for private imports provided they are strategically important.

If there is shortage of liquidity inside the country, the central bank of the country can print additional currency and/or ask the commercial banks to create additional credit. There are many measures which can increase the velocity of the currency through the promotion of transactions.

International liquidity is of "conventional" nature. There is no agency in the world which prints a currency common for all countries and all international transactions. Countries and trading interest accept the universally respected currency, which is dollar now. *Before the Second World War pound sterling of the UK was such currency.* **Gold** always was, still is and **shall remain** universally accepted, though it has been "dethroned" from the **IMF** system. [See the point later in this chapter itself).

International liquidity comprises of those currencies with which we can discharge the International liabilities. The US dollar and some key currencies of the highly developed countries have this position. The SDRs (special drawing rights of the IMF which are not in physical shape but are units of account) are important modes of settlement. *(See more about SDRs In this chapter itself).*

If the US dollar **(dollar written elsewhere, unless otherwise specified should be taken as the US dollar only)** is the main component of international liquidity, other key currencies are "near-International monies." **Reshuffling of the components of international liquidity is also there.** Most of the countries want to have dollars but as the value of dollar goes down due to the involvement of the US in **wars** countries swap dollars for other key currencies of which value is rising **or in gold.**

Therefore the components of the international liquidity become: Gold reserves + dollar reserves * other key currencies of the world + IMF quota rights + (see more about this in this chapter itself) +

SDRS + Swap arrangements + Standby Rights of the IMF (see ahead in the chapter itself).

The problem of international liquidity is faced by those countries which are developing. Those countries of which balance of payment is of deficit type face the shortage of international liquidity. Those countries which have balance of payment surpluses can provide loans (liquidity) to others. Receipts on international account exceeding payments, increase international liquidity of a country and vice-versa.

Developed countries do not face problems of international liquidity. The US certainly does not. **It can use paper to print** now dollar bills **(we call them "notes") and command the goods and services of other countries. If India wants to purchase something from abroad, it has to earn by exporting something first. But the US can use paper only to command goods and services.**

Of course, printing of excess dollars should cause inflation and then the exchange rate of the dollar will go down. But what actually happens is that a lot of dollar supply keeps on circulating In the world. This portion does not cause pressure on the prices in the US. If the countries which get dollars purchase goods and services from the US, then the liability is to be discharged with goods/services/monies of other countries/ gold etc. If the dollars are tendered to the Central Bank of the US then only the liability is to be discharged. This makes the US enjoy a status which no other country in the world; lucky due to being most powerful in economic and military terms.

Imblances in the demand and supply cause problems of shortage and excess of international liquidty. Those countries which have a higher demand for IL than supply will be deficient countries. They need assistance from IMF and all other possible sources.

Unconditional **international liquidity** includes gold, SDR, IMF tranches (Slices or shares of the countries) and key currencies of the world also come in this category.

Conditional international liquidity will include currencies of other countries than the most developed ones. If the currencies of certain countries are non-convertible they are the "most conditional." However, all currencies are to be respected. *[If one tears off a note in India publicly and throws it on the ground and stamples over it, one can be prosecuted for dishonouring the national symbol].*

Thus:

International liquidity is interpreted as the stock of resources within the hold of all the countries. It is used for meeting balance of payment difficulties. It is used to discharge past, current and future international liabilities. The reguirements of the international liquidity depend upon the demand and supply of the components of international liquidity for all commodities, goods and services which are not unecessary from the standpoint of the level of development and legitimate requirements of development.

We have used the word "legitimate" requirements. India cannot desire international liquidity which will bring it at par with the USA in one year. Similarly saying that India is short of international liquidity because we do not have sufficient IL to give one bottle of the best scotch whisky to every person of the country each day will be wrong.

There can be arguments about what is necessary and what is not. But the socio-economic development status and socio-cultural ethos decide. The use of IL In international transactions. *In short this is to say that we need not use IL for statis-fying the vanity of the super rich of the country before we have satisfied the minimum demands of the masses of India.*

The need for international liquidity is a combined function of the volume of international payments and the magnitude and duration of their instability. IL is increased if reserves are kept in assets of another country.

(A) There is no dearth of international liquidity in the world at the market price of loans.

(B) There is serious dearth of **cheap** international liquidity for the *developing economies.*

(C) Some countries have super abundant international liquidity: Japan is one of such countries. There are some countries which have serious dearth of international liquidity.

(D) After convertibility has been introduced in almost all the countries of **the world and the exchange controls** are all **but** gone, the possessors of international liquidity now include authorised dealers in foreign exchange also.

International Monetary Fund in recent years *has increased the depth of the dispensations but not the width.* In other words it is giving more but not for many purposes.

There is a tot of lot money circulating in the world. This is that money which moves from one country to another to earn profits on the interest rate differentials or making chance gain in currency speculation or bond investments.

Cloak room money is also there. This is that money which is taken from an unsafe and unprofitable country or centre to another which is atleast not unsafe. *If cloak room money finds a place of profit, then it becomes 'hot money'.* Cloak room money is in the temporary retirement of that much money.

If the deficits of the US and important countries increase, international liquidity increases automatically. But then their volitional dispensations (voluntry loans and transfers) get reduced. They increase when these countries have balance of payment surpluses. Then the less developed countries require more. *Match and mismatch in international liquidity (demand and supply) is an eternal problem.*

If a country has a high rate of inflation, it will face crunch (shortage) of international liquidity because its exports will go down due to being costly. It will require more money for cheap imports from abroad.

If a country has deflation, then its exports can go up but there will be so many problems associated with collapsing businesses and rising unemployment and falling income that the advantage cannot or may not be realised in terms of having high international liquidity.

The problem with economic states, variables, policies and corrective measures is such that nothing can be predicted. With luck the same thing can help or the same thing can bring a serious problem. This is due to what is happening to other countries.

World is dynamic-ever changing. Today's arrangements of international liquidity become insufficient for tomorrow. The problems are mostly faced by the developing countries. They have either one type of the problem or the other. Poor persons and poor countries are in continuous problems. The rich countries gain or extort gains from all situations of international liquidity. International liquidity should be so much that it is sufficient for a normal rising pattern of international trade, capital movement and moderate speculation in currencies.

IMF SCHEMES AND 60 YEARS OF HISTORICAL DEVELOPEMNT

1944-46 IMF was mooted, established, started functioning with total quotas of $ 1 billion. IMF does not give loans for development but for meeting temporary difficulties in the balance of payment. IMF allocated quota.

Quota is a responsibility **and** a right. If a country is allocated a quota of 1.98765 p.c. out of **100** then this much of the total quota of IMF will have to be contributed as funds. These funds earlier used to be in the form of *(i)* gold, *(ii)* dollars, *(iii)* currency of the country itself. *Their proportions differed; now the obligation to keep gold or contribute in gold has been abolished.* Some poorest of the poor countries can contribute their quota mostly in their own currency.

Quota as a right. One can withdraw from the **IMF** as much as is **its quota** ***but in dollars.*** **Here was the** advantage. Some poorest of the poor country could withdraw two times their quota or even more.

IMF cannot perform tricks. It cannot allow all countries to withdraw two times their quota. If one withdraws, other cannot. Hence some countries which were not borrowing from the IMF were enabling others to draw more than their quota. Quotas are released in instalments. Their recoveries are also in instalments. One cannot take out of a pot more water than what has been put into it.

The USA contributes more to the IMF but it can withdraw as the top loan taker.

The less developed countries want that the rich should put in more money and the poor countries should withdraw. The rich countries consider this "silly."

In the year 2003-04 the total quotas of the IMF were of nearly $ 400 b. INDIA's QUOTA was 1.916 p.c. in the year 2006 THE US QUOTA WAS 17 p.c. Quotas were revised 11 times. All quotas are out of 100. In 2009 IMF resources were equal to $ 600 billion equivalent in SD Rs. Quotas remain un changed in per centage terms.

1952-58 *Stand-by arrangements were introduced;* they arrangements are/were like providing an additional stapney to a car. In case of emergency *extra* loans could be promised and given.

1958-62 The total of quotas of $ 1 billion was raised to $ 15 b.

1962-63 GAB introduced i.e., "general agreement to borrow" was introduced. It was agreed upon by 10 top rich countries that they could lend 'more to countries than their quotas warranted. This amount was not related to the total quotas or *tranches/slices/shares* from the same for different countries. These rich countries realised that this additional lending helped their exports also.

1963 Compensatory Finance. Less developed countries suffered fall in prices when they had bumper crops. Higher exports too brought less income. Similarly when the crops fail, and the prices rise then also their total export incomes may fall. If the total income from exports falls, then IMF could provide the loans.

In the year 1966 India devalued its currency to cope with tardy growth in exports. That did not relate to the IMF but to India.

1966. The total of the quotas was raised, to $ 21.2 billion. That was done to provide more funds as the prices were rising everywhere in the world and the developing economies needed more funds.

1969 Buffer Stock Finance. Less developed countries are usually sellers of commodities i.e., produces of agriculture, horticulture etc. The less developed countries sell almost all marketable surplus immediately after the harvest as they remain in great "need of international liquidity. This makes the prices fall and the countries to sell at lower prices. This is known as "adverse net barter terms of trade." This leads to their exporting more goods to get the same imports (which is known as "adverse gross barter terms of trade). Ultimately "income terms of trade" i.e., income of exports over the imports falls. To avoid this IMF made provisions of giving loans s. that the developing economies have not to dispose off their exportable surpluses at low price. The holding power of the stock increases. The loans are to be returned within 3½ to 5 years. It is taken by the IMF that all countries will not have such problems at the same time.'

1970 SDRs created. (Special Drawirg Rights). SDRs are not currencies; they cannot be had in a hand. They are units of accounts. If India is given a loan of SDR 1 b. and India purchases goods from France, then the debit entry will be made in the account of India and a credit entry in the account of France. Suppose 1 SDR is to be created and suppose it is based on the dollar, pound sterling, EURO, yen and the currency of one more country (there can be ± 1 country, for example). Suppose the five currencies have weights of 50: 30: 10: 5: 5; If there is fall in the value of dollar by 20 p.c., then 50 p.c. of it will be 10 p.c. If the 1 SDR = 1 dollar was the earlier parity; it will now become SDR 1 = $ 1.10 and this way adjustments can go on.

This is an example. Actual position follows SDRs cannot be created unless the countries of whose currencies make up SDRs place funds with the IMF. The use of the SDRs is like the use of bank money through cheques and clearing house system. No cash is handled. Net result of the ± trade is settled ultimately with dollars (or gold or other currencies, if the countries so desire). SDRs help in bad times and help overcome short-term difficulties in balance of payment. Because of the availability of SDRs, the exchange rates do not fall or rise much. The actual position of the weights of SDRs was somewhat as under: (Mark and French France got submerged in Euro).

US Dollar	40 p.c. weight
German Mark	21 p.c.
Japanese Yen	17 p.c.
British Pound	11 p.c.
French Franc	11 p.c.

SDR is also known as "paper gold"

1971-73 This was the period of far reaching changes. The US was always involved after the Second World War in anti-communist alliances. There were SEATO, CENTO and NATO. US fought the communists in Korea, Vietnam and many other places. It was always having a cold war with the then USSR. Though NATO countries were on the side of the US but France was never happy with the "big brother" attitude of the USA. The value of its dollar was going down in the open market. Every country wanted to have dollars but not retain them. This was because the value (exchange rate of the dollar) was expected to fall due to its increasing supply. Both the USSR and Fiance which had huge gold reserves, wanted gold reserves prices to rise or the dollar prices to fall. The US dollars with the European countries were known as "Euro dollars." The dollars with the petroleum exporting countries were known as 'petro-dollars.' The USA wanted to dismantle the then USSR and it succeeded. Now there is no point in going in details. There were three main reasons for the collapse of the then USSR.

(A) The USSR could not innovate as much as the USA. Its production system became out of date. Productivity in all activities was low. People used to remain drunk with Vodka. Production was not as much as was shown. A lot of product was unusable and unexportable. Everybody's business was nobody's business. Production was down in farms and factories. The people of the USSR wanted levels of living as high as in the West. The incentives to become rich were not there in the then USSR.

(B) The USSR could not match military expenditure of the USA. The "Stars War" programme of Reagan made USSR's missiles mere toys. Military might was lost.

(C) The nationalities question cropped up. All Muslim regions of the then USSR wanted to become a separate country. Even some Christian regions opted out.

The countries which earned dollars began using them. They started buying gold fearing that rate of dollar will go down. They started buying other currencies. The holders of dollars started tendering dollars to the Central Bank of the US to demand gold/goods in return. The_US emptied 3/4th of the stocks of gold from Fort Knox where the gold is stored and which is under the sea to check price of gold from rising or to check the pries of dollar from falling. After that it could not. It made a feeble attempt to float dollar in the market and to maintain official parity in government to government relations. Then *dollar was allowed to get devalued. It came down to one-tenth of the previous rate immediately vis-a-vis the gold.* Gold instead of coming in $ 35per ounce changed to $ 440 per ounce. *It recovered thereafter, but never to $ 35 ounce.* In 2009 Dec, the rate was $ 1219 per ounce of gold.

The US dethroned gold from the IMF. No country was required to contribute **to its quota in gold. Gold was sold in** the open **market in a phased manner so that the** price **did not** fall. The **profit was used to increase the global liquidity.**

Oil Facility/: 1972 The Arab countries wanted to annihilate Israel-once for all. They raised the prices of petroleum crude from $ 1.2 a barrel to $ 42 a barrel. [Thereafter it came down to half that amount but again shot up to $ (nearly) 80 (position of September 2006) due to Iraq war]. The maximum was reached at $ 154 a barrel. In Dec. 2009, it was $ 74 a barrel.

While "Oil facility" i.e., special and extra **loans** were granted **by the IMF in the aftermath of 1972,** the same **facility** was not **given in 2004.** The earlier facility was withdrawn in 1974.

1976 Quota Adjustments (6th) in SDR and dollars were done. The accumulated 3rd to 6th quotas, the new quotas of the IMF were $ 44 b, equivalent to the SDR 39 billion.

1981 Seventh quota revision brought SDR quotas to 58.6 billion and in terms of dollar it came to $ 73 b.

As written earlier the SDR was made to base upon 5 currencies instead of 12 in 1970.

1982 Mexico, Brazil and Argentina were given very special packages of aid.

1983 Eighth quota revision took quotas to SDR 90 b. and in terms of dollars to $ 96 billion. [SDR and dollar rates do not remain the same in each year].

1985 Some very special schemes of writing off of the loans of very poor countries were taken. Not only interest but part or full principal was also written off. It was like a drop in a ocean, though.

1986 & 1987 Structural Adjustment Facility (SAF) and Enhanced Structural Adjustment Facility (ESAF) were introduced. *This was nothing but helping the countries in adopting LPG models of development.* **(Liberalisation,** privatisation and globalisation). The IMF **facilitates that. The developed** countries have vast scope of investing capital and exporting everything for the development of the private sector in-these countries.

LPG is **now the international model. One should have no objection. However, if corruption and unemployment** are there **LPG model will increase poverty and inequalities.** Theoretically "LPG with human face", as Government of India wants, is right *but is not a ground reality.* The high powered persons (politicians, bureaucrats, officialdom, economic vested interests and mafia groups) are hijacking India's development for themselves. IMF can do nothing against them.

Forty industrialised countries, contribute towards the loanable funds under SAF & ESAF.

1988 "Contingency Window" was "opened" in the sense that a special cell was introduced to examine the case of those who cannot repay IMF loans. Provision of writing them off is there.

1990 IMF quotas increased to SDR 135 b. or to $ 183 b.

1991-1992 Soviet Union broke up: and 14 break-away countries were made members of the IMF. *Quotas were suddenly increased by 50 p.c.* The adjusted quotas became SDR 202.5 billion or $ 275 b. This was the 10th revision.

1993 Systematic Transformation Facility (STF) was introduced for the benefit of those countries which left socialism and were to adopt LPG model of development. The loanable funds were increased by 20 p.c. for 14+1 (Russia).

1994 to 2000 ESTF and **GAB** were extended to the heavily indebted countries. **50 years of IMF were completed in 1994.**

2000 to 2006 The eleventh quotas got revised and revised to $ 400 b. **or SDR** 297 billion. **From 1: 1 parity,** now 1 SDR was equal to 2.0304566 dollars. IMF membership increased to 184 countries....the same as of the **WB.**

CRITICAL EVALUATION. We will be brief about our points. (1) IMF facilities are inadequate. (2) The developed countries have been put in win-win situations and the developing economies in lose- lose situations. (3) It is criminal on the part of the IMF to suggest down-sizing employment. (4) *Development and employment generation should go together.* (5) National governments of poor countries deserve condemnation for the massive corruption **and** unemployment they have brought in the developing economies. **World** Bank **and IMF** should help in solving problems associated with poverty.

IMF 2006–2009-2010 AND INDIA

IMF has now made it a habit that it advises the developing economies to_cut fiscal deficits and to cut down public expenditure. If public expenditure is cut down the axe falls on the expenditure for the benefit of the poor. India, except for some States, has now horrible roads. The primary public education has deteriorated in quality, notwithstanding the false "development reports" of the government. The general wards of the government hospitals are hell—if one wants to see what hell looks like. *Each State is keeping lakhs of posts vacant, though budgetary sanctions are obtained.* Some States are not paying even salaries to the employees for the last 10 years of so. Many governments came at the Centre; they too remained silent. Rate of reduction in the interst rates is transferring annually Rs. 90,000 crore from household sector to the rich through the nationalised commercial banks. On the deposits of Rs. 15,00,000 crore, the depositors are now getting 6 percentage points less. IMF has made even the future of the employees uncertain. The contractual provident fund rate has been slashed. **India did not** equalise the rates of interest **in rural India** where they are very high between 36 p.c.p.a. **to 60 p.c.p.a.** as the rates are quoted as Rs. 3 to 5 per hundred per month. IMF says that the governments are doing that themselves and blame the IMF and WB. There **is** truth in that because **for a few billions of dollars,** the economy **of** trillions of dollars is adjusted. Governments say that they are falling in line with the international strategy, **critics of the World Bank and** IMF say that **the** "best **thing they can do is *to* disappear"**

'We should, however, agree with the IMF and WB advise that all public sector undertakings must earn a commercial profits. If not, should not incur losses.

The President of the World Bank remains **a** US **person** while the **MD of IMF remains from the EU.** Though 160 of the 184 countries that are members are from the poor nations, their presence is neither reflected in the voting system nor in the distribution of upper level posts. Nearly 85 p.c. of the *top and influential posts go to the rich countries.* **Opinion of the less developed countries** *does* **not** count. They **opposed Iraq war after the US twin** towers **of economic** power were **felled down. Both were tragedies but the opinion** of the Secretary General **of** the **UNO who** does **not** belong to the US or **EU races too did not count. India's quota** was **4.1 p.c.** in 1958 and **1.95 p.c. in 1998. It was reduced to 1.916 p.c. in 2006.**

This was because of the entry of new members.

WORLD BANK ACTING IN TANDEM WITH THE IMF

* Top officials of **IMP** started demanding that the developed western countries **should dilute their** power over the IMF and if possible give it up altogether so that **IMF** can function independently of their influence. It is emphasied by the officials of **IMF** that though China is the fourth largest economy of the world, its share is just 3.72 p.c. **after 2006** revision. **Tiny Belgium has greater share than India and Brazil.** The UK and France have both 5 p.c. shares each and Germany has 6 p.c. share. **[Larry Elliott and Richard Adams, Guardian Newspaper Ltd. 2006: ToI in April 2006].**
* IMF was worried about the rising oil prices. As written elsewhere also in this book, the crude oil prices which were 1.2 dollar per barrel were $ 74 per barrel on 1st May 2006. The **oil producing countries were "magnets": they were sucking the wealth of the world. The US was using its printing press to print dollars but other countries were not having this advantage of having a "vehicle" currency of the world.** The developing economies were exporting more and more real goods to get the same quantities of oil. Oil producing countries want to take the price to $ 100 a barrel.
* IMF was also worried about the impact of'bird flu' on the economies of many countries. **IMF wrote off the entire IMF debt of Camoroon, one of the poor countries of Africa.**
* **IMF and the World Bank in their joint meetings in April 2006 emphasised that the big economies should practice 'transparency' in international trade, business and monetary flows. They also insisted that the fiscal deficits be brought down now over 3.5 p.c. of the GDP in** any case.
* **HIPC Initiative.** Both the Institutions are now engaged in **Enhanced Heavily Indebted Poor Countries (HIPC) Initiative i.e., 'relief from the old debts'. There were 29 HIPC countries for action of IMF and the WB on** the agenda.
* WB and IMF have now started monitoring the growth processes in developing economies. They predict that 7 p.c. growth rate per annum is possible in India and ASEAN countries. That will depend upon how countries can tackle the oil crisis.

* Control on inflation through fiscal discipline, freedom of flows FDI and FII, and pursuit of higher productivity norms a emphasised by them.

IMF IN SERIOUS CRISIS MODE: Doctor Heal Thyself Syndrome

IMF was/is supposed to help those countries which are in serioi talance of payment difficulties. IMF itself was in serious financial trouble, *so* much *so* that it had to freeze the salaries of its staff.

IMF was in serious deficits its deficit are expected to be of SDR 142 million in 2008-09 (SDR means special drawing right.

Three reasons can be listed for the present troubles:

1. IMF gives loans to very poor countries @ 0.5 p.c.p.a.
2. IMF was charging quasi-market rates of interest (Quasi means around half, but not exactly 50 p.c.), from the countries of Latin America and Eastern Europe which has countries which were formerly communist countries. Market mechanism has eased their troubles. Their periods of *crises* are nearly over. Now they borrow less from the IMF. Hence income of the IMF is down.

The biggest trade deficit in the world a massive $ 700 billion is run by the US, which can print dollars. The petroleum exporting countries may retain them. Or, the USA may succeed in selling them **arms to** recycle the dollars. Arms are very costly because of the destructive technology they embody.

When IMF was established, there was serious dearth of international liquidity in the world. The market rates of interest on loans were from 12 p.c. to 18 p.c. Now they are down to one-third level in the developed countries. The world is flushed with funds.

IMF lends too little with too many conditions. Hence governments prefer the market for non-concessional loans. (They can be raised by selling bonds).

It is clear that if the US deficits in "TRADE" (not in balance of payment) are $ 700 billion i.e., $ 70,000 crore or equivalent to Rs. 31,50,000 crore (1.2 times the India's money supply in May 2006). It can be imagined how much inflow are there in other countries. The bank of these countries are indundated with funds. The Government of India which is anti-domestic savers was feeling shortage of funds in its banks in April, 2006. These shortages were due to two reasons. One, as usual, the big borrowers were not returning the loans. Secondly, the depositors were diverting funds to financial Institutions like post offices (they are not banks), Like, mutual funds and share markets.

The GoI preferred to get equivalent of Rs. 15,000 crore from outside in a single week rather than increase the rate of interest on deposits by even 0.25 p.c. what to say by 0.5 or 1 p.c. GoI prefers to squander paying interest in dollars to foreigners rather than paying rupees to Indian savers, which amounts to more transfer of money inside the country.

When the IMF was established, dollar was the only convertible currency of the world. The capital market was not developed. Now it is highly developed. Even in the early years after 1945, the rich countries were borrowing more than the poor countries. Now the capital market is developed. The big savers of the rich countries invest not only in government bonds but in private bonds also.

The Importance of IMF Is not over because It lends at 0.5 p.c. rate of Interest/ and the poor countries find that very helpful.

A change that has taken places between (say) 1947 and 2006 Is the emergence of corrupt governments (politicians and administrator) which were not there In 1947. The fiscal deficits are squandered by the corrupt high powered persons on themselves and their cronies and relatives.

IMF voting rights depend upon GDP and per capita income also. US has 17 p.c. votes or quotas. UK, Germany, France and Japan have another 22 p.c. votes. Canada and Italy have 8 p.c. votes. Belgium has 2.1 p.c. votes higher than India 1.916 p.c. The above 8 Countries have 50 p.c. votes. China (3.72), S. Korea (1.35), Mexico (1.45) Turkey (1.55), UK (4.94), Japan (6.13) Germany (5.99).

India had forex reserves of $ 266 b. in the fall of the year 2007 and $ 256 in Dec. 2009. Now India does not need WB funds which come in a few millions of dollars. The WB has become/ sort of redundant/ in the global finance. The world has enough liquid funds that can flow across the continents in a jiffy through E'Banking. Now poorest of the poor nations need WB finance and that too at concessional rates.

The World Bank took the initiative in 2007 to provide funds to change the coal based power plants into modern ones which will have less breakdown and repairs and will have higher plant load factor (*i.e.,* the utilisation rates in 365 days with less number of days for shut down).

IMF AND INDIA 2007–08–2009–10

US economy was weaker in 2008 and 2009 due to various financial scams, real estate scams and huge military spending abroad. The result was that countries started preferring dollar less for keeping it as the reserve currency. Countries started preferring EURO and above all the gold. The demand for gold changed pattern; only one-fifth of the demand for gold was for jewellery and four-fifth was for keeping it as hedge asset. Its value rose and in November 2009, the price of one ounce of gold was nearly $ 1200. It was $ 444 in 1971 and $ 35 only in 1970. IMF sold gold in 2009.

IMF sold gold on preferential basis to China, India and Russia. IMF had 3217 metric tones of gold in 2009. It sold 403.3 metric tones in 2009 and 191.3 tonnes in 2010. Only the US and Germany had more gold than IMF. IMF decided in 2009 that gold was to be sold directly to the central banks of the countries. But the possibility of selling it directly in the open market was not discounted. The IMF had in mind selling about 2000 tons of gold in five years, may be up to the year 2013, (2009, 2010, 2011, 2012 and 2013).

The 403 tonnes of gold were worth $ 13 billion at the then prices. There were 186 big and small countries that were members of the IMF in 2009. The IMF informed the world that the gold was being sold to help the poor countries with finance. The top 20 countries known as G-20 decide this. IMF cannot get additional funds from the members by way of their increasing their quotas in absolute amounts. The position is that the poor countries want that the rich countries should provide fund and they should get it. That is not possible under IMF quota system. If quotas increase in absolute amounts they increase for all. Those who subscribe become entitled to get more loans from the

IMF. The poor countries can get more loan if rich countries do not exercise their rights to borrow. Selling gold was a better option.

India decided in 2009 to lend $ 10 b. to IMF. It is well known that India keeps at least 35 p.c. of its forex reserves abroad, including in the US to earn interest. India's lending to IMF was an exercise to ensure that it sets its quota raised so that it has higher voting rights. It is to be kept in mind (again) that the IMF quotas as distributed out of 100. Hence if India's quota will rise it will rise by a small percentage and at the cost of some other countries.

India bought as much as half of the gold sold by IMF in 2009 i.e., 200 tonnes for $ 6.7 billion. *By the end of 2009, India total forex reserves were of the order of$ 285.5 billion. Out of this sold reserves were of $ 10 b. only but with this purchase they became $ 16.7 b. i.e., nearly 6 p.c of the total forex reserves. India is the 10th most important country in the world which holds sold as official reserve to this extent.*

India reportedly is the biggest holder of unofficial reserves of gold in the world in the form of jewellery. It is held by the ladies of India!

In 2009, there was a NAB i.e., new agreement to borrow and it was to be taken to $ 600 b. after the IMF is having sale proceeds of the gold. Imagine that in 1972, the IMF had provided relief to the world to the tune of $ 1 b. only when the OPEC (Organisation of the Petroleum Exporting countries) raised the price of petroleum crude by 42 times i.e., by 4200 p.c. from $ 1.2 a barrel.

For the next ten years, unless something extra-ordinary happens in the world, the dollar is expected to retain the eminent position in the world as currency of reserve. Even if total holdings go down to less than half, the holdings will be the largest of any currency. The Renminbi of China will emerge at the margin to be followed by Indian rupee sometime in future. However, both of them together may not account even for 1 p.c. of reserve holding in the world. They may be currencies of future. The USA does not want the devaluation of its dollar that is happening in de facto way. It wants that other currencies should be revalued i.e., exchange par be hiked or raised so that they become costly. That will affect their exports adversely. The US is interested in seeing that Yen, Renminbi and Indian rupee go up. China exports much. It is establishing close diplomatic relations in Africa. It is holding its reserves tight and is miserly in importing. The US therefore pressurizes it to increase its imports. It soft-soaps it. It is a big market that is at the command of the leaders. Hence its leaders are pampered. The US pampers Pakistan also—ally of China. China has no fascination towards Pakistan except two. It also has claims over India's area and it keeps the Ughurs of China (Muslims) in good humour so that they do not revolt against China. Pakistan is a strange bedfellow thus. The US cannot pamper Indian leaders to increase imports because the importers decide about them.

China decided in 2009 to buy bonds of IMF to the tune of $ 50 b. In Sept. 2009 this was equal to SDR 32 billion. China exports a lot (but not the goods of good quality) and practises parsimony in utilizing the foreign exchange reserves. India is not regimented that way.

The dilemma of the US, as the US puts it.

"It is facing terrorism globally. The terrorist groups are not waging an open war but a war of pin-pricking and striking a blow or two too hard." The USA has (it seems) put all the eggs in one basket i.e., of Pakistan. It relies on it for helping it in catching the top terrorists and in dismantling their net work. Pakistan had been a member of SEATO and SENTO even in the 1950s onwards to encircle the communist USSR. It provided military bases to the US yet at the same time provided all that China needed to have contact with the rest of the world when China was not admitted in the UNO after its independence in 1949. The position had always been that Pakistan had nearly 50 p.c. of its foreign earnings by way of US grants. This was used in keeping the rulers rich, in forging anti-India defenses and a little bit in serving the US cause. Pakistan runs with the hare and hunts with the hound. That is its source of earning. Now Af-Pak policy of the US is costing it much. The US occupied Iraq for its oil rather than for WMD i.e., weapons of mass destruction". *In the year 2009 alone, the US dollar lost 12 p.c. value against EURO and SDR and more so against sold. Its fiscal deficit is 13.5 p.c. of the GDP (it objects India's 6.5 p.c. of the GDP). In 2009, 65 p.c. of the world official reserves were in the US dollars and 25 p.c. in EURO. Of the rest 10 p.c., nearly 90 p.c. were in gold.* Pak ISI outwits the US CIA. ISI creates terrorists.

US cannot lose a war to anyone but is losing prestige of the dollar. The US says it need not fear the Muslim world because they have only 3 p.c. of the GDP of the world. But it is at its wits end how to ensure that Pakistan does not remain a bottom-less sink of US dollars for it.

There were SDRs worth $ 317 billion in the world @ SDR 0.67353 per US $ and they were cumin seeds in the mouth of the camel. The US $ is in danger of losing its exchange rate further in future years.

In 2005, China was forced to revalue (upwards) its Renminbi by 2.1 p.c. but against a basket of currencies and not against the US $ only. For the last five years (2005-09), IMF "reforms" are under way. *Whenever the US goes on war, its dollar loses value and it forces strong countries to revalue their currencies so that dollar need not be devalued. The US is spending on wars and the supply of the US dollar is going up.* It sides with the US. The US errs. Others pay the price.

IMF also brings to the fore the fact that many countries which have high reserves also have high external debt. The following table gives the facts:

Country	Ext.debt. b.	Dec. 2008 Forex Reserves b.	External debt to GNP.percent.
Russia F.	485	4271	29.4
China	375	1946	11.6
Turkey	277	74	38.8
Brazil	263	194	18.7
Poland	242	62	47.7
India	231	256	18.9

This was the position by the end of the year 2008. It can be seen that China's forex reserves are 7.6 times that of India. Its debt/GNP ratio is also lower than India, just 61 p.c. *China's foreign exchange reserves are 520 p.c. of the foreign debt of China. India debt is 111 p.c. of the foreign exchange reserves. In other words if India were to repay all its debt, it cannot do so. It will have zero foreign exchange reserves. China is the only country with reserves being more than external debt to this extent.*

What India earns a good part of it goes to the Swiss Accounts also. Indian politicians are being caught with embezzlement; @ even 4000 crore per person. Reportedly the punters, corporate masters and even high officers are doing this work. India is rather poor; corrupt Indians are rich.

APRIL 2010

Global demand for gold was 3386 tonnes. USA was holding 8000 + tonnes, germany 3600 + tonnes, Italy 2200 + tonnes, France 2200 + tonnes. IMP, WB and Asian Development Bank will get $ 1100 billion or $ 1.1 trillion of resources in near future. IMF will get $ 750 b., out of which of 250 b. will be converted into SDRs.

EU has 32 p.c. IMF quota and USA 17 p.c. china had 3.2 p.c. India, as we sand, has *less than* 2 p.c. SDR had 44 p.c. weight of $ 34 p.c. of Euro; 11 p.c. of Yen and 11 p.c. of £ = 100 p.c. IMF now advocates that speculative capital flows need controls (2009-10). IMF estimated that $ 4.4 trillion will be needed in 2011 for stability and development. USA was pressing china in 2010 to revalue its currency, popularly known as Yuan.

China had the largest foreign exchange reserves in the world by the end of 2009-10, at $ 2.4 trillion or $ 2400 billion.

34 | European Monetary System and Euro Including Discussion on European Economic Union

Only EMS is the syllabus. We have given EMU also. We give something extra about EURO also.

HISTORY OF EMU

1920	The idea was first mooted for EMU and one currency by Mr. Gustav Strasemann. (See "Free" Wikipedia).
1957-1958	It was in 1957 that an agreement was reached about the common market for coal and steel between countries producing them. Lateron it was extended for atomic energy also. Thereafter there was a steady progress towards the EU. In 1958, the ECM (European Common Market) was formed by 6 nations namely, West Germany (East Germany was separated after the II World War and it was a communist country. Berlin its capital was divided and its western part was an enclave for West Germany), France, Italy, Belgium, the Netherlands (Holland whose people are known as Dutch) and Luxembourg.
1969-1972	Idea for monetary union was mooted. Preliminary details were worked out. There was serious crisis in **Europe following the collapse of the US $ in maintaining the parity of $ 35 = 1 ounce of gold. Dollar was devalued or got depreciated when even partial float was allowed. The rate became $ 444 = l ounce of gold !**" (Dec. 2009, the rate was $ 1219 per ounce). The leap-frog exercises were started in raising the oil prices in 1972, when the price of one barrel of petroleum crude was $ 1.2 only (It peaked up to $ 174 nearly in post Iraq war period after 2006.) In January, 2010 the prices were around $ 60 a barrel. The leap frog exercises were started by the Arab countries to get enough money (i) for annihilating Israel and (ii) for earning enough dollars to diversify development before the oil stocks exhaust. They may yet last for several centuries, but the world may have non-oil options of fuel and energy. EU tackled problems related to them.

1973	The UK, Ireland and Denmark joined.
1981	Greece joined.
1986	Portugal and Spain Joined.
1993	Sweden, Finland and Austria joined.

On 1, July, 1990, exchange controls were abolished and capital movements were completely liberalised In the EEU (as It was then).

The Treaty of Maastricht In 1992 established the completion of the EMU. Common agenda for convergence was there. It was related to inflation rate, public finances, interest rates and exchange rate stability. The Treaty came in force from November 1, 1993.

1994-1998.	European Monetary Institute (forerunner of the European Central Bank) was established. The name EURO was decided on 16th December, 1995. **ERM (exchange rate management mechanism) was decided.** At first the top 11 countries were to have ERM. On June 1, 1998 the ECB (European Central Bank) was established.
1999.	From 1st January 1999, the Euro as the real currency was there, **but the notes started being printed and the coins started being minted from 1st January 2002.** At that time the Euro was lower in exchange rate than dollar. The parity of 1:1 was not there. Then by 2006, the EURO started commanding nearly 1.4 dollars. During 2006-2009, the rate fluctuated between $ 1.6 $ 1.4.
2007	On 1st January 2007, Slovenia joined EMU.

See also the list of 27 countries where EURO is circulating: it is appended in this chapter itself.

EMU is known as EUROPEAN MONETARY UNION. Actually it is EUROPEAN "ECONOMIC AND MONETARY UNION". EEMU would have been better short form.

Not only there is a common currency but common economic policies. Now there is no problem of inter-country currency-differentials. There can be no trading in the currencies of the country. Exchange rates do not fall/rise and now the international or intra-bloc trade is on the prices of commodities, goods and services only. It is not additionally on the "prices of the currencies".

Under the ERM—I, the European countries used to follow the "snake in the tunnel policy". They wanted the upper and lower limits of the movements of the exchange rates of their currency vis-a-vis each other and more particularly vis-a-vis the US dollar to be within narrow limits. They targeted that inflation should not exceed 1.5 p.c.pa. and an insouciant attitude is to be taken towards unemployment.

There is a trade-off between inflation and unemployment. If a country wants to avoid inflation, there will be unemployment. If a country wants to avoid unemployment there will be inflation. Full employment without inflation could be had in highly regimented socialistic economies only.

European countries used to have nearly 12 p.c. unemployment of those who were seeking unemployment. It was a heavy price to pay. Interest rates were also controlled.

The EU countries used to buy back their own currencies and used to pump dollars in the economy), if the exchange rates of their currency fell. If they rose, they bought dollars to pump their own currencies in the market.

The European snake (ERM -I) was the decision of the original six members of the ECM (European Common Market). In March 1972, it was decided that the band of fluctuations would be 2.25 p.c. only. If the rate of any currency used to fall, then the member countries used to buy that currency so that its supply could be reduced and the supplies of other currencies could be increased.

EEC in 1979 agreed on the creation of the **ECU** i.e., European currency unit. **EMF** (European Monetary Fund) was formed for supporting ERM.

ERM-I became redundant with the introduction of the EURO. **ERM-II now manages the EURO against the US Dollar.**

There are rich and "poor" countries amongst the EU itself. A poor country is one where the public debt is a big percentage of the GDP. Luxembourg, Belgium, Ireland, Italy, Greece, Portugal and Slovenia exceed that norm. The norm is 60 p.c. of the GDP.

EU has 40 p.c. of the global trade. It has 40 p.c. of the gold (official) reserves of the world. It is now an economic power superior to the USA. However, the "national pride" of all countries remains. Just because countries are members of the EU, they do not yield an inch in football matches! This type of rivalry keeps them posing a challenge to the economic might of the USA.

EU is important for India. India is not important for the EU. India is not having even 0.4 p.c. share of the total trade of the EU. EU is slated to account for half of the global trade in a decade or so, particularly when the top car manufacturing companies of the USA were seeking advice from the Toyoto Company of Japan in 2007!

Most of the meetings of EU are held either at Brussels or in Luxembourg. There is a long term lending bank there known as the **EIB— European Investment Bank. It raises funds from the financial markets and gives loans and guarantees for enterprises for large scale projects, as well as to banks and other financial intermediaries for lending to small and medium sized enterprises. It is a non-profit making bank but does not subsidise its lending. The main objective of the Bank is to help in the balanced development of the EU. Priority is to be given to backward regions of the EU... e.g.,** East Germany is relatively backward to West Germany because of the past communist rule. EU is for convergence by ending the divergence.

EMC (European Monetary Cooperation Fund) is there. Members deposit 20 p.c. of their gold and dollar reserves with the fund and in return have access to a wide variety of credit facilities to settle payment imbalacnes in the **EC and to support the currency grid.**

ERM-II. It has to manage EURO rate vis-a-vis dollar and to allow 6 p.c. band to weak members or those who join late. The old band of 2.25 is still sacrosanct vis-a-vis dollar.

Germany has "veto power" in EU. The UK has not joined the EURO because of the national pride in the Pound Sterling. **EU and the USA are the most protective nations of the world. They form a strong opposition to protect themselves against the weak countries** !

EU, EURO and NATO are three aspects that are interlinked. The US and the

EU pulverised the erstwhile country Yogoslavakia into submission. The President of one of the Balkan countries was held captive and he died under captivity. Saddam Hussain (of Iraq) was hanged on 30th December 2006 so that he could not see the Id the next day and the new year of 2007 two days hence then). This was done by the USA and the E.U. connived. Destroying countries and then giving aid is big business for the USA and EU.

Turkey was to be admitted in 2007 but will now be admitted afterwards. If that will be so, then it will be the only Muslim country against the Christian **EU. Separate EU army is to be raised to full, other than of the NATO.** Russia is part of NATO but not of EU.

One shock to the **EMU** is the permanent withdrawal of the UK, which is of the same economic size as Germany or almost. There is a common **Parliament of the** EU but political unity is not there—still.

Advantages of the EU, EMU and EURO are: There is greater safety in trade and in international relations as risks that provoke fluctuations in exchange rates between the different currencies are reduced.

There is reduction of the cost of transactions within the EU.

There is greater transparency in the market that motivates the competitions between companies.

There is greater macro-economic stability through the harmonization of the monetary policy and of inflation rates.

There is disappearance.of the speculative pressures as compared to other currencies due to the importance of the EURO with respect to the currencies that it substitutes.

Thus: (1) The costs decrease for transactions within EU. (2) Uncertainty about exchange rates of member currencies goes. (3) All goods are labelled in EURO and price pattern is clear. (4) Finances are stable and efficient. (5) The single currency will be international reserve currency. (6) Inflation remains under control. However, unemployment rates are high in the EU.

The EU prefer to recruit the cheap labour from Turkey and pay the unemployment allowance to the natives. That is economical !

There is the loss of sovereignty and now the member countries cannot take independent measures to reduce unemployment in their country.

EURO

EURO was there in 31 countries and 27 "States" and "territories". (List appended).

EURO became the single currency of EMU and the currency and coins started circulating from January 1, 2002. EURO has 100 cents. Initially 12 billion bank notes were printed and 80 billion coins were minted. In France itself 7.6 billion coins had to be stored in 2 acres of land/surface.

For some months both national coins and EURO coins circulated, as the machines that dispensed the Coke and Pepsi and also the condoms could not be adjusted by that date !

Inflation limit was 1.5 p.c.p.a. Fiscal deficit limit was set at 3 p.c. of the GDP. Upper limit of the national debt was set at 60 p.c. of the GDP.

EU saved in the first year itself $ 65 billion in currency conversion exchange fees.

In the first year itself in Indian currency equivalent the saving was of Rs. 3,08,750 crore in conversion fees alone!

There is no buying and selling of currencies for price spread. There is no hedging or arbitrage for the erstwhile currencies. About four-fifth i.e.. 80 p.c. of the UK trade was with the EU and it was hoped that the UK will also have EURO. But it did not till 2009-2010 and there was no move to join EURO club and jettison the Pound Sterling. One great defeat of the USA was when the EURO crossed the value of dollar within two years. The USA had hoped it will never achieve 1:1 parity. If the conditions of joining EURO are fulfilled, the country can join the EURO Club merely by applying. The EURO Club wants to regain power equal to and then greater than the US $ in the world.

EURO started at 85 cents of dollar. Within one year it achieved parity. Now it is ahead of the US $. The USA, if it gains control over the oil resources, will emerge stronger. In Dec. 2009, one Euro was equal to $ 1.55 (cap) or $1 was equal to Euro 0.643. It was role seversal. In April 2010 one Euro was equal to $ 1.357.

The USA has offered India "joint efforts in discoveries of crude oil. If that is accepted, India will have to grant the US the rights to exploit India's oil fields. One is reading for the last 10 years that India has a "sea of oil" in Andhra Pradesh. In Barmer region in Rajasthan, people dig for water and the holes emit the gas. People cook food in punctiform space. There is super abundance of gas in India. India is asking for gas from Bangladesh and Iran. Is India afraid of the US offensive ? No one knows the mystery of India not exploiting its oil reserves.

The aim of IMF and the USA of US $ 1 = 1 EURO = 1 SDR does not seem possible now. The US dollar is going down. In desperation, the USA may resort to some drastic and unpredictable measures.

EURO IS USED AT THE OFFICIAL CURRENCY IN 31 "COUNTRIES" SOME OF THEM ARE "STATES" OR "TERRITORIES"

Sixteen more countries may join EURO by 2014.

It is to be noted that now 27 countries of the world peg their currencies to EURO.

Once upon a time, all countries which were under British occupation used to have Pound Sterling as the hinge currency. Then when these countries became free, they became members of the "Commonwealth Countries" - a group that still exists but is not politically active. The UK, Australia, New Zealand and Canada find more comfort with the Western capitalist world. Now Pound Sterling has lost the status of being the base currency.

Most important is still the US dollar but in future probably the EURO may become currency number 1 of the world. That may take a few decades.

TWELVE "COUNTRIES" where EURO circulates as official currency.

1.	Austria	7.	Ireland
2.	Belgium	8.	Italy

3.	Finland	9.	Luxembourg
4.	France	10.	Netherland or Holland (Duth)
5.	Germany	11.	Portugal
6.	Greece	12.	Spain.

Some islands are under some countries. Some of them are included and some are excluded from this category. They are not being mentioned here.

Four 4 Small European "STATES".

1.	Andorra	3.	San Marino
2.	Monaco	4	Vatican City

Seven (7) French Overseas territories where EURO is used.

1.	French Guiana	South America
2.	Guadeloupe	In Caribbean Islands. Some Parts use US $
3.	Martinique	Caribbean Islands
4.	Reunion Territory	Indian Ocean, South Africa.
5.	St Pierre-et-Miquelon	Off Newfoundland, North Atlantic.
6.	Mayotte	Indian Ocean, South Africa.
7.	Territory des Terres Australes et Antractiques Francaises	Southern Indian Ocean.

(In the above also some islands are included and some are exluded. though part of the main territory. Details omitted).

Five (5) Spanish territories in Northern Morocco.

(1) Ceuta (2) Melilla, (3) Some islands, (4) Islas Chafarinas (5) Penon de Alhucemas.

Two (2) Balkan Countries.

1. Kosovo and 2. Montengro. (Once part of Yogoslavakia).

31st Country.

CUBA. This is an important addition. The US is hell bent to destroy the economic-political system of Fidel Castro there. It is near the USA but adopted the currency of far off EU. The US hopes to change Cuba after (as it hopes) the death of Fidel Castro.

27 COUNTRIES/STATES/TERRITORIES FIXED TO THE EURO

Fourteen (14) West African Countries

1.	Benin	8.	Gabon
2.	Burkina Faso	9.	Guinea-Bissau

3.	Cameroon	10	Ivory Coast
4.	Central African Republic	11.	Mali
5.	Chand	12.	Niger
6.	Congo	13.	Senegal
7.	Equatorial Guinea	14.	Togo

Three French Overseas Territories (3)

1. French Polynesia.
2. New Caledonia
3. Wallis and Futuna Islands.

Two (2) African Islands where the currency was pegged to Portuguese or French Currency.

1. Cpe Verde
2. Comoros

Three (3) former communist countries where the currency was pegged to German Mark.

1. Bosina-Herzogovian
2. Bulgaria
3. Macedonia

One (01) North African country.

One (01) North African country

1. Morocco will become free trade area with the EU by 2012.

Four (04) European Union Countries (after 12 first group).

1. Cyprus
2. Denmark
3. Estonia
4. Hungary.

The Governments and the people of the following three EU countries did not still Join the EURO group (position as on January 2010). It Is also possible that they may never join.

1. United Kingdom.
2. Sweden.
3. Denmark.

Following countries EURO joined and the likely year is mentioned again their names.

2006-2007.

1. Croatia.
2. Romania.
3. Bulgaria.
4. Cyprus
5. Estonia
6. Lativa
7. Lithunaia.

2008-2010

1. Malta
2. Poland
3. Slovakia
9. Czech Republic

2010-2012

1. Turkey

For the latest get the information from the Embassy of the country concerned, if more information is wanted.

Currencies	*TT Buying*	*12.4.10*	*TT Selling*	*12.4.10*
U.S. Dollar	48.23	44.26	48.55	44.58
Euro	65.45	60.01	65.90	60.51
Pound Sterling	81.96	68.18	82.52	68.70
Jap.Yen (100 units37.34)	48.69	47.33	49.02	47.68
Swiss Franc	43.20	41.73	43.50	42.05
Singapore Dollar	32.56	31.81	32.79	32.06
Australian Dollar	31.86	41.05	32.10	41.36
Canadian Dollar	41.34	43.93	41.63	44.27
Swedish Kroner	6.78	6.17	6.82	6.21
Danish Kroner	8.79	8.07	8.85	8.13
New Zealand Dollar	28.72	31.48	28.96	31.73
Hongkong Dollar	6.22	5.70	6.26	5.75
Malaysian Ringitt	13.72	13.79	13.83	13.92
Kuwaiti Dinar	178.91	153.13	182.12	155.85
Uae Dirham	13.13	12.05	13.22	12.14
Bahraini Dinar	127.69	117.20	129.04	118.48
Qatari Riyal	13.23	12.15	13.34	12.26
Saudi Riyal	12.86	11.78	12.99	11.91
Ommani Riyal	124.79	114.56	126.58	116.28

On Oct. 10, 2008, The position was as under: (4.00 P.M) Euro 1 = 1.3594 dollars

Per dollar

1950	Rs. 4.79
1955	Rs. 4.79
1960	Rs. 4.77
1965	Rs. 4.78
1970	Rs. 7.56
1975	Rs. 8.37
1980	Rs. 7.86
1985	Rs. 12.36
1990	Rs. 17.50
1995	Rs. 32.42
2000	Rs. 44.94
2005	Rs. 44.09
Jan 8 2007	Rs. 44.60
April 12, 2010	Rs. 44.58

On PPP basis $ 1 was equal to Rs. 9.46 only. In USA the same basket of goods was 4.65 times costly.

Aug. 2008 Rs. 39.00
Oct. 2008 Rs. 48.00

NOTE

1. (Indian Bank publishes the rates of exchange DAILY at 4 p.m. Many newspaper* prorroduce the samel. Newspaper HINDU gives good commentary also). See last page of this chapter. India rupee appreciated against dollar, Euro and Pound sterling not due to India's strength but due to the weaknesses in the US, EU and U.K. economics. That was due to their involvements in war.

35 World Bank: International Finance Corporation and International Development Agency: ADB, Asian Development Bank

I. World Bank or International Bank of Reconstruction and Development. (WB or IBRD).
II. International Finance Corporation (IFC), 1956
III. International Development Association (IDA), 1960
IV. Multilateral Investment Guarantee Agency (MIGA), 1988
V. ASIAN DEVELOPMENT BANK

I. INTERNATIONAL BANK OF RECONSTRUCTION AND DEVELOPMENT (IBRD) POPULARLY KNOWN AS THE WORLD BANK.

EARLY HISTORY:

After the World War II (1939-1945), Prof. John Meyard Keynes (who was ICS officer but never came to India and worked in India House, London, before joining as Professor of Economics in Cambridge University), recommended the establishment of these twin institutions.

IBRD was to give loans to "reconstruct' war-ravaged countries and then to help in their development.

IMF was to provide short term loans to meet balance of payment difficulties.

The IBRD later on started being called as "World Bank" and that name has also become official. It does not give loans for balance of payment difficulties and the IMF loans are not linked to the development.

These two institutions are also known as Brettenwood twins as the decision was taken there. They were conceived in 1944. The World Bank was established in 1945 and started functioning from 1946. Lateron IDA (International Development Association) started giving loans of which repayment was to start after 50 to 35 years and which were given to cover operational expenses only. The rate of interest that could be charged was 1/2 or 3/4 p.c, only. IDA is the second window of the World Bank. For the loan taken in 1960, the repayment will start in 2010.[1]

The World Bank authorised India to receive Rs. 362 crore in 1980-81. That amount was Rs. 2219 crore in 1990-91. During the seven years from 1997-98 to 2003-04, the authorisation was for Rs. 23443 crore. The came to Rs. 3349 crore per year on average. Grant was given in one year only in substantial amount otherwise it remained between Rs. 1 to 6 crore only. The highest grant given was Rs. 392 crore in one year.

The loans taken from the World Bank are returned also and hence it is not to be assumed that all loans received are still to be paid. The total debt outstanding from external sources was about $ 120 b. in 2003-04, and over $ 136 b. in 2006. In 2008, world Bank sounded India that it was ready to give loan to India and India declined.—again as in 2007. In 2005, outstanding debt to world Bank was just $ 5.8 crore 2007, and in 2008, it was nil. In 2009 world Bank wanted to give $ 1 crore for cleaning ganga!

World Bank authorisation used was 72.8 p.c. only during these 10 years. All that is authorised is either not released or not used. In terms of dollars (the rates of exchange were different in different years), the amounts came to $ 458 million in 1980-81; $ 1237 m. in 1990-91 and $ 7027 million during the 10 years listed above. The seven year total thus was $ 7.0276 billion. It came to about $ 1 b. year: **$ 1 b. a year is now a paltry amount.** World Bank's total loans amounted to nearly $ 29 b by 2009.

The grant from the World Bank came to $ 94 million only

IDA IDA loans came to Rs. 1539 crore in 1980-81; Rs. 1698 crore in 1990-91 and Rs. 27173 crore during the seven years mentioned above. The average came to Rs. 3882 crore per year. These are concessional loans and 99 p.c. of the World Bank and IDA loans are used for the government projects or public sector. The share of the private sector comes to less than 1 p.c. infact. The total IDA loans in dollars came to $ 6.144 billion or 0.878 billion dollars per year. The utilisation of IDA loans was almost hundred percent. Now India does not get IDA loans.

ADB It provided a loan of Rs. 802 crore in 1990-91 and a total of Rs. 22404 crore in the 7 years mentioned above. Translated in dollars, it came to $ 5.493 billion in 7 years. ADB gave Rs. 242 crore as grants so far by 2003-04. Utilisation of ADB loans was to the tune of $ 3.816 billion only.*

Organization: It is of little concern for impact on economic development. The capital of the World Bank is raised periodically and is now nearly $ 200 b. There is a Board of Governors and big countries are represented by one nominee. The Finance Ministers of different countries, can be nominated to represent their country. The six permanent members are from the USA, the UK, Germany, France, China and India. The President is the executive head. There are several "functional committees" e.g., for loans, for special projects, etc. World Bank is a commercial bank and not a donor bank. One cannot take out of a pot more than what one has put in. The bank cannot create credit. It gives on loans the money provided by the rich countries. Market rates of interest are charged.

Commercial activities. World Bank charges 1/2 p.c. differential for itself between the rates of interest at which it borrows and lends. There are the usual procedures of evaluating the projects, seeking guarantees, examining the socio-economic profitability of the projects. The time pattern of returning the loans is settled. World Bank arranges loans. It seeks guarantees from the borrowing countries and gives guarantees to those countries which provide funds for loaning. The WB charges 1 p.c. commission on the overdue loans as guarantee recompense.

The Bank has personnel who can help in formulating projects, arranging the training of the personnel, provide technical know how and/or arrange the new capital goods that embody modern technology. It should be remembered that the World Bank had rejected the entire Amul project of India. It had advised India to import milk powder from the EU and oil from its favourite countries. Mr. Verghese, the founding father of Amul, gave India, not a project but a movement.

It is a big blot on the World Bank that it was against Amul project. The World Bank can settle economic disputes also which should, however, lead to World Bank stepping in with its loan to solve the problem. River water disputes can be solved between two countries, States of a country, for example, by funding a big irrigation dam.

Functions: Erstwhile World Bank President (who was one time defence secretary (Minister) of the USA) Robert MacNamara remarked once that the functions of the World Bank emanate from its view that 'poverty anywhere is a danger to prosperity everywhere', which words were spoken by the assassinated President of the US, Mr. Kennedy.

The main functions of the World Bank are:

1. To help in the reconstruction work of the war ravaged countries.
2. To assist in the development of the war ravaged countries in particular and all developing economies in general.
3. To help in the establishment of the projects in backward areas which will help in the establishment of the more supplementary and complementary industries.
4. To help in the development of infrastructure facilities like power, transport, communications, irrigation etc. so that there are maximum forward and backward linkages of projects and development schemes.
5. To upgrade the social infrastructure like public health, medical facilities, sanitation, education, professional education that makes people employable and public utilities.
6. To help in projects that ensure flood control, drought- proofing and to help regions after natural disasters. Also to help in the rehabilitation of wastelands, ravines etc.
7. To induce private investors of developed countries to invest in projects of developing economies by providing various types of guarantees.
8. To promote export promoting industries and to also help in the establishment of those industries which may be import substitution industries.
9. To give special assistance for environment improving programmes like social forestry, forestry proper, food forestry, environment forestry, grass land development, tourism development, housing projects, slum clearance, etc.
10. To help in modern projects like under-ground railways and to arrange loans even for the private sector for important ventures.

If war is won by nations; development is peace and is to be assisted by the World Bank. At least, so it says.

The World Bank publishes annual reports. Since its inception the WB has given about $ 450 billion, as loan to different countries. The percentage shares of different borrowing countries come to:

1.	India	12.0
2.	China	7.3
3.	Mexico	7.0
4.	Brazil	6.4
5.	Indonesia	6.0
6.	Argentina	3.5
7.	Korea	3.2
8.	Turkey	3.1
9.	Pakistan	3.0
10.	The Philippines	2.4
	Others	46.1

60TH ANNIVERSARY OF THE WORLD BANK AND THE IMF: APRIL 2004. POSITION 2009-2010 MARCH.

The twin institutions did not evaluate themselves in the 60th anniversary in the light of the evaluation done by developing nations of the world. The twin institutions are still working on the directives of the 7 advanced nations of the world and not on the basis of the suggestions of 184 nations that are the shareholders in WB. The President of the WB and the Managing Director of the IMF are still decided by the US, which as a courtesy consuls EU also—or rather a few important members of the same. Like WTO, IMF calls for transparency but does not practise the same in its selection of the MD or in its activities.

The World Bank has acknowledged that the UN targets for the year 2015 for Universalisation of the primary education, gender equality In schooling, and making significant reductions In maternal and child mortality will not be realised. No one criticises the US spending $ 500 billion a year on war. The proposals for even $ 1 billion., are kept pending for a long time In the WB and IMF. At present the US gives assistance to those which it "perceives" is aiding in fighting battle against terrorism. The US does not take any action against the country which is hunting with the dog and running with the hare! Any country not "okaying" all actions of the US and EU will figure in the black list of dispensations of the WB and IMF.

Real democracies suffer: real development efforts suffer: real poor are neglected. The nation or nations which pose as friends of these countries get largesses. The US and the EU do not recognize real and long term friends but "yes-countries" are treated true democracies by the WB and IMF.

India invested $ in IMF resources. In 2009-10, the world Bank wanted to participate in 68 projects in India with commitment of $ 19.57 billion. The world Bank wants to give $ 7 billion in 2010-2014.

INTERNATIONAL FINANCE CORPORATION (IFC) 1956.

World Bank gives loans for mostly public sector projects and IFC gives loans mostly for the private sector. IFC can invest in the equity capital of the private ventures and enterprises in different countries, developing economies in particular. All economies are designated as "developing", no country can now be called "backward". The countries resent such a designation. They infact retaliate by telling the countries which call them backward something as "decadent" or "uncivilized" or "imperialist". Hence offensive nomenclatures have been left. We designate countries as developed, moderately developed and developing.

The private industrial/business houses of repute or of promising nature can have loans or equity participation without the guarantee or the concerned governments of the countries. IFC can facilitate Indian entrepreneurs to receive foreign investment. At the same time it can help India in investing in foreign countries which are less developed than India.

If management is sub-optimal, IFC can help in improving all management functions. If management is good but capital is lacking that can be arranged. If necessary, both can be arranged for enlarging the scale and scope of enterprises.

"Scale" means making an enterprise bigger in economic size. "Scope" relates to producing a "broad-band" or related goods e.g., not merely TVs but DVDs also and then of various types. The IFC can arrange many bands of different lines of production.

IFC works in tandem with the WB but is not subordinate to it. As with other such institutions, the less developed countries think IFC as pro-rich of the capitalist world. The investors of the rich countries sometimes fear that IFC may lead them to blind alley and to unprofitable joint ventures or stakes in such countries.

IFC is not for minions. There is a critical minimum size or the projects; they should be big. They should be profitable. Above all, the foreign investors must not ever feel any snag in earning profits, repatriating them to their countries and retrieving their invested capital, if they so desire.

It is alleged that IFC Imposes "conditionalities". Such a criticism is frivolous. All those who give loans or invest will inquire about the soundness of the project.*

Starting from a capital of just $ 100 million, its present capital is nearly @ 2500 million or @ 2.5 billion. *Since its work is to act as an intermediary between the investors and those which desire investment, this capital is considered by it sufficient for the agency work and some stop-gap activities.*

For administrative purposes, the President of the World Bank is also a co-opted member of the IFC, as there are a few more members of the governing body or should be say, advisory body. However, as written earlier, IFC is not under WB. The WB has a large number of economic researchers, reporters, project evaluators from the formation to the state of successfully running the project or venture. No firm of any country which is not the member of the WB can take advantage of the services of the IFC.

The IFC does not help a foreign Investor to get control over other firms of foreign country by acquiring equity of more than 50 p.c. In other words, the involvement of the foreign investor has got to be not more than 50 p.c. This participation can be for establishment, expansion, renovation, upgradation, use of technological innovations, defensive investment for a product likely to become sunset product (as far as it can be defended) and investment in sunrise products. The IFC leaves the decisions to the investors and to the recipients. Rate of Interest charged ranges from 6 to 10 percent. The IFC supplements the ventures of the recipient countries and does not supplant them, not through IFC in any case.

IFC has no fixed lines of investment. There are investors who would like to invest in certain lines. IFC finds clients for them. There are firms which seek investment in their lines of choosing: IFC finds investors for them. IFC is the financial intermediary between financial intermediaries also.

We do not Agree with the Criticisms that are Found in Many Books that IFC Charges High Rates of Interest. All Financial Institutions of the World Cannot Become I.d.a.

IFC does the work of syndication of the loan. It is umbrella financier. Its partners share the profits and the risks also. It collects the funds and lends them in its name. Representatives of the investors, borrowers, IFCs can meet together and visit the investment sites also.

"A" loans are from its own resources; and
"B" loans are from the resources of others i.e., syndicated.

Between its inception and 2009, its cumulative financing was of $ 51 billion.

INTERNATIONAL DEVELOPMENT ASSOCIATION IDA (1960)

As we saw earlier this gives concessional loans for long term development and takes only a nominal service charge of less than 1 p.c. The repayment of loans starts after 50 years or 35 years. Hence replenishments were needed. When the developed countries gave money then only it could be lent. Since there was no recycling of the funds, the replenishments were necessary and are still necessary. Now it has been reduced to 35 years.

This is for "soft loans" as the interest is low. It is for social development because projects for people below the poverty line find great favour. Social infrastructure is regarded as more important for development of backward regions and people than high class economic infrastructure. If the IFC is for the "classes" (upper), IDA is for the masses.

On principle, all those countries which have per capita Income of more than $ 350 per year cannot get loans from the IDA. India "graduated" from that status. China was already above India. Yet both of them are getting loans: The reasons are China joined late and hence will be compensated for the period lost. India has highly skewed distribution of Income, the highest number of the persons below poverty line In any country of the world and the per capita Income on purchasing power parity basis is miserably low for a vast majority of population.

THE MOST IMPORTANT RECENT CHANGE IN THE FUNCTIONING OF THE IDA IS THAT THE EARLIER GRACE PERIOD IS NOW FOR 35 YEARS AND NOT FOR 50 YEARS, WITH WHICH IDA STARTED. IDA CAN GIVE LOAN ONLY IF DEVELOPED COUNTRIES BUT FUNDS AT ITS DISPOSAL FREE OF INTEREST AND FORGET ABOUT IT. IF NOT, IDA CAN DO NOTHING

There were 10 replenishments upto 1996 for $ 76 billion. The 11th replenishment is for $ 14.4 b. *From 1960 onwards there used to be massive International write up about each replenishment. The developing economies used to argue for high amounts and the developed economies were miserly.*

ONCE UPON A TIME THE UNO HAD PASSED A RESOLUTION THAT THE DEVELOPED COUNTRIES GIVE 1 P.C. OF THEIR GDP AS SOFT LOAN. THAT PERCENTAGE IS NOT EVEN 0.2 P.C. NOW.*

The loans of the developing economies are estimated to be $ 5 trillion i.e., $ 5000 billion. *When the WB and IDA write off loans of most indebted countries by amounts like $ 50 million or ever $ 500 million, they are cummin seeds in the mouth of camel.*

The rich countries cannot be blamed for all the ills of the developing countries. Most of the developing countries are "breeding grounds" of human beings. There is a great waste of high birth rates and high death rates. Dependency ratios are high. Unemployment rates are high. **Employment enables people to produce and then get purchasing power. Employment generation is not an expenditure only that the government/ employers have to incur. Employment is productive and income generating. It takes care of demand and supply both at the same time.**

Other than the malady of exploitation by the big powers and MNCs (who are contributing to development also), many of the rulers in developing economies are Satan Incarnate. They are the reasons for all the miseries of the developing economies. Hence the WB and IDA have become Indifferent to the case of development. The developed countries, WB and IDA consider developing economies as "bottomless sinks".

WB, IDA, and IMF offer suggestions or "structural reforms". These reforms are certainly reforms for development—but development of the already rich classes. India coined the term "reforms with human face", but that human face is not visible on grounds. Pro-poor and pro-employment programmes lack both national and international allocations.

IDA is known as the second window of the World Bank. Those countries which cannot get loans on commercial rates of interest can borrow from the IDA

One recent problem with the IDA is that the funding countries are not regular. All countries which are rich and are supposed to contribute to IDA replenishments, do not do so. Some have refused to contribute even a pence. Some contribute irregularly. Some contribute lesser amounts.*

MULTILATERAL INVESTMENT GUARANTEE AGENCY MIGA (1988) (Was Active In 2009–2010)

MIGA is an agency of the WB. The principal task of MIGA is to help the investors of the rich countries to invest in the investment lines that the developing economies want. It is concerned with foreign direct investment (FDI), which is considered to be investment in bricks, mortar and steel i.e., the real projects. Equity funds are utilised for establishing projects, erecting structures and installing machines. MIGA offers various types of services to the investors.

MIGA acts in tendem with WB, IDA, IFC and ICSID (International Centre for the Settlement of Investment Disputes.) MIGA cannot force the investor to invest in a country of its choice nor in the line suggested by MIGA. These things are not done. Nor can MIGA ensure a developing country that it can secure the necessary investment in the desired line from the prospective investors. It is simply an agent.

The gurantees to the investors are given by MIGA and MIGA first ensures from the countries/parties desiring investment. Projects, parties, governments and other factors are all evaluated by MIGA. Prospective returns/profits of the project are- evaluated and capacity to repay the loan or allow repatriation of profits to the investing country are guaranteed. MIGA says it reviews "environments": economic (returns), social (no hostility to investor) and legal (government maintains the law and order). No party can be a sucker of the other. Both countries have to act according to the laws of the other country. As modern information technology has developed beyond recognition, the aim of the MIGA that the work can be done within 4 months is being sounded for the work.

There are great political risks e.g., In the war-torn countries. A country can become "bankrupt" In the matter of repayment of international obligations. Such countries seek transfer moratoria i.e., postponement of the repayment. In rare cases a country can repudiate all external obligations. That is seldom allowed. The World Bank and the IMF ball out **but Invariably the rulers have to go and the economic policies are dictated by the WB and IMF.**

MIGA is related with the WB, but It has Its own Managing Director and policies. It acts In tandem.

Facts Sheet about The World Bank

- Between 1998-99 to 2004-05 i.e. in 7 years the authorisation (not utilisation) of loans to India was of Rs. 30484 crore. Average came to Rs. 4355 crore per year. Maximum was Rs. 8036 crore 'in 2001-02 and the minimum Rs. 368 crore in 1999-2000.
- Grants were nil in 1980-81, 1990-91, 1999-00. Loans in 1980-81 and 1990-91 were for Ra. 362 crore and Rs. 2219 crore respectively.
- Between 1998-99 (7 years the total grants received were Rs. 444...crore (average Rs. 63.4 per year). If we ignore the year 2000-01 (when grants were 392 crore rupees). The average came to Rs. 8.67 crore only. In 2001-02 only Rs. 1 crore came as grant !

IN DOLLAR TERMS

- For 7 years 1998-99 to 2004-05 $ 6.628 billion
- Grants $ 0.0353 in total
- Average of loans = 0.947 b per year
- Average of grants = 0.0050 6 per year

UTILISATION IN $

- Total Rs. 30900...utilisation is from past loans and hence it was more than 100% for 7 years.
- In dollar terms it was for $ 5.107 b. Exchange rate difference create differences in above two items.

IDA LOANS

- 1980-81 and 1990-91 $ 684 million and $ 744 million
- For the above 7 years $ 6.832 billion. IDA loans were concessional.

- In rupee terms, Rs. 31074 crore for 7 years.
  As exchange rates differed, the $ Rs. parity cannot be reconciled.

ASIAN DEVELOPMENT BANK

ADB, a multilateral development finance institution, was founded in 1961 by 31 member governments to promote the social and economic progress of the Asian and Pacific region. The membership increased to 57, of which 41 are from within the region and 16 from outside the region.

The Bank gives special attention to the needs of the smaller countries or developing economies of the Asian region. The main functions of the ADB are

1. To extend loans and equity investment for the economic and social development of the DMCs, (developing member countries).
2. To provide technical assistance for the preparation and execution of the development projects and programmes and for advisory services.
3. To promote and facilitate investment of public and private capital for development purposes.
4. To respond to requests for assistance in coordinating development policies and plans of its DMCs.
5. To reduce poverty, develop human resources, improve the status of women, protect the environment and to promote both growth and development.
6. The economic projects are 50 p.c. of the total projects and the socio-environmental projects have got to be the other 500 p.c.
7. Special economic areas are (i) agriculture and natural resources, (ii) energy, (Hi) industry and non-fuel minerals, (iv) finance and (u) transport and communications.
8. These projects are tailor-made for the DMCs and all project funding procedures are followed e.g., judging the feasibilities of the project, formulating and reformulating the same for maximum effectiveness, monitoring the execution of the projects that are financed by it and making changes if necessary.

ADB involves itself with such projects as AIDS/HIV control, controlling Avian flu, regional integration, trade development, employment and labour markets, health and education projects, competitiveness, and projects for future improvement in the technological upgradation. Macro-economic and fiscal policies are also reviewed.

ADB finances those projects about which guarantees are given by the governments of different countries.

Upto the year 2004, ADB gave assistance of $ 150 b. India got only 4 p.c. of the same. From the year 1988 to the year 2001, India got authorisation of $ 7.8 billion but It could utilise only 69.7 p.c. of the same. Nearly 30.3 p.c. could not be utilised by India. India supported a 200 p.c. increase in the capital base of the ADB in 2009, (free press Dec. 3, 2009).

This is considered Inefficient handling of the assistance of India. During the 7 years ending 2004, India got $ 5.5 b. (Rs. 22404 crore). Grants were for Rs, 242 crore only. The utilisation percentage during these last seven years mentioned above went down to 63.6 p.c. only.

India's subscription was $ 181 million i.e., $ 0.181 b.

All non-Asian members are from America and Europe. They are members of the ADB because They have a lot of investlble funds and they want to route them through ADB. They are not members to get aid.

Rich Asian countries get "OCRs" or ordinary capital resources. Poor countries like Nepal and Bhutan get grants. Short term loans are for 3 years on average. Medium term loans are for 10 years on average. Long term loans are for 30 years on average. The maximum period of grace can be 7 years. In other words, the repayment of loans can start from 85th month onwards.

ADB could not achieve much success Just as the World Bank could not get the success In all those objectives that tl reiterates. ADB cannot eradicate poverty In India. Indian Government alone can do It. ADB could not eradicate poverty even In Philippines where it is located.

Energy, transportation and communications are special economic sectors in which ADB is interested. ADB can finance all activities pertaining to the generation and distribution of power. It is also vitally interested in the rural electrification programmes. Thermal and Hydel both types of power projects are financed by ADB. ADB oversees power reforms also. ADB is giving extra importance for funding projects for the improvement of educational, medical, public health and family planning facilities.

ADB lends at LIBOR (London Interbank offer Rates).

The following table gives some important figures:

US dollars in millions.

	Region	2001-02	Annual average 1996-2002	Average Annual Share percentage
*1.	South Asia	2963	2149	34.2
*2.	South-East Asia	1365	2043	32.5
3.	China	882	1011	16.1
*4.	North Asia	38	619	9.9
*5.	Central Asia	385	254	4.0
*6.	Pacific	51	97	1.6
7.	Regional	191	107	1.7
Total rounded off		**5855**	**6280**	

The following table shows the ADB approved Loans by Sector in US dollars.

1. Transport and communications	1613	1328	21.7
2. Finance	865	1177	19.3
3. Social Infrastructure	670	1023	16.7
4. Energy	1018	835	13.7
5. Agriculture and Natural Resources	493	687	11.2
6. Multisector	155	454	7.4

Rounded off.

*See next page

There are activities and procedures galore in the ADB. They are to be followed. There are rules about subscriptions and about loans and about everything.

ADB mentions "three pillars of the strategy of reduction in poverty. They are (a) pro-poor sustainable economic growth, (o) inclusive social development and (c) good governance.

For each country the diagnosis is different. The programmes drafted are different. The strategy of implementation is different. ADB is following EPRS i.e., enhanced poverty reduction strategy. ADB is at present busy with enhancing the capacity of production, gender development programmes and the programmes of rural development.

ADB is assisting countries to be able to participate in global trade on the basis of competitiveness as required by the WTO.

ADB is promoting ventures in developing economies and effective partnerships. Knowledge based activities are being promoted. ADB is promoting portfolio management and regional economic cooperation. It is also guiding on credit risk management. As is known, production is "high value adding". ADB wants to assist in this. Even urban areas of many developing countries are in bad shape. ADB wants to assist the developing economies in improving urban development.

NOTE

1. If a question is asked on any one of them, others can also be discussed in brief is juxtaposition.
2. India received loans for the development of railways, ports and harbours, mining, steel plains rural and urban schemes was lowland development, big irrigation projects, air services, power projects, industrial finance etc.

   Cf world Bank Annual Reports

   Cf IMF's Finance and Development.
3. The reader can imagine giving a loan of just Rs. 1 lakh to someone. He will most certainly inquire (i) where will the money be used, (ii) what will be mode of return, (iii) whether the agreed upon interest will be paid regularly, (iv) whether the amortisation charges installment of the principal interest will be provided for and (v) whether the credibility of the borrower is right and/or be guaranteed.
4. The developed countries use world resources wastefully. The USA uses as much electrical) for neon-lighting and air-conditioning as India and China use for all purposes. The amount of tinned food which the cats and dogs of the US get is of high amount than the total ah that the US gives to the developing nations as loans. There are 7 shades of lipsticks for the bitches of the US. The pets have their mosquito nets, beds, pillows, mattress, burial grounds undertakers etc. But the poor nations which are corpulent and opulent, are miserly in concessional aid.

* Details of I to XI replenishments are not being here. Those who want to study in details replenishments of I to X can go through the book "INTERNATIONAL ECONOMICS" written by the same author, edition 1995. In the subsequent editions XI replenishment details are there.

South Asia means India, Bangladesh, Pakistan, Maldives, Sri Lanka, Nepal, Bhutan and Myanmar.

South East Asia means Cambodia, Vietnam, Laos, Malaysia, Indonesia, Philippines, Timor-Este, Singapore, Thailand.

North Asia means Mongolia, and Republic of Korea.

Central Asia means Azerbijan, Afghanistan, Uzbekistan, Turkmenistan, Tajikstan, Kazakhstan, Kyrgyz Republic.

Pacific refers to Samoa, Papua New Guinea, Cook Islands, Fiji, Kiribati, Marshall Islands, Micronesia, Nauru, Solomon Islands, Tonga, Tuvalu, and Vanuatu.

ADB: Website

36 India's International Trade Profile

A. India's export–Imports and BOP 1947–1961: 1950s first two five year plans period.
B. India's X-M and BOP during the decade of 1960s third FYP and three yearly plans period 1960–1969
C. India's X–M and BOP; decade of 1970s. Periods of fourth and fifth FYPs 1969–1974 and 1974–79.
D. India's X–M and BOP; Decade of 1980s. Sixth and seventh FYP periods upto 1991.
E. India's X–M and Bop: Decade of 1990s. Upto 2001-eight and ninth five YP periods upto 1997–2001
F. India X–M and BOP 2001–2008. decade of 2000. Statistical profile about gold reserves, SDR Reserves, capital flows, current A/C flows, capital account flows, exchange Rates, positions 1949–50 and decadal positions of X–M–BOP upto 2009, percentage sharer of imports and Exports, forex reserves decade 1990s and 2000s, External debt.
G. Top ten general export promoting and imports compression measures.
H. Old Exim policies 2002–2007; 2004–2009.
I. India's new Exim policy 2009–2014
J. India's BOP with selected countries.
K. Break up of India's External debt.

In 1947–48, India's exports were of Rs. 400 crore and imports of Rs. 388 crore. The values of exports and imports are different. Imports of foodgrains in early 1950s saved people from dying. Hence imports were of great value even if they cost a price. Hence aggregated trend rates and figures should be understood in broader sense. For narrow sense, the figures are here. BOP surplus was of Rs. 12. crore. BOP surplus was of Rs. 12 crore.

Exports bring foreign "hard" monies and are appreciated. However, they take away commodities, goods and services. Exports are leakages in real terms! They are additions in money terms. Hence *exports are important only if they are genuine marketable surpluses. Exports by depriving people of direly needed consumption by the masses will inflict pain.*

Imports are additions in the real economy because they bring vital commodies, goods and services. They are leakages in money terms. One need not mourn the loss of foreign exchange if imports increase our production and consumption bases.

DECADE OF 1950S WAS MORE OR LESS CORRESPONDING TO FIRST AND SECOND FIVE YEAR PLANS

The first five year plan (1951–1956) was more a rehabilitation plan than a development plan. India needed tremendous rehabilitation after the ravages of partition brought about by Pakistan. There were ill-effects of the Second World War (1939–1945) also.

The second five year plan laid the cornerstone of the development strategy of India. Jawaharlal Nehru wanted India to have basic and heavy industries as also to have big irrigation dams. He called them the "new temples of India". As such imports were needed during the first plan to ward off hunger and for rehabilitation works; during the second five year plan they were of the nature of "imports–replacing imports". Exports were traditional *i.e.,* of commodities like tea, mineral ores etc.

DURING THE 9 YEARS 1950–51 TO 1959–60, THE AVERAGES WORKED OUT AS UNDER

[Rs. crs.]

	Total	*Averages*
Exports	6505	722.77
Imports	8644	960.44
BoP Deficit	–2139	–237.66

The lowest imbalance of Rs. 2 crore was in the year 1950–51 and the highest was of Rs. 474 crore in the year 1957–58. *Four figure imports* were in this year (Rs. 1035 crore). During these years, exports never reached the four figure.

The UK was the main partner in the immediate post–colonial era under Commonwealth preferences. All jute mills except 1 were in India while almost the entire jute growing area was in the then East Pakistan (1947–1971), now Bangladesh. The Pakistan Government allowed the "golden fibre of Bangladesh" to rot so that Indian jute mills could be crippled. More crippled became the economy of the Bangladeshies. India had to divert area under rice to jute and import rice. Cotton textile machines were important item of imports.

Imports (cif) during the first plan were of Rs. 3651 crore; exports were of Rs. 3109 crore; and balance of payment deficit was of Rs. 542 crore. The yearly averages of imports, exports and deficits were of Rs. 730, 622 and 108 crore respectively. Imbalance of nearly 22 crore on average in rupee terms now will not attract attention.

1956–1961

Imports	5404	1080.4
Exports	3063	612.6
Deficits	– 2339	–467.8

B. DECADE OF 1960 THIRD FIVE YEAR PLAN 1961–1966 AND THREE YEARLY PLANS 1966–67 TO 1968–69

The Second Five Year Plan was based on Mahalanobis strategy of erecting the "new mandirs" of development and strengthening the public sector. Imports were imports–replacing imports. The same strategy continued during the Third Plan also.

Third Plan period was marred by two external aggressions (1962 by China and 1965 by Pakistan), in the aftermath of which two Prime Ministers died (Nehruji in 1964 and Shastriji in 1966), and there were two very severe drought years and two serious flood years. Nothing seemed normal during this period.

Imports compression and exports promotion remained main objectives of the period. *During the 10 years 1960–61 and 1969–70, the totals and averages of exports, imports and BoP were as under:*

Exports Rs. Crs.	9323	932.30
Imports Crs.	14901	1490.10
Deficit Rs. Crs.	5578	557.80

* For the first time in the history of India, the exports crossed the four–figure in 1966–67.

* For the first time the imports were higher than Rs. 2000 crore in this decade during the years 1966–67 and 1967–68. Thereafter they were down to figures of 1909 and 1582 respectively in the last two years of the decade.

* Not a single year of surplus BoP was there during this decade also.

Green Revolution was started in 1965. **Shastriji** [Remember his famous slogan *"Jaya Jawan and Jaya Kisaan"]*. Imports were to strengthen the industrial activities primarily and balanced growth as required in the agricultural and tertiary sectors. Imports were related to them and more to the defence needs.

Indian rupee was devalued second time (first time in 1949) by 36.5 p.c. against Pound Sterling. As we say devaluation makes the exports cheaper to the foreigner in their own currency; imports became dearer to Indians in Indian rupee. The intention was to promote exports and compress the imports.

Decades of 1950s and 1960s were marked by rigorous controls, conservation (economising atleast) of foreign exchange and socialist control. India followed "democratic socialism" and not "socialistic democracy". It was good at that time when (*i*) employment generation was needed, (*ii*) strengthening of public sector for ultimate help to the private sector was needed and when (*iii*) friendship with the men USSR was necessary otherwise UK and USA were hell–bent in rewarding Pakistan at the cost of India for Pakistan giving its space for anti–USSR activities.

C. DECADE OF 1970S MORE OR LESS PERIODS OF FOURTH AND FIFTH FIVE YEAR PLANS 1965–1974 AND 1974–1979:

(Here the Five Year Plans are not being discussed). The Fourth Plan was special because it incorporated the "consistency model" and first time laid special emphasis on minimum needs programme. In the Fifth Plan there was the new strategy of direct attack on

poverty. All plans used to aim at 5.5 to 6.5 p.c. annual growth rates and by 2008 there were assertions that India can achieve the growth rate of 10 to 12 p.c.

During the decade of 1970–71 to 1979–80 (not exactly coinciding with the above mentioned two five year plans), the picture of exports, imports and balance of payment deficits was as under:

	Total	Averages
Imports Rs. Crs.	45113	4511.3
Exports Rs. Crs.	37696	3769.6
BoP Deficit	– 7417	– 741.7

It was during this period that the leap–frog exercises in raising the prices of petroleum crude began. The Arab World decided to annihilate Israel with petrodollars. The prices of petroleum crude were raised from $ 2 (earlier contract price $ 1.2) a barrel to spot prices of $ 42 *i.e.,* 21 times. The entire world reeled under the impact. Money was getting sucked in the Middle–Eastern countries as if by a magnet. Fertiliser prices too rose. Imports of foodgrains became costly. (Lateron oil prices peaked to $ 174 a barrel by 2007-08 but were town to $ 84 in April 2010).

India's exports were the same traditional items like tea, jute, ready made garments, aqua–products, coffee, oil seeds (specially gound–nuts), live animals for slaughter in the Middle East, handicraft curios and some cottage industries items. Jewellery was also an important item.

1973 was the Watershed Year; Liberalisation Process Started from this Year Under Rajiv Gandhi. He Wanted

"Corruption to be out of politics: politics to be out of administration: and administration to be out of the economy".

1972–73 (Rs. 104 crore) and 1976–78 (Rs. 68 crores) were the two years when there were surpluses on imports and exports. However, the decade as a whole registered the deficit.

It *is to be remembered once again that yearly "balance of payment deficits" add up to "balance of international indebtedness"*

D. DECADE OF 1980S SIXTH AND SEVENTH PLANS

The Sixth Plan (1979–84) was revised again to be of 1980–85. Hence the Seventh. Plan was of 1985–90. This decade really included two five year plans to coincide with the decade of 1980s.

Oil imports which were around just Rs. 100 crore at the time of Independence were 125 times in the first year of this decade. This was relatively more due to rise in international prices than the rise in consumption due to increasing number of vehicles.

	Total	Averages
Imports Rs. Crs.	198976	19897.6
Exports Rs. Crs.	131746	13174.6
BOP Deficit	–67230	–6723.0

During the decade the first year itself started with the five–figure imports. The five figure exports could be achieved from 1984–85 onwards. There was not a single year of balance of payment surplus.

Liberalisation was resulting in excessive increases in imports. *The MNCs of the western capitalist world were pushing down their exports down the throats of India, but those who connived in the imports of superfluous things like cosmetics, fashion–designed clothes costing lakhs of rupees and many items of luxuries for the rich were Indians.*

It is to be kept in view that during all the decades, five year plans, and yearly plan periods there were "firm resolves" to have "sound" export promotion and imports compression measures. Self–reliance was also a slogan which never left India, atleast for putting it on the paper each time.

Scale and scope of international trade increased across the continents. India started seeking better economic relationships with African and Latin American countries.

E. DECADE OF 1990S

Two Yearly Plans Before the Eighth Plan: 1992–97 Ninth Five Year Plan (1997–2001).

Averages and totals for the decade of 1990s were Rs. crs.

	Total	*Averages*
Imports	1126838	112684
Exports	927290	92729
Deficits	–199548	–19955

It *we take the position of the Eighth Five Year Plan only. The imports were of Rs. 488045 crore and exports of Rs. 356507 crore and the deficit was of Rs. 531538 crore.*

NRIs of India were always sending money to India. A few years back in mid–2000, India was receiving $ 26 b. India had been the largest receiver of unrequired money is the world. India is expected to receive $ 34 b.

2008 July	India's external debt	$ 236 b.
	India's forex reserves	$ 286 b.

India's forex reserve rise due to upward price movement of gold increasing unrequited balances permanently. FDI flows still average $ 4.4 b per year for the last 10 years, F.I.I. inflows move between $ 11 b to $ 15 b.

	Exports *Rs. crores*	*US $ million*
2001–02	209018	43827
2002–03	255137	52719
2003–04	293367	63843
2004–05	375340	63536
2005–06	563800	124629
2007–08 Sep. 2007 (April–Oct. 6 month)	295233	72281

	Imports Rs. crores	US $ million
2001–02	245200	51413
2002–03	297206	61412

	Imports Rs. crores	US $ million
2003–04	359108	78149
2004–05	501065	111517
2005–06	660474	149184
2006–07	620568	181368
2007–08 (6 month)	446421	109204

	Payment Deficit (–1) Rs. Crores	US $ million
2001–02	–36182	–7587*
2002–03	–42069	–8693
2003–04	–65741	–14306
2004–05	–125725	–27981
2005–06	–204085	–46140
2006–07	–256768	–56739
2007–08	–151188	–36924

BOP deficit increase to 56.74 b. $ in 5 yrs *i.e.* 7,5 times. Exp. Imp. increasing very fast. BOP increasing faster. EPW Nov. 24,2007. 7.587 billion.

Statistical Summary of International Business: 2009 (for year ot year details see "Economic Survey" of Government of India-Latest)

* Gold reserves were 220 tonnes in 1950-51 and 358 tonnes in march 2009
* The value of these reserves increased from Rs. 113 cr. To Rs. 40793 crore due to price effect.
* SDR reserves were started in 1969-70 and were of 123 million which in rupee terms was equal to Rs. Crore. The lowest were in 1997-98 = SDR 1 million only, equal to Rs. 4 crore. The position in march 2009 was SDR 1 million, equal to Rs. 6 crore.
* Forex balances in Dec. 2009 were equal to $ 256 billions Rs. 12 *lakh–crore.* In 1950–51, the balances were $ 217 crore only. Equal to rs. 1029 crore.

		2007-08
$ Imports	257.8	billion
$ Exports	166.1	billion.
$ Deficit	91.7	billion.

* In rupee terms exports were 1670 times w.r. to 1950-51.
* In rupee terms imports were 2671 times w.r. to 1950-51.
* IMF transactions in 2007-08 were nil.
* Total capital by 2007-08 was $ 109 billion, in forign currency accounts.

* Total receipts on current account were $ 148.6 billion-on Invisibles.
* Total payments on current account were $ 74.0 billion-on Invisibles.
* Net receipt on current account were $ 74.6 billion-on Invisibles

The items were

(i) foreign travel,
(ii) transportation,
(iii) insurance.
(iv) investment,
(v) unilateral transfers and
(vi) government account and miscellaneous.

2007-08

* Total receipts on capital accounts were of $ 412 billion
* total payments on capital account were of $ 99 billion.

The main items were FDI, FII, Loans and baking transfer.

Receipts were 21 times; payments 23.5 times; net receipts were 15.6 times of what they were in 1990-91.

Exchange Rates

Exchange rate by the end of 2009 was Rs. 47 per dollar by the end of march 2009, it was Rs. 51.2 per dollar

		Euro rates E.1+	- Not in Existence
In 1980-81	Rs. 7.9		
In. 1990-91	Rs. 17.9	-	"
In 1999-00	Rs. 45.6	Rs. 44.8	
In 2007-08	Rs. 40.3	Rs. 57.3	
March, 2009	Rs. 51.3	Rs. 66.9	
Jan. 2010	Rs. 46.8	Rs. 67.6	
Aprial 2010	Rs. 44.0	Rs. 59.45	

	Exports - Imports - Balance X -	*M* -	*$ billion* *BOP*	*p.c. deficit to X*
1949-50	1.02	1.29	(-) 0.27	26.5
2969-70	1.87	2.51	(-) 0.64	34.2
1979-80	7.95	11.32	(-) 3.37	42.4
1989-90	16.61	21.22	(-) 4.61	27.8
2004-05	83.54	111.52	(-) 27.98	33.5
2008-09	168.70	287.76	(-) 119.06	70.6

Liberalization increased BoP deficit. It became 441 times. Exports were 168 times. Imports were 223 times. $ slided down and rupee appreciated in 2010. (April).

Percentage share	*Imports* *2006-07*	*2008-09* *2008-09*
1. Food and allied products	2.9	2.0
2. petroleum products,	30.8	33.8

3.	Coal	2.5	3.6
4.	fertilizers	1.6	5.0
5.	Capital goods.	154.	12.8
	(of this 54 p.c. were machines and tools		
	21 p.c. were transport equipment		
	17. p.c. elec. Goods and projects		
	8 p.c. others.		
6.	Gold and silver, pearls and precious stones	13.1	12.5
7.	Chemicals	5.2	5.3
8.	loan and steel	8.6	7.1
9.	Electronic good.	8.6	7.1
10.	Others	16.4	14.7
		100.0	100.0

EXPORTS

1.	Agricultural and allied ;	10.3	10.6
2.	Ores and minerals	4.8	3.6
3.	Manufactured goods	68.6	66.6
4.	Petroleum products and coal including for refinements	15.0	18.0
5.	Others	1.3	1.1
		100.0	100.0

Of the manufactured goods, 11.2 were gems and jewellery; 6.4 p.c. machinery 6.0 p.c. transport equipment, 5.6 readymade garments; S.O. drugs, U.S. p.c. manufacture of metals; 3.0 steel; 2.6 electronic goods; 2.5 p.c. cotton yearn etc; 1.6 dyes; 1.4 leather goods and 0.9 others = total 66.6

"Forex reserves". Gold is seldom sold, unless the country is in a very difficult position. The countries can increase the size of the forex reserves on paper if the prices of gold are rising in international market.

The following tablc shows the positions of foreign exchange reserves in certain years.

*	March 1991 (VP Singh PM) billion dollars	1
*	March 2001	40
*	March 2002	51
*	March 2003	70
*	March 2004	109
*	March 2005	146
*	January 2008	266
*	Dec. 2009	256

Reserve Bank of India has 358 tonnes of gold but the IMF reserves are just 10 million. (1000 m = 1 billion) and hence are insignificant.

India was getting a lot of foreign exchange investment. The FII investment is around 4 bilion a year on average. Most foreign investors invest in paricipatory notes. This is illegal type of work.

The investors may be those who are not permitted to invest. Or they may be those who are not permitted to invest in certain lines of investment.

They do it through Indian brokers. Most, if not all, brokers are those who make the commonmen, "broke" i.e., insolvent! Many brokers are not registered. The Government and the SEBI say that they do not know their names, phone numbers even!

There is a lot of proxy business by the brokers and for other brokers through participatory notes.

One Ketan Parekh was reportedly involved in winding Rs. 14000 crore. There are many Harshad Mehtas and Parekhs or others of different "surnames" who are bulls and bears and are cheating the "assess", the common men. Foreign exchange balances of India are not rising because exports are greater than the imports. In fact the position is opposite. Imports continue to be higher than exports. One is not sure whether Indians who earn illegal/corruption money first transfer fund surreptitiously and then bring back. India's foreign reserves are not "earned".

India's External Debt

India's external debt was $ 235 billion in 2008. It is to be kept in mind that the external debt of India is almost equal to the foreign exchange reserves. This is a recent phenomenon, Earlier debt used to be greater than the foreign exchange reserves. This 2008 position in rupee terms was equal to nearly 9.5 Lakh-crore rupees.

* Of the above nearly one-fifth 19.7 p.c. was concession debt.
* India's term debt to total percentage of debt was 21 p.c.
* Long-term debt to total percentage of debt was 79 p.c.

India was debt free in 1947. Infect England was indebted to India. It had imported goods during 1939-1945 world was II on credit and owed $ 3.87.33 at the then exchange rate was equal to Rs. 1743 crore.

India was the 8 th most indebted country in the world after; Russia, China, Brazil Argentina, Turkey, Mexico and Indonesia India's debt was 55 p.c. in US dollar; 17.5 p.c. in Indian rupee, 12 p.c. in Yen, 10 p.c. in SDR, 3.6. p.c. in Euro, 2.2 p.c. in Pound sterling and 0.3 p.c. in other in 2008. Positions can change.

TOP TEN 'GENERAL" EXPORT PROMOTION MEASURES AND TOP TEN 'GENERAL' IMPORT COMPRESSION MEASURES IN INDIA

TOP TEN 'GENERAL'EXPORT PROMOTION MEASURES

1. Government of India claimed that under its planning there were successful efforts to increase production everywhere. It was the endeavour of the GoI to particularly increase the exportable surpluses in all sectors, sub–sectors, activities, functions and facilities.

2. Inputs were arranged for export industries. Credit facilities were given on asking. In various industrial clusters, growth centres and growth poles infrastructure facilities like good roads, warehousing facilities, electricity, banking facilities, transport and telecommunications ' facilities were provided. Land and water were given at throw–away prices. Medical and educational facilities were also in place. They were given in all the States in the designated "backward" districts.
3. During the regime of fixed exchange rates, the exporters were given facilities to get foreign exchange for import of capital goods, technology and necessary inputs. Now the exchange rate is so managed that the exporters are not harmed; in fact they are helped to earn profits.
4. Taxes like income tax, production tax, excise duties and various types of duties / cesses were either not taken, or were refunded or were collected at very low rates (just to maintain services) from the exporters.
5. HPEPZ and HPEU (Hundred percent export promotion/production zones and hundred percent exporting units) were given massive facilities. Many subsidies were available.
6. Dry ports were "created" i.e., the costs of transport of goods to and fro between the factory and the ports were borne by the government. In simple words, the transport subsidy was 100 p.c. including handling and warehousing.
7. Innovative facilities were provided like container services. The embassy commercial members of the staff were at the beck and call of the exporting houses. "One–window" facility (at one place all formalities) used to be promised.
8. Quota restrictions against Indian exporters abroad were challenged.
9. Low tariff regime was introduced. OGL (Open general licensing) was geared to provide facilities to both the importers and exporters.
10. There was a general "provision". "Ask and you will get the concessions and help, if you are exporters of importance".

Top ten General Measues of Imports Compression

1. Government of India always claimed that it allowed the import of only necessary things, even when super luxury items, cosmetics, confectionery items, heady liquor, soft–drinks or their concentrates, high grade luxury cars etc. were coming. Government of India sometimes claimed that it imposed "across the counter" cuts on imports—i.e., by a fixed percentage on most of the imports, if not on all.
2. When it was permissible (WTO rules were not against that) high tariff duties were imposed on many imports.
3. When it was permissible (WTO rules were not there) quota restrictions were imposed.
4. When it was permissible (now WTO allows 3 p.c. dumping of the past average use) dumping invited countervailing duties. *Dumping means that the foreigner is selling below his own cost of production to oust the native competitor. Countervailing duty takes away that advantage and may even be so high that the foreign good may become costlier than the domestic product.*
5. Multinational companies were encouraged to open their branches and franchise in India rather than replace India's production with their exports (India's imports).
6. A list of "banned" imports always was there as of intoxicants narcotic and arms.

7. Administrative regulations were prohibiting unnecessary imports.
8. Foreign exchange was given at higher rate to discourage imports.
9. Imports that helped in production for exports were encouraged.
10. Government entered negotiations with parties to reduce import bill.

OLD EXIM POLICIES. PRE–LIBERALISATIONAND GLOBALISA TION EXIM POLICIES. EXIM POLICIES 2002–2007 AND THEN 2004–2009

EXIM POLICIES 2009-2014

* After 1950s, even export duties could be levied on the goods which were essential to the foreigners because they used to bear the duties and the volume of exports did not go down. These duties were abolished slowly.
* India used to levy high or heavy import duties, especially on those goods which used to compete with the then upcoming industries. India used to import bi–cycles even from the UK! Even al–pins and railway lines were imported. *Import duties used to be "protective". Scooters were not roads before 1968. There used to be advance booking for the same. Vespa scooter used to take about 15 years to be delivered and Lambretta about 8 to 10 years at different places. The GoI wanted low bill of petroleum products. In the early stages it used to be of about Rs. 200 crore only! Cars used to be owned by the royalty or big industrialists. Bhopal in the 1940s used to have just four cars—all owned by the royalty ! Now a car can be delivered at the same day at the house, if one so wishes. Many familes own 4 cars.*
* Indian industries were recommended to have protection for a period of at least 5 years, Imports–replacing–imports were preferred. BHEL and the four steel plants were established in the public sector with the foreign loans.

As there used to be deficit in the international trading account, the import duties used to be raised. However, slowly more items used to be permitted to be imported but with higher import duties. Imports of essential raw materials that used to be used in export industries were given preference.

As was seen earlier, Indian rupee was devalued in 1949 and 1966 and then two times in 1991 also. Now it floats.

There was license permit "raaj". Reportedly the big industrial houses were favoured. There was massive corruption also, reportedly.

India had to Import food–grains Also in the Past from the USA and it used to Export "Feed–Grains" to us i.e., those Grains which were Fed to the Animals there to Fatten them

India established State Trading Corporation in 1970 and once 75 p.c. imports were made by the Government of India through this STC. Now it is as good as dead. It says it earns 0.2 p.c. "profits" on the working capital.'

India had the system of quotas for the imports. Its anti–dumping measures were in place. It practised exchange controls. There was a time when the exporters were not entitled to even one dollar from the crores that they earned. The exporters were given equivalent rupees at the official exchange rate and the dollars used to be impounded by the Government. This was till 1991. *(See chapter on convertibility).*

Helping international business by helping producers was the important feature of the EXIM policies that used to be announced. All the districts of the country were declared as "A"."B", and "C". "A" stood for developed districts. They could be counted on the finger tips. Most of the districts of India were put in the category "C", i.e., most backward and "B" i.e., backward. Here concessions were given for industrialization like free land, free water, cheap and "adequate" (promised) power, labour training facilities, roads, linkages to the railway stations, dry ports, subsidies on transport to and fro ports and harbours to the industrial units in the interior areas and cheap capital. *An important feature of this policy was that even if a backward district became very advanced, its designation of being "backward" continued in the official books so that the industrialists could obtain concessions. Hundred percent exporting units were given what they wanted.*

Following top dozen points of the old EXIM policies can be listed: 2002-2009.

1. SEZ or special export zones were established. Here all infrastructure facilities were provided or at least promised. EOUs i.e., export oriented units were established here. They too were provided all facilities that they wanted on individual basis. Thus there were facilities that could generate "external" and (facilitate the generation of) 'internal" economies there.
2. Facilities were to be given from the OBU i.e., overseas banking units and more and more goods were put on OGL i.e., open general licensing. There was *EEFCA* i.e., exchange earners foreign currency account, under which the export earner could have retention up to 100 p.c. of the foreign exchange earned by them. *Under EPCG* i.e., export promotion capital goods, the status of "deemed exports" was granted in a year if the goods were in the process of being exported but had not left the shores of the country. This was for various concessions to the exporters. *DEPB* (duty entitlement passbook) system was also there. There were hundreds of items under it and the new items were frequently added. Various penalties and interest charges were waived for reducing various burdens. (China banned all abbreviations like OBU etc., in April 2010).
3. Targets for exports from agricultural sector or from handloom sector or from handicraft sectors were set year by year. *SSI had MAI for them.* This meant that small scale industries had "market access initiatives". There was no dearth of fixing targets e.g., for brass wares (say from Moradabad) for hosiery from Ludhiana and Tripur. "Export House" status could be granted to any exporter who could export for Rs. 5 crore or above. Artisans, producers of cottage industries and even small scale industrial units were suffering through out India for want of assured electricity and other help. Ground realities were very different from the claims made on the paper.
4. There were provisions in the EXIM policies for helping in the modernization of any production facility that could export. Promises in the EXIM policy are written in such a way that it used to appear (and it is still done) as if the entire administration will run at the beck and call of the small producers to help. *Sometimes the domestic sales were also adjusted against the exports, if exports could not materialize and this was misused by many producer.* Facilities for importing anything if the inputs

could be used for exports were promised. There were various schemes of reimbursement of the various types of fees and taxes. Export Houses were given licence/license or certificates for customs clearances both for exports and imports on self–declaration basis for EEFC.

5. In SION (standard inputs output norms), the rising fuel costs were included for relief. DEEC was abolished i.e., duty exemption entitlement certificate book was abolished and shipping bills or banks realization certificates were deemed sufficient. ***The hard** facts of the EXIM policies **were and continue to be that there are hundreds of provisions to be complied. One is bewildered in fillins up forms.***

4. *One foreigner observed that it is a peculiar situation in India that they ask for so many irrelevant details and when we seek assistance about how to comply with the requirement, the "babus "advise us "you can write "NIL "there'. These requirements are used to seeking bribes or for harassing the exporters importers.)*

6. India's peak rates on imports were brought down to 20 p.c. by 2009. They have to be brought down further as per requirements of the WTO. *SAD was abolished;* it stood for "special additional duties". Additional fees, cess, duties and taxes still abound in India. "On–line applications" facilities were introduced. Greater and better facilities were promised for export clusters and that means "clusters" had to be formed.

7. If exporters wanted to export food–grains to foreign countries, they had to buy the grains from the FCI i.e., Food Corporation of India. The grains that FCI keeps are usually kept in the mixed form and not in the well graded form. There are a lot of pebbles and mud–pieces in the bags of the grains taken from FCI. It was difficult for the exporters to tackle various problems. This requirement was abolished in the 2004–09 policy.

8. Many concessions were announced in importing the spare parts of the projects.

9. SSI units were permitted to have tie–ups with the big industrial units for the purpose of exports.

10. There were hundreds of separate policies e.g., for bio–technology, gems, telecoms, pharmaceuticals to n number of items.

India's Foreign Trade Policy EXIM 2009–2014 Major Highlights

(This is abridged from PNB's paper Aug. 2009. Cf; Deachen Palmo). Between 2003 and 2008–09 India's exports rose from $ 63 b. to $ 168 b. India's share in global exports rose from 0.83 p.c. 1.45 p.c. In services India's share in global trade was 2.8 p.c. India's exports in total of commodities, goods and services rose from 0.93 p.c. to 1.64 p.c. It was estimated that 1.4 crore jobs were created in the increased activity in IB.

The objectives of the policy are: (1) To combat decline in the exports, if there is recession in the world. (2) To increase the exports @ 15 p.c. per year with the annual export target reaching US $ 200 billion by March 2011 (equal to Rs. 9.8 trillion at the exchange rate (assumed) to be of Rs. 49 per dollar on average. (3) This target of increasing the exports @ 15 p.c.p.a. is to be taken up to 25 p.c.p.a. after 2011 to 2014. By 2020 the long term objective is to double the global trade of India. The Government of India mentions the usual measures that will be taken. It mentions fiscal incentives also.

About fiscal incentives there is a controversy. The corporate world of India raises the bogey of global recession adversely affecting India even when not even ripple effects may be felt. Shri P. Sainath (grandson of the. ex–President of India Shri VV Giri) has done great service to India by openly bringing to the light that "paid news" is there in the media. In December 2009, the Dubai grand plan of having real estates in the sea was in trouble and moratorium on debt was requested by Dubai builders. Government of India made it clear that Indians were not involved yet the press was making noises. Ordinary Indians were apprehending that as GoI gave Rs. 100000 crore in four months to the corporate world as fiscal bail out in 2008–09, it may do so in this case also. Development works for the ordinary citizens are downgraded.

Duty concessions will be there (lower duties and refunds). Production units which export 100 p.c. of their produce will be entitled for income tax exemptions. The old packages will be there. India Inc. and big-business Inc. get fiscal stimulas worth 4 lakh crore a year !

Promotional measures

Government can provide from 25 p.c. to 100 p.c. assistance to export promotion industries through various organizational setups. Exporters can be assisted to go to any part of the world for participating in export promoting fairs. There are EPCs i.e., export promotion councils and TPOs i.e., trade promotion organizations.

If the exporters have to incur expenses in the foreign countries for our export promotion in the form of meeting statutory charges, the Government of India can reimburse them.

If a town or city exports goods worth Rs. 150 crore each year from hāndicrafts, handlooms, agricultural goods or aqua–products and in other cases goods of Rs. 750 crore each year, then those towns can be • declared towns of excellence. Such towns get facilities for better infrastructure.

IBEF remains IBEF but with different meaning (India Brand Equity Fund to India Branch Equity *Foundation)* will promote business abroad. Research and Test houses are being upgraded.

FMS Focus Market Scheme

Under this, high freight costs are to be brought down. Credit entitlement has been extended from 2.5 p.c. to 3 p.c. Duty credit scrips will be available to the following: (a) SEZs, (b) service exports, (c) diamonds and precious stones, (d) all jewellery items of all metals, (e) all ores, (f) cereals, (g) sugar, (h) petroleum products (that usually go out for refinement), and (i) dairy products.

FPS or Focus Product Scheme

Big industries will also get higher credit entitlement from 1.25 p.c. to 2 p.c. and exports with high employment intensity will be "incentivized", (as the government puts it but does not specifiy).

MLFP or Market Linked Focus Product Scheme

Two per cent cost of "free on board" of export goods will be incentivized. This will be for countries like Brazil, South Africa and Australia or equally distant from India. *Directorate of Trade Remedy Measures* will be set up.

It is stipulated that there should be minimum 15 p.c. value adding for entitlement of any concession. Technological up–gradation will be reviewed. There should be technological up–gradation also. It has been pointed out to the exporters that 26 new countries have been added in the list where India's export presence should be seen. *EPCG scheme is for Export Promotion Capital Goods.* Fifteen p.c. value adding is the minimum. Technological up–gradation should be perceptible. Then 3 p.c. credit incentives will be available. Labour incentive industries will also get this concession.

* Merchant as well as Manufacturer Exporters,
* Service Providers, (SP)
* Export Oriented Units, (EOU)
* SEZs, (special export zones),
* AEZs (Agriculture Export Zones),
* Electronic Hardware Technology Parks, (EHTP)
* Bio–Technology Parks.(BTP)

These will be eligible for all the concessions listed above.

PTHs i.e., Premier Trading Houses will be required to export worth Rs. 7500 crore for FOB concessions. (Free on Board). Star Trading houses will be those which export minimum worth Rs. 2500 crore. Those which export minimum worth Rs. 500 crore will be known as "trading houses". Firm which exports worth Rs. 100 crore will be known as "Star Export House "but not "star trading house". If a firm exports goods of Rs. 20 crore and above but below Rs. 100 crore it will be known as "export house". (concessions will be according to the status).

Status holders are there for different industries e.g., the best status is the "Premier Trading House". There are lower requirements for giving concessions for products that come from agriculture or handlooms and handicrafts. Similarly there are different norms for marine/aqua products. Fish does not mean fish. There can be different norms for different types/items.

If imports are there for being used in the production of goods for exports, there will be duty free authorization. One change that has been introduced is that payment can be accepted through other means also rather than in cash only, as used to be done earlier.

There are many minor concessions that are shown as being of great importance. For example, much is made out of the fact that instead of 15 samples that were permitted earlier, now 50 can be permitted.

Once again there is mention of that "single window facility" i.e., everything will be decided at one place and numerous forms will not be required to be filled up nor the exporters/importers will be required to meet several persons.

This is being repeated since 1950s and that it self proves that the claims had always been false.

The 2009–2014 EXIM policy says *"We now aim to promote brand India "*. It is play of words only.

The fact remains that there will be as many problems as there are persons multiplied by the products! Indian administration, as the persons who are in IB say, remains as corrupt as it was and puts impediments as many as it used to put ever.

INDIA'S BALANCE OF TRADE WITH SELECTED COUNTRIES (US $ MILLION)

Region/Countries	2008-09			2007-08			2005-06			2000-01			195-96		
	Export	Import	BOT	Export	Import	BOT	Export	Import	BOT	Export	Import	BOT	Export	Import	BOT
1) Europe [37]	41620 (22.8)	55713 (19.1)	-14094	37257 (22.9)	51626 (20.5)	-14369	24910 (24.2)	33080 (22.2)	-8170	11433 (25.9)	13769 (27.6)	-2336	9235 (29.0)	11853 (32.3)	2618
1.1 Bi Countries 127]	38953	41653	-2700	34507	38432	-3925	23229	25998	-2769	10593	10530	63	8708	10753	-2045
i) UK	6595	5792	802	6701	4956	1746	5059	3930	1129	2272	626	1646	2011	1918	93
2) Germany	6344	11694	-5350	5119	9875	-4756	5586	6024	-2438	1884	2864	-980	1977	3145	1168
3) Netherland	6280	1876	4404	5228	1921	3305	2475	1050	1425	174	238	636	769	570	199
4) Belgium	4415	5441	-1026	4210	4360	-150	2871	4725	-1854	1454	3138	-1684	1120	1702	-582
5) taly	3776	4309	-533	3913	3900	13	2519	1856	663	1297	719	578	1014	1064	-50
6) France	2995	4588	-1593	2598	6256	-3658	2080	4113	-2033	1015	1749	-734	747	841	-94
7) Spam	2477	994	1483	2292	"994	1298	1606	573	1033	662	207	455	391	182	209
1.2 Other WE Countries 15]	7540	14079	-11489	2644	13157	-10514	1633	7046	-5413	826	3234	-2408	519	1090	-571
1) Turkey	1383	1444	-61	1750	1690	60	1010	194	816	437	43	394	172	51	121
1.3 East Europe [5]	127	31	95	106	36	70	48	36	12	14	5	9	8	10	-2
2) Africa (49)	11230 (6.1)	18586 (6.4)	-7356	11546 (7.1)	14949 (5.9)	-3403	5442 (5.3)	4041 (2.7)	1401	1801 (4.1)	1604 (3.2)	197	1513 (4.8)	1132 (3.1)	381
2.1 Southern Africa [9]	3115	7178	-40[illegible]3	3609	4835	-1226	1940	2636	-696	402	1061	-659	433	342	-91
1) South Africa	1966	5440	-3474	2659	3615	-956	1527	2472 "	-945	308	1018	-710	330	244	86
2.2 West Africa [23]	3353	10908	-7555	3477	9745	-6269	1899	1162	737	768	445	323	349	657	-308
1) Nigera	1528	8696	-7168	1084	7620	-6536	874	72	802	377	11	366	151	546	-395
2) Ghana	543	169	374	808	141	667	201	79	122	58	26	32	27	25	2
2.3 Central Africa [7]	383	139	244	258	49	209	165	19	146	76	4	72	64	5	59
1) Uganda	218	19	199	154	15	139	93	3	90	44	3	41	37	1	36
2.4 East Africa [101	4379	360	4019	4203	319	3884	1437	224	1213	556	93	463	523	128	395
1) Kenya	1335	81	1254	1580	87	1493	577	49	528	138	19	119	245	15	230
2) Mauritius	956	14	942	1087	10	1076	199	7	192	199	6	193	136	9	127
3) America (45)	28185 (15.4)	30358 (10.4)	-2174	27649 (17.0)	29564 (11.8)	-1915	21368 (20.7)	13037 (8.7)	8331	10865 (24 7)	3944 (7.9)	6921	6187 (19.5)	4835 (13.2)	1352
3.1 North America (2]	22176 (12.1)	20614 (7.1)	1562	21988 (13.5)	23003 (9.1)	-1015	18375 (17.8)	10375 (7.0)	8000	9887 (22.4)	3236 (6.5)	6651	5826 (18.3)	4242 (11.6)	1584
1) USA	20818	18163	2655	20722	21030	-307	17353	9455	7898	9236	2840	6396	5520	3861	1659
2) Canada	1358	2451	-1093	1266	1973	-707	1022	920	102	650	396	254	305	381	-76
3.2 Latin America [43]	6008 (3.3)	9744 (3.3)	-3736	5661 (3.5)	6561 (2.6)	-931	2993 (2.9)	2663 (1.8)	330	978 (2.2)	708 (1.4)	270	378 (1.2)	587 (1.6)	-209
1) Brazil	2550	1183	-1067	2518	949	1569	1091	893	198	223	142	81	86	261	-175
2) Mexico	651	1738	-1087	592	1184	-592	443	98	345	206	51	155	55	65	-10

3) Colombia	365	18	348	758	84	674	455	9	446	49	10	39	18	9	9
4) Argentina	347	510	-163	290	906	-616	200	754	-555	98	381	-283	38	131	-93
4) Asia & ASEAN [21]	95177 (52.1)	178958 (61.41	83781	84238 (51.7)	149841 (59.6)	-65603	49875 (48.4)	51573 (34.6)	-1698	17052 (38.7)	14296 (28.6)	2756	13106 (41.2)	16956 (46.2)	-3850
4.1 East Asia [11]	1733 (0.9)	9109 (3.1)	-7376	1410 (0.9)	8381 (3.3)	-6971	1005 (1.0)	5281 (3.5)	-4277	487 (1.1)	1152 (2.3)	-665	439 (1.4)	1092 (3.0)	-653
1) Australia	1426	8423	-6997	1151	7841	-6690	821	4948	-4127	401	1061	-660	376	1022	-646
4.2 ASEAN [10]	18891 (10.3)	25773 18.8)	-6883	16384 (10.1)	22675 (9.0)	-6290	10411 (10.1)	10884 (7.3)	-473	2875 (6.5)	4058 (8.1)	-1183	2739 (8.6)	2847 (7.8)	-108
1) Singapore	8207	7431	775	7371	8122	-750	5425	3354	2071	861	1433	-572	902	1113	-212
2) Malaysia	3431	7021	-3590	2569	6008	-3439	1162	2416	-1254	600	1150	-550	393	903	-510
3) Indonesia	2517	6674	-4157	2160	4826	-2666	1380	5005	-1628	394	903	-509	662	461	201
4) Thailand	1978	2656	-678	1809	2302	-493	1075	1212	-137	528	314	214	473	170	303
5) Vietnam Soc Rep	1729	404	1325	1603	173	1430	691	131	560	225	12	213	124	15	109
61 Philippines	734	253	481	619	205	414	495	236	259	201	63	138	144	21	173
4.3 WANA [191 (West Asia North Africa)	40835 (22.4)	85499 (29.3)	-44663	30372 (18.6)	71917 (28.6)	-41545	16685 (16.2)	10854 (7.3)	5831	5561 (12.6)	3047 (61)	2514	3081 (9.7)	8221 (22.4)	-5140
1) U Arab Emts	23921	20605	3316	15635	13477	2157	8592	4354	4238	2582	653	1929	1428	1607	-178
2) Saudi Arabia	4988	19493	-14505	3708	19411	-15702	1810	1632	178	808	618	190	482	2025	-1542
3) Iran	2509	12134	-9674	1949	10921	-8971	1188	702	486	222	211	11	155	598	-443
4) Israel	1439	2039	-600	1604	1428	176	1202	1031	171	471	432	39	217	243	-26
5) Egypt A RP	1631	2123	-492	1397	1984	-587	672	220	452	351	39	312	164	73	92
6) Yemen Rep	768	727	41	1018	1470	-452	2/9	10	269	157	15	142	80	20	60
7) Oman	771	1188	-417	938	1134	-196	408	266	147	144	6	138	110	20	90
8) Kuwait	788	9393	-8604	682	7694	-7012	514	462	52	198	112	86	136	1970	-1835
4.4 NE Asia [8]	25280 (13.8)	56785 (19.5)	31505	26450 (16.2)	44755 (17.8)	-18305	16226 (15.7)	23141 (15.5)	-6915	6248 (14.2)	5571 (11.2)	671	5108 (16.1)	4531 (12.4)	576
1) China PRP	9276	31334	27058	10834	27116	-16282	6759	10868	-4109	829	1493	-664	333	812	-479
2) Hong Kong	6662	6411	251	6308	2701	3608	4471	2207	2264	2631	838	1793	1821	388	1433
3) Japan	3001	7607	-4606	3856	6326	-2471	2481	4061	-1580	1779	1833	-54	2216	2468	-252
4) Korea RP	3990	8591	-4601	851	6041	-5190	1827	4564	-2737	446	890	-444	448	825	-377
4.5 South Asia [7]	8438 (4.6)	1791 (0.6)	6647	9622 (5.9)	2112 (0.8)	7510	5548 (5.4)	1413 (0.9)	4135	1881 (4.3)	461 (0.9)	1420	1740 (5.5)	265 (0.7)	1475
1) Sri Lanka DSR	2370	350	2020'	2827	631	2195	2025	578	1447	629	45	584	402	41	360
2) Bangladesh PR	2461	308	2152	2918	257	2661	1664	127	1537	873	74	799	1049	86	963
3) Pakistan IR	1418	362	1055	1945	288	1657	689	180	509	186	64	122	77	45	32
4) Nepal	1556	488	1067	1507	628	879	860	380	480	141	231	-90	160	49	111
5) CIS & Baltics [12]	1896	6558	-4662	1738	3780	-2042	1248	2953	-1705	1035	680	355	1136	1215	-79
5.1 CARs Countries [5]	256	262	-6	232	112	120	168	72	96	80	30	50	22	25	-3
5.2 Other CIS Countries [7]	1640	6296	-4656	1506	3668	-2162	1079	2880	-1801	955	650	305	1114	1190	-76
1) Russia	1078	4291	-3213	940	2470	-1530	733	2022	-1789	869	516	353	1045	856	189
Total (including unspecified)	18263	291475	1088144	162984	251562	-83578	103091	149166	-46075	44076	49975	-5899	36675	36675	4880

INDIA'S EXTERNAL DEBT (US $ MILLION)

								End-March								End-Junr	
Year	1991	1996	1997	1998	1999	2000	2001	2002	2003	2'004	2005	2006	2007	2008	2Q09	2008	2009
1 Multilateral 20900	28616	29218	29553	30534	31438	31105	31899	29994	29297	31744	32620	35337	39490	39538	39644	41236	
A. Government Borrowing	19887	26059	26369	26344	26967	27584	27414	28290	27271	26826	29204	29996	32514	36171	35725	16194	37062
i) Confessional	13377	17576	17636	1/8)6	18596	19269	19080	19713	21560	22674	24023	73731	24876	26859	25081	266/6	25908
a) IDA	13052	17263	17337	17541	18301	18964	18811	19440	21258	223S6	23693	23418	24548	26497	24758	26319	25570
b) Others	325	313	299	295	295	305	269	273	302	318	330	313	328	362	323	357	338
ii| Non-Confessional	6510	8483	8733	8508	8371	8315	8334	8577	5711	4152	5181	6265	7638	9312	10644	9518	11154
a) IBRD	6293	6938	6772	6430	6062	5810	5654	5742	4009	3144	3771	4400	5015	5660	5878	5716	6120
b) Others	217	1545	1961	2078	2309	2505	2680	2835	1702	1008	1410	1865	2623	3652	4766	3802	5034
B Non-Government Borrowing	1013	2557	2849	3209	3567	3854	3691	3609	2723	2471	2540	2624	2823	3319	3813	3450	4174
Non-Confessional	1013	2557	2849	3209	3567	3854	3691	3609	2723	2471	2540	2624	2823	3319	3813	3450	4174
a) Public sector	157	1353	1318	2216	2523	2793	2655	2609	1945	1770	1828	1908	2136	2589	2807	2666	2991
a.1) IBRD	157	860	929	1319	1495	1589	1525	1496	920	984	1020	1030	1043	1173	1395	1255	1525
a.2) Others	0	493	389	897	1028	1204	1130	1113	1025	786	808	878	1093	1416	1412	1411	1466
b) Financial institutions	657	721	665	550	641	710	722	766	668	651	637	589	554	587	730	648	793
b.1) I8RD	451	481	450	256	249	229	218	215	110	85	58	141	150	148	146	151	149
b.2) Others	206	240	215	294	392	481	504	551	558	566	579	448	404	439	584	497	644
c) Private sector	199	483	866	443	403	351	314	234	110 63	50	75 0	127	133	143	277	136	390
c.l) IBRD	371	364	456	334	309	269	246	190	63	0	0	0	0	0	0	0	0
c.2) Others	28	119	410	109	94	82	68	44	47	50	75	127	133	143	277	136	390
II Bilateral 14168	19213	17494	16969	17499	18175	15975	15323	16802	17277	17034	15761	16065	19701	20587	18724	21417	
A Government Borrowing	11936	15535	13652	12998	13447	11946	12176	11540	12664	12987	13132	12239	12344	14853	14655	13833	15169
I) Confessional	11936	15232	13394	12786	13286	13613	11898	11359	12547	17900	13074	12211	12344	14853	14655.	13833	15169
ill Non-Confessional	0	303	258	212	161	353	278	181	117	87	58	28	0	0	0	0	0
B Non-Government Borrowing	2232	3678	3842	3971	4052	4209	3799	3783	4138	4290	3902	3522	3721	4848	5950	4891	6248

i) Confessional	266	903	948	441	645	922	1196	1411	1685	1983	1708	1558	396	435	640	431	689
a) Public sector	0	110	293	49	124	341	635	877	1083	1287	1292	1185	285	307	227	294	238
b) Financial institutions	266	793	655	399	521	581	561	534	602	696	416	373	111	128	413	137	
ii) Non-Confessional	1966	2775	2894	3523	3407	3287	2603	2372	2453	2307	2194	1964	3325	4413	5310	4460	5559
a) Public sector	1530	1631	1453	1358	1224	1089	797	988	1076	1110	995	813	1702	2525	2959	2593	3006
b) Financial institutions	273	639	678	1067	1028	952	765	760	751	710	650	535	878	934	846	889	865
c) Private sector	163	505	763	1098	1155	1246	1041	624	626	487	549	616	745	954	1504	978	1688
III International Monetary Fund	2623	2374	1313	664	287	26	0	0	0	0	0	0	0	0	0	0	0
IV Trade Credit 4301	5376	5861	6526	6789	6780	5923	5368	4995	4697	5022	5420	7165	10358	14625	11030	15054	
V External Commercial Borrowings (Ebbs)	10209	13873	14335	16986	20978	19943	24408	23320	!2472	22C07	26405	!6452	41443	62337	62676	61058	S3153
VI NRI and FC(B&0) Deposits	10209	11011	11012	11913	11794	13559	16568	17154	13160	31216	32743	16282	41240	43672	41554	42612	14579
VII Rupee Debt 12847	8233	7511	5874	4731	4406	3719	3034	2822	2720	2302	2059	1951	2016	1527	1866	1607	
Gross Total Debt 83801	93730	93470	93531	96886	98263	101326	98843	104914	111645	132973	138133	171331	224573	229887	224264	227688	
Long-Term Debt	75257	88696	86744	88485	92612	94327	97698	96098	100245	107214	115250	118594	143201	177574	180514	174934	187047
Short-Term debt	8544	5034	6726	5046	4274	3933	3628	2745	4669	4431	17723	19539	28130	46999	49373	49330	410641
Memo: Confessional Debt as % of Total Debt	45.9	44.7	42.2	39.5	38.5	38.9	35.4	35.9	36.8	36.1	30.9	28.6	23.1	19.8	18.7	19.1	19.0
Short Term Debt as % of Total Debt	10.2	5.4	7.2	5.4	4.4	4.0	3.6	2.8	4.5	4.0	13.3	14.1	16.4	20.5	19.5	22.0	17.8
Debt Stock-GDP Ratio	28.7	27.0	24.6	24,3	23.6	22.0	22.5	21.1	20.3	17.8	18.5	17.2	18.1	18.9	21.4		21.4
Debt Service Ratio (%)	35.3	26.2	23.0	19.5	18.7	17.1	16.6	13.7	16.0	16.1	5.9	10.1	4.7	48	4.6		5.5

Index